MW00604609

THE LIZARD STAYS IN THE CAGE

Music, Art, Sex, Screenplays, Booze, and Basketball

By Anthony Smith

Published by Next Reinvention

Printed in the United States of America

First Edition: 2012

ISBN: 978-0-9859586-7-1

e-book ISBN: 978-0-9859586-4-0

Library of Congress Control Number (LCCN): 2012945796

www.anthonysmithcreations.com

Cover design by Eric Baxter

All illustrations by Anne Ormsby: www.ormsbyeditions.com

For my parents, Anne Ormsby and Len Smith:
Thank you for being there for me through thick and thin,
and for inspiring me to develop my abilities and make my mark on the world.
Without your love and support over the years,
I could have never done half the things I've managed to do in music and the arts.

Steve,

Hope you enjoy re-living some of our crazy days on the road. Good to be playing music with you again!

CHAPTERS

Introduction: The Lobster Suit Epiphany

PART I 1969-2000

PART II

PART III   2001-2007

AUTHOR'S NOTE

While preparing a final draft of the book you are holding, my main concern was to avoid coming off as mean-spirited, vindictive, or otherwise negative about the real-life people who have been included in the story. I realize this type of literary project is tricky business. Where is the fine line between candor and slander? Honest disclosure and incrimination? *The Lizard Stays in the Cage* has been kicking around for ten-plus years, first as a stack of handwritten notebooks, then a larded, un-edited jumble of chapters on a computer hard drive, and finally the version you are holding, which I hope amounts to a well-paced, entertaining read.

Looking for a final burst of energy to finish the project, after shelving it, returning to it, and repeating this process several times over the course of a decade, I turned to several published memoirs for inspiration. One in particular proved to be most helpful: Andre Agassi's *Open*, which achieved a level of self-effacing honesty I'd never previously observed in a memoir of any type. Agassi's book was entertaining, insightful, courageous and somewhat controversial. I decided that I wanted my book—although I am certainly different from Agassi in too many ways to count—to attempt to achieve some of those same qualities.

In order to do this, of course, an author must be willing to tell it like it is, and there are certain risks in doing that. For one thing, you run the risk of rubbing some people the wrong way; not everyone mentioned, either directly or through pseudonym, is going to like what is said about them. They might feel your characterization is inaccurate or unfair, and resent being included in the first place. Also, you must be willing to confess and concede unfavorable things about yourself. God knows, there are many moments within these pages that fail to paint the author in a particularly favorable light.

Many times, I asked myself what was compelling me to finish writing, to continue investing precious hour after hour in the editing process. I hadn't received an advance. I didn't have a publisher clamoring for my finished product. I finally came to the conclusion that the reason I wanted to get this work out there for the world to see, and hopefully read, was that I wholeheartedly believed I had a →

5

worthwhile story to tell. My experiences over the years as a person in the arts, along with a genetic propensity for storytelling, drove me to the finish line.

  Since the story spans many years and includes reference to hundreds of individuals, I have included a Cast of Characters, which also includes a few frequently used terms. Many (but not all) names have been changed to protect both the privacy and professional reputations of certain individuals.

CAST OF CHARACTERS/TERMS

I feel compelled to provide you with this partial, alphabetized reference list of characters, and a handful of terms, that appear in *The Lizard Stays in the Cage.* There are many people to keep track of through the following chapters—sometimes a character mentioned early isn't referred to again until much later, which could potentially be confusing. Along with the name, I've added a brief description. Many of the names have been changed, but these are all *real people*, except where indicated.

Andy Morton, a.k.a. "Woo"- JBS ambassador, close friend and ally during the touring years, road manager of Living Large, Global Funk Council.

Angela Marshall- director of West Side Second Chances group home in Santa Monica, where I served as a child care worker in the late nineties.

Ann Certich- my roommate in Santa Monica, an aspiring comedienne who ultimately landed a brief but memorable role on *Curb Your Enthusiasm.*

Anne Ormsby- my mother, a painter, devoted matriarch of a large, extended family, and someone who has always understood and encouraged my creative nature.

Arlen- colorful keyboardist for Los Angeles jam band Mama Sutra.

Augie- diminutive drummer from Canada, who flew down to Washington D.C. to audition with GFC. He didn't get the gig.

Baba- my grandfather, who lived in Orange County, and enjoyed a long, prosperous career as a keyboardist.

Ben Carson- second drummer in GFC, replaced Drew Reed.

Benny Green- precocious, baby-faced jazz pianist I met in the Bay Area a couple times.

Bill Nershi- Guitarist for the String Cheese Incident.

Bill Yeager- director of jazz studies at SDSU, where I studied in the early nineties.

Bluebird- New York drug kingpin, who hung around the West Coast in the late nineties and considered investing in Guppy, a funk band I was working with.

Bob Magnusson- San Diego jazz bassist, renowned for associations with many big-name artists.

Bobby Hutcherson- amazing jazz vibraphonist for whom Len and I named our cat. Lived in the Bay Area and performed at Garden City nightclub.

Brad Wood- hand-picked by Wildman, an East Coast drummer who played with GFC for a while.

Brett Sanders- San Diego jazz drummer, a creative talent and friend, with whom I toured in KD3 in 2006.

Brevan Maddox- hippie guitarist from Kansas, a kid I befriended and played music with during the Living Large and GFC days.

Brianna- journalist girlfriend who wrote a piece about me and fellow vibraphonist Dom Drake.

Bud French- San Diego bassist and friend, who led a Latin combo at Croce's for years.

"Captain" Ryan Callisto- Salt Lake City resident, a jam band patron and close friend during the GFC years.

Casy Cohn- owner of the Tone Shack, a music retail store in San Diego, and a friend and fellow songwriter.

Charlie Crompton- jam band buddy from Utah, who threw a big festival called Rolling Summer, which unfortunately resulted in disaster.

Chase Holtzclaw- third guitarist in Global Funk Council, left his home in Chicago to join the band for two years of relentless touring.

Chili Halprin- Park City-based jam band enthusiast, expert skier, friend, and "rising star of interstate bagel distribution."

Chip Cooley- aka Mr. Peepers, a young jam band journeyman who jumped on board with GFC to serve as a roadie/all-purpose homey and mascot.

Chris Taylor- One of my oldest friends, who settled in Texas after a stint in Hawaii as an Elvis impersonator, among other odd professions.

Chuck Metzger- our next door neighbor when I was growing up. Great guy, but he sure did a shitty Santa Claus impersonation.

Cobb Kern, aka Cletus- GFC drummer who briefly replaced Gruden, toured with me in the Western states.

Collin Smith- my younger brother, a former pro athlete, now a family/career man.

Crazy Joe Cahill- road manager for KD3, band I played in with Karl Denson.

Crystal from Bristol- a college-aged girl who hung out with Vick Barerra and me for a couple days, reinforcing the fact that grown men shouldn't consort with women fifteen years younger.

Dale Park, a.k.a. Tiny- guitarist, close friend, important character in the story. Contemplated a career in porn, decided against it, went on to tour with Rick James.

Damion Willis- R&B singer in San Diego, performed and recorded with Cult of Soul.

Dan Lebowitz- first guitarist in Global Funk Council, helped launch the band as a touring act, along with his girlfriend Jenna.

Dan Smith- my uncle, a terrific guy and one of my great supporters over the years.

Dave Veith- keyboardist for Karl Denson's Tiny Universe.

Debbie- friend and faithful supporter from the JBS.

Derek Fisher- infuriating member of numerous Los Angeles Lakers teams, whose every jumpshot was like a dagger to a vital organ.

Dick Merck- lawyer representing ex-NBA big man Jake Redwood, who sold me a lemon of an RV which would cost me tens of thousands of wasted dollars.

Dom Drake- well-known jazz vibraphonist, who settled in San Diego after living the jazz life for several decades.

Don Haas- my most important piano teacher, who guided me onto the right musical path during my teenage years.

Donnie Bus- kind but hapless road manager for Living Large, whose liabilities opened the door for Andy Morton, aka Woo.

Doreen Gunn- personal assistant to Shelly Yackus at A&M Records, where I interned in the early nineties.

Dr. Zimbalist- headmaster of Lawrence Academy, where I went to school through eighth grade.

Drew Reed- first drummer for GFC, after serving a stint in KDTU (Karl Denson's Tiny Universe).

Eric Levy- talented keyboardist for fusion superband Garaj Mahal.

Eric Shedlarsky- talent buyer for Harry O's nightclub in Park City, personal friend.

Fareed Haque- Midwest guitar virtuoso, member of Garaj Mahal, who performed and recorded with me in 2007.

Faze- hip-hop band I played in during the mid-nineties. Almost got signed by Jerry Heller, the godfather of West Coast gangsta rap.

Francois Bouffard- bassist and producer, a loquacious Frenchman who managed hip-hop group Faze, shopping the act to Jerry Heller and other L.A. industry bigwigs.

Fred Hersch- brilliant jazz pianist, a friend and source of inspiration.

Gary Klien- first bass player in Global Funk Council, who wound up suing me in small claims court.

GFC- short for Global Funk Council, the band I formed after being fired from Living Large.

Global Funk- the shortened version of the name, used after Drew Reed left the band and we went in a more experimental rock direction.

Gina Romero- aspiring pop singer/songwriter, hired Dale and me to produce a record of originals.

Gray Melton- my high school basketball coach; a guy I never fully got along with, and whose coaching tactics were in some ways rather questionable.

Greg Higgins- Memphis-based singer/keyboardist, enlisted by Lincoln Norris to front an all-star San Diego touring band.

Hal Diaz- owner and engineer of Crazy Licks Studios, a friend in the Santa Cruz area who recorded some of my projects, including an album with Fareed Haque and Roscoe Church.

Heath Alabaster- San Diego musician, created *Alabaster's Vengeance*, which became a cult classic among some of my musician friends.

Hollis Gentry- supremely talented saxophonist and good friend I worked with over the years in San Diego.

Ichabod- fourth or fifth GFC drummer, a nice guy who lasted only a few months.

Jack and Jessie- husband/wife managers of the apartment complex where my brother Collin and I lived in Northridge, when I left San Diego in 1997.

Jake Najor- second drummer in KD3.

Jake Redwood- ex-NBA basketball player, an acquaintance of my brother Collin; he sold me his RV, which turned out to be a horrible deal.

Jalen Jones- trumpet player and rapper for Faze, who went on to enjoy success as a musical director and producer in L.A.

Jarvis and Amir- the Abbott and Costello of jam band booking agents. Things were already heading downhill when they jumped on board.

JBS- the Jam Band Scene. The modern remnants of the hippie counterculture, fused with a hodgepodge of musical genres, including rock, funk, bluegrass, jazz, folk, and singer/songwriter.

Jeffrey "Wildman" Whitaker- third bassist in Global Funk Council, played in the band for over two years. Had a complicated relationship with the author.

Jim Gorman- roommate of Dale Park and the author in La Mesa, during the infamous Lizard period.

John Sinclair- well-known sixties activist, whom John Lennon wrote a song about. Hosted the Rolling Summer music festival in Utah one year.

John Staten- talented Living Large drummer, went on to play with Karl Denson's Tiny Universe.

Jonah Falcon- New Yorker film buff and renowned anatomical freak, apparently in possession of one of the largest penises in the world.

Karl Denson- popular saxophonist and bandleader, with whom I toured in 2006 and 2007.

KD3- the Karl Denson Trio, of which I was an original member.

Ken Dow- bassist for hip-hop group Faze.

Kurt Kimmelman- well-meaning but misguided music promoter, who wound up owing everyone money at Jazzfest in New Orleans one year.

Kyle Hollingsworth- keyboardist for the String Cheese Incident, a band I admired and in some ways emulated when I became immersed in the JBS.

LaTanya Lockett- neo-soul singer in San Diego, toured and performed with me starting in 2006.

Leland Hackworth- jam band mandolin player.

Len Smith- my father, a man of many talents, who supported me through thick and thin over the years.

Lincoln Norris- San Diego entrepreneur and music manager, with whom I worked at various points in my career.

Lunabelle Frost- friend from Missoula, Montana, harbored my bands many times, and ultimately relocated to Merced to live with us and serve as our traveling merchandise salesgirl.

Macy and the Lizard- Faze groupie and her pet, stars of the scene from which the title of the book is derived.

Manny Graham- one of many GFC drummers who ultimately failed to make the cut. Nice guy, though. Nice family, too.

Mario Walker- charismatic, colorful trumpet player and frontman for Living Large, the first touring group I ever played in.

Mark Reese- second guitarist for Global Funk Council, joined the band in Denver after Dan Lebowitz announced he was leaving the project.

Matt Schumacher- final Global Funk bassist, became a close friend.

Max Carver- owner and administrator of West Side Second Chances group home in Santa Monica, where I worked in the late nineties.

Micah- a friend of guitarist Chase, and one of many GFC drummers. Didn't stay in the band long.

Mike Blanco- close friend who moved to New York to pursue a career as a jazz bassist.

Mike Travis- drummer for the String Cheese Incident.

Mills Jamerson- Los Angeles record producer, deluded Dale Park and me into thinking we might get our original pop songs on major albums.

Mr. Reality- fictitious character created by Dale Park and me, while sharing an apartment in La Mesa in the mid-nineties.

Mr. Sunshine- cantankerous owner of the Top Hat, a popular jam band stop in Missoula, Montana.

Mrs. Baker- my first piano teacher.

Mrs. Pandolfi- middle school religion teacher, a heavy-set woman who liked to scream, "I said quiet!" during class.

Mullet- a very distinct hairstyle, in which the top and sides are short, and the back is long.

Nico Valencia- percussionist in Faze.

Olan Jarvis- duplicitous Texan trumpeter who moved into our house in Santa Clara, in the late eighties.

Orlando "Sparky" Stout- final Global Funk guitarist, could play superhumanly fast and was a fun guy to hang with on the road.

Otis "No Notice" Olsen- manager of Guppy. A friend in the late nineties who I had some good times with, but also a convicted felon who fired band members with no notice.

Page McConnell- keyboardist for Phish, the kings of the JBS, second only in stature only to the Grateful Dead.

Panama Mazakuza- smooth jazz guitarist.

Paula Smith-Arrigoni- my younger sister, an inspirational person who deftly juggles family and career.

Phish- kings of the modern jam-band scene, or JBS. A Vermont-based quartet that enjoyed phenomenal success.

Randy Lucas- owner and engineer of Blast Studios in San Diego, where Dale Park and I did lots of work in the nineties.

Raymond- Semi-retarded neighbor at Casa de Colina, an apartment complex where I shared a place with Wilbur Dugdale.

Red Sawchenko- grizzled laborer who drove me out to the rock quarry in Chino Valley, Arizona, where I worked briefly in the late nineties.

Ric Parnell- British session drummer who appeared in the film *Spinal Tap,* and whom I became friends with while he was living in Missoula.

Richard Sellers, a.k.a. Chef R&B- drummer in Faze, longtime close friend of the author.

Rick Helzer- my piano teacher and mentor at SDSU in the early nineties. A brilliant musical mind.

Ricky "Little Jesus" Perkins- roadie for Living Large and Global Funk Council, became a close friend of mine during my touring years.

Rob Sarno- Colorado-based booking agent who represented my groups, including Living Large and GFC.

Robert Horry- infuriating Laker, who hit perhaps the most nauseating shot in the history of the NBA.

Rochelle- friend in Chicago; a sophisticated city girl, who temporarily rescued me from the monotony of hanging with the band guys 24/7.

Rodney Bunker- bass player in Southern California funk band Guppy, who I suspected of undermining my position in the group.

Ron Jeremy- short, hairy porn icon, who I met in St. Louis while on tour.

Roscoe Church- colorful, high-maintenance drummer from New Orleans. Toured with me in Colorado, and later in California.

Roy Karch- L.A.-based adult film producer, who befriended Dale Park and offered him a chance to break into porn.

Sandy Steinman- RV salesman who sold me the Monaco Dynasty RV, which I would begin to refer to as the Travesty.

Schneider- property manager for an apartment I rented with Dale Park in La Mesa.

Shelly Yackus- Los Angeles recording engineer with many big credits. I worked for him—for free—in the early nineties.

Shouna Shoemake- first steady girlfriend I had after moving to San Diego in early nineties.

Simon Millburg- frontman for Southern California funk bar band, Guppy.

Sit in- to jump up on stage with a band and jam, as a guest.

Smith Dobson- my first jazz mentor, a fine pianist who played at Garden City nightclub in San Jose during the eighties.

Stone- Jalen Jones's cousin, a rapper/frontman in Faze.

String Cheese Incident- popular bluegrass-flavored jam band, a cross between Phish and the Grateful Dead.

Teena Singh- my girlfriend during the later Global Funk days, whom I met at an old friend's wedding in the Bay Area. We married in 2009, and now have two perfect little boys.

Terry Faylor- my stepfather, who met my mom Anne while I was playing high school basketball at Archbishop Mitty in San Jose, California.

Tim McMahon- One of my closest friends, and also one of the first musicians I played with upon moving to San Diego in late 1990.

Todd Sherman- hardcore JBS fan, angel investor for Living Large, co-founded Global Funk Council with me and continued to invest and support both me and the project for several years.

Travesty- the name I started calling my Monaco Dynasty motor home, after it became clear it was going to be a costly lemon.

Tristan "The Mayor" Dunlap- Phish diehard who served as sound engineer for Living Large and Global Funk Council.

Tyson- my cousin, a talented artist with whom I was always close, who moved in with me in Merced around 2005.

Vick Barerra- talented San Diego percussionist who toured with GFC.

Walt Williams- soul vocalist and friend from San Diego. Performed with Cult of Soul and toured with Trunk Fulla Funk.

Wilbur Dugdale- heavy-set roommate in La Mesa, one of my sidekicks during the mid-nineties.

Zak Najor- drummer in Greyboy All-Stars, Karl Denson's first touring band. Older brother of Jake Najor, who I toured with in KD3.

INTRODUCTION:

THE LOBSTER SUIT EPIPHANY

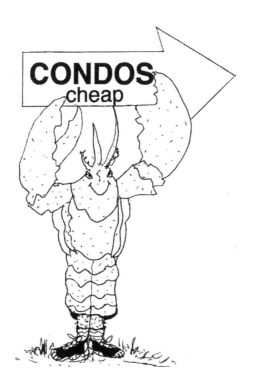

I was walking in downtown Portland, Maine, an hour before I was scheduled to play an outdoor concert with The Karl Denson Trio, a.k.a. KD3. It was rather humid, the final heat wave of the summer lingering longer than expected. I'd just enjoyed some stuffed *rotis* at a nearby Indian restaurant, and was getting mentally prepared to entertain the thousand or so people congregating in a public square for our early evening performance.

As I turned a corner I saw an image that made me realize how fortunate I was to still be in the music game, making some semblance of a living. You're thinking I'm going to tell you I was approached by a tattered beggar, a homeless mother or a legless war veteran in a wheelchair. No… what caught my attention was *a grown man dressed in a furry, red lobster suit, waving a sign at passing traffic in an effort to direct people to a brand new condominium complex.*

I imagined how hot it must be under that suit. I wondered what went through this guy's head when he woke up in the morning and had to climb into his lobster costume, stand at a busy intersection for hours, and jump up and down in front of passing cars. This wasn't a seventeen year-old kid we're talking about. The dude was in his thirties.

I realized that my frustrations and disappointments — the artistic and financial setbacks I'd lamented over the years — were largely irrelevant. Here, before my eyes, was a man whose job required dressing like a coveted creature of the sea in order to hawk overpriced McCompartments. I was not a struggling artist. I was one of the lucky ones. People paid me to do what I always wanted to do. This guy was getting paid seven bucks an hour to act like a lobster.

I suppose there are worse rackets than mimicking the movements of delicious crustaceans. I'm just glad I've been able to pursue a career in music for all this time. It's not always easy and doesn't always pay great, but it's a vocation society views with some measure of respect and admiration. Plus, it's something I still feel passionate about, twenty-five years after I first plunked out *The Indian Song* on my parents' upright Yamaha piano.[1]

Some would argue that it's too early for a memoir. I'm in my early forties, and my music career spans just over two decades. Sure, I've played in a wide variety of groups, probably written a couple hundred songs and taken a lot of creative chances, but it's not like I've won any Grammies.

I haven't exactly toured every corner of the globe, either. I did perform some concerts in Taiwan once, spending my free time wandering the sprawling night markets of Taipei, where I chugged snake blood from a shot glass, watched a family of five eat monkey brains, consumed a boiled frog, and zipped around at dangerous speeds on the back of a pollution-spewing moped. I also had a Taiwanese businessman ask me to please shut up, in a back alley dive bar, after concluding a medley of Billy Joel songs.

---

[1] I don't know if that was the actual name, but it was something like that. I think the whole piece consisted of four notes, repeated over and over.

I'm not divorced. I'm not confused, I'm not bi-curious, I don't have any tattoos, and I've thus far resisted the temptation to stick metal objects anywhere other than my earlobes. I am tall, slender but for a mostly hidden layer of abdominal excess, and am told I have decent looks. I'm losing my hair like a dehydrated Chia Pet, unfortunately, and it's getting harder to pull off the *comb down*.[2] I tried Nioxin, but come on... that crap doesn't really work.[3]

I'm not running for anything or running from anything. I'm not in recovery, and I'm not crusading for or against any particular cause. The only exception would be my intention of forming an organization whose sole aim would be to destroy all existing Kenny G, Dave Koz and Boney James albums.

I've yet to make wads of dough, only to squander those wads of dough on extravagant partying. I haven't battled any life-threatening illnesses. I make no claims to have ever been involved with the CIA, the IRA or the NRA. I never cared much for NWA, and I can count on one hand the unfortunate number of times I've had to play *YMCA*. I haven't procured a fat record deal, and numerous *Behind the Music* installments suggest this might be a good thing.

My story is largely devoid of the dramatic clichés which motivate people to write about their own lives. It's also free of the pitfalls that derail creative careers: drugs, failed marriages, bad business deals, writer's block, thoughts of suicide, and more drugs. I have managed not to sign my life away to crooked middlemen, haven't sunk too deep into debt, and have never turned to the crack pipe or smack syringe to escape my problems. I've acquired few enemies, but I've had my conflicts. These include run-ins with a small claims court-abusing bass player, a derisive Iowa City club owner, a volatile blow peddler-turned funk band manager, and a loudmouthed French Quarter weirdo—more on all this later.

---

[2] The prelude to the *comb-over*.

[3] Once you stop using it, the regrown hair falls out. Transplants, on the other hand, are a serious roll of the dice. Just like penile enlargement surgery. It might work out, or you might wind up like John Wayne Bobbit: check out Bobbit's porno, *Frankenpenis*, in which he flaunts his reattached, enlarged and misshapen package. You'll feel worse for him than you did when Lorraina hacked it off in the first place.

I never starred in any eighties MTV videos which, through sheer cheesiness, would have necessitated full immersion in the Federal Witness Protection Program. The best example of this would be Billy Squier, who managed to destroy his career with one lame video. I have no offspring I'm aware of, but I suppose the call could come from (insert talk-show-du-jour-host's name) one of these days. I guess I haven't made too big a mess of this fool's parade that is life.

Despite my lack of front-page fame, platinum records and drug-addled debauchery, I do believe I have a tale worth telling. In fact, I think you will find these pages to be at least as interesting, if not more so, than the memoirs of some individuals whose names bear a glossier patina of commercial success than my own. I've known geniuses, visionaries, virtuosos, saints, masterminds and beautiful people, along with hustlers, hucksters, charlatans, racists, compulsive liars, drug dealers, junkies and reprobates.

I've soared to creative heights and I've wallowed as a musical whore. I've warmed up the masses for luminaries like Earth, Wind & Fire, and I've sunk low enough to play stupid shit like *Songbird*. I've crossed paths with Springsteen, and I've butchered *Spring is Here* in Jenny Craig's living room. I've been screwed over, and I suppose I've done a bit of screwing over.

If you work in the arts long enough, you wind up a little crazy. It's the only way to cope. A musician leads an unpredictable existence. You don't know how you're going to get treated from day to day or gig to gig, so you learn not to take anything too seriously. You also learn to revel in the inherent absurdity of the human condition — especially if you spend a lot of time on the road.

The musicians who remain happy and fulfilled, through the constant vicissitudes, are the ones who believe their destiny is ultimately in their own hands. Those who feel the world owes them something, simply because they are artists, often head down a road of disillusioned bitterness from which they never return.

Just as life is by no means fair, success in the arts often relies on factors that have little to do with creative ability. There are people that become stars who, when it comes right down to it, have negligible talent.[4] Their ability to sell themselves, to fully believe even if they

---

[4]There are also those who have enormous talent, and deserve all the attention they receive. Great talent is rare, but it rarely goes unrecognized.

possess mediocre skills, be in the right place with the right look or the right sound, and/or leverage relationships and take advantage of nepotism brings them big success. Longevity, of course, requires actual talent. A break can put you on the map, but it can't keep you there if you're not bringing any substance to the table.[5]

The main reason many talented people remain unknown during their careers is that talented people tend to have little interest in promoting themselves or their work. They're too busy being, well, talented. But that's not enough anymore. The world has changed dramatically. According to Thomas L. Friedman, the world is now flat, meaning that resources and opportunities are now available to people in all corners of the globe. Anyone can market themselves or their products to just about anywhere, and they can do it cheaper and more efficiently than was previously possible.

This is both good and bad for the individual. It's good because you're not relying on some institution, such as a huge record label, to validate you and get your work out into the world. It's bad because now, any and every hack guitar player or singer/songwriter can make a record and market it, further saturating an already crowded landscape. Marketing savvy and networking chops, along with computer/internet skills, might be more important in our current age than actual content.

Even now, in Friedman's flat world, artists need help from larger infrastructures in order to have commercially successful careers. They must partner with people whose strength lies in the leveraging of artistic talent. The entertainment industry is predicated on and fueled by the efforts of such people: agents, managers, attorneys, etc. While the artist is busy trying to create something, the talent broker is busy building relationships with other business people.

To me, the great failure of art/music education in institutions of higher learning is the complete disregard of an entire half of the equation: What do you do once you graduate? How do you establish a niche for yourself? How do you parlay your skills into a profitable business? Schools churn out graduates with no idea how to proceed in the real world.[6]

---

[5] Just ask Pauly Shore.

[6] I say this with no intention of slighting my own college teachers, particularly Rick Helzer, who did in fact counsel me on numerous life matters, and remains, many years later, a good friend.

I learned nothing about business, management or finance in college. I realize that my music degree mostly prepared me to do one thing: Teach. But I didn't want to teach. I wanted to perform, compose, produce, and see the world. I left college armed with lots of academic information, as well as some artistic ability, but I hadn't a clue how to be successful in a professional sense.

If I had it to do over again, I would have double-majored in business *and* music; because in order to pursue your dreams in the arts, just like pursuing dreams of pretty much any nature, you have to go into business for yourself. There's no way around it. If you know zilch about business and make dumb decisions in that arena, your artistic dreams will be compromised, maybe even destroyed. You want to record an album of all your best songs, package it and market yourself? That costs money. That requires a business sense. Unless you're playing all the instruments yourself, engineering, mixing and mastering all by yourself as well, you will need people skills — an ability to manage the efforts of others. What I'm saying sounds obvious, but you will learn little of this in the average arts school. Most colleges prepare you for a world that doesn't exist outside the ivory tower.

I've made a number of mistakes over the years. I played in bands that were going nowhere, got stuck doing gigs that threatened to kill my spirit, chased unrealistic goals, and squandered what little savings I had on ill-advised projects. At times, I deluded myself into thinking I was better than I really was. Other times, I was better than I believed, and suffered due to self-deprecation.

My career as a musician and creative individual has been characterized by big swings from one end of the emotional spectrum to the other. There have been times I knew, without a doubt, I was doing exactly what I should be doing with my time and energy. I felt a purity of purpose, when both heart and mind were at peace with the chosen path. At times like this, I felt my life was the envy of those who toiled solely for financial gain. Such people would never experience such soulful joy.

Then there was the flipside — days of excruciating self-doubt, even self-loathing. Such days were filled with pangs of regret... *I should have gone to law school...* suspicions that I'd wasted the prime years of my life pursuing a futile course, a pipe dream doomed to fail from the beginning. On a few occasions, these waves of darkness metastasized into full-blown spells of depression. I wanted, on more than one occasion, to quit music and the creative arts altogether.[7]

In the arts, just like life itself, attitude is everything. If you feel good about what you're doing, if the passion is there, the shortcomings of your career are not as painful. The fact that you don't have a lot of money or security is not as disconcerting. If you feel lousy about yourself and what you're pursuing, there's really no point in continuing. There are much easier ways to make a living… careers that pay better and require far less of your blood, sweat and tears. If you're doing music just for money, forget it — get a straight job and just be a weekend warrior. You'll be able to afford nicer equipment, as well as medical insurance, and you won't have to play stuff you don't like!

The arts, for most of us, are not lucrative enough to merit the degree of difficulty you face in achieving success. That's why the majority of lifelong musicians and artists will tell you they don't really have a choice. They've been called to do this. I'm no different. I have a calling to do what I do, so it doesn't matter if it's worth it or not. It's what I'm going to keep doing, either way.

Thankfully, I feel my talents have evolved over the years. I get more pleasure now out of playing the piano than I ever did in the past, because I play better now than I did then. In another ten years, I'll play better than I do now, and it will be even more enjoyable to play. As Phish guitarist Trey Anastasio said in *Bittersweet Motel*, the harder (and longer) you work at your craft, the more satisfaction you get out of doing it.

If you set high standards for yourself, there is a considerable amount of attendant pressure. Many musicians turn into drug addicts. They feel they can't generate original ideas unless they alter their mind, thus escaping the limitations of the left-brain prison. Maybe they're right. Some of the Beatles music is wildly creative, and I doubt they would have written *I Am the Walrus* had they been sober. I myself have never used drugs to enhance creativity. I have used alcohol to calm my nerves, however, and it's certainly helped me to get up in front of a crowd that's about to stare at me like a goldfish in a bowl. Alcohol numbs the neurotic part of the brain, which is good sometimes, but I don't think it enhances creativity.

---

[7] I did try to quit music in 1997, but it wasn't long before I was playing gigs again.

I'm not saying I drink before every performance. I don't advocate that. But thank you, Jesus, for Captain Morgan spiced rum. The Captain has been my friend through some really hard stretches. The Captain has been my warm, fuzzy security blanket in a cold, harsh world.

I've touched on the difficulties of being in the arts, but there's also an upside. When you're doing something you're passionate about, you aren't in danger of suffering an identity crisis. Unlike those whose lives are compartmentalized into two distinct categories, work and play—an arrangement where the goal is to do as little of the former and as much of the latter as possible—your work and play overlap each other, giving your life a continued sense of freshness and adventure. You operate much differently than the conventional career person, who admires your resolve to set your own schedule, to do things your own way.

If I had five dollars for every person who's ever come up to me before or after a performance and said, "I wish I had the nerve to do what you're doing, when I still had the choice," I'd be setting these words from my private villa in Spain, instead of the Starbucks at the corner of College Avenue and El Cajon Boulevard. Some would argue that you always have a choice. In an idealistic sense I'd like to agree, but we all know it's not entirely true. You get a shot, and if you're not ready to take it, or are too afraid to take it, it might be a long time before you get another. If you don't take that shot, you have to live with the consequences. If you do manage the nerve to take the shot, and it bricks long off the back rim, you have to grab the rebound and put it up again. There's no rebound if you don't take the shot in the first place. I've fired a lot of bricks, but I've never been afraid to put the ball up. I've also gotten a lot of rebounds, and everyone knows that rebounding is the name of the game.[8]

As I look back, I realize I have lived by the credo, *Do what you love and the money will follow.* Okay, so I'm still kind of waiting for the big money to follow. Had I gone into the business of excising abnormal medulla oblongata growths or defending white-collar crime kingpins, maybe the green would have caught up with me by now. There's always the chance that I'll write a song that becomes an international

---

[8] If you shudder at the thought of more sports analogies to come, I refer you back to the title of the book.

27

hit, and then the royalty checks will roll in for years to come. Nobody I know has ever had this happen to them, or personally knows anyone who has enjoyed such a windfall, but these people apparently are out there somewhere.

Now that I've beaten the *do what you love* idea into your skull, let me add that it's important to figure out exactly what it is you love. A painter might be working in the broad field of painting, but that doesn't mean he's doing what he loves. He might be painting clown faces on kids at the local mall for tips. If you're a European automobile enthusiast, and I walk up to you as you polish the bumper of a 1994 Yugo down at the carwash, and say "Gee, it must be great to be following your passion in life," you're going to snarl at me with contempt. Just the same, Wolfgang Puck's not going to appreciate me interrupting him while he covers a shift for a buddy at Burger King, to say, "Guess it doesn't matter if you're whipping up a banana rum flambé with almondine reduction sauce or flame-broiling a batch of Whoppers, 'long as you're doing what you love, eh Wolfgang?"

It's the creative process itself that I love. Music is a vehicle for this, but there are others as well. I like to write short stories, treatments and screenplays, and I've enjoyed assembling this book, even if it seemed for a while there like it would never be completed. When I'm creating something, time flies. I don't even think about time. When I'm working for money, it's a different story.

People used to come up to me as I labored through the last set of some less-than-exciting gig and, recognizing my desire to be somewhere else, would optimistically offer, "At least you're playing your instrument… at least you get to have some fun!" Let's get something straight: Slapping on a monkey suit[9], getting stuck in nasty rush-hour congestion on the Interstate 5, interacting with obsequious valets in front of the Four Seasons as you climb out of your 1989 Dodge minivan, schlepping heavy gear down a putrid service corridor, apologizing your way through culturally irrelevant show tunes from the thirties and forties, annoying a small army of Nordstrom Rack poster boys as they nibble at imitation crab cakes in the Poinsettia Ballroom, slugging down mug after mug of watery coffee, just to stay awake long enough to finish the gig, lugging your stuff back the way you came, hassling with the valets yet again, removing your bow tie,

---

[9] Musicianspeak for *tuxedo*.

plucking the plastic black buttons from your sweat-drenched tux shirt, loading your crap back into the minivan, climbing in and hightailing back to your neighborhood Blockbuster, and renting a bad movie on purpose, because you need something mindless to numb your existential pain… is not fun.

Most of us musicians don't have this fate in mind when we first sit at the piano, or pick up a saxophone or trumpet at age eleven. We start because we're fascinated by the sound of music, with its infinite possibilities. As the years pass, we feel a burgeoning desire to express ourselves. Ultimately, we take the plunge to become full-time players. For a while, the sheer joy of getting to play music, instead of doing some boring job, is enough to keep us flying high. Then we realize how difficult it is to make a living playing an instrument. We maintain our spirited commitment at first, but the need to make money never diminishes. It only grows as we age, along with the amount needed to enjoy a comfortable existence.

Here is where the road forks. Some, like me, elect to stay the course.[10] Maybe we feel we have no choice, or maybe we have no interest in doing anything else. Others come to realize that the need to make money has superceded the need to be an artist. It doesn't happen overnight—it's a slow, insidious process, during which life's realities finally manage to squash the dream, to snuff the fire.

Ironically, the gig I described above, a typical job at a ritzy hotel, is beyond the ability of many big names in the rock and pop world. In other words, lots of the people you see on the cover of Rolling Stone could never get through a casual.[11] The same holds true for other mediums, such as theater. Some of the best actors out there wallow in anonymity for their entire careers, and some of the worst actors out there continue to browbeat you with their wooden style every time you go to the movies.

In mainstream pop and rock music, artists, particularly young ones, are groomed to fit a certain image: young, cute, sexy, dangerous, pissed off, etc. The job of writing and arranging albums is put in more capable hands. The music is tailored to fit a marketing image some

---

[10] And perhaps, as many would argue is the case with George W. Bush and Dick Cheney, our decision is an ill-fated one.

[11] Casuals usually require some sight-reading ability, stylistic versatility, and the technical ability to play an instrument well.

company thinks it can sell, or knows it can sell based on previous success. The most egregious example, albeit a dated one, is Milli Vanilli. At least Taylor Swift *tries* to sing.

That's the way the stale Starbucks scone crumbles, but it didn't always used to be like this. Think back to the seventies, when the biggest stars were also bad-ass musicians: James Taylor, Joni Mitchell, Bob Dylan, Carole King, Paul Simon, The Allman Brothers, Mario Santana, Frank Zappa, Jimi Hendrix, Eric Clapton, Led Zeppelin… the list goes on. Did anyone back then give a damn if James Taylor could bust some sweet dance moves? It was all about the music. Many of these aging artists are still stars on the has-been circuit, but they're not the important figures they were thirty years ago.

Put the aforementioned names next to, say, recent finalists or winners of *American Idol,* and we're not painting a pretty picture of modern pop culture. When you turn on the tube and someone's trying to convince you that Adam Lambert and Jordin Sparks are the present-day equivalent of Freddie Mercury and Mariah Carey, something's rotten in Denmark.

Don't get me wrong. There are plenty of great musicians out there going for it. I cross paths with them all the time, and am inspired by their enthusiasm. I do think, however, that we live in a society where it is very, very difficult to brave a career as a musician. The math just doesn't add up. Most people that do music full-time are constantly hustling and scuffling for new work, searching for opportunities… watching their friends and families drive Lexus SUV's while they're still tooling around in that beater from 1996.

Most of us take what work we can get. The Poinsettia Ballroom is better than nothing. Playing *Brown Eyed Girl* in Google's employee courtyard is a couple rungs above bagging donut holes at Winchell's. After a show in North Carolina several years ago, I asked the great guitarist John Scofield what he thought about the *jam band scene.*[12] He smiled and said, "I'm just glad to have a gig, man."

---

[12] The grass-roots musical subculture originally created by The Grateful Dead, which was inextricably linked to the hippie/anti-Vietnam movement of the late sixties and early seventies. I will refer extensively to this scene, which has enjoyed a resurgence in the last ten or fifteen years, largely due to the wildly successful Vermont band Phish.

I've taken many gigs over the years that meant little more than rent money. I've played coffee shops, malls, retirement homes, car dealerships, raceways, racetracks, prisons, nuclear submarine bases, political rallies, fundraisers, bait shops, bowling alleys, raves, rodeos, renaissance fairs, corporate training seminars, cruises, casinos, fashion shows, celebrity parties, and medical conventions for any disease you might imagine, including Irritable Bowel Syndrome.[13]

I never lost the conviction, through all those bizarre experiences, that I would try for something bigger and better. I always wanted to make my own mark — to offer some kind of creative statement to the world, whether the world gave a damn or not. This resolve led me to abandon Southern California freelance work in 2000, pack my belongings in storage and hit the road full-time. I was tired of spinning my creative wheels. I came across an opportunity to broaden my horizons in a nationally touring act, and jumped on it.

I once received some advice from Bill Nershi, the guitarist and bandleader of The String Cheese Incident, a once-popular, now-defunct Colorado jam band. Backstage at the Sanger Theater in New Orleans, Nershi told me: "If you want to build a strong, grass-roots following for your music, do as many shows a year as possible. Over two hundred, if you can. That's what we did." And that's what I did between 2001 and 2004. I formed my own band, Global Funk Council, wrote most of the material, and took responsibility for business decisions. I assembled a road crew, bought a massive RV, and set out to develop a national fan base through relentless, cross-country touring.

Global Funk Council canvassed almost every major city between San Diego, Burlington (Vermont), Atlanta and Vancouver, B.C. We hit a number of not-so-major ones, too. It was an epic American road adventure. I met amazing people, saw lots of incredible places, and gained a better appreciation of the myriad subcultures of the United States. I also came to understand, more than I ever had in the past, the transcendent power of music.

By becoming ensconced in the roots-rock/jam band scene, I had no choice but to embrace liberal ideas and lifestyles. I'd never been a pot

---

[13] The politically correct term is IBS, but either way, what it means is that your ass is raw. For an in-depth discussion of this misunderstood condition, refer to the Coen Brothers film, *The Ladykillers*.

smoker, a hippie, or a politically subversive individual, and yet here I was, constantly surrounded by hairy people taking bong rips followed by loud proclamations that "Bush is a fucking idiot!"

By the same token, the touring frequently led us to outposts of extreme conservatism, where every house has an American flag waving in the wind, and every other one has a large boat, motor home, or both parked in the driveway. I found myself getting confused at times. You can't call yourself a conservative when you wander around the country playing music with a bunch of free-spirited artist gypsies, following your heart more than your brain... and you can't call yourself a liberal when you believe in defense, the rights of individual citizens to acquire wealth through hard work and intelligence, and the need to put a stopgap in an out-of-control immigration crisis.

Musicians are expected to espouse extreme left wing ideology, which has never exactly been my cup of tea. I've also never been a fan of unquestioning, ignorant redneck patriotism. I consider myself a centrist, and thus felt, during my years of heavy touring, like I was always being pulled in one direction or the other. My skin crawled when some crystal-fondling Trustafarian in Arcata gave props to the *brave architects of 9/11*, just the same as it irked me when some Budweiser-swilling bubba in Nebraska said, "We should just nuke the whole Middle East and be done with those fuckers." It's hard to believe such polar opposites exist within the same country, and I'm not sure it's a positive outgrowth of a free society, or, as Patrick Buchanan contends, a sign of America's eventual demise.

The road gave me ample time to reflect on my entire life, and these reflections culminated in the book you are holding. At first, I scribbled furiously in notebooks, as the RV plowed through the Rocky Mountains during a blizzard, or leaked oil across the desert outside of Las Vegas. I was so consumed with writing that a couple guys in the band noted, "You're more into writing than you are into music, man." At one point in time it was true. I must have filled twenty notebooks between 2002 and 2003. When I finally got a laptop, I was really off to the races.

The road also allowed me to indulge my love of NBA basketball games. When I found myself in a city that had a team, and schedule permitted, I was there, as close to the court as possible, watching, enjoying... sometimes heckling. The chapter titled *Confessions of an*

NBA Heckler[14] chronicles some of my more notorious exploits in arenas like Salt Lake City's Delta Center.[15]

Storytelling is in my blood. My father, Len, has an extensive repository of anecdotes amassed during his eighty years of life, and I have long watched him regale listeners with tales from his childhood, career as a young radio and television actor, stint in the Air Force during the Korean War, time spent haunting the 1950's Los Angeles jazz scene, conflicted experience in the seminary, and decades as a high school English teacher. Over dinner, he'll unleash these gems on you in rapid-fire succession. He pulls the trigger on an old story and you never see it coming… it's so smooth you don't even detect the segue.

A good story never gets old. Sometimes it gets better with time, because you embellish it with new twists—things that didn't exactly happen in the original version, but that make the tale just a little more colorful. One of my favorite of Len's old Chicago stories goes as follows:

It was the forties, and times were tough in the neighborhood where Leonard Sr. and his wife, Helen, were raising their young family. One night, Len's younger brother, my uncle Dan, just a little tyke at the time, was playing with some toys on the living room floor. A neighbor came by unannounced, asking to talk to Leonard Sr., who was out playing an organ gig somewhere. The neighbor said he had business with the man of the house, so Helen invited him in to wait. She asked him what this business was, but he said he didn't want to talk in front of the kid. It was sensitive. Helen assured the neighbor that little Dan had no idea what was going on—the man could speak freely. He launched into an explanation of how he had come to ask Leonard Sr. if he could borrow some cash, since he was in dire financial straits. Dan kept playing with his toys down on the floor, paying no attention to the neighbor's lament. A few minutes later, Leonard Sr. walked in the door, and before the man could open his mouth to say a word, little Dan blurted out from the floor, "He wants money!"

The apple doesn't land far from the tree, as the saying goes. I've gathered plenty of my own distinct memories, most of which relate to my experiences in the arts. Many of the stories contained herein have been shared orally for years, prompting the suggestion, "You should put that stuff in a book." I finally took the advice.

---

[14] The title is a play on Joe Queenan's *Confessions of a Cineplex Heckler.*

[15] Home to the fans that tried and failed to poison Michael Jordan.

Beyond a desire to share stories, there were other reasons I pursued this project. People harbor misconceptions about artists and musicians, and my hope was to address some of them. This includes the notion that we are all flakes, burnouts and deadbeats.[16] Also, I aimed to voice my concern that while most people agree the arts play a vital role in our society, our society as a whole is doing less and less to nurture them. It's become increasingly difficult to live in America and support oneself playing music, writing, painting, or doing anything else artistic in nature. There is a feeling among some musicians I know that we are a dying breed. With all the D.J.'s, rappers and karaoke enthusiasts in the world, who really needs instrumentalists these days? *Let's just hire a D.J.!*

When I was dealing with club owners at the end of the night, I sometimes got the impression they viewed me as some kind of outmoded gladiator of the arts, battle-weary but not quite broken. It was like my band mates and I were sonic brontosauruses grazing the open plains, just before an extinction-causing meteor hits. We were like Clint Eastwood, minus the farting chimp, in *Every Which Way But Loose*—grizzled journeymen who knew we were near the end of the line, but had to trudge on another day.[17]

The thing is, I'm not an aging dinosaur, I'm not a broken down gladiator, and I'm not Clint. I'm not an old man yet. I should be enjoying the long career ahead of me, not living my days in fear like a crusty street pugilist trying to escape his past, or an old gunslinger waiting for that swift bullet to the brain when his back is turned.

Despite these causes for concern, I've come to believe that live music isn't going anywhere. People still frequent clubs to hear bands, new venues open all the time, parents still pay for their kids to take trombone lessons[18], and colleges across the country enroll thousands of new students as music majors every year. Plus, it still seems to be considered cool if you can rip it up on guitar, bash away on a drum set, or hammer out something impressive on the piano.

---

[16] Some of the book's most sensational moments, of course, revolve around the actions of flakes, burnouts and deadbeats.

[17] Actually, like Clint Eastwood in almost every movie he's ever made. Clint's always playing the old pro, that leathery sage muttering such humble words as, "Yeah…I'm the best there is."

[18] One of the cruelest things a parent can do to an unsuspecting child.

Live music will survive, but I do think that one day nightclubs will have holograms of classic bands instead of real musicians, so if you get sick of the jukebox, you can ask the bartender to switch to your favorite rock group for a while. He'll whip out his extensive hard drive library of classic concert holograms, and *voila*, you'll have Aerosmith right there, playing *Love in an Elevator*. This technology will incorporate aspects of karaoke, so that if you're feeling saucy, you can erase Steven Tyler, hop in there with Joe Perry and the gang, and sing *Janie's Got a Gun* yourself. You laugh, but are we not heading toward a day when you don't have to leave the house for anything? When your whole life will be set up so you never have to deal with another actual human being? When you don't even need the bar, because you can stage that hologram concert in the comfort of your own home?

I hope, through presenting this journey, to illuminate the plight of the creative musician in modern America, share my personal manifesto, and offer a few suggestions and caveats for aspiring artists. It takes guts to pursue a career so profoundly lacking in stability, and it takes conviction to stick with that career through extended periods of impecuniousness. People who manage prolonged careers in creative fields are some of the most resilient people around.

Have no fear. You won't find echoes of Tony Robbins, Deepak Chopra or Dr. Phil here; this is not another bromide-laden self-help tome. Nor will I bore you with sour grapes or bombard you with whiney grievances. My grapes aren't that sour and my grievances aren't that whiney. Furthermore, I promise this book will not fall into the category of *My Life Was Totally Screwed Up But Now I've Pulled It Together, Good Thing I Went Through That Screwed Up Period Or Else I Wouldn't Have Anything To Talk About, Buy My Book Because It's Got Lots Of Crude And Gratuitous Drug And Sex References, I Can't Write To Save My Life, But The Woman The Publishing Company Hired To Do The Actual Work Is Pretty Good.*

What I will do is drop names, dis a few numbskulls, offer up nuggets of hard-earned wisdom, give props where props are due, take the wind out of a few sails, dish some dirt, challenge conventional thinking, and shoot from the hip. I didn't seek the imprimatur of either the celebrated or the incriminated. I also elected not to disguise these events in a roman à clef. Using Truman Capote as an example, this technique just seems to infuriate people even more. If you were a jackass to me at some point and I've written about it here, rest assured… your name's been changed!

When I read a memoir, I want the truth; the grit, the gristle, the real stuff. Above all else, I wanted this book to be honest. Apologies to those who are offended by my candor, but don't confuse it with negativity. I have lots of hope, not just for myself, but for you, the reader, too. I encourage you to figure yourself out, while you still have time. And don't convince yourself that you have a lot of time. Tomorrow is not promised.

Despite my occasionally dark tone, I assure you that I like what I do. Nobody stuck an ice pick to my neck when I was thirteen and said I had to learn Bach's Two-Part Inventions, and nobody forces me at gunpoint to remain in this milieu today. I have no current plan to switch careers. Being a member of the artistic community is a privilege, and although it is an uphill struggle at times, I do cherish it. Had I elected to be Willie Loman instead of Willie Nelson, this curious literary odyssey wouldn't exist.

The following is a combination of personal history, social commentary, rants and diatribes, an attempt to be half as funny as Joe Queenan, acknowledgment of the many individuals who have impacted my life for better or worse, and the search for clarity and meaning in the midst of a career that offers no guarantees of either. This is my take on the world through an artist's eyes, and let this be my written legacy should I die tragically in a bizarre gardening accident or spontaneously combust on stage, leaving behind only a small, green globule.[19]

---

[19] A reference to the film *This Is Spinal Tap*, a favorite of many musicians, including myself. In one scene, frontman Nigel Tufnel, played hilariously by Christopher Guest, explains how the band's numerous drummers have been plagued by a death curse.

MILK COTTON

As a boy, I didn't aspire to be a musician. The thing that really grabbed my interest was skyscrapers. I was intrigued by the way they stretched up into the sky, sleek columns of resplendent glass and metal, symbolizing technological progress and modernism in their lunge for the heavens. Defying gravity and shunning practicality, skyscrapers were impressive models of daring and ingenuity, and when you stood at one's base and gazed up, its angular dimensions were testimony to the power of dreams. *If you can imagine it, someone can build it.*

I was also intrigued by cities. Not quaint, rural towns, but sprawling, cosmopolitan centers of culture and commerce. I borrowed books from the public library and poured through them, fascinated by the glossy color pictures of America's urban meccas. Each city had its own history, folklore and distinct flavor, and each had its own visual aesthetic, determined by the shapes and sizes of the buildings and monuments framing its skyline. I decided I wanted to be an architect. I wanted to design skyscrapers. Unfortunately, nature did not bless me with an aptitude for mathematical endeavors. By the time I reached adolescence, I was clearly a right-brainer. Sure, architects need imagination, but they also require a firm grasp of calculus. I wasn't in the hunt. Therefore, when I began taking piano lessons, it wasn't the classical repertoire, predicated on precision and correctness, which captured my youthful enthusiasm. If I couldn't employ my own stamp of originality I wasn't interested. I was attracted to the piano because, in it, I had discovered an outlet for my creative nature.

My mother Anne says I had early promise as a visual artist,[20] but that I, like many children, was a victim of the left-brain dominated curriculum of the American education system. School might have squelched any visual arts potential, but my right-brain predisposition was too strong to be stifled. In music I found a passion. The creative seeds were planted early, and blossomed for years until I made the monumental decision to pursue a career in the arts. The forces of pragmatism gnawed at me throughout my late teens and early twenties, but the music bug was relentless, eventually winning the war. If you are an artist at heart, there is no escape. You come to understand that this passion, whatever form it might take, defines who and what you are. You may realize this at eighteen, thirty-five or fifty.

I grew up in Santa Clara, California. Anne ran a daycare service out of our house at 2644 Barkley Avenue. The house sat across the street from a lovely park, where I spent countless hours playing sports and occupying my time with one innocent distraction or another. The park was attached to Bowers Elementary School, which I attended from kindergarten through third grade. Our neighborhood was in the heart of the area soon transformed into Silicon Valley, the hub of global computer technology. We were also just a few miles from Great America, a theme park in the tradition of Disneyland and Magic Mountain. The two signature rides at Great America were *The Demon* and *The Tidal Wave*, high-speed, twisting roller coasters that my friends and I rode over and over again. The park also had an amphitheater, where I saw concerts by hot contemporary pop acts like Midnight Oil and Richard Marx.

My father Len did not permit me to own a bike, which was the yardstick by which coolness and credibility were measured in my suburban enclave. This lack of wheels, along with a speech impediment that prevented me from pronouncing my r's with any success, facilitated an early environment of ridicule and persecution. If

---

[20] Anne is a successful West Coast painter.

I had been a tough-nosed kid, unwilling to take any flak from bullies, I would have risen above all this without event. Unfortunately, I was kind of a pussy. Leery of confrontation, as well as the prospect of an ass-kicking, I cowered pusillanimously from my detractors. An older kid overheard me one day, trying to pronounce the words *milk carton*, which came out sounding like *milk cotton*, and every time I saw the creep for the next two years, it was: *Hey, milk cotton… when you gonna learn how to ride a bike?* Such examples of psychological torment take their toll when you're ten.

There were some interesting little characters in the neighborhood, including many of the kids Anne supervised in her daycare service. I remember a quiet, Albino boy we'll call Lowell, who, having a hard time with the eighty-year transition between Pampers and Depends, soiled his Levis in our backyard, then bee-lined it for his mom's apartment a couple miles away. We drove around looking for the poor kid and found him sulking in front of the large complex, ashamed over his unexpected loss of bowel control.

Every now and then another kid used to come around, a greasy long-hair whose suspect hygiene habits had earned him the flattering nickname Smelly Eddie. One time he came to the door to collect for his newspaper route, looking more disheveled than ever, and my younger brother Collin shouted out, right in front of him, "Hey Dad… Smelly Eddie's at the door!" Eddie took it in stride. He knew he was funky.

There was a set of blonde, twin brothers, and I traded baseball cards with one of them. I bilked that sucker out of some choice cards. One day he showed up with a shaved head (after Anne informed his mother that he and his brother both had lice), carrying a big stack of Topps cards, ready to do business. I licked my chops. For some reason, this kid had decided that Jim Beatty, an obscure pitcher for the Yankees at the time, was the Second Coming of Sandy Koufax. I knew Beatty was an average, run-of-the-mill player, and I also knew his card wasn't worth squat. I scored a Vida Blue, a Rod Carew, and a Mike Schmidt rookie card… all in exchange for Jim Beatty.

I hung out with another neighborhood kid named Kevin Garber, whose dad, Bumps, had large, ugly tattoos on his arms. One day, Kevin, a string bean with glasses, was the recipient of an errant Sammy Sosa-style baseball swing, courtesy of me, that left his face looking like

Mickey Rourke in *Sin City*.[21] He screamed bloody murder, but the rest of us carried on with our game like nothing had happened. *Next batter!* Anne really chewed me out over that one.

On another afternoon, as curious kids are inclined to do from time to time, a few of the daycare runts and I decided to show each other our *stuff*. One adventurous participant stuck a Tonka Toy *where the sun don't shine*, and it got stuck in there. Word leaked to the parents that evening. The story got distorted so that *I* had shoved the toy in this kid's kiester, against his will. This claim, while entirely false, prompted a bare-ass beating from Len. There's an eye for an eye, and then there's *an ass for an ass.*

Another time, I got in trouble because I'd stashed some pictures from a Hustler magazine in my room. The pictures had a graphic, cunnilingual theme. A tame Playboy spread would have been more appropriate, since I didn't know the first thing about sex. I wasn't totally naïve to the ways of the world, however. I had been aware for a long time, for example, that there wasn't a Santa Claus—which is a story worth telling…

I must have been six or seven the year Len decided to enlist our next door neighbor, Chuck Metzger, to give me a Santa Claus surprise that I'd never forget. That he did. Chuck had a costume already, so all he needed was the beard. Len hooked him up with one, and the whole thing was set. Come Christmas Eve, old Chuck had a few too many nips of the *leaded* eggnog, and by the time he staggered over to make his appearance, not only was it the eleventh hour—but the guy was sloshed out of his mind.

It wasn't the booze that gave him away as he stumbled into our living room to stuff candy canes in my knit stocking. Sniffing out a drunk is beyond the savvy of your typical seven-year-old. No, it was the fact that Chuck had lost the beard Len gave him, and replaced it with a worn kitchen mop. I could see the mop's wooden handle as old Chuck pressed his chin down against the cloth strands in a pathetic attempt to cover his ass. "Ho ho ho," he said. "Hello there, Anthony." I gave him a suspicious once-over.

"Looks like Santa's a little early," Len offered. I wasn't buying it. Possessing a precocious sense of diplomacy, I did what any dutiful seven year-old would do: I covered for him. "Hi, Santa." Chuck sat

---

[21] Or Mickey Rourke in real life.

me on his knee and we played out the charade. "Have you been good this year?" he asked.

"Yeah," I muttered. A little honesty would have been nice. Something more along the lines of: *Hi there, Anthony. Yeah, it's me, Chuck, from next door. I'm not gonna lie, kid. I'm wasted. And by the way, there's no fucking Santa Claus. Chew on that, little fella!*

Chuck and I carried out the obligatory Yuletide protocol, then he stumbled home to get back to the sauce. Don't get me wrong—Chuck was a hell of a nice guy for all the years I knew him. He just happened to make a shitty Santa Claus. Anne was visibly disgusted, but Len hung in there. "You and Santa hit it off there, son."

"Jesus, Len, he knows." Anne was done playing games.

I may not have understood even the basics of sex and reproduction, but the Santa Claus revelation gave me an edge over other kids in the neighborhood, many of whom thought they were slick because their dads had broached the subject of sperm.

"Hey, Anthony, you don't know how to make a baby. I do because my dad explained it to me."

"Screw you, Jimmy. There's no Santa Claus. Your parents bought all that crap at Toys R Us."

Once Len brought me up to speed with the dirty secrets of reproduction, I was on a mission to enlighten as many people as possible with my newfound knowledge. I was a junior Jehovah's Witness of intercourse explanations. One day a lady in the grocery store was staring at my little sister, Paula, still in her stroller, and asked me a question: "Young man? Can I take your sister home with me? She's so cute." I set her straight.

"You don't have to, lady. You can have a child of your own. Just find a man to mix his sperm with your eggs. He'll stick his penis in your vagina, sperm will squirt out, and in nine months you'll have a baby of your own." How ya' like *those* apples, lady? I should have charged a consulting fee.

Anne's daycare environment provided plenty of color to my childhood. Kids were always coming and going. Just when a couple of them moved on, new ones would fill their spots. The parents of the daycare kids leaned on Anne in ways that exceeded the scope of her supervision duties. They would camp out in our living room after work, dumping their single-parent baggage and one-income tribulations on her as she transitioned back to mom/wife mode, preparing dinner for our family. Len was friendly and supportive when he returned home at the tail end of the daycare day, but due to his intellectual background and literary inclinations, there was a limited amount of stimulation he could receive from (or offer to) the majority of the daycare parents as they unloaded their grammatically suspect, broken-home lamentations. I used to look at the divorced daycare parents and their kids as somehow lesser than us, pitiable even. I was part of a healthy, model nuclear family. What I didn't know then was that Len, Anne, my brother and sister and I would have broken-home lamentations of our own in the not-so-distant future.

I was a natural leader in my youth—or maybe that's a euphemism for a bossy kid who intimidated weaker souls into subservience. I would organize games and events, and thrived on marshalling others like a military commander. I was a good athlete at a young age, becoming a proficient soccer player after a couple years of organized games. There was a kid named Arturo who lived nearby and played on an opposing team. He and his brother Sergio, who Collin nicknamed *Surgery*, found a wallet that I had lost one day. In the manner of a corrupt Third World government with a cocaine kingpin's savings account, the brothers appropriated my allowance money for their own uses. So, when my team faced off against Arturo's, I took the first opportunity to kick him hard in the shins, knocking him face-first into the mud. I remember those Saturday morning games… the smell of the freshly cut grass, parents standing on the side sipping coffee from 7-11, the trees lining a park that surely wasn't half as big as it seemed back then, and Len with his hands in his pockets, cheering me on.

I moved from soccer to basketball, baseball and flag football. Without a bike to secure neighborhood legitimacy, I had to turn to sports. I could easily beat anyone in the hood at basketball, so several of the snotty, bike-riding latchkey losers started referring to me as *Jock Anthony*. I was also a prospect in baseball, drafted as the first pick in little league one year. I dropped out before the season started, opting to do a community theater workshop instead. Standing out there at Cabrillo Park on windy, melancholy evenings, noisy traffic whizzing by along adjacent streets as I fielded groundballs but wished I was home, I'd found myself more attracted to the idea of acting.

I auditioned for a local theater group, and on the merits of an over-the-top, impromptu portrayal of a petulant cub in a family of bears, I earned a spot. Sadly, my early thespian foray was tainted by an instance of personal humiliation; during a well-attended amphitheater performance at Central Park in Santa Clara, I jumbled a monologue horribly and never recovered. One of my fellow cast members bailed me out, and I sulked through the rest of the show. During the drive home, looking for strokes, I turned to Anne and said, "I sure screwed up today, huh?"

"Yep, you sure did," she replied. The shame lingered for a long time and, I suspect, deterred me from attempting other dramatic projects.

I was a solid student throughout my early academic years, never sloughing off until college (which I would finish with a 3.0 GPA, having occasionally subscribed to the slacker motto, *D's get degrees*). My parents had high expectations of their firstborn son, and I tried hard to meet them. In fairness to them, I think I was driven by nature, and they just gave me a push in the direction I was already headed. I always had *A's* and *B's* in every subject. I wouldn't get a *C* until high school chemistry, when the prospect of upbraiding an acne-laden sap named Kirky was more gratifying than addressing the properties of covalent bonds.

Len and Anne were both English teachers, so I excelled at writing but more or less failed at math. I'm not the most technically inclined lad to ever come down the pike. I always enjoyed literary assignments, however, and would later ponder the idea of attempting to write as a career, particularly when *the topsy turvy world of rock and roll*[22] has had me in the dumps.

Len encouraged me to collect baseball cards, and used to take me and some other kids to a great specialty shop that had tons of rare, valuable cards. In turn, Anne would pile all the daycare kids into our rust-colored Pinto, which luckily never blew up,[23] and take us to Thrifty, home of the coldest fountain water in town and some pretty cheap ice cream. The younger kids would always make a mess out of their cones, ice cream dribbling down their fingers in the afternoon sun, and I would come to the rescue, eating most of it in the process. Both my parents were very generous towards the daycare crew and other kids in the neighborhood.

---

[22] Ian Faith, the perpetually frazzled Spinal Tap manager, describes the scene to Marty DeBergi, the *rockumentary* filmmaker played by Rob Reiner.

[23] Pintos were known to explode, for no apparent reason, in the late seventies.

It was a daycare kid, whose name I don't remember, who inspired me to try the piano. He'd taken a few lessons, and could plunk out this little Indian song on the upright Yamaha in our living room. I thought it was the coolest thing. Len, the product of a professional organist mother and father, sensed my interest and found me a teacher. Alice was soft-spoken and polite, but I didn't stay with her very long. I jumped from her brief tutelage to a hefty older lady named Mrs. Baker, who would teach me rhythm by singing *wa-ter-mel-on, wa-ter-mel-on.* Then, at the end of the lesson, she'd send me to the market to fetch her some breath mints. I don't recall her breath, good or bad, but she always had to have her mints close by. Mrs. Baker taught me to play pop songs, such as Phil Collins's *In the Air Tonight.* I also recall her lambasting Vladimir Horowitz for hitting some clams in a PBS airing of one of his final performances. I thought, "Give the guy a break, lady. He's eighty years old." That's what I remember: Breath mints, Phil Collins, Horowitz hitting clams, and wa-ter-mel-on, wa-ter-mel-on.

I had a friend from school who also played piano. His name was Leor, and he could play better than I. Leor and I decided to play a duet for the Bowers Elementary School talent show, but when his mother caught wind of the plan, she pulled the plug on it, snapping that Leor was "at a higher level on the instrument." Anne had no time for such musical snobbery, and set out to create an act for me that would blow Leor's skinny, advanced ass off the stage. We decided to abandon the piano. It's true, I wasn't very good. We came up with this dramatic performance art piece where I would draw symbolic images on big pieces of white paper, rip them down and furiously scribble again with large strokes of striking imagery. It was set to an upbeat rock song. At the talent show, Leor came out and played his modest ditty to polite applause. Then I came out, cranked up the volume and *threw down* with some performance art, blasting Leor and the other tame acts out of the cafeteria with the sheer spectacle of it all. *Rock and roll, baby.*

In the next few years, I concentrated on sports. I got pretty good at basketball, and spent most days after school shooting hoops in the park. While an attractive, older neighbor named Kathy Malcolm practiced a roller-skating routine to AC/DC's *Highway to Hell*, I was working on my dribbling and outside shot. Kathy babysat Collin and Paula sometimes, and Collin and I both had crushes on her. One time she went to take a shower at our house, and Collin, I'm guessing to have been about seven, asked if he could watch. When she asked why, he matter-of-factly replied, "So I can see your vagina." On a different occasion, I baited Kathy into saying the word *captain*. When she obliged, I squeezed her breasts with both hands and said *crunch!* At least Len and Anne Smith didn't have to wonder if their sons were gay.

There was a guy in the neighborhood named Nathan, a couple years older. He didn't play sports, but we both liked music and became friends. Nathan had mental issues, which you don't zero in on when you're twelve. He told me he worshipped the devil, and offered to initiate me into his sect. I agreed, and Nathan went ahead one day and started burning a pentagram into my hand using candle wax and toothpicks. I freaked out and told him to stop, but I still have a small scar on my right hand from that day.

Nathan's favorite band was Duran Duran, and he had converted his room into a shrine of worship, with giant posters of Simon LeBon, John Taylor and the rest of the band. At some point, Nathan started breaking into our house and stealing things, such as Len's expensive white raincoat. Somehow Len knew Nathan had stolen the jacket — he'd had a recollection of Nathan walking up Bowers Avenue in a long, white raincoat. Len showed up on Nathan's doorstep and asked his mother to retrieve the coat he knew Nathan had stolen. The poor lady was mortified. Sure enough, she returned with it in hand. She apologized profusely while Nathan whined in the background, "This is bullshit! I didn't do anything!" That was the last I ever saw of klepto, weirdo Nathan.

By sixth or seventh grade, I was a very good basketball player for my age. Actually, I was a *great* player for my age — the eleven year-old equivalent of a Dirk Nowitzki.[24] I was tall and could dribble, shoot and pass better than most twelve or thirteen year-olds.

One place I showcased this burgeoning talent was Stanford's annual youth basketball camp. You played basketball all day and well into the evening, and slept in a dorm. My roommate was a buddy from San Jose, Ollie Herning. Ollie's uncle happened to be the mayor of San Jose, but Ollie wasn't exactly a choir boy. A clever, conniving kid, he was always trying to corral me into joining him in some questionable activity. The first night in the dorm at Stanford, we decided it would be fun to grab a couple of the fire extinguishers off the wall and start

---

[24] Talented power forward for the Dallas Mavericks, who lopes up and down the court like an antelope, burying three-point shots or driving to the basket for thundering dunks. He also happens to be white.

randomly spraying things. After we'd had our fun, we covered our tracks and went to bed. In the morning, I was feeling guilty. It was a stupid thing to do, and Len was affiliated with the basketball program at the school.

"I hope we don't get caught," I said to Ollie.

"Relax, we'll be fine."

When the coaches gathered all two hundred of us together for the daily morning briefing, the head of the camp, Bruce Pearl, who was the assistant coach of the Stanford men's team at the time, bellowed in his characteristically hoarse voice: "Listen guys. There's been some vandalism in the dorm. We know who did it, and if you come forward on your own, the punishment will be less severe than if we have to pull you out of your morning drills. If you don't come forward we'll send you home." I started to panic. Len was going to kill me. I was ready to turn myself in and beg for Pearl's forgiveness: Please, Coach, don't send me home! I'll do anything! Don't tell my dad. Ollie remained completely cool throughout Pearl's spiel. When the coach was done, I looked over at Ollie. He whispered in my ear: "They don't know anything. Keep quiet and we'll be fine. If they knew who did it, they'd just grab us, not make an announcement to the whole camp. They don't know shit. Trust me." I followed Ollie's lead, and he was of course correct. Pearl was fishing, and thanks to Ollie's street-wise savvy, I didn't take the bait.

Pearl, I will point out, was a nice guy who was always friendly to Len, Paula, Collin and me at the men's games where Len worked as the public address announcer. Years later, Pearl climbed the NCAA coaching ranks to get the head job at Tennessee, a perennial top twenty contender. Unfortunately, he was implicated in a scandal in 2009 which forced him to resign. Maybe if he'd had Ollie in his corner, he could have weaseled his way out of trouble.

Around this time I discovered I had a good ear for music. I could pick out tunes from the radio and play them on the piano without looking at sheet music. I would write little songs of my own, and started to feel a growing creative desire.

A couple times a year we'd pile into the car and drive down to Orange County, where my grandfather lived. Grandma Smith had died of Alzheimer's Disease when I was a young boy, but Grandpa, or Baba as we called him, was still very healthy. Settled in La Habra for the golden years, Baba had enjoyed a long and fruitful career as an organist, and was still active in the community. He played in a local club, and also had a steady job at a progressive church in Whittier. He didn't much like it when I played the organ in his living room, because I would play too heavily on the keys, as if I were playing a piano. Baba would show me musical things, though, and encouraged me to keep studying music.

Len would play the piano, too. One time at Baba's place, Len was playing the piano after the elder musician had finished a couple tunes. Collin, just a little guy, came over and said, "Hey Dad, let me tell you something. Baba plays the piano better than you... *lots better.*"

Collin had a knack for such blunt witticisms at a young age. One time he returned from Bowers Park, after hanging out with some older guys who were apparently using profanity. "There are some guys over there using bad language, Dad. They said the *F word.*" Not convinced of his younger son's grasp of such taboos, Len asked, "What *is* the F word, Collin?" The little squirt leaned over, and in a discreet tone whispered..."*Shit.*"

A few years later, Collin and I were at a Stanford men's basketball game at Maples Pavilion in Palo Alto. Len was the public address announcer for all of Stanford's home games, so Collin and I got to see many future NBA stars while still in the college ranks. Chris Mullin, the Oakland Warriors' all-star sharpshooting forward, was in attendance at this particular game. Mullin was known to work out with Todd Lichti, Stanford's best player at the time, and was probably there to show encouragement to the younger athlete. Just the day before, it had been in the paper that Chris Mullin had checked into rehab because he had a problem with alcohol, specifically beer.

When Collin and I spotted Mullin in the crowd, sitting by himself, I said to my brother, "Look, Col, there's Chris Mullin!" Collin loved the NBA, and I expected him to react with star-struck admiration. The little chap was not as enamored of Mullin as I had anticipated, however, and instead turned in the direction of the six-foot-six swingman and jeered, "Beer alcoholic!"

Collin had early musical talent. He was on his way to becoming a fine clarinetist before he quit to concentrate on sports. One night Collin had a Christmas performance in the Bowers auditorium, and Len and I walked across the street to check it out. *Smitty*, as Len called him, was lined up on the stage next to several other kids. When they started playing, a curly-haired fat kid with a trumpet made a sound that could be likened to an underwater fart. Collin started cracking up uncontrollably and couldn't continue with his clarinet part. Once he composed himself, he noticed that the tiny Asian clarinetist next to him was way off, fouling up the whole piece. Collin started to berate the little guy right there in front of a packed auditorium of parents. Len and I broke into barely stifled laughter, and soon many others in the room were guffawing. For his encore, Smitty got up and nailed a nuanced, technically peerless solo rendition of *Silent Night*, quieting anyone who might have been wondering, "Can you do any better, kid?" *As a matter of fact, I can*.

Around this time, Len and Anne were having marital problems. The golden daycare age was over, and Anne was now working a stressful job as the regional training director for Orchard Supply Hardware. Don Henley's *End of the Innocence* didn't come along until the nineties, but its sentiments sum up what I was starting to feel in 1982.

I SAID QUIET!

In 1983, I attended junior high school at Lawrence Academy in Santa Clara. A divorce between Len and Anne was inevitable, and the custodial fate of me, Paula and Collin was uncertain. Even at thirteen, I was able to grasp how different my parents were. Len was into old jazz albums, Anne was into Neil Diamond eight-tracks.   Len's idea of a good time was scat-singing along to Blossom Dearie's version of *I'm Hip*, and Anne's idea of a good time was playing *Hey Jude* ten times in a row, singing along with the *na na na's* at the end.[25] That pretty much says it all. I believe the straw that broke the camel's back was not a particular issue or conflict, but a person. That person's name was Mary Calarudo.

Anne watched Mary Calarudo's two kids, Joseph and Ann-Marie, as part of her daycare service, and the two women became friends. Mary was a good-hearted woman, not sophisticated by any means, but a loving mom. She had been through failed relationships, had endured her share of heartbreak, and was now attempting to raise her young children without the help of a man. Anne sympathized with her, and her kids became friends with us.

At a family party at our house, Mary was introduced to my uncle Tim, Anne's younger brother. Tim had led an active life, had two young kids of his own, and had done all this while courageously dealing with a variety of severe, congenital heart defects. Mary and Tim bonded at that party and became romantically involved. Everyone viewed this as a positive development, as both people were in need of support and companionship.

So where was the problem, you ask? The problem was simple: Len thought Mary Calarudo was a loser; a rube. He didn't like her influence on Anne. I'm speculating, but I imagine he thought she represented an impediment to the health of his marriage. For Anne, Mary Calarudo was a breath of fresh air, a buddy, someone she could relax with and let it all hang out. Ultimately, Anne would drift away from Mary—but when I think of the time period when my parents' marriage crumbled, I always think of her for some reason.

The dress code at Lawrence Academy required boys to wear white collared shirts and blue corduroy pants. We were also required to attend Mass, and theology was included in the core curriculum. I vividly remember many of my teachers. There was Ms. Hartwick, a tall and geeky, blonde version of Olive Oyl, who taught history. Hartwick, like a few of the other female teachers, seemed like the kind of woman who still lived at home and had never gone on a date. She was too oblivious to notice a barrage of spitballs flung above her head

---

[25] I'm not making this up. One time I was home from school because I was sick, and as I ate some chicken noodle soup, Anne cranked the stereo and played *Hey Jude* ten times in a row.

and onto the chalkboard, as she rambled on about the Louisiana Purchase.

Then there was Mrs. Pandolfi, the plump religious studies teacher who routinely belted out the routinely ignored warning, *"I said quiet and I meant it, people!"* One day she discovered an unflattering portrait drawn by me and a couple buddies. We had elected to flex our meager art skills rather than listen to Mrs. Pandolfi's biblical stammering—which sounded like Julia Childs reading from Deuteronomy— and the resulting masterpiece featured her fat backside chasing after a Carl's Jr. delivery truck, as she screamed "Come back!"

There was Cedric Claxton, the physical education teacher who moonlighted as basketball and flag football coach. Claxton strolled into our basketball game against perennial powerhouse St. Simon in a full white tuxedo with top hat, tails and cane, for reasons never explained, only to watch from the sideline in humiliation as we got blown out by thirty points. Claxton's job, whether teaching P.E. or coaching hoops, seemed to entail rolling out the balls and kicking back. He was a good guy, cool and relaxed, so nobody took exception to his questionable diligence.

There was Mrs. Mervin, the Dean of Students, who said to me, "Look, I know you're not the kind of problem kid that defaces school property by writing dirty limericks in the men's room of the gymnasium. I know you're above that." She was wrong. I had gone into the gym bathroom the previous day, with a miscreant named Chaz Guzman, and scribbled profane rhymes all over a couple of the stalls.

Finally, there was Ms. Farnsworth, the hapless music teacher that looked like the character Pat from *Saturday Night Live*. She took so much verbal abuse from Sara Corsiglia, my best friend John Slanika and me that she walked out of the classroom to have a near-nervous breakdown one day. Mrs. Mervin came in and said, "You guys need to ease up on Ms. Farnsworth. She's trying very hard, and she doesn't appreciate you coming down on her all the time." This, of course, doesn't say much of Ms. Farnsworth's ability to control thirty smart-ass adolescents.

I always had a bit of a devious streak. Len was mostly concerned with my academic results, as well as the development of athletic and artistic talents, and I was excelling in each of these areas; so he didn't ride me too hard on the occasions when I had little discipline problems with teachers. Len was always on *my* side. If I was holding up my end of the bargain—getting good grades, furthering my development in various extra-curricular pursuits, and being honest with him—it was all good. We were buddies, from the time I was a kid; and like a loyal buddy, Len would defend me, even against some teacher who had an axe to grind.

For example, one time I got in trouble for snickering in church at old Father Wilkimeyer, during one of the self-aggrandizing, completely delusional monologues he passed off as sermons. These embarrassing promo campaigns were always concluded with a reminder that "WE CHOSE YOU! YOU DIDN'T CHOOSE US! LAWRENCE ACADEMY IS THE FINEST SCHOLASTIC INSTITUTION IN… IN… IN THE WORLD!" The punishment for my irreverence took the form of banishment from a Friday night dance in the gymnasium. I appealed this decision to Mrs. Mervin, who gave me permission to attend the dance and make amends in some other way. This information was not communicated to Dr. Zimbalist, the school's headmaster, who did not have a love connection with either Len or me.

I showed up at the dance with my friends, only to be rebuffed and turned away by Dr. Zimbalist. Len, the assistant headmaster, had made clear (within the confines of our home) that he viewed Dr. Zimbalist as a pompous douchebag. It was no more than ten minutes after I called Len, to alert him to my denied entrance, that I saw his light-blue Honda Accord ramble into the gymnasium parking lot. He was not pleased. He marched over to Dr. Zimbalist, his academic associate, and got in his puffy face. "What the hell is wrong with you?"

"Your son has been banned from the dance this evening," Zimbalist sternly announced.

"That's bullshit. He worked it out with the dean. And you…" Len inched closer to the stuffy, bearded headmaster. "You're an asshole."

I was confirmed in the St. Lawrence church, along with other kids from my class who were Catholic. My parents gave me some gifts, including the soundtrack to *Saturday Night Fever.* In my lifetime I can't recall a greater wave of hype surrounding the release of a film. John Travolta was huge. His picture was everywhere. The closest thing I can think of is Michael Jackson's *Thriller*, which came along several years later.

The *Saturday Night Fever* soundtrack featured the Bee Gees, whose signature singing style on such hits as *Jive Talkin'* was hot stuff at the time.[26] The music was so organically connected to the film that the Bee Gees became as big as the film itself. I wasn't just into the album... I was addicted to it. It was a great album! You had not only the Bee Gees gems, but also *Disco Inferno, If I Can't Have You, My Boogie Shoes*, and other catchy disco anthems. Len considered taking me to see the Bee Gees in concert at the Oakland Arena, but was dissuaded by a concert-savvy contemporary, Chris Bradford, who told him, "Don't do it Len. He's too young. It will be a zoo—people doing drugs, acting stupid." Thanks a lot, Chris.

A year later, Anne enrolled me in modeling school in San Francisco, and the Thompson Twins' *Hold Me Now* hit the airwaves with a vengeance. I refined my runway chops to this classic song, and was complimented by the teacher of the class, who said, "Good job! You have good posture, you're calm, and you smile. Someone must have told you to smile a lot. Keep doing that."

When I hear *Hold Me Now* these days, it conjures up everything I was feeling at fourteen. I'm transported back to those days of getting dressed up, rubbing gel into my copious brown hair,[27] driving with my schoolmate and friend John Wilson to classes at John Casablancas Elite Agency in San Francisco, clumsily trying to cop the *GQ* image, being interested in girls for the first time and trying to talk to them, learning how to present myself with style, and spending good times with Anne. Len took a hands-off, let's-see-what-happens approach to this venture—fathers aren't typically very supportive of forays into male fashion modeling. *Maybe my son is gay...*[28]

---

[26] It wasn't quite as hot in 2002, when the Bee Gees showed up on TV with tired faces, dance moves and vocal chords. Seeing three tired, fifty-something guys up there onstage in front of a bunch of yuppies, still trying to sound hip while singing "Whether you're a mother or whether you're a brother you're stayin' alive"... was a little sad.

[27] I would not use the word "copious" to describe what remains on my head at the current time.

[28] Len did provide some feedback, months later, when I completed the course and assembled my first portfolio. He took one look at my pictures—carefully arranged, posed shots—and said, "What the hell were they doing with your hair? It's sticking up funny." He was right. They had taken the money and delivered a bunch of shitty photos. "I'd re-do those if I were you," Len advised.

The first pop concert I ever went to was Wham, the wildly popular, British bubblegum duo, at the Oakland Civic Auditorium in 1984. *That settles it. My son IS gay, after all...*

Before becoming a George Michael fan, I had been obsessed with KISS, particularly Ace Frehley. I had stolen his name for a few years during elementary school, when I insisted on being called Ace. Anne had obliged, writing "Ace" on my brown lunch bags day after day, month after month. I was transfixed by the members of KISS because they were rumored to perpetrate truly sinister deeds. For example, it was rumored that Gene Simmons was spitting the blood of actual animals onstage. There were also reports that the band members used their imposing stiletto boots to stomp to death droves of live, baby chicks... while performing their show! This was the stuff that held my attention—that made me want to follow the band's every move. In all honesty, most of KISS's music pretty much sucked.

After KISS it was Ozzy Osbourne. I would study pictures of Ozzy in *Cream* and *Hit Parade* magazine, asking Len to take note of various aspects of the Ozzy phenomenon. "Look how much less he weighed when he was with Sabbath, Dad. Now he's all fat." Len, no headbanger, finally cracked one day and said, "Jesus, Anth, what is it with this Ozzy crap? Who the hell cares!"

"Well, Dad, maybe you don't realize that Ozzy bit the head off a bat during a meeting at his record label. Then he had to get seventeen shots in his stomach for rabies."

"Well, that's impressive. I stand corrected." John Slanika and I became obsessed with Ozzy's *Diary of a Madman*. The record explored mysticism and the dark spiritual world, and was given an extra boost of cachet when lead guitarist Randy Rhoads died in a horrible plane crash.[29]

Getting back to George Michael for a minute... his music, as was the case with lots of the eighties groups, was very kitsch. The songs were about love, emotion, and having fun. They were simple and felicitous, conveying messages some might consider pedestrian or naive. This is

---

[29] Chuck Klosterman reports on the crash as follows: "...the idiot flying Rhoads's plane decided to buzz the Osbourne's tour bus. He missed. The plane's left wing hit the bus at over 140 mph and flew into a nearby house, exploding on impact. They needed a dentist to identify Randy's 25-year-old corpse.

one of the main reasons the eighties got slammed so hard once they were over. By the gritty standards of the nineties, music suddenly had to meld scathing social commentary and nihilistic angst with screeching guitars, hip-hop beats or touchy feely acoustic riffs to be legitimate or, to use a contemporary catch-word, *resonant*. The stark contrast between the eighties and nineties was similar to that of the fifties and sixties, when the innocent, hokey sing-alongs of Frankie Valli, Buddy Holly and the Coasters gave way to the more rebellious, socio-politically driven work of Bob Dylan, Jefferson Airplane and the Grateful Dead.

I went from a diet of KISS, Ozzy, AC/DC and Aerosmith to the Bee Gees, Stevie Wonder, DeBarge, Prince, Michael Jackson and George Michael. It was quite a stylistic evolution, when you think about it. Furthermore, the jazz chords Len played at the piano started to make sense to my ear, where before they'd always sounded dissonant and weird.

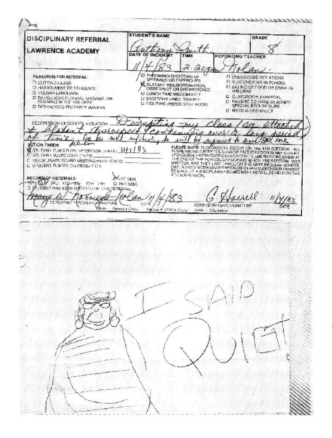

55

GOODBYE PEPPERONI, HELLO POPULARITY

At seventeen, my musical horizons were rapidly broadening. I began listening to and emulating people like Bill Evans, the influential jazz pianist who played on the classic Miles Davis album *Kind of Blue,* before going on to his own great career. I started to think I might be passionate enough about music to pursue it as a lifelong endeavor.

Senior year marked a considerable jump in my popularity. For one thing, my zits cleared up. Between freshman and junior year my face had more or less resembled a greasy pepperoni pie, as compassionately noted one day in English class by Dave del Fugo, a baby-faced football player with superhuman strength and nary a blemish—so I was delighted to have clear skin for my final high school campaign. This was thanks to Acutane, a miracle drug I'd started taking when my acne got out of control. Acutane dried out your sweat glands permanently, meaning you might wrinkle prematurely in later life. Oh well, it was worth it. Bring on the wrinkles.

The summer before, Anne had moved in with Terry Faylor, father of my friend Joe. Anne and Terry, a couple now, were sharing a house in Santa Clara. Terry was supportive of young kids socializing and even having some drinks in a controlled, safe environment; I threw a couple raging parties at the house, and knew I'd arrived in the upper echelon of coolness when I stood in the front driveway congregating with Craig Teschlag, Zack Gill, Pat O'Brien, Kevin Donahue and Dave Sardi in an attempt to determine how many beer kegs could realistically be planted in the backyard. By consorting with this cadre of well-connected partiers who comprised the social elite at Mitty High, I'd become inarguably *popular.* My newfound campus appeal aided me in crushing fellow candidates to become senior class vice-president.

I added trumpet to my musical arsenal of piano, keyboards, vibraphone and glockenspiel, and mildly wowed other kids in the jazz band by being able to pick out songs off the radio without looking at sheet music. The ability to hammer out Bruce Hornsby's *The Way It Is* and ABC's *Be Near Me* entirely by ear was impressive stuff. Since band was thought by cool people to be *for fags,*[30] I had to lead a surreptitious double-life as a slick, non-virgin jock ready to throw back a twelve-pack of MGD at any moment,[31] and a trumpet-wielding dweeb who accepted his place within the social fringe. It wasn't just fellow students I had to worry about, either. Gary Melton and the rest of the varsity basketball coaching staff thought playing musical instruments was for dorks, too.

For the school talent show, I assembled a line-up of players from the jazz band to rock out on Howard Jones' bubbly *Life in One Day,* not-so-humbly placing myself in the middle of the stage and taking the glory. Later in the year the school put together a Battle of the Bands. Joe Faylor, who not only played basketball but was also a good drummer,

---

[30] Not my term—and for clarification purposes, not a derogatory slur toward homosexuals, but a general character assassination.

[31] I only did this once, and it was with Budweiser, not MGD. My buddy Mark Austin and I puked the night away in Central Park, and to this day I loathe the smell, taste and very sight of Budweiser.

helped me organize a combo. After butchering our way through
Robert Palmer's *Addicted to Love*, with a miserable vocal performance
by yours truly, we finished *dead last*. Video footage confirmed that we
were in fact terrible.

I had an impressive campaign on the basketball court that year. I
averaged twenty-plus points, and also double figures in rebounds. I
set a record for three-point shot percentage in the West Coast Athletic
League, and also was named to the W.C.A.L.'s first team all-league.
We managed to beat Riordan, perennial all-black San Francisco
powerhouse. They were a better team but I had a big game, scoring
twenty-five points and dominating the boards. Len, discouraged with
both the team itself and Gray Melton's frustrating coaching style
(Melton liked to replace the starting five with subs, and make us watch
from the bench as they squandered whatever lead we'd worked to
gain), didn't come to the Riordan game out of fear of a disheartening
blow-out. I was sorry he missed it, since it was one of the best games
I'd ever played. Bill Delaney, head coach of the always-tough St.
Francis Lancers, approached me on the court after the game and said:
"I was worried you were getting discouraged, but after tonight I'm not
worried. You played a great game." I was never able to completely
reconcile my differences with Gray Melton, who occasionally threw me
out of practice for having a bad attitude, but we managed to co-exist
for the entire season.

I might have been the best player on my high school team, but all
eyes were on Jay Webb, the six-ten center who was being recruited by
the likes of coaching icons Bobby Cremins (Georgia Tech) and Jim
Valvano (North Carolina State). I had more of a work ethic in my left
pinkie finger than Jay had in his entire body, but Jay was nearly seven
feet tall, and Jay was black. He also happened to have legitimate talent.
Unfortunately for Jay, Gray Melton hated him with a passion. He
threw him out of practice even more than me.

One such occasion was the day before our second match-up against
St. Francis. After dismissing Jay from practice, Melton yelled to the rest
of us, "Fuck him! We'll play better without him." I knew I would have
to pick up the slack; fueled by an inspiring pre-game speech by one of
the assistant coaches, I came out bombing threes in the first quarter. I
fouled out during the third quarter with 22 points and a lot of
rebounds. We lost the game, but I made my presence felt.

Gray Melton was friends with the head coach at Harvard, and invited
him to watch me practice one day. Melton later called me and said,

"Good news... Coach liked your game." There were two problems, however: One, my SAT score was a bit low for Harvard, and two, there was no way I could afford to go there unless I got an athletic scholarship. My chance of going to Harvard withered away in the wind.

I was named the MVP of the varsity basketball squad. I was also selected to the West Coast Athletic League's varsity basketball First Team, an accomplishment that makes me proud to this day. I decided to write my college application essay based on my experiences on the basketball court. The piece was called *Oh, For Six Inches*, a humorous grievance about my lack of height for a basketball player. I made the compelling case that with another six inches all my athletic dreams could come true. As I would soon learn, the admissions boards of esteemed universities were not receptive to the rather blunt use of double entendre, in the form of *dick jokes,* as literary device.

KISS THIS, PAL

Once the basketball season concluded, Len, a showbiz veteran and now the head of Mitty's drama department, directed a production of William Inge's *Picnic* as the spring play. I auditioned for the male lead role, Hal, and got the part. We recruited Kassie Broyles, acknowledged as the *best looking girl in school*, to play the female lead. What Kassie might have lacked in thespian flair she more than made up for in visual appeal.

Hal was supposed to be a strapping stud, and in order to fit the part I had to pump some serious iron. I wasn't about to get up there in front the entire student body looking like a skinny wimp. Fearing a repeat of my early disaster with the Santa Clara Repertory Theater, I thoroughly learned my lines within the first week of rehearsal. Ellie Rock was less thorough in her preparation, and had to be spoon-fed her lines for a month, suggesting a correlation between her last name and retention skills.

The play ended up being a hit with the student body. I solidified my status as a well-rounded man on campus. *Picnic* was a nice cap to my high school experience, and I can only think of one thing I would have done differently if I had another chance…. I should have really gone for broke in those kissing scenes with Kassie.

I joined my buddies Jeff Watson and John Messier in performing a pair of pop songs, the first I'd ever written, at the senior graduation dinner. One was an up-tempo groover called *Don't Walk Away*, and the other was a ballad called *Step Across the Line*. The latter was reminiscent of a song called *Hands to Heaven*, by the eighties band Breathe. It was 1988, and most kids in our age group were listening to alternative rock. U2 was at the top of the heap. Here we are, twenty-plus years later, and things haven't changed much.

I saw U2 live in 2001, when they were touring in support of *All That You Can't Leave Behind*. My ears rang for at least three days after the concert, but it was one of the best rock shows I'd ever seen. U2 is a good example of the importance of chemistry in creative music. You can put together the most incredible players, but if they don't have a natural connection they won't make great music. Many of the best groups aren't comprised of the most individually gifted musicians, but ones who have complimentary talents and who understand their role in creating the overall sound.

Out of high school, I was rejected by Stanford, Harvard, and several other top notch universities. After working hard for four years, taking my academics seriously and avoiding the temptations of excessive partying and slouching off, I came up empty. I was crushed. Nobody knew how devastated I was because I didn't talk about it. To make matters worse I had earned disappointing scores on the S.A.T., a test I was sure to do well on. This made me feel intellectually inferior. People told me I was the *classic overachiever*. What the hell did that mean? I'd worked extra hard to overcome the fact that I was inherently dumb? My grades and accomplishments belied a basic lack of brains? I had busted ass for nothing, and now kids who hadn't done half the work I had, but had somehow managed higher test scores, were sailing past me and into the colleges of their choosing? This was a hard reality pill to swallow.

By 1988 admissions preferences were a fixture within the ivory tower. Yes, I had amassed an impressive resumé of extracurricular activities and a very good 3.75 G.P.A., but when my S.A.T. scores came back disappointing, I was basically sunk. I was a white male, after all, and had turned in a frustrated essay wishing for longer legs (or a longer *something*, depending on your take). My well-rounded accomplishments were not enough to turn the tide. Not with a last name like Smith.

It was the first major turning point in my life. In a screenplay this would be Major Plot Point One—the transition into Act Two. I know what you're thinking: *Kiss this, pal! You've had advantages your whole life.* You're basically right. I've had many opportunities to succeed in life, and I readily admit that. I've had supportive and intelligent parents, a middle-class upbringing and a reasonable work ethic instilled in me from a young age. I don't know why I'm telling you all this—maybe I've needed to get it off my chest for a long time. Maybe I'm trying to purge some ancient psychological baggage.

I made some obvious mistakes in my college planning. In only applying to the finest schools I left myself no second option. I remember the day the letters came in the mail. There were at least four of them, and they were all thin as hell. I knew what was inside before I opened them. If you were accepted, there was a whole brochure of information to sift through. The envelopes in *my* hand contained one piece of paper: a curt, sterile form letter expressing regret, assuring the rejected party that the competition was stiff, and he could always re-apply at a later time.

In the film *Risky Business,* lightweight Joel, played by a young Tom Cruise, pats Princeton admissions rep Bill Rutherford heartily on the back and says, "Sometimes you just gotta say what the fuck, Bill." Next thing you know, Bill, impressed with Joel's uncanny ability to run a whorehouse out of his parents' home while they're away on vacation, not to mention the fact that the kid has gotten Bill himself laid, changes his tune, offering Joel admission to the coveted Ivy League institution.

Real life didn't work out this way. I threw the rejection letters in the trash and registered at DeAnza, a junior college in Cupertino. Like a degenerate gambler in Vegas whose luck has run out, I accepted my pair of treys, gave up on the prospect of four ladies, pulled up stakes at Mandalay Bay and hopped the next geriatric express shuttle to Laughlin.

We all wind up on the wrong end of a situation at some point in life, by virtue of politics, racism, favoritism or simple bad luck. These, at least, are relatively comforting, out-of-your-own-control justifications for failure—ones which shield you from that dreaded suspicion which gnaws at you during your dark moments: *I didn't deserve it. I wasn't good enough.*

I don't blame anyone or anything for my personal failures and shortcomings, and I don't have a problem sticking by my choices and accepting their consequences. I should have studied harder for my standardized tests. I should have given myself a number of options. I made the choice to shoot for only the top schools in the country, and I came up short. I could have re-applied to those schools the following year, had I really wanted to attend them.

It's easier to blame the system, isn't it? The truth is, most of the time we have our own selves to blame for our failings. We create our own reality through our behavior, attitudes, and willingness or unwillingness to do the extra work necessary to excel. Other people are too busy worrying about their own lives and dilemmas to sit around thinking about how they might thwart or undermine *us*. Yet we're all prone to such narcissistic paranoia. I guess it's just human nature.

THAT'S WHY HE'S THE MANAGER,
AND YOU'RE THE BOX BOY

I began classes at DeAnza Junior College in the fall of 1988. I opted not to continue playing basketball; after dealing with Gray Melton for two years, I was jaded about athletics. Music had become the most important thing in my life. I began studying privately with Don Haas, a respected Bay Area jazz piano teacher. Don was a proponent of the *tough love* school. There were no strokes, no gratuitous pats on the back. Don made me painfully aware of weaknesses in my technical training on the piano. He knew there was no circumventing these problems if I wanted to become a professional.

I worked hard to improve, sometimes practicing eight hours a day. Piano technique never came naturally to me. I have long, double-jointed fingers that bend the wrong way. Certain exercises and passages, even basic ones, were difficult for me. Don was baffled at my understanding of advanced creative concepts, in light of my inability to execute some very rudimentary tasks. Technically speaking, I was an idiot savant… *minus the savant.*

My practice regimen included learning solos from albums, notating them on manuscript paper and playing them verbatim. I would even take bits and pieces of what somebody played and practice them in different keys and over different chord progressions. This was fun for *me*, but probably not too exciting for anyone in earshot. Even Len's patience would wear thin and he'd say, "Anth, could you play something else for a while… like an *actual song?*"

As my confidence improved I started jamming with, or *sitting in* with the bands at a San Jose nightclub called Garden City. The house pianist, a great jazz player named Smith Dobson, had encouraged me for years, allowing me to hover over him at the piano and scrutinize every movement of his fingers. Now Smith started hiring me as a sub. I was only nineteen, and this world-class player thought I was good enough to cover a whole night for him. I'm sure I wasn't the first guy on his list, but his faith that I could handle the gig made me feel good about my commitment to jazz. I got my first taste of dealing with drunks and opinionated jerks while playing at Garden City, too. Any musician who plays professionally knows exactly what I'm talking about.

I recall one guy coming up to me while I was at the piano who said, "You sound alright." I said thanks, the obligatory response to such high praise. "I'm just trying to learn from Smith Dobson." It was a humble enough reply on my part. The guy chuckled out loud, however, and said, "Let's get real. When Smith plays, it sounds like two pianos. When you play, it only sounds like one."

That's the kind of thing people in bars and clubs say freely and without compunction. They have no clue about what it takes to sit there and play an entire evening of music, but they'll be the first to judge you or even belittle your efforts. I got the last word with that guy… when I finished whatever song I was playing, I asked him his name. He said "Gordon." I stood up and announced, "And now, ladies and gentleman, the elegant piano stylings of *Gordon.*" He looked at me like I was nuts.

"You play, right?" I asked. He shook his head no. "I assumed that someone of your vast knowledge must be a pianist himself. Come on, how about a tune!" *Didn't hear a peep out of that guy for the rest of the night.*

I was recommended, on another occasion, by a fine San Jose pianist named Rich Turnoy. Rich had me cover a job for him with an old, square dude named Clay Sergeant. Clay had a large jazz ensemble, or *big band*, as they're called. We were all wearing monkey suits, despite the fact that the gig was outdoors and it was ninety degrees. After a song or two, my portable keyboard started having problems, and my amplifier began making an obnoxious crackling sound. I couldn't figure out what was wrong, so I kept hacking through Clay's lame arrangements. Shit might be blowing up, but *the show must go on*.

The grizzled old bandleader thought I didn't know what I was doing, like I was making the strange noise on *purpose*, and started screaming at me from across the stage. "Play, goddammit, play!" He got real sweaty, turning bright red and looking short of breath, and I feared this might be shaping up to be Clay's final *concert in the park*... the day he would get whisked off to that *big jazz gig in the sky*

"Play the chords, you.... you... goddamn you! What the hell's wrong with you! Comp... comp... comp!!!" He was like Fred C. Dobbs, on the verge of suffering a heat stroke while evading bandits in the Sierra Madre, or Ralph Bellamy getting rudely dismissed by Don Ameche, while having a massive coronary at the end of *Trading Places*. "*Sell... sell... sell!*"

Another time, a local trumpet player named Modesto Briseno hired me to do a two-day run "somewhere in Monterey." Cannery Row, perhaps? Seventeen Mile Drive, perchance? "Somewhere in Monterey" ended up being the infield at Laguna Seca Raceway. *During a race*. I, Modesto, Smith Dobson Jr., and an obscure bassist, whose relationship with me began with him spilling a bowl of stinky clam chowder all over my car keys, were cooped up in a tent, flies everywhere, cars roaring by at two hundred-plus miles per hour as we lumbered through *Satin Doll* and other tired swing turkeys in the blistering summer heat.

The gig didn't pay anything, either. We were supposed to get paid in *trade*, promised tickets to some sort of cruise. Musician's warning: this is always JIVE. Don't play a gig in which the compensation is trade. Also, if you ask how much a gig pays and then hear the words, *Here's the deal*, hang up the phone immediately.

Halfway through my first year of junior college, I decided to drop out and get a day job. Len was less than thrilled. He gave me some cash and said "Good luck, son." Joe Faylor and I, eager to take a stab at living on our own, found an apartment in Sunnyvale and made a go of being roommates. Joe was working at Price Club, a big retail warehouse that sold wholesale goods to the public. I did a brief stint there as well...

One day at Price Club, we ran out of boxes for people's groceries, as was prone to happen, and a customer hassled me to go find him some. I flat-out told him to forget it, demonstrating a desire to please that certainly had me on a fast track to middle management.[32] The guy got angry and bellowed for a supervisor. The supervisor was no older than me. He came over, allowed the very overweight guy to vent, and then assured him he'd get his boxes. As the supervisor hurried off to appease the customer, the lard-ass turned to me and said, *"You see... that's why he's the manager, and you're the box boy."*

My next job was in the payroll department at Lockheed Missiles and Space, a huge military contractor in Silicon Valley. How people can do this kind of work for thirty or forty years is something I'll never understand. My boss was a middle-aged guy named Al, mustached and soft-spoken. He was Big Gay Al, long before *South Park.*

One month of shuffling papers and crunching numbers in a tiny cubicle was enough. I began hanging out with the night shift, running around Lockheed delivering something called Pony Mail. This was more fun than sitting there during the day, learning the intricacies of payroll accounting, which in my estimation must rank among the most boring occupations in the history of humankind. Big Gay Al got wise to me and warned against continuing my defiant participation in Pony Mail delivery. I ignored him and was ultimately called into the head honcho's office. The boss smiled and calmly said, "I hear we're having lots of problems with you, Anthony. I was impressed with your interview, so I'm surprised." I told him I'd try harder, but I had no intention of trying harder. I hated the job.

I was going to quit, but got canned before I had the chance. Big Gay Al called me up and said, "We don't need you to come in anymore." What a relief. I took advantage of my sudden hiatus to visit Uncle Dan, Len's younger brother who lived in the San Diego area. Dan was a huge jazz fan, like Len, and had always encouraged my piano playing. The two brothers had many great stories from their years spent

---

[32] When I look back on the straight gigs I've had, I must concede the following: excluding my noble stab at social work in the late nineties, I have been a relatively mediocre employee.

frequenting jazz clubs in the fifties, when you could hear world class musicians playing seven nights a week in both Southern and Northern California.

There's a ton of good Miles Davis stories out there—many true, others exaggerated or downright apocryphal—but here's one, a great one, that's never been told before, and is entirely true...

Miles Davis had many fans, none more enthusiastic than Len, who preferred the brooding trumpeter's playing to even that of the king of bebop, Charlie Parker. Not only did Len love Miles' playing, but he also dug him personally, and would chat with him at nightclubs here and there, when the opportunity presented itself. Miles had been a boxer in his youth, as had Len, and both shared a love of the sport and its major figures; they would talk about an upcoming fight, and who had the upper hand, or who was the best fighter in a certain weight class... that kind of stuff. The point is, Len loved Miles, and jumped at any chance to hear him perform.

One night, Len went to some club in San Francisco to catch Miles with his quartet. It so happened that before the show, Len found himself having a conversation with the owner of the place.

"It's great that you were able to get Miles to play here. He's sounding as good as ever."

"Yeah, I guess," the owner sighed. "Miles is a pain in the ass to deal with."

"But he's Miles Davis. He's one of the greats. You have to put up with a little bullshit with a guy like Miles. He's under a lot of pressure. He's in the spotlight."

"I don't know if it's worth it, to be honest."

"Oh, come on. Do you know how many people would love to have the one and only Miles Davis performing in their club?"

As Len was championing the cause of his favorite trumpet player, he felt a hand on his shoulder, followed by a firm shove. Someone was pushing him out of the way. Len turned to see who it was, and there was Miles, a scowl on his face as he brushed Len to the side. Miles got in the club owner's face and growled, "Motherfucker, where's my money?!"

I got my chance to see Miles live around 1988 or 1989, when he brought his electric fusion group to the Paul Masson Winery in Saratoga. Miles wasn't really playing shit at that point, barely blowing his trumpet at all. He would play the horn with one hand while he plunked out some simple chords on a Fender Rhodes with the other. There was a funny quote around then, by the famous jazz trumpet player Nat Adderley, who said: "Miles plays trumpet with his right hand and keyboard with his left. And you know what? He ain't sayin' shit with either." It was true. The iconic jazz master was far past his prime (he would only live a few more years, in fact), but as was his trademark throughout his storied career, he always had an amazing band. This one was no different. Kenny Garrett was on saxophone, Kei Akagi on keyboards, and the rest of the lineup was equally strong. I was thrilled to get to see Miles in person, just one time.

Len and I decided to split when Miles exited the stage, the band still playing. As we made our way to the exit, Miles and his handler walked right past us. I'll never forget the moment, because the man had an amazing presence. He was dressed in colorful showman's garb, of course, but it was something much more than that. Miles had very dark, rich skin, and piercing eyes. His aura was huge and undeniable, and I felt it as he walked past us. You knew you were in the presence of something special.

As he passed, Len said "Thanks a lot, Miles." This caught Miles slightly off guard, and I wasn't sure if he was going to blurt out something like "Shut the fuck up!" But no, he looked at us, nodded in thanks and said, "All right." I remember that like it was yesterday, and I always will. Now that I think about it, I've been very lucky to have had at least brief brushes with some of the absolute giants of modern jazz: Miles, Chick Corea, Herbie Hancock, Bobby Hutcherson, Art Farmer, Joe Henderson, Freddie Hubbard, Cedar Walton, Kenny Barron, and others. Many of them aren't with us anymore, sadly.

Getting back to 1990 and my trip to San Diego, Dan wanted to show me the campus of San Diego State University, particularly the music department. I was there for about thirty seconds when I decided I wanted to transfer to SDSU as soon as possible. There were beautiful blonde girls flitting about in tight shorts, the weather was perfect, and the music program was strong and suited to my background. The jazz ensemble had just returned from performing at the Montreaux Jazz Festival in Europe.

I spent countless hours in those developmental years transcribing (copying) the solos and musical ideas of players I admired. I learned a great deal from this process and recommend it to any young musician who wants to play creative music. It not only opens your ear to new sounds but also helps you develop an improvisational vocabulary. Much like language, the ease with which you express yourself musically depends on the depth of your vocabulary. Not all great players endorse transcribing, however. I once told the master pianist Kenny Kirkland that I'd learned one of his recorded solos, note-for-note, from start to finish. He wasn't impressed: "Oh... you copied that?" he said.

Another time, I approached the jazz vibraphone giant Bobby Hutcherson, one of my musical heroes, about publishing a volume of transcriptions of his solos. This was work I had slaved over painstakingly. Hutcherson shook his head. "Nah. Once you play it, it's gone. It belongs to the universe." Okay, Bobby, whatever. Sometimes with great musicians, you ask a concrete question with the hope of gleaning something about the craft, and what you get back is some pseudo-metaphysical bullshit that only confuses you further. The master, having mastered technique to the point that he doesn't think about it anymore, has the luxury of thinking abstractly, of expressing his thoughts through metaphors or oblique language.

Genius is a peculiar phenomenon. I don't toss the word around liberally, as is fashionable in our age of hyperbole. I do find a small number of people to be worthy of the label, though. There is an intangible ingredient that factors into the criteria for real genius. I think it has something to do with originality. For me to consider someone a genius, they have to be an innovator. Geniuses are the rare people who get imitated and emulated because they have forged an artistic identity that is undeniably their own. But it is more than that. A genius has to push the envelope of what is possible in their medium.

I once interviewed jazz bassist Bob Magnusson, a fellow San Diego resident, for an article in a European bass player magazine. He had worked with Sarah Vaughn, the virtuosic jazz singer who many consider the greatest of all time. Sarah Vaughn was most likely a vocal genius. She could do things with her voice that had never been done before.

Magnusson had also done some work with Madonna, so I thought it would be interesting to ask him to contrast the two experiences. He laughed and said, "Working with Sarah was one of the greatest experiences of my life. Next to that, doing a session with Madonna means nothing to me." That's the kind of honesty I appreciate.

One thing to consider about genius is the fact that some artists are able to tap into it for a moment in time, or for a brief period in their careers, but then return to mortality for the remainder of them. Or, in some cases, it's hit and miss throughout an artist's career. I think of the example of Steven Spielberg. In the genius column, I offer:

1. *Duel*. Spielberg's first feature film. A masterpiece. The movie was a one-man performance by Dennis Weaver, struggling against a diabolical truck driver you never actually see. *Duel* has been widely imitated since it was released thirty years ago.

2. *Close Encounters of the Third Kind*. The creativity and vision behind this movie is still staggering today. It also has been copied and borrowed from *ad nauseum*.

3. *Jaws*. The first mega-blockbuster. It changed the way movies were made, and further demonstrated Spielberg's ability to create an anthropomorphic nemesis (a truck in *Duel*, a shark in this case) and build an entire film around it.

4. *Raiders of the Lost Ark*. The avatar of all comic book movies. If it's possible to make a genius action/adventure film, this is it.

Spielberg's work is always technically excellent, but that certain, unmistakable magic isn't always there. What about *Jurassic Park*, you say? *Jurassic Park* was a blockbuster, but far from a great film, in my opinion; and it's hard to believe the director who brought us *Close Encounters* is also responsible for *Jurassic Park: The Lost World*. Especially when you consider a scene like the one where the daughter of Dr. Ian Malcolm, played by Jeff Goldblum, swings from a beam and kicks a velociraptor in the head, sending it flying from a building. This highly plausible event is followed by the quip, "And you got cut from the gymnastics team?" One wonders if Spielberg broke out his Ouija board and summoned the ghost of Groucho Marx to help fine- tune the script's dialogue. How about *Saving Private Ryan*, you say? I found the plot a tad far-fetched, myself.[33]

Doesn't it seem that in many cases an artist's best work is their early stuff? Prince's *Purple Rain* is a work of genius. Has he matched it in

---

[33] The actor that played the elderly Private Ryan, Harrison Young, turned up as a character in Rob Zombie's twisted *House of a Thousand Corpses*. In the director's commentary, right after the character gets skinned and turned into a disgusting body suit, Zombie proclaims, "We finally did what nobody else could... we killed Private Ryan!"

the last fifteen years? No, probably not. Pearl Jam's first album, *Ten?* Pretty brilliant. Since then, nothing even close.

You see this with actors, also. Robert DeNiro and Al Pacino, for example, cemented their legacies with the work they did in their thirties and forties. Some would argue that the pair of them have been reduced in recent years to playing caricatures of themselves. Is it really the same guy in both *Taxi Driver* and *Godsend?* Is it the same guy in classics like *Serpico* and *Scarface* that later showed up in *Gigli* and *The Devil's Advocate?*

Among my musical friends and associates over the years, there are a few that stand out as geniuses. Fred Hersch is one artist I feel is worthy of the distinction. I first met Fred, an internationally respected jazz pianist who lives in New York City, when he was touring the West Coast with saxophonist Jane Ira Bloom, in the late eighties. We kept in touch via phone and mail, but it wasn't until the mid-nineties that I earned Fred's respect on a musical level; I recorded a Fred Hersch tribute album, playing his original compositions along with several of my own—songs crafted in the spirit of his music.

Fred was moved by the gesture, sincerely liked the album, which he kindly said was better than some first efforts on major labels, and we became friends from that point on. He would send me his new albums, and I'd send him my music also. Occasionally, we'd meet up for lunch when his travels brought him out west, or me out east.

Having a close relationship with an individual of such immense talent has been an important experience for me, providing me insight into the ingredients and intricacies of greatness. Fred is a jazz musician who never got distracted by the peripheral excesses of the entertainment industry. He's always directed his energies toward being a quality artist and making great music, period. Pop fads and trends have come and gone, as they will, but Fred continues to produce beautiful albums and push himself in new directions.

Guys like Fred can also fuel one's self-doubt. Back in the forties and fifties, the era when jazz thrived most in America, great pianists like Bud Powell, Art Tatum, Oscar Peterson and Bill Evans were famous for scaring more than a few lesser piano players into giving up the ghost and finding *real* jobs. While I never wanted to quit playing altogether, I've certainly had times when I harbored feelings of inferiority when listening to the greats.

This is a natural feeling to experience for anyone who is sensitive about what they're doing, but to overindulge it is to miss the whole point of jazz, as well as the creative process itself, which is to develop your own identity. The artists we celebrate, study and analyze are the ones who accomplished this, not those who were carbon copies of someone else. Even a guy like Ornette Coleman, whose saxophone playing and composing were dismissed and ridiculed by critics, fans and other musicians for decades, ultimately emerged as a heroic, progressive figure in the evolution of improvisational music, because he followed his own path and had the courage to be unique.

At some point, you realize you are never going to be Fred Hersch, Herbie Hancock or any of the other greats you admire. You will have to look for your own thing. This is scary, because there are no guarantees the search will yield something the world likes or wants. Still, this is the cross you must bear if you want to be a creative artist.

The majority of us are not geniuses. We rely on hard work and perseverance. I'm blessed with a pretty good ear for music, but beyond that I don't feel I possess any innate, extraordinary musical gifts. If I have a gift, I think it's imagination. Composing has never been a struggle. I don't remember ever suffering writer's block. When I get into the *right brain zone,* I can stay focused for many hours. I don't think about food or anything else. There have been times when I've written the better part of several songs in one day. One of the secrets is that I don't allow myself to judge what I'm creating, while I'm creating it. When I go back to evaluate the work later, some of it will be good and some of it won't, and hopefully I'll know the difference.

I inherited this instinct from my mother Anne. It's a certain reckless creative abandon, an ability to just *go* without over-thinking. I offer two thoughts to support this approach: First, you get better just by doing something, so do it as much as possible. The process of writing five bad songs hones your chops for the great one you're on the verge of discovering. Second, it's a numbers game. Crank out as much work as you can, and some of it just might have value. The more mature you become in your craft, the quicker you get at determining what's good and what goes in the trash bin.

Prince, who I mentioned before, is a great example of this; nobody in pop music has been more prolific than the diminutive, reclusive showman from Minneapolis. The sheer volume of Prince's songwriting catalogue is the stuff of legend. Much of it remains in a "vault," apparently, waiting for its day in the sun. Having listened to and also studied quite a bit of his music over the years, I'd have to say the range of quality in his songs is pretty wide. There are some that are inarguably brilliant, so much so that they've had a lasting impact on pop music as a whole. But there are also a number of his tunes that go nowhere, lyrically or musically, and are thus forgettable. When you've cranked out as many albums as Prince has, you're not going to hit the bull's eye every time. I imagine that he would disagree about which songs are his best. Some of the ones I think are average might be among his favorites, and a few I think are pure genius are ones he might have hammered out in twenty minutes. I also think Prince — although I am in no way comparing myself to him, to be clear — shares my approach to writing: *write, write, write… crank it out, go with the flow, let it rip… come back and evaluate later.*

Songwriting is a very personal process. I remember an interview with Sting years back, in which he explained that he can't collaborate well with other writers, because the lyrics, as well as the process as a whole, are such a personal thing for him. I read a much more recent Sting interview in which he also argued, quite interestingly, that pop songwriting is not about creating as much as collating. Re-arranging what already exists. He went on to question the originality of two of his biggest hits, *Roxanne* and *Every Breath You Take.* If Sting is a collator rather than a creator, it must be said that he is among the best collators in the history of popular music.

Getting back to the notion of good and bad in the arts, I will argue that *good* is a highly subjective term. It's hard to argue that something isn't good. If it has even a tiny kernel of artistic value, and somebody out there likes it, then who's to say it isn't *good?* It's good to *them.* To deny this is to veer into the territory of artistic snobbery. Some people have simple taste, and that's fine. Often, simplicity is more effective than complexity. Why does everyone rave about the Beatles as a timeless, classic group? Because above all else, their music is *simple.* The songs, especially the early stuff, don't challenge your intellect. They're simple, catchy, accessible and fun; and that's what pop culture is all about. The Beatles did push the envelope as they evolved, and their later work was more compelling. *Revolver,* for example, was way ahead of its time. The Beatles, thus, are an example of a group enjoying massive, unparalleled success while also breaking some new ground.

Bad is also a highly subjective term. When I say something is *bad,* I'm saying I don't feel it has artistic merit or substance. When someone else, who might not have as developed an ear, says something is bad, it's perhaps for the simple reason that it grates on their nerves, or isn't sufficiently melodic. Using these criteria, landmark albums like Miles

Davis's *Bitches Brew* and John Coltrane's *Ascension* could be considered *bad* — in fact, with pleasantness and harmoniousness as your firm barometers, you could even make a case that all Twentieth Century classical music is crap.[34] When it comes to artistic criticism, good and bad are broad terms that need to be qualified and defined.

Unlike the general (and hopelessly subjective) notions of good and bad, the idea of *greatness* is not hinged upon the tastes of the individual. There is inherent objectivity in the perception and recognition of greatness. For someone to be great, their contribution must be undeniable. They must have proven it over and over again, maintaining a level of excellence that, to large extent, defies criticism. In sports, nobody questions Magic Johnson, Joe Montana or Wayne Gretsky's legacies. In the thespian world, you will never hear a single soul second-guess Laurence Olivier, Meryl Streep or Marlon Brando. Within the annals of timeless literary fiction, the talents of William Faulkner or John Steinbeck are not argued, and the jury's in on the philosophical and scientific contributions of Socrates, DaVinci, Darwin and Einstein. Why? These individuals elevated their chosen discipline, and they did it over and over again. They were great, end of story.

---

[34] Of course, it would be an absurd, totally misguided case.

SORRY IF THE HOUSE
SMELLS LIKE BARBECUE

Around 1988, Len met a guy named Olan Jarvis. Olan had wandered into Garden City nightclub one night, announcing that he was a trumpet player from Texas. He was around fifty, talked with a thick southern accent, was mostly bald on top with long wavy strands on the side and back, and was short and slight of build. Olan talked a mean game, citing associations with numerous big names from the jazz world. He seemed to have an impressive resume, particularly for someone living out of an old, beat up car in the Garden City parking lot. Len struck up a friendship with Olan, and invited him to stay at our house until he could land on his feet.

Olan had some catchphrases that still work their way into family conversation, many years later. For example, he took a liking to our cat, Bobby.[35] Every time Bobby strutted by, Olan would exclaim,

---

[35] Named after vibraphone great Bobby Hutcherson, since the little guy liked to hang out underneath Len's vibraphone while one of us was playing it. Len approached the jazz giant one night at Garden City to inform him of the

"Baaaaaaad Bob-by." Bobby was a good pet, affectionate when he felt like it, but Bobby didn't take any crap. You could horse around with him a little, but sooner or later he would let you know that playtime was over. *The fun and games are done. Leave me alone now.* You could either heed Bobby's warning or prepare for battle. If you jerked around with him beyond this point, you were going to pay the price. Like Sugar Ray Leonard, you might outlast him, but you were never going to match his sheer *speed.*

For all his southern, scholarly wisdom, Olan couldn't grasp this simple dynamic. One evening, after lubing up on a healthy taste of generic Stolichnaya, the old Texan decided to test Bobby's limits. Len and I were watching intently. Instead of intervening we decided to let nature take its course. The laws of the jungle will not be denied. Bobby had the gleam in his eye—the gleam of a wrath to be unleashed in full. *Bad shit was about to happen.*

Len warned Olan to back off. I had an old scar on my nose from such miscalculations, and also admonished the liquored vagabond against further teasing of the animal. Olan ignored us and continued waving his arm in direct striking distance. WHAM! Bobby nailed him with a quick right cross. Blood trickled from Olan's trembling hand. Len and I shrugged our shoulders, assuming Olan had learned his lesson and would walk away. But no… Olan held his ground, that bloody hand quivering as the evening breeze blew across Bowers Park and in through the family room window. Bobby lashed out again, this time with a combination. Olan's funky red sweater sleeve was shredded, and his hand and arm were now bleeding in several places. "Get out of there, Olan!" Len shouted, now genuinely concerned. "You can't pull on Wilson… er, Bobby! He's too fast!"[36]

"That's alright, Zoot,"[37] Olan calmly responded. "He can't hurt me." Like a Great White after the first taste of flesh, Bobby transformed into a bloodthirsty mini-tiger, lunging savagely at our houseguest, who

---

honorary christening, and Hutcherson responded with stony silence. Perhaps this slap in the face, coupled with my grandfather Arwin's lackluster reaction to Len's announcement of naming me Anthony Arwin Smith, back in 1969, deterred Len from further attempts to celebrate individuals through this particular method of veneration.

[36] Olan was no Shane.

[37] Olan nicknamed Len "Zoot," after jazz saxophonist Zoot Sims.

stood there taking punishing blow after blow, the vodka coursing through his veins, numbing the pain. When it was all done, Olan crumpled into a chair, picking at his wounds… fucked up. All he could mutter was "Baaaaad Bob-by, baaaaaad Bob-by."

Olan's tall tales were generally unfounded in truth. He liked to boast about how Freddie Hubbard, the legendary jazz trumpeter, had tried to hustle his wife right in front of him, years earlier in Texas. Len and I dismissed this as jive, along with his many other ridiculous stories. Once in a blue moon, however, Olan would prove you wrong…

One night, Olan, Todd Poyner and I drove up to Oakland to hear Joe Henderson, Cedar Walton and Freddie Hubbard play at Kimball's East. The whole ride up there, Olan kept saying, "Hey A, when Freddie sees us, watch what he says to me. He'll say, 'Don't blame me, man, don't blame me.'" I knew there was no way Freddie Hubbard was even going to recognize this clown, much less remember some drunken instance years ago when he'd hit on the guy's wife.

Freddie showed up late for the gig, something that was not a departure from his shaky reputation over the years. Afterwards, Olan somehow got us all backstage. First, we approached Joe Henderson, who did in fact recognize Olan. Was he interested in having a conversation, in catching up? Hardly. Olan jabbered at the docile saxophone master, as Todd and I lurked nearby, hands awkwardly jammed in our pockets. All old Joe would say was, "Yeah, okay… okay, man… yeah."

Then we headed down the hall toward Freddie's dressing room. When we walked through the door, we might as well have been wearing white, hooded robes and carrying little burning crosses. A half-dozen militant-looking, large black dudes looked at us like, *What the fuck?* I thought we were about to become Reginald Dennys of the jazz world, but Freddie took one look at Olan, and what do you think he said? "Don't blame me, Olan. Don't blame me." Olan grinned over at me and Todd and proudly proclaimed, "Baaaaaaad Fred-die." Having one of the world's great jazz trumpeters come on to his wife, once upon a time, had apparently been quite an honor for Olan.

Aside from his connections in the jazz world, Olan fancied himself the consummate ladies' man. He had a habit of likening a particular woman's charms to foods associated with her ethnicity. If an attractive Asian lady walked by, Olan would turn to you and say, "I'd like to get me some of that sweet n' sour, Zoot." One time, Len and I were heading on a short vacation, and Olan bragged that he was going to bed a certain black woman while we were gone. When we returned, he greeted us with, "Hey A, Zoot… Sorry if the house smells like barbecue."

"Ahh, that's bullshit, Olan," Len shot back. There was no way he had lured some chick back to the house while we were gone.

After a while, two things were clear about the Texan. One, his amusing tendency to stretch the truth was not so amusing anymore. You began to wonder if you could believe anything he said; he exhibited the behavior of a compulsive liar. Second, Olan was a serious alcoholic who needed help. His room was littered with empty vodka bottles, and he would begin shaking if he didn't down several Screwdrivers every evening.

One day Olan announced that he was up for a Pulitzer Prize in literature. Len and I knew he'd been a college professor for many years, but this was an outlandish claim. He'd shown us some original poetry one time, which, though pretty good, we doubted he'd written himself. When we asked to see his Pulitzer nomination letter, Olan told us he'd "thrown it away." That's not the kind of thing you just throw away. A couple nights later at Garden City, a local pianist named Martan Mann stopped his set when Olan walked in. News of Olan's scholarly accomplishments had spread, so Martan announced into the microphone, "Ladies and gentlemen, we have in our presence a Pulitzer Prize candidate in literature, the honorable Dr. Olan Jarvis." The place erupted in applause.

At the set break, Len, taking a certain pleasure in debunking such a load of B.S., approached the piano and quietly took the wind out of Martan's sails. "Hey Martan, I'm sorry to break it to you, but that Pulitzer prize thing is bullshit. There's no nomination, no letter. Olan made it up." Martan was furious. He yelled at Len, "Why didn't you tell me before I announced it?!" Len just shrugged as if to say, "You're the one that fell for it."

The Garden City scene was as much social as it was musical. There were more than a couple single, middle-aged female regulars. Olan came into the house one night and told me and Len, "I met a little dumplin' tonight." Her name was Ann Cummings. She would get up and sing sometimes, and Len had seen her in there on occasion. Olan recounted a conversation he and Ann had at some point: "You know, I think you like me," he'd told her. According to Olan, Ann had blushed and replied, "Big time."

Ann quickly tired of Olan's act, and wound up commiserating with Len about the situation. This, of course, is always a good ice breaker in itself. Soon Len was seeing Ann, who emphatically denied the "big time" line.

I inherited a strong sense of loyalty from Len. If you're in the inner circle of trust, we'll fight for you. If you cross us, adios! Len revealed this characteristic one day when he and Ann were discussing the fate of Bad Bobby. Len was asking how Bobby would fit into their plans, when Ann nonchalantly said, "I don't care about that cat." Without batting an eye, Len shot back, "Alright, Annie. We can just call it quits. He matters to *me*." Ann, shocked, swiftly retracted the statement. The man was loyal to his cat, and nobody was gonna mess with that, not even his *little dumplin'*. Olan wound up hightailing it back to Texas, his West Coast support group fed up with his duplicitous antics. Nobody knows what happened to him. Len and Ann got married, thanks at least in small part to her rejuvenated interest in bad Bobby's future.[38]

---

[38] Kind of a funny coincidence that both Len's wives would be named Ann(e).

I'M SURE YOU REALLY WANNA HEAR *ME* PLAY, BENNY

I decided to sell my trumpet in order to pay for studio time, so I could record some pop songs I'd written. One of them was called *Writing for the Radio*, and was about a guy trying to reach his old girlfriend by getting his song on the radio. I didn't have an ex-girlfriend I was trying to reach, but I was definitely trying to get my song on the radio. My cousin Bill Haller was working for M.C.A. Records in L.A., and had heard some of my songs. He liked *Writing for the Radio* and a few others. "The singing totally sucks," he said, "but there's some good writing there." He was right about the singing.

I met Tom Ford, an engineer with a recording studio in San Mateo, and started working with him. I recorded six or seven songs, including one called *You Can Do Better Than That*, which I swear should have been on a Paula Abdul record. Another was called *Into You*, a Gloria Estafan-inspired ballad with a strong hook and a nice vocal performance by Anita Ochoa, a girl I was working with in a band called Flashpoint.

The leader of Flashpoint was a Milquetoast guy named Jesse. We rehearsed at his Mom's house. Jesse wasn't a kid — probably in his mid-thirties. This was long before *The Wedding Singer*, but the band could have provided the movie's inspiration. Jesse hired this male vocalist who was a real bullshit artist. The guy had all the nerve in the world, but no chops. He sang the Bobby Brown song *Every Little Step* with strained affectation, so bad it was embarrassing to endure. I knew the guy couldn't sing a lick, but I didn't say anything; I was the youngest, greenest member of the band. Eventually, some guitar player we were auditioning had the gumption to say, "I like the band, but this guy can't sing. Get another singer and I'll do the gig." Right in front of him.

My cousin Bill liked my song *Intuiton.* He agreed to shop it, along with *Into You*, to MCA for a publishing deal. *Intuition* was sung by a tall, androgynous woman with bleached white hair, whom I'd met through Tom. I don't remember her name, but I remember her bragging about working with Narada Michael Walden, the big-time producer who'd put Whitney Houston and Mariah Carey on the map. One night, Tom was joking about how Aretha Franklin, despite her obvious legacy, was now a major has-been. It so happened that Aretha was this woman's idol — without saying anything, she just packed up her stuff and bailed. I never saw her again. Good thing she'd already finished the track!

MCA passed on my songs, but Anne encouraged me to keep going. She loved my demo and told me I was "going to make it." She always believed in my songwriting ability. Tom hooked me up with a gig producing a track for some aspiring R&B artist, a Filipino girl with a black manager named Isaac. Isaac came across as a smooth, well-traveled music industry veteran. About halfway through the production, Tom informed me that Isaac hadn't paid us a dime. I told Tom to collect before we continued, but he begged me to finish the song, assuring me he'd get the money. Len warned me not to do it, that his guy was playing us, but I went ahead out of loyalty to Tom. Then, Tom did a dumb thing. He gave the finished master recording to Isaac before he'd come up with the money. Isaac stopped returning calls, and never came through with the dough. It was the first time I got stiffed in my music career, but it certainly wouldn't be the last.

Len sat me down to give me some advice: Keep doing music, but get something else, a back-up. The arts are too difficult to rely on exclusively for your livelihood. I respected what he was saying, but I'd made up my mind to be a full-time musician. I didn't need a safety net. I was going to make it. Sensing my passion and my resolve, Len finally said, "Well, son, you probably won't ever make very much money." Who cares about money at eighteen?

One of life's cruel jokes is the fact that some of the most defining decisions you make in your entire life occur by fifteen. A friend of mine once said, "I was just a naive kid. I picked up a trombone and nobody warned me. Nobody said anything. How was I supposed to know?" We gravitate toward certain pursuits early in life, often just because it's fun and fulfilling. But we don't realize we might be stuck doing it for fifty years! Yeah, yeah, you can always change careers… people say that, and you read it in magazines. But can you, really? When you've spent your teens and twenties, perhaps even your thirties, building up a certain skill set through education and life experience, can you just stop doing it one day and start doing something entirely different? It sounds refreshing, but does anyone actually do it?

I was splitting my time between jazz and pop music. I assumed I'd eventually settle into one niche or the other, but here I am, two decades later, still riding that fence. In the late eighties, the Bay Area was a great place to catch world-class jazz artists on tour. I heard the McCoy Tyner Trio, Oscar Peterson, Horace Silver, Marcus Roberts, Elaine Elias, and many others. Seeing Chick Corea's Akoustic Band at Yoshi's had a particular impact on me. Chick's incredible playing, along with that of bassist John Patittuci and drummer Dave Weckl, blew me away. When Chick exited the stage, I extended my hand to shake his. He stopped and looked me in the eye, then reached out and grabbed my hand, saying "Thanks, man." I'll never forget that.

Another night, I went to catch piano legend Herbie Hancock, at the opening of a new club called Kimball's East. As I stood in the lobby looking at promotional posters, I felt a hand on my shoulder. I turned around, and it was Herbie. There I was, face to face with the bespectacled giant of jazz. Looking back, I wonder how I had the dough to attend all those concerts by famous jazz musicians. Oh yeah, it's coming back to me now… *Thanks, Len.*

There was a jazz club in Santa Cruz called the Kuumbwa Center. There, I caught Art Blakey and the Jazz Messengers, who were featuring a baby-faced pianist named Benny Green. Halfway through the set, Benny played an unaccompanied medley of songs, showcasing his virtuosity on the instrument. I approached him after the set to pay my respects. The first question I asked was how old he was.

"Twenty-five," Benny said. "How old are you?"

"Nineteen."

"You look older than me," he joked. We had a nice conversation about piano players we liked, and then I said goodbye, shaking hands and thanking him again for his music. His hands were soft and pale, like he'd never done anything with them other than play the piano. As I was about to walk off, I threw in: "Hope to hear you again sometime soon."

"I hope to hear you too," Benny said with utmost sincerity. For some reason, rather than just say "Okay, great," I did a stupid thing. I laughed. Not a gracious, humble laugh, but a mocking, insolent one. *I'm sure you really wanna hear ME play, Benny.* He stared at me, shocked. I walked away, still snickering. When I got to the door, I took one last look back at him—he was still staring me down in disbelief. He was genuinely *hurt.* He'd taken the time to talk to a young, aspiring pianist, and was rewarded by having the kid laugh in his face.

I can't say why I laughed. I was probably so insecure about my own playing that the prospect of sitting down to play for Benny Green seemed like a joke. Whatever my motivation, I felt terrible about it for a long time. It makes me uncomfortable to think about to this day. When I met Benny again several years later, he didn't remember the incident.

The following week, a trumpet player friend named Todd drove with me up to San Francisco to see Art Blakey play again. After the concert, Todd and I walked back to the parking lot to discover that his car was locked inside for the night. A cop drove by and said, "I advise you to get out of this area as quickly as possible." We took a cab to a hotel, opting to share a room until we could get his car in the morning. The desk clerk gave us a wink... *You two sweethearts have a good time, now.* We were like, "No, man... our car got locked in a parking lot." *Of course it did, sugar.* Todd and I were forced to share a queen bed, and found ourselves in an awkward *Planes, Trains and Automobiles* moment, praying that each other's hands were wedged between two pillows, not something else.[39]

---

[39] My hand was in fact wedged between two pillows…but Steve Martin's character, Neal Page, was not so lucky.

DEAD PEOPLE'S MUSIC

The first major hurdle of my adult life appeared right after I moved to San Diego. I developed an acute anxiety disorder. I'd experienced some minor heart palpitations in Northern California, but the condition became aggravated once I relocated. Somehow, I believed I was going to die; have a heart attack, specifically. Maybe a month after moving into student housing on the campus of San Diego State, I had a major panic attack inside a record store. The manager, following *how to avoid a lawsuit* corporate protocol, called an ambulance immediately. I didn't feel like I needed to be hospitalized, but I was freaked out and nervous, so I waited. The ambulance came roaring into the shopping complex. Two paramedics stormed in, grabbed me and shuttled me away to Alvarado Hospital. As we flew down College Avenue toward the freeway, my blood pressure shot up further. One of the guys told me to "Hold on." It was a weird feeling, for sure.

When I made it to the hospital, a doctor hooked me up to an EKG machine to make sure my heart was okay. I was fine, he said. It was all in my head. I was told I had an anxiety disorder. Since I was shaken up by the incident, the doctor recommended I check into a psychiatric hospital for a few days. I reluctantly agreed.

The psych ward at Alvarado Hospital bore resemblance to Ken Kesey's colorful microcosm in *One Flew Over the Cuckoo's Nest*. The nurses were uptight squares, the patients were basket cases. Like Jack Nicholson's character in the film, I didn't believe I needed to be there. My mind was fine. With anxiety disorders, you convince yourself there is something *physically* wrong with you, something even medical experts cannot detect, and you truly believe you are in danger of dying. If you're really caught up in it, even a clean EKG reading isn't going to alleviate your fear.

I received phone calls and visits from family and friends. It was comforting to know people cared, even if they couldn't understand what I was going through. This was 1990, when anxiety disorders still suffered a stigma of illegitimacy. Now, all you have to do is say the words *panic attack* and you're given a lifetime supply of Prozac, and flown out to L.A. for a guest spot on Dr. Phil.

A pair of girls from school came to visit me in the hospital, and I was romantically interested in both of them. A gay male nurse walked into my room and caught me kissing one of the girls. He reprimanded me, when I thought I had a high five coming. Later, the other girl came for a visit. She was supportive and nice, but I'd made my decision; I was going with Contestant Number One. There I was, having panic attacks, breakin' hearts on the funny farm.

I attribute the anxiety disorder to a Type A personality. Being the firstborn child only reinforced what I believe to be a genetic predisposition. Growing up, my parents not only expected me to be active and productive—they expected me to excel. The relentless drive didn't come from them, however. I was born with it. I've never been someone to sit around doing nothing, even when I was a little kid. I've always spent the majority of my free time trying to make something happen, as opposed to being the kind of person who kicks back and takes it as it comes. I don't like to take it as it comes. This implies that your destiny is not in your own hands, and I believe it mostly is. I'm driven, and as a result, I'm too hard on myself sometimes; but I'd rather be too hard on myself than not hard enough. The latter is synonymous with mediocrity.

When I first arrived in San Diego, the landscape of popular American music was dramatically changing. The innocent, upbeat kitsch of George Michael's pop eighties was giving way to rawer, angst-driven idioms like grunge rock and hip-hop. Groups like Public Enemy, N.W.A., Digable Planets, Arrested Development, A Tribe Called Quest, Snoop Dogg, Pearl Jam, Soundgarden, Nirvana, Alice and Chains, Stone Temple Pilots, the Red Hot Chili Peppers, Living Colour, Sublime, Nine Inch Nails, and Metallica were at the vanguard of this transformation. The more urgent music and gritty lyrical content of these groups created a new milieu in which pop music was now evaluated socio-culturally, rather than on the merits of lighthearted, musical catchiness. After the innocent abandon of the eighties, this was a major departure.

The grunge movement, for example, was an outgrowth of Generation X nihilism, and a reaction against the ridiculous hair metal bands (Poison, Ratt, Def Leppard, etc.) and primped, preening pop acts that preceded it.[40] Grunge's point-blank examination of psychological and environmental encroachments upon the psyche of the modern individual was, in some ways, a refreshing departure from the shameless hedonism and trite party sentiments of all the vapid hair bands. Let's face it, as spokesmen for a generation, Eddie Vedder and Kurt Cobain had more interesting matters to discuss than Brett Michaels and Joe Elliot. The former were exploring the dark recesses of their tortured psyches, asking difficult existential questions, while the latter were more or less saying, "Hey bro, let's go score some drugs and hustle some pussy."

If grunge superseded hair metal, then new, edgier rap and hip-hop artists had the same effect on the British-influenced pop of the preceding decade. The unsentimental grittiness of Ice Tea and Dr. Dre evoked a sense of urgency and urban realism that made the juvenile longings of the Thompson Twins, Howard Jones and Duran Duran seem altogether banal.

On purely musical terms, however, I believe, as I have mentioned, that things went downhill in the nineties. The artists of the eighties

---

[40] Try saying that five times in a row, really fast!

concerned themselves with melody, harmony, song structure, and singing. Their collective message might not have been ultra-deep, but they were more musically interesting than what followed.

The audition seemed to go okay. I played a couple songs, sight-read some music, picked out a few chord voicings, and that was it. The faculty thanked me and I left without further ado. Within a couple days, there was a buzz around the music building that some new guy had really made an impression at the auditions. Though I found it hard to believe, they were talking about me. The faculty had placed me in both the top ensemble and top combo for the upcoming semester.

I felt proud. I had won something. Being picked as the top guy at the school, as a new student nonetheless, was an accomplishment that offset the lingering disappointment of being rejected by all those colleges a couple years earlier.

When the jazz ensemble convened for the first time, the other twenty band members eyed me, curious to see if I could live up to the hype. The first piece we rehearsed began with a piano solo. Bill Yeager, the ensemble director, flashed me a look that said: *Let's see what you got, kid.* I represented myself well, confirming the positive buzz. My reputation in San Diego was off to a good start.

At San Diego State, I felt like I'd found my place—an environment that was challenging and also creatively rewarding. I was pursuing both jazz and classical music, a decision met with some resistance by my teachers. The classical camp looked down on jazz as a less refined musical idiom, and the jazz camp referred to the classical world as *dead people's music*. I would eventually narrow my focus to jazz, but I stuck to my guns and juggled both styles during my first two years at SDSU.

Rick Helzer, my jazz piano teacher, became a good friend and source of musical inspiration. He'd visited me in the hospital, offering spiritual guidance as an extension of his devout Christian faith. Rick asked me to consider becoming Born Again, and I did think it over. One day, I was invited to participate in a small prayer group in his office. The ritual consisted of each person mustering an impromptu supplication to the Big Guy Upstairs, citing Scripture while baring the contents of his soul. After a pair of eloquent offerings by Rick and a fellow student, brimming with astute biblical references and inspired personal testimony, it was my turn. I was out of my element. I didn't have the theological chops to hang with these Born Again champs. My strained attempt came across like a blurb from a Beavis and Butthead episode. *Uhhhh, Jesus… huh-huh… you, like, do some cool stuff, and uh…*

like, make me a tool of your, uh… huh-huh, huh-huh… I said tool." My awkward appeal went over like a silent-but-deadly squeaker in Sunday school.

When it came down to it, I just wasn't ready to put a moratorium on the carefree whims enjoyed by a twenty year-old, away from home for the first time. I hadn't experienced life yet. Once you've dissipated yourself into a state of moral bankruptcy, *then* it's time to dip your head in the water. I wasn't planning to ever sink to that quagmire. Luckily, Rick wasn't like the religious zealots of various faiths who impose their beliefs on anyone who will listen (and even those who are not listening). He just put it out there and allowed me to decide for myself. Furthermore, when it seemed I wasn't going to follow that spiritual path, he continued to be my friend.

I was raised Catholic, but found that my assumptions were challenged when I arrived at an institution of higher learning. I wrote a song about this awakening, titled *A Fashion of Belief*. The lyrics reflected the new philosophical ideas I was being exposed to, mainly those of Sartre, Nietsche and Freud:

It was a logical progression
From acceptance on to doubt
Youth spent under a shroud of
Conflicting truths and ideologies
The more we learned the less we knew
As logic and science
Became dark clouds looming over the easy landscape of faith

I spent countless nights during that first year at SDSU holed up in a practice cubicle, hammering out exercises and songs on the student grand pianos. I would hear the faint sounds of kids partying at one of the nearby fraternity houses or sororities. Sometimes I wanted to join them—slug down beer, engage in raspy drunken exhortations, try to get lucky—but I was completely consumed by music. I sacrificed sleep, neglected social opportunities and shirked my academic responsibilities in the quest for greater mastery of the piano.

My first college roommate, Doug Dickstein, was a bright kid from New Jersey. He wanted to be the next Quentin Tarantino. He had a good sense of humor, and we got along well. Our next door neighbor Pat Buchelli was also a cool guy. One night, the three of us rounded up a handful of dorm dudes for a trip down to Tijuana. Being a junior transfer and a couple years older, I figured I would be the voice of reason, the enforcer of moderation; a mature counterbalance to these green college bucks. This noble stance lasted for about twenty minutes.

As we walked across the border, I looked down in the dirt and spotted a dollar bill. When I picked it up, it was not George Washington's stoic mug staring back at me. It was a studious Ben Franklin's. The combination of being eighteen, drunk, and wandering aimlessly in a Third World country was not a fortuitous one. In a gesture of considerable generosity, I led the boys to a strip club (read: brothel) and treated each of them to a poke at the proverbial piñata. We were lined up in restaurant-style booths, giving the impression that the place had been some kind of a restaurant before being converted to a den of iniquity.

To cap a lovely evening, the guys and I decided to chant the chorus of Bruce Springsteen's *Born in the U.S.A.,* as we strode past pissed-off *federales* en route back to the border. What I didn't realize is that there is a mandatory Mexican tax imposed on stupid-ass American teenagers, especially ones playing the role of patriotic vocalists. This tax amounts to *whatever you have left in your wallet.*

Rick's mini-campaign to convert me to Christian fundamentalism might not have worked out, but the piano lessons were very productive. He expanded my musical palette by introducing me to the concepts of Ornette Coleman, sixties-era Miles Davis, Anthony Braxton, and others associated with post-bebop and the avant garde movement. Rick also directed Combo #1, comprised of the school's best players, including myself. It was a very good band, everyone pushing each other to improve. The repertoire was difficult, as Rick was happier to see his students struggling with complex music than coasting over basic blues chord changes. The guys in that group all became my personal friends, and I would continue to work with some of them in professional situations for years to come.

Kevin Delgado, the bass player in Combo #1, invited me to join a Latin jazz group he was forming outside of school. Koro Libre featured a line-up of top notch local players, including drummer Mark Lamsen and percussionist Tommy Aros, who was in a popular smooth jazz group of that time, Fattburger. Tommy also toured the world with pop singer Luis Miguel, and told stories of packed stadiums in South America. The music was all based on complex Latin and Brazilian rhythms, and the specificity of the piano parts forced me to grow as a player. There was a great deal of freedom when it was time to solo, but when comping (providing chords and rhythms) for other instruments, there were certain things you had to do in order to be stylistically accurate, and to thus treat the music with integrity. The instruments in the rhythm section—piano, bass, drums and percussion—all fit together like pieces of a puzzle. Unlike in some other styles, the drums and percussion typically played very syncopated, polyrhythmic grooves, which meant you couldn't fall back on those instruments as a *crutch* to support or correct your personal time feel. You had to have a rock solid sense of time and rhythm on your own, or you would throw off the rest of the band, exposing yourself as a weak link. It was an honor to be in Koro Libre, and another affirmation that my hard work was paying off.

Koro Libre played steadily at a downtown San Diego club called Croce's. Named after the late singer/songwriter Jim Croce, and owned and managed by his widow, Ingrid, Croce's offered live music seven nights a week, and was a fixture of the downtown scene. Some local musicians resented Ingrid Croce, a couple going so far as to refuse to play there. The feeling (among some) was that she didn't pay well enough, and had little loyalty to local musicians. The latter wasn't true—pianist Shep Myers, a friend of mine although he was much older, had kept his steady weekly gig at Croce's for years. Ingrid, at that time, was investing in the development of her son, A.J. Croce, who was attempting a national career as a pianist/singer in the Harry Connick, Jr. style, only more bluesy. My personal experiences with Ingrid Croce were favorable. She was always cordial, and seemed to be a smart business owner.

Across the street from Croce's, there was another nightclub—I don't remember its name. One day, Glen Fisher hired me and some other musicians to show up at this place for an all-day movie shoot. It turned out the film was a made-for-television account of the Menendez Brothers story: *Menendez: A Killing in Beverly Hills.* Lyle and Erik Menendez shot their parents to death with a shotgun in 1989. Their father, a music industry executive named Jose, was played in the film by Edward James Olmos. Sure enough, when I walked in for the shoot, there was Olmos, the mustached Hispanic actor perhaps best known for playing inspirational schoolteacher Jaime Escalante in *Stand and Deliver,* and also Beverly D'Angelo, who was playing the wife. Olmos walked the walk in real life—I had heard him give an uplifting speech at SDSU several months earlier, during which he implored students to take a stand and do something positive with their lives. My favorite

Olmos film was *American Me,* the gritty tale of an aging, Mexican gang member in L.A. who tries to go straight, but finds in the end that his die has been cast, and there is no escape. Olmos was friendly and approachable at the shoot, so I walked over, shook his hand and said, "I really enjoyed *American Me.* He sighed and shook his head—I'd said something wrong. I realized after the fact that he felt the film was intended to sound an alarm, to wake people up to the realities of the barrio, the urban jungle, or whatever you want to call it. You were supposed to learn from its message—but you weren't supposed to enjoy it. Nonetheless, Olmos was a music fan, and a musician himself, so he took an interest in the band gathered for the shoot, a local all-star Latin ensemble.

The scene, it turned out, was pretty cheesy. We played in the nightclub, and then later, while we were lounging backstage in the green room, Jose Menendez (Olmos) came back stage and said something like, "I like your sound. How would you guys like to have a record contract?" We were instructed by the director to crack big grins, turn to each other and say, "Wow! Record contract?" I remember looking over at drummer Danny Campbell as we did a few takes, thinking to myself, *we might be good musicians, but we're crappy actors!* I never did find out if our scene made it into the movie. There are some clips on youtube, but I couldn't find any with Edward James Olmos.

IF YOU CAN'T BRING US OUR LUNCH...

Over the summer of 1991, I decided not to go home to Northern California, and instead accepted a music industry internship in Los Angeles. I'd heard stories about people who started as underlings and worked their way to remarkable accomplishments. A notable example was David Geffen, who began in the mailroom and wound up a billionaire, and Jimmy Iovine, the Interscope mogul who also started with nothing.

My initial contact at A&M was Doreen Gunn, assistant to an accomplished, semi-famous recording engineer named Shelly Yackus. Yackus had worked on albums for John Lennon, Joe Cocker and other big names. My job was to assist Shelly and the various recording artists who came to work in the studios. My official title was *runner* — as it turned out, *runner* was a euphemism for *fart catcher*.[41] If anyone

---

[41] A term coined by my Cousin Bill, who had done his fair share of entertainment industry fart catching.

said jump, you asked how high. If anyone needed their nose wiped, you said "Here's the Kleenex." If anyone expelled gas, you made like Yadier Molina in Game Seven. Being a runner put you on track to become an engineer, however, and I figured that, although I didn't want to become a full-time recording engineer, I definitely wanted to be a songwriter and producer for big-time artists, and this was where all that was happening.

After taking me on a tour to show me the lay of the land, Doreen sat me in her office and said, "Did I mention that the job doesn't pay anything?" The rationale with internships is that you, the young apprentice seeking entry into an otherwise closed world, gain invaluable career experience while having new doors opened to you. Then, the theory suggests, you should be able parlay the initial opportunity into an actual career. Upon first glance, I wasn't convinced this was going to be the case with my A&M gig, but I was there, settled in L.A. for the summer, so I figured I might as well go for it.

Worried about not having cash, I looked for a second job, one that actually paid something. I tried Thrifty's, Blockbuster, and even walked into a gelato shop. It was *Lost in America*, only I was lost in Los Angeles. In the gelato place, I was met by an acne-riddled underling who asserted, "I'm the assistant manager here. Come back in two hours. I want you to talk to the manager." I agreed, but he wasn't done talking. "Don't get your hopes up. You see that?" He was pointing at a pile of papers. "That's a stack of applications from people that wanna work here. A lot of 'em are highly qualified, too." Visions of Robert Townsend's *Hollywood Shuffle* flashed through my mind. *Say it with me now… Winky… Dinky… Dog!*

I promised the assistant manager not to get my hopes up, and returned later as instructed. The manager, sixtyish, was standing behind the counter, watching vanilla bean gelato ooze from a dispenser and into a Styrofoam cup. Once he had served a pair of impatient baby boomers their afternoon treat, he turned to me and sighed. "Your lack of experience in the field concerns me."

"I'm a musician, just kind of looking for a part-time side gig this summer."

"If I take a chance on you, I expect you to treat this like a big deal. Not just some side thing you're doing. You have to believe."

"Believe in what… the merits of gelato?"

"Are you being a smart-ass?"

"No, no, not at all. I do believe in gelato. In fact, I've enjoyed it on many occasions. They say if you want to sell something, you've got to love the product, right? I certainly love gelato… and if you give me the opportunity, I'll prove it."

"I don't know. You're asking me to roll the dice here." He was understandably conflicted. If I didn't pan out, it was going to be his ass on the chopping block. The Corporate Gelato Brass was going to need a fall guy, and he would most likely be it.

"Hey, if you don't think I've got the right stuff, there's a smoothie place next door I can try."

"Yeah, it's just that we're running a tight ship here, and I need people who are passionate about the cause."

"Did I not just say I love gelato?"

"Thanks for stopping in."

Never tell anyone you're a musician when applying for *anything*: a job, a loan, entrance to a homeless soup kitchen. You can stagger into a hospital emergency room with a machete in your chest, your leg cut off at the knee, and several bullet wounds — and if you identify yourself as a musician (a.k.a. loser with no medical insurance), the nurse will grimace, turn away from you and ask, "Where's that girl with the ingrown toenail?"

I abandoned the search for paid employment and decided to put my all into being a fart catcher at A&M. My first day began with a sit-down with Shelly Yackus. We'd already had a preliminary phone chat about studio gear, during which he'd determined that I wasn't a complete buffoon, in terms of my knowledge of studios and recording equipment. Now, it was time to learn what Shelly wanted me to do for him. He explained, in so many words, the somewhat disheartening truth: I was going to be fetching shit for people. When I feebly asked if there was some scenario in which I might make a few bucks for doing this, he sighed and said, "I don't want to be difficult, but I thought Doreen made it clear there would be no money involved." Just a few minutes earlier, the guy had pulled up in a shiny Jaguar. There was money involved, all right. It just didn't involve *me*. "Can your folks kick you down some cash to get through the summer?" Shelly wondered.

By the end of the first day, it was clear that my work would not entail helping mix the next Joe Cocker album with Shelly, much less doing keyboard sessions for Sting. Instead, it would consist of scurrying around L.A. on my own nickel, catering to the whims of pretentious tools like Lars Ulrich of Metallica. In addition to Metallica, the studio's clients included The Cult, Tina Turner, Melissa Etheridge, and the bad boys of Motley Crüe.

A typical order from central command was as follows: *Go get Ian (the Cult singer) a copy of Billboard and two copies of Pollstar, get a case of Pepsi and another two of Mountain Dew for the Turner entourage, take this pre-amp over to Studio C before Mick Mars (Motley Crüe guitarist) blows a gasket, grab some sandwiches for Metallica at Jerry's Deli—the one on Ventura Boulevard and not the other one—hurry on that part of it, because Lars doesn't like to wait. Then, go find out what Melissa Etheridge's life partner needs from Sav-On, and go give Shelly's daughter and her boyfriend a ride to the Galleria in Encino. And get your ass back here quick!*

One day I found myself in luxurious Studio A, after Motley Crüe had finished a session. As you might expect, there were empty booze bottles and dirty magazines scattered around the room. Feeling scandalous, I ventured upstairs into the private lounge to have a peek. What I found was better than the bootleg Tommy Lee/Pamela Anderson videotape, Vince Neil's personal diary, or anything else one might have hoped to stumble upon. Lying on a coffee table was the script for a proposed Motley Crüe music video. The song was called *Primal Scream*, and the script laid out a detailed scenario in which the camera would cut between shots of the band, jamming away, and a pack of savage, slathering dogs chasing some poor son of a bitch through a satanic cemetery. This would have been a great concept, had it not already been done in *The Omen*, back in the seventies. As I pored through the "script," I realized it was the embodiment of every lame heavy metal cliché in the book. I contemplated stealing it, but chickened out. My non-paying internship was on the line, after all.

If nothing else, working at A&M gave me ammunition for some epic name-dropping. And drop I did. Everybody loved my story about Jon Bon Jovi passing me in the hallway, coming up to my waist (chest, if you count the hair). Or Bruce Springsteen and I having a quick chat as we both reached for a pretzel, while a gospel vocal group called Sounds of Blackness wailed away in the studio parking lot. I had a few cordial run-ins with Bruce, who was working on a pair of new albums to follow up his spectacular success in the late eighties. The Boss even stopped and asked me a question or two one time, which was more than the snotty chick at the reception desk could ever manage. Tracy Chapman, on the other hand, had become angry when I'd had the audacity to ask her where to put some equipment she'd requested. Her career cooled off in subsequent years—perhaps she's more humble now, and thus more compassionate toward studio flunkies. I had friendly exchanges with both Melissa Etheridge and Tina Turner, the latter being one of those star-struck moments when you don't know what to say, so you stand there with a smile on your face, frozen.

One day I had the good fortune of crossing paths with acclaimed heavy metal producer Bob Rock. I'd been asked to assist on a Motley Crüe session, so I was chilling in the studio while Nikki (*I died and came back from the dead to still not give a shit*) Sixx was doing some kind of sloppy warm-up on his electric bass. Bob Rock walked in and said hello to everyone, exchanging some chit chat with those he knew and recognized. Then he turned to me and said, "Who the hell are you?" I explained what I was doing there, Rock nodded and turned away. After a few minutes, he made a subtle gesture to the head engineer, who walked over to me and said, "Thanks for your help." Translation: *Bob wants you to get the fuck out now.*

A fellow A&M *go-fer* named Ralph befriended me, and we would hang out in between food runs. On one occasion Ralph brought lunch back from a fancy restaurant for some big-name band working with Shelly. Errantly, he had forgotten their credit card at the restaurant. Shelly walked over to the guy, in front of the whole band and crew, and said, "Well, Ralph, it seems you can't bring us our lunch… that much is clear… and if you can't bring us our lunch, Ralph, I have to ask… what exactly *can* you fucking do for us?!"

I didn't have much interaction with Shelly. More often I had to deal with Doreen and her flaky co-worker, Faith, who yapped on the phone all day—what else was there to do?—and gossiped about frivolous developments in the business. One such morsel was the earth-shattering rumor that KISS was *back in the studio, writing*.[42] I asked Faith if she knew what they were going to call the new album. "*Lick it Up,*" she whispered, proud to have such coveted insider knowledge. One day Faith was on the phone with Tom Petty's wife—the two were apparently friends. Faith had called to see if the woman would mind paying Faith's way when the pair went out on the town, later that night. Sensing my silent judgment after she hung up Faith barked, "She's Tom Petty's fucking wife, man… I think she can afford it!" It

---

[42] KISS has done some things worthy of the attention over the years… but writing ain't one of 'em.

was gold-digging once removed, I guess. Between Faith and Doreen, I'm not sure what (if anything) was accomplished in that office. *So... what would you say it is you do here?*[43] Doreen played up the role of industry mover and shaker, but it seemed to me she was more or less a paper shuffler. She took every chance she could to give me the old *this is a tough business, kid* routine. *You've got a long road ahead of you.* I took it with a smile, and I don't think Doreen ever had a clue how cynically I viewed the whole situation.

One day at A&M I made the acquaintance of Eduardo del Barrio, a gifted pianist and composer. Del Barrio was Herb Alpert's musical director, and took me to check out Alpert's private recording kiosk. I had introduced myself as a piano player, so the older man asked me to play a tune on Alpert's keyboard. I played an original jazz piece, which del Barrio seemed to like. Shortly thereafter, I met Alpert himself. While I was assisting the legendary Tijuana Brass trumpeter on a session for some large gospel choir, he asked me, "Are you a good player?" I replied that yes, I thought I was a good player, but I didn't sell it, didn't drive it home. It wasn't the time for humility. It was the time to say: *I play my ass off, Herb! You need to work with me, man.* I was still a little green at that point, both musically and business-wise. Had I been in the same situation a few years later, I could have capitalized more on the opportunity.

As the summer was winding down, I contemplated my options. I realized that while the go-fer gig at A&M put you on a (slow) track to be an eventual engineer, I had no desire to be a full-time engineer, and not much natural aptitude to be an engineer. I was a piano player and songwriter. I needed to go back to SDSU and perfect my craft, so I could have a career like Eduardo del Barrio. So I could produce big-name butt rock like Bob Rock. So I could enjoy a bloated sense of self-worth while bossing around hapless interns.

The week before I returned to San Diego, Doreen said she had a surprise for me. Had Shelly decided to dip into his personal coffers and kick down some chump change for all my scuffling around? Or, had Bruce Springsteen pulled Doreen aside and said, "That Anthony seems like a cool kid. I wanna try using him on a keyboard track for this one song."? As it turned out, Doreen's brother and his sons were

---

[43] The classic question asked by the pair of officious, corporate axemen brought in to trim the fat at the fictitious Initech in the film *Office Space*.

visiting from the Midwest. They had an extra ticket for a Dodger game. You're laughing, right? You think I'm kidding. No. I'm being serious. Doreen's big "gift" to me, after three months of working for free and listening to her lectures about the music business, was the incredible opportunity to accompany her brother and his kids to see a baseball game.

Fearing I might insult Doreen if I said no—who knew, maybe knowing her and Shelly would somehow help me in the future—I agreed to go. Doreen's brother turned out to be a good guy, the kids were nice, and I ended up enjoying their company. Also, I felt like I had done her yet another favor by keeping her family company for an evening. When I said my goodbyes at A&M later that week, Doreen said, "Hey, things worked out pretty well, huh?"

"How do you mean, Doreen?" I asked.

"Well, you got to go to a Dodger game." I looked at her like the jazz pianist Benny Green had once looked at me—with utter disbelief. This woman actually thought this was my big pay-off, my reward for three months of toiling around L.A. for a bunch of ego-inflated assholes with giant hair.

So, you're wondering, what did I learn from my music industry intern experience? I'll tell you what I learned. I learned that there are ways to profoundly waste one's time in life, and doing cartwheels for a carrot-dangling, music biz bottom feeder, while entertaining the delusion that it's actually going to get you somewhere, qualifies as one of them. I must say, however, that while my A&M stint was musically a waste of time, it was valuable life experience. It took the wind out of my sails, helped me understand how things work out there in the real world; and, truth be told, it was sort of cool to exchange pleasantries with The Boss, and catch a smile from Tina Turner.

Before returning to school, I attended a jazz piano master class in San Francisco, taught by Fred Hersch. Many excellent pianists showed up to both listen and play. I was clearly the youngest. Fred played a couple pieces, and then invited anyone to come up and play something for the group. I'd always grappled with performance nerves, and this was about as nerve-racking an environment as one could imagine: playing for a group of fellow pianists, in this case older and more experienced, who are listening intently to every note.

I figured I needed to prove to myself that I could do it. I raised my hand and was picked. I played *Have You Met Miss Jones* and *The Peacocks*, two songs I knew well. Under the tense circumstances, I was happy with how I performed. Fred gave me a fair-minded critique, saying he liked my pedal work, but my time feel needed improvement. Looking back, it was a pivotal experience. I proved to myself on that day that I had the balls to brave a career as a pianist. I had gone for it, for better or worse. Like the saying goes, it's the chances you *don't* take that will come back to haunt you.

SHOULD BE *FORTY*

Shortly after returning to San Diego to begin my second year at SDSU, I met Shouna Shoemake, an opera major. While cramming with fellow students for an awful music history exam, we found ourselves commiserating. Shouna was tall, African-American and attractive. Our first date was on my twenty-second birthday, at a restaurant in Mission Valley called Bennigen's.

Shouna was a promising opera singer, a star of the school's vocal department. I had never dated a black girl before, and had slight insecurities about it at first. Once I got to know Shouna's mother, Earline, I realized that Shouna had been raised in an environment where racial issues were of little importance. Shouna's sister was married to a white man, and her brother was married to a white woman. I was impressed by the open-mindedness of the Shoemake clan.

Shouna was my first serious girlfriend. Hard to believe, considering I was twenty-two, but I'd always been too busy with sports and school to get involved in a long-term situation. Shouna was caring and loyal, and it was a nice change of pace to have a young woman in my life for once. Race, believe it or not, never even came up between us. My family didn't care what color my girlfriend was—they were just happy I had one. Her family, in turn, liked me and supported the relationship.

There was only one group who ever expressed disapproval over us being together: young, African-American males. One day while walking across the campus, Shouna and I passed by a group of black football players. Their jeers were loud and clear: *You don't have to be with that white boy, girl. Let me take care of you. Lose that chump.* Shouna ignored them, but the incident pissed me off. I felt like firing back, "How are you going to take care of her? By getting her knocked up then taking off?" I know, it was a racist impulse to even contemplate retaliating in that manner, but let me shoot from the hip: These guys were acting like major assholes, disrespecting both of us for no reason, and I couldn't say anything in return, at least without risking getting my ass seriously kicked. Imagine the tables are turned and a bunch of white athletes are hanging out somewhere on campus. An interracial couple walks by, and they start to lay into the white girl: "Come on baby, what are you doing with that black guy? You should stick with us. Stick with your own kind." Was something like this to go down, the culprits very well might be *expelled from the university* for engaging in *blatant racial harassment.*

I had a couple other experiences at SDSU that challenged my sense of racial harmony with African-Americans. One took place during an intramural basketball game, between my dorm and one of the campus fraternities. Our team, a bunch of gangly white guys, with a pudgy Asian kid thrown in for good measure, wasn't very good. Our all-black opponent quickly established dominance, running up a huge lead in a matter of minutes. This was a low-key intramural contest, with nothing at stake; but rather than make it a laughable situation, these guys chose to make it ugly. They humiliated us with surly remarks. After they'd racked up a thirty-point lead, I said to one of the guys, in an effort to lighten things up, "Come on, you're up by thirty." He scowled and said, "Should be *forty.*"

Another time, I attended a campus discussion about racial issues. The scholarly panel included an articulate, middle-aged black woman, who went to great lengths to bemoan the racism she believed ran rampant throughout the university. I raised my hand and asked how she thought this specifically manifested itself, adding that I, excluding a couple minor instances, hadn't personally seen evidence of this epidemic. She argued that it was invisible and institutionalized. I went on to state my belief that the vast majority of students and teachers at SDSU were not racists, but rather were committed to getting along harmoniously with all ethnic groups. I finished my testimony by asking the question: "In an environment of supposed higher learning, why can't we move past such small thinking to a more evolved state of racial enlightenment?"

"Because most people are not like you," she said. "Most people aren't really interested in harmony and equality. They only say they are." Maybe she was right. Either way, I left the discussion feeling sad.

I decided to take a Black Studies course, hoping to expand my understanding of racial issues. I was one of two white people in the class. *Good*, I thought. This will be a reality check. I'll know how blacks feel when immersed in an all-white environment. The professor presented his ideas from a neutral position, with the occasional tilt toward Afro-centric ideology. The students were vocal with their opinions, their arguments fueled by emotion and experience. I mostly kept my mouth shut, hoping to expand my racial consciousness. Until one day…

The professor launched a discourse, á la Dr. Harry Edwards, about how black athletes excel over other ethnic groups because of environmental conditions. He maintained that young black men had no other avenue to escape the poverty of the ghetto, so they played basketball night and day, dreaming of the fame and fortune associated with the NBA. Was this a valid point? Of course it was. It's a true statement, and it does *partially* explain why blacks are so successful at the sport. But to say this was the *only* reason blacks dominated the game of basketball, and to some extent, other major sports as well, was a serious affront to reality. I couldn't maintain my silence any longer.

"Professor, have you ever played basketball?" I asked. He shook his head no.

"I played competitively for a number of years, and my experience leads me to conclude that blacks have a natural edge, in terms of sheer athleticism. They run faster, and they jump higher and more explosively. They also move more gracefully on the court." The class reacted as if washed over by an invidious wave of racism. The idea that there might be physical differences, be they advantages or disadvantages, was inherently evil, the group seemed to think. I believe my comment elicited this reaction for two reasons: One, the suggestion that black athletes excel through more abundant physical gifts implies that they don't work as hard for their accomplishments; it downplays the struggle to transcend low socio-economic status. Second, any hint of physical differences between races seems, for some people, to open a Pandora's box of more unsavory possibilities, such as the notion that there could be intellectual differences as well.

I'm convinced that all ethnic groups work equally hard, and *must* work equally hard in order to meet the demands of professional athletics, an arena in which there is scarce room for favoritism and quotas. Only the best and most qualified get the job, regardless of color or creed—and regardless of the sport, for that matter. So, to be clear, I am saying that I believe blacks, whites and other ethnic groups work equally hard to succeed in basketball. Blacks just happen to be genetically predisposed, as a group, to excel more at this particular game than whites.

While I am convinced of the above, I am also entirely *unconvinced* that differences or discrepancies exist regarding the inherent brainpower of various ethnic groups. To argue to the contrary is to support the kinds of dangerous ideas that resulted in the notorious eugenics movement, which in turn encouraged the ethnic cleansing campaign of the Nazis in World War II. Furthermore, there simply is no evidence of this in the world in which we live. Look at all the great scholars and intellectual visionaries of various ethnicities. No one group can lay claim to being intellectually superior. I think a more interesting study would be to look at how cultural and environmental factors have affected the development of intellectual faculties, both historically and in the modern world. We'll save that for another book.

TWENTY BUCKS,
AND ALL-YOU-CAN-EAT CHIPS AND SALSA

Looking to expand my stylistic horizons, I joined a reggae group called Fried Bananas, comprised of fellow SDSU music majors. The band included a horn section, and the songs were mostly covers. We performed in San Diego's rock-oriented venues like Winston's, Blind Melons and the Belly Up Tavern. There wasn't much money, but the gigs provided a way to blow off steam, after dealing with the rigors of academia all week. Shouna and her girlfriends would come to the gigs, and we'd all drink, dance and have a good time. One of the band's steady engagements was at a bar in Pacific Beach called Diego's. The pay was *twenty bucks, and all-you-can-eat chips and salsa.*

I shared a house in Allied Gardens with two of the Fried Bananas guys: guitarist Jamey Byers, and bassist Adrian Ahearn. Like me, they were both jazz majors, but liked pop and rock music, and seriously questioned the prospect of making a living playing only jazz. At some point, the three of us decided to revamp the band and really try to make something happen. We replaced drummer Randy "Scalded

Dog"[44] Seals, who had been a member of Strawberry Alarm Clock back in the hippie days, with a much younger, more technically proficient kid named Jordan Dalrymple. We were inspired by popular Southern California bar bands like Common Sense and the Gnarly Bras, and abandoned our ska-flavored sound in favor of a harder hitting, reggae/rock sound. This entailed losing the horn section; Jamey and I both played in the jazz big bands at SDSU, and were tired of trumpets and saxophones blasting away all the time. We wanted a tighter, leaner sound.

Excited with our new direction, the three of us set out to look for new places to play in San Diego. I got on the phone and started calling bars and clubs, and heeding the (misguided) advice of some fellow musician, decided to *highball* the band's asking price. One particularly memorable negotiation took place between me and the owner of an Irish dive bar. The guy spoke with a thick brogue, like he'd just arrived from Dublin days earlier. After a brief chat, it was time to get down to brass tacks. "Sounds like we can do some business. So, there, Tony, tell me how much yer band is askin' for a performance fee?"

"We don't leave the house for less than a five hundred dollar guarantee."

"Five hundred dollars, you say?"

"Yeah."

"Well, I'll tell ya what, Tony. For that kinda money... why don't you take yer fuckin' band to the Sports Arena."

That wouldn't be my last confrontation with a guy that spoke in a thick brogue. Years later, I was out in Arizona touring with a funk band, and met a young woman who expressed an interest in spending some time with me after the gig. Next thing I knew, some pasty guy with a beanie, looking like Ed Harris with those beady, menacing eyes, was in my face punishing me with pungent Guiness breath.

"I see you made the acquaintance of me little sister," he said.

---

[44] I gave Randy this nickname because he would do a signature drum solo, without fail on every gig, in which he abandoned his sticks and started beating on the drums with his hands. By the end, he'd be sweaty and out of breath, his face red as a tomato. I joked to the guys that Randy looked like a dog that had just been scalded by boiling hot water. I had borrowed this expression from a used car salesman in San Jose, who took me for a test drive in an old BMW, and shouted as I sped down Stevens Creek Boulevard, "She runs like a scalded dog, eh? An old, scalded fucking dog!"

"Huh?" I asked.

"I know your type. Yer wearin' yer intentions on yer face."

"What the hell are you talking about, man?"

"I'm tellin' yew here and now, lad. You shant be leavin' with me sister."

"We're just talking, man. Relax."

"I don't know ya. Don't know ya from Adam. And you won't be leaving this fookin' bar with me baby sister." I thought it over, and while the girl was enjoyable to talk to, decided it wasn't worth getting my knees broken in the back alley over. I *told yew not to mess with me sister, yew fook! Now yer gonna pay!* WHAAAM! Who knew the IRA had established a branch in Flagstaff, Arizona?

Some of my jazz friends and mentors were less than enthusiastic about my forays into pop and rock. They felt I was wasting my time in Fried Bananas, and should just stick with jazz. I liked rock, however. I wasn't a jazz purist, in my heart of hearts. I liked songwriting. I liked playing synthesizers and keyboards. I enjoyed performing for people who wanted to hear what I was playing. I liked singing. When I played jazz, most people in the audience were three times my age. I wanted to feel like I was playing music that people of my own generation could relate to. There was also the matter of older local musicians I knew — guys twenty or thirty years my senior, still living in tiny apartments by themselves, eeking it out month-to-month. We were playing the same gigs, making the same dough. I took some long looks in the mirror.

At the behest of my Fried Bananas bandmates, I decided to grow my hair long for the first time in my life. As it grew out, I realized it was much curlier than I'd thought. I got it long enough to put in a ponytail, and discovered that some girls really liked the look. I was now a *long hair*, a term Jamey had coined — he himself had worn long hair since I'd first met him, and firmly believed it enhanced not only one's stage presence, but also one's chances of securing the company of a young woman once the gig was through. I also put together a wardrobe of funky, reggae-esque clothing: colorful shirts, baggy corduroy pants, jewelry with peace/anti-establishment symbols, and quirky hats. If I was going to be in a reggae band, I had to walk the walk. The only thing I didn't do was start to smoke pot.

The three of us began working hard on our songwriting. Rather than write tunes together, we would each retreat to our rooms, sit alone with our instruments and craft melodies and lyrics. When we thought we had something good—a nugget, as we would call a promising hook—we'd show it to the rest of the band. If, when you demoed your latest idea, the other guys started smiling and coming up with parts on their instruments, you knew you had a potential winner. If, on the other hand, you announced "Guys, I've got a nugget," then played your new ditty only to be met with awkward silence, as Jamey had the misfortune of doing one day at rehearsal, you took your lumps and went back to the drawing board.

After a while, we were convinced we had enough great tunes, among the three of us, to hit the studio and record a great album. Since we played live shows regularly, we were able to try our original stuff on audiences, and see what moved people and what didn't. I was enjoying a fertile writing period at that time, and penned several songs the guys in the band felt were pretty brilliant: *Strong Love, A Question of Time, Six Times Around the Sun, A Fashion of Belief, Tomorrow's Children,* and *Human Interest.* Jamey and Adrian collaborated on a catchy tune called *Love One Another,* and individually also contributed some good tunes. We had a nice thing going. There were only two elements we were missing: a convincing lead singer and a reliable following.

As we swam uphill for a couple years, trying to build a fan base and secure better opportunities, our relationships with each other deteriorated. Jamey and I locked horns regarding the creative direction of the band. He envisioned a hybrid of Lenny Kravitz and (guitarist) Joe Satriani, while I was shooting for a sound closer to Sting and Tears for Fears. Meanwhile, Adrian was imagining himself as a West Coast Jimmy Buffet, with a bit of a punk edge. The three visions did not mix in the end.

They say a first album either brings a band together or breaks it up. Not long after we received our finished CDs in the mail—what should have been major turning point —Fried Bananas broke up. We'd bickered throughout the studio process, not one of us willing to face the fact that we were mediocre lead vocalists. We had a group of pretty good songs, but not one emerged as a surefire hit you could hang your hat on. Sadly, the singing just wasn't good enough. Jordan, disgruntled with the whole experience, had more or less phoned it in, playing solid drum parts but not giving a shit about the final product. Jamey and I came to realize we had different ideas about the band's direction. He and Adrian also were now constantly locking horns. We'd all borrowed money from our families to finance the album; now we had an album all right, but we had no band. We kind of looked like idiots. After Jamey and Jordan quit, Adrian and I remained roommates, and contemplated replacing them and keeping the band alive. Upon more reflection, we realized it was time to wipe the slate clean. Time to take Kenny Rogers's timeless advice.

Despite the failure of Fried Bananas, Jamey and I remained friends. Beyond the band, we had bonded through presenting an ambitious jazz concert of originals and difficult repertoire, in partial fulfillment of requirements for our performance degrees at SDSU. We were both big fans of Los Angeles pianist/composer Lee Gregory, so I transcribed, with help from the composer himself, a daring Gregory original piece. I also got to take a private lesson with Gregory, at his modest apartment in L.A.

The lesson with Lee Gregory was a colorful experience. When I got to his place Lee didn't want to chit chat, which is what happens at a lot of lessons. He wanted to hear me play. I played a couple songs for him, and he played a couple for me. Then we played together. He was a great pianist, in the tradition of McCoy Tyner disciples like Joey Calderazzo and Mulgrew Miller. His piano touch was clean and angular, his right-hand lines inventive and energetic.

We took a break to listen to McCoy Tyner's famous recording of *Surrey With the Fringe on Top*, the Rodgers and Hammerstein standard from *Oklahoma*. We both waved our hands along with the record, playing *air piano* with McCoy's improvisation. We both knew the solo note-for-note. I'd heard Lee could play great over the classic John Coltrane song, *Giant Steps*, which contains a series of rapidly changing chords, played at a fast tempo. I said, "Lee, word on the streets is that you can really play the hell out of Giant Steps."

"Yeah... I can," he replied. Then he sat down and played the absolute shit out of it. I've still got the recording somewhere. As the lesson shifted to the realm of composition, Lee trotted out a classical vocal piece he'd written while studying at USC, years earlier. "Here's the flute part," he said as he played a single line on the piano. "Now, the French horn." He added another line. "And right here..." He squinted to read the page. "Okay, here's where the bitch comes in... Laaaaaaaaa!"

I GREW UP WATCHING YOU WORK

One of the bonuses of braving a career as a musician is the multitude of humorous, entertaining and even bizarre circumstances you find yourself in, just by freelancing and accepting random jobs from people you might not know very well. By choosing to spend your days interacting and collaborating with artistic types, you are virtually guaranteed a wealth of colorful material to share with friends, family, and anyone you might meet during your travels. Here is but a smattering of examples from my early gigging days…

The first gig I ever did upon arriving in San Diego was at a joint called Café Bravo. The leader was a trombonist named Dillon Bromley. It was a low-key gig on an off-night, so there wasn't much pressure. When I got there, the stage had some equipment on it. I asked Dillon, "Is it okay if I move this crap over a little so I can set up?" He shot back, "That's not crap! That's someone's personal property, and if you don't want to respect it, maybe you should go home."

I took it on the chin, but a couple years later it was payback time. I was accompanying scholarship applicants for the jazz studies faculty at SDSU, when a familiar face walked through the door: Dillon Bromley. *You're on my turf now, buddy.* He stood before the faculty panel and announced that he would like to play *Moose the Mooch*, an old Charlie Parker song. Anyone who's ever flipped the pages of a real book[45] knows that *Moose the Mooch*, based on the chords to George Gershwin's *I Got Rhythm*, is a bebop riff to be played at a fast, cooking tempo. But Dillon decided to get creative. "Let's do it as a samba," he said. Simply put, this is an idea that downright stinks. One of the lamest tricks in the book is to turn a well-worn jazz tune into some jive Brazilian mash-up. The only thing worse is to take the party on down to Jamaica… *reggae stylie, mon!* Where's the barf bag?

Instead of suggesting a different approach, which might have spared Dillon humiliation, I decided to *roll with his vision.* "That sounds like a great idea, Dillon," I said. He grabbed his trombone, counted off the band, then blurted out a flurry of notes at the wrong tempo. We sounded like we were playing two different songs. His eyes got wide as he stared over at me, wondering what was happening. I played dumb. I let him bury himself, as the brows of the faculty members furrowed with disappointment. After Dillon packed his horn and sauntered out, presumably denied the scholarship he had come seeking, Bill Yeager, head of the jazz department and a fine trombonist himself, approached me. *Oh no*, I thought, *he's going to let me have it.* But Bill, one of my main allies at SDSU, smiled wryly and whispered in my ear, "You sure got him good."

One afternoon, I showed up at the Mission Valley Radisson for a blues job in the main ballroom. I was the first one there, and had no idea who the client was. As I set up my keyboard I heard a robotic monotone nearby. I looked up and saw an elderly man whose throat was fitted with some kind of voice amplifying device. The clinical term, for the record, is *laryngectomy*. The diseased larynx is replaced with an artificial box allowing the recipient to vocalize, though only in a monotone. In other words, there are no inflections in the voice. It sounds like a robot talking. Or Stephen Hawking.

I returned to setting up my gear, interrupted again a few minutes later by another peculiar sound. I looked up and saw an older lady,

---

[45] Book of jazz standards written in musical notation.

also speaking through an artificial voice box. Hers was tuned a bit higher but had the same characteristic monotone. *Now there's a coincidence*, I thought. Two of those babies in the same room, within a matter of minutes. I finished setting up my keyboard, then left to grab some dinner before the downbeat. As I approached the ballroom door upon my return I sensed something ominous. A magnificent rumble was emanating from within. I opened the door with caution, not knowing what lurked inside. Then I saw them. *Two thousand of them,* pitched with slight variations that resulted in a cacophonous din I can't begin to describe. My jaw dropped as an announcement was made over the public address system: "Good evening, and welcome to the National Laryngectomy Convention!"

We played some quiet jazz standards as dinner was served. Then, as the second set commenced, one of the guests/survivors approached to ask our bandleader a question: "Can I sing one?" The bandleader almost chuckled, thinking the guy was some kind of wisenheimer who'd had a couple glasses of wine and was now making a self-deprecating quip about his condition. But this guy wasn't kidding.

"What would you like to sing?" the leader asked.

"I-would-like-to-do-*Moon-River*," the septuagenarian answered in a robotic, unwavering tone. I couldn't help thinking that Jobim's *One Note Samba* would be a better choice... but *Moon River* it was.

The leader of the band that night was a nice guy, but maybe not Michael Brecker's rival on saxophone. His day job was serving as mayor of a San Diego suburb, and he booked a few gigs here and there, mostly for fun. The rest of the musicians were nice guys as well—but I must point out that it can never be assumed that a group of nice guys, as pleasant as they are to be around, are certain to achieve musical greatness. There's a running joke I have with a few of my more accomplished musician friends:

So, how does (insert guy's name) play?
Well... he's a real nice guy.
That's not what I asked you. How does he play?
He's real down-to-earth, easy to get along with.
You're not answering my question.
He's a family man. Cut him some slack.
But can he play his instrument?
You're not hearing me. This man is a provider! He's got mouths to feed!

One time, the leader of the blues band… nice guy… mayor of National City… provider… landed us a Christmas gig at the Del Mar estate of Jenny Craig, the famous diet guru. The place was something else—right on the beach, surrounded by large, marble pillars that gave it the appearance of an ancient Greek temple.

The guitarist waltzed in with his gear, and the first thing I noticed was that he was missing his front teeth. The next thing I noticed was that he seemed to have the musical ear of a water buffalo. Once the music began, he felt little shame in butchering the most primitive of chord progressions. As I quietly lamented the musical mess we were making all over Jenny Craig's immaculate living room, I spotted a familiar face in the crowd. Not just a familiar face, but a veritable icon from my youth.

Dick Van Patton was to my generation what Kiefer Sutherland is to today's television audience. The man was a god. Sure, *Eight is Enough* was an ensemble cast, with various subplots woven into every episode, but Van Patton was the glue that held it all together. Everybody knew that. Without Shaq, there would have been no Laker three-peat. Without Tom Petty, there couldn't have been any Heartbreakers. Without Wolf Blitzer, scratch CNN. Without mighty Dick Van Patton, *Eight is Enough* probably wouldn't have ever made it from page to screen in the first place. And think about it… without *Eight is Enough* re-runs, just where would we be in the world today?

There was no way I was missing out on a chance to get in Dick Van Patton's face that night. I was in the presence of greatness, and I wanted a piece of it. "Mr. Van Patton," I said as I approached, "I grew up watching you work."

"Oh?" he responded, thinking for a moment that perhaps I was versed in the more obscure reaches of his four-decade ouvre.

"I never missed a single episode of *Eight is Enough*," I assured him. His face sank. Not that shit again. Twenty years later, and this guy wants to talk about *Eight is Enough*. I knew I had one chance to come up with something clever to regain Van Patton's interest, or he was going to dis me and head for the bacon-wrapped scallops in the corner.

"Remember that guest spot you did on *The Streets of San Francisco*?" I asked. I saw a flicker of hope in his eyes. "You were one of the hostages, and Karl Malden was trying to find all you guys… but you were stashed in this warehouse, down by the wharf." Van Patton was back with me now, engaged. "So then Karl Malden and Michael Douglas ran out of time to meet the kidnappers' demands, and they decided to make you an example. I remember the look of consternation on your face, right before you bought the farm, Dick. They shot you in cold blood, there in that abandoned warehouse. It was a sad TV moment. America cried that night."[46] I shook hands with Dick Van Patton, and skulked back to the bandstand to blow some more chunks with toothless six-string butchers and squawking local politicians. At the end of the evening, Jenny Craig approached the stage, turned to the guitarist and loudly proclaimed, "You are the greatest of guitar players!" Clearly, Madame Craig's ear for talent was not as keen as her nose for winning diet formulas.

KIFM, San Diego's proud purveyors of smooth jazz, held a downtown music festival every year, during which they would always throw in some local, cheaply acquired talent to round out the roster. One year they asked my jazz group Blueprint to back a New York guitarist named Panama Mazakuza. We agreed, and the station gave me a copy of Panama's latest album to check out. After checking out the first track, in which Panama more or less desecrated the sultry, sensuous Al B. Sure ballad *Nite and Day*, one of my favorite jams of the entire eighties, I'd already heard enough. My band had committed to the gig, however, and so we had to go through with it.

We had met with Panama for a quick rehearsal, and I immediately noticed that his classic, Asian visage and gray, flowing hair made him look like the arch-villain from a bad kung fu flick. He was a very nice guy,[47] but his playing sounded like melodic diarrhea... super-fast noodling, up and down the neck of the insrument, with little musical logic behind it.

Smooth jazz concerts are often even worse than the pablum you hear on the radio. Live, the musicians take on an air of feigned, golly-shucks enthusiasm to cloak what in reality is a completely cynical view of the genre's fan base; these capable but calculated hucksters hammer repetitive phrases and rhythms, resorting to a predictable vocabulary of shopworn gimmicks in an unapologetic attempt to elicit Pavlovian reactions from a crowd which, excluding a tiny minority of sophisticated listeners, is all but unaware that it's being subjected to an

---

[46] Okay, so I'll admit I'm creatively re-imagining the actual conversation... just a little.

[47] I'm making the argument that, when it comes to artistic ability, this distinction is often the kiss of death.

insincere onslaught of pre-fabricated sonic hype. Like illusionists, such musicians have a grab bag of tricks they know will get over with their typical audience. Smooth jazz seemed to peak in the nineties, but even today I hear certain artists resorting to these tactics to curry favor. It's sad that the audience is still suckers for these tricks, but it's also sad that some musicians don't have the creative pride to avoid such threadbare clichés. I'm not just talking about smooth jazz. It runs rampant in hip-hop, reggae and pop also.

We took the stage to accompany Panama at a crowded, downtown venue. The audience, as you might imagine, loved the show. Bassist Ken Dow, who would go on later to find success as the original bassist for the global phenomenon *Jersey Boys*, shot me looks throughout the set: *Are people really buying this?* Not only were they buying it... they were standing and cheering for it. As we finished the last song, Panama waved off the band, having decided to punctuate his performance with a solo guitar cadenza. The crowd hung on every note as he bridged the broad, stylistic gap between Hiroshima and Sepultura... Peter White and Whitesnake... Boney James and Ronnie James Dio. Before our eyes, Panama was creating a new genre of music: *heavy metal lights-out jazz.* Long, gray wisps flowing, he threw his head back with Yanni-esque magnificence, landing on a final, triumphant chord. The audience went wild. Ken and I had seen (and heard) enough. We both lost it and began chuckling out loud.

Later that night, I wound up hanging out with Panama's manager, a Caribbean woman in her forties who'd flown out from Florida to see the show. After spending a couple hours socializing with her, she made me an interesting offer: *Tell me when you're free, and I'll fly you down to Miami to hang out for a week in my condo. All expenses covered.* I gave the sugar mama proposition some thought. I'd never been to Miami, and it sounded pleasant, but wasn't convinced I wanted to spend a week smearing Coppertone lotion on some Japanese smooth jazz guitar player's manager's cottage cheese thighs, in exchange for a plane ticket and a couple steak dinners. I told her I appreciated the offer, but I passed.

Another time, I got a call for a jazz orchestra job at the Sheraton Harbor Island. It was steady every week, but required that you be a member of the local musicians' union. I joined so I could do the gig. When I showed up the first night, there was a big box of white tuxedos, and the leader told me to "Grab a monkey suit, man." The gig consisted of reading through arrangements out of a massive songbook, while elderly couples cut the rug. There were good players in the band, but I found myself wondering, as the leader loudly barked the numbers of the charts he wanted us to pull from his compendium of corny classics, *what am I doing here?*

One night on this particular job, there was an elaborate tray of finger food desserts laid out near the bandstand. An older trumpet player and I stood nearby on the break, salivating. We checked to make sure the coast was clear, and then we made our move. As we stood there devouring cream-filled confections, we were accosted by a walkie talkie-wielding chick with a Sheraton nametag pinned to her pantsuit, who came out of nowhere. "What do you think you're doing?!" she snapped. "Those are not for you! They're for the client!" The veteran player and I stood there in our cheap, white monkey suits, nothing to say for ourselves. Chocolate dripped from our guilty fingers as she ripped us a new one for shoplifting a couple miniature éclairs.

We were reduced to clowns, just like the Bridges Brothers in *The Fabulous Baker Boys*. It was at that very moment that I had an epiphany: I was never going to be happy with my life by making a living this way. I had a choice. I could play as many weddings, bar mitzvahs and private parties as humanly possible, a move that might insure a workable income for a single guy. If this was my choice, I'd never know the highs of playing for an audience who paid to hear me perform my own music. I'd never distinguish myself as a creative artist in the world. I might manage some stability, but the ceiling was low. The alternative would be to veer off the safe path and pursue the frontier of original music. This would be much more of a crapshoot. There would be no guarantees, and I might very well wind up broke in the end.

The day was coming when I'd no longer be able to ride the fence between these two very different paths. There was no way I was going to commit my entire existence to playing corporate events. My initial attraction to music had been spiritual, and I wasn't going to spend my adult life slowly killing the passion that had consumed me as a young guy.

In the corporate world, the very cornerstone upon which all is built is *the client*. You hear these words over and over, always muttered with a deferential tone. The client is the reason you're there. The reason you have a job. The client is going to get what he wants, because the client is writing the checks. I'll tell you a few more things about the client…

The client would prefer that the band members remain out of sight when they're not playing.

The client prefers that the band loads in five hours earlier than the guests arrive, to avoid the embarrassment of one of the guests seeing someone walk past them with a hand-truck.

The client has requested that the bride's brother get up and sing Gloria with the band, 'cause everyone knows Jim's a real wildman!

The client requires that the music never actually stop. It must keep going all night, with no breaks, so the musicians will have to work out some kind of rotation that prevents silence at any point in the party.

The client has provided a list of songs that will be appropriate to be performed. The client wanted a DJ instead of a band, truth be told, but was assured by friends that an actual band would look more classy. The client wants this night to be special, after all.

The client has provided ham sandwiches for the band, which are to be eaten only in the designated musician area. The client and guests will be having filet mignon.

The client has expressly forbidden the musicians from interacting with guests of the client's party. Should it come to the attention of the booking agency that any musician has violated this agreement, there will be dire consequences for all musicians on the job. Thus, each musician is encouraged to take personal responsibility to ensure that the client and his guests feel the proper sense of division between themselves and the hired help.

The musicians are also discouraged from fraternizing with the catering staff. There have been past reported incidents of sexual indecency perpetrated by musicians and catering employees, and this type of transgression will not be tolerated.

The client doesn't really want the musicians here at all, but realizes no party is complete without some putzes in tuxes making inconsequential noise over in the corner.

While discussing the needs of the client one day, my drummer friend Tim McMahon and I came to a conclusion:

The client could kiss our ass.

BIOTECH FIRM SEEKS JAZZ PIANIST

In early 1994, Shouna broke up with me. It was disappointing, but I realized I was too into music to be any good as a boyfriend. My senior recital, the equivalent of final dissertation, was coming up, so I practiced piano longer and more intensely than I ever had in my life. I really wanted to impress people with my final recital. I selected material that would force me to make a quantum leap to the next level of virtuosity. This included a note-for-note transcription of Art Tatum's version of *Sweet Lorraine,* and also a transcription of James P. Johnson's famous stride piece, *Carolina Shout.*

The older you get, the more you see patterns in your behavior over the years. The more you get to know who you are, as reflected by the way you've conducted your life. I've always been a guy who bites off a bit more than he can chew. As the recital approached, I realized I lacked the ability to pull off some of the music I'd chosen. Even with great preparation, I was still going to struggle to get through parts of the recital.

Unlike a bar gig, a concert recital is heavily scrutinized. The audience is quiet, sitting still, listening carefully to everything you're doing. There's much more pressure. You're expected to nail every intricate passage, and the only thing anyone is going to remember is if you make a big mistake. The main goal is to not screw up bad enough that anyone will notice. The following story illustrates this notion beautifully…

The SDSU big band, under Bill Yeager's direction, landed a prestigious job backing acclaimed, blind jazz singer Diane Schuur. The concert was set to take place at the East County Performing Arts Center in El Cajon, and there was a rehearsal the afternoon of the show. This was our only chance to learn Diane's material. Schuur, undeniably a great vocal talent, arrived at the rehearsal cranky and impatient. After a while she warmed up a bit, making a couple crude jokes and some friendly small talk.

In addition to the SDSU jazz ensemble, the rhythm section was rounded out by the late John Guerin on drums (once married to Joni Mitchell), and Bob Magnusson on bass. One of Schuur's arrangements started out with a short piano lick. She told me to insert a four-bar drum intro that wasn't written in the original score. Instead of doing what I should have done—promptly jot the new instructions down—I opted to make a *mental note*. We were going through music so quickly, everyone struggling to keep up with the headliner's requests and demands, that I figured I'd just remember the note, come concert time.

Later that night, the concert got off to a good start. My mom and sister were in the audience, rooting me on. Schuur's voice sounded excellent, as expected. After a few numbers, we got to the song where I was supposed to have inserted the four-bar drum intro. Schuur snapped her fingers to count off the band, and I forgot to wait before playing the piano lick. I came blazing right in, along with Guerin's drum fill, prompting Schuur to wave us off. "Wait!" she shouted. There was an awkward silence as the whole band realized I had fucked up. The audience didn't know I was the culprit, but they knew something had gone wrong.

Schuur, bless her, covered me by blaming herself and making light of it. Meanwhile, John Guerin was growling at me in a hushed whisper, "You forgot the four-bar intro, man!" I remember very little else about the concert—the song selection, the musical highlights… What I remember is that I screwed up. After the show, Bill Yeager came over to me and quietly said, "I sure wish you had written that down." Yes, it was my fault, but I will say this—had Schuur been more patient during the rehearsal instead of barreling through everything so quickly, I might have taken better notes.

As my college days were rapidly coming to a close, I began to have concerns about the future. I started to wonder how my creative ideas were going to fare in the real world. One afternoon, the university hosted a job fair in the main courtyard, an opportunity for graduating seniors to test the waters with potential employers. I shuffled past booth after booth, asking myself: *What exactly am I going to do with my life now?* I looked around, but there were no banners reading:

BIOTECH FIRM SEEKS JAZZ PIANIST.

I got through my senior recital okay, but overall was disappointed with the result. I didn't play my best, the program was too long and self-indulgent, and Chip Fuji, a vibes player I'd hired to play throughout the concert, butchered several of my original tunes, failing to take the gig seriously. I didn't have the chops to play an Art Tatum transcription, and some of my original writing at that point was just, well, weird. This was one moment in my journey when I wondered if I was good enough to make it. There would be other such junctures down the road, but this was a tough one, because I had yet to leave the academic nest, to prove that I could be successful out in the real world.

I was confronting, for the first time, the difficult marriage of art and commerce. How was I going to make money playing esoteric, original music? What kind of gigs was I going to get? Was my playing really any good? My songwriting? Had the university duped me into thinking I had what it took, just so I'd keep paying tuition?

I wasn't ready to throw in the towel, however. I was just getting started. My skin thickened up a bit, and I decided I was going to continue in the arts, for better or worse. Other musicians might give up after graduation and get a day job, but I wasn't going to be one of them.

Most people never know the intense ups and downs associated with the creative process. There is the high of creating something meaningful, possibly achieving greatness, and there is the low of completely failing to do this. When you create something, you have to embrace the possibility that the finished product might not be valued by other people; and you might not be the best person to judge why.

How is an artist to weigh his own instincts against the feedback he receives from other people? How does he know when to embrace or dismiss criticism? It's a tough dilemma—one that is sometimes resolved only through hindsight. At times you're right to stick to your guns, but sometimes you're better served to listen to what people are telling you. The wisdom of your choice, or lack thereof, is only revealed after the fact... after the world decides whether it likes your stuff or not.

In a band it gets more complicated, because you're part of a collective. Being in a band is like being a painter, but instead of just going with your instinct, you have to consult a committee for approval with each and every brush of the canvas. *What do you think about this? This color look okay to you?* The marriage of democracy and creativity can be exciting when it works, but when it doesn't, it's frustrating and stifling.

There were so many kids graduating the day I received my Bachelor of Arts degree that Len and Ann, who had driven all the way from Prescott to witness the event, were forced to watch on TV from a nearby lecture hall. One of the university's Deans, whom I'd traveled with to Taiwan, handed me the prized piece of paper. It felt good to be finished, but the whole day was anti-climactic, to tell you the truth. Len rewarded my academic perseverance by giving me his car, a white Dodge Caravan. This allowed me to sell my ugly brown truck, a.k.a. the Chimichanga[48], to a pair of illegal immigrant gardeners in the neighborhood. I was hoping for better luck with the Caravan.[49]

---

[48] Prior to this, the Chimichanga had been ripped off in the parking lot of the jazz club Elario's, while I was inside playing a gig. When the police found it near the Mexican border, there were empty beer bottles and women's panties strewn around the back.

[49] Not only was the Chimichanga stolen, but in another earlier bout of misfortune, *all my musical gear* had been stolen from the Chimichanga. I'm talking about multiple keyboards, stands, cables, and an amplifier. I swear that vehicle was cursed.

WHITE MEN CAN'T JUMP,
BUT THEY *CAN* RAP

Even though Fried Bananas, *San Diego's premier all-white reggae band,*[50] had fallen apart, my desire to be involved in creative projects was stronger than ever. I showed up for a downtown gig with a trumpet player named Jalen Jones, who led a hip-hop jazz project called Faze. Jalen, a charismatic young black guy who was popular with the ladies, fronted the group with the help of his cousin, a strong, bespectacled guy who went by the name Stone. I immediately got along well with the guys in Faze, particularly drummer Richard Sellers, who seemed to know what I was going to play before I did. By the end of that first night, Richard and I had connected like we'd been playing together for years. We cracked huge grins and hugged each other. It

---

[50] Haha.

was the beginning of a strong friendship and musical partnership that has lasted to this day.

The bass player in Faze was Ken Dow, my co-conspirator in the previously discussed Panama Mazakuza debacle. There was also a percussionist, Nico Valencia, whose mild manner belied a rough-and-tumble past. The equal distribution of black and white members gave Faze a desirable ethnic blend. Before playing the first note, a multi-racial band makes a statement simply by walking on stage together: It *is* possible.

Faze rehearsed at a rented house near SDSU. The address was 5292 Gary Street. Jalen and Stone lived there, along with Richard and a very large, funny guy named Wilbur Dugdale. The rehearsals would turn into mini-parties, with young women parading in and out. The scene looked like an MTV video—a low-budget video, that is. Jalen and Stien juggled a small stable of girls between the two of them, and their rap lyrics reflected this. Songs like *I Gotta Have a Mom* and *Much Respect to the Ladies* ran the gamut from proud philandering to worship of all things feminine.

I came up with a nickname for Richard, which he still has on his business card today: *Chef R&B*. When someone calls Richard for a gig that doesn't pay anything, he waits until they're done talking and then says: "Take a closer look at the card. It says Chef R&B… not Chef R & free."

Faze had steady work at a club in La Jolla called Taxxi. The Malibu of San Diego, La Jolla is a beach community that accommodates both wealthy locals and tourists with abundant play money. The main thoroughfare is lined with overpriced art galleries, restaurants and women's clothing stores. Taxxi was La Jolla's version of Studio 54. Coked out, synthetically enhanced Amazon blondes mingled with stogie-smoking, Armani-wearing Italian guys. You would see the occasional celebrity, such as Malcolm Jamal Warner (Theo from the Cosby Show). Warner was a fan of the hip-hop scene, and a musician himself. One night he and I got into an in-depth conversation about music. Inevitably, we were interrupted by a female fan. "I just had to say something to you," she giggled. "I appreciate that," he replied, "but can you see I'm in the middle of a conversation?"

Jalen was a poised, rather stoic individual—a good listener who thought carefully before throwing around his opinions. After we became friends, he confided in me details about his troubled youth—stories of brutal, gang-like activity. He wasn't proud of it, but it was part of his past. One of his stories reminded me of a particularly harsh scene from the film, *American History X*. I found Jalen's story fascinating, and years later would base the central character of one of my screenplays on what I knew of his life. It was called *Skill*, and told the story of a jazz/hip-hop band trying to make it in Los Angeles.

Jalen and I made a powerful musical duo. He had great ideas for grooves, beats, hooks and instrumental melodies, and also good rapping ability. In turn, he admired my improvising and composing talent. One day, I played and sang him an R&B song I'd written, and Jalen said "Anth, you're going to be rich."[51] When I expressed an interest in rapping, he offered instruction. He dissected my rhymes and my delivery, suggesting I add a slight accent of some kind, so as not to sound so… white. My rapping debut in Faze was in a song called *P.D.A.* (Public Displays of Affection, not Personal Data Assistant). I still remember part of it:

Don't get me wrong, much respect to the ladies
There's a girl out there who's gotta be down to have my babies
And I'll find her some day, my prince will come to verify
The accuracy of my ever cautious eye
But until that time my heart belongs to hip-hop, jazz and rhyme
I'll be kickin' it on the Soul Bus
That's because I'm a member of the Six from Gary Street
You all are in for such a treat, but don't compete for my affections
Mistaking love for your physical intentions

You know the drill, step off my grill
You know the drill, step off my grill
You know the drill, step off my grill
I ain't down with no P.D.A.

My relationship with Faze's other frontman, Stone, wasn't always amicable. Stone was a great guy to party with, and like Jalen, had clever musical ideas and a lot of charisma. Stone also had a dark side, however, which surfaced from time to time. When he was emanating this vibe, his body language said: *Give me a reason and I'll fuck you up.* Most people, me included, didn't want to give him that reason. He

---

[51] A nice sentiment, but in retrospect a bit of an overstatement.

was a fearless, muscular dude. One night we almost came to blows, after a disagreement over the guest list for a particular show. He begged me to hit him, but instead I backed away, my legs trembling. He had no fear, but I certainly had some.

Soon, Stone was not the only one in the band I was at odds with. Jalen and I had a falling out over a girl I'd been seeing, and he *then began* seeing. As you might gather, there was a bit of *overlap*, and I was not tickled by this fact. Things were sadly never quite the same between us after that.

We did, however, temporarily bury the hatchet one night at a wild rave called Narnia. This two-day free-for-all took place on an Indian reservation and included bands, DJs, and thousands of kids doing every drug imaginable. After we played a set, Jalen and I got liquored up. Feeling no pain, we walked around the reservation in almost predatory fashion. A pair of massive white guys bumped us when passing by, and we detected a bit of an attitude from them. We stopped walking. Jalen backtracked, got up in one of the guy's mugs and said, "Is there a problem?" The guy, much bigger than us, seemed terrified.

"No, there's no problem," he meekly replied. Jalen had a crazy look in his eye, and in that moment I realized he had not been bullshitting about his past. And in that moment, I was ready to join him in brawling with those big cornfed motherfuckers. I wanted it to happen, dare I admit. Maybe I subconsciously believed that kicking some ass with Jalen would allow us to sweep our baggage under the table and start fresh. The guys weren't interested in a fight, and so, still on the prowl for shenanigans of some kind, we made our way into a random trailer—a den of drug-infested excess, as it turned out. Kids staggered around, mumbling unintelligibly to themselves. We quickly decided it wasn't our scene, and got up to leave. Before we were out the door one girl asked, "Where are you two going?" Jalen and I shot each other a look. The olive-skinned girl was wearing a curly, white wig and some sort of glittery retro costume. She was not unattractive. "I'm going wherever you guys are going," she said.

A steady wave of attractive young women had been parading by all night, tantalizing every straight guy with lurid outfits and suggestive dance moves; and here was one that apparently wanted to take the party to the next level. Jalen and I led our new friend off the beaten path, into an area laden with brush and trees. The hypnotic pulse of techno beats thumped off in the distance, as I found myself writhing around in the woods with this uninhibited vixen of Narnia. She blurted out phrases of encouragement, in a voice reminiscent of a forgotten era of the silver screen—kind of a combination of Jenna Jamison and Greta Garbo.

I'd lost track of Jalen, until I glanced over and saw him prepping for action, revealing nothing that might encourage the dismissal of black anatomical myths. At some point we switched roles, he now serving as the object of our psychedelic nymph's anachronistic coaching. The booze had taken its toll, however, forcing Jalen to throw in the towel prematurely. I pulled myself together as our friend, disheveled and tripping on one substance or another, picked at the twigs and foliage that had lodged in the strands of her synthetic wig.

We returned to the festivities, said our goodbyes to *Greta Jamison*, and chanced upon Chef R&B. Once we'd given him some indication of our previous whereabouts, he asked if we planned to continue hanging out with our new friend for the remainder of the evening. We informed him that alas, we did not, at which time he pointed directly behind us and said, coining a classic new phrase of the era, "Then y'all ain't walkin' fast enough." There she was bringing up the rear, trying to keep up. Without thinking Jalen and I morphed into hip-hop's interracial answer to Michael Johnson and Donavan Bailey, rounding the final stretch in a record-breaking race for the finish line.[52]

I had a guitarist friend at that time, Dale Park, who I thought would make a great addition to Faze. Dale joined the group and immediately improved its sound. He also made suggestions that tightened the focus of the material. Faze started to develop a distinct musical identity.

Dale, in turn, had a friend in San Diego named Francois Bouffard. Francois was a bassist and producer, and had worked with many well-established artists and songwriters. A wild Frenchman with a thick accent, Francois was also an irresistible raconteur, passionately recounting tales that combined high-level musical interaction with sexual frivolity. I would be lying if I said I wasn't fascinated by the colorful, lascivious details of Francois's globetrotting excursions.

Francois came to a Faze show to check out the band and was struck by what he saw. He believed there was some magic there, and offered to shop us around L.A. using his connections. We accepted, and recorded some songs in Francois's home studio. Then we entered

---

[52] Only in this case, neither of us faked pulling up lame.

Discmaker's Unsigned Band Contest. We were selected as finalists, and played for industry insiders at The Troubador in West Los Angeles. We performed well but did not win.

Francois landed us a gig at The Roxy, another high-profile L.A. venue. The Roxy, like other Hollywood clubs, required you to pay money to play there. If you sold enough tickets you could make some money yourself, but you were doing the gig for the chance to showcase your music to industry people, who came in search of fresh talent.

We rehearsed diligently for the Roxy show, realizing the band's future might be hinged on its success or failure. We created clever segues between songs, fine-tuned all the arrangements, and considered our visual presentation. We also recruited a group of friends to make the trek to L.A. with us. It was important to have a crowd cheering you on when you played in front of industry people.

The show went very well, the band playing to its full potential. I was proud of our performance. Francois told us there were some record executives in the crowd, but for whatever reason no deal discussion came of it.

Dale talked me into moving in with him at his parents' house in Lakeside. Since his folks were living in Long Beach, we would have the place all to ourselves. I agreed, and the first thing we did was hit the local Cost Plus and stock up on all kinds of cool amenities—beads, tapestries, lamps. We transformed the place into a bachelor pad extraoirdinaire, removing doors and replacing them with beads, rearranging the furniture to maximize the *feng shui*, and lighting candles and incense. Now all we needed was some free-lovin' hippie chicks.

For a couple weeks everything was great. Aside from his parents' two hulking, unkempt dogs, Dale and I had the whole house to ourselves. We could play music as loud as we wanted, and leave the kitchen a mess without worry. The honeymoon abruptly ended when Dale's parents announced they were returning to Lakeside. Now I'd be living with Dale, his parents, his down-on-her-luck older sister, and the two dogs.

The main difficulty with this new arrangement was the fact that I had taken the door off my bedroom and replaced it with beads. This allowed twenty-four-hour access to my sanctuary, rendering it more of a *common area*. Both dogs and humans now wandered in and out of my room at will. The dogs sniffed and licked me at sunrise each morning, and Dale's father Arnold, a jazz enthusiast, stood by my bed and launched lengthy discourses on the illustrious legacy of improvised music in America.

"Art Pepper... some say he was the best. I myself do not agree."

For obvious reasons, Dale and I began searching for an apartment. We found a third roommate, a saxophonist friend of Dale named Jim Gorman, and settled into the second story of a house on La Mesa Boulevard. La Mesa, an eastern suburb of San Diego, was a nice residential town. It got very hot there in the summer, however.

Dale got a teaching job at a music store across the street from our apartment, and Ed worked a horribly degrading telemarketing job. I, meanwhile, did as many local gigs as I could string together. Sometimes the gigs were challenging, like the time I was hired to accompany Don Menza, a respected tenor saxophonist from L.A. It was a two-night run at Elario's in La Jolla, and the rhythm section consisted of Bob Magnusson on bass, Jim Plank on drums, and me. I had seen these two men play, in this very club, with such greats as the late guitarist Joe Pass and pianist Kenny Barron, so the opportunity was a personal milestone of sorts.

Magnusson, who had worked with countless luminaries from the jazz world, warned me that Menza could be difficult at times. I didn't want to suffer the same fate as a certain pianist who, a few years earlier, had been ridiculed and driven from the stage in this same club, by a truculent[53] Freddie Hubbard. As it turned out I got along fine with the much older saxophonist, and knew the majority of tunes he called during both nights of the engagement. He didn't melt down until the end of the second night, when, after being handed a check when he had expected cash, he yelled, "This means nothing to me!" Bob Magnusson turned to him and said, in a tone of voice reflecting the accumulated wisdom of literally thousands of gigs, "Let's take it easy now, Don."

I was working regularly at that time with Hollis Gentry III, a very talented sax player with a great following in San Diego. Hollis had done major international tours with artists like Larry Carlton and David Benoit, and was considered the most visible jazz musician in the city. Hollis and I rarely discussed musical theory, but he provided mentorship in other ways. We had engaging conversations that covered many topics, from general life struggles to philosophy and

---

[53] ... and most likely high.

women. If I tried to steer one of our chats toward musical specifics, Hollis might sigh and say, "That's between you and God, my friend."

I admired Hollis's approach to being a bandleader. He hired guys whose playing he respected, then allowed them to approach the music in their own way. He didn't micromanage. He wasn't going to sit there and tell you what or how to play. I later incorporated this idea into my own musical philosophy. When putting together my own groups, I would try to get the best players I could find, and then give them the freedom to put their own *thing* on top of my ideas. Don Haas, my most important piano teacher, had first steered me down this path when he said, "You're not a drummer. You're not going to think of anything as cool as what a good drummer is going to come up with on his own, so just give him a sketch to work with."

Hollis Gentry's rhythm section included my pal Tim McMahon on drums and Sven McKibbon on upright bass. Tim and I would hang out after the gigs, frequenting late-night eateries like Etna's, Hong Kong, and Rudford's Diner. Etna's could lay claim to some of the best pizza and pasta in San Diego. From the outside it looked like a dump, stuck in a bad neighborhood, but once you walked inside the place was humbly charming. It was a perfect first-date spot: great food, quaint, unpretentious.

 Hong Kong was in the heart of Hillcrest and stayed open very late at night—an important consideration for gigging musicians. Often, I didn't leave a job until one or two in the morning, and being a young man with a healthy appetite, was ready for some fresh, hot chow. The amazing thing about Hong Kong was that in the dozens of times I'd been there with various friends, *we were always waited on by the same lady.* She didn't speak English but she was always in good spirits, and had mastered the Asian-pioneered art of nodding and laughing at every word muttered by a customer. Given her tireless commitment to her job, I came to view this little woman as the Cal Ripken, Jr. of late-night Chinese joints. If one-night stands were *pu-pu platters,* she would be the Wilt Chamberlain of wontons.

Sven, Hollis's bassist, was a good player, capable of executing fluid solos and walking confidently lines at fast tempos. If you wanted to know how good Sven was, all you had to do was *ask him.* As we stood in front of Croce's during a break one night he said, "I heard the new Keith Jarrett album today. Gary Peacock's bass playing is really great on it... he's playing lots of stuff that *I* would play." On another occasion, I told Sven I was planning to record a CD of my own jazz piano arrangements and then press up a thousand copies.

"Oh yeah? Who are you planning to give them to?" he asked.

"Family and friends, mostly," I replied. Sven snickered.

"Do you have a thousand family and friends?"

Hollis, like so many brilliant musicians, had his demons. The man liked to drink. On a club gig, this was no big deal. We all had a drink or two when playing Croce's or a number of other night spots. But was it cool to throw back a few when you were doing, say, a wedding? *Not so much.* I showed up at the La Valencia Hotel in La Jolla one early afternoon for a very upscale reception. The band was solid: Glen Fisher on bass, Carlos Vazquez on drums, me, and Hollis on sax. There might have been a couple other guys, too.

When Hollis arrived, he was already feeling no pain. While we set up our equipment in an immaculately decorated ballroom, the tall reed man started stumbling around looking for a bar. He found one, and grabbed himself a glass of Merlot. We knew trouble was brewing—we weren't supposed to drink—but hoped Hollis would keep it together. He was one of those guys who got a lot of passes, thanks to his undeniable charisma.

There was a big buffet spread already set up, and it goes without saying that we were absolutely not supposed to start digging in. Hollis, however, was taking cues from his own script, and wandered over to the food, waving his full glass of wine around precariously. You can guess what happened from here... the glass slipped out of his long fingers, the wine splattering not only the long, white tablecloth but also the food itself. The only thing worse would have been *dropping trow* and pissing on the cake in the corner.

The wedding coordinator saw what had happened—she saw Hollis staggering, and put two and two together. Rather than lay into him, or into all of us, she pulled out her phone and *called the police.* "There's a drunken man disrupting the peace at the La Valencia Hotel," she said. It wasn't long before a pair of officers arrived at the scene.

"He's in here somewhere," the coordinator said. The rest of us played dumb. Hollis had been whisked by one of the musicians into the storage room where we were keeping our empty cases. The cops were no dummies, and walked right back to the room. *Oh shit, this is bad,* we thought. They returned to the ballroom empty-handed, a puzzled look on their faces.

"Where did he go," one of them barked.

"He must have split," someone lied. Frustrated, the cops left the scene. We walked back to the storage room and beheld a hilarious sight: Hollis climbing out of Glen's upright bass case, where he had been hiding the whole time.

Jalen and the gang were having financial issues at the house on Gary Street. Shit was starting to get shut off. One day, Wilbur—all three-hundred-fifty-plus pounds of him—and I were watching cable TV in his room. Suddenly the screen went fuzzy. Wilbur opened the blinds on his window, and there he was, up on the telephone pole: a Cox Cable employee in a hard hat. Wilbur yelped out the window, "Pleeeease, fool! I gotta have my cable! Come down off that pole!"

"Then give me the four hundred and thirty-seven dollars and forty-two cents you owe," the guy yelled back.

When it was time for the crew to move to a new spot, I volunteered my Dodge minivan to help with the process. Chef R&B threw his box spring on top of the van, and I tied it down with a bungee cord. That's right—one bungee cord. "Should do the trick," I said. The Chef and I were a quarter mile down Montezuma Boulevard when I heard the unmistakable twang of a snapped bungee, followed immediately by the screech of tires. Afraid to look back, I pulled the van to the side of the road. I climbed out slowly, looked behind my car, and saw Chef's box spring plopped there on the street, inches from the car it had almost creamed. Let me clarify that: the *cop car* it had almost creamed. The pissed off cop got out and marched over, wagging his hairy finger near my chest as I caught the glare from his sunglasses.

"You almost caused a major accident!"

"Sorry, Officer. Thought I had the mattress secured pretty good there."

"With one bungee cord?!!"

"You think I should have used two?"

I received a multitude of traffic citations in my mid-twenties. There was a certain judge at the Clairemont courthouse, Judge Millington, who I appeared before on a few occasions. One time, Judge Millington wasn't buying my story about how road construction had impaired my ability to spot a stop sign.

"I'm not trying to be disputatious here," I assured him.

"Disputatious? Look at Mr. Big Vocabulary over here!" he bellowed, rousing the entire courthouse to laughter. I now wonder if Mike Judge had been in the audience that day, because a very similar scene turned up in his hilarious movie *Idiocracy,* in 2006.

THIS GUY'S A GENIUS

By my mid-twenties, I started to wonder how I'd ever make a substantial income as a freelance musician. I was providing for myself, keeping a roof over my head, but not putting anything away. I did what most keyboard players do under these circumstances: I got a sales job in a retail music store.

Jerry Olsher knew me from the San Diego scene, and was enthusiastic when I approached him about a job at his store, Music Mart. Jerry played and sang himself, and liked to have sales guys who could perform—guys who were actual professionals. He figured he'd sell more instruments if the customers heard them being made to sound easy and effortless. People would figure, "Hey, I can do that." Also, it just looked better to have experienced pros showing the merchandise than pimply teenagers who couldn't play *Chopsticks.*

I've said it before, but I'll repeat, *I'm not the most technically inclined lad to ever come down the pike.* It was somewhat difficult for me to figure out all the electronic parameters within modern keyboards and synthesizers. Reading instruction manuals was a hair-pulling experience—I must have read quite a few of them, because I don't have much hair left now.

While Jerry supported my efforts to confront the techie learning curve, his customers were not always so patient. One time, a composer friend of Jerry's came into the store looking for troubleshooting help with a keyboard he'd purchased. The guy rattled off a litany of problems, none of which I had the slightest clue how to remedy. When he was done talking, I said:

"Let me get this right... the keyboard stores data on memory cards, but you're not able to organize the data the way you want, and you're trying to figure out a better way to store your multi-track song sequences... am I right?" The guy's eyes lit up real wide, and he turned to address the entire store, customers and employees alike:

Hey Jerry...This guy's amazing. Where'd you find him? Hold on to this one. He's something special. This guy's a regular frickin' genius! My problems are solved!

After I'd been working at Music Mart for a couple months, Jerry brought in a guitar player friend of his to manage the whole store. Marvin Kravjansky, mid-forties and pudgy, wore thick glasses, square clothes, and possessed a formidable finger-picking guitar style. I, meanwhile, bored to tears with this new career path, had developed a formidable *nose*-picking style. Jerry had given me an opportunity to expand my horizons, but let's face it—sometimes in life, we begin to expand a particular horizon, only to realize it is better left *un-expanded*.

Marvin liked to work the *family angle* of music sales. He recruited young kids and their eager parents, playing to dreams of musical grandeur... visions of sold-out future concerts at Carnegie Hall, tours of Europe, etc. Before their kid could take the musical world by storm, Marvin assured the parents he'd need a guitar he could grow into—an instrument that could keep up with his progress. Therefore, in Marvin's mind, it made sense to start out with the most expensive, meticulously crafted instrument in the entire store. Some might have questioned the decision to unload a $1500 Takamine custom six-string on a ten-year old with clumsy fingers and a tin ear, but not Marvin, who had a commitment to quality and excellence. He would literally spend hours with one family, building a relationship, planting the seeds. Marvin assured the parents that on that glorious day, years in the future, when little Lee set foot on the stage at Carnegie Hall, premiering his three-part concerto for wind, brass and classical guitar, Marvin would be there in the front row, grinning from ear to ear.

This sales approach was demonstrated beautifully on one particular occasion. Marvin had been working all afternoon with a young, affluent couple and their small son... let's call him Billy. After much deliberating, these folks decided to heed Marvin's advice and go with a $3000 guitar. Marvin closed the deal, wrote up the receipt, then ceremoniously trotted to the front of the store. The couple followed as Marvin, good shepherd of guitar sales, held little Billy's hand. I, along with the several other people in the store, stood nearby witnessing the spectacle. Marvin gazed wistfully in my direction, and I responded with a tender smile. Then, realizing he had the entire store's attention, Marvin dropped to one knee, to speak face-to-face with the tike.

"Now, Billy, I want you to make me a promise." The kid stared at Marvin nervously and then glanced at his parents. They nodded their heads in approval.

"Okay," Billy nervously muttered.

"I want you to promise me that you're going to practice that guitar faithfully every day. Can you do that?"

"Yeah," Billy croaked.

"Say it... *I promise.*"

"I promise to practice my guitar every day."

"Good. Now I want you to turn and face your parents." Little Billy complied.

"Now you're going to make a promise to your mom and dad, okay?"

"Okay."

"I want you to say, 'Mom, Dad... I honor and appreciate you. I promise to make you proud for giving me this wonderful guitar. I promise to take care of it, and to play it to the best of my ability, now and for as long as it is God's will for me to do so.'"

It was like the poor kid was marrying the damn guitar.

"I promise... to do all that stuff."

136

"Okay, great." Marvin rose again to his feet, patted little Billy on the head, and turned once again to the parents.

"I think he's ready, Mike... Lisa."

"We think so too, Marvin. I don't know how to thank you for everything you've done."

We all watched as Marvin walked the young family, $3000 custom guitar in tow, out to their Range Rover, and waved, enraptured with the bittersweet melancholy of the moment. He watched them drive off into the Claremont Mesa sunset, then returned to the store, walked in triumphantly, and looked me in the eye. Then, Marvin raised his right arm high, pulled on an imaginary cash register handle, and said one word:

Ch-ching.

Jerry was a good singer and songwriter, and participated in a local organization called the San Diego Songwriters Showcase. The group brought in a publisher or other type of music industry insider, often from L.A., to screen songs written by San Diego locals. I had recently recorded some pop song demos, and Jerry encouraged me and Dale Park, my co-writer, to enter a few for consideration.

Over hot and sour soup at Hong Kong, Dale and I had planned the next five years of our songwriting/producing careers. We were going to place our songs with successful artists, develop a thriving publishing company called Major Ears Music, and build a home studio where we could develop artists and crank out hit songs, all while solidifying a production team under the handle *A.D. 2 Million.*

We had some very good songs. The first one I penned was called *Vicarious,* and told the story of a guy dreaming about his ex-girlfriend, while he's making love to his *new* girlfriend. The lyrics were somewhat clever, if I say so myself:

Association
Can be such a dangerous word
Imagination takes over
When I feel your warm, tender skin
As I'm touching her
Baby you walked right on out of my life
Said you want me to keep in touch
But bein' friends with you

Is just not enough

She wears the same perfume
She does her hair the way you used to
I know it just ain't right
To play these games no girl deserves to be put through...

I'm vicariously loving you

I shopped *Vicarious* at the annual Songwriter's Convention in Los Angeles. It was a two-day event with featured panel speakers, such as John Passenheim, attorney and author of the popular book, *Everything You Need to Know About the Music Business,* workshops, and pitch sessions, where you had the opportunity to present your material to publishers and major label executives. My song was well-received, and stood out as one of the more promising offerings at the whole convention. I thought, *this might be my break.* All you needed was one hit to make a name for yourself.

At that time Alanis Morissette was all the rage—the brightest new star on the pop horizon—and many of the record label representatives were saying the same thing: *We're looking for the next Alanis Morissette.* I couldn't understand why everyone wanted to copy what was already out there, rather than light upon something fresh and original. Shows you how naïve I was...

A few years later when I began trying writing screenplays, a great truth of the entertainment industry would be revealed to me. As William Goldman famously said, *nobody knows anything.* When a singer or a film breaks through somehow, everyone scrambles to imitate the hot new commodity. If you think you're going to bowl everyone over with your bold, original vision, think again. You'd be better off trying to peddle something tried-and-true, which perhaps just a splash of originality, and wait until you're successful before you try to reinvent the wheel. There are those who would disagree with me, but hey, *the world is full of idealists.*

One of the people I hooked up with at the convention was a guy named John Wilson,[54] whose claim to fame was being Janet Jackson's producer before Jimmy Jam and Terry Lewis came along. Wilson had

---

[54] No relation to my junior high school friend.

penned one of the lesser known songs on the singer's first album, which became a blockbuster smash; he had been overshadowed by Jam and Lewis, who wrote the all big hits, but he still had platinum credentials. Wilson agreed to meet Dale and me at a Denny's in Sherman Oaks, to discuss our music. We were fired up. This guy was on the inside and he could open doors. After some casual conversation we presented him with a compilation tape of our best songs. Wilson took our tape and told us he'd call.

While in L.A. we also had a meeting with a prominent entertainment attorney named John Yarmoski. Yarmoski had listened to our music and agreed to set aside a few minutes to meet with us. You might be wondering what good it would do to give music to a lawyer, as opposed to a producer or label executive. At that time in the business, entertainment lawyers had the clout to shop for publishing and artist deals. Since they worked constantly with the labels and publishing companies to broker deals and negotiate contracts, they had personal relationships with influential decision-makers. Of course, these days it's a whole new ballgame. Digital downloading, piracy, and the general collapse of the big label model have changed everything.

Yarmoski wasted no time in telling Dale and me that he thought our music was great. He liked the songs, heard the commercial potential, and was curious what we wanted to do with them. We didn't know how to respond to that question. Wasn't it obvious what we wanted to do with our material? We wanted to get the songs recorded on major label albums by big-name artists. Wasn't that where Yarmoski came in? Selling our stuff and taking his cut?

Yes, he said, that was essentially his role. But the thing was, guys like John Yarmoski, as much as they liked your material, weren't just going to shop your stuff for free. He would be happy to make the rounds on our behalf, pitching us as promising new songwriters... for a price. And that price was not cheap. Dale and I had barely scraped together the money to make the demo recording. We didn't have thousands of dollars to shell out to a lawyer to pitch our stuff, with no guarantee of anything coming of it. This leads me to a general point I'd like to make about the arts...

There is a strong case to be made for establishing a reliable means of making money outside of your artistic realm. If you make enough where you can save a nest egg, doing something other than playing music or writing or whatever it is you do, then you can take some of that nest egg and invest it wisely in furthering your artistic pursuits;

because no matter what you do... paint, write scripts, compose music... it all costs money. It costs money to produce the work, and it *definitely* costs money to develop the relationships with those who might help you get your work out into the world. If you're always struggling financially, you won't ever have the money you need to open doors. Also, when you're relying exclusively on your artistic pursuits to make money, it's very hard not to compromise the integrity of the vocation. You wind up doing things you'd never do if money wasn't a factor, and in the process damage that delicate, sacred passion which lies not only at the heart of your work, but the heart of *you.*

A clear distinction must be drawn between being a serious artist and being successful in the real world. Being a serious artist means you strive for excellence and originality, and you are uncompromising with your work. It might also mean you are poor, if it's the only thing you do for money. If you don't care about being poor, and the joy of following your artistic vision, unhindered by the constraints of commercialism, is enough to keep you going, that's great. You might have a cabinet full of Top Ramen, but you've also got your principles. If you want to be *recognized* and *rewarded,* however... the minute you decide these things are important, you've entered a whole new arena. Now you have to play ball. You've got to be a strategist, a diplomat, a politician, a hustler. You might have to be a whore. You've got to do things the uncompromising purist would never stoop to consider. The entertainment world, like the world itself, is competitive, crowded, chaotic, and in the end, more or less uncaring about your little dreams. If you're going to take your shot out there, you're going to get dirty, and it's going to get ugly.

Dale and I got a follow-up call from John Wilson, one week later. He liked our songwriting but felt the production value was weak. The music would have to be much more slickly produced if he was going to shop it to labels and artists. If we wanted, he would produce a new demo for us, re-recording everything in order to make the songs really shine.

"That sounds great, John. Let's do it," Dale enthused.

"Great. My price is five thousand dollars, plus the studio time."

There are very few people out there who will commit their energy to helping your career without expecting something tangible in return, usually money. If you find that rare person—they do exist, believe it or not—who admires your talent enough to invest time, money and resources in your career, without demanding something in return, please...

Hold on to that person for dear life.

Back in San Diego, Dale and I set our sights on the upcoming San Diego Songwriter Showcase. The guest of honor was Mills Jamerson, a Los Angeles producer. Mills, black and around fifty, had supposed ties to hot R&B artists of the day. We polished our soul-oriented material, including a catchy, Babyface-style track called *Ten Locations*, in which a male singer tells his girl about his favorite ten locations on her body. There was a Prince-like ballad called *Take Me With You*, a pretty crossover pop/country tune called *The Sun Won't Rise Without You*, a Cher-inspired power ballad called *You've Done Enough*, and a Luther Vandross-flavored love song called *Let's Enjoy the View*.

Many local songwriters turned out for Jamerson's pitch session, and Dale and I were excited to play him our material. After hearing some entries from fellow San Diego writers, we realized our stuff was a cut above. Some of the local offerings were downright embarrassing, but we knew our stuff sounded like music you might actually hear on the radio. Dale leaned over to me and whispered, crudely but astutely, "Mark my words. This guy's going to be blowing us by the end of the night."

As our first song played, Jamerson's ears perked up, his eyes frantically searching the room. We sat back, arms folded across our chests.

A couple hours later, Jamerson had played several songs from the production team of A.D. 2 Million, and was now lavishing high praise on us, in a crowded banquet room of aspiring San Diego tunesmiths. "Everybody take a minute to go meet these guys," he said. "They understand the ingredients of a good song. These guys are going places."

We followed up the big night, at Jamerson's suggestion, with a meeting in Los Angeles. This time it was a Denny's in Hollywood. I invited Jalen Jones, who also aspired to pop songwriting success, to make the drive with us up to L.A.[55] Jalen had reservations about

---

[55] Jalen, in the end, has been the one to find real success as a pop songwriter. His credits include the Black Eyed Peas hit *Where Is The Love*, co-written by Justin Timberlake.

Jamerson's authenticity, after talking to him on the phone. He wanted to check the guy out in person.

Jalen served as our street smart, hip-hop counterpart, there to bridge the racial/cultural gap and also cut through any jive. We got to the Denny's, went inside and took a booth, and waited for Jamerson. Jalen stood up.

"Where you going?" I asked.

"Outside. I wanna see what this motherfucker rolls up in."

When Jamerson arrived in some kind of Toyota sedan, we had our first red flag. After some discussion about placing songs with artists, it was apparent to all that the man had little to offer us. He talked big, but when you tried to pin him down to specifics, or to steer the conversation toward actual plans and goals, he started shifting in his chair. He said he'd played *Vicarious* for Phillip Bailey, the singer from Earth, Wind and Fire, and the owner of one of pop music's most distinctive falsettos had apparently liked it. That was the big news Jamerson brought to the table. *So what? If he's not interested in recording the tune, who cares if he likes it?* Jalen, meanwhile, didn't say a word the whole time. He just sat there, studying the older man. We drove home, nothing to show for an evening spent shuffling back and forth on the 405. Jalen told us he thought Jamerson was a hustler and a bullshit artist.

After a couple more fizzled attempts to hook up with Mills Jamerson, I wrote him off. Jerry Olsher, my boss and fellow songwriter at Music Mart, hadn't trusted the guy from the beginning. When I told him how things had panned out, he sighed and said, "Yeah, I figured he was just another *schwartze blowin' in the wind*." Years later, Dale called me one night and said he'd heard a song on the radio that sounded suspiciously similar to *The Sun Won't Rise Without You*. Dale had done a bit of research, and guess whose name was on the credits as a writer and producer? That's right… Mills Jamerson. Jalen had been right.

Around that time, I had re-established contact with Dale Tedesco, a publisher I first met while still in school at SDSU. Dale had attempted to place a couple of my early demos with artists, but nothing had materialized. Now, I made plans to meet with him and have him check out some newer songs. I drove up to his house in Grenada Hills, and we sat in his home office and listened to my stuff. There was a huge pile of tapes and CD's on Tedesco's desk. Most of them were unsolicited submissions from people like me.

"You see this pile? I get this much music *every week* from people I've never met or heard of. And you know what? Most of it is garbage." After listening to my songs, Dale stopped the machine, clasped his hands and gave me the truth: "You have some talent, you know. But I have to tell you, this is a hard racket, man. It's not very glamorous. You just keep slugging it out, and eventually you'll get something recorded by someone."

One of the problems with trying to get the attention of the industry was the fact that these people were inundated with a steady barrage of unsolicited product, most of which wasn't very good. Many of the bigger fish didn't even accept unsolicited work in the first place, because they would run the risk of a plagiarism lawsuit just by admitting they'd accepted someone's ideas for consideration. The last thing Shania Twain needed was to get dragged into court by Bobbie Sue Mulgrevey of Anamoose, North Dakota, who claimed the singer stole the melody from a song called *Teardrops on the Cowpie of My Heart...*

Judge: How do you suggest Ms. Twain might have heard your song, Ms. Mulgrevey?
Bobbie Sue: Well, I've been playing my guitar and singing at Jesus n' Java, every Tuesday evening for the last six years.
Judge: That's a Christian coffeehouse?
Bobbie Sue: Hottest spot in Anamoose.
Judge: Well that's saying something, isn't it?
Bobbie Sue: You bet.
Judge: Ms. Twain... Have you ever been to Anamoose, North Dakota?
Shania Twain: No. I've never been to North Dakota period.
Judge: So then, Ms. Mulgrevey, how could Ms. Twain have stolen your song if she's never even been in the state where you perform it?
Bobbie Sue: She might have sent in a spy. There's lots of good songwriting coming out of Anamoose these days.

I got a call from Bob Chini, the recording engineer who'd helped me put together the demo for *Vicarious.* Bob had some exciting news: the producer for Colour Me Badd, a platinum-selling boy band of that era, had heard the song and loved it. He wanted to use it on the new Colour Me Badd album. Was I interested? Yes, of course, I told Bob. Tell him that I'd love to have a song on that album. Bob relayed the message, and then called me back a few days later. "There's just one catch," Bob explained.

"What's that?"

"He wants to change the name of the song. He doesn't like the word 'vicarious'. He says he had to look it up in the dictionary… and if *he* doesn't know what it means, how the hell are teenage girls going to know?"

"I didn't realize 'vicarious' was such an esoteric word."

"Are you willing to change the lyrics?"

"I'll give it a shot." I tried to rewrite the song, but hit a wall. The whole thing was constructed around that very word. Inaccessible as it might have been to fifteen year-olds, *vicarious* was the whole hook. Besides, I didn't agree with the producer. Bobby Brown had enjoyed a major hit with *My Prerogative*. How many teenagers knew what *that* meant? Or cared? It was a catchy tune and it didn't matter. In fact, that was part of the song's novel success—the inclusion of a "big" word in a simple pop song. The same thing could work with my tune, I felt. Nothing came of it, needless to say. I guess the moral of the story is that boy band producers are in the business of getting adolescent girls hot and bothered enough to buy albums, not improving their command of the English language through the use of advanced vocabulary.

Pop songwriting was not proving to be very lucrative for me at that point, but another opportunity fell into my lap that had the potential of being *highly lucrative.* Jalen and I had met a couple older Hispanic women, who happened to be roommates, at one of our shows, and we would go over to their pad to hang out on occasion. This was long before the term *cougar* had been coined. The woman I was friends with, Lucita, had been raised in Mexico before moving to San Diego and becoming a U.S. citizen. After we'd known each other a while, Lucita told me that her father, who was deceased, had at one point been the *President of Mexico.* I looked up his name and it was true. Well, a little further down the road, Lucita got an interesting phone call. Her father's best friend had been a high-ranking general in the Mexican military, and he had always treated Lucita like his own daughter. The phone call informed Lucita that the general had passed away, and that she was named as a beneficiary in his will. I gently pried for more information, curious about the details.

"You're not going to believe this," Lucita said.

"Try me."

"The general specified that he wants me to move back to Mexico City. Oh yeah, and he wants me to be married."

"Married to who?"

"Whoever. A man of my choosing."

"Why would you agree to such a thing?" I asked. She paused and smiled.

"I guess because if I do, he's leaving me a million dollars." Lucita and I were not a couple, but I was the only guy she was hanging out with at the time. For a brief minute there, I seriously contemplated the possibility. Would it be so bad to relocate to Mexico City, learn to speak Spanish, co-habitate with Lucita and enjoy the inheritance of a million dollars?" Maybe not… but I was a young man, and I had other plans in life. Faze was going to blow up and become a global hip-hop phenomenon; and I was going to be the token, white rapper and keyboard player in the band's music videos.

CLAUDIUS ON THE LEFT,
LISBETHA ON THE RIGHT

Faze landed a gig at a major Hollywood club, opening for a hot R&B singer who had a huge single on the radio. The band rehearsed thoroughly, recognizing it as an important opportunity. The green room at this well-known club was plush. You had your own food and drink server the whole night, and got to enjoy being treated like a successful artist. Some of our San Diego friends were hanging backstage, and also a certain well-known film actor named Claudius, who'd brought along his wife Lisbetha. In order to explain why it was awkward to be sitting with Claudius on the left, Lisbetha on the right, I've got to back up a little...

A friend from the East Coast had told me a story about a legendary jazz musician, rumored to be carrying on an affair with the wife of a television actor, both parties based in New York. The jazz great would pick up the wife in the afternoon, while the actor was working on one of his projects, and they'd drive to an industrial area of Brooklyn, where he'd find an inconspicuous place to park his Ferarri. He would then administer service of the oral variety, and according to the scandalous wife, his talents in this department could rival his nimble, artistically groundbreaking fingers. Why she would divulge this sensitive information to my friend, I can't tell you. Why he would further divulge it to me, I *can* tell you—it was too good not to share.

Anyway, there I was in the green room, sitting on a couch between Claudius and Lisbetha. I looked over at Lisbetha and imagined her skulking off to some back street littered with bleak warehouses in a sketchy part of Brooklyn, allowing a celebrated jazz giant, whose solos I had once studied, to use his tongue to spell the entire alphabet on a certain part of her body.[56] Claudius sat there sipping his cocktail—he hadn't a clue.

Around that time, Faze also got the chance to play the House of Blues. The crowd was surprisingly appreciative, considering we were just the warm-up act for a much bigger name. As mentioned, Jalen had taken me under his wing as a rapper; I now had several raps polished and memorized, and I'd tested them on audiences in San Diego. My decision to rap had been a ballsy one, considering my roots as a suburban white kid with a comfortable upbringing. I had negligible street credibility—which is everything, if you're going to pass yourself off as a rap personality. Even Eminem, with verified urban experience, or at least white trash experience, took a lot of crap in the beginning for being a white boy rapper. Since he was backed by none other than the iconic Dr. Dre, he was able to weather and transcend this criticism en route to fabulous success.

Before the set, Jalen and Stone had given me the green light to drop my rap on *The Age We Live In*, a song I'd written for the group. Knowing this, I took the stage, uncertain if I would have the courage to actually follow through with it. The place was sold out. The crowd was on fire. We played our first couple songs, and people cheered and danced. This was a big moment for us. Then, we broke into *The Age We Live In*, my moment of truth. After the chorus, Jalen and Stien looked over at me, perched behind the keyboard, and motioned for me to come out front. I walked to center stage, took the microphone from

---

[56] I lifted this description of a rather creative approach to oral sex from an old Sam Kinison stand-up routine.

Stone, pushed my long, curly hair brown back with my hand,[57] and started my flow. In case you're not clear about what I'm saying, let me put it like this: I rapped at the House of Blues, in front of a packed house. And here's the kicker... *They liked it.* That's right, the mostly urban (black and Hispanic) crowd accepted my white, formerly suburban, college-educated mojo, for that glorious three minutes while I stood before them rocking the mic, waving my free hand in the air, the way you have to when you're a rapper. Nobody can ever take that away from me. If someone tries to put me down, I can always say: *Oh yeah? Well I rapped at the House of Blues... and they liked it!* How many people of Caucasian descent can say that?

Here's the first verse of the rap, as I recall it:

I never thought I'd see the day
So many people on the streets, nothin' to say
"Could you spare a little?"
I don't even know how to play that
'Cause I'm just getting' by myself
I do what I do because I love it
I ain't above it to be a week or two from chillin' solo in my ride
Twenty-four seven, steps to heaven
Too many to count at this point
You need somethin' more than just a fat-ass joint
To escape sad reality here in the nineties
Our creed is truculence atomically framed
The feared tao of Mad Phat is safe as any Indian cow
Allow me to introduce my little friend
A la Pacino at the end of a saga
Quite derogatory, sorry if it's over your head, Jed
The television pop of the brain dead
Freddie came to town to play his horn but he got high instead
Sometimes it seems like hope is dead

With the hopes of reaching an audience in other regions, Faze booked a little tour in the Bay Area. One of the shows was at Ajax

---

[57] Yes, I had very long hair for a couple years there. I'm glad I grew it out once in my life, while there was still enough to pull off the vibe convincingly. These days, I'd be lookin' at a *skullet*... and we can't have that now, can we?

Lounge, the early home to artists who went on to bigger things, like guitarist Charlie Hunter. During these short road trips, I would hang out mostly with Nico, the percussionist. Nico looked like a smaller, less pretentious version of Fabio, with the long brown hair and chiseled features, and was thus quite a hit with the ladies. Nico was also a tough guy, a bad boy—he'd been in gangs and he'd kicked a lot of ass. He wasn't looking for trouble now, but he wasn't about to run from it either. Lots of girls were (and are) attracted to that package.

One night in Santa Cruz, Nico and I were chilling in a bar. We invited a pair of young ladies to join us back at Anne's house in Aptos. They accepted, and we consumed some drinks while enjoying the Jacuzzi. Later, we all crashed in the living room, pairing off and taking different sides of the room. I could hear everything Nico was whispering to his new friend:

"I know it sounds crazy, and I don't know how to say this, but... you make me feel special. There's something really different about you. I haven't felt this way for a long time. I'm not good at expressing my emotions, but... *I think I love you.*"

In the morning, Anne marched into the living room, flung open the window shades to flood us with the harsh rays of the sun, and announced, "Okay, guys, up and at 'em! Let's get going!" In other words, *Anth, wake your ass up and get these women out of my house.* The frumpled girls splashed water on their faces and headed for the door. I walked them out, but Nico, uninterested in chivalry, kicked it on the couch. Mandy, the girl I'd been entertaining, was understandably embarrassed. "Great... the dreaded Walk of Shame," she quipped.

It turned out Mandy was a cocktail waitress at Ajax Lounge, where we were playing the following night. Modesto Briseno, the old trumpeter friend who'd once dragged me to Laguna Seca to play jazz during an actual race, showed up and played a couple songs with us. After the show, Mandy invited me to her apartment. I accepted, and we relaxed in her candlelit room, listening to soft music. After some wine and pleasant conversation, we became aware of an olfactory disturbance: the litterbox in the corner was funky. Mandy got up, replaced the kitty litter and re-joined me. We shrugged and smiled, hoping this minor reality check wouldn't spoil a promising night of romance.

We finished off a bottle of wine, exhausted the chit-chat, and now it was time to move things along. A loud *meeeeow* stopped us in our tracks. I looked over by the bedroom door, and there was this big, furry creature staring into my eyes, glaring at me with what seemed like contempt, as if I was the latest in a string of prospective male suitors with designs on stealing his thunder. He fixed his sights on the immaculate litterbox in the corner.

"That's Proust," Mandy offered.

Why do people name their damn pets after dead French authors?

"Hey there, buddy," I lamely muttered. Proust sauntered over to the corner and climbed into the box. Mandy chuckled nervously and watched as Proust stretched and began pawing and licking at his underside, eyes on us the whole time. Then, the competitive fur-ball settled on his haunches, shot one last surly glare in my direction, and took a dump the size of Nebraska. *So much for romance.*

In addition to trips to the Bay Area, Faze also did a couple runs out in Arizona, specifically the Phoenix area. One time Jalen, Chef R&B and I stayed at Len's house in Prescott; Len had sold his place in Santa Clara and moved out to Prescott in the early nineties. We had a nice hang, listening to jazz records, even doing an impromptu jam in Len's living room.

When Len and Ann said they wanted to come see the band play in Phoenix, I had reservations. The Roxy was a hardcore hip-hop and rap venue with a pretty rough clientele. There had even been a gang-related shooting or two in the parking lot in recent months. Despite my warnings, my father and stepmother decided to make the two-hour drive to Phoenix to make the show, and I of course was happy to have their support.

As I had suspected it would be, the Roxy was extremely loud inside, with hardened-looking urban characters sauntering around in the dark, the oppressive thump of a monotonous bass drum pattern rattling the walls. Len perched up on the balcony to check out our set, the oldest person in the joint by thirty-five years. The emcee was a young black guy with baggy pants, a sideways baseball cap and a loud, bellowing voice, which caused the house P.A. system to distort. "Yo, give it up for Faze, all the way from Cali! Give it up, y'all!" After our set was done, he jumped up on stage again and said, "Yo, that shit was large! Give it up! Make some noise! That shit was very large!"

Out of respect, Jalen and Stone walked over with me to say hello to Len and Ann, who were really going the extra mile to support their hip-hop-playing son from California. Stone shook Len's hand and said, "Thanks a lot for coming all the way down here to see us, Mr. Smith. I know it's probably not your cup of tea, so we appreciate it." Len replied, in his crystal clear, famously articulate English teacher's baritone: "We're happy to be here, man. And that shit you guys dropped tonight… *that shit was large.*" Stone, Jalen and I almost cried we laughed so hard.

TINY N' ANTH DO LA MESA!

Schneider

There are times in life when finances necessitate sharing a small living space with one or more people. Yes, you'd like to have that two-bedroom apartment all to yourself, but no, you don't have a thousand bucks a month to throw away on rent. You hope and you pray that the individuals you've decided to roll the dice with, whether good friends or random strangers from Craigslist, don't turn out to be deadbeats or psychos in the end. Even if your roommates are totally cool and completely trustworthy, there's going to come a point where you realize you know more about them—their warts, their quirks, their foibles—than you know about yourself.

Apartment dwelling also forces intimacy with those above, below and on either side of you. You may never hang out with your neighbors, but you probably know exactly what's happening in their lives. You find yourself in the hallway bumping into Mrs. Dombrowski, someone you've never exchanged a single word with, but who you've listened to trudging around above you for the last eighteen months. You blurt out the following: *Can you maybe not vacuum at seven a.m. on Sunday morning? And how 'bout lightening up on Gus. Yeah, he likes to throw back a few Coors Lights and watch WWF after work, but he's not a bad dude. You know, if you didn't have to have the last word all the time, maybe things wouldn't be so tense up there. I get the impression that the love life could use a tweak or two, also. When Gus takes those real long showers, what is it you think he's doing, washing between his toes? One more thing, while I'm venting... Can you please, please pop in a new CD? If I have to endure the monotonous bass lines to Rod Stewart's Greatest Hits one more time, there's a good chance I'm gonna upchuck my Healthy Choice pot roast entrée. Thanks, Mrs. Dombrowski. Have a nice day.*

As a duplex, quadraplex, or too-many-freakin'-plex dweller, you also have the challenge of dealing with that curious animal known as the property manager. This person is supposed to be your security blanket... your Rock of Gibraltar, or at least your Rock of Frigidaire. He's your beacon of hope through a tempest of broken toilets, stalled air-conditioning units and cockroach armies.

In 1995, I moved into an apartment with friends and fellow musicians Dale Park and Jim Gorman, on the second floor of a house in downtown La Mesa. The property manager was a silver-haired, fifty-something good ole' boy with bad chompers and sun-mottled forearms. We called him Schneider, in honor of the fix-it man from *One Day at a Time*. Everything started out peachy with Schneider. A leaky faucet, a problem with the phone jack... no sweat. Schneider and his 24-Hour Complete Property Management were all over it. The service was twenty-four hour, and it was complete.

This honeymoon, as it turned out, was short-lived. One night I called Schneider at three in the morning, after an unsuccessful attempt to address a small *plumbing concern*. He stormed over, wielding his plunger like a light saber in the hands of Count Dooku. "How can a man live twenty-six goddamn years and not figure out how to plunge a frickin' toilet?!" he snapped. It was a fair question.

"I had a pretty good idea what to do," I explained, "but common sense dictates that you leave this kind of situation in the hands of experts. That would be you." He sniffed resentfully then proceeded to execute some serious, septic legerdemain. Make that Count *Dookie*.

Relations with Schneider deteriorated from there. While we'd once relied on our property guru to brave the most daunting of domestic contingencies, we now found ourselves more or less on our own. I would call with minor, reasonable requests, only to be gunned down like a Japanese trainee pilot at Leyte Gulf. Things came to a head one

154

hot day in July, when our refrigerator conked out. We'd just bought enough groceries to feed the whole Latvian army — about four bags — so we were a bit bent out of shape. We demanded that Schneider replace the fridge immediately and also reimburse us for the food that had spoiled.

Before I go any further, I should probably mention that Schneider was a big-time lush. He'd come over to collect the rent reeking of a sour mix of sweat, Old Spice and Fleishman's Vodka, gussied up in a loud Hawaiian shirt and white painter pants, greasy hair matted down against his splotched, weathered dome as he hurried to hit Hooter's happy hour[58], with its giant-screen Nascar spectacles, disgusting fried appetizers and curvaceous young lasses in fluorescent orange butt-huggers and meretricious nylons. The girls were trained to not only tolerate but even *encourage* the advances of lecherous geezers like Schneider, so long as he didn't try and slide those crusty, property manager paws from his mozzarella sticks over to their... well, you get the picture.

The morning after the fridge busted, Schneider came laboring up our old wooden stairwell, one of his Hooters cronies assisting him. They had precariously mounted a replacement fridge on a rusted, lightweight hand truck. Schneider glared up at the three of us with contempt. We were really putting him out with this one.

La Mesa is a number of miles inland and gets quite hot in the summer. This day was a particularly sweltering one. I'm not sure if Schneider expected us to give him a hand, but like Steve Harvey at a

---

[58] I had to call the Hooters in the Gaslamp District to confirm that the restaurant did in fact exist during this time period. I was told by a kid named Jackson, who announced upon answering that "Hooters is the home of NFL football in downtown San Diego," that this particular Hooters franchise, the first in San Diego, opened in "around 1994 or 1995." So my Hooters reference does work in this context. Even if it had not, I was planning to leave it in and offer a creative license disclaimer. Whether true or not, I love the image of Schneider ogling young female servers, stuffing his face with larded snacks and screaming at the TV during Monday Night Football. The Hooters company began in 1983, the first location being in Clearwater, Florida. The original six owners opened the restaurant on April Fool's Day, because they were convinced the idea was going to flop. Twenty-five years later, they have created an empire — one which perfectly captures the contemporary American zeitgeist.

rap concert we weren't about to *help out*. We were paying too much for this cramped rat-trap as it was. Now, we were supposed to expose our pallid butt cracks to the oppressive rays of the East County sun, in order to help this codger do *his* job? *Ish don't think so,* as Bruno would say.

Schneider and his pal managed to hoist the new fridge, which he had acquired earlier that morning from a used appliance joint on El Cajon Boulevard, up the remainder of the steps and into our kitchen. He swapped it with the junker, checked to see if the new unit was in fact working, then strapped the dead one to his dolly and dragged it back down the stairs. All this required a Herculean effort, and Schneider grunted and groaned in agony the whole way down. Neither Dale, Jim nor I, all fit as a fiddle, sporting muscles we'd been chiseling at the gym for months, lifted so much as a finger throughout this process. In fact, we never even got up off the couch. The whole time Schneider was slaving away, we might as well have been draped in togas, getting fanned by a harem of exotic beauties while munching on fresh grapes.

Once Schneider left, Dale and I ran out and bought a bunch of groceries to celebrate our new lease on refrigeration. Alas, 24-Hour Complete Property Management had come through in the clutch. Maybe this was the beginning of *white trash Glasnost*, a period of improved communication and eased tension between demanding tenants and disgruntled property manager. I looked out the kitchen window and glimpsed a rainbow stretching all the way from 7-11 to the Chevron station, as birds began chirping quaint little melodies of hope and renewal. For a few days, everything was calm. Life was good. No broken stuff, no antagonistic exchanges with Schneider.

But the winds of change shifted again, as quickly as a black El Camino could screech down La Mesa Boulevard at three in the morning, bumping some Wu Tang Clan for the whole neighborhood's pleasure. My fantasy was blown out of the bong water as I sat up in bed, nose alerting me to the stench of food starting to go bad. The stench of promises broken, and trust snatched back into the void of apartment dweller's hell... a fetid combination of Schneider's Old Spice commingled with rotten milk, spoiled meat and Dale's stinky sock pile.

The replacement unit had died a quick death. Schneider's resentful climb up our stairwell had been in vain. The following morning we watched as he labored, yet again, up our rickety stairs with another used refrigerator. He was alone this time; his grizzled buddy must have been out at one of the Indian casinos, yanking nickel slots. Out of breath and sweating like an overworked pig in the south of Texas, Schneider halted halfway up the stairs to gather himself, and to glower at us with his most menacing *I despise you sons of bitches* scowl. Dale, Jim and I remained devoid of sympathy for the man, however. We weren't about to risk our delicate fingers hauling heavy shit up some crumbling staircase on a hand truck. It wasn't like any of us had medical insurance or anything.

Realizing we had again elected to pull a Steve Harvey, to *watch from the sidelines*, Schneider mustered a surprising surge of adrenalin and manhandled the big appliance up the rest of the stairs. Before a dentally disastrous grin of satisfaction could finish metastasizing across Schneider's reddened, puffy face, Dale saddled him with some more bad news: Sadly, our water heater had bought the farm.

Upon returning home from a weightlifting session the following afternoon, Dale and I found Schneider sprawled out on our kitchen floor, drunk as a skunk. Littered around him was a mountain of empty Budweiser cans and defective water heater parts. Schneider let out a raspy chuckle and growled, "Can't do this kinda work without sluggin' back a few brewskis!" While Dale and I found Schneider and his shenanigans at least moderately amusing, Jim was *over it*. Tired of property manager drama, and tired of cleaning up the mess Dale and I were constantly leaving in the kitchen. One night, Jim stormed into my room and announced, "If you don't want to wash my dishes after you use them, maybe I should just pack them up." I thought about it for a minute and responded, "Yeah… maybe you should pack 'em up." Jim moved out a week later.

Wilbur

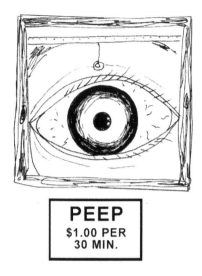

The vacancy left by Ed's swift departure was filled by our friend
Wilbur Dugdale, from the Faze crew. Wilbur weighed well over three
hundred pounds, and was further distinguished by a purple birthmark
which covered half his face. He was quick-witted and colorful, but
without any semblance of a promising career path. He bounced from
one lame telemarketing job to the next. When home, Wilbur tended to
stay in his room, zoning out in front of the tube and consuming box
after box of Little Debbie snack cakes.

Living with Wilbur was interesting because he always brought
home new stories about his telemarketing exploits. In one of the offices
he worked—and when I say office, I mean a slapdash bivouac of
phones, cheap tables and partitions that could be disassembled on the
fly, to evade the wrath of the Better Business Bureau—there was a
mean, witch manager who would walk over and slap Wilbur's hands
with a ruler, whenever she thought he was slouching off. She had a
variety of such punishments for unproductive employees: stomping
your foot, poking you in the neck with a finger, or slamming a fist
down on your desk if you were dozing off. I told Wilbur she should
just outfit each telemarketer with electrodes and shock them from a

remote control device. It would be kind of like that episode of *The Simpsons* from the first season.[59]

Unlike the rest of the guys in the Faze crew, Wilbur did not have a natural rapport with women. His lack of confidence was exacerbated by the fact that he was roughly the size of a D8 Caterpillar bulldozer. Let's face it, it's hard to *get some* when you resemble the Michelin Tire mascot or, on a really bad day, a twenty-five year old transmogrification of the Gerber baby.

There was a round-the-clock XXX spot called Jolar, not far from our apartment. Dale would drop in there from time to time, and one night invited Wilbur to join him. I also happened to be along for the ride. Jolar, like your typical adult bookstore, was divided into two sections. The front portion contained magazines, videos and sex toys. The back area had private booths, as well as live shows, where you could interact with real girls.

Once we got to Jolar, Dale and I encouraged Wilbur to blow off some steam with a solo visit to the private video booths. He hastily disappeared into a dark, seedy cluster of cubicles. The problem with Jolar's private booths was that they weren't completely private. There was only a partial barrier separating the patron from the main area, which made it possible for someone to drop in on you during your *viewing experience*. Wilbur was about to learn this the hard way.

While Wilbur engaged in *viewing*, a guy poked his head in to catch a peak. Wilbur waved him off (using his free hand, presumably), and the guy took the hint and disappeared. *Viewing* resumed, but a minute later the same intruder popped by again. This time Wilbur snapped, "No, man, no! I don't need any help here! Get lost!"

"You need to stop doing that," the guy said. "Right now."

"Hey, I paid my money. Leave me alone," Wilbur fired back. That's when *peeper non grata* pulled a badge.

"That's illegal. Pull your pants up, son."

"Please, officer, cut me a break. I just needed some relief."

"I'm a detective, not an officer… and I can't let you walk. I gotta write it up."

What I'd like to know is, how bad did this detective guy fuck up some major homicide or narcotics investigation, to wind up HERE, skulking around in

---

[59] *There's No Disgrace Like Home.* Season One, Episode Four.

porno purgatory, busting frustrated outcasts choking the chicken to Christy Canyon videos?[60]

Poor Wilbur... tried to take matters into his own hands and still couldn't get no satisfaction. Wilbur came moping over to the front of the store, citation pronged between his pudgy fingers like Holden Caulfield's pathetic term paper on ancient Egypt.

"Son of a bitch gave me a ticket. I gotta appear in court."
The guy at the front register handed Wilbur a business card with a lawyer's number on it.

"Call that number, bud. We got people to handle these types of situations. You probably won't have to do no time."

Wilbur did have to appear in court, but he was acquitted of any wrongdoing. After some deliberation, the judge found that Wilbur had acted within his inalienable rights, and that the partitions at Jolar, incomplete as they were, had indeed been constructed to facilitate... *viewing*. Wilbur's attorney had turned the tide when he cleverly contended that, "If the patron buys his tokens, Your Honor, it's his right to do some strokin'."[61]

Wilbur's ordeal reminds me of something that happened when I was in college. It must have been about 1992, and I wandered into a porn bookstore on El Cajon Boulevard. As I ventured into the video arcade I felt someone tap my shoulder. I turned and was greeted by an unattractive, middle-aged schlub I knew from the San Diego State music department. He flashed me a creepy smile. I surveyed the area and realized there were a number of guys milling around... not one woman.

"Don't be frightened," the music department weirdo said, inching closer. "You have nothing to be ashamed of. It's perfectly natural." I tried to sidestep him and get to the exit, but out of nowhere, some buffed guy in a tank top was blocking my path. His muscular arms were folded across his chest in intimidating fashion, his mustache making John Oates look downright pre-pubescent. The accompanist was still jabbering at me: "Just go with it. Accept it. There's nothing wrong with it." People can do what they want, and far be it for me to judge someone's lifestyle and sexual choices, but... let's be real clear

---

[60] I always loved Christy Canyon. I gotta be honest.

[61] I'll admit it... I made this last little bit up. Not the part about Wilbur in the booth, but the part about the lawyer's Johnny Cochran-inspired remark.

about this... *There was no way in hell I was going to get bent over in the shadowy recesses of some smut cubicle, by an aggressive, ex-member of the Village People.*

"Let me by," I demanded. He didn't budge. Now I felt a twinge of genuine fear.

"What do I have to do, fight you in order to get out of here?" He still didn't move. I started to raise my fist, nervous that we might actually be coming to blows... err, I mean punches. Finally, the guy relaxed his posture.

"It's cool, man. You can leave. Don't say anything to the manager, okay?" I bolted out of there, never to return.

Tiny

Dale and I weren't having much luck with our musical careers at this time. Gigs were sporadic, and despite writing some catchy, marketable pop tunes, we were yet to generate any significant interest in our songwriting. We began channeling our creativity in offbeat ways, such as dreaming up fictional characters to reflect the absurdity of our experiences. The first of these characters, a miniscule convict with impressive pugilistic skills and skinhead allegiances, was based on Dale himself...

We had been looking over some Faze promotional band photos, from a shoot that took place in an industrial area near downtown San Diego. In one picture, the six of us were waxing tough, bare-chested and brooding as we posed on some railroad tracks with the skyline as a backdrop. For some reason, this particular shot had distorted in a way that made me, with my long hair, black sunglasses and puffed-out upper torso, appear to be about seven feet tall and menacing. Dale, standing right next to me in the picture, came out looking about *four* feet tall. His nose appeared to be flattened down against his face. He was sporting a wife-beater, flexing his compact muscles like a circus strongman, and affecting a curious grimace that made it look like he was the owner of a befuddled, possibly inbred brow.[62] He looked, in summary, like a mutant extra on the set of *Time Bandits*, while the whole shot suggested a post-apocalyptic, hip-hop take on *The Little Rascals*.

"Dale, your nose looks smashed in this picture, and you look like some kind of little midget bad-ass," I chuckled.

"That's not me, Anth."

"If it's not you, then who is it?" Dale paused, smiled and said: "Tiny."

We broke into a belly laugh, writhing around for several minutes. An alter-ego was born, and from there on out I would often address my friend not by his given name, but as Tiny. We decided this new character needed a backstory, so we created the Legend of Tiny. It went something like this:

Tiny was the toughest fella in our whole gang. He wasn't the smartest, and he sure as hell wasn't the tallest, but what he lacked in intelligence, stature and looks, he made up for in heart and character. I once watched Tiny singlehandedly dismantle a crew of twenty violent thugs from our rival cross-town gang. People think Tiny's retarded or somethin', but the real reason his nose is smashed against his face is that he's broken it forty-three times.

---

[62] A look perfected by Iced Cube, master of the half-confused, half-pissed off glare.

Tiny's notoriety grew much bigger when he went to the penitentiary for running a huge crystal meth plant out of an abandoned house in the outskirts of Alpine. He had been using the Wednesday Night Men's Scratch League at Parkway Lanes as a front, but some kid workin' the pro shop ratted Tiny out, when Tiny cut off the kid's credit after his debt got too high.

Tiny's the only inmate who's ever walked the yard at Pelican Bay alone. Years later at Fulsom, where he did his second big stretch of time, they named a whole wing after him, when he united the Aryans and the radical Muslims for a prison-wide weightlifting competition. The evening almost ended in a bloody riot, after Lefty "One Nut" Nuremburg deadlocked with Mohammed Abdur Mugatu for first place, but Tiny squashed the whole beef by taking the bench himself. With the entire yard watching, Tiny clean-pressed nine-hundred-and-sixty pounds, shattering the national maximum security facility record. The two rival factions hoisted Tiny in the air, and the warden, watching from a surveillance tower with binoculars, a sniper at his side, issued an immediate pardon for Tiny and his cellmate, Toothless Kalolo, a heavily tattooed Samoan former international black market kidney broker. Toothless Kalolo had once rescued Tiny from being pulverized in a cafeteria meat grinder, when the South Block overlords mistakenly thought Tiny had intercepted an anally smuggled shipment of black tar heroin. Once they were sprung, Tiny and Toothless Kalolo set up a tattoo shop in Pacific Beach. Things didn't work out with the business, so they sold their interest to a big, white biker named Ruben.

This is where the lines of fiction and reality blur, for one of Ruben's first customers was…

Snuffleupagus

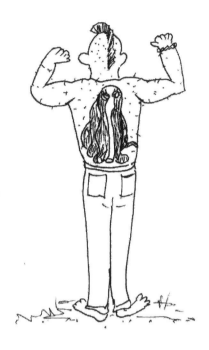

...Jim Gorman. Jim was the roommate who had bolted when I told him what he could do with his dishes.[63] He had his own place now, and he'd socked away a nice chunk of dough to blow on some whim yet to be determined. He was vacillating between a vacation in Europe, a Harley, and a full back tattoo. When I saw he was toting around a stack of tattoo magazines, scrutinizing the work of master inkers from South America to Australia, I knew which way he was planning to jump: Forget the Eurorail pass... to hell with the Harley... Jim was going to brave the needle.

Had he scouted top-flight artists in Southern California, or made arrangements to visit Europe and seek out a distinguished ink master to create his *piece de resistance*, I would have understood and endorsed

---

[63] Jim and I ultimately reconciled our conflicting standards of kitchen cleanliness. Alas, time heals old dishwashing wounds.

Jim's decision. But instead of pursuing a magazine-caliber craftsman, Jim opted to get the work done locally. There must have been a few good tattoo artists in San Diego… Ruben, a mean-spirited One Percenter who was running an ink shop/meth distribution warehouse in Pacific Beach, was not one of them. I still could have stood behind Jim's plan, had he at least enlisted a professional illustrator to provide the blueprint from which Ruben would do his inking. But this is where Jim made a crucial mistake; he entrusted his good buddy Tiny with the task of designing his full back piece.

Tiny might have been one tough little cuss, with street credentials longer than Fifty Cent's rap sheet, but he was no illustrator. Nonetheless, the smash-nosed convict created a very ambitious concept. He sketched out a wild scene in which flame-spitting dragons guarded a spiraling, other-worldly pathway to the heavens, flaring out from the nostrils of a Gandolfian wizard, whose antiquated visage encompassed what could only be described as a brave, Tolken-esque vision.

Sometimes the best laid plans can lead to disaster, as we all know. When Jim returned from his first inking session with Ruben, I knew he was in trouble. Tiny now found himself in the shoes of Mary Shelley's notorious madman, faced with the sizable chasm that can exist between noble intentions and their physical realization.

"Check out the dragons," Jim instructed us. "How do they look?" Tiny shot me a concerned glance. I took a moment to search for a response.

"Well, Jim, the left dragon is okay, but the right one kind of looks like, well… Snuffleupagus."

"Like *what?*"

"You know, Snuffleupagus from Sesame Street… with the big trunk. Big Bird's best friend."

"I always liked Snuffy *better* than Big Bird," Tiny added.

"I've always had the impression that he connected more naturally with the kids," I agreed.

Jim didn't take this too well. His bold, edgy ideas were being reduced to comparisons with a furry creature from a children's television program. I'd like to tell you the situation improved from here, but that would be a lie. Ruben worked for a mere forty minutes at a clip, then he'd send Jim to the market for beer, work another measly ten minutes and call it a night, announcing with no possibility for debate, "I'm done. See you next time." Tiny watched his original blueprint deviate further and further toward a grotesque display of biker tattoo butchery, and there was nothing he or anyone else could do about it. Jim, in turn, found himself playing out the role of a disfigured Calibos in *Clash of the Titans*, crying out to the sky, "Look what your God has done to me!"

We all knew that any protests directed at Ruben would be met with sadistic reprisal, so we allowed the charade to continue. Meanwhile, Jim's back was beginning to look like the Sunday funnies left out in the rain. He'd dropped thousands on a tattoo that, to my untrained eye, looked like Snuffleupagus emerging from the nose of a pissed off gargoyle, drawn in bright, flourescent colors like the ones on the Matchbox racecars I played with as a kid, with stairs winding into a labyrinthine dystopia reminiscent of Fred and Lamont Sanford's junkyard, all splashed against a backdrop bearing more similarity to an electrical fire in a Medieval Times gift shop than an enchanting, mystical passageway to eternity. But this story has a nice ending…

Jim allowed Ruben to finish his horrible design, and then, after allowing himself a break from the discomfort of having a needle tearing into his back for the previous several months, found himself a truly talented artist he could trust. Jim proceeded to have his entire back re-inked, sticking loyally to Tiny's original vision. After this miraculous transformation, the dragons actually looked like dragons, the wizard appeared Gandolfian, the spiraling stairway no longer looked like somebody spilled a large order of nachos on Jim's bare back, and the whole presentation made a lot more sense. Jim had finally acquired the best tattoo that thousands of dollars and a year of excruciating agony, at the hands of a homicidal biker, can buy.

Mr. Reality

There was another character Tiny and I created, this one born of not only our imaginations, but our subconscious fears as well. He was a short, bald Italian guy in a beanie, and we called him Mr. Reality. A cross between Joe Pesci and Steve Buscemi, Mr. Reality was a little man that popped up on your shoulder when you were in need of a reality check. He always had a bottle of *reality pills* handy, and he wasn't going to sprinkle any sugar on your situation. Instead, you could count on him to give you the bare, ugly truth. Mr. Reality's raspy wake-up calls always began with the same profane, condescending salutation: "Hey d-bag!" Tiny and I received frequent visits from Mr. Reality. Most of our musical jobs were artistic dead ends that meant nothing but a little dough to keep the monkey off our backs. We often wondered if we'd made a grave mistake dedicating our lives to music.

I had a steady gig in a posh restaurant in Tijuana, playing jazz with a Russian drummer named Ivan. I think his wife was playing in

Orchestra Tijuana at the time. The restaurant was always empty, leading me to suspect it was serving as a front for a drug cartel. One night I was sitting there between sets, when… *bing!* There he was in his little cardigan sweater, Rayon slacks and beanie, kicking it on my shoulder…

Hey d-bag! Let's take a look at this situation. You're drivin' down to Tijuana every week, risking your ass in a violent Third World country, so you can play background music with some Russian drummer that looks like Dolph Lundgren in Rocky IV, in a completely empty restaurant… and whadda you get for your trouble? Ninety bucks. That isn't very much, is it, d-bag.

All you could do was sit there and take it. He wasn't done, either.

What do you think your father would say if he could see you right now? He'd say, "Where did I go wrong? How did my son turn out to be such a loser?" Sometimes I'd talk back to Mr. Reality…

"But Mr. Reality, I'm making an honest living. I'm doing my best."

No, d-bag. This ain't your best. You're just eekin' your way through life. At this rate you'll be an old man without any savings, holed up in a studio apartment somewhere. I strongly advise you against starting a family.

"I have a right to follow my dreams, Mr. Reality! I have dreams, you know."

Those aren't dreams, d-bag. They're delusions. Way I see it, you got two options on the table: get a real estate license and start over, or take a nosedive off the Coronado Bridge.

Cut to the Coronado Bridge on a cold January night…

Bing!

Well, well… Here we are, d-bag. Can't take it anymore, huh?

"I can't bring myself to do another Top 40 gig at the Marriott."

I don't blame you.

"I tried! All those original projects, all the money I invested in my musical career: promotional materials, recordings, equipment… it's not fair!"

Now, now, d-bag. You ain't the first guy to go through life and wind up with the short end of the stick. Nobody can say you didn't try. Look at what happened to the Sacramento Kings in 2002. Look at what happened to Kobe Bryant in Colorado.

"Yeah, but he makes twenty million bones a year."

True. Kobe makes more in one season than you're gonna make in your entire life.

168

"Maybe I won't jump. Maybe I'll go back and give it another try. I know I have talent. I can't give up now!"

Come on, already.   It's cold up here. I got other losers to ridicule. What's it gonna be?

"I'm not jumping. I'm gonna return to my life, and I'm gonna make it. I'm outta here, Mr. Reality."

Alright, go back to serenading the busboy at El Mucho Dinero Laundero on Tuesday nights. But watch your back—those cartels are getting pretty violent these days.

Mr. Reality, of course, was a representation of what Shelby Steele once described as the *anti-self*.[64] He personified the insecurities and self-doubts that haunt us all. Mr. Reality gave Dale and me a vehicle through which to make light of our anxieties about a difficult future as musicians. That brings us to a pivotal moment in the story…

---

[64] Steele writes about this in his book, *The Content of Our Character*.

The Lizard

After two years of performing around Southern California, Faze had earned a modest but respectable little following. Attractive women were starting to hang around at the shows. One was a young tax secretary named Macy.

Tiny, avid conspiracy theorist and fledgling ufologist, had been entertaining suspicions that Macy was an alien. If creatures from other planets were among us here on Earth, scheming behind facades of human flesh, Tiny was convinced that Macy was one of them. It was true, there were some odd glitches in both her physiology and speech patterns; it was as if her H.S.P.C. (Human Simulation Program Chip) would hiccup from time to time, causing actual humans in the room to scratch their heads and wonder, "What was that?"

Nonetheless, Macy was a cute alien. She might have been a hybrid descendant from the original days of the Annunaki, the very ancient alien race that first populated and civilized planet Earth, long before creating *homo sapiens* to serve as nothing more than their slave race[65],

---

[65] Just like the *shoggoths* in H.P. Lovecraft's *At the Mountains of Madness*.

and long before allowing that slave race to branch out and become the custodians of their own culture and society.[66]

After a Faze concert one night, Jalen threw a wild party at his house. All the guys in the band were there, along with an assortment of extra-terrestrials masquerading as women. Macy, who was looking rather sexy, had not come alone. She had brought a friend. A green, slithering, scaly friend.

Tiny and I spotted her across the room as she talked to this friend, a lizard that was about a foot long and confined to a metal cage. Theories abounded. Was the lizard one of *them* too? Maybe the lizard was calling the shots, controlling Macy's body. Maybe Macy *was* the lizard, her body just a decoy so it could hatch an evil alien plot without arousing suspicion. Maybe the lizard was a conduit for Macy to transmit important data back to the mother ship. Maybe Macy was a clone prototype, a sort of body snatcher- style replacement for a real human being, and the lizard was there to monitor her effectiveness, then report back to the alien authorities. Or... and this was really, really going out on a limb... *Maybe it was just a goddamn lizard.*

We approached Macy, aware that we might be called upon to save the entire planet, making this a pivotal night in human history. Macy suggested that the four of us—me, Tiny, her and the lizard—excuse ourselves from the party, and spend the remainder of the evening in the comfort of our humble loft in La Mesa. What was she up to? Was she going to pull some Natasha Henstridge moves, lulling us into a compromised state of arousal, then trick one of us into impregnating her with a half-human, half-alien hodgepodge? Was the lizard going to slither down my throat while I lay sleeping, only to grow to five times its size by morning and pop out of my chest in a gory, Gigeresque bloodbath? Whatever was about to unfold, one thing was clear: Tiny and I had a responsibility to the human race to reveal Macy and her lizard as the impostors they were. We would have to play this scene out to a possibly grim, gruesome conclusion. Humanity was counting on us.

During the ride home, my car broke down several blocks from the apartment. We walked the rest of the way, taking turns carrying the lizard through the late-night fog. Once we got home, Macy placed the lizard's cage on the coffee table in our living room, a clever vantage

---

[66] The Sumerian civilization.

point from which it could survey its surroundings and signal her with further instructions.

Anyone who watches Hollywood movies knows that aliens have some surefire ways of ingratiating themselves with humans, usually in their quest to infiltrate the population here on Earth. For starters, they can tug at our heartstrings (*E.T., Starman, A.I., K-Pax*), winning us over with warm, fuzzy qualities that make them seem even more human than us *real* humans…

These aliens are supposed to be cold, creepy and mean, but now that we've gotten to know and love them, and now that they've exposed us to the cruel barbarism of our pathetic little world as we slouch our way toward Gomorrah[67]… we've come to realize that WE'RE the problem. WE'RE the dangerous ones.

Aliens can also just pummel the snot out of us with incredibly advanced firepower (*War of the Worlds, Independence Day*). That is, until the tandem of Bill Pullman and Will Smith defeat their entire warship fleet single-handedly. *Yeah, that could happen.* Aliens can bury a bunch of deadly machines deep underground, leave them there for centuries, and activate them at some arbitrary point in the future, setting them loose on the vulnerable human masses… and as cool as this sounds, instead of following these killing machines around and witnessing them wreak havoc, we will be relegated by the dictates of a cheesy screenplay to watch Tom Cruise bicker with his alienated son for two hours. Aliens are also adept at capitalizing on that most exploitable of human weaknesses: sexuality. (*Species, What Planet Are You From?*).

Tiny and I had no way of knowing which angle Macy planned to work, though we were beginning to suspect it would be the latter. We sat there in the apartment, eyes darting lambently from lizard to Macy, Macy back to lizard, waiting for one of them to make a move. "Let's get comfortable," Macy suggested. *Uh oh, here we go.* Soon, I found myself stripped of all garb, disoriented and on the verge of contributing to the creation of a new hybrid intergalactic species. I realized Macy and her accomplice were, as feared, in possession of manipulative alien powers. Tiny also fell prey to Macy's allure, eagerly peeling off layers of clothing to reveal:

Nothing to support myths of black anatomical superiority
Quite a bit to refute myths of white anatomical inferiority

---

[67] Thanks to Robert Bork, by way of the poet Yeats, for that metaphor.

The considerable irony inherent in his nickname

Hours later, after a strange, phantasmagorical experience, I would awake from a haze[68] to find myself plopped on the couch, still naked, hair tousled and family jewels withered. I was seated next to the lizard, which appeared relaxed and in a state of repose. Jim Gorman, who had stopped by for a cup of coffee before work, sat on the other side of the lizard, dressed in pressed slacks and a tie, legs folded as he split his attention between Macy and the morning newspaper. We watched in amazement as Tiny, showing no signs of fatigue, and clearly still beguiled by Macy's Roswellian charms, conducted a spirited campaign to insure the success of this fascinating new synthesis of races.

Suddenly the lizard began to stir in its cage, darting from side to side and squirming wildly as its tongue flicked in and out like a reptilian Gene Simmons. It must have sensed that the moment of conception was near, or worse, was trying to signal Macy that it had detected a fault in Tiny's DNA. If the lizard rendered Tiny unsuitable for procreation, it might command Macy to snap his neck, rather than carry the funk guitarist's flawed offspring.

I reached over to free the lizard, realizing that I must now do everything in my power to allow this event of monumental global importance to run its course. The lizard was thrashing violently, pressing its body against the cage while uttering noises unlike anything I'd ever heard. It wanted out. I began to open the cage door, convinced this was what must be done, although a bit concerned that the thing might bolt over to the bed and burrow its way in between Tiny's buttocks. *Haven't seen that one in a movie yet.* The lizard was almost free when Tiny aborted his gymnastic display to issue me a direct order:

"Anth... the lizard stays in the cage."

"But Tiny, I think it wants—"

Tiny repeated the words slowly and carefully...

---

[68] Regressive hypnotherapy led me to believe that the events of this evening were not limited to what transpired in our apartment, but also involved some kind of medical examination and interrogation on board an alien vessel, conducted by a handful of Greys in contamination suits. I'm convinced they kept a tiny chunk of my pancreas, as well as a short piece of my large intestine.

THE LIZARD STAYS IN THE CAGE.

We never saw Macy again. To my knowledge, neither has anyone else. She and her scaly sidekick seemed to just disappear from the face of the earth. That was a number of years ago, and who knows… they might be halfway home by now.

Alabaster's Vengeance

That brings us to the curious case of a man we'll call Heath Alabaster. In the mid-nineties, Heath released a self-produced album: *Alabaster's Vengeance.* I became aware of this work through Richard "Chef R&B" Sellers, who was preparing to enter the studio with Heath to record a follow-up album. Heath had given Richard a copy of *Alabaster's Vengeance* to study, so Richard would be *familiar with his vibe.* Richard came to a Faze rehearsal one afternoon saying, "I'm supposed to do a studio date with this guy. You gotta hear this stuff." *Alabaster's Vengeance,* my fellow Faze members and I were amused to discover, was a colorful tour through the history of rock and roll; but this tour was being guided by a guy who was clearly a couple *samosas* short of a vegetarian Gujarati sampler.   This fact, coupled with some strange liner notes and bizarre artwork, prompted Tiny and me to expand our ever-growing menagerie of fictitious characters…

Miroslav and Ula Alabaster, first-generation Russian immigrants (a janitor and a schoolteacher, respectively), detested their son Heath's rock and roll aspirations. They had always dreamed of Heath becoming a dermatologist or an anesthesiologist, but he was more interested in becoming El Cajon's answer to Tom Petty. Heath had gotten mixed up with Wolfgang, a scheming "producer" who played heavy metal guitar and sang raspy, Satanic-sounding back-up vocals. Wolfgang had served a few years hard time in the late eighties, for embezzling thousands of dollars from Casey Cohn's Tone Shack, where he had been an ineffective, underachieving salesman and teacher.

At some point, Heath came into some money (which is why Wolfgang was hanging around in the first place). The speculation was that Heath had been diagnosed with a rare, medically fascinating but not life-threatening neurological disorder, and by donating his body to research, while still alive and young, he had raised the cash to finance a big-budget studio album—the great ambition of his life. He hired such San Diego heavyweights as Max Welford, the world class jazz pianist who had worked with numerous musical legends over the years. Welford insisted on quadruple union scale, which Heath was happy to pay. Heath's only professional music job, up to that point, had been playing for tips at Bean There Done That, a short-lived coffee cantina in Jamul. Heath had been fired from the gig after smashing his guitar against a wall and injuring a couple high school kids, when the barista had insisted on making blended drinks while Heath was singing his intricately arranged Nirvana medley.

Feeling he was in need of a business manager/personal handler, with all the exciting things suddenly happening in his musical career, Heath enlisted Talbot, his hunchbacked East European cousin, who was cursed with an inordinately large, misshapen head à la the Elephant Man, and had long ago been abandoned by a morphine-addled aunt in the suburbs of Warsaw.

Talbot immediately locked horns with Wolfgang, convinced the German guitarist was a charlatan intent on swindling Heath out of his medical guinea pig nest egg. Wolfgang, in turn, noticed in Talbot certain behavioral red flags, which he suspected were evidence of homicidal tendencies. Wolfgang had the keen street instincts of a career criminal… it was true that Talbot had gone on a murderous rampage upon his arrival in El Cajon, slaying several transients and meth freaks in cases that remained unsolved. Talbot hid the heads of his victims under the Alabaster residence, where Miroslav and Ula were quietly living out their days—Miroslav still reporting faithfully for his custodial duties at Granite Hills High School. Heath knew about the heads, and promised Talbot he could sing some back-ups on the album… provided Talbot curb his horrific need to spill East County blood, which was, after all, a major distraction while Heath was trying to perfect his musical arrangements. Heath's quiet bargain with Talbot angered Wolfgang, because it was HIS job to sing back-up, as agreed in the original production deal. Wolfgang proceeded to erase Talbot's vocal parts and sing them himself, all behind Heath's back.

Max Welford had just polished his piano track on People Say It's In the Stars, Heath's emotional tribute to The Muppets, and was still hanging out in the studio when Wolfgang started replacing Talbot's guttural, atonal parts with his own multi-track vocal performance on To Stay, Today, To Stay. Max knew a shit storm was brewing, and was also disconcerted by the evil timbre of Wolfgang's singing voice, which, when layered several times on top of itself, sounded like an eternally damned barbershop quartet, whose collective larynxes had been violently ripped out of their throats, and were now relegated to howling in tortured misery in the wretched bowels of Hell. Max was, however, getting quadruple scale, as mentioned, so he decided to keep silent on the matter. When the album was released, and he realized Wolfgang had deceived him, Talbot, strong as a chimpanzee, pummeled Wolfgang's already hideous face, re-arranging his grotesque hook nose, which actually looked better after the beating. "This time for Talbot!" he screamed. "This time for Talbot!"

I could go on, but you get the basic idea. Perhaps *The Complete Adventures of Heath Alabaster* will be published in a future volume.

It is a verity that all important artists, somewhere along the way, produce a magnum opus; one work which best exemplifies their genius. The Clash had *London Calling,* Prince hit his pinnacle with *Purple Rain,* The Doors gave us *L.A. Woman,* Paul Simon graced us with *Graceland…* and Heath Alabaster has further blessed us with *Alabaster's Vengeance.* This eclectic collage of pop and rock songs borrows stylistically from a wide variety of artists, including Poison, The Grateful Dead, Glenn Frey, Bruce Springsteen, David Byrne, Richard Marx and Kermit the Frog. It also contains the most compelling lyrics this side of early Miley Cyrus.

Alabaster's Vengeance is one of those albums where, upon your first listen, you just *know.* It's like the first time you heard *The White Album, Synchronicity* or *The Chronic.* My reaction was so strong that I immediately sought out more information about this mysterious, underground artist. I scoured the weekly Reader, hoping Heath might be performing somewhere in town. I asked musician friends if they knew his whereabouts. Sadly, my investigation turned up nothing. All I was able to learn about Heath was the information provided in the album's liner notes, leading me to the following conclusions:

Worldwide accommodations were provided *exclusively* by The Radisson.
Ibanez guitars were used *exclusively.*
The album serves as a vendetta against the entire planet, as well as an *I-told-you-so* diatribe directed at Heath's parents for pressuring him to get a real job.
The word "baby" is the album's central leitmotif.
The song *Sullenly* earns Heath the unique distinction of being the first artist, as far as I know, to integrate the vocal styles of Luciano Pavarotti and Johnny Rotten within the same piece of music.

If you want to hear this masterpiece for yourself, you'll have to contact me directly. It's not available in stores or on any websites I'm aware of. The excellent jazz bassist Marc Johnson once said, "Take your stand and let the universe react as it will." Heath Alabaster took his stand, God knows.[69] It's hard to say how the universe has reacted, because his work has not been distributed, to my knowledge, beyond Southern California. I can, however, tell you how *I* have reacted, and how a number of my musician friends have reacted: with sheer wonder and amazement. It is one thing to be bad... okay, to be really, really bad. It's another thing to be so bad that the listener becomes convinced the music is so bad that it is brilliant; so bad that its entertainment value, as an example of how awful music can be, catapults it into heavy rotation in your i-Tunes library.

Should you feel I am being excessively harsh, let me assure you that my own music has, at times, been skewered brutally. For example, a jam band follower from Chico, a kid named Jersey Joe, once expressed the opinion that my Living Large song, *Feel the Sun*, was "a great song to change your tampon to." He said this to my face... and he was a *friend* of mine.

---

[69] One of Heath's most memorable lyrics includes a chant of: "Oh God, I know," which is mimicked satanically by Wolfgang.

The Faith of Roy

One day, Tiny and I were brainstorming ideas about employment. We needed more gigs, and we needed better paying gigs, so we were trying to think *outside the box*. My friend Noel, a schoolteacher and salsa dancer who would pop by on occasion, was at this time dating a Mexican woman he had come to believe resembled the Taco Bell chihuahua... so I guess he, in turn, was thinking *outside the bun.*[70]

Anyway, Tiny had a sudden brainstorm.

"I know someone who can hook us up," he said with a smile.

"Who?"

"Roy."

Roy... it was a comforting name. Roy sounds like the kind of guy that can help your cause. Roy sounds like the kind of guy who's going to be in your corner, who's going to do you a solid just because that's the kind of guy he is. He does favors for people. Not because he has to, but just because he's Roy.

"Roy who?" I asked.

---

[70] In case you forgot, that was the slogan of those old Taco Bell commercials, featuring the talking chihuahua. I have heard it said that Penelope Cruz also resembles a chihuahua... but if so, that's the best looking damn chihuahua I've ever seen.

"Roy Karch."

"What is he, a booking agent or something?"

"No. He's an adult film producer. I met him in Vegas a couple years ago."

"So what're we gonna do, be in pornos?"

"Let me tell you how I met him. I was playing a Top 40 gig in the lounge of a hotel, and I started recognizing the faces of everyone hanging out at the bar." Tiny was becoming animated. This was a subject of great passion for him.

"I saw Peter North, Debbie Diamond and other people I knew. I realized they were porn stars, and they were there for the annual adult awards convention!" Yes, these were household names in adult entertainment. Names, I must confess, I was familiar with.

"So the band was on a break," Tiny continued, "and I got talking to Ron Jeremy, one of my idols. I asked him about breaking into the business."

"Doing what?"

"Soundtracks."

Ahh. Tiny and I had discussed doing adult soundtracks on more than one occasion. Seemed like easy work, and with the hundreds of new releases every month, it seemed like it might be abundant work.

"Ron said I should star in a couple scenes first, put myself on the map, and then try to do soundtracks. Said it's easier to break in that way."

"Hmmm, interesting," I said.

"Ron introduced me to this guy Roy, a producer/director. Roy Karch. He gave me his number, said to look him up some time. Seemed like a nice dude. I still have the number."

"Well, what good's a number if you never use it?" With that, Tiny found Roy's number and proceeded to call him. I listened in from another phone, and marveled at the fact that not only did Roy answer quickly, but he remembered Tiny immediately from Vegas.

"David... sure I remember you. How the hell are you? You're the guitar player, right?"

"That's right, Roy. We talked for quite a while that night."

"Yeah, we did. So what can I do for you?"

"Well, I'd like to meet up with you, have a chat about a few things." This seemed like a stretch, but Roy didn't hesitate.

"That sounds great. Why don't you come up Monday and hang with me here at my facility in Reseda?"

"Sounds good. You mind if I bring my friend Anthony along?"

"No problem. We'll have a good time." So it was planned. Tiny and I would drive to Reseda and have a meeting with Roy Karch. What business did we possibly have with the man? I had no idea, but it sounded like a fun hang. Who would turn down the opportunity to visit a thriving porn movie plant? Okay, maybe I can think of a few people, but I wasn't one of them.

With even slight traffic, it takes the better part of three hours to get to Reseda from San Diego. Reseda is plumb in the middle of the smog-caked Valley, and to get there you must endure the congested 101, and even worse, the dreaded 405. The Valley was, and still is, *world porno headquarters*. My brother Collin and his Cal State Northridge brethren had made frequent porn star sightings in the area, including one exciting brush with the redoubtable Neanderthal swordsman Buck Adams, who was sucking down a late-night chili dog at 7-11.[71]

Come Monday, Tiny and I made the trek to Reseda and arrived at Roy's compound, a plain white building shaped like a typical industrial warehouse. The building was nestled between similarly non-distinctive structures, each of which concealed the nature of its business by virtue of a homogenous facade.

"Here we are," Tiny announced, sounding like Clark Griswald at the gates of Wally World. The place might not have been much to see from the outside, but once we entered the lobby we realized there was a major operation going on. The building was bustling with activity. Girls with great bodies hustled by, along with computer geeks, slovenly middle-aged producer types and lithe cameramen. A paunchy, sweaty character approached us. He immediately knew who we were, and we knew who he was.

"Roy..." Tiny said, extending his hand, which the puffy-faced guy accepted as he responded, "Dale... glad you made it." Tiny introduced me, and Roy gave us a tour of the entire facility, which included an inventory warehouse, a post-production studio, a leisure lounge, cafeteria, and of course an elaborate series of mini-sets, each designed for a particular theme. There was the auto garage, the convent, the

---

[71] A few years later, Collin and I, roommates in Northridge, spotted the entrepreneurial porn actor-turned auteur Sean Michaels, known in adult biz circles as Tootsie Pole, hanging out at International House of Pancakes. Visionaries have to eat too, I guess.

hospital, the gym locker room, the barn/horse stable, and the standard romantic bedroom layout. Tiny and I were impressed.

"We're an entirely self-contained operation here, guys," Roy boasted, leading us into a room with some guys hunched at computers.

"Here's where we design the cover art... what ends up on the box. The box is really important. If people dig the pictures on the box, they'll buy the video." We nodded in agreement. Roy grabbed a couple video boxes and held them up for us to see.

"I'm known in the industry as the king of the funny word-play titles."

"Like *Saturday Night Beaver*.... *Flashpants*... *Blown on the Fourth of July?*" I chimed in.

"Yeah, exactly."

"I've got a good title I thought up, Roy," I said.

"Oh? Try me."

"You've heard of Pocahontas..."

"Of course."

"How about..."

I grinned devilishly.

"Poke-a-Hot-Ass."[72]

"That's terrific, Tony. You go by Tony?"

"Not really, but I've been thinking about adopting an adult industry handle. I'm leaning toward Tony Sebastian."

"I like it. It says class."

Roy completed the tour and led us to a conference table. Behind it, there hung a large dry-erase board. We sat down, and I noticed that the board had names scribbled across it, connected by brackets that made it look like the match-ups for the NCAA Sweet Sixteen. At the top, large letters spelled: *UP-ENDED*.

"So what's on your mind, Dale?" Roy asked.

"Well, Roy, Anth and I would really like to do some soundtrack work, try and make a few bucks." Roy frowned.

---

[72] I'm pretty sure Roy stole my title. I saw it on an adult video box many months later. I'm still waiting for my first royalty check. If Roy even thinks of stealing any of my other titles, such as *Yerassisdark III*, an interracial extravaganza which takes place on an obscure island that happens to be populated with live dinosaurs, I'm coming after him.

"I use canned music for all my movies. I've got over five hundred hours of stuff I outright own. It saves a lot of money. I don't really need new soundtracks." Tiny and I sat there quiet. There wasn't much else to say. That is, until Roy threw us the most unexpected curveball imaginable:

"But that's not really what you came here to talk about... *is it*, Dale." Tiny paused, leaned forward a bit and said, "No, it's not Roy." I spilled whatever I was drinking. What were they talking about? My understanding was that we had come to discuss soundtrack work, nothing more.

"So what is it we're here to talk about, Dale?" Tiny looked Roy confidently in the eye and said, "Roy, I wanna make movies. I'd like to be an adult film star." Roy sat there for a minute, considering Tiny's confident statement. I was speechless. None of this was in the script. It was all improv.

"Balling on the screen isn't like doing it in your living room, guys... even with your buddy watching you. I got grips, gaffers... fluffers... there's lots of people standing around staring at the action. And you have to perform in front of all of them, while following my strict instructions."

"What kind of instructions?" I asked.

"I might say to switch positions, or move a limb or two so I can align the camera for a close-up. When I get enough footage, I give you a signal, then when you're ready to pop you call out, 'Okay, Roy. I'm gonna pop now.'"

Isn't that romantic, I thought. You're making love to a woman, and suddenly you're supposed to stop and scream out to some schlub across the room, *I'm gonna pop Roy! Move into position!*

"What if the guy doesn't give you enough warning to catch the money shot, Roy?" Dale asked.

"That screws everything up. The money shot is a critical piece of footage. Without it, I have to get real creative to pull the scene together in the editing room. Proper warning for the money shot is the mark of a real pro." I felt like I needed to go to bat for my bro. I had seen him in action, after all, and knew he had the right stuff.

"Dale's got the goods, Roy. You should use him. He's got what it takes." Roy seemed to be buying what I was saying.

"I suppose I can hook you up with the talent agency we use, Dale." Tiny was getting more brazen by the minute.

"That doesn't interest me. What interests me is working directly with *you*, Roy."

"Well, as you can see, I am casting a new film, *Up-Ended*, to start production next week. I need someone to work with this gal named Esa Marie. Only thing is, it's a *backdoor* scene. Know what I'm saying?"

We did.

"How do you feel about that, Dale?"

"I feel fine about it, Roy. Think Anth can come along for support, hang with me on the set? If I'm going backdoor, Roy, I could use someone in my corner." It was looking like I was going to need some pom-poms.

"Yeah, sure. I can only give you a hundred bucks. The guys make a lot less than the chicks in this business. But if you become one of the guys the ladies wanna work with, you get bumped up to three hundred a scene."

"Okay, Roy. I'm in."

"What's your stage name, Dale... you got one picked out?"

"Yes..." Tiny and I had agreed on stage names during the drive up from San Diego.

"You can call me Dale Streak."

"That's good. I like that, guys. Nice visual implications. I can even see a little gob hanging off the end of the *k,* you know, when it's written. That'll be your logo. We'll trademark it."

"That's clever, Roy. You're a true innovator," I offered.

So it was settled. Tiny would launch his career as a porn actor. Once he showed his stuff in that first scene, I was sure he was going to get picked up to appear in more movies. I'd seen him in action with Macy and the lizard, and I knew his capabilities better than anyone. The guy had some serious chops.

 We said our goodbyes to Roy and drove home, prattling the whole way about future possibilities. A series of Dale Streak features: *9 ½ Streaks, Streak and Eggs, Shooting Streak, Twin Streaks*, etc. We decided I, Tony Sebastian, would be Tiny's manager and agent in the porn business. I would negotiate his deals. Also, I would serve as Tiny's personal fitness trainer.

For the next couple weeks leading up to the day of the shoot, we ran the hills of La Mesa, did crunches and sit-ups, and lifted weights like madmen. Tiny wanted to be fit as a fiddle for his fifteen minutes in the seedy sun. I played a youthful Burgess Meredith to his French/Jewish

Rocky, working him hard, day after day. Tiny ate vitamins and low-fat grub. I tested his mental readiness. I pushed him and he delivered. I was proud of the kid. Like Roy said, not everyone could do this kind of work. You needed swagger in your step, ice in your veins, and elephant balls in your pants.

A couple days before the shoot, I found Tiny hunched over in his bedroom, stoic and introspective. He had his hand propped on his chin like The Thinker, perhaps contemplating an ignominious future as The Porker.

"What's wrong, Tiny?" I asked.

"I'm kind of having a hard time with this thing, man."

"You don't have to go through with it. It's your call."

"I want to go through with it, I do. It's just that it's about the hardest goddamn thing I've ever had to face in my life... screwing some strange woman with all these people gawking at me, shining lights, barking instructions." I understood Tiny's dilemma. It would take a certain cold detachment to strip naked and waltz onto a movie set, proceeding to engage in the most intimate of acts with a total stranger, knowing each moment was being captured on film. Every grunt, thrust and gyration was being preserved digitally, carved in cinematic stone for posterity and its moral judgments. Yes, I understood Tiny's apprehension. And just what had compelled the venerable porn mogul Roy Karch to go out on a limb for an unknown, someone who'd never even hung around the set? For all Roy knew, Tiny's equipment was the size of a jalapeno. Roy had never pulled a *Colonel James*,[73] asking to take a gander at Tiny's goods. It was a mysterious thing, this blind faith... this Faith of Roy.

The night before the shoot, Tiny was psyching himself up, resolved to go through with the scene, when the phone rang. It was Roy. I could hear the disappointment in his voice.

"Dale, I've got bad news. My business partner caught wind of the fact that I was using a total newcomer... in a *backdoor* scene, on top of that... and he doesn't like it. This Esa Marie chick is kind of an up and coming star. We're gonna have to pair her with a more proven commodity. But if you really want to pursue this as a career, I can—

---

[73] Robert Ridgeley played Colonel James, a perverted old character who bankrolls Jack Horner (Burt Reynolds)'s porn films in *Boogie Nights*.

"That's alright, Roy," Tiny interjected. "I'll get in touch with you another time. Thanks for the opportunity." That was that. Tiny was off the hook. There would be no second drive to Reseda, no Dale Streak… no exciting new porn career launched. I believe Tiny took comfort in the fact that he had been ready to go through with it — he'd had the nerve to give porn a try — but I also believe he was relieved when the porn gods pulled the rug on his epic, backdoor scene with Esa Marie.

Schneider Wins

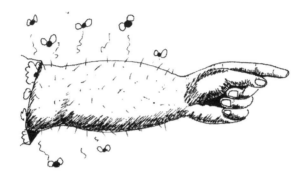

Relations further deteriorated with 24-Hour Complete Property Management. Schneider now hated us, because we had consistently forced him to do his job — replace faulty appliances, fix things that were broken — oh, the audacity! We had come to hate him too, and at Tiny's urging, I called the owner of the property and left a scathing message. I condemned Schneider as disagreeable and incompetent. Before the call, I had written out several scripted pages, and recited a ridiculous litany of grievances on the owner's voice mail… at three in the morning. The message culminated in a demand that 24-Hour Complete Property Management be relieved of duty… fired, in other words.

Tiny and I were certain the owner would side with us. We were convinced he'd realize we were good tenants, and would replace Schneider quickly. Thus, it was a surprise when Schneider came gimping up the steps a couple days later, a self-satisfied smirk plastered across his face, and handed me a piece of paper: Thirty-Day Notice to Vacate Premises. It was *signed by the owner himself*. You could see that this was a big moment for Schneider… one of the crowning achievements of his life: Ousting a pair of young musicians from their crummy apartment. What had the old coot told the owner? Which lie did he tell?[74] How had he poisoned the guy against us? It didn't matter now. Schneider had outmaneuvered us. Checkmate. We had no choice but to pack up and bail.

Instead of just collecting our things and moving out, Tiny and I made the misguided decision to attempt to get our deposit money back. At that young age, I sincerely believed that when you move out of an apartment, it is in fact possible to get your deposit back — that you're not automatically and invariably going to get screwed out of that money by your shady property manager. I didn't understand that deposits are part of the whole hustle, part of the property rental racket. Damn, there was so much I didn't know back then.

We cleaned that crap apartment like our lives depended on it. We scrubbed, washed, scraped and scoured for hours, making the place so spotless that there was no way this guy was going to be able to deny us our money. We even took pictures, in case we'd need to prove how clean we'd left it. The downstairs neighbor inspected the apartment, and said he'd testify as a witness if we needed him. So we moved out and waited for our check. And what do you think we received in the mail? A letter that said: *Tenants left the apartment filthy. Unit requires massive cleaning and repairs. No deposit to be refunded.*

The fumes from the ammonia were still irritating the hairs in my nostrils. My hands and back were sore from all the scrubbing. Old Schneider had gotten the last laugh. Sure, we could have taken him to court, and we might have won, but who the hell wanted to go to the trouble of all that? Tiny and I were too lazy to file a claim. We had better things to do, or at least we told ourselves we did. We decided to take it on the chin. Schneider pocketed our lousy seven hundred bucks. It was the end of an era. The Lizard days were coming to a close. Dale Streak and Tony Sebastian's glorious La Mesa run was finished.

---

[74] William Goldman, the legendary screenwriter, has a funny Hollywood trenches book called: *Which Lie Did I Tell?*

SAN DIEGO-ITIS

Tiny moved back in with his parents in Lakeside, while Wilbur and I migrated to a La Mesa apartment complex called Casa de Colina. Given my unfamiliarity with the Spanish language, I translated this to mean *House of the Colon*. The unit was small and the walls were thin. Wilbur was still hopping from one telemarketing dead end to another, and I continued to do a variety of gigs — some good, some bad, and some ugly.

The good: Tim McMahon, bassist Bob Magnusson, saxophonist Paul Sundfor and I put together a jazz quartet called Myriad. I practiced hard, since the other three guys were older and more seasoned. I wrote arrangements for a studio recording, which included a post-bop version of *The Lady is a Tramp*, and an odd-meter take on pianist Cedar Walton's *Bolivia*. Myriad performed shows at the Horton Grand Hotel and Ki's Coffee on Top. I was proud to work with such high-caliber musicians; these guys wouldn't play with just anyone.

You can't B.S. your way into a great band. If you can't cut it, good musicians won't want you on the stage. In rock, the standard is a little different. You've got to fit the group's visual image, which might be more important than the music, whereas in jazz and classical, it's all about the playing. None of your cohorts in the San Francisco Symphony are going to care about your sweet stage vibe, if your oboe work bites.

The bad: One night I was doing a wedding reception with local bandleader Bill Shreeve at The Prado, a nice area of Balboa Park. I was just sitting there in my tuxedo, playing my keyboard and minding my own business. The next thing I knew, an old man was onstage, right in my face. "Stand up!" he screamed. I stood to address him, fearing there might be an emergency situation in the crowd. *Uncle Marvin just keeled over! Call 9-1-1!*

"What can I do for you?" I asked. He grabbed my tux jacket and started *shaking me.* Yes, actually shaking me.

"It's too loud! You turn that shit down! Turn it down!"
I kept my cool and said, "Please take your hands off me." He continued to buttonhole me while screaming, "I'm paying for this whole goddamn wedding! You turn it down now!"

"Take your hands off me," I repeated. "I won't ask again." He gathered his wits and backed off. *The client sensed he was in danger of receiving a right cross to the jaw.*

"I'll tell the bandleader you want the volume down," I added. He nodded and walked away. During the break, Bill walked over to me and said, "You sure handled that well. I would have kicked the guy in the nuts." Corporate Gig Rule #1 specifies: *never, ever kick the client in the nut sack.*

This kind of situation occurs often at weddings. The party is divided into numerous camps. First, the young people: siblings, cousins, and friends of the bride and groom. They want loud dance music. It's bad enough they have to endure an entire day with all these old farts they have to pretend to be nice to, so you better play some cool music to ease their suffering. *None of that corny swing shit.* Then you have the bride's mother and her sisters, who are spoiling for that choice Neil Diamond or Michael Bolton cover. *Do you guys know Forever in Blue Jeans? Or hey, how 'bout Love Is A Wonderful Thing? Maybe I can get my husband's lazy butt out here on the dance floor. He's not bad once he let's go*

and gets into it… he just starts out a little self-conscious and embarrassed.[75]
Then there are the old folks. They think everything is just too damn
loud…

*What ever happened to the days when pop music was still real music? I don't
know what to call that crap on the radio now, but it sure isn't music! How
about some Tony Bennett, for God's sake? I'll slip you a twenty if you go over
there and tell those bastards to stop playing the Black Guy Pee Pees, or
whatever the hell their name is.*

You mean the Black Eyed Peas, Grandpa.

There is no way to make everyone happy, so you resign yourself to
being browbeaten all night by the client and his insatiable, multi-
generational posse.

Now it's time for *the ugly:* I was playing every week at Croce's with
my bassist friend Bud French and his small Latin combo. It was a fun
scene, with local musicians dropping in to jam with us. A trumpet
player we'll call Julio Castillo was one of the guys who would stop by
to play with the band. Julio was a ratty burnout character whose best
days were in the distant past. Once upon a time, he'd recorded jazz
albums with famous people like Freddie Hubbard, and he himself had
been a world-class player. Now, he was a world-class druggie who
crawled out from a rock in Tijuana every now and again, to blast a
couple sloppy solos and cause some sort of hassle.

The Croce's gig, dubbed *Monday Night Madness,* incorporated the
shtick of Larry Lowy, the restaurant's quirky, long-serving bartender.
Larry and Bud had little routines worked out, and even though they
might have gotten stale for the musicians, the weekly influx of fresh
tourists ate them up without fail. There were jokes, special songs, and
Larry even had a makeshift percussion rig behind the bar. Bud had

---

[75] Your husband's instincts are correct, his embarrassment justified. His
dancing sucks, and the guys in the band are shooting each other looks while he
makes a fool of himself, attempting to distract people from his utter lack of
rhythm with quirky, disjointed mannerisms à la a poor man's Mick Jagger. Do
the right thing—let him sit it out with the boys, while you and the rest of the
girls do the old estrogen shuffle, punctuated with the requisite, occasional
group *wooooooos* that, unbeknownst to you, make most males want to smash
delicate, inanimate objects with a sledgehammer.

designated certain spots in the show where the band would stop playing long enough for Larry to bang, typically out of rhythm, on either a wood block or set of bells. The crowd always loved it.

One busy night at Croce's, Julio Castillo skulked into the club with his horn to play a couple tunes. There had been rumors spreading that he was dead—one report speculated that he'd been iced over a south-of-the-border drug deal gone bad—so when he showed up, alive and kicking, it was a bit of a surprise for everyone. Julio pulled out his trumpet and began warming up. Meanwhile, the band was in the middle of playing a sensitive ballad. Bud motioned to Julio to stop warming up until we were done with the song. He was ruining the vibe.

"Wait for the next song," Bud said. Julio set his trumpet down, and started mumbling Spanish insults under his breath. Within a minute or two, he picked his horn up again and started playing scales in the wrong key—a blatant challenge to Bud, who repeated his words: "Wait for the next song." This time, Julio pulled the trumpet from his mouth and put it back in its case. He closed the case and looked like he was going to split, like he was giving up on playing with the band. Bud was taking a bass solo, paying no attention when Julio got up and walked over to where the bassist was standing on stage. Thinking the trumpeter had something to say to him, Bud leaned closer to his face. Julio opened his mouth, but instead of words, it was a *giant loogie* that flew from his lips, scoring a direct hit that began dribbling down Bud's nose. Julio bolted out the front door and down 5th Street, as Bud threw down his bass to chase after the slimy vulgarian. The rest of us continued playing like nothing had happened. Julio was thin and wiry. He could still move quickly. T.J. Hooker[76] might have been able to catch him, but Bud French could not.

"Little fucker got away," Bud lamented upon his return.

That reminds me of one time when I was a kid, and some older jerk, for no reason whatsoever, spit at me from several feet away. It landed right in my eye. I started crying and ran home. When I saw the same

---

[76] Len and I used to laugh at episodes of T.J. Hooker, when William Shatner, fat and out of shape, would run down some stereotypically cast, skinny black guy who looked like a world class sprinter. Shatner was always struggling for breath, laboring with every stride, and yet somehow he closed the gap, winding up close enough to execute a standard TV cop show lunge/tackle.

guy a week later, hanging out with some other neighborhood regulars, he grinned and said, "I spit in your eye." I had no comeback. I put my head down in shame. Don't you ever wish, as an adult, you could exact revenge for such moments from your childhood, when you didn't have the courage to stand up for yourself? That loser probably never gave it a second thought, but I have to live with the memory for the rest of my life…

I walk into a nice restaurant in some random city, and continue over to a table where several modest-income businessmen sit having lunch. I've done my research, planned this mission carefully, and am here specifically for this moment, which I have rehearsed in my mind a hundred times. I zero in on one guy in particular and walk right up. I grab a chair and sit next to him, real close, violating his personal space. He's got a receding hairline, crow's feet, half-assed goatee and cheap suit. I smell lousy cologne on him. Old Spice, I think. He doesn't know me, no idea who I am, and shoots a surprised look, first at me and then at his friends, who are equally puzzled.

"Can I help you?"

"No."

"Then whadda you want?"

"You don't remember me?"

"No. I've never met you before."

"Are you sure?" I gather saliva from the back of my throat, swirling it around in my mouth. Deliberately. Demonstratively. When I'm ready, I fire one right between the eyes. A big one. High volume. Couple crusty boogers lodged in the goo. Shock. He and his friends can't believe what just happened.

"Why did you do that?!" he whines. I grin, reciprocating the exact facial expression that has haunted my memories since 1981. I wait a few priceless, awkward moments, then say:

"I just spit in your eye. Now we're even." He looks at me like I'm crazy, like I'm some lunatic perpetrating a random, senseless act against an innocent citizen… but then his face changes. His pupils dilate with a faint mnemonic glimmer. He remembers. He knows that I know he remembers. Oh yes, he remembers. I am, at long last, satisfied. Vindicated.

It's not like I really want to spit in anyone's eye. It's just one of those absurd little fantasies we all entertain, kind of like that scene in *Take the Money and Run*, when Woody Allen, waiting in line for a movie, silences a quasi-intellectual blowhard by presenting Marshall McCluhan, in the flesh, who proceeds to tell the guy on behalf of Allen, "You idiot! You know nothing of my work." Allen then turns to the camera, breaks the fourth wall and says, "Don't you wish real life was like that?"

Wilbur and I had a neighbor at Casa de Colina named Raymond. Raymond was functionally retarded—self-sufficient enough to live on his own and hold down a job, but challenged with considerable mental hurdles. He would leave his apartment early each morning, old metal lunchbox in hand, to catch the bus out in front of the complex.

Raymond must have been a deep sleeper, because he had an elaborate system of alarm clocks that all started going nuts at 5 a.m. There was the one that went *oop, oop, oop, oop, oop*. Then the one that went *bluh-luh-luh-luh, bluh-luh-luh-luh, bluh-luh-luh-luh, bluh-luh-luh-luh*. Yet another that went *eewn...eewn...eewn...eewn*. And, of course, there was the standard *BEEP! BEEP! BEEP! BEEP!* Sometimes this symphony would blare away for fifteen or twenty minutes before Raymond stopped it. It was hard to believe he was sleeping through all this noise, so I imagined Raymond just staring at the ceiling, blocking out the noise as he mustered the will to face the day.

Wilbur and I talked about what we should do, since the situation was really messing with our sleep. Throw a bowling ball through the wall? Corner Raymond on his way to the bus stop and hector him? Threaten to steal his lunchbox if the noise persisted? We concurred that it was bad karma to mess with a guy like Raymond, even if he was waking us up at the crack of dawn every day. Raymond had enough to deal with already, including an abusive jerk in a ten-gallon hat who picked him up in his battered old El Dorado, every Wednesday night, and took him roller skating. I couldn't figure out the relationship between the two men... was he an uncle? A sponsor? A con artist somehow manipulating the retarded man, or embroiling him in some twisted, co-dependent relationship? I know I'm not painting a pretty picture here. It's *Xanadu* meets *I Am Sam,* with a smidge of *Midnight Cowboy.* Given Raymond's obstacles in life, we tolerated *oop, bluh-luh-luh-luh, eewn* and *BEEP*. It could have been worse. We could have had Heath and Talbott living next door, writing songs for the follow-up album and looking for a place to hide the severed heads.[77]

---

[77] If you missed this reference, please refer to *Tiny n' Anth Do La Mesa.*

In 1996 the odds of Faze making a big music industry splash were getting slim; we were all growing older. I was tired of San Diego. I had been semi-blacklisted by a pair of female singers seeking to punish me for trivial mishaps (coming back late from a break on a gig... not returning a phone call). This hardly seemed like justification for slandering my name around town. Suddenly, in the eyes of the jobbing community, I was a flake. After playing hundreds of gigs with dozens of people, making the occasional mistake, yes, but always taking my work seriously and trying to be professional, I was stuck with the worst rap a freelance musician can have: *He's unreliable.*

I began to wonder if the San Diego scene and its petty recriminations was the place I wanted to be. I wasn't even sure I wanted to continue as a professional musician. Where had it gotten me? Into a cramped, stuffy apartment with a blimp-sized telemarketer, who sat around eating Little Debbie snack cakes and bopping old Bozo to back issues of Lingerie Lard-Asses... while living next door to a mentally challenged forty-five year-old with seventeen different alarm clocks and an abusive, urban cowboy sponsor. *I wasn't exactly setting the world on fire.*

Despite becoming disenchanted with the local scene, my commitment to the creative process never wavered. I sat in that apartment and wrote songs on my Ensoniq TS-10 keyboard, day after day. Something was still driving me. I put a new group together. This time, it was going to rock. I called it Ransom Kings, and recruited Tiny to play guitar. We recorded a demo of seven songs: *Fools Covet, Artifacts, Pieces of My Broken Mirror, Ugly, No More Room in Heaven, Whipping Boy* and *Six Times Around the Sun.* The writing style incorporated everyone from Sting to Pearl Jam.

Looking back, the songs were interesting but the project lacked focus. This has always been my Achilles heel. I try to do too many different things. I'm overly ambitious. I aim to pull off a synthesis of Sting, Herbie Hancock, Peter Gabriel, Bruce Hornsby, Bobby Hutcherson, Chick Corea, John Medeski, U2 and Dr. John. Talk about all over the place...

Even though the Ransom Kings songs were stylistically scattered, the lyrics were an improvement over my previous stuff. Also, the production was more intricate than anything I had done before. *Fools Covet*, probably the best of the lot, was an epic pop arrangement with string lines, horn punctuations, clever guitar riffs and layered vocal harmonies. The song had Beatles and Yes-inspired touches, and the lyrics, somewhat autobiographical, had an effective storytelling quality:

Seemed like a good idea at the time
So anxiously I stood in line
For my turn to paint the fence
He said it was small price to pay
So I gave all my pennies away
For the chance to paint his fence
I wasn't the only one left in the summer sun
Paint spilled across my pockets

Fools Covet what they cannot have
I found I had been foolish
Wise people seem to understand
That fools covet

Time passed until I finally came of age
Much smarter, still no gifted sage
And I found a woman's eyes
Could change my sense of who I thought I was
Blind hope became the master of my heart
As reason's seams all came apart
The ones I wanted the most,
The ones I couldn't have
A pill I never learned to swallow

CHORUS

Everywhere I turn it seems there's someone, something I desire
If only I was more equipped to handle these emotions
I keep searching for the knowledge that I'll need to get beyond this world of wishing
The same mistakes will haunt me, haunt me time and time again
Until I learn the truth, until I learn from smarter men
I've fallen in this trap before, well I should know by now…
Fools covet

While recording this and other songs, I made the pleasant discovery that my singing had improved. I was figuring out how to write for my voice and range. Great singer/songwriters — and I'm by no means saying that I am one — have the ability to merge their voice and writing into one distinct entity. Jerry Garcia, Bruce Springsteen, Joni Mitchell and Marvin Gaye come to mind as just a few examples.

Singing takes a certain amount of courage. Any chump can get up at the local dive and belt out *Old Time Rock and Roll* after pounding a few Jaeger shots. But fronting a band in a concert situation, or even just a club gig, where people are paying money to be entertained, takes confidence. It's somewhat daunting to present yourself to the world as a singer, because everyone and their grandma is a self-appointed expert on singing, and there are widely varying ideas of what good singing sounds like. Someone might say, "You're not bad, but you're no Stevie Wonder." Well, there are already ten thousand imitators copping *his* style. Why would you want to be number ten thousand-and-one?

Singing, like playing improvised music, is largely about finding your own style and delivering it with conviction. Pitch is paramount, also. You can have a so-so natural tone, but if you sing with excellent pitch, you're going to sound like a pro. That's what separates the men from Karaoke/Foosball Tuesdays.

While I was writing the lyrics to *Six Times Around the Sun*, a peculiar thing happened. The lyric had begun around this idea: *What would you do if you only had six days to live?* I had been sharing this high concept with people for a couple weeks when a friend said, "Sorry to break it to you, but the earth rotates around the sun in a *year,* not a day." Oops. Fortunately, this led to a more poignant theme: Children who are taken from the world before their time. *Six Times Around the Sun* became about a fictitious six year-old girl who dies tragically. Shortly after I'd finished the song, I struck up a conversation with a woman who had just lost her young daughter to a rare illness. She had sat by the little girl's side as she took her last breaths, unable to do anything to help her. I asked how old the girl was, and the woman paused for a moment before saying: "Six." Given that I had just written the song, it spooked me out a bit. Her story became the second verse:

She was born with two strikes against her
And still a beautiful child
A longshot to reach the age of reason
Because her mother had lived a little wild
She had a smile for everyone

So much love to give, so many reasons to live
But the little girl would only make it
Six times around the sun

Six times around the sun
Six times around, six times around
Six times around the sun

We sat in a pale yellow booth
As the woman pointed to a small tattoo
The name for both her greatest joy and sorrow
Kissed by the wings of an angel
And she tried to explain to me the point when a mother's touch
Can't ease the wrath of nature's will
Watching her child's last breaths
There would be no birthday cake with the number seven

Ransom Kings never got around to doing any live shows. I had notebooks full of unfinished ideas, and plenty more songs to record, but I'd run out of money. The studio is an expensive environment, and I was paying for everything myself. Whenever I managed to save some cash I would throw myself into a new project, once again draining my personal resources. I had to do it. Mine was the burden of having bountiful ideas without a record label to back them. I am, at heart, a risk-taker. I will keep going for broke until I run out of ideas, and I will run out of breath before I run out of ideas.

One night, Wilbur and I were relaxing in the hot tub at Casa de Colina.[78] I started telling him about a concept I had for a movie screenplay, centered around a pair of bumbling FBI agents, forced to infiltrate the world of rodeo by masquerading as rodeo clowns. As I laid out the basic plot, Wilbur started adding funny twists and bits of dialogue. I got psyched about the whole idea, and started sketching a first draft the next day. I didn't know how to format a screenplay, so I bought a few books on the subject.

---

[78] Unlike Kathy Bates in *About Schmidt*, Wilbur did not try to attack me sexually. Wilbur's breasts, incidentally, were about the same size as Kathy Bates's in *About Schmidt*.

Soon I had a big stack of books on screenwriting, some dealing with style, others character development, and a few that contained interviews with successful writers. I also got my hands on actual screenplays. I was going to write *Clowns,* and it was going to be great. The seeds of my San Diego discontent, planted months earlier, were now sprouting from the soil. Steady work had dried up. Despite the strengths of *Fools Covet*, Ransom Kings wasn't going anywhere. Faze was all but dead. I wasn't sure I believed in the band concept anymore. It was time to do something that relied only on me; a solo effort. If I couldn't find success in a collective environment, maybe I could find it by pursuing the most solitary vocation known to man: literary writing.

If I was going to be serious about screenwriting, there was only one place to do it: Los Angeles. I'd have to plan it out. I would need money, a pad, and a course of action. In the meantime, Tiny and I picked up a gig writing and producing a pop record for a local singer named Gina Romero. She was in her thirties, and had dreams of being a star.

Gina started coming to my apartment for writing sessions, and we collaborated on several songs, including a catchy funk tune called *Reciprocate.* I appreciated Gina's relentless drive, a rare quality in our, sunny, Southern province, but Gina also suffered from a bit of *San Diego-itis*. This was a self-coined term Tiny and I used to describe the inability of local musicians to see the bigger music industry picture, and to set realistic goals that reflected this understanding.

Gina had socked away a nest egg to finance her ambitions, so the album had a green light. In the world of entertainment, *anything* gets a green light if someone's willing to put up money to back it. People assume that if something is being financially supported it must, on some level, be good. This is false. There is no correlation between the amount of money spent on a project, and the artistic success or intrinsic value of that project. History is littered with examples of great artists being neglected and dying in obscurity, as well as charlatans enjoying commercial success and material spoils well beyond what their talent merited. If you aspire to have a life in the arts, *get over it.* There's no point fighting it. It's how the world works.

One thing I know about musicians, including myself, is that we all have our price. If a project gets a green light, and there's a piece of the pie with our name on it, and the music isn't so horrible that we couldn't possibly live with ourselves after playing it, count us in. We might start out our careers clinging to some impenetrable sense of integrity, but in the end, most of us do what's necessary to survive. Some might call this being a whore, but long ago I realized that flexibility and versatility, as well as open-mindedness to take on work outside of my comfort zone, are the main reasons I've worked consistently for twenty years.

I'd like to explain why I've so stubbornly avoided a full-time job outside the arts for so long. It stems from my basic belief that you are what you do. If you spend your life working as a lawyer, that's what you are. That's how you define yourself, and that's what you project to the world. You hang out with other lawyers most of the time, and the challenges you face on a daily basis, at least as far as your career is concerned, are legal in nature. You're not sitting around thinking about mechanical engineering or chemistry, because you're not an engineer or a chemist. If you're a singer, let's say a very good one, but you work full-time as a software designer, this is your title: *software designer who sings on the weekend.* That might sound harsh, because maybe your heart is really in your singing, and you're just doing software design to pay the bills—but the fact is that you're spending the majority of your creative energy, the prime hours of your fleeting life, doing something other than sing, which is the thing that actually matters to you.

The point is, don't deceive yourself into thinking you can spend the majority of your life doing one thing, but somehow define yourself in terms of another; or believe that some magic day is going to come when you will do a complete one-eighty, abandon your career and start over doing whatever is in your heart. Sure, it happens, but it's rare.

This isn't to say that working a day job, or having a career lucrative enough to facilitate some other pursuit is wrong for everyone. It doesn't work for me, but I've known people who have pulled off this juggling act, still managing to be productive in their artistic endeavors. I also used to know musicians who subsidized their dreams by slinging marijuana or other illegal substances. Based on my observations, this can be an effective (though obviously illegal) way to keep a financially unsuccessful band in business.

Tempting as it might be if you're a young, struggling musician, it's probably not a wise idea to sell drugs. I'm reminded of an old acquaintance named Potato, a wiry, energetic guy with beady eyes. He was always nice when I bumped into him at festivals around the country. I wondered how he was able to afford passing his days flying around, attending music festivals, eating out and staying in hotels—but it wasn't my business, and I never asked. There were lots of kids pulling off that lifestyle.

All of a sudden, I stopped bumping into Potato. West Coast? No Potato. East Coast? No Potato. Know why? Because the only place you were going to bump into Potato, for a few years there, was in the yard at San Quentin Penitentiary. Potato's house in Northern California had gotten raided by feds, and he had been unlucky enough to be sitting on a huge stash. Not just drugs, either. He also had guns and a big pile of dough. Not good, Potato. Not good.[79]

Perhaps we should talk about drugs for a minute. I myself have never been a user. I do have an appetite for liquor, specifically Captain Morgan rum, and as I'm quick to admit when discussing the *trajectory* of my years on the road, the Captain has been a loyal friend through trying times. I'm not much of a pot smoker. I never felt like it did much for me. Never dug the high. I've taken a puff here and there, but more out of camaraderie than anything else. I only got really stoned one time, when I was seventeen and trying it for the first time. Erik Vaishville, a childhood pal, brought some pot to the Century Theaters in San Jose. It was Thanksgiving night, and Vaish, Derrek Mason and I were checking out the original *Child's Play*. Vaish showed us how to smoke out of a soda can. I'm pretty sure that's the hardest I've ever laughed in my entire life. *Child's Play*, on that occasion, was the funniest comedy of all time.

I never felt much temptation to use harder stuff. I was always spooked by the stories you'd hear about someone keeling over. A great example was Len Bias, the college basketball star who died from smoking crack on the same day he was drafted into the NBA.

I did try coke once, after a show in San Francisco. I was hanging out at someone's apartment, having a drink or two, and suddenly there were lines spread out on a glass table in front of me. For some reason

---

[79] Sometime later, I was playing a show in Davis, California. My buddy Woo came out to the show from Chico, bringing several friends. One guy in particular helped us load in and out of the venue. I didn't pay him much attention, and simply thanked him for lifting our gear. I did notice he was in good shape—thin but muscular, clean cut, healthy. After we'd loaded out and were preparing to leave, I asked Woo:
"Do I know that guy from somewhere?"
"You sure do. That's Potato." He'd done his time and was clean now. I couldn't believe it was the same person.

on this night, curiosity got the best of me. I took a toot in each nostril, and split a third line between both of them. It did not kill me, and in fact, I liked the high. I have to be honest. It was short but intense. It made me feel in complete control of everything, my senses super-charged in a way I had never experienced. In the morning, after getting no sleep, a wave of depression washed over me. I don't know if it was guilt over breaking a lifelong resolve to never touch the stuff, or the standard next-day crash. Either way, I felt awful, and at that moment I vowed I'd never touch cocaine again.

Over the years, people have asked me how I managed to avoid doing drugs while immersed in a livelihood that, let's face it, is teeming with every substance under the sun. I think the answer is that I'm stubborn. I've avoided drugs for the same reason I've never caved in and started eating mayonnaise, mustard and relish. I'm picky about what I ingest. Furthermore, I've suspected, despite the morbid visions of premature demise we all entertain, that I might be stuck on this planet for a while. (Having two of four grandparents live to ninety reinforced this notion). And however long I'm here, I'd like to hold on to my brain. I shudder at the thought of slowly frying my mental faculties, then spending the golden years as a worthless vegetable.

With Tiny and me serving as producers, Gina began recording her album at Blast Studios. The engineer and owner, Randy Lucas, had recorded some of my original songs in the past, and was a friend. He was full of energy and ideas, a joy to work with. Tiny and I assumed he and Gina would get along just fine. To borrow a line from Spike Lee's *Malcom X: don't assume anything.* From the minute we all arrived at the studio, Gina rubbed Randy in all the wrong ways. She was demanding and tactless, complaining that everything was taking too long. She wanted to spend ten hours on each vocal performance, while Tiny and I wanted to spend two or three. We could see Randy's patience rapidly wearing thin.

Gina was turning into a studio nightmare. She explained to us one day: "I may be a singer, but I'm also a predator. When I'm on stage, I stalk my prey." At one point, the Predator spent three hours going over the same vocal line. Randy hit his breaking point. Tiny and I haplessly attempted to coach her through the track, but she refused to continue on past the one problematic phrase. She sang it at least two hundred times. Finally, Randy called for a break and pulled Dale and me outside. He was sweaty and flustered.

"Jesus, guys… I don't think I can do this anymore. This chick is pushing me over the edge. And something stinks in there."

"You mean the song? Her vocal performance?"

"No, something actually stinks."

"It's the food she brought in that Tupperware container," Tiny said. Some kinda organic, vegetarian shit."

"I don't care about the money, guys. This isn't how I wanna spend my time on the planet. This chick is driving me nuts. I want to go home and be with my wife."

Randy had paid his dues. It wasn't easy running your own studio. You had to deal with every wannabe that owned a guitar. Every juvenile punk within a fifty mile radius. Randy had shared some past experiences as a studio owner, including one memorable tale…

A band of teenage skater/thrash musicians got dropped by their parents, and planned to record a few songs with Randy. It was their first time in a studio, and Randy had laid out some basic, reasonable rules to both the parents and the kids, who promised to behave themselves. The name of the band was Excrement—a good indication of the musical magic to come. The tracking went okay, and then it was time to mix everything down. As they all sat in the control room, Randy manipulating knobs and faders on his main console, one of the kids stood up, stuck his butt in the older man's face and *let one rip.* The rest of the band broke out in juvenile laughter. Randy was the one person in the room who didn't find it funny. He threw the members of Excrement out into the street to wait for mommy's shuttle service.

The story is reminiscent of Tom Wolfe's novel, *I Am Charlotte Simmons*, which brilliantly indicts the American collegiate environment for being crude and barbaric. Wolfe's book was sandbagged by critics who felt threatened by Wolfe's dead-on honesty, or who didn't want to acknowledge that such crudity runs rampant in modern American society, not just on college campuses. If you doubt Wolfe's accuracy in capturing the pulse of modern pop culture, check out *Jack-Ass, the Movie* and get back to me.[80]

I myself endured some ridiculous moments while working at various studios around town. Golden Track was a comfortable space, but not located in the best of neighborhoods. Homeless people would wander

---

[80] I admit I laughed hard at a few of the scenes in *Jack-Ass.*

in, or random drug addicts who'd migrated west from El Cajon. One time, I was in the middle of some session when a transient man staggered in to interrupt us. He was missing many teeth and smelled funky. The guy started yelling from the front hallway.

"Yo, playa! I need to speak to the C.E.O.!"

"I'll be with you in a minute," Chad, the engineer replied.

"Y'all wanna blow dis shit up? I got rhymes! I need the C... E... O!"

"Excuse me, sir? How can I help you?"

"Y'all wanna blow dis shit up or what, playa? I just need some beats to go wit my rhymes, knowudahmsayin'?"

"Uh, we're in session right now. Can you come back another time?" Homeboy's hoarse, Ebonics-laden rodomontade got confrontational.

"I'm tellin' you, man... wit my crayzee rhymze an mad flow, and yo beats... y'all got beats, right? Dawg, we can blow dis shit up! Blow it up like the World Trade Center! Nahmean, yo?"

No, buddy, I don't know what you're referring to... the World Trade Center? What happened there?

Rap and karaoke, at their worst, are co-conspirators in a disturbing modern trend. Suddenly, everyone thinks they're an *artist*. It takes a lot for a rapper to impress me. Guys in different cities used to come up to the stage saying, "Let me jump up with y'all and spit some rhymes." Most of the time, it was the usual *strugglin' on the streets* tirade. *Yawn.* It's gonna take more than some hackneyed urban harangue, peppered with lightweight, lefty colloquialisms to make me spill my caramel latte, home skillet.

As for karaoke, it would be one thing if people just got up there to have a little fun, harboring no delusions of grandeur. The fact is that there's a whole competitive subculture where people take karaoke very seriously. It's a parallel universe in which the audience and the performer become one and the same, harkening back to our old friend Kenny G, who was brilliantly skewered in Joe Queenan's pop culture classic, *Red `, White Trash and The Blue Lagoon*:

> I bailed out of Radio City Music Hall long before
> Kenny G had finished his set. One reason, among
> many, that I left so early was my disgust at his shit-
> eating patter about how much he owed to his public —
> the mythical "you guys." His populist demeanor

stood in sharp contrast to a great saxophonist like
Sonny Rollins. Sonny Rollins never dismantles the
essential wall between performer and spectator.
Kenny G's prancing in the aisles bleats: "I'm just like
you. I'm just a lucky guy. But any one of you could be
up here, too." This smarminess repelled me. If Kenny
G was just an average guy with a horn, why did I have
to pay $60 to see him?

A few years ago, I had my own infuriating run-in with one of the great
musical frauds of modern times. Maybe *the* greatest...

I share an enthusiasm for NBA basketball with my brother-in-law,
Massimo. While both living in the Bay Area a while back, we decided
to catch a Golden State Warriors game. The Warriors were taking on
the Houston Rockets, led by 7'5" behemoth Yao Ming. It was a good
crowd, well over ten thousand. The game was enjoyable, and when
halftime arrived, we waited to discover what entertainment treat was
in store. The arena became pitch black, as the public address
announcer's overwrought baritone growled, "Ladies and gentleman,
for your halftime pleasure, please welcome national recording artist...
the one, the only...

Williaaaaaaaaam Huuuuuuuuuuuuung!

For those of you who don't recognize the name, William Hung is the
Asian guy that went on *American Idol* and performed a tone-deaf,
moronic version of Ricky Martin's *She Bangs*, accompanied by
schizophrenic dance moves... a spectacle so outrageous that Hung
landed himself an agent, got a recording contract, and started making
international publicity appearances. Of course, it was all a joke, right?
Right?

When the NBA announcer said Hung's name, a spotlight located him
at center court, flanked by hotties from the Warrior cheerleading
squad. This was followed by the deafening roar of thousands of
people. It sure didn't seem like a joke. Hung started singing his
signature song, *She Bangs*, and people went nuts. This *going nuts* was
not distinguishable from when people go nuts over something that is
actually good. It had the same exact feel. I found this troubling.

Massimo is a well-mannered, classy guy who goes out of his way to
be supportive and upbeat. He is not prone to negative, emotional

outbursts. When William Hung finished butchering Ricky Martin, and broke into a *second song*, Elton John's sappy *Can You Feel the Love*, my brother-in-law lost it.

"What is this shit, Anth? Who is this idiot? What's he doing out there? Why is he being featured?"

"He's a star, Massi. He got his break on American Idol, now he's pretty big."

"But he can't sing! He's... he's fucking terrible, Anth!"

"Yes, he is, Massi. I agree. But none of these thousands of people seem to care."

People were dancing and cheering in the aisles, celebrating Hung's triumph of the human spirit. *You can do anything you set your mind to, if you want it bad enough. You just have to believe in yourself. You can make your dream come true. Don't let anyone take away your dream.*

I became pissed myself when Hung insisted on doing the entire Elton John song, bellowing with no sense of pitch whatsoever. I started booing. Next thing I knew, people were scowling at us. Someone even threw something at us. *What's wrong with you? He's doing his best, you jerk! William Hung is an inspiration to us all!* Once Hung finished, having been center stage for a good fifteen minutes, the announcer said, "Be sure to pick up your copy of William Hung's new album, *Inspiration,* available in the lobby on your way out of the arena tonight!"

One thinks of all the truly talented people out there, who for one reason or another never get a break, who never get much recognition. Then there's this lame-o who can't sing, can't dance, and looks like... I'm not going to say it. He's got an agent, he's flying around making paid appearances, and he's hired to entertain me at a professional sporting event I've shelled out eighty bucks to attend. And it's not his fault. He's just a pawn. He just thinks he lives in a great country where dreams come true. He doesn't understand that he's little more than a circus act, with a very short shelf life.

I guess I should hop down off my high horse and tell you that I've been known to grab a karaoke microphone from time to time. It is, after all, good clean fun. Wait, let me rephrase that: it's good, clean, drunken fun. There's only one way to do karaoke, and that's microphone in one hand, glass of booze in the other.

Tiny and I had a favorite spot near SDSU, a Chinese restaurant called Li's Garden. We'd eat cracked crab, drink beer and witness some of the worst vocal performances this side of a Kowloon watering hole (or an

NBA halftime presentation). I remember one gem sung by a Jackie Chan lookalike:

My luuuuuuhv, I will always love you, my luuuuuuuhv.

Another time, I remember ruining the family-oriented atmosphere of karaoke night at a restaurant in Dana Point, California. Adrian Ahearn and I started freak-dancing with a couple girls we'd just met, while a soccer mom was wheezing through some insufferable Cher anthem. As we rained on the PG-13 parade, a guy came over and said, "This is a family establishment. Let's keep it tasteful, guys." Talk about lobbing a watermelon up to plate with Albert Pujols standing there…

"Taste? You're ruining your children's musical tastes for life, sir, just by being here. Don't talk to me about taste." I went on to explain how his generation had malt shops and sock-hops as pre-mating-ritual environments. In the new millenium, we have skateboard parks, strip malls, X Box parties, chat rooms and karaoke. He shook his head and hit the stage to tackle some Limp Bizkit.

After a disastrous attempt to reunite Gina and Randy in the studio, Gina became disgruntled and fired Tiny and me as the producers of her debut album. Outside of the recording studio environment she was a nice person, very cool and fun to be around. When it came to Gina's musical ambitions, however, the humility one would have hoped for, given her modest singing and songwriting ability, was entirely superceded by delusions of subtle artistry. This is one of the things that makes the music business difficult. Everybody wants to be a star in this celebrity-driven culture. They don't want to pay the years of dues it takes to be great, mind you, but they want to be a star. They want the trappings of success without doing the work, without developing the craft. What's unfortunate is that this delusion is fueled by real-life examples to support the lust for stardom. In other words, the delusion is no longer a delusion. It's a tangible opportunity. You can take William Hung and make him a star for fifteen minutes. And if you can do that, anything is possible. I tackled this subject in the lyrics to a song from my most recent studio effort:

Exciting time in human history
Everything's up for grabs
And most of it is free
The world is flat, like the book suggests

We're all the same
There's no more worst or best

Past the days of monopolies
What's mine is yours
Ain't that democracy
You're free to change whatever I create
Just take the parts you like, and cut and paste
I was tired of my obscurity
So I took matters into my own hands

Got my own show
Where we talk about me
It's written, directed and produced
And stars yours truly
I'm really takin' off
Blowin' up huge
Next comes the book, the movie
Then I'll start my own YouTube

Celebrity fixation hits most of us on one level or another. Living in America, you can't avoid it. I'm susceptible to it like anyone else. I realized this years ago, while visiting my younger sister Paula at UCLA. Paula was working toward an eventual Masters degree in Urban Planning and Development, and we would get together to have dinner or see a flick. We were walking around Westwood, when we noticed a big movie premiere was about to take place at the Westwood Theater. We decided to stop and watch the stars arrive in their limousines. I'd never done something like this before—gawk at celebrities—and had always looked down on such behavior.

Soon, there were a couple thousand people crowding the street, hoping to catch a glimpse of the stars of *The Last Action Hero*, most notably Arnold Schwarzenegger.[81] I couldn't believe how many big names showed up. Most weren't even in the movie; they were just making an appearance. Dozens of stars milled around in front of the theater, schmoozing, doing interviews. Mingling with the common folk from behind the barricade across the street, I thought to myself:

---

[81] The film would go on to be Arnold's first major flop.

I'm above this. Who cares about these Hollywood people? I wasn't going to make googly eyes at stars. I was simply here to conduct an experiment—to do a little field research on the American public's celebrity fixation. Just as I was thinking this, a stretch limo pulled up directly in front of my sister and me. Security guards surrounded the vehicle as the passenger door opened. *Must be someone big.* A broad, chiseled guy hopped out. Arnold. Conan. The Terminator. Commando. Kindergarten Cop.[82]

I crumbled. "Arnold!" I screamed, clawing my way to the front of the pack, greedily craving a handshake with the screen legend. "Arrrrrrrrrrrnold!" When I emerged from the melee, Paula was laughing at me, the commoner, the Philistine who claws until he's close enough to sniff his favorite screen idol. I might as well have been a housewife from Armadillo.

The fiasco with Gina was the final straw for me in San Diego. L.A. was looking better all the time. My brother Collin was there, Paula was there, the music industry was there, the movie industry (hence the market for my screenplay) was there, and most importantly... Arnold was there. Collin was looking for a roommate to share an apartment in Northridge, where he was going to school and playing Division I men's volleyball; so I bid farewell to Wilbur and Casa de Colina, Raymond and his Alarms of Many Cacophonous Noises, The Predator and her organic tofu and her two hundred attempts to sing the same line, and the San Diego music scene. It was time for a new adventure.

---

[82] 2010 update: The Governator.

THE WORLD MAKES US THAT WAY

If you're planning to move to Los Angeles, it's a good idea to know a few people before you get there. Just showing up with nothing in place, no plan and no prospects, is not recommended, especially if you're moving there to establish yourself in the entertainment industry. Los Angeles is not so much a city as a sprawling, seemingly infinite megalopolis. A tiny, concentrated phalanx of skyscrapers, cloistered so closely together and in such meager numbers that it is almost humorous, serves as the focal point around which hundreds of suburban enclaves string together, to form the vast stretch of development between Irvine and the edge of the San Fernando Valley. In truth, there no longer remains much barren land between Los Angeles and San Diego to the south, nor Santa Barbara to the north. One day, the megalopolis will stretch from the border of Mexico to Hearst Castle and the shores of San Simeon, or perhaps all the way to the quiet, northern reaches of Eureka. Everyone wants to live in California, after all.

The massive labyrinth of freeways, overpasses, underpasses, industrial complexes, billboards, beaches, restaurants, ghettos, movie theaters, housing tracts, gated communities, boulevards, film studios, amphitheatres, museums, mausoleums, arenas, stadiums, universities, hospitals, cemeteries, correctional facilities, research labs, plants, factories, post-production labs, hills, valleys, piers, boardwalks, bookstores, clothing outlets, mega-malls, mini-malls, tourist attractions, rehab centers, auto garages, junkyards, car dealerships, dive bars, diners, hotels, roach motels, more freeways and even more billboards, all of which coalesce to form a gigantic supercity that seems like its own sovereign nation, can be a bit overwhelming.

L.A. is a place of connections. You can't do anything without them. You're either on the inside, you're plotting to get on the inside, or you're nowhere. During my brief *tenure* at A&M in 1991, I had gotten my first bitter taste of life in L.A. as an outsider. I was an outsider working on the inside, but was constantly reminded I was an outsider, which is worse than being an outsider who doesn't realize it or doesn't care in the first place. Now, in 1997, I was returning to try my hand again, with no one to call, no one to ask for a favor. I had no juice in a place where juice is everything. It wasn't much of a plan. I just wanted to get the hell out of San Diego.

I didn't know what I was looking for anymore. My interest in music had waned, the dream of mainstream success hadn't worked out, and I had lost the fire. The passion that had always perpetuated itself in the past was now something I had to consciously manufacture. Music had become boring. I had done so many different things—sideman jobs, my own groups, school, composing, recording—and I was spent. Screenwriting was a new frontier, a fresh challenge that required all of my intellectual energy. I wasn't naïve enough to think I would start selling scripts right away, but I did have long-term hopes. I'd already developed, from that first conversation in the Casa de Colina hot tub with Wilbur, a completed 120-page first draft of *Clowns*.

I had other concepts for scripts, too. With patience and perseverance, I hoped I might turn this hobby into a vocation. In the meantime I would need a day job. Collin and I moved into a two-bedroom apartment, not far from the Cal State Northridge campus. He had a full athletic scholarship to play men's Division One volleyball, and wasn't available to hang out much. On my own in L.A., a little fish in an endless pond, I began the hunt for employment.

Despite Collin being tied up on campus all the time, I cherished the chance to share a place with my younger brother. For much of our lives, we'd been separated by circumstances beyond our control. Still, we'd remained close. Now we were able to be buddies again. It had eaten at me for years that I hadn't had the opportunity to really be a big brother—the kind who's there all the time, leading the way, supporting in ways a parent cannot. Sure, Collin was doing fine in his life now, and I was finding my way, but there were scars from our adolescence that had never healed. We'd both had a tough time growing up, and we'd mostly dealt with it alone.

The apartment was nothing special, but at least comfortable. The building was managed by a middle-aged couple named Jessie and Jack. Jack was a real character—racist and unabashed. You passed by his maintenance cage on the way from the underground parking garage to the elevator, and he was always waiting there with a ribald story or joke. One time, Jack launched into a rant about the Winchester Mystery House: "That bitch was crazy, I tell you! Didn't have nothing to do but sit in that big mansion thinking up all kinds of crazy shit to do to the place. All those secret compartments leading nowhere, trap doors, staircases running into the ceiling…" Then the monologue would take a different direction, and Jack was now talking about self-defense: "Let's say you get into a fight with a really big black guy, a big tough son of a bitch from Compton or some place, and you need a way to bring him down, know what you do? Whack him in the knee-cap… either kick it, or better yet, whack it with a baseball bat. That'll bring that big son of a bitch down in a hurry, and he won't get up!" People like Jack are hard to ignore, because aside from their prejudices and insensitivities, they're entertaining raconteurs—and their lack of self-awareness makes them even more interesting.

Jack provided politically incorrect comic relief, while Jessie was the *enforcer.* She was among that distinct breed of American women with short, frosted hair, a high school diploma and a twenty-years-and-running, two-pack-a-day nicotine addiction. Her gravelly windpipe had been sucking in carcinogens since Gerald Ford was in the White House. Jessie projected a tough attitude, but once you got to know her she was a pleasant person. She and Jack took a liking to the Smith boys.

The place didn't come with a refrigerator, so I had to go out and buy one. After my tribulations in La Mesa, I certainly had the experience to make a wise consumer choice. Collin and I went to Sears and picked out a model from their new appliance showroom. My credit application, however, was rejected. We left empty-handed, forced to settle on a used unit from a second-hand shop. I wrote a letter to TRW requesting a copy of my credit report.

The report contained fraudulent transactions—unpaid purchases that were not mine. I wrote a series of letters to TRW to get the items removed from my record, and after several months, it finally worked. My report was now clean. I didn't know it at the time, but good credit was going to play an integral role in furthering my music career.[83]

One evening, I was returning to the apartment with some groceries and accidentally dropped and broke a large, glass jar of spaghetti sauce all over the garage floor. The stuff was everywhere. I went up to Jessie and Jack's apartment to tell them what happened and see if I might borrow a mop. Jesse came to the door, and when I explained what happened and asked her for something to clean up the mess, she became fraught with emotion. She almost started to cry.

"Don't worry, Jessie, I'll clean it up," I promised.

"It's not that," she said, fighting back the tears.

"It's just that... nobody's ever done this before."

"Nobody ever spilled spaghetti sauce?"

"Nobody's ever come to me and *admitted* it. You could have just left that sauce sitting there for someone else to worry about, and I would have never known it was you who did it. But you said, 'I'm not gonna do that. This is my mess and I'm gonna clean it up.' Thank you so much. The world would be a better place if more people were like you."

You would have thought I'd forked over a kidney to her ailing granddaughter, coughed up a nut for her eunuch stepson, or personally muled several grams of high-grade blow, wedged between my butt cheeks, from the slums of Bogota to her doorstep in Northridge... not spilled a jar of Ragu in the parking garage. What kind of deadbeats did this poor woman have to deal with?

Another time, I was passing Jack's cage and I saw out of the corner of my eye that he was irritated. I stopped to see what was wrong.

"Think it was those junkies on the third floor again."

"What happened?" I asked.

"Someone took a dump in the elevator."

"People really need to look after their pets better," I offered.

"I said some-*one*, not some-*thing*. I ain't talkin' about pets."

"What are you telling me here, Jack?"

"I'm tellin' you it wasn't done by no dog."

---

[83] Or, one could argue, leading me further into the abyss.

"A cat then?"

Jack sighed and shook his head.

"I had Jessie go in there n' corroborize (sic) my suspicions. Came back and she says 'Yeah, Jack, you're right...

enter X Files music...

...judging by the shape... and consistency... it's *human.'*"

"Jesus, people live like animals," I concurred.

I could have sat in the cage every day and listened to Jack's stories, but it was time to get out there and make some money. I had no gigs, no income. Paula was working at an employment agency, and hooked me up with an interview at a continuation school in Santa Monica. The school was called West Side Second Chances. The owner's name was Max Carver. I met Max in his office on the campus, and he explained that he was running both a school and a group home, which was right across the street. He was looking for child care workers for the group home.

Max was an intelligent, literate man, and we got along well at the first meeting. He sent me to meet with Angela Marshall, director of the group home program. She was a confident black woman in her late forties, who took a no-nonsense approach to raising the six young men who lived in the house. Angela said Max had liked me, and though I didn't have any experience, my college degree made me hirable. This was the one and only time in my life that anybody has ever asked to see my degree.

I was offered a position as a child care worker. The job entailed supervising teenage boys who were in the State of California's custody. Duties included cooking, administering medication, supervising chores, chaperoning group outings, and counseling the boys individually. I would be a surrogate parent, in other words. The money was bad and there were zero benefits. Still, I felt compelled to give it a try. Angela warned that it would not be easy. The kids would push my buttons in ways I couldn't imagine. She also said I was going to take flak for being a white boy. The kids were almost all Latino and black. I silently concluded that Angela was being negative, and knew I would have no problem getting along with these guys. I could hang... I could be a homey. I accepted the job.

The group home opportunity was attractive for several reasons. First, lousy pay or not, it was a job that required my college degree. During all the bar mitzvahs, clambakes, street fairs and random shindigs I'd plodded through for years in San Diego, the Bachelor of

Arts degree had collected dust on my bedroom wall. Second, I had found an opportunity to do something for someone other than myself. While you like to think you're providing the universe with a service it needs by making music, the truth is that your motivation in the arts is mostly selfish in nature. You're doing it for *you*. Third, the job seemed low-key. There was no uniform, no corporate protocol, and unlike my previous investigations of the bottom-rung job pool in Los Angeles, you didn't have to answer to cranky gelato scoopers with power complexes. Fourth, it seemed like a job that wasn't going to drain me psychologically or spiritually. I needed to save my creative energy for writing.

On my first day, Angela threw me into the trenches. I'd never been much of a cook, but there I was wearing an apron, preparing a meal for six hungry teenage boys. I related well to them right off the bat. As I'd hoped, my interest in music and sports bridged the racial and generational gaps. After a couple weeks, the guys and I were comfortable with each other and on good terms. I disciplined them as I was instructed to, but left plenty of slack on the rope. These kids weren't going to respond to a heavy hand.

Commuting every day from Northridge to Santa Monica proved a hassle. The only way to get there was the 405, the most congested freeway in the entire country. Although the distance was only ten or fifteen miles, the drive would take a minimum of an hour, but often longer.

I'd see people cursing at each other, occasionally even jumping out of their cars to settle matters with their fists. One time a guy got out of his truck, walked to another vehicle and started beating up the driver, as I and the rest of the people sitting in their cars watched. Then the guy walked back to his truck, hopped in and drove off, like nothing had happened. This was right on the freeway, during rush hour. The gridlock was so extreme that he had time to do all this without obstructing traffic. Congestion is such a problem in L.A. at almost any time of day or night that people have nervous breakdowns right there on the road. People lose their minds before your eyes. Ask anyone who lives in L.A., and they'll tell you that this is how it is.

Despite severe traffic and other concomitant manifestations of urban malaise, L.A. excited me in some ways. There was so much going on all the time. If you were interested in art and culture there were endless outlets. I was proud of myself for getting out of San Diego; while I had no immediate prospects in either writing or music, I had at least put myself in an environment where good things could happen. I'd escaped the small-town mentality of San Diego for a major metropolitan melting pot.[84]

One of the cool things about living in L.A. was the inevitable brush with fame, here and there. I started casually dating a woman named Korena, an aspiring actress who tended bar at a trendy spot right on Sunset Boulevard, not far from one of the major film studios. One night I was hanging at the bar while Korena worked, and the cast of a popular TV show of that time, Broadcast News, came in to relax after filming an episode. I found myself sitting right next to Phil Hartman, the great comedian and Saturday Night Live alumnus. Hartman looked drawn and haggard. He was drinking hard. After ordering yet another drink in a short period of time, he quipped to Korena, "I drink to forget." I didn't think much of it; show biz is a lot less glamourous than people think, regardless of the level of success. Hartman was probably just weary from being in such demand.

Only a few days later, I was jarred by a disturbing headline: *Phil Hartman Found Dead in His Home… victim of an apparent murder/suicide.* The actor's wife, who had a history of mental illness, had completely lost her mind, using a gun to end both her and her husband's lives. It was a sad end for a very talented guy.

I particularly liked the West Side—Santa Monica and everything west of it. This is the nicest part of L.A., excluding the mansions in the hills. This is where stars live. The affluent neighborhoods are here, and this part of town has a hip, sophisticated feel. After a shift at the group home, I would spend the rest of the evening hanging out in bookstores and record shops along 3rd and Promenade, a retail/restaurant thoroughfare that runs adjacent to Santa Monica Beach.

One time I attended a lecture and book signing by one of my favorite authors at the time, crime fiction guru James Ellroy. Listening to Ellroy discuss his writing process, then meeting him and expressing appreciation for his work, was the kind of experience that made L.A. a stimulating place to live. It was also exciting to know I was in the screenwriting capital of the world. If I had talent, it would be discovered here. Or so I thought.

---

[84] After watching various prison documentaries, I must say that I prefer the term melting pot to *tossed salad*.

I had finished a second draft of *Clowns*, and was trying to figure out how I might coerce someone into actually reading it. Writing is not easy, but the process of crafting words and story pales in difficulty next to the daunting task of marketing the completed script. I learned of a service that offered analysis of your screenplay from industry experts, with the possibility of getting a deal if they liked your material. For two hundred bucks you could present your work without having a door slammed in your face.

The story analyst who evaluated *Clowns* had some positive comments. Before I share those, here is an excerpt from the screenplay.[85] It's a scene between the two main characters, Mike Seskis and Gil Washington, incompetent young FBI agents who head to Arizona to disguise themselves as rodeo clowns in order to crack a case:

```
INT. AIRPLANE - NIGHT

Mike and Gil kick back, the plump guy fast asleep.
The CAMERA pans to them from across the plane,
revealing that there is a rich cross-section of
ethnic passengers on this flight.

                    GIL
        Look at this: a damn freakshow.

                    MIKE
        That's pretty judgmental, Gil.
        America's a melting pot.  All colors
        and creeds are entitled to pursue
        happiness, wealth and power.  It's
        what the country's founded on.

                    GIL

        What the country's founded on is
        bullshit. Look at our national
        symbol— the bird they should have
        picked is the wild turkey.
```

---

[85] Chris Taylor deserves some credit for this scene, since it is loosely based on a conversation he recounted to me over the phone.

                    MIKE
The wild turkey.

                    GIL
A hard worker that has something to
contribute to society.

                    MIKE
So you don't like the bald eagle.

                    GIL
The concept of the bald eagle is all
wrong. Look at him. He survives by
stealing from all the other *honest*
birds.

                    MIKE
You're trippin', man.

                    GIL
Say there's a falcon—another honest
bird—out hunting fish. He finally
catches one, and heads back to the
nest to feed the young falcons. The
bald eagle circles around, waits for
just the right moment, then BAM! He
swoops down and takes that fish right
out of the falcon's mouth.

                    MIKE
Sounds like a stupid falcon.

                    GIL
The eagle lives off the hard work of
other birds, which is exactly what
white people do in America. The bald
eagle is *White America*.

                    MIKE
Well if the fucking falcon is that
hungry, why doesn't he fight harder
to keep his fish?

                    GIL
        'Cause the bald eagle is a crafty
        mofo.

                    MIKE
        Tough shit then. The falcon should
        quit his bitching and get on with
        life.

                    GIL
        That's what he's trying to do.

                    MIKE
        No, he's pecking the bald eagle in
        the ass after he got his fish back.

                    GIL
        The falcon wouldn't be pecking the
        bald eagle's ass if he hadn't stole
        the fish in the first place.

                    MIKE
        Look, he gave the fish back, said
        sorry, and promised not to steal it
        anymore! Why is the goddamned falcon
        still pecking Away like there's no
        tomorrow?

                    GIL
        Because the falcon is still pissed
        off.

                    MIKE
        Then he should expect to keep getting
        his ass kicked.

CUT TO:

So there's glimpse of the characters, and here's what the industry
analyst had to say about the entire script:

*This well-written, engaging screenplay has the potential to be a very funny
action comedy, with likable main characters and a setting we haven't really
seen in this type of film. The writer has a keen sense for subtle comedy, though*

he occasionally flounders, usually when indulging in bathroom humor or cheap sight gags. Unfortunately, the script doesn't live up to its overall potential, primarily due to a weakly structured plot and unevenly developed characters, though these problems could likely be solved in a rewrite.

Dialogue is strong and frequently funny, if occasionally overlong and expository. Descriptions are smartly written, crisp, and spare, appropriate to the genre and markedly better than most.

In sum, despite any elements which are either misplaced or missing, there is much here which merits consideration as well. There's a lot of talent on these pages, and further work on plotting and character development are called for in order to really let it shine.

PASS

Not bad for a first effort. I was encouraged by the analyst's feedback, and set out to rewrite the script.

I told Angela I was writing screenplays. She said that one of the group home's private benefactors was a successful screenwriter named Jane Alexander. Angela gave me the woman's address and suggested I contact her and introduce myself. I did a little research and learned Alexander had written the screenplays for *How to Make An American Quilt*, starring Winona Ryder, and *It Could Happen to You*, starring Nicolas Cage and Bridget Fonda. I rented the movies and liked them both. The writing was strong.

I wrote Jane a letter saying hello, complimented her writing and asked if I might meet with her sometime to discuss the craft. She didn't respond. I wrote a second letter, apologizing for the "presumptuous nature of my first letter." This time I got a response. It was terse, stating that she didn't have time to meet me or even talk to me, but whatever I did, "Never, ever, ever, ever give up."

With due respect to the woman's busy schedule, how can you be too swamped to chat with someone on the phone for five minutes? Would a half-hour lunch meeting, planned well ahead of time, with a young person who had taken the time to become familiar with her work, and was aspiring to do the same thing she was doing, really be logistically impossible? Everyone has to eat, don't they? Would it have been a major imposition to pencil me in for a short coffee or lunch, a couple weeks or even a couple months down the road, on a lazy Wednesday afternoon?

She said *I can't help you*, but what she really meant was *I won't help you*. I had been warned; unsolicited queries get you nowhere in Los Angeles. I wasn't asking her to read my screenplay, I wasn't asking her to put in a good word to her literary agent. My intentions were humble. All I wanted was a little support, maybe a couple suggestions about how to go about the whole thing. But, like I said before, I was on the outside. Had I been a friend of a friend, or the offspring of an industry colleague, I'm guessing she would have found a few minutes to meet with me. I vowed that if I was ever in such a position, I'd make time for somebody who appreciated my talent and had gone out of their way to contact me. I'm still sticking to that vow, years later. Send me your CD and I'll listen to it. Send me your book or your screenplay and I'll give it a look. I'll even meet you at Starbucks for a VBF.

Back at the group home, things became more complicated. Angela's original warnings were becoming a reality. I had made a mistake getting buddy-buddy with the kids. It made for a non-confrontational environment in the beginning, but when it came time to buckle down and implement discipline and structure, the guys resented me and felt I was betraying them. I was not presenting consistent character, and as I was learning, working with kids is *all* about consistent character and expectations.

The group home was like a family. You got to know the kids and the staff as if you had grown up with them. There was DeRon, a quiet, skinny black kid who was an excellent athlete. He could really shoot the basketball. I used to take him and some of the others to Lincoln Park on the weekends. We'd play pick-up basketball games, mostly with grown men.

One day, we had an entire team consisting of group home kids and me, and got on a big roll. We won four games in a row, beating teams made up of guys in their twenties and thirties. DeRon and I were on fire, burying long jumpshots all day. Even a husky, Ritalin-popping kid named Brick (great name for a basketball player) came up huge, rebounding hard and getting crucial steals in the clutch.

DeRon had a smart mouth on him. During one game, he gave some lip to a real hard-ass, gangster guy. When the gangster heard the skinny kid insult him, he swung at DeRon with everything he had. "Shut your mouth, young-ass nigga," the guy said. The punch missed DeRon and hit *me* instead. I stared at the guy for a second. He laughed and shrugged his shoulders. *What are you going to do about, bitch?* It goes without saying that I wasn't going to do a damn thing. This was one guy I didn't want a piece of. Not even a sliver. I may not like to take crap, but I also have a self-preservation instinct. As a strict rule, I don't mess with buffed, knife-scarred black dudes from the hood... even if they accidentally punch me in the face during a pick-up game.

Despite getting smacked in public by a remorseless thug, these were positive times. I was making a difference in the lives of disadvantaged kids, and it felt good. The job forced me to take a look at myself. It brought flaws in my personality to the surface, putting them on display for the kids, the staff, and most importantly, me. I would need to evolve into a better person if I wanted to be an effective child care worker; it was a situation where you had to put others' needs before your own. I was so used to living for myself and thinking about my own interests that I didn't know how to be selfless. It had always been about *me*. Now it was about DeRon, Brick and the others.

One kid, Hugo, had a real impact on me. Hugo was a short, Hispanic eighteen year-old, always in trouble. We got along well, in a big brother/little brother way, excluding one time when I sent him to the juvenile detention center in Sylmar. Hugo had cursed me in front of the others, and the only way I could save face was to punish him. Backing down would have looked weak. Another staff member, a Hispanic guy named Thomas, had reluctantly driven Hugo to the detention facility.

Thomas was a smart guy who wanted to do some good with his life, but he was also an administrative ass-kisser. I didn't like the way he clung to his Latino roots as a defining badge of honor. I've always been uncomfortable when people define themselves by race. It just doesn't seem right to me. In fact, it seems hypocritical for a society to promote and celebrate racial distinctions under the guise of multiculturalism, then turn around and decry the rampant *racism* that supposedly pervades every aspect of that very society. The way I see it, there's an awfully thin line between racial pride and racial prejudice. Why is it hip if your mom was a Black Panther, but horrible if your pops was a white supremacist? It's all the same ugly, destructive shit, isn't it?

Miguel was the youngest kid at the group home. This kid, whose parents were from South America, had some tough problems. He was on heavy medication that failed to curb violent mood swings and frequent outbursts. He was picked on constantly by the others, who called him *man hole* instead of Miguel, and would constantly antagonize him to get a reaction. Miguel also had a bed-wetting issue, which didn't help his cause. There was a popular R&B song on the radio, and the chorus went: *Somebody's sleeping in my behhhhhhhd.* When it got to that part of the song, however, the boys would all point at Miguel and start wailing, *Somebody's PISSING in my behhhhhhhd!*

Angela fancied herself a leader and nurturer, but she was in fact neither. She played the mother hen role, but the boys feared her wrath more than they sought her comfort. Over the course of one week, she forced me to show the entire *Roots* series on videotape. She thought it was the greatest TV show of all time. The thing was, the boys didn't give a rat's ass about *Roots*. They nodded off, threw pencils, and made farting noises the whole time it was on. I wasn't that excited about it myself. This was 1998, and *Roots* felt like old news. The scene that got the greatest rise out of the kids was the one where O.J. Simpson comes hauling ass across the tundra in a loincloth. O.J.'s agent must have insisted on a clause in his contract stating: *There must be a moment in the film where O.J. runs full-speed. His audience demands it.* The kids all perked up.

"Hey, holmes, there's O.J.!"

"That nigga is fast!"

"O.J. straight punked the court n' shit, yo! Got away with killin' that white bitch and her friend."

The poignant themes of *Roots* were really *resonating* at West Side Second Chances.

Imagine O.J. turning up in a Jean Claude Van Damme movie... I've even got a basic plot worked out. Jean Claude, alongside his computer-generated identical twin brother, plus Dennis Rodman, thrown in for a few laughs, fight off a small army of Armenian martial arts experts/anthrax smugglers. Out of nowhere, and just in the nick of time, PLOW! O.J. comes crashing through the wall in a missile-equipped white Bronco, proclaiming over a thumpin' gangsta rap soundtrack, "The glove may not fit, but I'm 'bout to blow up some shit!"

Angela had been right about some things. I was learning quite a lot from the group home experience. Discovering what it means to be disadvantaged. These kids were products of broken homes, poverty, drug abuse, and a perpetual lack of adult supervision and healthy role models. Without fail, they were starving for a strong father figure, and hadn't been exposed to much of anything beyond their immediate urban surroundings. They were streetwise, yes, but most lacked the reading skills to deliver a convincing rendition of *Green Eggs and Ham*. Their cultural surroundings had encouraged intellectual ignorance, instead glorifying the life of the pimp, the hustler, the criminal. Despite all this, you realized they were basically good kids with good hearts. I wrote a song about it a few years later, called *The World Makes Us That Way*:

Twenty-five, I decided it was time for some kinda change of pace
Packed my life in a U-Haul, landed in a harder, faster place
Realized that I'd have to start over, not a damn soul knew my name
Took a job in a group home just to stay ahead in the month-to-month game

Six boys thrown together 'cause they'd flunked out of polite society
Each with his sad story, no stranger to the planet's harsh realities
Some angry, some bitter 'cause they knew they'd been given a raw deal
They were now in the state's custody 'cause all they knew was how to cheat and steal

We don't start out thinkin' it's a rat race
Everybody livin' for themselves
We're not born believin' that it's all about money
Everyone's got somethin' to sell
We don't leave the womb
Just assuming most people gonna somehow let us down
We don't begin our lives with hate
The world makes us that way

It's hard to re-program a kid when you get him at sixteen or seventeen. By that age, he's hard-wired to be the person he's going to be for the next sixty years. Once a kid is sixteen, his environment has left a permanent impression on his personality, and his life experiences have begun to define who he is as a human being. Also, if he comes from unfortunate circumstances, by sixteen he's probably angry, confused and disillusioned. You're going to fight an uphill battle with this kid.

While I believe most people want to do the right thing in life, there is also the occasional rotten apple with which you must contend. At West Side Second Chances I remember two examples. First, there was Felix. This kid, at seventeen, had already determined that the world is a terrible place, where people suffer and dreams don't come true. He was conflicted, aloof, and sometimes hostile. He treated the others meanly and callously. Felix was also very close-minded. Everything sucked. Nothing was cool. He took me on a few times, after successfully ruffling the feathers of other staff members like Efrin Kubo, a bumbling Nigerian who stuttered in broken English. Efrin had no control over the kids, but what he *did* have was some breath that could knock you all the way to Bakersfield.

Felix came up to me one day and said, "How old are you? Twenty-seven, doing this shitty job? You don't have anything going in life." This would have crushed me had I been thin-skinned, because let's face it—his words contained an element of truth. What *was* I doing here at twenty-seven, working for the chump change these people were paying me? I wasn't disadvantaged, my mother hadn't died of AIDS... I had a *lucky* upbringing, and yet here I was. What did I have to say for myself? How was I supposed to be an example of what a person can accomplish in life, when I was working in a group home for eight bucks an hour?

I've always liked being intellectually challenged, and Felix's attack prompted me to put on the mental gloves. I had a few things I'd been waiting to tell him about *his* character, and here was the perfect opportunity.

"You don't have shit, so why should I listen to you?" Felix continued, on a roll. He thought he *knew* me, thought he had me *nailed.* I was some white pussy who'd lived a life of privilege. He probably thought I was about to cry. "People trying to tell us around here that we shouldn't copy Biggie and Puffy and Tupac, like they bad influences or somethin'... and you n' the other staff people is supposed to be our models. *Those* guys are rollin', makin' millions, gettin' bitches, livin' large, and y'all don't have shit. So why the fuck should I care what *you* think?" Felix was proud of himself. I contemplated my response and fired back.

"You're right, Felix. I don't make much money here, and I *never* will, if I choose to stay in this line of work. But you want to know what's really sad?" I had his attention now, and continued. "The fact that the State of California pisses away taxpayers' money, giving a loser like me eight bucks an hour to wipe the ass of a worthless kid like you, someone that has no future whatsoever. You're a complete waste. A statistic. They should haul you back to the barrio and bring someone in here that at least has a chance of doing something with his life.

'Cause you ain't it. You're not worth eight bucks an hour of supervision. They should dump you back on the corner where they found you and forget you even exist. We need some population control, motherfucker, and *you're* what needs to be controlled."

I wasn't sure where it all came from, and had another staff member overheard this conversation I might have been fired, but it felt good saying it. I waited for Felix to lash back. He paused to think, then smiled and extended his hand for a high five. "Yeah, man, you're right. We're both losers. We're both fucked," he chuckled. From that moment on, Felix and I had no problem getting along. We understood each other. By standing up for myself I had earned his respect, and he was henceforth more cooperative around the group home.

My second group home nemesis, and a craftier one, was a small white kid named Albert. In contrast to the others, Albert was educated, artistic, and respectful of the care workers. At staff meetings, we would wonder why he was even in state custody. The kid was a model group home resident.

When Albert finally fell from grace, however, he fell hard. I received reports from the school that he was getting into fights and causing trouble with teachers. I initially blamed this on the intolerance of his classmates, since I had always observed Albert as well-behaved. I had become a big brother to him, encouraging him to develop his talents. When Albert demonstrated interest in music, I brought in my keyboard to give him a lesson. When he showed an interest in writing, I took him to the office of the screenwriting analysis service I was retaining, hoping he'd realize that the world offered more productive pursuits than stealing people's credit cards.[86]

Sadly, Albert went the wrong way. My creative crash course didn't take root. The other kids had been spreading rumors that Albert was homosexual, further intimating that he had expressed sexual interest in *me*. I ignored this talk, but then Albert began to divulge the details of his weekend home visits. He bragged that he liked to perform fellatio on grown men, and said he was making some money turning tricks during his time at home. Albert even tried to demonstrate his fellatio technique in front of the other boys one evening, while I was driving

---

[86] As I read this passage now, I have to admit I'm not sure what I think is a more dignified use of one's time: attempting to sell a screenplay in Hollywood, or stealing people's credit cards.

them all home from an outing. When Hugo saw this he started to unzip his pants and shouted, "Fuck the demonstration, holmes! Let's go for real! You look like you know what you're doing. *Andale!*"

When we got back to the house, I told Albert it was not cool to teach the other residents how to give a blow job, nor was it acceptable to actually offer them such services. He agreed to back off, then asked me if I knew what a *feefee* was. I did not. As it turned out, all six of the boys were in the process of making their own feefee, to see who could come up with the best one. They were having a *feefee contest*, and I, Albert explained, was expected to be the judge. So I guess I better tell you what a feefee is. If you're easily offended, you might want to stop reading…

A *feefee,* according to the boys at West Side Second Chances Group Home, was a homemade device made in juvenile detention centers, using a sock, a rubber glove, and a couple other items I can't remember now. It was supposed to mimic the contours of a (female sex organ), so that the detainee might provide relief for himself without having to use his own hand, or worse, the orifice of another detainee. Albert boasted, "I can put together a *feefee* that'll make you cry." You might be thinking: *How could you allow such activities to go on?* *These boys were in your care.* But you have to understand something—this is what they knew. This is how they lived. If I was to thwart every questionable activity they engaged in I would have been doing so nonstop. Instead, I picked my battles. Blow jobs got shut down, feefees got a pass. I allowed the feefee contest to run its course. The winner was Hugo.

My good rapport with Albert was irrevocably undermined one night after I reprimanded him over a pointless altercation with Miguel. Albert brazenly defied me, and when I tried to calm him down he exploded, saying, "Fuck you, cracker! You stupid cracker white-boy motherfucker! I had never received this kind of racial barrage from the black or Hispanic guys. Here was this little homosexual white kid, barely five feet tall, calling me a *fucking cracker.* I revoked Albert's extra-curricular privileges and alerted the staff that he was in a bad way.

I should have known the kid was eventually going to blow.[87] I'd read his file. He had been implicated in credit card fraud, which is not

---

[87] So to speak!

like breaking a car window and snatching a Blahpunkt. This type of white-collar crime requires some conniving and some brains.

In an effort to exact revenge on me, cracker disciplinarian and discerning judge of feefee quality, Albert called upon his mother. I had met the woman at therapy meetings, and had quickly gathered that her social graces made Roseanne Barr look like Princess Diana. Albert lied and told his mother I had assaulted him in the group home—that I'd put my hands on him in an inappropriate manner. She reported this to the State Board. Of course, I had never so much as laid a finger on the kid.

The staff recognized this as an obvious prevarication. I never received so much as a phone call from the State Board. I had embraced this child worker experience with idealistic fire, determined to be a positive role model for underprivileged young men. To some extent, I did that; but one year later, that idealism had been wrenched out of me. The pay was inexcusably bad. The kids, though mostly good-hearted, were incorrigible and damaged. The people running the place weren't doing it for the right reasons. It struck me as a smarmy business venture in flimsy humanitarian clothes.

I realized this one morning, when I was read the riot act by Max Carver's wife. She was furious that I'd bought the boys a cheap breakfast at McDonald's, before school. We were supposed to feed them with store-bought groceries, but the staff from the previous evening had failed to stock the kitchen with the basics needed to prepare a meal. When Carver's wife found out I spent money on food from a restaurant, she let me have it. I had defied group home policy, and I had squandered her money.

What a pitiful situation. These kids had been dumped on their entire lives and now they were stuck in this miserable place, at the mercy of the owners' Machiavellian agenda. The owners were milking the system, using the kids as pawns to facilitate their personal financial goals. The State of California was the breast and the kids were the nipple. I remained on the staff, but started looking for another job.

Collin and I had been living in Northridge for about a year, and we were sick of it. We were determined to migrate to the other side of the hills. We found a place in Santa Monica and said goodbye to Jessie and Jack. Jack left me with one last monologue about all the things that were screwed up in the world, and I left him with a final rent check, some beat-up furniture and a cockroach infestation.

Our new place was just inside the Santa Monica city limits, on Centinela Avenue near Colorado Street. It was a mere block from the house Paula was sharing with her Italian boyfriend, Massimo Arrigoni. Collin was training for the AVP Pro Beach Volleyball Tour, and I was working harder than ever on my screenplays. I had finished a few more, including *Deviance*, a black comedy about a sex addict in San Francisco, and *The Man Who Couldn't Miss*, a fantasy adventure about a Milwaukee used refrigerator salesman[88] who acquires the mysterious ability to shoot a basketball and never miss.

Despite my reluctance to pursue them, new musical opportunities presented themselves. I began working with a blues singer named David Basse. David was a nice guy,[89] and we did gigs together around Southern California, including an upscale party at Atlas Bar & Grill. The party, thrown somehow in conjunction with the National Football League, was for the participants in Robin Williams and Billy Crystal's annual Comic Relief fundraiser at the neighboring Wiltern Theater.

During the band's first break, the comedian Jon Lovitz was standing next to me at the bar. I had considered Lovitz as someone who could possibly play the lead character in my screenplay *Deviance*, so I initiated a conversation. He gave me the old Hollywood *half-glance*, processed a couple of my questions and responded curtly. Lovitz was busy pounding drinks with Bill Maher and a couple women that were both a head taller than either of them.

Richard Sellers, still going by *Chef R&B*, was also on the gig, and together we approached Warren Moon, the journeyman NFL quarterback. Moon was cool, talking to us for a few minutes and answering a couple questions. Later in the night, Darius Rucker, the lead singer of Hootie and the Blowfish, came onstage and did a couple Sinatra tunes. Rucker had told me earlier at the bar that he would give me his card before he left, so I could send him my original music to check out. I was certain he'd blow it off—but sure enough, he made a point of finding me later, gave me the card, and told me to send whatever I had.

I also worked at that time with an older lady named Marti Lynch. Marti lived in Carlsbad, which is between San Diego and Los Angeles.

---

[88] You gotta write what you know.

[89] Unlike some of the other *nice guys* we've discussed, this guy had legit talent—he could sing and play drums.

Marti was a retired teacher and an aspiring jazz vocalist. Her son was the respected New York trumpet player, Brian Lynch.

Marti planned to record a jazz album, and hired me to arrange the music and play piano. The band included a line-up of heavyweight jazz musicians, including the terrific drummer Willie Jones III. Brian Lynch, whose resumé included a stint in Art Blakey's Jazz Messengers, was on board also. He flew out to San Diego to rehearse and help make the record. At the first meeting, I could sense Brian thought I might be a poseur. He was probably thinking: *Who's this local hack, and why's he taking my mom's money?* Had I been a charlatan, Brian would have figured it out inside five minutes' rehearsal time. Fortunately, I was prepared. I had written good charts, put a lot of thought into the arrangements, and came in ready to play; and while I wasn't Mulgrew Miller from a pianistic perspective, I also wasn't John Tesh. We recorded the album, and it was a treat to spend two full days in the studio with this excellent band. I returned to L.A. with a nice credit to my name, as well as a few dollars in my pocket.

While working with Marti, there was an unfortunate miscommunication that occurred with another musical associate, a tenor saxophonist from Orange County named Pete Floyd. Pete lived next door to my Aunt Mary Lou in La Habra, and I had gotten to know him over the years when we visited Mary Lou and my grandfather. During my junior high and early high school days, I had been friends with Pete's daughter, Dee, a very pretty girl about my age. As I got older and my musicianship grew, Pete would occasionally hire me to play with him at Steamer's, a jazz club in Fullerton.

One time I had to back out of one of Pete's gigs. As we say in musician's parlance, *I was double-booked.* I had subbed out on Marti Lynch a couple times in the past, and didn't want to let her down again. She was providing me with regular employment. Pete only called from time to time, so I decided I would have to bow out of the Steamer's show with him. I didn't trot out some mendacious excuse for Pete, but instead told him the truth: I had made a mistake and double-booked myself. I hoped he would understand, but instead Pete screamed into the phone, "No, man! No way!"

"I'm sorry, Pete. It's not okay, I know that."

"No, it's not okay! I can't hire you anymore."

"I realize that. I'm very sorry." I felt bad about it, but mistakes happen, and we do what we have to do. My error was not maliciously intended. I felt bad to lose a friend like Pete, because I knew it was my fault for letting him down. But he had a choice. He made the decision to sever our relationship over the incident. I believe you should try to preserve as many relationships as possible as you make your way through life, but I also think you've got to be fatalistic at times. Some relationships are there for the long run, some fall by the wayside; and sometimes it's out of your control.

I've often thought that if I could clone myself, I'd actually make a decent living as a musician. What makes freelance gigging so hard is that your income is derived solely through labor. If you are not there, in the flesh, you can't make the bread. People in career paths that offer the possibility of residual income have a real advantage.

Richard Sellers brought me along to a weekly jam session at Chadney's, a spot in the Valley. There, I met George Gaffney, a good piano player and leader of the house band. After I sat in on a couple tunes, George came over and complimented my playing. We became friends, and he started recommending me for jobs. Through George I met Tony Dumas, the well-traveled and oft-recorded jazz bassist. I got the chance to play with Tony on a couple gigs. George introduced me to other top notch players, also.

As I was starting to get involved in the Los Angeles jazz scene, I got an unexpected offer from Tiny to audition for a Southern California funk cover band called Guppy. In real life, the band was named after a *different* fish, but I don't have particularly nice things to say about this organization, so we'll go with Guppy.

At this point in my life, I was not excited about cover bands. I was all about creativity. No, at that time, I would have rather administered bikini waxes to transvestites than play in a cover band. Guppy was a different animal, however. They had a solid following, played better rooms than your average cover band, and according to Tiny, were looking to become an original project. Bingo. That was the magic word: *original.* Also, the money wasn't bad, and you got paid in cash after every gig. You didn't have to wait two months for a check from some agency that left your money sitting in a bank account, accruing interest while your gas and water were getting shut off.

I did a couple shows with Guppy as a trial, and was given the permanent job. The lead singer was a gangly, forty year-old freak named Simon Millburg. Simon was a compelling frontman in a bizarre, disquieting way. He had a healthy head of black, shoulder-length hair, googly Marty Feldman eyes, and not an ounce of fat on him. He wanted every show to be a circus, so he would come out in strange, gender-bending costumes.

One night in Santa Monica, Collin came to watch Guppy perform. Simon walked onstage in a checkered blue skirt and bobby socks. His wavy hair was pulled up in pigtails. The second keyboard player, Sydney, a chronic stutterer, was decked out in a vintage white wedding dress. After the set, Collin came over and said, "Anth, the singer came out looking like a Catholic schoolgirl with a dick. I didn't know what to do." I laughed as he continued, "Plus you got that fruitcake on the other side of the stage, looking like he just emerged from some kind of sixties bridal boutique time warp." A Guppy show was a curious spectacle.

The most intriguing individual in the Guppy organization wasn't an actual member of the band—he was the manager. Otis Olsen was re-acclimating himself to the free world after a prison stint. Somehow he'd emerged from his incarceration with a burning desire to break into the music business. Now, Otis was Simon Millburg's *yes man.* Otis was edgy and volatile, but also passionate about music and generous with his resources. He wanted to help the band move on to bigger and better things than the Southern California club circuit. I was down with that.

It turned out Otis lived only a mile or so from my place in Santa Monica, so we started hanging out socially. He was a few rungs up the lifestyle ladder, and I figured he had stashed away a bunch of money before he went into the slammer—it was common knowledge that his prison time was a result of drug dealing. Now, Otis had the freedom to enjoy the cash and share it with his friends. It didn't dawn on me that he might be dealing again, but I was seduced by Otis's fast lifestyle, and the recipient of some of the mentioned generosity, so I can't say it would have mattered much if I *had* known. As long as Otis wasn't asking me to make drop-offs or pick-ups, and I didn't feel like I was going to wind up like Tony Montana's friend in the shower in Scarface, I was happy to be the recipient of Otis's largesse. I never had much extra money of my own, and here was a guy who threw it around like he was playing Monopoly.

Otis lived in a nice condominium in Brentwood, zoomed around in a slick yellow Porsche, ate in nice restaurants and had tall, sexy women hanging around him. The guy kind of had it going on. He would pick me up and take me to a strip club in West L.A., where he was both a V.I.P. regular as well as a personal friend of many of the ladies.

As a general rule, strip clubs are for suckers. Guys drop large amounts of cash in these places and don't get anything out of it but a bad case of blue balls. The women that work these joints are real pros. They create the illusion, through seductive dances and suggestive talk, that if you play your cards right, you might actually score; but if you were to hear what they say behind closed doors, if you caught them backstage or behind the scenes, you'd never look at strip clubs in the same way again. These girls make major bucks—six figure incomes, and they know exactly how to play to the weakness of the horny, heterosexual male: by teasing him and getting his sexual hopes up.

Exotic dancing[90] is a refined racket. I've heard off-duty stripper acquaintances say the majority of guys who frequent strip clubs are clueless idiots. Girls learn how to manipulate them and empty their pockets, encouraging the erroneous conviction that *if I keep coming back here, maybe she'll eventually hook up with me.* She's never going to hook up with you, dumb-ass.[91] You might wind up paying for it, but you're not getting it for free. And do you think she's looking for the guy that's going to share her life in this place? *Hey Dad, meet Dennis. He comes in to Squatters to get a couple lapdances, throws his hard-earned money down the drain, then goes home to relieve himself. I think he's the one.*

Stripping is a way for young women to make great money and establish independence, and I guess in the interest of fairness it should be noted that many of the girls do take pride in their dancing. I'm not trying to dismiss the entire institution, but I say this to the random male patron out there: If you think you're going to waltz into a strip club, pay your measly twenty bucks for a lapdance and walk out with a beautiful girl under your arm a few hours later, it's time to take your reality pills.

There are exceptions to this, of course. When you're a slickly dressed, ostensibly rich guy zipping around in a chic sports car, throwing cash around like Planter's dry roasted peanuts, the rules change a bit. When I walked into that strip club in Santa Monica with Otis, we weren't stooges ripe for the picking, or just another pair of

---

[90] A dubious label, really; some of these women will have sex with you if the price is right... and is it really that much of a jump to go from putting it right in someone's face to actually letting them touch it?

[91] And even if she did, you think she's going to look in the morning like she does when she's up there straddling that pole, wearing five layers of makeup?

blue collar bubbas set to get swindled by a crew of wily pros. No, these ladies knew Otis personally, and since I was tagging along, I was immediately vetted and approved. After kicking and scratching in L.A. for over a year, I finally had some juice.

Within moments three women sat down to talk to us, and didn't pressure us to buy lapdances. Fifteen minutes later, I had hooked up a date with one of them.[92] The whole time we were there, I never even pulled out my wallet. Otis paid for everything, which made it difficult to judge his checkered past.

One time my car broke down at home, and I was in a hurry to get to San Diego. Shouna, the ex-girlfriend I still saw from time to time, was giving an opera recital. I called Otis to ask if he could help, and he was there five minutes later, jumping my battery and making sure I was covered. The guy was becoming a good friend.

Otis had attracted me with his car, cash, nice apartment, stripper friends and basic generosity, but I had begun to realize something about him: he was a master of appearances. He'd cultivated an attractive image, but most of its layers were fabricated. The more I got to know Otis, the more his personal life seemed like a mess. For a band manager, he didn't have much understanding of the music business. This fact made him defensive and irrational. Also, it was obvious Otis was dealing drugs again, and had no desire to go straight. With his two strikes in the California legal system, he was a ticking time bomb, and didn't seem to care. It turned out that he didn't have the money to maintain the lavish existence he flaunted, and I was detecting signs of a volatile temper. Years later, when I saw the film *Blow*, I thought of Otis.

Guppy was rounded out by Cecil McBee, Jr., a bassist I knew from San Diego, a black, female singer named Wanda, and a drummer named Demetrio. Shortly after I joined the band, we flew to Orlando, Florida for a show at the House of Blues. The performance was not particularly inspired, and what I remember most about the trip to Orlando is sitting in a hotel room for two days straight, watching pay-per-view movies with Tiny.

Word had spread through the band that Cecil was going to be fired. That is, word spread to everyone but Cecil. I found it disconcerting

---

[92] Even after I declined an offer to "purchase" the panties she was wearing at the time.

that Simon and Otis weren't going to give Cecil any notice. They were just going to pull the rug on him.

The flight from Orlando back to L.A. was one of the scariest experiences of my life. The turbulence was so extreme that several passengers began reciting tearful, eleventh-hour invocations. You could see fear in everyone's eyes. I closed mine, clenched my fists and waited for the ordeal to pass. It didn't. I reflected back on the highs and lows of my life as the plane jarred back and forth—a five hundred MPH punching bag taking a major atmospheric drubbing. I wasn't ready to buy the farm. I'd just spent two days wasting away in a Best Western in Orlando with Tiny and a ragtag assortment of funk musicians... hardly a defining moment. Somehow the plane pulled through, and the pilot acted as if it was no big deal.

Cecil got the boot back in L.A., and was replaced by Rodney Bunker, a massive, African-American bass player from the Valley. Rodney had done big tours, and had many suggestions for tightening up the band. Rodney also knew how to play the L.A. schmooze game to great effect, quickly usurping my status as Otis's new best friend.

One of Rodney's first Guppy gigs was an opening set for Earth, Wind & Fire. Along with the legendary group, we were part of the pre-Super Bowl festivities being held in a huge tent outside of Qualcomm Stadium. Shouna was back in my life, and she came with me to the show. She was looking quite attractive that night, and Rodney started drooling when he saw her. "Yo Ant[93]... your girl is *off the hook*," he said. I hadn't heard that expression before, so I looked at him with a blank face. Nowadays, a Mormon librarian in Provo knows what *off the hook* means.

Rodney and I had differences. I felt he was trying to take control of the group, even though Simon was the leader. Rodney wanted things the way he wanted them. Simon, of course, was taking most of the money, and probably didn't care if Rodney threw his abundant weight around. It just meant less work for Simon. Rodney wanted to turn Guppy into an R&B act, while Tiny and I were aiming for more of a *Red Hot Chili Peppers meets David Bowie meets P-Funk* mix. I wrote a few

---

[93] It seems that among the white friends I've had over the years, the preferred shortening of my given sobriquet to a less syllabically challenging name-byte has been "Anth." Among my black friends and acquaintances, it has been even further abbreviated to "Ant."

tunes for the band, one of which had genuine hit potential. It was called *Freaky Revelation,* and was built around a simple but brilliant guitar riff by Tiny.[94] I had a complete set of lyrics for the song, but Simon wrote his own quirky words to go with my chorus, groove and horn arrangement, and we realized we had a potential breakthrough song on our hands.

There were other strong songs as well. One was co-penned by Gavin Christopher, a songwriting journeyman who'd enjoyed a radio hit in the eighties with *One Step Closer to You.* For a while, Cristopher hung around the band; I think he was waiting to see if it was going to take off or not, and if it did, he wanted to be involved somehow. Cristopher lived in an apartment in Venice Beach, and his neighbor was the punk rock legend Johnny Rotten. One day, as he told it, he walked over and knocked on Rotten's door to say hello. The Sex Pistols frontman wasn't looking to make new connections, apparently. Before Christopher could finish introducing himself, Rotten sent him steppin'. This is reminiscent of one of the best Miles Davis stories of all time (and there are many good ones):

Miles was in his later years, painting in solitude in his Malibu beach house. There was a knock. Miles stopped painting and answered the door. There stood Mick Jagger. "Hey, Miles. I've always been a big fan, and I just wanted to meet you and pay my respects." Miles glared at the Rolling Stones legend and said, "I don't remember inviting you over here, motherfucker," then slammed the door in Jagger's face. Classic!

For reasons not explained by management, Demetrio joined the ranks of *band members fired with no notice.* Demetrio had two kids and needed the gig. He at least deserved notice so he could make other plans. Otis was afraid that a fired musician would get payback by not showing up for a gig, so he just dropped you on the fly to insure that wouldn't happen. Tiny and I started calling him *No Notice Otis.*

Otis called me right after he dropped Demetrio. When I picked up the phone, he blurted, "Guess what? I just fucking fired Demetrio." He was gloating, and wanted me go along with it. If I knew then what I know now I would have just said, "Oh, really?" and changed the

---

[94] Tiny's main strength as a guitar player is his ability to come up with great parts in the studio—a prized skill.

subject. Back then, I was of a mind to gallantly defend the concept of right and wrong. It bothered me that first Cecil and now Demetrio had been canned without warning, so I put it back in Otis's face. "Why aren't you giving him any notice? Do you think that's fair, after the guy's made a commitment to this band?" Otis hadn't called to have his authority questioned. He started screaming at me.

"I don't have to give anyone notice! I'm the fucking manager! It's none of your fucking business!" He slammed the phone down. I knew I had crossed a line, and if I wanted to stay on his good side and keep the gig I would have to call back and apologize, saying I realized I had been out of line and Demetrio had it coming. I wasn't going to do that. Both Cecil and Demetrio were nice guys and good players, and they didn't deserve such bullshit treatment. I wasn't going to kowtow to some loose cannon just to keep my little keyboard post.

Otis had started bringing around a black guy named Bluebird, who'd migrated west from New York. While just your average looking Joe, Bluebird was supposedly a New York drug kingpin worth a hundred million big ones. Otis hosted a couple parties at his place, and I kicked it with Bluebird there on more than one occasion. I never brought up anything to do with drugs, but the guy liked to talk about the music business and the creative process. We got along well. While Bluebird talked, I found myself coveting the brand-spanking-new, beige Timberland boots he was sporting.

It turned out that Otis and Simon were grooming Bluebird to be a major investor in Guppy. With even a tiny fraction of his fortune, the band would be able to make a record, assemble a promotional campaign, put every member on a comfortable retainer, and buy a tour bus. Had Bluebird offered the cash, let me say that I wouldn't have been the one to raise an ethical objection.

I always wondered why Bluebird would routinely peel back the curtain, while in the middle of a conversation, and peek out the front window of Otis's condominium in Brentwood. One day I learned the truth. Bluebird had come to L.A. to escape the heat of the D.E.A., which was pursuing him on the East Coast. They'd tracked him down out here, and were hot on his trail. I also learned that he'd desperately sought the protection of the local chapter of the Nation of Islam, but they had turned him away.

Without any kind of a struggle, Bluebird was apprehended in front of Otis's place. The feds just waltzed up, put the cuffs on him and dragged him off to jail. The next time I was at Otis's pad, I noticed something enticing near the doorway… there sat Bluebird's pristine Timberland boots. Otis saw that I was looking at them. "Go ahead," he said. "He ain't gonna be needing them anymore." I picked up one of the boots and took a closer look. Size 13. Perfect. Only worn a couple times. I rocked those bad boys for the next six months.

The last significant Guppy show I played was at Rimac Arena, on the campus of the UCSD. It was promoted as an evening of alternative rock, and we were sharing the bill with a couple popular ska and neo-swing bands. Guppy was rehearsed and tight, but one thing was for sure: we were not alternative rock.

In 1998, college kids were not checking for an eighties funk/disco revival act. The reaction when Wanda took the stage and started singing *Ain't Noboby*, from the *Breakin'* soundtrack, was not merely one of indifference. The crowd was downright hostile. A handful of large, inebriated male students decided to make Rodney Bunker their whipping boy for the evening. Somewhere in the middle of *Brick House* they started yelling, "Hey you, you on the bass, you suck! And your band fucking sucks! But you suck the most!" The drunken louts were offended that a casino-caliber cover band had infiltrated their collegiate turf with some weak, blast-from-the-past Top 40 shit. Rodney was a big guy, and he stared them down in disbelief. Surely, they couldn't be talking to *him*...

"Yeah, *you*, motherfucker… *You!* Youuuuuuuuuuu suck!" Rodney had a look on his face like he was ready to kill someone. These bloated university bubbas were clearly ready to throw down. They didn't just want us to stop playing—no, they wanted our cheesy asses out of their building immediately. I had little ego invested in Guppy. I was a sideman, finding the whole incident somewhat entertaining. It was also instructive. If an audience wants alt rock, you don't give them Morris Day and the Time. If they want Fuel, you don't force feed Frankie Goes to Hollywood. You don't push Sister Sledge onto the stage at Lollapalooza, in front of ten thousand kids that just moshed to Hoobastank, unless you're determined to start a riot. I was quietly amused that Guppy got booed off the stage, and that Rodney had been vociferously dissed by frat meatheads. I *agreed* with them. What we were playing was, for the most part, jive, and some of the people involved, I had come to believe, were jive. I wondered if Tiny and I were turning into jive-asses just by playing in this group.

One very non-jive thing happening around this time was my younger sister, Paula, graduating from UCLA with a Masters in Urban

Planning and Development. This was a big deal; Paula would be the first person in our family to obtain a graduate degree, and we were all very proud of her. We all gathered at the campus of UCLA to witness her receiving her diploma. It was Len, Ann, Terry and Anne, Collin and me.

The keynote address was given by Antonio Villaraigosa, the Democratic Speaker of Assembly, who would go on to become mayor of Los Angeles in 2005. Villaraigosa was clearly a charismatic orator and an inspiration to the Hispanic community—but my brother Collin, once again demonstrating his legendary, keen eye for bullshit, took exception to a passage from the politician's speech. Villaraigosa said to the crowd, "Graduates, I challenge you. I challenge you to go out into the world and make a difference..." etc, etc, etc. Collin turned to Len and me and quietly huffed, "Give me a break, man. I challenge you? Couldn't this guy come up with some more original shit than that?" Len and I laughed.

Then, when Paula walked to the stage and was handed her diploma, it was quite an emotional moment. All four of our parents had tears in their eyes, and Collin and I smiled from ear to ear. Paula had always been a successful person—good student, good athlete, social butterfly, president of her high school student body—and she was surely going to do great things in her professional career.

Collin also had a bright future, as he would soon parlay his collegiate volleyball success into a fruitful Pro Beach Volleyball (AVP) campaign. He would establish himself as one of the premiere athletes in the sport, training regularly with all-time great Karch Kiraly, and teaming up with such heavy hitters as former Olympian Brian Ivy.

One time, Collin was playing the big annual Manhattan Beach tournament, with the six-foot-eight Ivy as his partner. Len and Ann made the trip, and I was also there on the beach to check out the action. Unlike other professional sporting events, where there is considerable distance between the athletes and the fans, Pro Beach Volleyball allowed spectators to be right on top of the action, mere feet away from the players and the court. Thus, I was sitting courtside to watch Collin and his partner square off against the AVP veteran Tim Hovland and his partner, a guy named Bill Boulliane, who people called "Beef." Hovland, who had previously enjoyed a very successful run with Mike Dodd, was a big name in the AVP world.

Collin's team fell behind quickly, and it looked like Hovland and company were going to sail to an easy victory and advance in the tournament. When things got desperate, the score 13-5, Collin a mere two points from elimination, a switch flipped inside me and I knew what I had to do. I started heckling Tim Hovland, and cheering loudly for Collin and Brian.

Good things began to happen. Collin's team rattled off several points in a row. I announced to the beach crowd, "We've got a changing of the guard, folks! A changing of the guard!" I also threw in, "You gotta bend those old knees, Tim!" I was clearly getting under Hovland's skin, a fact which was made plain when he turned to me and flipped me the bird. I didn't care. I just wanted Collin to find a way to come back and win, and if I could help the cause by getting this guy out of his comfort zone, that's what I was going to do.

Professional sports, in a psychological sense, are very nasty. There's an unspoken energy between opponents, a cutthroat, *I will do whatever I can to crush you and leave your carcass to the vultures* kind of mentality. Let me clarify: Tim Hovland might be a great guy off the court, but when he was competing, trying to win a tournament, as he was against my brother that day, he was a merciless son of a bitch. All great athletes are. Even a guy like Roger Federer, the tennis great known for his calm demeanor and wonderful sportsmanship, is, while in the heat of battle, a remorseless assassin who feels no sympathy whatsoever for his opponent. You think he's going to give you a game here or there, just to bolster your self-esteem? Bullshit. He wants to bagel you, 6-0, 6-0, 6-0. Guaranteed.

Collin and Brian came back and won the match, and I half-expected Tim Hovland to walk over and challenge me to a fistfight. He didn't, fortunately. Little did I know that by engaging in psychological warfare with an aging AVP legend, I was preparing for future battles in professional basketball arenas. More on that later.

Back at the group home, word spread that the facility was closing down permanently. I and the rest of the staff had a whole, whopping week to make other employment arrangements. First there was No Notice Otis, now there was *One Week Carver*. Just in time for Christmas! I was so jaded over the shady agenda of the group home that I adopted a *laissez faire* policy in my final week of duty. It was obvious the administration didn't care about the kids or the staff, so why should I care if the kids were following the rules? There was no mention of referrals to other employers or other opportunities. It was just *have a nice life*.

That leads us to a series of pivotal events in the author's saga, a crossroads of sorts. It all started during my final overnight shift at the group home, with Hugo begging me to let him drink a beer. He had been asking for weeks, and I had always quickly said no. On this final night, however, I couldn't think of a single good reason he shouldn't have one. Hell, I wanted one too. Incidentally, Tiny had stopped by to hang with the boys one last time; they knew him from a few previous visits, which, by the way, were in violation of California state policy.

Hugo asked if Tiny might drive him to the market for a forty.[95] I said yes, he might. When they returned, Hugo was carrying the forty, and Tiny was carrying a case of Budweiser. I wasn't in the mood to protest, so I cracked one of those puppies open and started guzzling. Naturally, everyone else wanted one too, and like I said, I was not of a mind to give a damn.

I don't recall who it belonged to, but someone in the house happened to be in possession of a pornographic videotape. While DeRon popped in the porn, Hugo and the other homeys cracked themselves a cold Bud, Tiny pulled out his *peace pipe*, which contained a freshly packed bowl of ganja, and the party was on. You might be wondering what in God's name I was thinking, drinking booze with guys barely old enough to drive, allowing them to watch X-rated movies, and letting my buddy smoke them out — all while they were in my state-authorized custody. I grant you, it's a valid question. I don't know that I have a good answer for you, but I do know that it is a story worth telling.

This full-blown bacchanal of booze, smoke and drinking games continued into the wee hours, as we blasted profane hip-hop, smoked Tiny's chronic and watched Peter North pull off some inspired, acrobatic swashbuckling. I had been listening to the group home guys utter their shared mantra, *I don't give a fuck,* since the day I first came to work there. This was their shield against a world that, in their eyes, didn't give a fuck. If *they* didn't give a fuck either, it neutralized the fact that the world didn't give a fuck; and after hearing them repeat these words over and over again for twelve months, during which time I had come to understand both the hopelessness of their collective

---

[95] A forty-ounce bottle of beer.

predicament and the futility of the system itself, you know what? I didn't give a fuck either.

Tiny was having the time of his life, the kids were finally free to say and do whatever they wanted, and I'd found a way to flip the bird to the powers that be. By the time the first beams of sunlight penetrated the upstairs loft where we'd been carousing for hours, several of the residents were pretty wasted. While the three or four beers I'd consumed didn't have a major effect, the same quantity had all but plastered the seventeen and eighteen-year olds, who were due in the classroom in another couple hours.

I headed back to my apartment to get some sleep, and when I woke several hours later, there was a message on my machine… from Max Carver. It went something like this:

Anthony, this is Max Carver. I'm sitting in my office, staring at a stack of sworn affidavits from the residents of the group home, who say you allowed them to drink alcohol, watch pornographic movies and smoke marijuana. They also say there was an individual named Tiny, apparently your friend, who was there partaking of the same activities. Call me immediately. I need to get your side of it before I talk to the police.

Oh shit, I thought. *Maybe that wasn't such a bright idea. Maybe I could have aired my grievances in another manner. Can I go to jail for this?* I decided to seek advice from someone who would know exactly what to do in this situation; someone who could provide the criminal's perspective. I called Otis. He listened to the whole story and said the following: "All right, Anthony… this is what you're gonna do." I was hanging on every word, ready to follow Otis's lead. Whatever he said to tell Carver, that was exactly what I was going to say.

"First off, don't admit anything."

"Shouldn't I at least say, man, I'm sorry for—"

"Are you hearing me? Don't admit *anything*. Nothing happened. The accusations are bullshit. Who are the cops going to believe, these little probationary delinquents or you, an upstanding child worker with a clean record? Don't admit a goddamn thing. You understand me?"

"Yeah, I got it, Otis."

"Okay, now that we've got that straight, this is what you're gonna do next…"

"I'm listening, man."

"You're going to say, 'Let's be straight with each other, Max. I saw a lot of stuff that you and I both know violated the state's group home licensing code. I'm not gonna waste your time specifying things now. You know what I'm talking about. You could go down for *half* the shit I saw. I can call the state board and have a chat about all this, or I can just forget about it. Of course, that depends if you forget about everything too. So, I'm gonna ask you one question: Is this a conversation we really want to continue having?'"

I was writing it all down. This was great stuff Otis was feeding me. Like something out of an Italian gangster movie. I was going to regurgitate it word for masterful word. My double line beeped. It was Carver. I thanked Otis, said goodbye and clicked over. Carver repeated the stuff about affidavits, and I faithfully read Otis's script, capping it off with, "So, Max, having said all that, is this a conversation we really want to have?" There was a long pause. Uncomfortable silence. Then Carver quietly said, "No. I don't think it is."

"Good. You have my final check?"

"Yes. It's waiting for you in the office."
And that was that. I hung up, and it was the last time I ever talked to the guy. Otis had been right on the money. Never go on the defensive. *Deny, deny, deny.* Don't let anyone get you on the ropes. Somebody accuses you, accuse them back. If they threaten you, threaten them with something worse. It worked perfectly.

Otis bailed me out of a tough jam, but my next conversation with him, a few days later, would not be as productive.

"Hey man, I've got some bad news."

"What's that?" I asked.

"Guppy is letting you go."

"No notice?"

"Nope."

I had been keeping my schedule clear for Guppy, so I didn't have anything else booked. It wasn't like I had income from other projects, either. That sale offer for *Clowns* wasn't coming any time soon. Also, I'd turned down an opportunity to go to Rio de Janeiro to work on a Brazilian album with bassist Glen Fisher. Why? It had conflicted with a Guppy show I assumed I'd be playing.

I called Simon and explained to him that I felt I deserved some compensation. He agreed, and promised to send me two weeks severance pay. In the meantime, I called Jimmy Macon, the guitarist from the Gap Band. Tiny and I had gone over to Jimmy's house a couple times to smoke cigarettes, drink Coronas and talk shop about the music business. I told him Guppy fired me and I needed work. He hooked me up on a weekend gig in Mammoth. I hoped there would be a check from Simon waiting for me in the mailbox upon my return, but as you can imagine, the box was empty.

My mother Anne, concerned about my situation, called Simon herself to ask him to send the two weeks severance pay. After talking to him, she called me and said he'd apologized, and hadn't realized I needed the dough. He'd get it to me right away. That money never came. Not a penny. I contemplated dragging the guy into court, going against my conviction that such actions are trifling and a waste of time, but Tiny told me Simon had moved his family onto a boat with no address. Maybe I wasn't the only one he owed money.

For many years after my forced departure, Simon Millburg and his lounge act continued limping around the lower rungs of the Southern California bar circuit, playing their same tired repertoire from the nineties. Now, the guy's in his fifties, still singing in the same clubs, and, as I recently learned, attempting to groom teenage girls for pop singing stardom. Simon made an appearance with one such acolyte in the retirement home where my father Len happens to live. Is it me, or is there something a little pathetic about a fifty-something dude who stills sings *Play That Funky Music, White Boy* in dive bars, while trying to get over, in his spare time, as a poor man's version of another, much more successful guy named Simon?

EGOMANIACS, BACKSTABBERS
AND BULLSHITTERS

My sudden departure from Guppy, a band that, while not my ultimate creative vehicle, was a project I'd worked hard for and written original music for, left me feeling a bit down. I had moved to L.A. to take a break from music, had found my interest rejuvenated, and now was in the same type of losing situation that had led me to abandon Faze and the San Diego scene in the first place. How many times can you dedicate yourself to a project, give it your best shot, and then watch it flounder, before you begin to doubt yourself? Time and again, you establish goals with a group of creative people, and something goes wrong. Maybe it's a combination of *several* things that go wrong, but the bottom line is this: the group falls on its face. It fails. You fail. Doubt creeps in again.

This is where you determine your true reasons for being in the arts. If they're the wrong reasons, this is where you figure that out and quit. You're not twenty-two anymore. You don't have limitless time to squander. Life is no longer a vast ocean of possibilities. The world is no longer your oyster. You are now one lowly oyster among millions of others oysters, past the point where you can wave the banner of youth to defend your circumstances.

I was still hungry in 1999, but for the first time in my life, the hardships of the path were planting seeds of cynicism. A romantic notion of the entertainment industry—that starry-eyed wonderment with which I'd gazed at the Hollywood sign and the Capitol Records building, when cruising down the 101 to visit relatives in Orange County as a teenager—had been whittled down to a begrudging acceptance of the way the world really works. Most people were watching their own backs and looking out for number one, and there was no environment in which this was more apparent than the arts and entertainment industry, which I had discovered was full of egomaniacs, backstabbers and bullshitters.

I decided that despite all the obstacles in my path, I wasn't going to be deterred from pursuing the things the things I cared about. Difficult people and situations were only potholes in the road. I knew I had something original to offer. Even Simon Millburg knew that. He'd told me, early in my Guppy days, that I was "too talented to be in this band." If I'd listened I wouldn't have wasted so much time.

You have to cultivate a strong sense of self-belief if you wish to have a prolonged career in the arts. People will dismiss you and your work. They will attempt to demoralize you. Some will try to convince you the cause is hopeless. You'll never get anyone to listen to your songs, read your scripts, or consider your paintings. You're not worthy. You're not good enough. Nobody cares. You have to realize that being a naysayer, for many, is a power trip. Having negative, condescending opinions makes them feel strong and in control

When it comes to criticism you have to consider the source. When coming from someone you admire and respect, listen carefully. Check your ego at the door and look to learn a thing or two. When criticism comes from a source you don't trust or value, swiftly dismiss it. I'm not suggesting you should inure yourself against negative feedback altogether, because negative feedback, if constructive, can be very helpful in refining your work. But you need to be careful who you listen to, when it comes to identifying weaknesses and making improvements.

At the end of the day you have to go with your vision. Only one person has laid everything on the line for this work, and it is you. For everyone else your work is one miniscule entity, orbiting around in a solar system cluttered with millions of other entities. For you, that work is the center of the universe—and nobody else, not even your supportive parents, who have backed your dreams with both moral and financial support, or your husband or wife, who would like nothing more than to watch you take the podium to accept a prestigious award one day, are capable of understanding that. The only one who's every going to truly understand why you create your work, and how much it means to you, is *you*.

Artists are a different breed of human being. Their mental eccentricities and individualistic quirks make them seem troubled and difficult to the outside world, but those qualities are also woven into the mysterious fabric of their gifts—a fact lost on most people. If you're completely normal—free of all dissatisfaction, angst and conflict—you probably aren't the kind of person who's going to spend the majority of his or her life obsessively searching for creative inspiration. If you're perpetually happy and content you're probably a likable person, but maybe not perceived as being an incredibly interesting one. *Happy* implies free of conflict, and freedom from conflict does not result in compelling art. How many riveting dramas can you think of that center around content, happy people?[96]

Some people live a relatively content, un-conflicted life, and counterbalance this emotional and psychological stasis by dropping down a waterfall in a barrel, or tight-rope walking between two hot air balloons at 25,000 feet. I'm sure it's exhilarating when you live to tell about it, but the potential downside of such thrills seems a bit perilous from my side of the sandbox. I'd like to live a long life and have the chance to produce as many creative works as possible, and this isn't going to happen if a bungee cable snaps and I crack my skull on the bottom of the Columbia Gorge. I guess there are different kinds of risk-taking.

---

[96] I can think of one: *Happy Go Lucky,* a 2008 film which features a wonderful performance by Sally Hawkins.

PACKAGE FOR SPIELBERG

Disappointed but undeterred, I braced myself to bounce back from the latest setbacks in L.A. The first order of business was to make some cash, now that both my day gig and band had fallen apart at the same time. I got a lead from my brother, and took a job with a courier service. The prospect of scurrying around greater Los Angeles with a stack of someone else's movie scripts may not have been ideal, but I figured it would have a plus or two. For one thing, the company catered to Hollywood directors and producers. This meant I would be rubbing elbows with people who might be interested in my own screenplays. Maybe I could do the occasional switcheroo, exchanging my script with the one I was supposed to deliver. *What the hell is Deviance? I'm supposed to be reading Home Alone 3.*

What the job actually amounted to, as I was about to learn, was hustling around town all day annoying receptionists, locking horns with parking attendants, and squaring off against lobby security guards. Nobody perched comfortably atop the upper reaches of this elite totem pole would even acknowledge your existence as a delivery boy, unless you were somehow getting in the way.

There was one cool thing about the courier job: the fact that I didn't have to wear a uniform. This is always priority number one with any job. When you get to set your own hours and work as a contractor, that's a positive too. With few exceptions, having a boss is a drag, and after languishing under the iron-fisted aegis of Angela Marshall I was looking for a situation where I could steer my own ship. So, armed with a walkie-talkie, pager, Thomas Guide map of L.A., stack of packages and the ulterior motive of getting my screenplays in the hands of movers and shakers, I embarked on a new mission.

I delivered packages to Hollywood people like Mickey Rourke and Shari Belafonte. I wandered the lots of all the big film studios, hoping to connect with powerful executives and their malleable underlings. Someday I would tell the story of how I'd gotten my humble start, schlepping scripts around town for a few years, then parlaying this low-paying racket, against the odds, into a fabulous screenwriting career. *Now that I've got my Oscar for Best Original Screenplay,* I would tell Vanity Fair's Christopher Hitchens over an expensive lunch, *it's time to direct.*

I would be the David Geffen of screenwriting, beginning as a scrambling, walkie-talkie wielding flunky and winding up a celebrated big shot. While all this was outlandish and lacking any connection to reality, the fantasy at least squelched pangs of insignificance and helped me kept hope alive.

After a few weeks as a courier, it was clear that just because you were standing in the *doorway* didn't mean you were in the *door*. High-ranking execs were not as eager as I'd hoped to discuss *Clowns* during the elevator ride down to the lobby. To them, I was just a schmuck with a nametag and holstered radio. I would have to cleverly bamboozle these people into paying attention to my random, lost-in-the-shuffle ass.

Finally, I got what looked like a big break. It was… drum roll, please… *a package addressed directly to Steven Spielberg.* Now, I would have the chance to pitch my stuff to a true giant, to someone who could make major moves with one phone call. If Steven Spielberg picked up the phone and said, "You know, I'd like to do a movie about a one-legged Indian midget schoolteacher, who rises up against the Nazis, infiltrates Hitler's inner sanctum and begins converting Heinrich Himmler and his minions to the teachings of Sikh Hinduism," rest assured that within a couple years, that movie will be showing on screens across America. I'm just not sure what it will be called. *Patel's List? Teaching Heinrich?*

I sped over to the Universal lot, whizzing through a labyrinth of buildings and sets, and on past an agglomeration of tram-riding tourists who eyeballed me as a potential celebrity sighting, and down a hill into the quaint, hidden nook of Amblin Entertainment. My mind raced with possibilities…

I would march past the reception desk and straight into the Hollywood icon's office, where he'd be grubbing a bagel, sipping a macchiato and shooting the breeze with Tom Hanks. I'd tell Spielberg I wasn't crazy about the Jurassic Park trilogy, but considered Duel, Close Encounters and Jaws true masterpieces. I'd hand him the tube with his name on it. He'd look it over, set it down on his desk and say, "Thanks for the tube. I've been waiting for it. But that isn't what we're really here to talk about… is it, Anthony." Roy Karch meets the creator of E.T.

"No, Steven. It's not."

At once, I'd launch into an eloquent pitch of Clowns, riffing on plot beats and character traits, slipping in hip pop culture references, explaining how nothing like this had been done before, and how the script fused the best elements of City Slickers and Lethal Weapon, and I'd do all this while demonstrating an encyclopedic knowledge of cinema, dating back to the 1930's. With every word, the two heavyweights would become increasingly enthralled with my project, to the point that when two security goons burst into the room to rearrange my face, Hanks would wave them off. "It's okay, Vitali. This guy is good. We gotta hear this." By the end of the lunch hour, I'd have an attractive offer on the table, and the three of us would be discussing the strong possibility of Hanks playing Mike Seskis, my bumbling rookie F.B.I. agent, who must disguise himself as a rodeo clown in order to case the suspected ringleader of a malicious gang of rodeo cowboy Christian zealot psychos.

"I'm not sure about the scene, prior to the denouement, where you've got the two leads jumping in slow motion, to avoid being incinerated by a giant fireball," Spielberg would say. "Is it necessary?"

"Yes," I'd answer. "Jerry Bruckheimer made the slow motion fireball jump an industry standard, and you have to throw it in there. Without it, we've got nothing to put in the trailer." Hanks would chime in with his two cents:

"You've got that scene where the waiters pull out M-16s from under their silver serving platters, then try to take out the archbishop, who turns out to be packing some serious heat himself, and mows those bastards down singlehandedly, finishing by looking to the heavens and making the sign of the cross, that pair of Glock 9 millimeters still smoking in his hands. We can use that in the trailer. We don't need the fireball." But I'd hold my ground.

"We're keeping the fireball, Tom. Live with it. This is my vision, okay?" Spielberg and Hanks would nod their heads in understanding, and we'd move on. We'd work out a few more wrinkles of the deal, then the dynamic pair would lead me into the main lobby to make an announcement: "It's the strangest thing, everyone. This courier guy just marched into my office to deliver a package, and next thing Tom and I know, he's pitching us the best damn movie idea we've heard in a long time. I haven't had chills like this since Alice Walker came in here with The Color Purple. Get the lawyers in here ASAP, and get this kid a literary agent. We're doing this deal right now, before any other studio hears about it. I don't want to hassle with a bidding war on this one. I want it all to myself. We've just discovered an exciting new talent, people!" The Amblin staff would break out in applause, and my writing career would be launched.

I pulled into the Amblin lot and parked my black Honda Civic. I grabbed the cylindrical package addressed to Steven Spielberg and marched confidently toward the front door. I went over variations of the Spielberg spiel in my head…

Can you sign for this, Mr. Spielberg? By the way, I've got this awesome idea to combine City Slickers and Lethal Weapon.
I'll need your John Hancock here, Mr. Spielberg. The sooner we get your signature, the sooner we can start talking about my screenplay.
Let me get your autograph on this thing here, Mr. Spielberg. I'll bet you started out delivering packages too, huh?
Got a joke for you, Mr. Spielberg. Why did the insomniac go to the drugstore for sleeping pills? Because he lost his DVD copy of Amistad. Now that we've broken the ice, can I tell you about my screenplay?

I decided to drop the rehearsed opener and just improvise. As I approached the front lobby I was accosted by a humorless security guard. I waved the tube in the air, waxed nonchalant and announced, "Package for Spielberg." The guard snatched the tube out of my hands and started poking at it suspiciously. Then he started poking at *me* suspiciously. The redoubtable director had been stalked in recent months by some wacko, and here I was, a courier yahoo waving a tube in the air, praying I was the next Joe Eszterhas.

Amazingly, I was allowed to enter the building with the tube. A receptionist motioned me over with a curled finger, snatched the tube from my clutches and barked, "Sign here." I obeyed, looking down the hall for signs of *the man*. No luck. No signs of Steven.

"Thank you," she snapped.

"Sure. My pleasure. I hope this is the first of many packages I'll be delivering for Mr. Spielberg. Next time I'll be happy to take it right to his office."

"Thank you."

"No need to thank me. I'm just doing my job, right?"

"THANK YOU." She was like Bob Rock during that Motley Crue session at A&M, only better looking and bitchier.

"Oh, right, I get it. You're trying to say *Get your ass out of here*."

I started to wonder if this courier job was really going to get me noticed in Hollywood. Nobody wanted to so much as catch a whiff of my perspiring armpits, much less accept an original screenplay. Perhaps I had overestimated the networking potential here. The difference between me and a Pizza Hut delivery driver was that *my* back seat held prized intellectual property… but based on the way I was getting treated by Hollywood's power players, I'm pretty sure I would have curried more favor had I been toting around the Meat Lovers Special.

The gravity of my position was further laid plain when a receptionist at one of the studios said to me, "Thank you for speaking intelligible English. It's so rare with you people, and it's really refreshing. Don't you dare quit now, okay?"

Maybe I was spinning my wheels again, but there was always the chance that during my next round of deliveries Shari Belafonte might invite me in for an iced tea, or Ice Tea might invite me into his crib to look at naked pictures of Shari Belafonte. Maybe Mickey Rourke would come out on his porch and beat the crap out of me for no good reason, then feel bad about it and read my script. Down at courier headquarters, the boss would say, "Hey Smith… Mickey Rourke's on the phone. He wants to talk to you."

Mickey: Sorry about the other day, man. I did some blow the night before and I was in a real shit mood. But hey, I read your stuff. Very cool. I was wondering if you could see me playing the psycho Christian terrorist ringleader?

Me: Absolutely, Mickey. In fact, I wrote the character with you in mind.

Hey, that could happen, right? *Something* had to happen, damn it. I continued speeding around L.A., disseminating scripts at the various studio lots, braving traffic jams and traversing winding roads to hunt down reclusive moguls in their hilltop sanctuaries. *When the Big One hits*, I fantasized, *all these exorbitantly priced domiciles are going to break off their stilts and start sliding down to sea level. Then we'll all be stuck in this smoggy, chaotic cesspool together.*

One afternoon I was hustling around Beverly Hills, slinging scripts for the courier company. A Molly Ringwald sidewalk shoulder-brush had me kind of pumped up, I'll admit. Just past the intersection of Rodeo and Little Santa Monica, I looked down to double-check some directions. When I looked back up, cars had come to a standstill in front of me. I slammed on my brakes, but was unable to avoid smashing into the vehicle in front of me, which in turn smashed into the vehicle in front of *it*. I buried my head in my hands and sat there for a moment, in my crumpled ride. The scene turned into a nightmare of honking horns, cops and robotic lookie-lou's, the latter gawking at me, the admitted culprit in this fiasco, as if I was some freak.

The lady I'd hit was old and completely out of it. She complained that she was having chest pains. Since there was already a dearth of compassion in the Beverly Hills air, my first thought was: *That's just great. She's having a heart attack. My premium's gonna go through the roof now.* Plus, my car was totaled and, like an idiot, I was only carrying liability insurance. The courier company was providing no additional coverage to their employees. *Drive and deliver at your own risk, asshole.*

I already had a hefty monthly payment, and now I was going to have to cough up six grand for the repair job. As you might guess, I was a little short. Len agreed to cover the repairs, but in exchange for his bailout he wanted to know what I was going to do with my life. This was a fair question, and I didn't have a compelling answer. I was writing scripts and slowly meeting people in L.A. I was where I wanted to be, doing what I wanted to be doing. It just wasn't working out.

Right after the accident, I did a couple jazz gigs in Kansas with David Basse. We played a fair in a small town called Salina. I liked the slow-paced, simple feel. People weren't complicated, and they weren't rushing around like the frazzled denizens of Southern California. After the gig, we ate butter-drenched, cracked crab and got drunk at Red Lobster. David had previously lived in Kansas City, and planned on moving back there soon. He took me to a couple jazz clubs and told me that if I ever wanted to relocate to Kansas City, I'd have all the work I could handle.

Back home, Len presented me with another option: Move to Prescott, live with him for a while, and enroll in graduate school at Arizona State University. I didn't really want to leave Los Angeles. It was the place to be for a writer. I *wanted* to be a writer, of course. A musician is what I actually *was*.

There was one last turn of events that convinced me I had some bad juju working against me in L.A. I was playing a gig with David Basse at Lunaria, a nice jazz club not far from my apartment in Santa Monica. There, I met a cocktail waitress named Celia. She said she was a singer. We hit it off, and she came back to my apartment for a nightcap after the gig. We listened to music, I played piano and she sang, and we drank some red wine. Collin had moved out, and I now shared the place with a friend of my sister, a social worker and aspiring comic named Ann Certich.[97] She wasn't around that evening, so I had the pad to myself.

Things got interesting with Celia, there on the living room floor, right next to a black iron burn branded into the cheap, brown carpet.[98] As we lay there, exchanging your typical *wow, this is all happening so fast* throw-away lines, interspersed with the equally clichéd *I'm usually not like this… you're really casting a spell on me* banter, I realized nature was calling. "Hold that thought. I'll be right back." I hurried to the

---

[97] Ann had a bit of a breakthrough many years later, when she was featured in a memorable scene on *Curb Your Enthusiasm.* Larry David is waiting in line at a buffet, and Ann's character uses the fact that she barely knows some guy, who happens to be ahead of Larry in the line, to cut in front of Larry. Larry, of course, sees right through this ruse, and a humorous argument ensues.

[98] Courtesy of Mike Blanco, a bass player friend of mine.

bathroom to handle my business. It turned out to be an involved project. Once finished, I lit a match, blew it out and tossed it into the waste can.

I returned to Celia, hoping as we all do under such circumstances for a grace period before my guest might need to pay her own visit to the *bomb site*. Sulfur can only do so much for you, after all. We resumed our previous activities, and everything was going smoothly. That's when I looked over and saw smoke billowing from under the bathroom door. I jumped to my feet, pretty much free of clothes at that point, and rushed back over there, swinging the door open to see flames shooting from the trash can and up the wall.

We can all agree that lavatory freshness is important, but I had allowed it to compromise fire safety. My roommate Ann, in her quest for flawless skin, had discarded a large mound of Stridex acne pads in the trash can. I should have realized that even a blown-out match might ignite the entire pile.

"You've got to put that fire out... quickly," Celia said, impressive in her calm collectedness. I sprinted to my room, grabbed the comforter off my bed, raced back into the bathroom and threw it over the flames. As smoke wafted into the rest of the apartment I saw that the fire had left large, black burn marks on the wall, and the toilet seat was partially melted.

The combination of getting fired from a mediocre funk band by its mercurial, ex-convict manager and *Catholic-schoolgirl-with-a-dick* frontman, being threatened by the unscrupulous owner of a group home in Santa Monica after treating the residents to an evening of beer, weed and pornography (all in the service of some kind of ill-conceived *screw you* to the powers that be), getting frisked by a suspicious rent-a-cop on the lot of Amblin Entertainment, when all I wanted to do was shake hands with Steven Spielberg and pitch him my original screenplay, ramming an elderly woman's vehicle in Beverly Hills and triggering heart palpitations in the old bird, while trashing my own car in the process, then nearly burning down my crummy apartment while bumpin' uglies with a cocktail waitress/Diana Krall clone[99] I'd seduced

---

[99] I hired Celia to sing with a band I'd assembled for a New Year's Eve gig in Long Beach. Needless to say, she had sounded considerably better while interpreting *Peel Me a Grape* in her birthday suit, back at my apartment that first night.

while backing up a random blues singer from Kansas, led me to the conclusion that Los Angeles did not want me at this point in time. I accepted Len's proposal to move to Arizona.

Before I left town, I did a couple final gigs. One was with an R&B singer who called himself Sexy Jamar. Sexy Jamar had a good band, and popular singers would stop by to sit in, such as El DeBarge, one of my adolescent musical idols. On this particular night, I was less than pleased to look across the stage and see Rodney Bunker standing there with his bass. He had been instrumental in my getting fired from Guppy. Nobody had told me this—I somehow just knew it. Rodney was a rotund, narcoleptic arriviste who'd browned the right noses and jockeyed me out of position so he could assume control for himself. I sure didn't want to play a gig with him *now*.

I never made eye contact with Rodney the whole night, and hoped he wasn't going to try to talk to me after the gig. As I was packing up my keyboard gear, I heard his raspy voice mumble, "I know you hate me." I didn't answer. He pressed the issue.

"I said, I know you hate me, but do you wanna talk about it?" I finally looked over at him and said, "You screwed me, man. I don't have anything to say to you." The bass player's tone shifted from reconciliatory to confrontational.

"You screwed yourself!" I didn't say anything else, and resumed packing up my equipment. It was pouring rain outside. As I moved for the door, Rodney stepped in front of me. This was a very big guy we're talking about. He just stood there. I wasn't scared, though. It's physiologically impossible to be angry and scared at the same time. "Get your fat ass out of my way," I said. Surprised to hear these words coming from my mouth, Rodney stepped to the side. I could see he was now furious. As I carried my keyboards to the car, he followed me outside and got in my face. We stood nose-to-nose, getting soaked by the downpour. I stood there inhaling his pungent breath, insult to my injury after he'd already expedited my departure from Guppy. He finally said, "If I hook up any gigs, do you wanna do 'em?"

"If you got something, give me a call," I answered.

I had made the mistake of telling Sexy Jamar about what happened with Guppy—how I'd been dropped by No Notice Otis, and how Simon had promised me some dough and then totally flaked. I must have made some comment like, "I should sue those bastards," because the very next day there was a message on my machine from Otis. It said: "You wanna fucking sue me? Go ahead. You'll see what happens if you try to fucking sue me! You'll never get another job in this fucking town!" As usual, Otis was incapable of constructing a sentence without throwing in an *f bomb* or two.

I slept on it before deciding how to react to the threatening message. I decided it was in everyone's best interest to smooth things over — that I should prevent this conflict from escalating further. Otis was capable of anything. He was the kind of character who gets in a drunken argument over baseball stats, bashes someone's head in at a bar, and winds up doing time for second degree murder. Otis lived his life like he didn't have anything to lose, and that's not the kind of guy you want to have an unresolved beef with. I called back and assured him I wasn't planning on suing anybody, which was the truth. I might have made some remark to Sexy Jamar in frustration, but I've never been the kind of guy that drags a relatively petty financial matter into small claims court, then sanctimoniously boasts of triumph when the other party fails to appear. I've got better things to do with my time.

"Look, man, I'm not going to sue," I said to Otis. I *do* think it's lame that you and Simon didn't give me some money at the end, though. I was loyal to Guppy. I never missed a rehearsal or a gig. I was writing songs for the group. It's bad karma on your end, and I deserved better than that."

Later that night, I happened to run into Otis one last time at Luna Park, a West Hollywood club where I'd gone to check out some band. In bizarre fashion, he cracked a big smile when he saw me, came over and slapped my hand. It was a weird moment. The guy had been screaming at me less than twenty-four hours earlier, like Mike Tyson at a press conference (*I'm gonna eat your children!*). It was then that I realized Otis was somewhat crazy, and I felt relieved to no longer be a part of the Guppy organization. There were bad vibes surrounding that group of people, as would be evidenced a few years later, when Sexy Jamar was murdered over a dispute with drug dealers. Either unwilling or unable to pay a debt, the pretty-boy R&B singer was shot multiple times in his L.A. apartment, then set on fire and left to burn. Let's just say there are probably more pleasant ways to go out.

I prepared to move out of my apartment in Santa Monica, and you're going to be shocked to hear this, but... I was informed that I wouldn't be getting any of my security deposit back. The landlord, Ivan, was a young Japanese guy managing the complex for his parents. He was married and had a baby. I liked him. I remember our conversation about the deposit.

"I realize there's a bit of damage, between the iron imprint on the carpet and the burn marks in the bathroom," I said.

"Yeah. It's pretty extensive."

"I figure you can just patch up the carpet, and the bathroom is salvageable, right? How much does a plastic toilet seat cost? Fifty bucks?"

"What about the burn marks shooting up the walls, all the way to the ceiling?"

"I tried to wipe the walls down, but that black stuff's on there pretty good."

"That's because those aren't stains. The walls are actually *burned*."

"Yep, guess that's true."

"Did you clean the kitchen?"

"Uh, not really."

"Hmmm."

"Look, Ivan, if I can just get back half of the deposit I'll be happy."

"That might not be realistic."

"I could really use some cash for the next place."

"I hear you, but it's going to cost me like two grand just to make the apartment rentable again."

"Really?"

"Yeah, man. I mean, what the hell happened in that bathroom?"

"Well, I dropped a deuce, and tried to cover it up with a match. Then I returned to entertaining the promiscuous cocktail waitress I'd met earlier that evening at a nearby jazz bar, and lo and behold, suddenly the bathroom was engulfed in flames. That sort of thing must happen all the time, right?"

"Uh, not really. Anyway, it's unfortunate, but someone has to pay for it. How about I just use your deposit to fix the place up, and I won't charge you any extra for nearly burning down the whole building. I can do that for you, because I like you and you've always paid your rent on time."

"Okay, man. I guess that's fair."

I packed a U-Haul and cruised out to Arizona. I knew I wanted to write, and figured the best way to go about it was to pursue a degree. I decided I would get my double masters in creative writing and piano performance. That way I'd have options. I could continue my career in music and ultimately break into the literary world. The days of scuffling were a thing of the past. I was turning a new leaf. Things could only get better from here, right? *I'm not going to say it…*

ROCK BOTTOM

Despite the misfortunes I'd experienced in Los Angeles, I was yet to reach my absolute nadir as an aspiring artist. No, I had further depths to plumb, and they were right around the corner. I didn't know it at the time, but I was going to Arizona to bottom out.

After abandoning Southern California, my goal was to enroll at Arizona State University and pursue graduate work in music and writing. The soonest I could start school was the fall, so I had an entire summer to kill. Len was happy to house me in Prescott, but made it clear he wasn't going to allow a twenty-eight year-old man to lounge around from June to September. He wanted that man to find a job. I made a quick attempt to find work playing piano in local restaurants and bars, but I was putting most of my energy into writing—short stories, screenplays and CD reviews for an underground L.A. jazz magazine called *Bird*.

Len was pleased that I was honing my writing craft, but this pleasure was eclipsed by the sobering reality that writing wasn't earning me a dime. I was supposed to get paid for the jazz reviews, but the money never came, and the magazine folded with barely anyone noticing. I had credit card debt, and Capital One wasn't of a mind to care that I was busy perfecting a piece of short science fiction about a disturbing future society, where children brandish firearms, and a non-fatal gunshot wound is the equivalent of a scrape on the knee.

The day I visited the campus of ASU, it must have been 110 degrees. After walking around for only a few minutes I was drenched in sweat, and scrambled to find the air-conditioned music building. I sat down with Chuck Moronic, the director of jazz studies, to discuss my academic future. He explained that jobs like his were scarce. There were only a handful of such positions out there to begin with, and the guys who had them were hanging on for dear life. Moronic said he knew people with doctorate degrees who couldn't find a university gig. That was not what I had moved to Arizona to hear.

My scholastic agenda now in question, I returned to Prescott with one option: figure out how to make some cash. Many a musician has had to look in the mirror and face a hard truth: *I have one marketable skill in life. It's music or Jack in the Box.* I wasn't anxious to sit in a corner and bang on an out of tune piano in a local watering hole, for fifty bucks and half-priced pub grub, but I was *dead set* against slinging curly fries and barking into a drive-through intercom. I perused job listings, hoping to spot an opportunity in a field I hadn't previously considered. One ad caught my attention; while the wording was vague, the job seemed to have three things going for it: No uniform, you set your own hours, and you worked by yourself. The only thing missing from the description was: *Don't do any actual work. Just collect check.*

I called the phone number and spoke to a guy who told me the job involved physical labor. He wouldn't get any more specific than that. "You'll have to come out here and check it out for yourself."

"Come out where?"

"The site."

The site…

For someone of my background, who had averted blue-collar grinds his entire life, *the site* was a term which conjured unease, perhaps even mild fear. You weren't going to flex your mental muscles while participating in a progressive think tank at *the site*. Maybe at the lyceum, the center, or the institute, but not *the site*. At *the site*, you were going to fasten your boots, roll up your sleeves and do a man's work for a man's wage. You were going to break your back and make zero excuses, and nobody was going to give a damn if you could quote Dante's *Inferno*. It was all about accountability at *the site*.

Accountability, reliability, and results. There weren't any free rides at *the site*, and there wasn't room for some sarcastic candy-ass. Most guys had handlebar mustaches and hairy forearms, lookd like Wade Boggs or Bill Buckner, and would eat you for breakfast if you showed the slightest weakness. If you were heading out to *the site* and didn't have balls, you would have to grow some quick.

The next morning I woke up at five-thirty a.m., kick-started my ticker with a quad mocha, and drove to a big strip mall complex, racing the bright, orange ball ascending into the sky above the RV-littered Wal-Mart parking lot. There, I waited for a guy named Red Sawchenko, who was supposed to take me out to… *the site*. After a few minutes, a leather-skinned, pock-marked character wobbled into the parking lot in a clunker pick-up. It was safe to say Red's vehicle wasn't going to be featured in any Sunday afternoon football commercials. I hopped in.

"Morning, Mr. Sawchenko."

"Call me Red."

As we rolled out toward Chino Valley, Red's weathered visage, calloused hands and greasy *skullet*[100] threw up some red flags. If this workplace, whatever it turned out to be, was providing its employees with the slightest measure of financial comfort, it was not evidenced by the visual presentation of Red Sawchenko; and beyond my chauffeur's ragtag appearance, I realized we had veered off the highway and were now rambling over the rough surface of a winding backroad. I squeezed Red for information about the job but he remained silent, focusing his attention on the swirl of dust obfuscating the view ahead.

Red spit a chunk of tobacco from his mouth and out the half-open, driver-side window, missing the mark enough so that a little gob hugged the edge of the glass and began dribbling down like a gooey, chocolate-covered snail. This act triggered a barrage of phlegm-riddled, gurgling paroxysms, the kind you expected from a lifelong cancer sticker like Red. As he struggled to clear his throat, I played a bit of *Conspiracies While You Wait*, a game I had created to entertain myself when caught up in bizarre, possibly life-threatening scenarios…[101]

---

[100] A mullet sported by a mostly bald person. Also check out the *sku-drullet,* or *sku-dreadlocket.*

[101] Such as the previously discussed lizard incident.

Maybe Red worked for someone who was privy to the fact that a giant meteor was going to obliterate life on earth in a matter of days, and I had been chosen, for reasons unexplained, to survive in a subterranean bunker.[102]
Or...
Red had preemptively kidnapped me because he knew a distant relative of mine, a great uncle living in Europe, was about to kick off, leaving me a huge sum of money I had no idea about. Red was taking me back to his motley crew of accomplices, who were hiding out somewhere in the boonies. Hillbilly madness would ensue, in a crude, Deliverance-inspired comedy of errors.[103]

As I glanced over at Red, he looked more like a mass murderer than a dimwitted kidnapper. If he was a psychopath, I'd have to figure out his next move before *he* did... get inside the mind of the killer. Become him. We all know this drill, and we all know how it winds up: *Having untangled the complex web of Red's string of grotesque, brilliantly conceived massacres of individuals who, due to a variety of moral transgressions, clearly had it coming, I chase him here to the roof of this skyscraper, where he hangs from a ledge, scowls, loses his grip and utters the final words: "See you in hell." He plummets to his splattery demise, but can miraculously hear me loud and clear as I whisper under my breath, "Ditto, asshole."*[104]
This comeback makes no sense whatsoever, since I'm not planning on going to hell, but it sounds cool to thirteen year-olds, the target demographic for the film.

The most plausible theory was that Red was a member of some backwoods, Satan-worshipping sect, and had been burdened with a monthly human sacrifice quota to satisfy here in Chino Valley. It was a perfect trap—put an ad in the Prescott paper, shanghai some dope into thinking you're taking him to *the site*, and herd him into the middle of nowhere to cut his heart and liver out. Paranoia on my part? Perhaps, but we were now several miles off the highway, and had been lumbering along this roughshod path for over half an hour. The National Anti-Vivisection Society was nowhere to be found.

Red pulled the truck to the side of the road as we turned a bend, and I thought, *here it comes. What first? The liver?* I waited for a retinue of

---

[102] John Cleese jokes about this at the beginning of *Rat Race*, while in *Deep Impact*, the filmmakers were, unfortunately, being serious.

[103] Sounds like a good plot for Adam Sandler and Will Ferrell, huh?

[104] Combining the patois of *Ghost* and *The Terminator*.

hooded, chanting nut jobs to emerge from the neighboring brush. Instead, I heard a loud explosion. *The meteor, hitting a little early?* I spotted a row of parked vehicles—big trucks and raised 4 X 4's, the kinds of ass-kickin' mean machines that would make Bob Seger wail like a howling jackal in the night—and guys wearing hard hats, with tools hafted in bulky utility belts, pacing around, arms akimbo, speaking a jargon as unintelligible to my ears as Hangul.

Red climbed arthritically from the pick-up, grabbed a bucket of tools with one hand and a twelver of PBR with the other, turned to me and said, "Go get 'em, tiger. See you at the end of the day...that is, if you're still here." I watched him disappear into a cloud of blast particles like the mythical Charon, paddling across the fog-blanketed Styx after ferrying dead souls in his dingy.

"You the one I talked to on the phone?" I turned in the direction of the new voice, sizing up a tall, mustached guy in his late twenties.

"Yeah, that's me."

"I'm Jay, the foreman. Welcome to the site." I surveyed the area, scoping bulldozers as they manipulated chunks of earth in their anthropomorphic jaws. Stout, bare-chested yeomen hammered slabs of clay-colored stone, as intermittent *kabooms* sent tornadoes of dirt whipping through the air. Suddenly it was clear. *I was in a rock quarry.*

"What were you in for?" Jay asked.

"In where?"

"The slammer. You're on parole, right?"

"No. I'm an out-of-work piano player, which is probably worse."

"So how did you find out about this place?"

"Newspaper ad. It was pretty vague, you know, about what the actual job was." Jay flashed a knowing grin.

"That's the only way I can get guys up here to check it out. If I tell them on the phone it's a rock quarry, they hang up before I finish my sentence. But if they come up here and take a look, half the time they end up liking the work and sticking around." I found that hard to believe. How could anyone like this work? It seemed horrible.

"Most of our guys are ex-cons, looking for a chance to turn their lives around," Jay continued. "Is that why you're here? Looking to turn your life around?"

"I'm looking to make some cash, more than anything. I came out here because it appears the hiring criteria aren't too strict."

"This is man's work, buddy. You think just anyone can cut this job? You're kidding yourself. Is that what you think?" No, I did not. I harkened back to that day at Roy Karch's porn compound in Reseda, when the old veteran explained to Tiny and me that it was no walk in the park to waltz onto the set of an adult feature film, get fluffed, and drop some drain babies, on command, for a crew of camera-wielding sleazebags. Working in this rock quarry would be no picnic either.

"Here, these will be yours." Jay handed over a bucket of hammers and wedges, just like the one Red had in his truck. "These are the tools of the trade." Sensing my trepidation, Jay tried to lighten the situation by saying, "So, you play the piano pretty good?"

"I've been playing a long time. I have a college degree in music performance, and I'm also an aspiring writer of screenplays and short fiction." He frowned and shook his head…

What kind of cruel world is this, where artistic people with college degrees are forced to accept back-breaking jobs mostly done by former convicts, in scorching hot rock quarries nestled deep in the bowels of Chino Valley?

"Well, Jay, I've accomplished just about everything I can in music, and the next logical step in my life is to tackle a new challenge. You know, put myself in a situation where I might maim, disfigure or dismember a critical part of my body, such as my hands or fingers." Jay chuckled and patted me on the back. At least I had a sense of humor. He led me to my personal work area. My *office*.

"This is your little corner, my friend. When you're ready, give a whistle, and one of the Cats'll come over and drop a rock for you. When he said rock, what he meant was boulder. Big, hulking boulder that could crush a rhinoceros.

"Let's get it going," Jay rallied.

"Let's get it going," I agreed. Jay let out a piercing whistle, and sure enough here came one of those massive tractor monstrosities, dangling a giant, brown meatball in its incisors. The Cat backed into my work station, its abrasive BEEP, BEEP, BEEP taking me back to the glory days of Casa de Colina and my old semi-retarded[105] neighbor

---

[105] I've been recently corrected when using the word "retarded" in public. "*Special needs* is the appropriate term these days," someone barked at me. Okay, but if George Carlin were still alive, I imagine him saying, "…and while we're on the subject of politically correct bullshit expressions, here's one for you: *special needs*. Now that, my friends, is a real bullshit expression!" I can understand how "retard" is a derogative and offensive word, unless being muttered by Matt Dillon's character in *Something About Mary,* in which case we can all agree it's rather funny, but "retarded?" When I was growing up in the

Raymond.[106] Meanwhile, a series of explosions blasted in random spots all around us. It was like a rough day in Jalalabad out there. Once the monster dropped its meatball, Jay shook my hand, wished me luck and disappeared. This was the real moment of truth. *Dear God, what in hell am I doing out here? Am I completely insane?* I looked at that rock, I looked down at my hammer, I looked over at all the ex-drug peddlers, murderers, whatever they were, and I realized: In order to do this, I was going to have to become temporarily insane. I was going to have to lose my mind like a soldier in battle, and dive in without any fear. This was the only way.

So that's what I did. I grabbed that hammer and started pounding on that rock. I pounded on it like I'd never pounded on anything in my life. The sun was beating down, my heart palpitating in my chest, sweat pouring off me, and I pounded away, hour after hour. I didn't know what I was doing, and I proceeded to hack the rock into big, ugly slabs that wouldn't fit on the palette. I had no form, no chops, but I didn't give a shit. I was out of my mind. Either I was spiritually cleansing myself or having a complete meltdown. Whatever it was, I have to be honest—it felt good.

After several hours, Jay returned to check up on me. He laughed when he saw the mess I'd made out of my boulder.

"Well, you've got the spirit. Now we need to work on the technique." Jay stayed with me for a good hour, teaching me the subtleties of the craft; there was an art to wielding these chisels, chips and wedges. I watched Jay exert a minimum amount of effort and achieve a maximum result. He was a master flagstone cutter. This was a family business, and he had grown up out here. He'd probably been doing this since he was sixteen. He patiently explained basic principles of physics and geology, and how they applied to flagstone. The idea was to cut the rock into very thin slabs, which were then transported to

---

seventies, you were either normal, "hyper-active," or "retarded." Each group had its own bus.

[106] According to celebrated actor Kirk Lazarus (played by Robert Downey Jr.) in *Tropic Thunder*, if you're going for an Academy Award, you can't go "full retard." Only half. Or, as Ricky Gervais would point out, you can also play a priest or a nun who courageously fought against the Nazis during WWII. I would like to add my own archetypal suggestion: the tortured but brilliant crooner, either of the blind, African-American variety, or the French, free-spirited, women-behaving-badly variety.

supply companies who sold the flagstone to building contractors, who used it to assemble pool decks, walkways and other surfaces. It was big business.

Jay taught me how to position the various wedges at different points on the rock, applying equal pressure to ensure a symmetrical split. Each rock, he explained, had a unique personality, and the moment you thought you could predict a rock's behavior was the moment you floundered.

"A piece of flagstone's like a woman, my friend. The Caterpillar's like your best friend, the guy who comes over and introduces you to her. You think you already know what to expect, because, well, this isn't the first piece of flagstone you ever tackled, now, is it?"

"No, Jay. I've tackled a fair amount of flagstone."

"Right. So you get your wedges in there, thinking you know how she's gonna respond—the rock, that is. But she doesn't. She's got her own ideas about things, and you're gonna have to adapt and improvise if you wanna make her happy. You following me?"

"Yeah, completely."

"So you give a little chip here, wedge it in a little over there, and you see what's working. More important, you see what *isn't* working and you make adjustments. Pull a wedge, re-position it, nurse this other one along until it feels right. The thing is—and you may not want to accept this at first—she's the boss. It's her show, and you're just a facilitator. Stay out of the way and she'll be good to you. You force things, you try to take charge and do it your way, and she'll make your life a living hell."

"We still talking about flagstone here, Jay?"

I took Jay's words to heart and put my all into cutting flagstone. He was right, there was an art to it. When you did it correctly, physics kicked in and the rock started popping from somewhere deep in the middle, pieces flaking off in smooth, thin layers. It was a thing of beauty. I piled up stacks of perfect slabs, my pride mounting with each completed palette. I slipped into a meditative state out there in Chino Valley, my breathing steady and my mood tranquil. The monotony of the work allowed me to reflect on aspects of my life. I got in great shape fast. And while there was always the chance I'd smash my fingers with one of those hammers, I could not deny a surprising truth: I liked working in a rock quarry. I didn't know it, but I was renewing my spirit for the next ten years of my journey in the arts. It was *Zen and the Art of Splitting Flagstone*.

Working at the quarry was physically harder than any sport I'd played or any job I'd done. At the end of the day I was sore, cramped and sunburned. All I wanted to do was slug back some beers at a downtown dive bar. One night, happy hour transformed into a karaoke jam. My interpretation of Seal's *Kiss from a Rose* garnered the interest of young lady who, while pulverizing *What If God Was One of Us*, compensated for it by being attractive and intelligent. I snuck her back to Len's pad later that night. If I was going to haul my bones out to Chino Valley to work in a rock quarry by day, I was going to drink beer and, if the opportunity presented itself, have a little fun at night. Len couldn't begrudge me these basic vices.

I realized that if push came to shove, there were a lot of jobs I could do. I wasn't some piano prodigy nerd whose parents had sheltered him from physical activity since he was six years old, frightened he'd hurt his fingers. It was obvious I didn't give a damn about my fingers! Working at the quarry should have been my lowest moment, the experience I'd look back on one day and think, *that's when I bottomed out*. I mean, could it get any worse than working at a flagstone plant? But cutting flagstone turned out not to be so bad. It was far from the crappiest job I'd ever done.

As my thirtieth birthday approached, I relaxed atop a boulder at my rock-splitting station in Chino Valley and took inventory of the various difficulties I'd weathered thus far in life: My parents' acrimonious divorce, the college rejections, the panic attacks and hospitalization, the roller coaster of the artistic life and the frequent disappointments of the music scene. I was finally finding myself; and my skin, which had always been thin, was getting tougher.

While I was working at the quarry, I got a call from Gilbert Castellanos, a jazz trumpet player friend in San Diego. Gilbert was looking for a vibraphonist, and invited me to join his jazz quartet for some upcoming gigs. I had learned my life lessons in Chino Valley. I had pounded a few brews and exploited my karaoke ability in local dive bars. I'd hung out with Len for a few months. I knew I couldn't make Prescott my permanent home. So, replenished like Malcolm X after his pilgrimage to Mecca, and wiser for his struggles, I decided to return to the front lines of the Southern California music scene and resume the good fight.

RANDOM RIFFS

Earth Day

I showed up for Earth Day in Chico wearing an imitation leopard hat. I didn't even think about what I was doing. After the set, a couple hippies walked over to me and said, "Nice tunes. And we just wanted to tell you, that's a terrific fashion statement you're making on Earth Day. You're obviously committed to making the world a better place." Next year I'm taking the stage in a fur and some alligator skin pants.

The Convalescent Ghosts of Eureka

At one point, the GFC organization contemplated setting up headquarters in Eureka. We found a house that had something like eleven bedrooms, if you can believe that. It was all by itself out in the middle of nowhere—perfect for our needs. It turned out this place was an old convalescent hospital that somebody had bought, converted into a residence, and was now renting out. If we took the place, Woo was going to be living there alone for a while, until we finished our tour.

Wildman and I got a great idea for a practical joke. We decided we'd go to the community theatre in Eureka, find some really old actors, and hire them to sneak into the house while Woo was there alone. They would hide in various parts of the house and whisper to him while he was lying in bed.

"Woo... Woo... For years we were mistreated and abused. The doctors gave us the wrong meds. They killed us through their negligence. And now *you're* going to pay."

Vocabulary Abuse

It's funny what happens when you introduce a new vocabulary word to your friends. Either they ignore it, or they start using it too. When I was in Faze, I used the word *alleviate* one time. Pretty soon, *alleviate* was not just a verb but also a noun, an adjective, and a cure-all for any linguistic stumbling block:

Man, I don't think you truly alleviate the nature of this situation.
Sure I do, I just choose to accept a different alleviation than you do.
That's not very alleveatory for you to say that, my man.
Just stop over-alleviating every detail, alright?
I'll try to take into alleviation what you're saying, but I can't alleviate any
promises.
I alleviate you on that, my brother.
Cool. Let's alleviate some lunch.

Grass Roots Marketing

Global Funk Council was driving to a show in Springdale, Utah, just outside Zion National Park. Sadly, a man had been knocked from his old, beat-up motorcycle by a car. We couldn't pass, as the man lay in the street waiting for help to arrive. There were a bunch of people standing around, some trying to help, some just watching with morbid curiosity. Mr. Peepers spoke up: "Would it be wrong if I passed out some fliers for tonight's show?"

Family Loyalty

A friend of mine, Zeki, launched an independent record label, fulfilling a lifelong dream. A rich uncle of his, Uncle Umut, agreed to bankroll the business for the first couple years. Uncle Umut had been generous, allowing Zeki to build a state-of-the-art recording studio with lots of high-end gear. There was also a considerable budget provided for the development of talent.

After a couple years, Uncle Umut decided he was completely unhappy with the progress Zeki was making with the label. He not only decided to stop funding it, but he also announced to Zeki that he was going to sell the building and liquidate all the equipment. Needless to say, Zeki was very disappointed and disheartened. He felt that Uncle Umut was really screwing him on the deal.

After all this went down, I didn't talk to Zeki for a number of months. When I finally did catch up with him, he was in great spirits.

I asked him what had changed, and he said, "There have been some developments since we last talked. Things are looking up."

"What happened?"

"Well, there have been some changes, and my circumstances are not what they were when we last spoke."

"Zeki, you're beating around the bush. Cut to the chase. What happened?"

"Okay, well, Uncle Umut went out for his morning swim in the lake, and uh…"

"Yeah? What?"

"He didn't come back."

"Oh, that's terrible. I'm really sorry to hear that."

"Due to this unforeseen circumstance, I've been able to hold onto my equipment and keep the label going."

"Well, that's good, but I'm so sorry for your loss. Poor Uncle Umut."

"Oh, no, no… *fuck him*. He was trying to crush my dreams."

Woo, a Bottle of Crown Royal, and the Merits of Youthful Shrubbery

"I got lucky," Woo sighed as I answered the phone. For a moment I thought he had ventured back down to Tijuana on his own to engage in activities that had nothing to do with the Travesty, and I responded, "That's not luck, Woo—that's capitalism." But the big guy's sullen tone quickly suggested otherwise, and I realized he was on a completely different wavelength. "I'm talking about my car," he said. "I crashed it."

Woo's cell phone is a real turkey, distorting his already high-pitched voice to an edgy squeal that sounds like the Pillsbury Dough Boy with a mouthful of helium. Through much practice, I've learned to filter out the warped gibberish and glean the gist of whatever he's talking about at a given moment, but it took me a while to master this ability.

"Are you okay?" I asked.

"Yeah. Like I said, I got lucky."

"How so?"

"It was a young tree."

"Meaning what, exactly… it was capricious? Impressionable? Malleable?"

"Exactly. It was malleable. And pliable. Had some give to it. If it had been a two hundred year-old redwood, I'da been toast."

"Were you hammered?"

"Yeah, but I can't figure out why."

"Could it be that maybe you drank too much?"

"It was the usual amount. Nothing more."

Don't be deceived by this statement. If you've ever seen the Biography Channel special on Andre the Giant, which I caught at a roach motel in Bozeman, Montana, you know that certain rare individuals possess extraordinary powers of consumption. The famous wrestler, whose head was literally the size of a large watermelon, was known to routinely down many full-course dinners, a large handle of whiskey, and at least a few bottles of wine, all in one sitting.

As is documented in the GFC Timeline of Significant Events, I saw Woo polish off an entire bottle of Crown Royal at an otherwise forgettable Living Large show in Klamath Falls, Oregon, a town steeped in GFC/Living Large lore. Woo had crossed the line with a female bartender, fondling her without invitation to the point that she walked over to me and snapped, *We have to establish some boundaries here with your manager.*

"You only drank one handle?" I asked.

"That's it. And I was blitzed."

"That's peculiar, Woo. Maybe you should see a doctor," I offered, concerned and confused. As the conversation progressed I was relieved to learn that Woo hadn't injured himself—only the tree—while also managing to finish off a Dodge minivan that appeared to be on its last legs anyway. There is a lesson in all this, of course: Crashing one's car while driving wasted is only acceptable if:

The recipient of the crash is an inanimate object.

That inanimate object is a tree.

That tree is young.

The members of MADD don't find out, because they'll crucify your ass.

Woo summed up the experience with two simple quotes from pop culture figures. The first is from a Jerry Garcia/Robert Hunter song called *Bertha:*

The road went around a corner, and I went straight into a tree.

The second is from Krusty the Klown: "Glug glug, vroom vroom, crash crash."

The Watching and the Licking

"I hate that little fucker," Anne confided in a hushed voice as we stood in the kitchen of her house in Aptos.

"Who?"

"That dog."

"Sadie?"

"Yes."

Sadie is my brother Collin and his wife's small beagle/Chihuahua, which I have only met on one occasion, and seemed harmless enough to me.

"Why do you hate it?"

"It makes me nervous. I don't trust it."

"Seemed pretty harmless to me."

"Yeah, well you obviously didn't look into its eyes."

"What do you mean?"

"Its eyes... are evil. It looks at you like it knows things. It studies you and it makes very specific judgments."

"Judgments?"

"Specific, intelligent judgments."

"I think you might be giving the dog a little too much credit, there, Mom."

"Those aren't the eyes of a dumb, incapable animal."

"So you don't like it because of its eyes?"

"Not just the eyes."

"Well what else, then?"

"The licking. It's always licking everything. I don't like that."

"That's what dogs do, Mom. They lick stuff."

"Well, I don't like it. All that licking makes me nervous. The watching... and the licking."

"And what is it you think the dog is capable of doing?"

"Going after the baby. It knows it's going to play second fiddle to the baby from now on, and it doesn't like it."

"You think all that's going on in that little brain?"

"I'm telling you, that dog is brilliant. And it's evil."

The *baby* referred to Collin's newborn daughter, Madeline, who was just home from the hospital.

"I made a deal with Collin," Anne continued.

"What kind of deal?"

"If the dog makes any kind of move, and so much as scratches the baby on the arm, it's out of there."

"Out of there?"

"Back to Texas with Stacey's parents."

"I see... I guess that sounds fair enough."

"I'm gonna bait it when I'm down there next week."

"The dog? You're gonna bait the dog?"

"Yep."

"And how, may I ask, are you going to do that?"

"I'm going to trick it into biting me."

"Oh, I get it. You want it to bite you, so you can use that as ammo to get it out of the house and away from the baby."

"Exactly. I'm going to antagonize the little sucker until it lunges at me in anger."

"Good plan. You know, you could attach little pieces of raw meat to your legs... that'll get her to bite you for sure."

"That's a great idea. I might try that."

A couple weeks later, Terry, my step-dad, also weighed in on the matter...

"It's not so much the capacity for violence I'm worried about with that dog, but I have to agree with your mom."

"About what?"

"The licking."

"You don't like being licked by a dog?"

"Well, I watch it licking its own balls and butt, and then when it's outside, it's eating other dogs' crap..."

"But Collin and Stacey don't let it lick the baby."

"Generally speaking, this is true... but it still gets a random lick in here and there."

"So it's that sneaky, occasional lick that troubles you."

"Yeah, because I just watched it licking its own balls, now it's up in the baby's face."

"I don't think it has balls, Terry. Its name is Sadie, after all."

"Well, it's got an ass, doesn't it?"

"Yes. It does have an ass."

Anne decided to chime in at this point.

"You know, I will say that despite my dislike of all the licking the dog does, I don't mind it so much when it licks my toes."

Terry turned back to me at this point, eager to defend himself.

"I would be happy to lick your mother's toes myself, Anth, but she's apparently more interested in having the dog do it."

Anne shrugged her shoulders and responded, "Your tongue's not as small and as warm as the dog's. The dog's tongue feels better. At least on my toes."

These are the kinds of conversations that take place in my mother's kitchen.

Conversation in my Kitchen

An exchange between my wife and me, while our two very young sons were eating their dinner…

Me: I'm worried about Raja having that fork.
Teena: Why?
Me: I'm concerned that little Jaan is going to get stuck by it.
Teena: Well… why don't you give Jaan your knife, so he can defend himself.

Conversation in my Living Room

The following exchange took place with my wife, while watching NBA basketball on TV.

Teena: These guys aren't that good, are they?
Me: Why do you say that?
Teena: They just seem like they need to work on their gerbil penetration.
Me: Their *what?*
Teena: Their gerbil penetration.
Me: I think you mean *dribble* penetration, babe.
Teena: Yeah, that too.

Band Solidarity

A guitarist friend of mine, Jack, played in a popular touring band from L.A. called Nuclei. After canvassing the States with considerable success for several years, a promoter stepped up and offered to arrange a European tour. The band enthusiastically accepted and the deal was done. After the plane left LAX, the promoter walked over and sat next to Jack.

"There's a bit of a complication," he said.

"Okay, what?" Jack responded.

"Well, I kind of forgot to hook up the work visas."

"That seems like a pretty big problem."

"I think we can fudge it when we land at Heathrow."

"How are we going to do that?"

He proceeded to explain his plan, which, it must be noted, was a terrible one. The plane landed in London, and Jack and the rest of the band made their way through the customs line. When Jack got to the front of the line, an officer asked him what his business was in London.

"I'm just going to hang out. Check out the city."

"What's the guitar for?"

"I'm going to busk... for extra money. You know, play on the street."

"Can you come with me, please?" The officer led Jack down a corridor and into an interrogation room.

"Okay, let's start over. Why are you in London?" The promoter had warned Jack that he could possibly get grilled, but if he stuck to his story, he'd eventually get through. Jack had no idea if the others had been admitted.

"I'm busking, man. I told you." The officer wasn't buying it, and soon there was another guy in the room, this one bigger and seemingly more pissed off.

"What do you say we cut the bullshit now, Jack. Tell me what you're doing here." Jack was starting to get nervous. Somehow, he stuck to his guns.

"I don't know why you're hassling me. I'm just here with my guitar." The imposing agent leaned closer.

"What if I told you that you're a member of a band called Nuclei, and that I know you're lying to my face right now?" Jack broke into a sweat. "And what if I told you that you've got a whole European tour lined up, and you're making up some bullshit about busking because you don't have the proper paperwork?"

Jack was dead in the water.

"I'm sorry I lied. I was just trying to get through without any complications."

"Here's what I'm going to do. I'm going to make an announcement to the entire airport, summoning the rest of your band to return to customs and help you straighten out this mess. If they come back, I'm sure we can work it out. If they do not, I'm putting you on the next plane back to Los Angeles."

The agent left the room, leaving Jack to wait it out. After a while, he returned, brow furrowed.

"Bad news, Jack. Your buddies left you high and dry. You're going back to L.A."

Jack was ushered onto the next available flight to LAX. When he got home, he was unable to reach the rest of the band, who had somehow gotten through customs and elected not to go back and take accountability for the visa blunder. Jack decided to buy a new flight on his own nickel and fly right back to London again. He'd miss the first couple shows, but he wouldn't miss the whole tour. It goes without saying that he was a bit pissed off at the rest of the band.

He made it to Heathrow again, this time with the proper work visa, and eventually rendezvoused with the rest of Nuclei, somewhere in Europe. The band's keyboardist was the first to greet him.

"Hey man, you made it," he said.

"Yeah. It was a real nightmare."

"I know, bro. We totally would have come back for you, but we took a vote and decided it would be best if we kept cruising. We figured you'd eventually catch up with us. Way to take one for the team, Jack. You're a real trooper. *High five...*"

The White Man's Jig

After playing bars, clubs and wedding reception halls for over twenty years, I've made many observations about human nature. Yes, I've learned a great deal by watching people of all ages, colors and creeds interact in festive settings. Having amassed all this experience, there is one burning question I have... one puzzle whose answer still eludes me. I'm hoping you, reader, can help me with this:

WHY ARE MEN SUCH SHITTY DANCERS?

What is it that makes women dance so much better than men? Why is it that the average woman, even if she is terribly out of shape, moves so much more gracefully and effortlessly than her average male counterpart? I myself am a bad dancer. I know I'm not good at it, and I've managed to put together a few basic, humble moves over the years that I can count on if summoned, against my will, to the dance floor — little steps, gestures and bullshit arm movements that will allow me to at least get by, and avoid being that anti-social jerk who refuses to get off his rump and go with the program.

It's not guys like me that are annoying. The guys that fall into my category — the *I can't dance but I'm out here doing my best, trying to be a good sport* male dancer category — are sympathetic to each other's predicament. We see each other doing the white man's jig, while our lady is effortlessly busting crazy-ass hip-hop moves in perfect rhythm, and we have an unspoken understanding: *Hey man, way to hang tough. This sucks, but hey, gotta keep everyone happy, right?*

Guys like us minimize the damage by staying mellow and controlled, sticking with the few rudimentary moves we know we can pull off without looking like a spaz/douchebag. We don't dance, really... we kind of waddle back and forth, snapping our fingers here and there, silently singing along even though we don't know the lyrics. We're miserable out there, self-conscious of every calculated twitch and spasm, but we pretend we're enjoying ourselves. *Cool vibe in here, baby. I'm having a nice time tonight.*

Women know that dancing is their domain. All you have to do is look at the expressions on their faces to realize that women are in their element, completely in control, on the dance floor. Yeah, I'm sexy, I'm uninhibited, I have rhythm, and I *own this shit.* Not the case for ninety-eight percent of the men out there. Most of us men, when forced into this most uncomfortable of environments, are simply trying to not look like a complete moron.

I say most men, because, excluding the two percent who actually are good dancers, there is a minority of males who take a different approach. They suck just as bad as the rest of us, if not worse, but instead of downplay their inteptitude, they try to distract from it by overcompensating; they get out there and bust awkward, unnatural moves: strange gyrations, thrusts, spins, weird, schizophrenic arm swings, and of course plenty of goofy, fun-loving faces intended to say, *I'm a carefree, crazy kinda guy!* These guys think people are watching them thinking, "That Bob… what a quirky, zany character. He sure lives life to the fullest." What people are really thinking is, "What the hell is Bob doing out there? Does he know how bad he looks? I mean, I've seen some lousy male dancers, but he's off the charts. Somebody should do something."

Being a veteran of too many club gigs and receptions to count, where my musical cohorts and I have suffered through many a miserable dance performance, almost invariably involving the male species, I would like to offer the following advice to all men out there: If and when you are forced out onto a dance floor against your will, resist the temptation to be quirky and offbeat. Resist the belief that if you jump around like a schizophrenic nut case, trying to approximate tricks you saw mullet-sporting Kevin Bacon pull off twenty years ago in *Footloose,* or Patrick Swayze in *Dirty Dancing,* people are going to think you're the life of the party. You've heard that saying: *forget what people think… just dance!* Bad advice, guys. Don't embarrass yourself unnecessarily. Either tone it down and keep a low profile… stay off the radar by remaining chill and self-controlled… or, and this might be the better choice, just take the position of my dad Len—no Gene Kelly, and well aware of it—and inform people, when they're trying to drag you out there to flail around while some wanker DJ blasts an annoying techno remix five times louder than it needs to be: *Sorry. I don't dance.*

Cheat Your Way to a Great G.P.A.!

During my first year at SDSU, I had a political science course in which the teacher was an elderly man named Professor Crumb. Along with most of the other students, I viewed the course as somewhat of a joke. Professor Crumb stammered on and on, to the point that a couple guys began bringing the newspaper to class, brazenly perusing the sports page during the lecture. Old Man Crumb got wise to this eventually, and stopped his soporific spiel to bicker, "I can't imagine why you'd think it's perfectly okay to read the newspaper during my class."

It was one of the courses where you're supposed to be keeping some kind of running journal every week, in this case a chronicle of current events. I completely blew this off for most of the semester, thinking I'd just slap something together a couple nights before the whole thing was due. The problem with this strategy was that I made a mistake writing down the deadline. I showed up for class one day thinking I still had some time, and Professor Crumb announced, "Please put your final journal project on my desk today before leaving class." *Oh shit. How am I going to weasel out of this one?* I walked to the front of the room at the end of the class, a nervous grin on my face.

"Hey Professor... how's it going?"

"Fine. What can I do for you?"

"Well, I kind of made a mistake in my planning. I need some extra time to get my final assignment to you."

"You've had all semester. I haven't even been assigning any other work. What have you been doing?"

"I'm taking a pretty heavy load right now. I'm kind of swamped." Professor Crumb was entirely unmoved, and suddenly not seeming like a doddering old man.

"You're not going to pass the class without your journal, and I'm not inclined to grant an extension." I walked out of there bummed. All I had to do was jot down some weekly crap about current events, and I would have skated through the class with a good grade. But I had blown it. I resigned myself to getting a crummy grade, maybe even failing, and moved on.

The following week, when finals were over and teachers were compiling their grades, I got an unexpected phone call. I recognized the voice on the other end.

"Hello, Anthony? This is Professor Crumb from San Diego State."

"Oh, yes. How are you, Professor?"

"Okay, except that I have a bit of a problem."

"What's that?"

"I can't find your final project... your weekly journal. I must have misplaced it somehow."

You can't find it because I didn't turn it in, buddy.

"Oh, that's a shame. What are you going to do?"

"Well, can you tell me what grade I gave you?"

Are you serious? You're asking what grade you gave me? Pinch me, I'm dreaming. I'm sorry for what I'm about to admit. It doesn't say much for my moral fiber at age twenty. It does, however, say a great deal about my understanding of how the world works, and my ability to embrace the Malcom X school of getting ahead in life: *by any means necessary...*

"Uh... let's see... you know, Professor Crumb, I'm pretty sure you gave me a B+ for the final project."

"B+, you say?"

"Yep."

"Okay, well, nice work. Looks like you've got an A- in the class. Have a good summer."

"You too, sir. Have yourself a wonderful summer."

I pose the question to you, reader: Put yourself in my shoes. What would you have done? Would you have admitted that you didn't turn in the work, knowing you'd fail the class and have to take it all over again? Makes for quite the moral dilemma, doesn't it.

I Heard Comp, Not Cap

One of the perks of being a touring musician is the free stuff people give you, because they think musicians are cool—or they are affiliated with a venue where you're performing, and thus feel obligated to try and make you happy. This hospitality can take the form of numerous things, but the ones musicians tend to appreciate the most are food and drink. When it comes to meals and bar tabs, the magic word is *comp*. When I discovered that we were being fed *and* given a generous bar tab at a given show, I would walk back over to the guys in the band with a smile on my face and say: "I heard comp, not cap."

The following is an illustration of *comp* being completely abused. My band was playing a wedding for a good friend, in the Lake Tahoe area. This friend had generously helped the band in the past with merchandise and other things, but for his wedding we weren't being paid a whole lot. I realized this was fair, given his previous largesse, but the other guys were kind of bugged about it. Thus, when the friend told us, after we'd soundchecked, to go to the hotel's (fancy) restaurant, get a table and order whatever we wanted, everyone's eyes lit up.

It was a fairly large band, maybe seven or eight people. We got our table and everyone immediately ordered wine; and when I say ordered wine, I mean everyone ordered their own bottle. One guy took a small sip, spit it out and demanded a new bottle. It reminded me of the crusty old Mafia boss in that scene in *Mulholland Drive,* regurgitating the espresso which has failed to meet his exacting standards.

Rather than pick one appetizer from the extensive menu, every guy ordered at least three. Then when it was time to decide on entrees, everyone ordered two or three of those, too. There wasn't enough room on the table for all the food and bottles.

Nervous that we might be abusing our host's generosity, I left the table and found him. "Hey, man, we're going kind of crazy at dinner. Do you want me to tone it down?"

"No, no! Have anything and everything. Don't sweat it. Whatever you guys want." I returned to the table, gave a thumbs up, and the gluttony continued. After a small mountain of dinner plates had been cleared, and everyone was sitting around in a state of food-induced lethargy, our cocktail waiter—not to be confused with our personal *sommelier*—stopped by to ask if we would care for an after-dinner *digestif.*[107]

"Of course," everyone said, almost in unison. By now, the bill must have been inching its way toward a grand, but we had a green light... why stop now? The server made his way around the table taking everyone's drink order. Finally, it was my turn.

---

[107] An after-dinner drink designed to relax the stomach after a heavy meal.

"I'll be having Courvoisier," I said with smug confidence, as if I dined regularly in such elegant establishments, and not in various Burger Kings and Der Wienerschnitzels scattered around the country.

"Very good, sir. May I point out that we carry two types of Courvoisier. The regular brand… and the XO brand." He directed my attention to the page on the cocktail menu dedicated to top-shelf items. The Courvoisier XO being offered was a special, extra-aged cognac with a ridiculous price of sixty bucks a taste, or something like that.

"Have you made a choice, sir?" I looked back up at the guy and said with a straight face, "Do I look like I drink regular Courvoisier?"

"No sir, absolutely not."

"Bring me the XO."

"Absolutely, sir." Once the server was out of earshot, the whole table broke out in laughter.

I heard comp, not cap.

Bridging the Racial Divide

KD3 Tour, 4:02 pm 10/28/06, Virginia/North Carolina border

Sighting of a black man walking into McDonald's wearing a vest patterned after the Confederate Flag. Now there's a man doing his part to bridge the racial divide in America. That's a truly progressive American.

Too Much Stuff on My Pizza

I come from a family of entrepreneurs. My mother Anne has multiple siblings, and each of them has gone into business for himself at one time or another. A few years back, two of my mom's brothers, David and Charles, decided to open a pizzeria in Sacramento, California. They did their due diligence researching the many elements that go into creating and managing a restaurant, and ultimately launched Pop's Pizza, operating out of a rented space in a strip mall.

The place had been open for a while when I finally got the chance to stop in, say hello and sample the pizza, which I'd heard was very good. My cousin Tyson and I were driving our grandmother, Lulu, to her house in a small town called Mt. Aukumn, and decided to pop in at Pop's, unannounced.

The three of us walked in and were greeted by our uncles David and Charles, and also David's sons Ben and Andy, our cousins. It was a real family operation. Everyone was happy to see Grandma Lulu, and David wasted no time preparing a pizza for his mother and two nephews. The place was crowded, which made us happy. Word had spread in the local area, and Pop's Pizza was doing well in its first year.

After a few minutes, David, who stands six-foot-five and is built like a former NFL lineman, proudly walked over and placed a hot, fresh pizza on our table.

"This is what I call The Works. Hope you like it." Tyson and I eagerly dug in, but Grandma Lulu took a closer, suspicious look at her son's culinary creation.

"What's wrong, Mom?" David asked.

"There's an awful lot of stuff on this pizza," she noted.

"That's why it's called The Works. I need to get back to the kitchen. Enjoy." David left us and we started chowing. The pizza was delicious. Yes, there were a number of toppings liberally sprinkled throughout the pie, but it was a very tasty pizza. Tyson and I noticed that Lulu was shaking her head, not happy. Suddenly she called out to the kitchen, in earshot of all the restaurant's patrons.

"David…" David stopped what he was doing and looked over at us. "Yeah, mom?"

"There's too much stuff on this pizza."

"So pick off what you don't want."

"I don't want to pick anything off. I want a pizza that has the right amount of stuff on it." Tyson and I started quietly chuckling, as David made his way back over to our table. Our uncle took the opportunity to share his mission statement with the entire pizzeria.

"When Charlie and I first came up with the idea for Pop's Pizza, we agreed on one important thing. Let me tell you what that was. I was so sick and tired of going out for pizza, only to be disappointed by the amount of topping, whether it was pepperoni or mushrooms or peppers. I decided that my pizza place would be different. You might walk out of Pop's Pizza saying, 'You know, there sure was a lot of stuff on my pizza.' But you know what you will never walk out of Pop's Pizza saying? 'There wasn't enough stuff on my pizza.'" Lulu took a minute to finish chewing her bite of overpopulated pizza and find the right words. She wiped her mouth and said, "Well congratulations,

David. You certainly accomplished your goal. There's way too much stuff on this pizza."

Tyson and I howled with laughter. When we were done eating, Lulu walked to the cash register and pulled out her wallet. Her grandson, our cousin Andy, shook his head.

"Hey Dad, Grandma's trying to *pay* for her pizza. Can you believe that?" David, however, saw an opportunity to settle the score.

"She's trying to pay?"

"Yeah."

"Great. Ring her up."

I have a colorful family.

Exciting New English Words and Phrases

It's rare that you hear an exciting new English word or phrase that makes its way into the lexicon and somehow sticks. My wife and I have the fortune of knowing someone who has coined not one such example, but several. The first of these gems was revealed as follows: Our friend, who we'll call Linda, saw that Teena, my wife, had a splitting headache. She handed her a bottle of painkillers and said, "Here, honey… pop a couple of these ibu-proteins. You'll feel better in no time."

On another occasion, Linda and I were engaged in one of the quasi-philosophical conversations you have with someone in your kitchen, when you're just trying to pass the time. I was offering up some tired cliché about taking life as it comes, when Linda really hit it out of the park: "I hear you. No matter what challenges you face, you've just gotta learn to take everything with the greatest of salt."

On yet another occasion, I came home and Linda was sitting on the living room couch. Teena was upstairs working, and I could smell that she'd been doing some Indian cooking earlier, using lentils and various spices. Linda saw me sniffing and said, "She's been making them lentos again."

I offer one final example of Linda's humorous challenges with the English language. One day Linda showed up to babysit our kids, and was obviously in a bad mood. I asked her what was wrong. She shook her head and answered: "My husband got real mad at me today. He went to buy a new computer on credit, but I had maxed out his card, and so…"

She paused for dramatic effect.

"… his credit card was… *reclined.*"

Steve Francis and the Special Shoes

If you have read from the beginning of this book, you'll recall the author's passage about African-Amercian athletic prowess. I argued that while yes, blacks dedicate their lives to the game of basketball from an early age, and have the motivation (in some cases at least) of greatly desiring to rise above challenging life circumstances and make it to the NBA, where they will enjoy wealth and fame, this is not the only factor which explains professional basketball's majority-black demographic. No, I contended, we must also acknowledge that African-American athletes tend to possess certain natural advantages, such as a higher concentration of fast-twitch muscles and otherwise superior physical ability—running faster and jumping higher and more explosively, for example.

When I was arguing this point back in those days, I would often use myself, a Caucasian, hard-working athlete in my youth, as an example to defend my position. I would explain how as a teenager I had worn these special "jumping shoes" which I'd ordered from some catalog—shoes which put your foot at an upward angle, forcing the calf muscles to stretch and, at least in theory, increasing your jumping ability. I wore the shoes day after day, month after month, and nothing really changed in terms of my vertical leaping prowess. I concluded that "you either got it or you don't." I would quip, "I don't think (former NBA guard) Steve Francis wore some special shoes to acquire his forty-inch vertical jump. That's just ridiculous."

Steve Francis seemed like a good example to use, because he was
  A) African-American
  B) An incredible leaper
  C) He made it look effortless, like he was born to do it.

Anyway, there's the essence of the argument. Fast forward many years, and I'm in my thirties, on the road somewhere along the East Coast. I'm in some bar, playing a gig with my touring jam band, and I get into a discussion between sets with some random guy. We start talking about basketball. Somehow, whose name comes up? Steve Francis. I mention how great the guy is, and what a natural athlete. The guy says… I'm not making this up… "Yeah, I went to high school with Steve. He used to work his ass off to be a better athlete, all the time."

"Really? What kind of stuff would he do?"

"Well, he practiced all the time. And he had these special shoes. They put your foot at an angle, and they were supposed to make you jump higher. Steve used to wear those things for *hours* every day. Guy was really determined."

So much for my theory.

I COULD GET USED TO
YOUR BACTERIA

Quotes, Quips and Conversational Tidbits from the Trenches

As a touring musician, I tended to hang around colorful people who said funny things. The following words are the product of many thousands of travel miles. Some came from the mouths of those in my immediate circle of friends and peers, and others came from random strangers. A few also originated from the flapping gums of your humble author.

Sexual experimentation:
It's like jamming a solo. Every now and then, you gotta take it way out there.

Having your own teeth. There's nothing quite like it.
-Pock8

The generation gap:
You're not my elder. You're just old.

Left-hand compliments:
For some reason, you look handsome this morning.

I don't think anymore... I just use the Internet instead.
-Pock8

I'm the Stephen Hawking of jazz.
-Fareed Haque

You're right, Todd, the band has really been neglecting the retarded demographic. That's a market we should be capitalizing on.
-Wildman

Bitch, you just ran over my foot with your car. Now you gonna catch up with an old friend?
-Walt Williams

Yeah, I realize you're having a seizure right now. I see the foam oozing from your mouth. But did I not tell you to stop drinking? Peace, I'm out.
-Anonymous

Look at her. You see how beautiful she is? What makes you think I wanna talk to *your* dumb ass?
-Karl Denson

Women just ain't funny.
-Karl Denson

Golf:
Just hit the damn ball already. If it goes in, great. If it doesn't, say fuck it and move on to the next hole.

Measurements:
We've certainly got length covered. Now all we need is some girth.

Making dates in bars:
I can see setting that up when you're drunk at three in the morning... but to actually follow through with it the next day? That's mind boggling.

Hanging out with the guys:
What kind of pussy orders French onion soup in a sports bar?

Patience:
I don't mind waiting. As long as there's some eventual having.

Saying goodbye:
She was basically breaking up with me, and I was basically saying "That sounds great."

Short-lived flings:
It was a one hit wonder. I hit it once, then I wondered why.

Sharing close quarters:
Your bowels are *your* business. Please don't make them mine.

The mentally challenged:
I'd rather have him tearing my ticket at the multiplex than drooling on my hamburger.

Loyalty:
I was there for you in the beginning, I was there for you in the middle, and just a heads up… I'm gonna take off in the end.

Motor home hygiene:
It's either you or someone very close to you that stinks.

A concert experience:
These guys are good. It's really loud, plus they let you get hammered in here.

The East Coast:
It's hard to feel hip when you're in South Carolina.

The other half:
I find that the best way to deal with corporate people is to mock them and insult their intelligence.

Advanced physics:
Rocks are heavy.

Last words you hear before getting your ass kicked in Texas:
So, you fellas in some kinda little band or somethin'?

The thinning of the herd:
After 2, fat chicks gonna have to do.

Diplomacy:
You're the only one I have to keep happy. Everyone else can screw off and go to hell.

Advanced business strategy:
When it comes down to it, this is the thing, and I want to make this real clear... I'd rather make three dollars than two.

Being a non-morning person:
Jesus, you look like somebody kicked you in the head.

Community service:
Seeing all these people recycling makes me feel better about not doing it myself.

Striking out:
I listened to her whole life story… for *nothing.*

Thinking too much:
Stupidity is a form of therapy.

Deep thoughts:
It's really hard to feel inspiration sometimes. Especially when you try and you try, but when it comes down to it you're just not inspired.

Wimpy music:
Don't get me wrong, man. I didn't mean to insult your music. I think it's the perfect song to change your tampon to.

Questionable musical guests:
My grandma's a nice guy too, but you don't see me bringing *her* up onstage.

Healthy diets and vitamins:
Why's everybody so into longevity these days? What's the big deal?

Annoying people:
It's better to be aloof than to be a fool.

Navigation:
Out of Washington D.C., the roads are laid out very logically. You can go any direction other than north, east or west… and you're guaranteed to be heading south.

Settling an account:
Which one of y'all is the big dick around here?

Being remembered:
I realized today that I better start making some friends, or my funeral's really going to suck.

Destiny:
If I wasn't living here, there's just no way I would have been here to meet you at this time.

Antiquity:
I saw Louis Armstrong's first trumpet at the Smithsonian. It looked really old, because, you know, he started playing at a very young age.

Culinary subtleties:
What the hell are you doing? You can't microwave hummus!

Mechanical savvy:
Hello, people! It's a *twelve bolt* battery. Count 'em: One, two, three…

Beverages:
I wish water tasted like Coke. That would be awesome. People would think you were living healthy, but to *you* it would seem like you were drinking Coke, which would be better.

Working with the autistic:
I love those people, and I love my job. I really do. But I count my blessings I don't have to come home to any of them.
Observation:
Forgive me, but do I detect a hint of condensation in your tone?

Sibling duty:
At my brother's graduation ceremony, the speeches were long and awful, so it was more like a *gragitation* ceremony.

Family parties:
Thank you so, so much. It's so rare to come to one of these family events and have a conversation of significance.

Conflicting agendas:
Put me on a lake during the summer, barbecuing, fishing and watching the sunset. I'll live in a tent and I'll be one happy dude. My wife, now that's another story. She's not gonna leave the big house on the other side of the lake.

The morning after:
How'd she look in the light, you ask? Let me tell you... Like she needed to get back into the dark.

Cleanliness and kindness:
I'm just a much more compassionate person when I shower.

Guys waiting for a free toilet:
Hurry up, dude. I think my water just broke.

Meeting that someone special:
She didn't smell too bad for a jogger.

Breaking it gently:
I've got some bad news, and some more *really* bad news. The bad news is, the Celtics were getting the crap kicked out of them at halftime. The really bad news is that after that, they eventually lost.

The shortcomings of a certain white wine:
I ain't gonna lie, bro. This isn't the best Merlot I ever tasted.

Word choice:
When you've started to use the *f word* as a conjunction, it's time to clean up your language.

Sizing up an RV mechanic:
Once I heard his shitkicker country accent, I knew we were in good hands.

Classroom etiquette:
I was a teacher for eight years, and I never once cursed in front of the fucking children.

Roots:
I was born in New York. My first word was *fuck* and my second word was *you asshole.*

Parents calling the classroom from their cellphones:
Are you kidding me? Park your goddamn Range Rover and walk your ass in here, soccer mom!

Deep thoughts:
As long as you tell the whole truth, you'll never, ever lie.

Left-handed compliments:
I happen to think you're pretty talented. But truthfully, I don't know shit.

Exercise:
If you're sucking wind after a quick game of air hockey, it's time to hit the treadmill.

The road:
You're gonna get sick of *anyone* after that much time together. Even God.

Sex and animals:
Is it asking too much that you keep your dog out of the room while we're having sex?

Sex and animals:
Let him watch. Maybe he'll learn something.

Sex and animals:
Better yet, let's have him jump in and I'll watch for a while. Then maybe *I'll* learn something.

Song titles:
Come On Irene? It's actually *Come On Eileen.* You've been hanging out in Chinese karaoke bars too long.

Tolerance:
Is there someplace I can go to hide, before another idiot materializes to regale me with useless gibberish?

Food:
Sometimes you can just look at a piece of bread and know it's going to be awesome.

Differences:
Some people have so little in common that even a horrible addiction like cigarette smoking has no bonding effect.

Attempting to identify a black actor in the 007 film, Die Another Day:
Please, God. Don't let that be Snoop Dogg.

Finding that special someone:
I'd say something, and, get this... she'd counter with something intelligible. Can you believe it?

Under-appreciation:
You're giving me the runaround, when you should be giving me the *reach around.*

Undesired houseguests:
This guy's a good musician. He deserves to be here. *You* just wanna lay on my fouton, dude.

Picking up quality women:
As you're aware, it's all relative to your particular degree of desperation.

Bathroom inspiration:
I'd have to say that while I'm sitting there in the morning, some of the greatest stuff comes out.

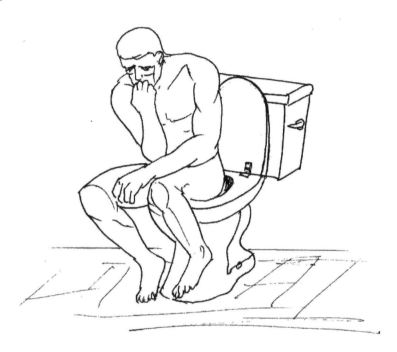

Observation:
One thing I realize is that you see lots of interesting stuff, just being alive.

Musical ambition:
I'll open up for Ass on a Plate, if it's good exposure.

Materialism and Valentine's Day:
If you like hangin' with someone, shit, just tell 'em. Do you really need chocolates?

Bisexuality:

I don't understand it. What you're saying is, "I'll screw anything that walks." So, does that include farm animals? *They* walk...

Getting jilted:

You develop a thick skin over the years from women screwing you over. In that sense, I'm kind of like a dragon.

Intellectual prowess:

The thing with me is, I get bored really easily. It takes a lot to hold my attention. That's why I watch soap operas.

Reaching a younger audience:

I can't tell you how happy I'm going to be, playing in front of a crowd that's not ninety and sharing teeth.

Joining the band and jumping on the road:
Thanks for the opportunity, guys. So at what point are we going to, like, bathe?

Laying it down in the studio:
I told you, I'm playing it safe in here, man. I'm not trying to get my juices off.

Collaboration:
I'll have to give you credit for that. Unless, of course, it makes money, in which case I'll deny your involvement completely.

Scoring:
He's a product of the Malcolm X School of Getting Laid. *By any means necessary.*

Musical knowledge:
If there's one thing I bring to the table every time, it's my ignorance.

Limitations:
Yeah, sure, it's possible. Just not by me.

Losing a parking space to a handicapped citizen:
Oh, that's just great. That's just fucking great! He's got those goddamn gimp tags!

Female flute players:
Forget about what, when or how to play. She didn't know *why* to play.

The realities of a musician:
So, are you actually living somewhere these days?

Work ethic:
Retirement is wasted on the old.

Performance evaluation:
There are some definite questions as to what the fuck you're doing around here.

The miracle of birth:
I kept getting these phone calls from my mother about my sister's labor, and I would answer them... out of courtesy.

Bad trombone playing:
You sound like a garbage truck with a flat tire.

Burn out:
I've been around so much horseshit, it doesn't even stink anymore.

A romantic conquest in the Rockies:
Looks like our friend Steve scored himself a snow hag.

Progress:
I wasn't very good then, and I'm not very good now, but I'm sure a lot better than I was back then.

Customer service:
I want to make sure you're happy here. If I have to coddle you, if I have to stroke your balls… just say the word. That's what I'm prepared to do.

Thin walls:
You sounded like you were wrestling a bear in there, man.

Carrot-dangling:
If that pie ever actually makes it out of the oven, there's going to be a big slice with your name on it, my man.

Memory:
I was about to open my mouth and say something stupid, but I lost my train of thought.

Beer:
Man, beer is like the best thing ever… because you need it, and it's always there.

Equipment:
I thought the keyboards worked well tonight. Not the broken one so much, but the other ones that were working okay to begin with.

Bad musicians:
Let's face it. He couldn't play shit if I sat him on the pot.
-Uncle Joe Gallagher

Frustration:
Just a heads up, guys… One of these days, I'm going to punch my fist through that thing, and there's gonna be blood everywhere, and it's not going to be good.

Racial generalizations:
Gosh, black people are fast, huh?

Drinking:
Somewhere in between that fourth or fifth Captain and Coke, my commitment to fashion went out the window.

Aging:
Nobody looks good in their fifties.

The chain of command:
Here's how it works. You're the colonel, I'm the captain, and he's the dumb-ass.

Poorly recorded Phish bootlegs:
I'm not saying you have to turn it off. I'm just saying that listening to it makes me want to pick up a sledgehammer and cave somebody's head in.

Henry Rollins's tedious prose:
I'm getting tired of reading the same contradictory shit from this miserable schmuck.

Afternoon boozing:
You say it's time for sound check? Fine, but why should that stop this gentleman from pouring me another cocktail?

Advice about dating a madam:
I understand your concern, but I don't think you should make any rash decisions until you've entertained at least a few of her employees.

Inside the RV:
I woke up wanting some hot breakfast, but instead I got some breath-ass.
-the Mayor

Mark my words. They're gonna make a mortar out of this guy.
-Little Jesus

White people infiltrating the hood:
He look like dat nigga Bono!

Touring:
I don't want to be high maintenance, but I've had to piss since Indiana.

Being self-taught:
I can *hear* that you haven't had any lessons, asshole. You don't need to brag about it.

Dating:
You know, I've been thinking… I could get used to your bacteria.

More on aging:
By sixty, everybody looks like shit.

Eloquent Metaphors:
Rehearsing is kind of like taking a dump. You know you're done when the paper starts coming up clean. You know you're done rehearsing when there aren't any more stains left on the songs.

Drinking:
It's good to have vodka. It's good to have a friend in life.

Drinking:
If you're in it for the vodka, you're definitely in it for the right reasons.

Nobody wants to watch some drunk guy playing keyboards.
-Hank Easton

I'll allow you to continue your train of thought for now. If at any point you want to hear the actual truth, let me know.
-Joe Cahill

When someone is willing to sign away their rights to an entire album of music for five nuggets in a plastic bag, you probably don't have to worry about things like copyright infringement lawsuits.
-Your author

Inside the RV:
It's one thing to break wind. It's another thing to not have matches.

Drive us to drink? I think we've proven we don't need to be driven to drink. Hell, we can bike there.
-Joe Cahill

I'd really love to hang with you guys, but I've got to sit in the hotel and write horn arrangements for this French dude named Cornelius.
-Karl Denson

For that kind of money, you can take your fookin' band to the Sports Arena!
-Owner of an Irish pub in San Diego

Hospitality:
I heard *comp,* not cap.

You wanna make things right? Then I need to hear a please, a sorry and a thank you, all in the same sentence.
-Joe Cahill

Is there a Telluride law against parking with your lights on? No? Then piss off.
-Joe Cahill

TV:
With Springer, there's a lot more than meets the eye. You gotta read between the lines. You gotta *look beneath the surface.*

TV:
I watch Jerry Springer because it makes me very happy about my life.

Groupies:
As fine as you girls are, I just want to let you know in advance that I won't remember any of you the next time I see you.
-Karl Denson

We sat in a van, drank gallons of Captain Morgan rum, and did terrible things to terrible people.
-Orlando Stout

I need to be able to maintain eye contact with you onstage at all times, so I can shoot you dirty looks when you make mistakes.
-Your author

Every day is New Year's Eve to *me*, brother.
-Hal Cabrera

There's not much left in the... what do you call that thing? Oh yeah...
the time sand jar.
-Vin Barerra

What's the big deal? Every city has a Liberty Bell.
-Vin Barerra

I put the moves on a priest last night. You would have been proud of
me.
-Todd Sherman

I don't mind workin' for free. But every now and then I gotta do
somethin' for *me*.
-Bradshaw

It's a short fall from green to jaded.
-Woo

I covet your George Foreman grill. It's way bigger than mine.
-Little John Chrisley

You open your mouth, and music comes out. Or it doesn't.
-Ann Williams

Positivity:
In this life you have to keep looking forward, not backwards, but let's face it... is there really that much to look forward to?

Finding a polite way to say "no":
Well, thanks for thinking of me. I'm open to talking about it.
-Pock8

Ever since my iguana took a crap on my Roland D-50 keyboard, middle C plays louder than the rest of the notes. It's the strangest thing.
-Little John Chrisley

For some reason, whenever I'm having kinky sex, my iguana starts freaking out and climbs on the woman's back. What should I do?
-Little John Chrisley

Sometimes when you're out with your girlfriends, you don't want answers. You just want to bitch and complain about stuff.
-Pock8

It's very hard to get lesbians to part with their money.
-Kat Danser

The fact of the matter is this: You just don't have any clout in the state of Idaho.
-Lunabelle Frost

It's not every day you see a nun aggressively driving a Hummer.
-Your Author

You know your day's not going well when you're wasting multiple hours trying to track down some flaky asshole in Pocatello, Idaho.
-Lunabelle Frost

I replaced the swastikas on my forearm, from back in my Arian supremacist days, with a large purple dildo. That way, every time I look at my arm, I remember how stupid I was back then.
-Anonymous tattoo artist in Moscow, ID

Please don't hold me personally accountable for the ferret, which at the current time is regrettably unaccounted for.
-Anonymous

Self-Effacing Honesty:
I repulse women. They find me grotesquely unattractive.
-Bill Shreeve

Variations on a theme:

How much longer are you going to be working on this book?

Can you move on to something else soon?

What are you editing *now?*

You need closure on this project, and you need it very soon.

I need closure on this project.

ARE YOU FREAKIN' DONE YET???

-My wife

Natural born leader.

Demonstrating an early flair for the dramatic.

Boxing lesson with Dad.

With Dad and my Sister
Paula.

Early Days in NorCal.

With Grandpa Ormsby, a lifelong entrepenuer.

With Grandpa Smith (Baba), a career musican/keyboardist who always encouraged my musical pursuits.

TimesTribune
BOYS
ATHLETE OF THE WEEK

Anthony Smith
Mitty, basketball

Anthony, a senior, led the Monarchs to two victories in the Fremont tournament by scoring 54 points, rebounding well and playing excellent defense.

High school basketball glory days.

All-league basketball team

BOYS

De Anza Athletic League

First team

Most valuable player — Ron Reis, Monta Vista.

Name	Position	School
Enrique Cebildo	Guard	Fremont
Matt Chavez	Guard	Lynbrook
Steve Robinson	Center	Fremont
Matt Romig	Forward	Cupertino
Curt Siwek	Forward	Monta Vista

Second team

Name	Position	School
Greg Fujii	Guard	Homestead
Kevin Kraft	Guard	Saratoga
Chris Senkeresty	Center	Lynbrook
Jack Slavik	Forward	Monta Vista
Brett Thorp	Forward	Cupertino

Honorable mention

Matt Bokemeier (Homestead); Jim Burns (Lynbrook); Steve Daetz (Homestead); Dan Haughton (Cupertino); Lance Kameda (Fremont); John Nora (Saratoga).

Peninsula Athletic League

First team

Most valuable player — Eric Williams, San Mateo.

Name	Position	School
Eric Williams	Forward	San Mateo
Craig Henderson	Guard	San Mateo
Tony Sylvestri	Guard	Capuchino
Denard White	Guard	Menlo-Atherton
Gary Lundgren	Guard	Hillsdale

Second team

Name	Position	School
Atiba Williams	Center	Menlo-Atherton
Cedric Reed	Guard	Menlo-Atherton
Kendric Reed	Guard	Menlo-Atherton
Doug Stewart	Forward	San Mateo
Marcus Turner	Guard	Woodside

Santa Clara Valley League

First team

Most valuable player — Lindsay Pettis, Milpitas.

Name	Position	School
Lindsay Pettis	Center	Milpitas
Derrick Parmer	Forward	Wilcox

Joey Taylor	Forward	Gunn
Matt Magee	Center	Palo Alto
Jeremy Everett	Guard	Santa Clara
Darrin Connolly	Forward	Milpitas

Second team

Name	Position	School
Leo Johnson	Guard	Los Altos
Greg Imahara	Guard	Wilcox
Todd Smith	Center	Gunn
Dan Filer	Guard	Gunn
John Dietz	Forward	Mountain View
Troy Prather	Forward	Milpitas

Honorable mention

LaRon Johnson (Palo Alto), Jim Marchant (Gunn), tom Cheli (Los Altos), Joe Vu (Milpitas), Peter Chmyz (Palo Alto).

West Catholic League

First team

Most valuable player — Wayman Strickland, Riordan.

Name	Position	School
Wayman Strickland	Guard	Riordan
Anthony Smith	Forward	Mitty
John Brown	Guard	Sacred Heart
Darren Brown	Forward	St. Francis
Vince Manfreda	Center	Sacred Heart
Mike Flohr	Guard	Bellarmine

Second team

James Jackson	Forward	Serra
Mike King	Guard	St. Ignatius
Damon Pierson	Guard	St. Ignatius
Tony Gillette	Forward	Serra
Lance Roehl	Forward	St. Francis

Honorable mention

David Benton (Riordan), Troy LeBlanc (Riordan), Cas Banaszek (Serra), Jason Stamps (Serra), Shanan Rosenberg (St. Francis), Jay Webb (Mitty), Ray Kelly (Riordan), Greg Walker (Bellarmine), Greg Paulson (St. Francis), Casey Courneen (Bellarmine), Derrek Mason (Mitty), William Young (Serra).

GIRLS

De Anza Athletic League

First team

First team All W.C.A.L., the same league that produced Barry Bonds Jr., Tom Brady, and many other world class atheletes.

Senior year at Archbisop Mitty High School in San Jose, CA (1988).

Starring in "Picnic" opposite female lead Kassie Broyles (play directed by Len).

My cat Bobby, named after jazz great Bobby Hutcherson.

With my brother Collin. Guess which one is the athlete and which one is the musician?

With Mom and Step Dad Terry in Santa Cruz, early nineties.

My first orginal band, Fried Bananas (Jamey Byers, Jordan Dalrymple, me and Adrian Ahearn).

Publicity shot for Blueprint, my jazz quartet with (from left) Richard Sellers, Prince Board, Mike Blanco and me.

In the studio, making a jazz record with Richard Sellers, Rob Thorsen and Brian Lynch.

Posing and jamming with La Vibra, a Latin jazz all-star group (from left): Chuck Prada, Lynn Willard, Tim McMahon, me, Kevin Hennessy and Hank Easton.

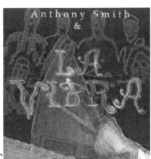 

Album art for two creative projects I was particularly proud of.

Cult of Soul publicity shot "trying to look tough." Vocalist Damion Willis on far right.

Celebrating my 30th birthday with my mom Anne in San Diego.

The effect I have on people.

Hitting the road in 2000.

Jam band festival somewhere in the Northwest.

Making funny faces at the Fox Theater in Boulder, CO.

Early shot with Karl Denson in Boise, ID. David Veith on my left. I would later tour with Karl in KD3.

Showing off the new album, Keep on Pushin', on board the infamous "Travesty."

My friend and keyboard roadie, the one and only Ricky "Little Jesus" Perkins.

Global Funk Council inaugural gig at Dizzy's in San Diego. Let the madness begin.

With my wife Teena: early dating days in Manteca, CA (the halfway point between San Francisco and Merced).

Relaxing with Dad Len and Step Mom Ann in Rancho Bernado, CA in between tours.

Rocking the turban in New Delhi, India.

On tour with KD3, guess where?

My pilgrimage to the mecca of rock: Stonehenge!!

At the San Diego Zoo with my sister Paula.

Publicity for "Life As We Know It," released on Terresterial Records.

The happy family man.

With The Mighty Untouchables in San Diego.

Posing at home with my vibraphone mallets.

DANCING AROUND THE HOUSE NAKED

I gathered my things and moved back to San Diego, where I was certain of at least one thing: I would find plenty of work playing music. Gilbert Castellanos used a B-3 organ player in his group, so he didn't need me to play keyboards. Instead, I played vibraphone. Also known as *vibes*, this instrument looks like a xylophone, but has metal bars, a sustain pedal, and a motor, which creates an adjustable *vibrato* sound. The vibraphone is a somewhat obscure instrument, but a few big jazz names have played it over the years; Lionel Hampton's career spanned almost the entire epoch of traditional jazz. Milt Jackson rose to fame as a member of the Modern Jazz Quartet (MJQ). Gary Burton played on the landmark album *Getz Au Go-Go*, which brought *bossa nova* music to the U.S. in the late sixties. Roy Ayers made forays into funk, exposing vibes to a larger audience than ever before.

I had been tinkering on the vibes since I was a teenager, but this was my first chance to play the instrument in a band, and a good band at that. Gilbert, organist Joe Bagg and drummer Mark Ferber were all excellent young jazz musicians. I hadn't secured a place to live yet, so I holed up temporarily at my aunt and uncle's home in Encinitas. I quickly found opportunities to work and make money, picking up weekend engagements at La Casa del Zorro in Borrego Springs, and also re-connecting with people I'd worked with in previous years. After a while, I moved in with a guitarist friend, Hank Easton. Hank and his wife Leslie had just bought a house in La Mesa. Hank, a great musician, seemed like he had life figured out; successful marriage, nice house, recording studio. There I was, the wandering bachelor renting a spare bedroom. Quasimodo without the cool tower.

I'd stood at the top of the mountain—right before it was blasted to unearth some choice flagstone— thrown my arms into the air, and exalted in a glorious affirmation of self-worth, a blossoming feeling of machismo, and a renewed sense of purpose in life. Yeah, I'd done that. But in all honesty, returning to San Diego felt a little demoralizing.

I wasn't a kid anymore. No, I was pushing thirty now, and that romantic sheen which glosses the struggles of one's twenties was rapidly losing luster. Friends my age were buying homes, starting families. They were living stable lives with material comforts. Sure, there was a sense of freedom that accompanied the life I'd chosen. The freedom to follow any passion, to take any detour in the road. This freedom came with a price, however.

Looking back, that was a hard time in my life. I was looking for purpose. I'd started seeing a girl I was pretty into, but after getting a taste of the musician's life, she kicked me to the curb. Then, after only a few months in the band, Gilbert fired me from his jazz quartet without offering a reason. He didn't actually fire me—he just stopped calling me for gigs. I was replaced by a Los Angeles guitarist named Anthony Wilson, the son of bandleader Gerald Wilson.

Not one to sit around feeling sorry for myself, I decided to put together two new bands. La Vibra was a Latin-flavored jazz/rock ensemble. Cult of Soul was an R&B/hip-hop project. If I was going to be ensconced in the San Diego music scene once again, this time I would lead my own groups.

I hit the studio with both new bands, setting out to make a pair of albums. Keep in mind that when I speak of *making albums*, I was doing everything myself. Paying for the studio, assembling the musicians, writing charts, refining the arrangements, mixing and producing the finished product. There was no record label. I never sat around waiting for some big break to happen. If Artie Fufkin and Polymer Records[108] had decided to sign me up, and the contract looked legit, sure, I might have jumped on it. It would have been nice to have access to the resources a label could provide—studio budget, distribution, promotion, tour support—but I didn't mind getting by without one, as long as I could continue to document my creative ideas.

Excluding the burden of having to tap my own financial reserves, being self-contained provides fulfillment on levels a major label artist might not enjoy. By having a hand in each step of the process, you ensure the finished recording will turn out the way you want it to. You're not answering to anyone other than yourself, so you don't have to make compromises. There's nothing on the line but your own standards and expectations. The bottom line is not money, so the purity of the process is maintained.

The instrumentation of La Vibra was drums, percussion, piano, guitar, bass and vibraphone. We recorded in Hank's home studio, and finished all the basic tracking in a couple days. I was going for a hybrid sound combining traditional Latin rhythms with elements of jazz, pop, and rock guitar. The combination of Hank's aggressive guitar playing and my jazz vibraphone lines made for a fresh sound. I had never heard these two idioms combined before.

We recorded some standards and cover songs, including an intricate treatment of *Out Of This World*, which caught the ears of flautist Holly Hoffman and pianist Mike Wofford, two of San Diego's best jazz musicians. Holly and Mike performed the arrangement live, and recorded it on an album as well.

I was, at that time, also completing a demo for Cult of Soul, working closely with Tim McMahon. Cult of Soul was borne out of our mutual interest in R&B. We were both big fans of the underappreciated Minneapolis group, Mint Condition, a six-piece vocal unit who were also good instrumentalists. Their albums, most notably *Definition of a Band*, had a serious impact on my musical ideas, as I developed a passion for soulful melodies and deep grooves.

I was also listening to Busta Rhymes, Lauryn Hill and KRS-One, and found these influences creeping into the mix. Since the days of Faze, I had maintained an interest in rapping; not the superfluous elements of

---

[108] Paul Schaefer's character in *Spinal Tap*.

it, like gold caps, baggy clothes, and orgiastic MTV videos, but the craft itself. I wanted to take another stab at it, and Cult of Soul provided a good vehicle.

My previous bands had adhered to the *collective* model—a democratic environment where everybody's ideas carry equal weight. This is a rewarding format when all parties are simpatico, but in Cult of Soul I saw an opportunity to follow my own vision, unobstructed by the input of others.

Tim and I really clicked. We were hearing things the same way, and worked out a system that fulfilled us both: I would write the basic songs—melody, lyrics, chords—and Tim would add drum grooves and arrangement concepts. Then, we would flesh them out to completion. After a while, we had about twenty good songs. Like me, Tim had spent years toiling away, often stuck in musically unfulfilling situations. We felt this was our chance to develop a band with both a creative and commercial upside.

We worked with a black, male singer named Damion Willis. Damion was tall, handsome and had tremendous stage charisma. Also, he sang great. The guy had star potential. During an early gig at the Marriott Hotel on Coronado Island, we were approached by a guy who introduced himself as a record label executive. His name was Kent Anderson, and he was sitting with other people from the staff of Virgin Records. Kent dug what we were doing, and said, "I might be able to help you guys."

I told Kent we were developing an album, and would send him some music when it was finished. I'd been around the block enough not to overreact to the first hint of interest from someone in the music business. People talk a mean game, especially when they're half drunk, but as Richard Marx put it, *It don't mean nothin' 'til you sign it on the dotted line.* Nonetheless, it was a promising exchange that fueled my resolve to finish the album.

Recording the instruments in the studio, also known as *tracking,* proved an enjoyable experience. I played Fender Rhodes, synthesizers, piano, organ, vibes, and even dragged in my four-octave marimba for a couple songs. Tim and I had carefully mapped out the arrangements before we recorded, but once we had a basic skeleton of the songs, we allowed ourselves the freedom to experiment with sounds and parts. When this kind of childlike sonic exploration is possible, it's a blast. Many of the Grateful Dead's early recording innovations were stumbled upon in this manner, including those on their seminal album, *American Anthem.*

The instrumental aspect of the recording was highly enjoyable, but when it came time to lay the vocal tracks, I hit a stumbling block. Damion didn't want to sing some of the songs as they'd been written. Instead, he wanted to ad-lib his own melodies.

Tiny once offered me some sound wisdom when he said, "You shouldn't try to be a perfectionist in your life in general, but you've got to be a perfectionist in *something.* For us, it's music." The recording studio is a perfectionist environment. While you hope to capture some of the same spontaneity and vitality you would get in a live performance, you hold yourself to a higher technical standard in the studio. Once it's on tape, it's there forever. It's not going to change. If you don't go back and fix that mistake in bar seventy-three, it's going to haunt you and anyone else who hears the song, whether it's the second time hearing it or the two thousandth.

One of the micro art forms within the recording process is the ability to recognize when something needs to be re-done, or when something is a *keeper.* This is the job of a producer, and a good one understands the subtleties of music on an intuitive level. A tight technical performance with no emotion behind it is as bad, if not worse, than the opposite: a heartfelt performance that lacks execution.

If you listen to your favorite records with an acute ear for idiosyncrasies, even mistakes, you'll discover things you never heard before. You might realize that the overall performance wasn't as tight as you thought. You come to understand that it's the the spirit or the *vibe* behind the song that really grabs you. A producer who is too intent on perfection often winds up expunging the humanity, the warmth and character, right out of a song.

I spent many hours sculpting the melodies for the songs on *Walkin' My Planet.* Everything was where it was for a reason. Just as a writer needs a purpose for every word, and should be able to justify any passage, I had whittled away the melodies until they were as polished as I could make them.

Damion was a gifted singer, and I wanted him to come up with his own interpretations, but he confused interpretation with *revision*; he thought it was okay to rewrite my melodies to his liking, and he came to the studio not really knowing the material. I think he felt that since he was the lead singer, the melodies should be a reflection of *his* vocal sensibilities, not mine. To some extent, it was a valid point, and herein lies the problem with writing for a singer other than yourself. I had a distinct vision, but I didn't have the vocal chops to deliver the songs in the R&B style in which they'd been written.

Damion and I came up with a compromise, and we managed to capture good vocal performances on a handful of the songs. I wound up singing the rest of them myself. I didn't have Darnell's God-given talent — his rich tone, or his ability to ad-lib gloriously in that gospel manner that blesses only the rarest set of Caucasian vocal chords, but I was able to do a respectable job. Had I been blessed with a great natural singing voice, I sometimes wonder how far I could have gone in pop music. I had the ambition, and I had the writing ability. I just didn't have the sweet pipes.

I sang many of the back-up vocal parts on the album, and did raps on several tracks. Despite my concern with being dismissed as a lame white rapper, I wound up happy with the hip-hop tracks. I'd managed to infuse them with a bit of intellect as well as vocal style, without trying to sound black.

Songwriting gave me a platform to express views without sounding preachy. Most people don't care about your personal take on the world, if you just start throwing around your opinions in a given conversation, but through song lyrics you can express the same ideas and beliefs with a sense of urgency and social purpose.

By the time *Walkin' My Planet* was completed, Damion had quit the band and we'd replaced him with Walt Williams, another young, talented singer. Like Damion, Walt was a raw talent. He hadn't studied music, but possessed a naturally pleasing voice. Walt and I, though from completely different backgrounds, become good friends. We shared a love of basketball, and had both played competitively.

Once *Walkin' My Planet* was pressed, I sent copies to some well-known musicians and industry people. The musicians loved it. Joe Locke, the New York vibraphonist, called me to sing the album's praises. "As I listened to it, I was dancing around the house naked," he said. The music industry, however, was not as enthusiastic. Kent Anderson, the Virgin executive I'd met in Coronado, told me there were "strong tracks," but he wouldn't know how to market the album, because the music didn't fit into an established niche. It wasn't hip-hop exactly, it wasn't R&B enough to fit *that* mold, and it wasn't exactly jazz or pop. Personally, I liked this fact. When your work can't be easily pigeon-holed, you know you're doing something interesting. This, of course is one of the great artistic dilemmas: reconciling your creativity with the rigid demands of the marketplace. More than anything else, *Walkin' My Planet* was a singer/songwriter album. It was a personal showcase. After Len had listened to it, he said to me, "It's the story of your life."

Finishing and releasing the album was cathartic, both musically and psychologically. I'd created something I'd wanted for a long time: a calling card. Now, when people wondered, *what's your creative statement to the world?*, I would have an answer. Within our means, Tim and I had delivered the best album we were capable of making. There's a lot of satisfaction in that; in creating something you can present to people without disclaimers.

There wasn't a scene in San Diego to support the ambitions of a soul/hip-hop/jazz act, the same as there hadn't really been one when Faze was trying to make its mark. Tim and I hoped, however, to at least find a deal to distribute the album. We organized an album release party at a local club called The Juke Joint. In typical fashion, I went overboard, assembling a ten-piece band with a horn section, multiple vocalists and other instruments. I also enlisted a classical violinist to open the show, as well as a local artist to present an exhibit in the club's lobby.

We rehearsed thoroughly, and I even paid certain musicians for their time. I dropped considerable cash promoting the event, including mass-printing a color flier to advertise the art exhibit. The day of the release party, I was stressed. I'd expended a great amount of energy and personal resources, first on making the album itself, and now on organizing this event. Those old demons, the heart palpitations of my late teens and early twenties, came back to pay an untimely visit.

The show went okay, but there were numerous snags. The club was unaccommodating, making it difficult for our friends and patrons to relax and enjoy the music. The band was unfocused. There were too many people onstage, some who didn't know the songs very well. This was my fault. I wanted to blow people away with a big production, but I wound up presenting a band that was discombobulated. Still, *Walkin' My Planet* was an important personal accomplishment, and it merited a party. Both sets of my parents were in supportive attendance. We sold a few CDs, too.

My inability to remain enthusiastic about a project, once it is completed, is one of my main problems as an artist. I have little interest in promoting and pushing the finished product. Since I'm not in it for the money, really—you must have gathered this by now—my interest wanes when the creative work is done. I've always embraced the notion that somebody else should handle the task of brokering the work. I'm not much of a salesman.[109]

The trouble with my career so far is that there's been nobody to do this. Therefore, *Walkin' My Planet* and my other projects have not enjoyed widespread exposure on even a regional level. For this, I must again blame myself. I make an initial thrust to pitch my work, contacting agents, executives or whoever holds the keys to the kingdom, but if this brief campaign yields no results I quickly throw in the towel. I'm not a relentless badgerer of industry contacts, or a thick-skinned hustler of commercial opportunities… *and that has been my downfall.*

Around this time I got an out-of-the-blue phone call from Bill Yeager, my old teacher from SDSU. Bill started the conversation by saying, "Anthony, I've got something for you that seems like it's too good to be true." *That should have been my warning…*

Bill explained that he had been approached to put together a jazz group to represent SDSU at a university in the heart of China. This school was going to host a global creative symposium, lasting for a whole year, which would bring together dozens of cultures and artistic disciplines. Each participant would have all expenses covered and also receive a generous monthly stipend, while living in China and participating in the event. Bill was right—it did sound too good to be true.

"It's gonna happen," Bill said. "I'm on the committee to put the whole thing together. I'm going, and I wanna take you and some of the other standouts from the program." I hadn't been at State for years, so it was flattering that Bill had thought of me as his first choice on piano; and, of course, I was thrilled at the chance to go to China for a year. Why wouldn't I be? It sounded far more rewarding than anything I currently had going on in town.

"We gotta get some rehearsals together, and then play for the committee… but the committee is just a formality. It's a done deal."

"Sounds great, Bill. Count me in." We rehearsed a small jazz combo, including my good friends, guitarist Paul Imperato and drummer Richard Sellers. Then, it was time to play for the committee.

---

[109] I've revisited this thought lately. I've come around to the idea of being more involved in the business side of things.

I'd already told everyone I knew that I'd be soon spending a full year in China.

The committee was comprised of deans from SDSU and also a few representatives from the sister university in China. The Chinese representatives spoke little English, smiling nervously and whispering to each other while we set up our instruments. When we were ready, saxophonist Paul Sundfor launched into the first tune from our traditional jazz repertoire. I couldn't help but notice that the Chinese representatives weren't smiling anymore. One of them muttered something to Bill while we played.

Once we finished the song Bill walked over, his face slightly red. "Guys, you think you can play something a little more upbeat?" We were confused.

"What do you mean, Bill? That was pretty upbeat."

"Yeah, but more, uh, you know, more with a backbeat. Funky." Paul furrowed his brow. He was a man with absolutely zero tolerance for anything resembling bullshit, and this was quickly starting to smell like bullshit. I took the lead.

"Okay, let's do a Monk tune, but with a funk groove, guys." We played again, and the Chinese panel was still visibly unmoved. Again, Bill walked over.

"Hey, Anthony, remember when we were in Taiwan?"

"Yeah?"

"You played that Elton John Medley at the karaoke bar that night?"

"You want me to play Elton John songs for these Chinese academic dignitaries?"

"Yeah. I think that's more what they were expecting." We were all dumbfounded. Paul had heard enough. He walked over, stuck his sax in its case and headed for the door.

"Where you going, Paul?" Bill called out.

"They don't want what we're doing, right?"

"Well, not exactly."

"Then I'm out of here. I'm not interested." I valiantly plodded through my Elton John medley, Richard drumming along. When I stopped, the head representative walked over to explain himself, speaking in barely understandable English.

"We looking for more dancing… and jumping… and, uh, smoke…"

"Smoke?"

"More singing, and jumping, and smoke. What we want is… *Amelican lock band.*"

"What did he say? Amelican what?" He repeated his words slowly.
"A-ME-LI-CAN LLLLLOCK BAND!" Bill was now bright red.
"Obviously, there's been a miscommunication."

Needless to say, the trip didn't happen.

SLEEPING IN VS. MIRACLE EAR

Arguments For and Against the Musician's Life

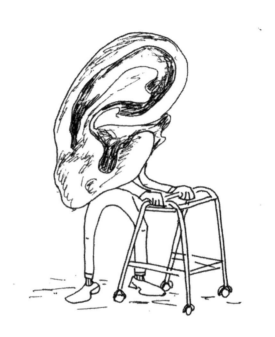

By now you might be asking: *What about the upside of this whole arts and music thing? If it's so taxing, with such limited rewards, why stick it out? Why not take Mr. Reality's advice and get a real job?* I guess I could have walked away, tried something else. Eventually the arts would have pulled me back. It would only have been a matter of time. You see, I'm a creativity junkie, and to my knowledge, there is no Twelve Step program for people like me.

I never said this was a fairy tale. I want people to understand how much persistence it takes to survive the arts and entertainment industry. There's this idea that you pay dues for a while, acquire experience and create demand for your talents, and then one day you don't have to pay dues anymore. The truth is that most of us keep paying dues throughout our careers. Behind the show, no matter how glamorous it might look from the audience's perspective, is a lot of hard work. Jumping on stage and performing is the easy part.

But you're right; what about the upside? I've discussed the struggles, and maybe it's time to put on a happy face for a minute. Here's a list of some things that make a life in music worth living…

Reasons It's Cool to be a Musician

SLEEPING IN

Oh, how nice it is to wake up not when some grating alarm sounds at 6 a.m., but when your eyes open because you are no longer tired. Most people are afforded this luxury only on weekends. Imagine enjoying it every day…

NO UNIFORMS

The first thing that comes to mind is Hot Dog on a Stick's humiliating uniforms, but a suit and tie is a uniform too.

EXPRESSING YOURSELF

There is no need to be a weekend warrior, or to manufacture outlandish, beyond-the-pale ways of expressing your individuality. This basic human need is satisfied by your livelihood.

PANACHE

You might be broke, but you're not a faceless member of the hoi-polloi. A lot of people think you're a flake, a social pariah, or a seedy ambassador of decadence and debauchery, but others think you're courageous, mysterious, and culturally indispensable. Either way, you're making a splash.

NO BALL AND CHAIN

You're working for yourself, man. You're free. The lack of consistent employment that cements your indigence also ensures your mobility. You can get up and go at any time, without forfeiting a 401K plan, benefits package, or sense of financial security. You can't miss what you never had!

WORKING WITH INTERESTING PEOPLE
It's true, the music industry overflows with scoundrels, cheats, degenerates, druggies, losers, snake oil salesmen, crooks, hustlers, sharks, freaks, head cases, opportunists, psychos and otherwise confused, conflicted, contradictory, dubious and deceptive individuals. It is remarkably free, however, of rubes, bubbas, chumps, doodlebugs and insufferable bores. Druggies, losers, and the other mentioned groups may be a pain in the ass to deal with on a regular basis, but they sure keep life interesting.

WORKING WITH TALENTED PEOPLE
There is great satisfaction to be had in collaborating with bright and gifted individuals, many who also exhibit the characteristics detailed in the previous paragraph.

THE SOCIAL ELEMENT
You meet new people every day. Sure, some are annoying, but some are really cool; and you don't have to pull *A Night at the Roxbury* to get your social kicks. All you have to do is show up for work and be yourself. Your music is your introduction.

LOW EXPECTATIONS OF FAMILY AND FRIENDS
Come Christmas time, you're off the hook. Everyone knows you're broke, and they're just *happy to have you home*. This latitude, of course, starts to lose its charm once you hit thirty.

NO T.P.S. REPORTS
(See the movie *Office Space*).

COURTESY, COURTESY, COURTESY
People are always giving you free stuff. I don't know if it's because they feel pity, or they just want to be able to say they know you when you make it big. Either way, you're the recipient of frequent acts of generosity, which you're in the position to reciprocate only through your music.

NO DRUG TESTING
Not a biggie for me, because I only drink, but a major boon for most of my friends. Conventional society assumes you line your innards with

every substance under the sun, so why bother to make you piss in a jar?

A CUBICLE-FREE WORKING ENVIRONMENT
I have known this fate, the fate of the legions that constitute the Cubicle-Shackled Workers of America. I swiftly extricated myself from this suffocating predicament and never looked back, but I understand that others, for whatever reason, cannot. They're resigned and confined to a lifetime in the cubicle.

SEXUAL HARRASSMENT A BADGE OF HONOR, NOT SHAME
Got a weakness for mixing business with pleasure? No problem! Music is the career for you. Your carousing and philandering, should it reach epic enough proportions, will actually be a *cause celebre* in the eyes of the media, as well as the forum of pop culture perception. In the corporate world, you'd be a pervert and a criminal, but in the world of rock and roll, you're a swordsman extraordinaire.

GETTING TO SEE AMERICA
While flying is much faster and less tedious, driving around the country gives you the chance to really see and experience the United States: The people, the geography, the cultural distinctions and varying climates. It's the grass roots method of travel, and it requires patience. I'm not sold on flying, anyway. My dark coloring and eyebrows seem to throw up red flags all over the place, and I'm tired of taking off my shoes during security check-in.

CELEBRITY/STAR POTENTIAL
The odds are overwhelmingly against you, but does that stop people from buying lottery tickets? You're in a field that offers the possibility of fame and fortune, and while these are not things to be pursued with any degree of seriousness, it's nice to know at least you're in the hunt for a life less ordinary. Plumbers can't say that.

PEOPLE ACTUALLY ENVY WHAT YOU DO
While Harry Shearer's Derek Smalls character had his tongue firmly in cheek when he told bandmate David St. Hubbins that "People should envy us," the fact is that it's *true*... people envy you. They want to be like you. You're a person who follows your dreams and forsakes security, that great sanctuary of the masses.

THE SITTIN'-ON-THE-PORCH-IN-FRONT-OF-THE-GENERAL-
STORE FACTOR
When you're an old fart, your best days far behind you, and you're
sitting on the porch in front of the general store reflecting on your life,
boring young people with your stories, you're going to have so many
fond recollections of your life in music. You're going to forget a lot of
the negative stuff, like we are apt to do as human beings, and fixate on
the enjoyable aspects of your career. You'll relish in the wisdom that
prompted you to choose passion over the almighty dollar, since you
now understand, as an old person, that life on Earth is fleeting.
Whether your general store is in Mendocino, Monrovia or Mogadishu
will depend on how many Top 40 hits you charted back in the day.

There you have it: Eighteen reasons why it's good to be a musician.
Now, I feel like I've gone off the Pollyanna deep end. There are two
sides to every coin—no yin without a yang—so here they are, the...

Reasons It Stinks to be a Musician

THE QUESTIONS
People always want to pick your brain, and often ask the most
irritating questions. Some of my favorite:

*So, do you just like drive around all the time and play your keyboard and
stuff?*[110]

What's your REAL job?
I don't believe in real jobs

Can you play the black keys too?
No, I can't play the black ones yet. But it's something I'm planning to
work on in the future. [111]

---

[110] Popular on first—and only—dates with women.

[111] Forgive the sarcasm.

Can you put me on the guest list?
(sigh) I guess so.

So, do you just make it up as you go?
Yes, that's exactly it. We just make it up as we go. We have no idea what we're doing, any of the time. That way we don't spoil our natural talent.[112]

Are you classically trained?[113]
Yes, and I'm potty-trained also. Pretty impressive, huh?

Do you have groupies in every town?[114]
If what you're asking me here is if I'm going to keep your picture by the bed in every hotel room, pining away while acknowledging my overwhelming obsession with you, I'm gonna have to go with… no!

Do you guys all crash in the RV? How does that work out?
It's awesome. Seven sweaty guys flopped around the inside of a motor home, sniffling, snoring, and… you can imagine.

Will you remember me when you're famous? No.

My brother does a mean Elvis. Can he jam out a little Hound Dog next set?
Sure, but tell him this practice could very well lead to him getting his ass kicked.

You're not bad—ever think of playing at Nordstrom's?
Baby steps, my friend, baby steps. First you play the clubs, then the theatres, then the arenas, then maybe you get into Carnegie Hall… then you can start to think about Nordstrom's.

You ever hear of (insert random name of some obscure group in North Dakota)? Yeah, I've got all their albums.

---

[112] Again, forgive the sarcasm.

[113] A cliché that makes it sound like you're a dog doing tricks.

[114] Asked frequently by insecure groupies.

Wanna puff some nuggets, brother?
Would that mean that I and my band can crash at your house for a couple days?

Where are you guys from?
This is a reasonable enough question, but why does it really matter, and why is it the first thing people always want to know?

How do you guys get gigs? You just call the club or something, and tell them you have a band?
We just show up somewhere with our instruments and see what happens.

Who's your favorite Beatle?[115]
How can you pick just one?

THE GAWKS
For some reason people like to drop their mouths open, let some ooze drool out, and stare blankly at you for long, awkward periods of time. This happens without fail when we drive into some town for a show. At moments like this my old soundman Tristan Dunlap would lean out the window and shout, "Hey, Britney Spears is in here!" This would get a rise from teens, middle-aged housewives and dirty old men alike. Sometimes the gawks come while you're onstage, too. Makes you feel like you're part of a zoo exhibit.

THE GRIND
Just like being a pro athlete or anything else that requires extensive travel, being on the road for two hundred-plus shows a year will wear you down. There are nights when you can't find one compelling reason why you should get up on stage and perform. Still, perform you must, so you suck it up and do your job. Strangely, these can sometimes be the best nights.

---

[115] I've seen Medeski, Martin and Wood deal with this question beautifully, but those guys are real pros.

MIRACLE EAR

Rock music is loud. Sometimes, it's excruciatingly loud. I don't know any musician who wants to wear earplugs all the time. Furthermore, good rock drummers are loud rock drummers. Over the years, your ears are going to take somewhat of a beating. There's no way around it other than to have something stuffed into your ear your whole life. If you're careful you can minimize the damage, but the vast majority of touring musicians do have some hearing loss.

ASSUMPTIONS

People assume since you're a musician, you're a die-hard liberal. Your mission in life must be to hoist the disenfranchised upon your shoulders, fight against the evils of all corporations and conservative politicians, eat organic tofu, smoke pot, and spit invective at The Man. If you don't toe this line you're a curious disappointment. I've always made a clear distinction between what I do for a living and my opinions and views about things. I became a musician because I loved music. There was no political or social agenda attached to it.

NO MORE HOOPS

I've already got one permanently crooked finger from playing basketball. Now, I have to be very careful not to mangle my fingers, so I don't play hoops much anymore. But I've been loving tennis lately.

TOO MUCH OUT THERE

There's just too much music in the world these days. A lot of it's not very good, but the distinction between good and bad is obscured by the sheer glut of product in the marketplace.

OWW, MY BACK[116]

You end up lifting a lot of heavy equipment—at least as a keyboardist or a drummer. That takes its toll on your back and your joints over the years.

---

[116] Not to be confused with *Oww, My Balls!*, the most popular TV show in the year 2505, according to the narrator of Mike Judge's film *Idiocracy.*

SAME GROOVE, DIFFERENT DAY
Music is inherently repetitive, and when you play the same songs over and over, week after week and month after month, it can get pretty stale.

SOCIETAL DISCONNECT
At the end of the day, most people just don't get you. And you don't get them.

MARIO WALKER AND LIVING LARGE

In early 2000, I got a call from Mario Walker, a trumpet player from the local scene. Mario, black and in his mid-twenties, was a natural talent on trumpet. He had a strong, warm tone and good range, and reminded me of a young Freddie Hubbard. I'd hired him on occasion for local gigs, and we had natural rapport. Mario spent half his time in San Diego, the other half on the road with Karl Denson, a popular funk saxophonist. Denson had made his name as a founding member of Greyboy All-Stars, a group that helped pioneer the acid jazz movement in the early nineties.

Mario made the decision to break away from Karl and form his own project, a collective featuring the best players from San Diego's funk/jazz talent pool. He asked me to join on keyboards and vibraphone. I hadn't done much touring yet, and was attracted to the idea. The new band was called Living Large.

Mario gathered an impressive group of veteran players, including Hollis Gentry on saxophone and Ignacio Arango on bass. In addition to good musicians, Mario had the support of Lincoln Norris, an aspiring entrepreneur, and Todd Sherman, a music lover and angel investor. Lincoln, a light-skinned, six-foot black guy who was handsome, well-dressed and in his early thirties, had served during the Gulf War in 1991, and now looked to make his mark in the music business. He was articulate and ambitious, and when he wasn't expounding on the future of the entertainment industry or strategizing moves for Living Large, Lincoln was an engaged listener, open to everyone's ideas.

Todd Sherman, also around thirty, was white, medium height, and sported an East Coast preppy look. He'd been successful in the computer industry, and was a great supporter of the Jam Band Scene, the genre of music first created by the Grateful Dead in the sixties, later carried on in the nineties by Phish and other groups. Todd was living a rock star life, flying around for various consulting jobs, and also jetting in and out of different cities to attend concerts by his favorite groups.

Lincoln and I got along well at first, our nascent partnership a study in contrast. He was the product of a single-parent household in urban Chicago, and a war veteran. I was a suburban jock white kid turned freelance musician. Surprisingly, we had a great deal of common ground. We both loved soulful music, reading and the pursuit of knowledge, playing basketball, watching movies, and the therapy of humor. We were also both major dreamers. We shared the belief that greatness is only possible through daring vision and great risk, and we were willing to put our money where our mouth was.

At the first Living Large rehearsal, Lincoln and Mario laid out their master plan, which boiled down to one simple goal: conquering the world. I thought they were getting a bit ahead of themselves, talking about marketing plans and elaborate merchandising concepts, but in a laid back town like San Diego, you had to tip your hat to these guys for being highly motivated.

After playing through Mario's musical arrangements, it was clear he would need help as both an arranger and bandleader. Hollis and I struggled to make sense of Mario's songs, which lacked a logical sense of harmony or basic theory. He had good ideas, but they weren't developed.

Living Large played its first show at Winston's, a club in Ocean Beach where I'd performed many times over the years. I played a Korg Triton keyboard, purchased with Todd Sherman's money. Lincoln loved the Triton. In his mind, it was not only one of the great keyboards of all time, but perhaps one of the great *inventions* of all time. He would go on and on about the Triton, with its futuristic silver paint and fancy touch-screen display, to the point that it was comical. "That Triton is a motherfucker, dawg!" he would say. When I suggested that I might be better off with a real Hammond B-3, Lincoln countered, "I don't wasn't us to sound like everyone else."

"But Lincoln, the B-3 is the real deal. That's what the Triton is mimicking," I said.

"You mean with that spinning wheel and all that? That shit is crazy, man."

"Yeah, that's a Leslie speaker. That's *the sound*: A B-3 with a Leslie."

"Forget all that bullshit. The Triton, now *that's* a motherfucker."

Trousers for John

At rehearsal one day, Mario announced the dates for Living Large's first tour. We would start by flying to Utah to play a few shows in Park City, the affluent ski resort nestled in the mountains above Salt

Lake City. We rehearsed in an old building called the Community Actors' Theatre. Drummer John Staten, the younger brother of jazz drummer Brett Sanders, looked like a six-foot version of Shaquille O'Neal. He was twenty-one and had promising talent. John was a funny, good-hearted guy with an enormous laugh, unlike any I'd ever heard. He and I became fast buddies.

John and I flew together to Salt Lake City to commence the Living Large tour. After meeting us at the Salt Lake airport, a promoter took us to lunch at a Vietnamese restaurant. I couldn't wait to see what this kid, who'd barely ever left the city of San Diego in twenty-one years, was going to order at some random Vietnamese restaurant in Salt Lake City. John opened the menu only to discover it wasn't in English. It was one of those menus with little pictures of various foods, and John pointed at some nasty looking fish concoction and asked, "What *is* that?" These were dangerous waters for a guy who ate steak and fries for almost every meal.

After scouring the menu in vain, John decided to order something that (sort of) resembled fried chicken. I went with a bowl of pork noodles, a far safer choice. The food arrived, and John, ravenous from the flight, split open the belly of this strange, crispy little creature, all by itself on the big, otherwise empty plate in front of him. A meager puff of steam shot from its innards as it collapsed like a punctured lung. The promoter and I laughed, John sitting there with a look of disappointment. I gave him a pat on the back and said, "First rule of the road is, don't order fried chicken at a Vietnamese restaurant, my man."

On another funny note, the airline had lost John's luggage, forcing him to scramble for whatever clothes he could find—he performed the first show in a hodgepodge ensemble consisting of a horribly out-of-style, brown terrycloth sport jacket and some very tight, shiny leather pants. The pants looked so absurd that I was inspired to dedicate a song to my sartorially challenged friend: *Trousers for John*.

The Canyons Resort in Park City was much classier than any dumpy motels I'd stayed in during previous musical travels. We played a couple low-key gigs at the resort, ate gourmet meals, worked out in the gym, and chilled on Main Street, with its smattering of B-list movie stars and affluent locals. Park City had established itself as a smaller scale version of Aspen, the king of all American mountain towns, through hosting the annual Sundance Film Festival, also steadily building its reputation as a world class ski destination.

One night, I sat in Lincoln's room watching extreme skiing on TV. Some guy was plummeting down an almost completely vertical cliff, defying physics by not only staying on his feet, but also executing difficult tricks. Lincoln stared at the screen with a quizzical, almost irritated look. Finally, he said, "Anthony, white people are insane."

"Do clarify," I responded.

"Look at this motherfucker. He's trying to kill himself. I'm convinced."

"What does being white have to do with it?"

"Y'all got a monopoly on that extreme sports shit. Black people don't do that crazy shit. Black people got a strong self-preservation instinct."

"But I've seen black guys skiing double black diamond courses. More than a couple times.

"They might *look* black, but they're not *bruthas*. The black guys that do that stuff talk like white dudes from Orange County."

"You're right," I agreed. My man had a point. Here's a conversation you don't hear too often:

What up, yo?

Chillin', son.

What you feel like doin' this weekend?

I dunno, hit up a barbecue, watch some football n' shit like that.

Nah, fuck that, bro. I ain't feelin' that. I got a better idea...

What up?

Let's go motherfuckin' bungee jumpin'!

Yeaaaah, buuuooooy!

We played a nightclub called Mother Urban's, and were happy to learn that Roy Hargrove, the famous jazz trumpet player, was in the crowd and wanted to jam with us. Hargrove soloed over a blues, building to a spectacular climax that made the crowd go crazy. When the set ended, he got up to leave, carrying not only his own trumpet case, but also Mario's.

"Why is Roy Hargrove taking your trumpet, Mario?" I asked.

"I gave it to him... as a gift."

"So you have another one to play for the rest of the tour?"

"Yeah, I have another one." This move left me puzzled, but was the kind of capricious behavior I came to expect from Mario.

The stint in Park City was a comfortable kick-off to my touring experience, though a highly inaccurate measure of how life would be on the road. Playing your first-ever shows in the Jam Band Scene (which I will hereafter refer to as the JBS) at a tony resort in Park City, was like having your first car be a brand new Maserati, then switching to a used Hyundai for the rest of your life.

We continued the tour in a fifteen-seat passenger van. If you've spent any time in one of these, you know the notion of squeezing *fifteen people* inside is laughable. The seats are crammed close together, and not designed for tall guys. There are four benches behind the driver area, each supposed to seat three people, except for the final bench, which is supposed to seat… four! With no room to stretch your legs or take a nap, it doesn't take long to become a cranky band member. You might wind up in such a fragile mental state that by the time the van closes in on the next city, something as trifling as an inadvertent passing of gas can trigger an emotional collapse. I've seen it happen.

The Living Large van contained a colorful group of characters: Mario, with his schizophrenic flow of ideas and mercurial mood swings, John, with his provincial manners, wisecracks and never-ending belly laughs, Lincoln, the articulate Gulf War veteran who had survived a barrage of mortar blasts in the Saudi Desert, but now struggled to embrace the improvisational nature of the touring life, Bradshaw, a real-life Fred Sanford, recruited by Lincoln to serve as driver and fix-it man, Ignacio, the docile, elder statesman from Cuba, whose automatic response to almost any question was a shrug of the shoulders and the words, "I do not know, my friend… I joss play my bass," Hollis, the brilliant, baritone-voiced sax man with a big heart and even bigger personal demons, whose storied career had all but derailed, leading him to this humble juncture as a jam band sideman, and me, the token white keyboard player, with my boundless creative energy, ambitious musical ideas and intense, driven nature.

In addition to the qualities I mentioned, Lincoln and I had one other personality trait in common: we both had a temper. I'd learned to keep mine in relative check over the years, and it would only flare on occasion. Lincoln, however, was a short-fused time bomb. One comment could send him into a rage. Even a small bump in the road, be it a misguided comment or a random instance of stupidity on someone's part, would infuriate him, because it was a distraction from the ultimate goal, which, I remind you, was to conquer the world.

Thus, Lincoln was not destined to have a harmonious relationship with Mario, who, for all his raw talent and charisma, in some ways still behaved like a little kid. Mario could do something musically brilliant one minute, then turn around and do something else you would expect of a ten year-old. This was problematic for Lincoln because Mario was, at least in theory, *the man in charge.* He was supposed to be setting an example for the rest of us, artistically and professionally. Lincoln had been the catalyst in Mario's decision to break from Karl Denson and start his own band, because Lincoln believed Mario could be his *own* Karl Denson—an organized, successful bandleader with a busy schedule and national following. It was true, Mario had the same innate gift as Karl, an intangible magnetism that made people watch his every move on stage, that made an audience *love* the guy before he'd even put the horn to his mouth. Mario had that rare thing, yes, and Lincoln was wise to realize it. But that was where the similarities between Mario and Karl ended.

Things Are Not Going Well

The escalating conflict between Lincoln and Mario came to a head somewhere between Salt Lake City and Jackson Hole, Wyoming. Exactly where, I can't tell you, because the van was on the freeway, going 80 mph at the time. Lincoln was sitting up front, suggesting to Mario that he arrange a certain song in a certain manner. Mario nodded his head in seeming agreement, but when Lincoln finished talking, Mario said, "That's cool, but I'm gonna do it the way I wanna do it." Lincoln sat there in silence, Mario reclined in the seat directly behind him, wearing goofy sunglasses and effecting a Lenny Kravitz-inspired air of nonchalance. Suddenly Lincoln lunged into the back seat, grabbing Mario and wrestling him to the floor of the vehicle. Bradshaw kept trucking along the freeway as the two men punched at each other's heads. The rest of us sat there, frozen, watching. Someone said, "Hey Bradshaw, maybe you should pull over." Once the van came to a stop, Mario extricated himself from Lincoln's clutches and hopped out of the van. His sunglasses were mangled, the frame bent like a pretzel. Bradshaw delivered what would become a classic, oft-repeated line: "Things are not going well."

Indeed, they were not, as we continued our trek from SLC to Jackson Hole, in the middle of a growing snowstorm. Under favorable conditions, this is an eight-hour drive. Throw in icy, winding roads and poor visibility, and now you're looking at an easy ten. We were supposed to play that evening at the Mangy Moose, a popular club in the resort village of Wyoming's world famous ski town, and it was obvious we were going to be very late due to the weather. When we finally made it to Jackson Hole, it was after eleven p.m.

The manager told Lincoln it was too late. The night was a wash, and we shouldn't bother setting up our equipment. But Lincoln wasn't having it. He ordered us to drag the gear inside, set up and play, assuring the manager, "We *will* play, and you *will* pay us."

"We'll work out a compromise," she said. I could see Lincoln's point, and I could also see hers. It wasn't our fault we got caught in a blizzard, and it wasn't the club's fault we were so late. After we played a few songs, to a mostly empty room, the police showed up. I assumed the manager had made the call, but it turned out that it had been Lincoln, who wanted to make sure we didn't get stiffed out of our guarantee. The club coughed up a grand, but Lincoln had forced a Pyrrhic victory—our bridge with the Mangy Moose was burned for future business.

Mario's marquee value might have been the reason we were out on the road in the first place, but somebody was going to have to take control of the musical direction, or the project was going nowhere. That someone was me. Lincoln asked me to assume creative control, but do so without threatening Mario. I was happy to, because the music needed help, and it also meant I'd have more of a chance to develop my ideas and establish my value to the group.

I was getting inspired by the grass roots music scene. By scene, I mean the bands, the fans, the venues, and the history and philosophy behind it all. The JBS was a world I'd known nothing about, prior to touring. I'd been aware of the Grateful Dead, but didn't know their music, and knew very little about the massive countercultural movement they'd spearheaded decades earlier.

I had no clue this movement had continued through the nineties and into the new millennium, galvanizing a whole new generation of modern bands and musical ideas. I knew so little about the Dead's legacy that when I, as a teenager in Santa Clara, had stumbled upon a music video featuring Jerry Garcia, the man who'd amassed a huge following of fanatic disciples, I wondered, *Who's this grizzled old fart with the cracking voice, and what's he doing on MTV?*

I also knew little about the band that inherited the Grateful Dead's throne in the nineties, building on their musical and socio-cultural innovations while creating an equally phenomenal following: Phish. Sometimes in life, you look directly at something without seeing it. This was true, in a very literal sense, of my first experience with Phish. The year was 1994, and I was playing in San Francisco with Fried Bananas; we were opening for Common Sense, a fellow Southern California reggae act, in the courtyard of the fabled Phoenix Hotel. After our set, I sat at a table with some friends, next to a group of white guys in their late twenties. They looked kind of like geeks. After a while, I got up and walked to the bar with a young woman I'd just met that afternoon. Somebody came over and said, "You were sitting right next to Phish out there in the courtyard! They're playing the Warfield tonight." I didn't know anything about Phish, and didn't much care, since the girl was attractive and a good conversationalist, and didn't seem to notice that I was wearing a beard to cover some weird rash that had enveloped my cheeks.

As I dropped the name Phish in casual conversation the following couple days, mentioning that I'd crossed paths with them, it was brought to my attention that these guys were some kind of big deal. I'd had no idea. I decided to buy a Phish album to see what all the hype was about. Considering that the quartet from Vermont is viewed as an important link in the evolution of rock/jazz and improvised music, and also the fact that they've sold millions of albums, obscene amounts of merchandise, have commanded a live audience of over a hundred thousand people in certain parts of the country, and continue to boast a vast army of fans who worship the ground they walk on, what I'm about to admit is difficult: I didn't get Phish.

I listened to *Picture of Nectar* from start to finish, several times, waiting for a tingle, some feeling of excitement. It never came. I thought: *Yeah, they play their instruments well, but the music is nerdy and contrived.* The songs meandered, and it was all so... *white.* The singing was wimpy and lacked soul. I threw *Picture of Nectar* in a pile and didn't buy any more Phish albums. At that time, they just weren't my cup of tea.

Living Large had a couple short tours under its belt in late 1999, but I was about to get my first real taste of the hardcore JBS crowd. Lincoln booked us to play a late-night boat cruise in San Francisco, billed as an after-party for Phish's show at Shoreline Amphitheatre in Mountain View. Phish had announced their retirement prior to the concert, so my jam band career was beginning just as theirs was ending.

As was evidenced on the cruise, Generation X (my generation), as well as its successor, Y, had produced more than enough hippies to keep the Dead's original grass roots movement alive. These hippies were, by and large, products of good homes and higher education. Many had trust funds[117], and hence the financial freedom to do whatever they wanted with their time, but others were just broke kids who loved the scene and the music, who scraped by and survived somehow from one tour to the next. The JBS celebrated open-mindedness and a strong sense of community, promoting a festive environment in which drugs and alcohol were the sideshow, music the main attraction. Or maybe it was the other way around.

The boat show was a big success for Living Large, despite the fact that bassist Ken Dow[118] got terribly seasick, and couldn't make it through the gig. I had to cover his bass lines on keys, then jump over to vibraphone, then jump back on the keyboard and try to pull off some exciting solos. After it was over, I felt I'd played well and picked up the slack for Ken.

Mario, however, informed me that one of the dudes from Jive, a small-time Colorado band playing in another area of the boat, had come up to him and said, "Your band sounds good, but that keyboard player isn't happening." That stung. I knew my theory inside out, had a college degree, was a veteran of many bands, and was now working

---

[117] They're sometimes referred to as *trustafarians*, because they incorporate an earthy, non-materialistic lifestyle and political agenda, while continuing to exploit the benefits of their parents' fat bank accounts.

[118] Ken would later become the original bassist for the worldwide Broadway phenomenon, *Jersey Boys*.

in a scene with musicians who, in many cases, didn't know a scale from an arpeggio. Who the hell was this punk to tell Mario that *I* couldn't play? Pissed, I went back to San Diego and practiced harder, wrote more music, and upgraded my keyboard rig. I was going to prove this jerk from Jive was wrong about me. Months later, Jive posted an internet missive, stating the band was breaking up due to the persistent difficulties of the road. I felt a vindictive jolt of Schadenfreude.

As I spent more time on the road with Living Large, my freelance San Diego career became increasingly difficult to maintain. If new Living Large shows were booked, I had to be available. My commitment to the road meant making less money, but I realized the band provided more of a long-term opportunity than my work in San Diego. On the road, I was playing for people paying money to hear original music. We weren't merely playing gigs in Living Large. We were playing *shows*. There's a big difference.

The road did require some lifestyle adjustments. I no longer got to sleep in my own, comfortable bed every night. Nor did I kick back in my apartment with a movie and some take-out, or go for a jog anytime I felt like it. On tour, I had to abandon all semblance of a daily routine, and instead embrace an environment characterized by a lack of comfort and familiarity, where everything constantly changes, and one never knows what's coming next. A touring musician conditions himself to derive pleasure from the uncertainties of the journey. When things work out well—a great show, a connection with a respected musician from another band, a classic incident (for the memoir), a satisfying dinner with friends, a spontaneous fling with a cute female fan—you revel in the unpredictability of it all. When things go to shit, you try to laugh, shake it off and say, "Well, that's the road." Or, as my buddy Matt Schumacher says, "strikes and gutters."

Hanging with String Cheese

In the early spring of 2000, I was introduced to a bona fide star of the JBS. The String Cheese Incident, a bluegrass/rock quintet out of Boulder, Colorado, was doing a two-night run at the Wiltern Theater in Los Angeles. Mario and I both showed up separately, and he was invited to jump onstage with the band and play some trumpet. The sold-out crowd loved him, which prompted Don Strasburg, owner of the popular Fox Theater in Boulder, to book Living Large for a future date. SCI had packed the place with enthusiastic fans, and though the band meandered through long, static jams that went nowhere[119], I generally liked the music. After the show, I hung out in a hotel room with Woo and a bunch of JBS kids, including Rye Palmer, aka Mr. Peepers, and Eric Thompson, two guys who would become good friends in the future.

The Living Large van headed north for Oregon, where we crossed paths again with String Cheese. Mario had been friends with them ever since he and Karl Denson toured with the band a year earlier. They were happy to see that Mario, who (SCI) guitarist Billy Nershi had hailed as *the new Miles Davis*,[120] was now leading his own project.

During a day off in Eugene, I was introduced to Kyle Hollingsworth, SCI's keyboardist, who I immediately clicked with. After an in-depth conversation about music, Kyle and I checked out Jazz is Dead, an all-star Grateful Dead cover band performing at the Wild Duck. Jazz is Dead included keyboardist T Lavitz, bassist Alphonso Johnson and other established players.

The next afternoon, before SCI's show at the Holt Center, Kyle and I got together to do some playing. He quickly demonstrated his good chops and a strong work ethic. We talked about our "lick books" — most jazz guys have one of these, a music notebook filled with phrases and ideas either "lifted" from other players, self-created, or a combination of both. The lick book is something you keep adding on to for years, so it's very personal. When a melody in the middle of someone's solo catches your ear, you transcribe it and add it to the book.

That night, SCI show's was impressive. The band combined bluegrass, funk, techno and rock in a fresh and engaging way, offering up both intricate passages and free-form funk explorations. People went nuts the whole evening, dancing in the aisles.

For the first time in a long while, I felt I was reaching people in a positive way with my music. Being a member of a rising, regional touring act bolstered my sense of artistic self-worth, and touring also satisfied my desire to see the country. I experienced not only big cities and the urban skylines that had fascinated me my entire life, but also

---

[119] A trademark of the Grateful Dead.

[120] More a reflection of the young trumpeter's enigmatic persona than any musical similarities.

rural areas, natural wonders and national landmarks. The more of the country I experienced in person, the more I felt a sense of pride in it. I don't mean this in a cornball, clichéd way—it's just that when you take the time to really travel and experience the U.S., exploring its varied regions and contrasting subcultures, you gain a new appreciation of the country as a whole.

Living Large gave me a perfect vehicle for self-expression. I was writing songs, playing a variety of keyboards, taking long solos and singing leads. The vibe on the road had lightened, because Lincoln had decided to stay in San Diego to handle administrative tasks. It was just the band and a couple roadies in the van now.

Todd Sherman flew out to join the party on occasion, and was appreciative of my efforts. After one show, he pulled me aside and said, "T... it's *your* band." [121] I was writing lots of new tunes and filling much of the solo space, Mario settling into his role as a colorful frontman (as opposed to a musical director). John had developed into an exciting drum talent, crafting innovative beats and getting large crowds moving with his infectious style. John and I were bringing much to the table, but neither of our names was ever mentioned on the marquee. The band was being billed as: MARIO WALKER AND LIVING LARGE. Perhaps this was rightfully so, because as much as the rest of us were adding, Mario remained the focus of attention. In terms of pure stage presence, he was the star.

Lincoln had recruited Danny Bus, a black guy in his late twenties, to serve as road manager in Lincoln's absence. Danny was a nice cat, but he wasn't always the swiftest dude on the scene. One night, some young lady was coming on to him at a show, telling him in very specific words what she wanted to do to him later that night. Somehow, I was in earshot of this conversation. When she was done explaining her plans, the lady asked Danny, "So what are *you* going to do to *me?*" Danny was befuddled.

"Uh, I'm gonna, ummm, I'm gonna make it feel real good."

"Make what feel real good?"

"Uh, you know. The stuff I like to do."

"No, I don't know. That's why I'm asking."

---

[121] Todd was the first one to call me *T.*

"Well, I'm g'on like, uh, do some real nasty stuff. 'Til the break of dawn, girl." At a loss for words, Danny was resorting to bad R&B lyrics.

Our fledgling road manager's run was short-lived. One afternoon in Victor, Idaho, he gathered everyone in the lobby of the Super 8 Motel, and informed us that four hundred dollars were missing from the band's petty cash fund. Mario went on the warpath, accusing everyone of stealing from him. When he pointed his irrational attack in *my* direction, I challenged him to a fight. Luckily it didn't go that far, but grudges were formed. The seeds of future antagonisms were planted. And, of course, the missing money never showed up.

Big Daddy Woo-Woo

Danny's failure as a road manager was significant, because it opened the door for Andy Morton, known to most at that time as Big Daddy Woo-Woo (who I will refer to as Woo). Woo was a heavyset guy in his late twenties, with a ponytail, glasses and a high-pitched voice. He had been a fixture on Phish tour over the years, a ubiquitous mascot of the JBS. Woo was generous with praise for new bands he liked, and equally critical of ones he thought were mediocre or over-hyped. His mind was like an encyclopedia, and he could support his far-left political leanings with facts and well-researched insights. He and I would pass the time, during long van rides, with engaging discussions about current affairs. Woo genuinely loved music, and through collecting recordings and attending hundreds of shows, had developed a refined appreciation of various genres. Like Todd, Woo had gotten to know Mario through the trumpeter's association with Karl Denson and his band, Tiny Universe. The acquisition of Woo, wily JBS mover and shaker, was a major boost to the Living Large organization.

After a run through Utah and Nevada, we decided to take on a new roadie, Salt Lake City native Ricky Perkins. Ricky was such a Phish loyalist that he had the band's logo tattooed across his heart. He was in his early twenties, and a good-looking kid, though short, long-haired and scruffy. Ricky would become one of my best friends and closest allies on the road. Night after night, month after month, he helped me set up and break down my keyboard rig, lugging everything up and down stairs, to and from venue after venue. Often, he would break everything down by himself after a show, allowing me to relax and unwind.

In the beginning, Lincoln had genuine affection for both Woo and Ricky. While en route to a gig in the Bay Area one day, Ricky poked fun at Lincoln, saying his rather small head and broad shoulders made him look like "a black Beetlejuice." Without batting an eye, Lincoln shot back: "You look like a motherfucking midget Jesus in a Christian circus sideshow." We all broke into spasms of laughter. It was one of the greatest comebacks ever. From that moment on, Ricky Perkins was *Little Jesus*.

Living Large also secured the services of Tristan Dunlap, a.k.a. *the Mayor*. The Mayor was a fledgling soundman and, it almost goes without saying, fanatic Phish devotee. He wore glasses and sort of a bowl haircut, and he was bright and technically adept. Things were really rolling now. Mario was an unpredictable, compelling showman. John was laying it down on the drums, and I was writing catchy original jams that were going over well. The buzz around the JBS was strong, and promoters were paying attention. When we cruised into the Rolling Summer Festival near Ogden Utah, to participate in a star-studded, three-day event organized by a thickly dreadlocked friend named Charlie Crompton, the band was poised to make a major breakthrough.

Charlie had assembled an impressive line-up that included Galactic, the popular funk group out of New Orleans, Robert Walters' 20th Congress, Jerry Joseph, John Bell (singer from Widespread Panic), and Ween; but despite this roster, the festival quickly became a nightmare. The sound was terrible, the schedule poorly managed, and brazen interference by law enforcement cast a dark cloud over the entire event. It turned into the *Rolling Bummer*.

Feedback was so bad during Ween's set that the band began mocking the soundman in the middle of their show. Then, during a late-night jam combining Living Large and another promising group, Particle, the police shut down the music after just twenty minutes, ordering the crowd to disperse, despite the fact that Charlie had the required permits. By that time, a bunch of kids had already gotten busted for drug possession, and a lot of people were splitting the festival early.

We stayed at Charlie's house in Eden, a tiny community in the mountains above Ogden. When I walked into the place at four in the morning, there sat an aging, bearded dude, a spitting image of Colonel Sanders, sitting in the living room, typing away at a computer. I'd never seen him before, and he just seemed like a random straggler. I walked past the guy, up the stairs, and retired to the same room I always took when the band stayed at Charlie's. I realized there was somebody's stuff strewn around on the floor, but didn't think twice about it, and passed out as soon as my head hit the pillow. The door creaked open a while later, and there stood the straggler from downstairs.

"That's messed up, man," the Colonel barked. "You bogarted my room."

"Sorry, bro, early bird gets the worm," I shot back. The Colonel bailed back downstairs, and I fell back into slumber. The next morning I told Charlie that "some Colonel Sanders-looking character tried to claim my room, but I wasn't havin' it."

"Oh no," Charlie sighed. "You stole John Sinclair's bed."

John Sinclair was a prominent liberal activist in the sixties, enjoying his fifteen minutes in the controversial sun after being incarcerated for marijuana possession. This injustice pissed off more than a few dope-smoking hippies, and would take on legendary status when John Lennon recounted the ordeal in his song, *Free John Sinclair*.

Charlie had brought in Sinclair to host the festival and boost its cachet. In addition to hippie street cred, Sinclair brought to the table a barrage of unintentionally comedic beat poetry riffs to fire up the crowd between musical acts. In exchange for his emceeing chops and literary gifts, Sinclair had been offered, along with an unknown (but most likely paltry) sum of money, the perk of getting to hole up in Charlie's less-than-luxurious guest bedroom. Now that I had denied him this pleasure, sleep-deprived Sinclair had a chip on his shoulder, and would exact revenge by refusing to acknowledge Living Large for the remainder of the festivities.

I've long harbored guilt over "bogarting" the bed of a historical figure of John Sinclair's magnitude, and I think it's time I make amends. I figure the best way to right the ship is to further immortalize Sinclair in song, so I've re-written the lyrics to John Lennon's stirring call to action. Here goes…

GIVE JOHN SINCLAIR HIS BED BACK

It ain't fair, John Sinclair
In Utah, yeah, what happened there
His bed got jacked without a care
Won't you help out John Sinclair
Let him be, set him free
Do it for my man, Charlie
I stole his room, I took his spot
While he was downstairs smoking pot
Now he's gotta, gotta, gotta, gotta
Take the couch, yeah
Gotta, gotta, gotta, gotta take the couch

If I'd known just who he was
I'd still have snaked his room because
He treated me and my band rude
He looks like Colonel Sanders, too

I walked into the house that night
Marched past the man without a fight
Went upstairs and hit the sack
His shit was strewn around unpacked

He came up later, barged right in
Said, "Can I have the bed back, for a fin?"

I said, "Hell no, take the couch you fool"
In a hippie drawl, he said "That ain't cool"
"Early bird gets the worm," I crowed
So John Sinclair skulked back below
And snubbed my tribe the next two days
Refused to announce us 'fore we played

Was I punished for what I'd done?
For bogarting the man's bed, just for fun?
Don't know, but I sure slept like a rock
He banged and banged, but the door, I locked
Now I gotta, gotta, gotta, gotta
Gotta, gotta, gotta, gotta
Give John Sinclair his bed back

Living Large was making progress in the JBS, but reports of Lincoln's aggressive business tactics were reaching the band. He'd booked us in a large San Francisco hall called the Russian Center, working with the promoters of High Sierra Music Festival, the West Coast's premier JBS gathering. Lincoln insisted we were worthy of a high guarantee, but the Russian Center show bombed. Then, when the lineup for High Sierra was announced a couple weeks later, Living Large was conspicuously absent from the roster. Though his intentions were good, Lincoln was rubbing people the wrong way, throwing his weight around as if we were on a par with KDTU. We were rising, but we couldn't draw enough of a crowd to back up the demands.

A division began to form within the organization. Woo, a guy who truly had his finger on the pulse of the JBS, expressed frustration over how the band was handling promotion, tour strategy, and the cultivation of a loyal fan base. He felt that by allowing Lincoln to strong-arm potential allies, be they booking agents, promoters, or various other important players, the band was making a grave mistake.

Lincoln wasn't just the manager, however; he was largely responsible for creating Living Large in the first place. It was his passion, his platform, and he was determined to run the organization the way he saw fit. Unlike Woo, he didn't define himself through the milieu of the modern hippie movement, nor the grass roots music scene of which groups like Phish and Widespread Panic were king. Instead, Lincoln saw the JBS as a stepping stone in Living Large's quest to become a global musical and marketing force. Lincoln was committed to maintaining an African-American identity, in terms of the music, the image of the band, and even the public persona he was attempting to cultivate. Being recognized by the black community was important to Lincoln.

Karl Denson, it seemed to me, had realized his grass roots national fan base was not just a means to an end, not just some temporary reality to be tolerated until his act evolved into something bigger and better. No, these were the people buttressing Karl's career, whose investment in his music would one day pay his kids' college tuition. He understood and respected this. Perhaps part of Karl's brilliance was his ability to effortlessly bridge the gap between black and white. Nobody would ever accuse the man of selling out to a mass audience, or of kowtowing to anyone—but Karl also avoided marginalizing himself. He didn't narrow his market by making race an essential part of his artistic identity.

As time passed I started to sense that Lincoln and Woo were polar opposites, pulling the band and its music in different directions. Lincoln envisioned the band winding up, stylistically speaking, as a spin-off of Incognito or Meshell Ndegeocello. Woo's vision combined Maceo Parker, the Meters and Phish. Had Lincoln and Woo worked together harmoniously, it's frightening to imagine what the band might have been able to achieve, given all the talent involved.

I'M RIGHT HERE

In the late summer of 2001, Living Large played a show in Boise, Idaho, a *late-night* for a tour featuring Karl Denson's Tiny Universe, DJ Logic, Rusted Root, and Bob Weir's Rat Dog. Late-nights were an important tool, as they gave a band the chance to win over the audience of a more established act. This particular late-night turned into a rock star party, as members of the aforementioned bands started pouring in. Karl Denson jumped up to play with us, marking his first reunion with Mario since the trumpeter had abruptly left Tiny Universe.

As we relaxed in the V.I.P. room during a break, Little Jesus spotted Grateful Dead icon Bob Weir. He approached Jerry Garcia's right-hand man to ask if he could take a picture with him, and Weir, clearly inebriated, shrugged his shoulders and grunted, "I'm right here." This seemed to mean *I guess so.* The moment inspired an ongoing road joke, in which one guy would say "I'm right here," and another would add, "like Bob Weir."

Before leaving Boise, I had a lengthy phone conversation with Lincoln. He was disillusioned, and confided in me that he was considering quitting as manager of Living Large. He felt Mario didn't appreciate his efforts and sacrifices. I assured Lincoln that good things were happening in the scene; people were speaking favorably about the band, and it was worth hanging in there. He seemed reassured by my words, and I hung up thinking everything would be okay.

The band cut back across the Northwest, stopping in Bingen, Washington to play a bar along Hood River. Mario was in rare form that night, wandering around the joint before and after every trumpet solo, talking to girls. We all did our fair share of talking to girls, of course—just not while actually *performing*.

I got fairly drunk that night, slugging back my medicine of choice, Captain and Coke,[122] with the also-drunk bar owner, a middle-aged lady who played some piano. She had an out-of-tune upright in the bar, and we sat there playing songs and throwing back cocktails until sunrise.

The next morning, I slept it off in some kind of hostel, located within a set of buildings that had previously served as Bingen's high school. I was roused from slumber by a knock. I rubbed my eyes, rose to my feet and opened the door. Ignacio was standing there in his boxer shorts, a troubled look on his face. "My friend," he said in characteristic *Cube-lish*, "They are blowing up buildings. We are at war, my friend."

It was the morning of September 11, 2001. The members of Living Large gathered in a lounge, watching in disbelief as the second World Trade Center tower crumbled. It was our era's equivalent of watching the JFK assassination on television in 1963. You knew you were witnessing events that would impact the rest of your life as an American, and you knew you would remember exactly where you were and what you were doing when it happened.

Living Large was scheduled to play a show that same night in Eugene, Oregon. I was certain it would be cancelled, and in no mood to perform after what I'd witnessed on the TV. Like most Americans, I was quite upset about what had happened. The venue in Eugene, however, decided to go ahead with the show. They expected us to be there and were holding us to our contract. I anticipated the club would

---

[122] My medicine of choice remains Captain and Coke, only now, in an ongoing battle against the abdominal spare tire of middle age, it has been modified to Captain and *Diet* Coke.

be a ghost town that evening, but it wasn't the case. Lots of people showed up and proceeded to drink and party as if it was just another day. I looked out at tables of rowdy college kids, loud and loaded, and thought to myself, *Are you really this numb?* Near a university campus you would expect a more sensitive reaction to events of such profound implications. The kids in this bar didn't give a damn about what was happening on the East Coast, no matter how earth-shattering.

The next day we stopped for gas on the way to Santa Cruz. We'd been listening to a radio show discussing the projected backlash against Middle Eastern people in the U.S., sure to result from 9/11. A few of us walked into the convenience store, where the clerk was clearly Middle Eastern. There was a moment of tension as we exchanged glances with the man. Then he flashed a grin and said, "Hello guys! Welcome! How can we help you today?" It was the first time I could recall receiving such a warm salutation from a minimart clerk. I made a point of smiling and being kind, realizing this man, along with many other Middle Eastern people in America, had suddenly been put in a very awkward position. Germany would never entirely escape its association with Hitler and the Nazis, whites in America would always be tainted by their historical role as oppressors and racists, and Arab-Americans would now be stigmatized as a result of a few murderous, suicidal individuals.

As we continued the drive south to Santa Cruz, Mario called Lincoln and began discussing the Living Large studio album, which we'd been recording for the past couple months. It had only been a week or two since I'd first talked Lincoln out of quitting as the band's manager, then into giving Mario another chance. I thought Lincoln and I were solid, and had no reason to believe we were on the verge of a major falling out. Mario passed the phone to me and I expressed some minor concern about the recording process; were we, the band, going to have creative input in the mixing and sequencing of the songs for the album? Lincoln's tone became stern as he replied, "I want to be very clear here... *I'm* producing the album. You're staying on the road."

We had comforted each other in times of frustration, and our relationship had been built on mutual respect... or so I thought. I didn't view Lincoln as my boss, nor the proprietor of my music. Living Large had evolved as a start-up business, with various people bringing complementary talents to the table. Now I was sensing that some kind of power play was being made, and I didn't like it. I was a vital part of the vision, not a flunkie.

"I'm not comfortable with that," I told Lincoln.

"*I'm* the producer," he repeated. "I'm gonna put the music together in a way that I can sell it."

The next four words that came out of my mouth opened the floodgates for a battle of wills that would derail the Living Large organization, and force my musical career in a new direction: "That's not your place," I answered.

"What?" Lincoln screamed. "Not my motherfuckin' place? Let me tell you something. Mario *is* the band. You got that? He *is* the band." Not only was this the ultimate insult to me, John and Ignacio, but the fact that Lincoln actually believed it was all about Mario called into question his grip on reality.

"I already signed Mario to a record contract, dawg," Lincoln continued. "It has nothing to do with you. You're expendable." When I heard this I knew my days in Living Large were numbered. If Mario *was* the band, and the rest of us could go at any time—if this charismatic but highly unorganized, impulsive trumpet player, who had written two songs in as many years, and whose unpredictable antics had tarnished his personal reputation—if *he* was the whole band, then Living Large was a band I didn't need to be a part of anymore.

Woo saw the writing on the wall. He knew that if *I* was going, he was probably on the way out, too. He had openly defied Lincoln, questioning the manager's marketing strategies and overall leadership ability. Together Woo and I had quietly formed an alliance, and now that Lincoln and Mario's balance of power was being threatened, we were the ones who would be deleted from the equation. Lincoln had encouraged Mario to walk from Karl Denson's Tiny Universe during its height of popularity, a decision that had paved the way for my initial opportunity, but one that also flew in the face of logic. Furthermore, Lincoln prided himself on making bold, swift moves. If he was going to rise to the elite ranks of an entertainment mogul, more than a few people were going to get bruised along the way. Mario and Lincoln had started Living Large. It was their vision, their baby, their dream. In the end it was their table, and Woo and I had just been sitting at it.

Once we got to Santa Cruz, Woo and I dropped Mario at a hotel, and we went to my mother Anne's house in Aptos, along with John, Ignacio and the Mayor. In the morning we gathered to discuss the future of the project. A guitarist friend from San Francisco, Dan Lebowitz, called as we were having this discussion, and told me Lincoln had called *him* and asked that he play the next couple Living Large shows in my absence, because I was having *technical difficulties*. Right then and there I knew I was probably going to get screwed somehow. I had Woo pay me a thousand bucks from the band fund, a portion of what I had earned per my agreement with Lincoln. Seasoned enough by now to have been fucked over (in terms of money) more than a couple times, I couldn't take that chance this time. Woo also gave Little Jesus and the Mayor some money for their work in the crew, but John and Ignacio refused to take any.

I was hoping John and Ignacio would join me in defending our collective right to have creative control of our music. If we presented a united front, Lincoln would have to acquiesce on some level. Anne pulled me aside, however, and laid down the truth: "Anth, these guys aren't going to side with you. They're going to stay with Lincoln. You're going to have to do this alone." She was right, but not *entirely* right: When it all hit the fan a couple days later, I would find that I wasn't all alone... there *were* people in my corner. Just not the guys in the band.

I went ahead and played the Catalyst show in Santa Cruz, with Dan Lebowitz sitting in on guitar. The next day Lincoln announced that he was flying up from San Diego for the band's show at the Elbo Room, in San Francisco. A showdown was brewing, and I met with Woo and Todd to figure out a plan. Todd had his own issues with Lincoln. The two had become estranged a few months earlier when Lincoln, who'd accepted Todd's start-up capital to get Living Large off the ground, told Todd, in so many words, to stay out of his way. Lincoln had supposedly said, "You have to submit to me, Todd."

An intelligent computer consultant who'd made a mark on his industry, Todd was willing to help financially and also play a minor role in charting the course for Living Large, but he wasn't going to stand by and get steamrolled by Lincoln and Mario. Todd and I had become close, and if Lincoln now intended to fire me and Woo, while cutting the band's benefactor out of the picture as well, Todd simply wanted to be paid back. He said, "T, I've got your back, regardless of what goes down. Just do me a favor."

"What's that?" I asked.

"After the show, grab the Triton. It's yours now. I paid for it, and I want you to have it."

That night, the Elbo Room was raging by 11 pm. The band played great, maybe the best show we'd ever done. Mario put the trumpet in

378

his mouth and blew with poise and charisma. The rhythm section, joined by percussionist Vick Barerra, dropped nasty grooves all night. I saw Lincoln in the crowd, but we hadn't spoken since his arrival. He'd been too busy, I would later learn, corralling John and Ignacio in an effort to turn them against me and hasten my departure. During the show, Lincoln and Todd nearly came to blows. Todd approached him to have a chat, and Lincoln said "Get out of my face." Todd reciprocated this warm greeting with "Give me my fucking money." It was a conversation going nowhere fast. When Todd repeated his request for payback of the ten thousand dollars he'd invested in Living Large, Lincoln's response was, "You'll have to take that up with Mario. That's *his* business."

The show was so slamming, so promising that Woo and I were lulled into thinking there might be a chance to salvage things. If we all sat down when we got back to San Diego, we might clear the air and work everything out. The band was moving too fast to allow petty squabbles to destroy it; but practically the moment I walked off stage, Lincoln was in my face, handing me a piece of paper. It said, in so many words: *Your services are no longer required by Living Large.*

Lincoln, whose personal bible at that time was a book called *The 49 Laws of Power,* had elected to decapitate the two-headed serpent of dissention; Woo was handed his walking papers also. I stood there on the dance floor at one-thirty in the morning, reading my termination letter. I was not invited to ride back to San Diego with the band, and would have to make my own travel arrangements. (I was provided a bit of money for a one-way flight). My instruments and equipment would be returned to me once we were all back home.

There was no way in hell I was going to part with my musical gear, and just *hope* it would be waiting for me when I got back to San Diego. I stored my keyboards backstage, including the Triton, which somehow slipped off Lincoln's radar. This was a move that took some balls, because I knew push would come to shove when Lincoln realized he didn't have the Triton in the band trailer.

I arranged with the club to come back the next afternoon for my equipment, and walked outside as the manager locked the door behind us. I stood with Woo on the street, watching as Lincoln pleaded his final case to the remaining band members inside the van. He said, "Those who wish to move forward with Mario Walker and Living Large remain seated. If you would like to follow the vision of Anthony Smith, Andy Morton and Todd Sherman, now's the time to get out of the van." *Creeeeak!* The van door slid open. Out jumped the Mayor. Behind him was Little Jesus. Suddenly Anthony Smith, the ousted traitor, was not alone on the street. I had Woo to my right, the Mayor and Little Jesus to the left. My new splinter group was four deep on that San Francisco street corner. Sadly, but I suppose not entirely surprisingly, Living Large had been divided along racial lines.

It was time for the coup de grâce. Lincoln came marching over to the front of the Elbo Room, peering inside from behind the locked steel gate. "Open this gate. We still have equipment inside." *He had remembered the Triton.* The iron grill at the club's entrance prevented anyone from entering, but you could see what was going on inside. Several employees were sitting at the bar, tallying cash. They looked up when Lincoln issued his command, but quickly returned to their work, ignoring the request. Lincoln shook the gate. "Open this gate immediately. I have equipment inside!" This time nobody even looked up. They just kept counting money. Lincoln turned in my direction, furious.

"Where's the Triton?" he asked.

"It's inside still. Todd told me to keep it. He says *he* paid for it, and it's mine now." This made Lincoln livid. He moved to get up in my face, but Woo saw this coming, took off his glasses, and stepped in between the two of us. If Lincoln wanted to take a swing at me, he was going to have to swing through Woo first. Now, *that's* a good friend. In one fell swoop, Woo had earned his place in *T's Circle of Lifelong Trust.*

Lincoln decided to back down. "You know what?" he said, "Keep the Triton." He hopped in the van, and the remaining members of Living Large sped off into the night. On the surface, the blow-up seemed to have a racial component, but in reality it was more about power. There had been several big egos jousting for power (not excluding my own), and something had to give.

The next day I grabbed my equipment at the Elbo Room, rented a minivan to transport me and the other three defectors, and we hit the road for San Diego. It was one memorable ride. We laughed, bitched, smoked pot, and agreed we were going to keep moving forward, someway and somehow. We had been good friends before the previous evening's developments, but now we were blood brothers—a low-budget, hippie version of the Corleone Family.

We'd had a promising thing going, and Woo and I believed all five of us had been integral to the rise of Living Large. The way we saw it, I had been the main songwriter, Woo had been the JBS mastermind, the Mayor had been responsible for the band's quality live sound, Todd had been the principal supporter, in both a financial and moral sense, and Little Jesus had been a hard-working roadie and loyal JBS homey. Lincoln and Mario were pulling the rug out on *themselves*. We had everything we needed to keep the ball rolling on our own. All we needed was a new name and a few new musicians.

We set up shop in my San Diego apartment and began organizing our new project. Literally *two days* after the Elbo Room, I was well on my way to establishing a new touring group. The Mayor, holed up at his parents' house in Murietta, drove down during the afternoons to help with the overall plan. Woo sat on my computer making contacts, following up with promoters we had worked with in the past, and began to piece together a maiden voyage for the new band.

Woo had just been offered the road manager gig with Project Logic, which would have meant a jump in pay, perks and credibility, but he opted to hang with his boys. This lit a fire under my ass to get the new ensemble together quick; I reached out to my extensive network of San Diego musicians. I had a good reputation in town, had many friends who were good players, and knew I'd be able to rally a handful of cats hungry to hit the road and break out of the local same ole'.

The initial band included alto saxophonist Nash Masters, who was also my roommate. I was converting our quiet, two-bedroom apartment in University Heights into headquarters of the new organization, and saw no way of justifying this without offering Nash a gig. He was paying rent, and it wasn't fair to infringe on his space unless he had an interest in what was happening. Plus, he was an excellent sax player, and I imagined the confident sound of his alto working well with the funky material the new band was going to play.

On bass, I called upon Gary Klein, who I'd known for years in San Diego. Gary had written original music and recorded a couple albums, and his versatility appealed to me. Through a stroke of good timing, Drew Reed, Karl Denson's drummer for the past couple years, was also suddenly available. Without knowing much about the circumstances of his departure, I called Drew to talk about the new band. After a couple phone conversations, he committed to joining. He too was anxious to get back on the road and follow his own vision.

It was an exciting time. More than ever in my life, I was laying it all on the line, risking everything. I was driven by pride, eager to show not only Lincoln, Mario, John and Ignacio, but the JBS as a whole that I was not expendable—that I deserved to be out on the road, playing big shows in prestigious venues. *That was where I belonged.*

It was also a scary time. I believed in what we were going after, but was also pragmatic enough to recognize the risk. There were no guarantees this whole thing was going to fly. I knew this, but I was going to follow through with my vision come hell or high water. I've never been more driven to do anything than I was to launch that band. It was the culmination of everything I had been through, everything I had worked for over the years, and everything I hoped to get out of my future career. I was jumping without a net, and it was damn invigorating.

My frustration with Lincoln and Mario, who I felt had sabotaged a potentially great band, also spurred me on. Rather than whine about what had happened, I wanted to take action. By moving forward without blaming anyone for anything, Woo and I would show the JBS community that we were committed to the scene and committed to our music. Truthfully, I also realized that what had happened to Living Large wasn't completely Lincoln or Mario's fault. In my heart of hearts, I hadn't wanted to be a sideman, for Mario or anyone else; and Woo just wasn't cut out to be someone's road-managing yes man. I had my own ideas about music and about running a band, Woo had his own ideas about the scene and its culture, and it was time to take our shot, on our own terms.

Using Little Jesus's Salt Lake City connections, Woo started putting together dates for a band that still had no name. After a bit of deliberation, we made a decision. We were going to be *Global Funk Council.* The name jumped out at you on the page, had a nice ring to it, and packed the kind of wallop that would get people who had never heard of us into clubs. I realized, even then, that the day might come when a name with the word *funk* in it might backfire, leading people to pigeonhole the act, but I was willing to take that chance in order to generate immediate market interest. People were going to dig the idea of Global Funk Council, especially when they learned it featured former members of Karl Denson's Tiny Universe and Living Large. If we had to milk the *all-star funk band* angle to get ourselves on the map, so be it.

Woo nailed down a run of Utah and Idaho dates for early November, leaving us little time to get our music together. I wasn't worried, as I was convinced that if the business side of things was organized well, the music would be fine. I still believe this. Throw good musicians together and they're going to make good music. The presentation and marketing of that music? That's a trickier can of worms. That requires real ingenuity.

In order to rehearse with Drew, who lived in San Jose, Woo and I made plans to be in the Bay Area for a while. We brought Nash with us, and quickly realized the guy was going to struggle to *make the road*. A mere two hours into the eight-hour drive to San Francisco, Nash complained that he was uncomfortable. He was tired of sitting in the car. You expect this from a child, yes, but not from a full-grown man. "Are we almost there?" doesn't sound quite as cute coming from a twenty-four year-old dude with stubble.

For Woo, the distance between San Diego and San Francisco was the equivalent of driving up the street to the 7-11 near your house, to pick up cream for your morning pot of coffee. He had once driven the Living Large van straight from San Diego to Little Rock, Arkansas, stopping only for gas—the guy had major road chops. When the Red Bull (or whatever was fueling his extraordinary abilities behind the wheel) wore off, he would start cranking CD's at loud volume, and also roll down the driver-side window to get a continual blast of cold air. If you were riding shotgun, the moment the CD ended Woo would yell "CD! CD!" This meant you needed to pop out the one that had finished and replace it with something else, as fast as possible. If you chose something not to his liking he would say, "Not that candy-ass shit! Give me some Meters or James Brown!" He had his quirks, but Woo's stamina was comparable to that of a seasoned truck driver.

Little Jesus stayed at my apartment in San Diego, holding down the fort. In Little Jesus Land, *holding down the fort* translated to nursing an old bag of freezer-burned chicken breasts, getting in fistfights at the dive bar on the corner, and pissing off my neighbors by chain-smoking cigarettes in the courtyard and carrying on profane cell phone conversations. Come to think of it, I don't remember how he was able to even afford a cell phone!

Once we got to San Francisco, the plan was to stay with Dan Lebowitz and his girlfriend, Jenna, in their second-story flat in the Mission District. I was hoping Dan would join Global Funk Council on guitar, but he wanted to check out the vibe before he made a commitment. After we'd crashed there a couple days, Dan and Jenna's roommates made their wishes clear: *Get yo asses out.* We had to find another place to set up shop. I called my friend Debbie.

Debbie and I had first crossed paths a year earlier at the Rolling Summer Festival. She saw me standing there, artist laminate hanging from my neck, backwards baseball cap and scruffy stubble, and was somehow impressed. With her cherry-highlighted black hair, made up face and short skirt, Debbie distinguished herself from the dreadlock-shaking, patchouli-doused crowd. She said hello and offered me some spiked lemonade, back at her car. I accepted, and told her not to make it too stiff. I had a show to play.[123] Her response was, "Fine. I'll do that later." Had this been on the set of a porn production in a rented duplex in Van Nuys, it would have amounted to brilliant, award-winning dialogue. In the dirt parking lot of some fledgling hippie festival in northern Utah, it was pretty cheesy.

I invited Debbie to crash at Charlie Crompton's abode that night, along with me and the rest of the band. I had given the mighty John Sinclair his bed back, so everything was cool, save the activist's irritation due to the nocturnal frivolities taking place in adjacent rooms, while he attempted to concentrate on his unique brand of shopworn, quasi-Kerouacian prose.

Debbie and I kept in touch after Utah, becoming good friends. She welcomed the idea of me staying at her place in San Francisco for a few days. It was testimony to her kind nature that when I told her I'd be dragging along three grown men, including one with a tendency to bicker like a five year-old serving "time out!" in the corner, her enthusiasm did not wane. Woo, Nash, Gary (who flew up from San Diego to rehearse on the weekends) and I showed up on Debbie's doorstep, offering nothing more than a Ziploc bag filled with shitty pot, and our magnetic personalities.

It may sound as if I brokered my affections in exchange for a roof over our heads, but I liked Debbie. She lived a hard lifestyle and had the guffaw of a sixty year-old sailor, but she also believed in my talent, and had no doubt I was going to get this new project off the ground and be successful. God knows, I needed that belief. Others saw in Debbie a smoking, drinking groupie, an unabashed hedonist—but I saw a solid, generous person, and my instincts were pretty good in such matters.

---

[123] That shows you how early this was in my touring days. Later on, when things really went to hell, I would have wanted that drink to be as stiff as possible, regardless of whether or not there was a show to play.

Nash complained about moving around between people's pads, about winging it the way one does when trying to get something done on a shoestring budget, and also about Debbie herself. "Okay," I thought, "Let's stay at *your* friends' houses for a while. Here's the ball... run with it." Had we relied on Nash's "social network" for lodging, we would have found ourselves scurrying for shelter in some sketchy park near the Presidio.

The first GFC rehearsals, held in Dan's apartment, went well. Everyone clicked for the most part, and the groove felt solid. We drew upon a pre-existing catalogue of my original songs from the old Living Large repertoire, with the goal of eventually including everyone's compositions. I wanted the band to operate as a collective, and hoped to avoid the ego battles that had precipitated the Living Large meltdown.

In Living Large, Mario had clung to the belief that he was *the guy*, the focus of everything we were doing. I wanted to create a situation with my new group where everyone got their chance to be *the guy*. I believed that each member of the group should feel like a valued part of the creative process—like he or she was indispensible. I wanted everyone in GFC to feel a sense of creative ownership. I was determined not to be a control freak.

It was a noble goal, but in retrospect I realize it was somewhat misguided. An egalitarian approach fails in the arts for the same reasons it breaks down in other areas of life; some people are equipped to contribute more than others. Some hold themselves to the highest of standards, while others are lazy underachievers. Here's another thing: Some people have original, brilliant ideas. Whether it's innate or learned, they come up with inspired gems, time and again. Other people, bold as they might be to chime in with their two cents, have mediocre, pedestrian ideas. If you sit around entertaining everyone's input with an equal investment of time and energy, you waste a lot of time on bad ideas.

Andrew Ridgeley, part of the eighties pop duo Wham!, was shrewd enough to recognize that his own musical talent was negligible, but his partner, George Michael, was a pop songwriting genius. Ridgeley had hit the jackpot and he knew it. He got out of his buddy's way, let him write a couple multi-platinum albums, and was rewarded immensely for understanding the reality of the situation. Of course Michael dumped him after they made it big, but let's just say you're never going to see Andrew Ridgeley folding your burrito at Chipotle.

THREE MEN AND A DOG

We spent a few days at Debbie's place, hanging out during the day, partying and hitting clubs at night. Debbie and her roommate, the singer in an all-girl cover band called Thunderpussy, were cool with us staying longer but I didn't want to wear out a friend's welcome. Luckily another friend named Candida, a Bay Area concert promoter, was taking off for the weekend and needed someone to watch her dog Muca.

I dragged Nash and Woo over to Candida's apartment near the Haight District, buying us a couple more days off the streets. From the moment we arrived our hands were full. Muca, affectionate but horribly behaved, ran amuck in the small apartment, trying to break anything he could get his paws on. Woo wasted no time in reprimanding the unruly animal, while Nash, impervious to his surroundings, stared like a stoned zombie at the fuzzy TV screen. (There was no cable). I was worried that Woo's high-pitched, abusive cackle would prompt some neighbor to call to the S.P.C.A. "Muca! Muca! Sit the fuck down!" I had witnessed Woo take a much softer tone with his own dog Petunia, a fat little bulldog with horrible breath and a snore so loud it rattled the walls of the ranch house in Durham.

Muca's relentless digestive system necessitated frequent trips to the Golden Gate panhandle. On the way back to the apartment, I would stop at a local grocery mart for things like gnocchi and canned tomato sauce. As I stirred the cheap sauce in Candida's kitchen, Nash and Woo lounging on the couch taking endless bong hits, a voice in my head wondered: *What the hell are you doing slumming in San Francisco? You had plenty of local work in San Diego. You had a decent life. Are you nuts?*

Sleeping provisions were limited. Candida had asked that I take the bed, since I was the one she actually knew. "Sorry, guys," I said. "Candida wants me to sleep in her bed. You get the floor. We should respect her wishes."

One night, Woo stayed out late partying at the nearby Justice League club. When he returned I was in the bed, Nash sprawled out on the couch. All that remained for him was the cold, hardwood floor. In the morning I found Woo in the fetal position on the ground, attempting to balance his large mass on two tiny cushions from the couch. A dirty sweatshirt served as his blanket, while Muca gently gnawed at his face. It was both funny and sad.

We caught several shows, including one by Garaj Mahal, a driving rock/jazz quartet in the spirit of the Mahavishnu Orchestra. Woo, I and even deadpan Nash were impressed. The bassist, Kai Eckhart, had toured with John McLauglin, and guitarist Fareed Haque was something of a minor star in international jazz circles.

We also caught Rodney Jones's Soul Manifesto, with Fred Wesley on trombone and Idris Muhammed on drums, and Project Logic, a cutting edge funk/electronica group. Another night we checked out Charlie Hunter, the innovative Bay Area guitarist, who augmented his Fillmore show with a guest appearance by Norah Jones, at that time unknown. Jones sang *Tennessee Waltz,* which, while not unpleasant, left me wondering *what's the big deal?* Shows you what I knew.

Another night, I scored a free ticket to see southern rock gods Widespread Panic at the Greek Theatre. I wasn't impressed with the band that night; they struck me as one-dimensional and boring. What *was* impressive was their fanatical following of fans who screamed the words to every song. Guitarist Michael Hauser, seemingly immune to the crowd's energy, sat in a chair looking down the whole show. Hauser would die of pancreatic cancer in 2002.

My previous trip to the Greek Theatre, to see The String Cheese Incident, had been quite memorable...

For some reason, SCI shows always brought out my wild, impulsive side. I had gone with a group of friends, and decided to smoke some herb during the first set (something I would do only on rare occasion). I was feeling good, coming off the previous String Cheese show in Santa Barbara, where Mario Walker and I had joined the band for a couple songs, him on trumpet and me on vibraphone.[124]

As I hit the pipe handed to me, there amongst the earthy crowd at the Greek, I asked the Mayor, "Why is the nugget red?"

"Because it's really premium shit, T," he responded. That was good enough for me, ganja novice that I was, and I took another two or three healthy rips off the pipe, cashing it. As I sat watching the show, an unfamiliar feeling of euphoria rippled through my body in smooth, pleasurable waves. Marijuana never had such a soothing effect on me—it usually made me edgy.

"Damn, Mayor... I'm pretty high," I mumbled.

"Yeah," he chuckled. "Opium will do that to you." *Opium?* I would have protested the Mayor's trickery, but was too relaxed to complain. As I sat there feeling no pain, I suddenly became aware that I really had to take a whiz. In fact, I had never had to take one so desperately, except for perhaps one time when I was nine or ten, and was forced to relieve myself, *in my pants*, in a drugstore that didn't have a public bathroom. Now, twenty years later, the opium high had disconnected me from that reliable awareness of bodily needs that prevents one from wetting (or soiling) themselves. It felt like my bladder was going to burst.

I stumbled to the nearest bathroom, ducked into a stall and prepared for the leak of a lifetime. As I was squaring myself away, I noticed something down by the toilet. Overlapping into my stall was the bare foot of some hippie dude, peeing in the next booth over. Why would he come into this filthy bathroom barefoot? What kind of person did that?

---

[124]Mario had angered SCI mandolin player Mike Kang during a version of John Coltrane's *Impressions,* when Mario transformed, in mid-solo, from trumpet player to Solid Gold dancer, abandoning his horn to bust some strange moves.

I began to manipulate my wrinkled firehose toward the bowl in front of me, but couldn't take my eye off the guy's foot. In an opium-induced state of delirium, that fungus-ridden foot became my whole world; the focus of my existence. Something strange began to happen. My arm moved left, re-directing my equipment so that the trajectory of the coming stream was now in line with the naked, exposed hoof. Like that classic scene in *Evil Dead II*, it was like my hand now had a mind of its own, or was possessed by some kind of demented gremlin. This guy was taking one hell of a leak, and his foot seemed like it was planted there to mock me, to snicker at me in my drug-addled stupor. I clenched my bladder muscles in desperation, but that foot screamed out at me, its hairy toes, overgrown nails and crusty calluses all issuing a clear demand:

PEE ON ME

A powerful stream shot from my loins, first blasting the toes then dousing the entire foot in a yellow puddle. "Jesus!" the guy screamed, his deep voice reverberating off the walls as his foot shot back under the stall, like a reptile darting under a rock. *You mock me, oh stinky, defiant hippie foot? Then feel the wrath of the opium rain.*

As the deluge continued, I felt a slap on the back of my head. I finished the job, zipped up and stumbled outside. Spotting the guy up ahead, I raced to catch up.

"Hey man, why did you slap my head?"

"Cause you pissed on my foot, bro."

"Maybe you should think twice about slapping people."

"Maybe you shouldn't urinate on people's bare feet."

"Maybe if your foot was covered up it wouldn't have got peed on."

"Try pissing on my foot again and see what happens."

"You want to settle this in the parking lot?"

"Let's go."

We both started striding toward the parking lot, ready to square off. The absurdity of the conflict hit us both at once. We looked each other in the eye and couldn't help cracking a smile.

"Dude, I'm sorry. My friends got me wasted on opium."

"No worries, bro. Didn't really wanna fight anyway. Have a good one."

I returned to the concert and grooved to the rest of String Cheese's bluegrass-flavored set. You think beer makes white men dance better… you should see the effects of hard drugs. I was a regular Fred freakin'Astaire out there.

It was time to return to San Diego. We had two more weeks to rehearse and make preparations for our first tour. When I got home, there were messages on my machine from Lincoln, Mario and John. They wanted me to re-join Living Large for rehearsals at the downtown Children's Museum, and then hit the road for a lengthy East Coast tour. Had I missed something? Was I only imagining that Woo and I had been fired after the Elbo Room show?

The ramifications of Lincoln's hasty decision had started to hit home. Mario would be steering the ship now, and given the quirks of the trumpeter's personality, Lincoln must have realized the challenges this would present. Living Large now faced the prospect of heading out on tour with a mere twenty minutes worth of material—I'd asked John and Ignacio to stop playing my songs.

I told Lincoln I'd consider the tour, but only if it included Woo. Lincoln balked at the idea; he believed the JBS mastermind from Northern California had undermined his leadership, and had no love for the big guy anymore. I pointed out that Woo had watched my back and stuck with me, not to mention how much he had done to help Living Large. There was no way I was doing anything further with Mario unless it also involved Woo. Lincoln acknowledged that we were at an impasse, and that's where the conversation, and the idea of me returning to Living Large, ended.

Woo and I finalized the Global Funk Council tour and finished assembling the new band. My apartment was pretty crowded, with Drew, Dan, Little Jesus, Woo, Nash and I all crammed in there together. I began to realize that Little Jesus and Nash were something less than a match made in heaven. Nash, who had been my roommate for maybe six months, griped that Little Jesus wasn't respecting our living space—he felt that my Salt Lake sidekick was a slob, and acted like it was *his* apartment. The fact of the matter was that it was *my* apartment, and I had invited to Nash to live there in the first place. Since nothing would compromise my newfound loyalty to Little Jesus and Woo, in the wake of their valiant Elbo Room stand, Nash's trifling quibbles fell on deaf ears. I didn't care what he thought. I was giving him a chance to be part of something bigger than his provincial San Diego world could offer, and he would to have to suck it up if he wanted to hang.

Nash was not the only person Little Jesus was rubbing the wrong way, unfortunately. My Christian circus sidekick had provoked complaints from other tenants in the complex, and the property manager, a gay school bus driver named Vernon, was starting to lay into me. Vernon called me to his apartment one day and warned me that I was on some kind of informal probation, stemming from his distaste with Little Jesus, as well as the fact that someone had complained about a hefty black woman "screaming at the top of her lungs" in my unit one afternoon. It's not what you think... I was having a rehearsal with a classically trained singer, and she was only capable of belting at full volume.

Given the assortment of characters living in that complex, it seemed unfair that Vernon was singling me out. Right below me lived a gay couple—very nice guys, but who occasionally paraded through the courtyard wearing cheekless leather pants, the ones which leave your entire ass exposed, as if to say *come on in, check it out!* Or: *feel free to have a crack at it!* These guys had carefully arranged the common living area of their place, so that one wouldn't know the particulars of their private life, but if you ventured into the back bedroom, as I did one day in between games of billiards, there were strange contraptions and mountings... it was *Hostel* meets *Milk*.[125]

Truthfully, the apartment didn't matter much to me anymore. Many things now seemed disposable—the apartment, my savings, my privacy, my sanity. I was going to make Global Funk Council successful, and nothing would stand in the way. Looking back on all this years later, what was going to matter? This dumb little apartment? Some modest creature comforts? My boring local routine? The illusion of security? My intolerant, gay landlord? No. What was going to matter was that there was an opportunity to do something real, something big, at a point in my life when I could truly seize it, and I was going to grab that son of a bitch with both hands. *That* was what would mean something in the end.

One night, after several days of hard work on the new project, the guys piled into my minivan and we made a late-night run for the border. We had closed down the American bars, and now Tijuana, that sleazy 2 a.m. afterthought that beckons many a drunk male, was calling us with its siren Mariachi song.

---

[125] Two excellent movies, by the way.

I am proud to say I can count my trips to Tijuana over the years on one hand. Some guys I know would need a calculator. You'll recall my earlier account of leading a posse of horny eighteen year-olds into Mexico in 1990. Now, ten years later, I was poised to lead a posse of horny twenty-eight year-olds.

There isn't much to do in Tijuana at 4 am on a weeknight but get in trouble. Adrian Ahearn and I had come to this conclusion the hard way, years earlier…

My bass-playing *compadre* and I, both single and suddenly desiring not to be, had gone lookin' for love in all the wrong places, and the only hook-up that took place was a hammered Mexican guy's fist connecting with my chin. It was a sucker punch I never saw coming, no doubt encouraged by the ridiculous Robin Hood bowl cut I was sporting at the time. Adrian, mostly bald on top with long strands on the side, had covered his head in a rainbow bandanna, rendering him a curious cross between Andre Agassi and Aunt Jemima. In the pugilistic Mexican's defense, we must have looked like a pair of fruitcakes. I was more than ready to fight back, but Adrian wisely reminded me that we had wandered down some funky back alley in Tijuana, and a group of local guys was gathering on the corner, grumbling in our direction. Perhaps this wasn't the time to take a stand.

So here I was, thirty-one years old, the memory of the sucker punch still fresh in my mind, but still game to party in Tijuana. I steered the mini-van south, parking on the U.S. side of the border. We all stumbled across on foot, and as it tends to go down there, a watering hole was located, and multiple *cervezas* were consumed. As it also tends to go down there, the propositions of Tijuana's hardest working labor force did not go unacknowledged.

Nash, as usual, was light on cash. Woo lent him some dough and he disappeared to do his thing. Little Jesus made his selection and also broke from the group. Woo proceeded to negotiate some kind of package deal with a pair of ladies, involving a creative commingling of sex and narcotics, for himself and one other guy who shall remain nameless.

"Okay, this is what we'd like to do…"
(Please use your imagination)

Woo's sordid vision did not come to fruition that evening, mainly for financial reasons. *Yes,* the ladies said, it was possible. Anything is possible. Just not for thirty-seven bucks.

The first Global Funk Council show took place on Halloween night at Dizzy's, a downtown San Diego club. Months earlier I had staged a concert at this same venue, featuring dueling vibraphones. The colorful Dom Drake and I were the two vibes players. Allow me to again digress, reader, for this is a story worth telling...

I had been dating a young Jewish woman named Brianna for a few months. She was a journalist by day, devoted salsa dancer by night. We'd met at the Red Fox, a cool little bar/restaurant on El Cajon Boulevard.

The Red Fox attracted an unusual cross-section of young and older people, as well as artists and musicians. Most nights, a white-haired, spirited lady named Shirley hammered out show tunes on a piano in the corner.

Brianna was writing freelance articles for small magazines and newspapers. One day, I told her about my idea to put together a two-vibraphone concert with Dom Drake, the locally residing but internationally recognized bebop veteran who had, once upon a time, recorded with Bill Evans and other jazz heavyweights. I realize that before I can continue with the Brianna/Dom story, I have to back up even further and share the circumstances surrounding my very first introduction to Dom—*a story within a story*, and also worth telling...

After moving back to San Diego in 1999, to play vibes in Gilbert Castellanos's jazz quartet, one of my first gigs was the annual KSDS Jazz Festival. We were scheduled for an early afternoon slot, followed by the headliner, Dom Drake. Dom, who I'd never met prior to that day, called me in the morning to ask if he could borrow my vibraphone for his set. I said of course, as I was happy to help out such an accomplished jazz veteran.

After I finished playing with Gilbert, Dom walked over and said hello. He was a short guy with a scruffy face, hair pulled back in a ponytail, and a weathered face suggesting multiple decades of hard living. Dom complimented me on my playing, a nice gesture, then took a look at the vibraphone. "Hey, do you think I can use your mallets, too?" *Sure, man. You wanna borrow my car... maybe some cash, too?*

I reluctantly handed over my cherished, purple Bobby Hutcherson mallets, and Dom got ready to start his show. He had been somewhat soft-spoken and reserved up to that point, but once the music began Dom transformed into a new animal: a feral, vibraphone-pounding madman, hammering the shit out of my poor Yamaha vibes. Before the end of the first tune he was drenched in sweat. Also, he'd somehow managed to knock the instrument completely out of alignment.

Dom ran over to me at the side of the side of the stage and screamed, "Something's wrong, man!" I walked over to the vibes and realigned the frame. Dom smiled, said thanks and got back to work putting an absolute hurtin' on those shiny silver bars. Like many jazzers, Dom was in the habit of singing along with whatever melody he was playing—and like the most notorious practitioner of this quirk, pianist Keith Jarrett, Dom did not possess a pleasing singing voice. As he grunted along with his solo (which, in the interest of fairness, was pretty burning), he suddenly decided to do a full three-sixty spin, finishing his move with an exaggerated low-note whack! Liberated of its hipster ponytail during this mallet-wielding spasm, Dom's long hair now waved freely in the wind.

He might have been smacking my vibes like a red-headed stepchild who just totaled the Range Rover, but I had faith Dom wasn't causing any permanent damage. He was, after all, a distinguished vibraphone legend.

After finishing his set to warm applause, I noticed Dom was wiping the surface of my vibes with a paper towel. I was too far away to see exactly what he was doing or why he was doing it—I assumed he'd dripped sweat on the bars, and was cleaning up before handing the instrument back over. I walked closer, getting a sick feeling in my stomach as I approached. Dom looked anxiously in my direction then returned to his frantic wiping. When I got to him I saw that it wasn't his sweat that had drenched my vibes... it was the man's *blood.* It wasn't just a trickle, either. No, Dom had bled profusely on my axe, puddles of crimson splashed across the bars like a Jackson Pollock original. My jaw dropped. *This guy just bled all over my vibes!*

"Don't worry," Dom said, sensing my shock. "I don't have AIDS."

The passage of time had mitigated the horror of *Blood on the Vibes.* Now, a year later, Brianna thought the dueling vibes concert was a great idea. She pitched it to the San Diego Union Tribune, and got the green light to write the piece. Dom agreed to do the event, and I booked a date at Dizzy's. After I'd hired a band and chosen material, Brianna scheduled an interview/photo shoot at Dom's house in Del Mar. Actually, it was Dom's attorney girlfriend's house, in an upscale beach neighborhood.

In the spirit of preserving her journalistic integrity, Brianna and I agreed there was no reason Dom needed to know we were involved romantically. Instead, we would pretend we were meeting for the first time, just as he and she were. We arrived at the house in separate cars, spacing our knocks on the front door over a few minutes to make it look like we were strangers. Dom's girlfriend welcomed us inside, and led us to the back where Dom had his music studio. I surveyed the interior of the pad, determining that these plush surroundings were not the spoils of Dom's career as a jazz vibraphonist. With all due respect for his impressive resumé, he'd obviously hooked up with a chick that had some bread.

Dom, the sixty-something jazz journeyman, was waiting for us in his studio. "Hey, man," he said, shaking my hand. Then he saw Brianna. "Ohhhhhh," he gasped. "You're beautiful." Fair enough. The guy appreciated an attractive young woman. Nothing wrong with that, right?

Brianna began the interview. I was sitting next to her, Dom in a chair facing both of us. She threw out preliminary questions, but Dom more or less ignored them. His mind was somewhere else.

"Are you Jewish?" he asked.

"Yes," she said.

"You're just beautiful," he repeated as he rose up out of his chair and placed his hands on Brianna's cheeks, his face inches from hers. "Beautiful!"

She smiled nervously. Dom was more or less hitting on my girlfriend, in *his* girlfriend's house, and all I could do was sit there like a jerk and ride out the charade.

A photographer from the newspaper had also showed up, so Dom and I posed for a few pictures. Dom and I talked about some tunes we might want to play at the show, then it was time for me, the photographer and Brianna to leave; our business was done. In Dom's mind, however, it wasn't time for *us* to leave. It was time for *the photographer and me* to leave. Dom's girlfriend had split to run some errands, leaving him free reign to operate... if he could just get rid of me and the other guy.

Brianna tried to follow me out, but Dom stepped between us. "Stay a minute," he told her. I got to the door, worried about leaving her in there. "See you at the gig, man," Dom called to me as I reluctantly left. I drove up the street and pulled over, waiting a few minutes before calling Brianna on my cell. "Are you out of there?" I asked.

"Yeah, I just made it out," she said. A fine journalist, she did what she had to do to get her story, sacrificing personal safety in the process. The show with Dom was a big success, Brianna's article generating local interest in both of our careers. I was up for doing it again, but Dom confessed after the performance that he "wasn't comfortable with the format." I dug playing with him, and appreciated the chance to work with such an accomplished fellow vibes player; and to be fair, it's possible that I misread Dom's intentions with Brianna... but I understand musicians, be they young, old or whatever, so in the words of Sir Charles Barkley... *I doubt it.*

After an inaugural, low-key Dizzy's gig, GFC hit the road. I'd bought a trailer to haul equipment and luggage, and rented a fifteen-seat passenger van to haul *us.* The crew included me, Nash, Gary, Little Jesus, the Mayor, Woo, Drew, Dan and Jenna. That's nine people in one van. The driving was all being done by Drew, the Mayor and me, with an occasional shift by Dan. Jenna tried to take the wheel at one point, to pull her weight as road manager, but that lasted about twenty minutes. She was scaring the shit out of everyone, the van weaving in and out of its lane. The wheel looked like a foreign object in her hands. Dan stepped up and said "Hey, babe, I'll take over." Once the switch was made, Drew spoke up, employing his characteristic lack of tact: "Sorry about that Jenna, but I was afraid I was going to die." (Jenna took it in stride, and ultimately got her driving together enough to be able to take occasional shifts).

Our first stop was the Lazy Moon Saloon in Salt Lake City, a club owned and operated by a trio of Little Jesus's friends. As luck would have it, guess who was also in town to play at the nearby Zephyr Club? That's right, Mario Walker and Living Large.

The Lazy Moon show was a big success. The club was packed and the band sounded strong. We had miraculously managed, in only a month since the Elbo Room, to create merchandise (t-shirts, sweatshirts, CDs and stickers) bearing the new Global Funk Council logo, assemble a good band, and book an out-of-state tour. The merchandise sold like hotcakes, and I realized we had co-opted the

Living Large buzz and fan base. John and Ignacio came by the club to say hello, and were dumbfounded by the fact that I, Woo and the gang had not only created a new band, but had started to build a new scene in such a short amount of time. I could hardly believe it myself. It was an amazing accomplishment.

John and Ignacio invited me and the GFC crew to come to the Zephyr the following night to catch Living Large. I wasn't crazy about seeing Mario again, and I'm sure he didn't much want to see me either; nonetheless, I rounded up the troops to show support for John and Ignacio, who despite the rift were still my friends. We walked into the Zephyr around 10 pm, expecting to see a lot of heads. Instead, there were maybe five people inside, and *four of them were wearing new Global Funk Council sweatshirts*. We perched up on the balcony to watch the show, and Mario walked past us on his way to the stage. In a bizarre sartorial turn, the trumpeter had accessorized his usual button-down shirt and dress pants with a mask and cape. He stopped to offer a lukewarm hello, leaving on the mask and cape the whole time. I said "Hey, Mario, what's happening?" What I *really* wanted to say was "On guard!"

Living Large took the stage. We looked and listened from the balcony, Mario leading the new lineup in an opening number that could be summed up as *Loony Tunes* meets *Sketches of Spain*, with a pinch of *Two Mules for Sister Sara*. Drew and I looked at each other, confused. Mario held long, melancholy notes as the rhythm section percolated along with what sounded like a variation of the Casio CZ-101 tango (rhythm preset #39). When the guitarist let out a cactus-flavored twang, it would not have been a surprise to see young, stubble-faced Clint Eastwood saunter through the Zephyr on horseback. Was this Mario Walker and Living Large, or Miles "Zorro" Davis and the Spaghetti Western All-Stars?

After this bizarre opening, Mario broke into a Stevie Wonder cover and returned to form, laying down soulful lines over a smooth R&B pocket. The band found its stride, and the rest of the set was pretty good. Mario might have been an eccentric guy, but I always loved his trumpet sound, and always believed he had a real gift for interpreting a melody.

The GFC tour moved to Ogden, a college town forty minutes north of Salt Lake City. Ogden gave the impression that you'd stepped into a time warp and were back in the year 1976. The buildings were old, the general atmosphere that of a place that stopped modernizing decades ago. The show was at Beatnick's, a small blues club. We packed it, and you could sense in the crowd a feeling of excitement about the band. We were new and we were good. We had a grooving drummer, a talented saxophonist, a capable keyboardist/songwriter (if I may say so myself), and a pair of young but seasoned pros on guitar and bass. The band had great potential, and people in the JBS felt it immediately. Kids were pushed up to the stage, hanging on every riff, every jam; I realized I'd made a wise decision to break out on my own. It was a blast to play for an audience like that. The adrenaline got pumping, and it brought out the best in you. Afterwards, people came up to talk to us, digging what we were laying down. Jenna sold merchandise like hotcakes. Good things were happening.

A friend of mine, Kyra, who had driven up from Salt Lake City, invited me to her hotel room to hang after the show. Kyra and I had gotten to know each other during my Living Large days, first meeting when I was writing a new tune on Charlie Crompton's porch, a reggae ditty called *Chillin' on the Mountain*. Kyra was an artistic young woman who loved live music. She had expressed hope that our friendship might evolve into something more, but these were not the days of exclusivity. Driving around in a van, roaming from town to town, playing shows in bars, throwing back a few cocktails, hitting an after party at someone's house, going to sleep at five-thirty in the morning… this was not the stuff of stability nor monogamy. If you're going to pay the price to live the dream—and pay I did—you might as well live it to the fullest.

I was beat after a long night at Beatnick's, but also buzzing on positive energy. I decided to make an appearance at Kyra's room, in the same hotel where the rest of the band was staying. I didn't realize Kyra was sharing the room with her friend, a fellow music lover who also happened to be named Kyra. I knew Kyra #1 to be a liberal, open-minded person. Her roommate in Salt Lake City was an exotic dancer, who had developed a "friendship" with Mario during earlier Living Large tours of Utah; she had a preference for "friendships" with African-American guys, and would also indulge the occasional "friendship" with a member of the same sex, including her roommate, Kyra #1. Are you following this? Anyway, what I'm getting at is that when Kyra #1 and Kyra #2 began expressing their "friendship" in that hotel room in Ogden, while I was relaxing and sipping a cold beer, my first reaction was not to jump up and bolt out of there.

As I worked on this book, wondering if it would be wise to acknowledge such activities, and also wondering if my wife would ever speak to me again should I elect to do so, certain trusted (male) colleagues suggested that these moments, collectively speaking, represent a fundamental aspect of the touring musician's life; to omit all reference to them would not only be dishonest, but would also deprive the reader, looking first and foremost to be entertained, of a certain vicarious enjoyment. In the end, I decided on a compromise; morally questionable events are sometimes mentioned, yes, but in an oblique manner that does not incriminate the author or his accomplices any more so than necessary.

While perusing *The Moral Animal*, Robert Wright's astute overview of modern evolutionary psychology, I noticed convincing parallels between the sexuality of males in the great ape family and human males, or for our specific purposes here, *traveling musician males:*

> Orangutan males are drifters. They wander in solitude, looking for females, who tend to be stationary, each in her own home range.

He continues:

> A male may settle down long enough to monopolize one, two or even more of these ranges, though vast monopolies are discouraged by the attendant need to fend off vast numbers of rivals. Once the mission is accomplished, and the resident female gives birth, the male is likely to disappear. He may return years later, when pregnancy is again possible. In the meantime, he doesn't bother to write.

Wright goes on to say:
> The goal is to become leader of a pack comprising several adult females.

And also that:
> As a dominant male, he will get sole access to the females.

Applied to the traveling male musician, much of this rings true, with the following exceptions: First, Wright contends that "vast monopolies are discouraged by the attendant need to fend off vast numbers of rivals"… the truth is, the traveling male musician needn't be concerned with rivals. He can co-exist with rivals harmoniously, because by the time a rival has been alerted to his establishment of a new monopoly, the traveling male musician is asleep in the van, already halfway to the next gig in Klamath Falls.

Also, Wright says that the male "may return years later, when pregnancy is again possible." Actually, the traveling male musician goes to great lengths to avoid *initial* pregnancy—that is, unless he wishes to follow in B.B. King's footsteps; or Shawn Kemp, if you are a hoops fan. For that matter, it is unlikely that the traveling male musician will make enough money to still be out there on the road, "years later."

Wright also slightly misses the mark with this comment: "As a dominant male, he will get sole access to the females." The traveling male musician is not seeking sole access. He's merely hoping to acquire *temporary* access.

We were only a week into the tour when I noticed a troubling chink in the armor. Nash and Gary had formed some sort of *complainer's alliance,* and it was becoming clear they weren't willing to make the sacrifices necessary to build something with the rest of us. The Mayor had warned me about Nash from day one: "T, I don't think this is the right kid."

Our next stop was a hippie commune near Zion. We'll call it Rustic Wells. Nestled within an obscure, middle-of-nowhere town in central Utah, the place combined the psychedelic atmosphere of a Grateful Dead lot with the eerie isolation of the Branch Davidian compound in Waco, circa 1991.

The facility included natural hot springs, a gift shop with glasswork and knick-knacks, a small music stage, and some humble lodging. After surveying the scene Little Jesus said to Tom, the owner, "This place is cool, man. It could grow into a nice thing."

"Nothing's growing, man!" Tom snapped, thinking Little Jesus was insinuating that something was *growing* in the basement.[126] Despite Tom's occasional passive-aggressive flare-ups, I liked the guy. He supported creative music, and not just stuff that sounded like the Grateful Dead. He liked funk, rock, and mainstream jazz.

---

[126] It wasn't, as far as I know.

Tom had enjoyed a successful graphic arts career in California, designing artwork that wound up on a variety of Grateful Dead merchandise. Here at Rustic Wells, he'd constructed a hodgepodge of old, junked video cameras and lights, tangled in a web of wires, with the hopes of creating videos performances of the groups who came there to play. You almost expected Christopher Lloyd to emerge from the shadows and shoot you back to 1955.

Tom was inclined to take in stragglers and vagabonds, thus the place was staffed by a combination of aging ex-bikers and vegetarian hippie drifters. The kitchen was manned by a paunchy guy named Clyde. In exchange for cooking, Clyde earned a humble wage and was allowed to live, along with his dog, in a broken down school bus next to the main building. Clyde had been a touring rock bassist, Clyde had been a biker, and in my estimation Clyde had been some kind of serious bad-ass. One could only imagine the brutal scraps which had led to Clyde's conspicuous lack of teeth. *You shoulda seen what happened to the other guy, hoss...*

Along with Clyde's dog, there were half a dozen pooches on the property, and the entire lot of them appeared to be on their last legs. When you arrived at Rustic's ramshackle entrance, these animals were strewn out before you, heads resting on the hot concrete, unkempt manes covered with flies. Brian Jordan, guitarist for Karl Denson's Tiny Universe, was less than pleased when he showed up to play a gig with his own project. "What is this shithole?!" he bellowed in disbelief. One of Jordan's sidemen, equally unhappy with the booking, voiced his distaste to Lincoln Norris, who was home in California: "The music's good, the music's great. No problems with the music. Everything else? *Straaaaaaight dookie!*" [127]

I always enjoyed a day or two at Rustic Wells, myself. I would take long, solo walks into the hills, play a little ping-pong, write screenplays or journal entries, and soak in the hot springs under the stars. Plus, there were usually a few interesting characters who showed up out of nowhere to hear the music and hang out—like random souls wandering into a dark, desolate bar in an old western flick.

During GFC's visit to Rustic we tried, unsuccessfully, to work out an odd-meter arrangement of the Dead song *Eyes of the World*. We also failed to make sense of one of Gary's original compositions. After

---

[127] In other words, straight dog shit.

learning the melody in excruciating, note-by-note fashion—Gary didn't have it written out, so he had to teach it to us this way—I was the one to say, "This just isn't working, man. We can keep trying, but I have to be honest. I'm not feeling this tune."

Little Jesus and Woo continued to lock horns with Nash, who acted like a sullen loner. He passed his days on the road pacing, smoking cigarettes and affecting a jaded stance that was not, at twenty-four years old, an organic outgrowth of hard life experience, but rather a pretentious affectation gleaned from keeping the company of older and more accomplished musicians.

Woo was pissed at Nash, because the sax man still owed him money from that night in Tijuana. I'm not going to say what Nash had spent the money on, but I'm pretty sure it wasn't street tacos. He claimed his pockets were empty at the moment, so Woo wryly suggested: "Maybe you can borrow the cash from your girlfriend back in San Diego."

After Rustic Wells, we continued on to Park City, Living Large's old stomping grounds. I'd made a few good friends there in the previous year of touring, such as Chili Halprin, a rising kingpin in the world of interstate bagel distribution,[128] and Eric "Shed" Shedlarsky, a talent buyer for the concert venue Harry O's. I always cherished a day or two in this upscale mountain village.

Park City was already very cold in November. The ground wasn't covered in snow yet, but you could feel the bone-chilling freeze of a mountain winter lurking. As I stood on the street in front of Starbucks, I spotted a couple minor celebrities: First, Tracy Ullman, the comedienne. Then, Stephen Baldwin, the Baldwin bro who'd flirted with minor cinematic stardom after roles in *The Usual Suspects* and *Fled*, but now was looking like a stuffed chipmunk in Patagonia wear. Baldwin was fighting back a throng of feverish disciples (read: a pair of middle-aged housewives from Provo).[129]

---

[128] Seriously… the guy was building an impressive bagel dynasty. He had distribution deals worked out all over the Western states. I'm not making this up.

[129] Stephen's career, spotty as it might be, must be recognized as significantly more distinguished than that of his brother Daniel, who was once the subject of the following press blurb: *Actor Daniel Baldwin was arrested in Santa Monica on suspicion of stealing an SUV. Officers saw him in a white GMC Yukon reported stolen in neighboring Orange County, authorities said. The actor was taken to jail for grand theft auto and bail was set at $20,000. "The car belongs to an acquaintance of Mr.*

As I watched Baldwin tend to his ravenous public, I felt a tap on my shoulder. There was Nash, covered in a wool cap and parka. He wanted to talk, so we ducked into Starbucks to escape the cold. Nash said he was fed up with Little Jesus and Woo. "I can't work with these amateurs, man. I'm a top level professional."[130] The thing was, we were just getting started. The road ahead would be long and arduous. If Nash was already struggling, it didn't bode well for his future in the project. I decided to be dead honest.[131] I told Nash he didn't seem cut out for the touring life. It's not for everyone. This would be a good experience for him, no matter what happened from here. A band needs chemistry, and if it's not there, changes are in order. I was trying to be supportive, but my words were only bumming the guy out further. He walked off, dejected. I figured he'd sulk through the rest of the tour and bow out when we got home.

I was wrong. That night, before the gig, Nash and Gary announced they were *bailing after the show*. Furthermore, they wanted to be paid for the tour, right then and there. Forget the fact that we'd all agreed to do the tour in its entirety, honoring the commitments made to various promoters and venues. Forget the fact that we'd agreed, before leaving San Diego, to wait until getting home to assess what happened on the road. Forget the fact that the most unprofessional thing a musician can do is bail in the middle of a run, leaving a band high and dry. It was an unreasonable position Nash and Gary were taking, but I wasn't in the mood to argue. I just wanted to be finished with their negative energy, and the easiest thing was to cough up some money and move on. I instructed Jenna to go ahead and pay them out.

The remaining band was Drew, Dan and me: drums, guitar and keyboards. We headed north toward Idaho, and let me point out that besides disgruntled sidemen, vehicular issues and garden variety financial concerns, there are other things that can derail a traveling band. One such thing is stray animals. You hear people talk about hitting deer all the time. It's sad but also inevitable. There's also coyotes, wild cats, squirrels, raccoons, skunks, etc. People don't tend to feel as bad about these smaller critters, which all potentially fall within

---

Baldwin, but he had no permission to take it," an O.C. sheriff's department spokesman said.

[130] Inspiration for the title of a future Global Funk Council song.

[131] Rarely a wise idea in life… in my opinion.

the category of *roadkill*. The creature you don't hear people talk about much, when it comes to highway hazards, is birds. This is because one, people don't hit birds very often, and two, if you do hit one, a pigeon or other small bird probably isn't going to mess you up too bad. But pigeons aren't the only thing flying around out there. No, there are other, much bigger winged specimens zigzagging around in the sky, occasionally dipping down into highway striking distance...

The rental van was making its way north on I-15 in the middle of the night, the Mayor driving and me riding shotgun. We were having our usual enjoyable post-gig conversation about one thing or another, when I caught a glimpse of something out of the corner of my eye: a big, white mass, traveling in our direction from the side of the road. It wasn't moving fast, but appeared to have a *potentially problematic trajectory*. I was only subconsciously aware of this as the Mayor and I continued chatting; but then a few seconds later, I turned and saw it again, only now it was much closer—so close that it was about to smash into our windshield.

"Shit!" the Mayor shouted. "That's a giant snow owl!" With that, the huge bird flew right in front of the van, which was going eighty MPH, and indeed smashed right into the windshield. Feathers flew everywhere. The glass cracked into a massive spiderweb. We didn't stop to check on the snow owl, but I have a hunch he didn't make it. Unfortunately, this would not be the last of God's creatures to have direct, high-speed contact with my various touring vehicles.

We would play the last few shows of the tour as a trio, in the tradition of the East Coast group Soulive. Bryce Nelson, owner of the Knotty Pine in Victor, Idaho, wasn't tickled when we showed up with half a band. He reluctantly allowed us to play the two-night run, and it went better than expected. We played the same songs but stretched them out, taking creative chances while reimagining everything on the fly. The music sounded rawer and less arranged, but at the same time tighter and more cohesive. We congratulated ourselves for getting through the rest of the dates under challenging circumstances.

There was a feeling of uncertainty among the remaining band and crew, but I wasn't deterred in the least. Until you've got the right nucleus, you can't be too sorry to see anyone cash in their chips—they're probably doing you a favor in the long run. It's better to cut losses with people who don't jibe with the project, than to keep putting band aids on a situation that's unlikely to improve.

Back in San Diego, I returned the rental van to discover that the bill was *twice the amount we had netted on the tour.* I slapped down my American Express card and crossed my fingers. This was the beginning of an unavoidable abuse of credit cards that would last the remainder of the band's life; it would take years to dig myself out of the hole born on that day.

While that first tour might sound like a disaster, it was actually a great moral victory— at least that's the way I felt about it. In just a couple months' time, I'd broken away from a negative situation, started my own group and kept my music career rolling. This time, I didn't have to answer to anyone. The ship was mine to steer. This time, it was *my* table.

TRAVESTY OF JUSTICE

As a replacement for Gary, Dan recommended his roommate, Steve Adams. Steve was a cool guy; not flashy on the bass, but easy to get along with and a good team player. I didn't try to replace Nash. I'd had it with high-maintenance sax players. We would do the next leg of touring, through Utah and Idaho, as a quartet.

A new problem emerged. Drew wasn't having fun playing with the current line-up of guys. He didn't think Dan and Steve were digging into the groove. I asked him to give it some time, but Drew flat-out warned me, "If something doesn't happen to make this situation more musically satisfying, I don't know how long I can do this." I didn't appreciate the ultimatum, but I also knew I didn't want to lose Drew, and would have to do something quick.

Coincidentally, I had just received a call from Vick Barerra, the percussionist who'd joined Living Large around the time I left. Vick was fed up with Mario and the crew, and had just quit. He was available. Since I knew Vick to be a confident performer who worked hard at his craft, I made plans to bring him on board. Drew agreed this might be the musical boost the music needed.

It was mid-December, and we decided to take a short break. Drew and I spent our free time looking for an affordable touring vehicle, so we could stop throwing away every penny we were making on van rentals. Half the battle for a traveling group is getting from Point A to Point B, efficiently and safely.

Drew and I had made a pact to do as many shows as humanly possible in those first couple years. We felt this would be the key to building a national fan base and growing a business on the level of The String Cheese Incident or Karl Denson's Tiny Universe.

After enduring the previous few months in a cramped van, we were both thinking the same thing: motor home. With a motor home or RV, we figured we'd have more space to move around during long trips, and the kitchen would save us lots of dough in the long run. Also, we'd all have a place to crash, eliminating the continual need for motel rooms.

The problem with buying an RV was that you first had to get approved for a loan. I had decent credit, but it was more difficult to get a loan for an RV. I got turned down at a dealership in San Jose.

Not convinced the RV plan was going to pan out, Drew and I visited a couple car lots, and looked at fifteen-seat passenger vans identical to the ones we'd been renting. If we owned it, we wouldn't be coughing up four or five grand every month. Warning to first-time road musicians: DO NOT RENT A VEHICLE FOR TOURING. Excluding the rare deal through a friend or family member, companies charge you for mileage on top of the daily rate. This compounds quickly, and you wind up owing more than you made on the tour—just for the vehicle rental. After a hard month of roughing it, eating gas station food and sleeping on people's couches, winding up in the red is not exactly a morale builder.

I got a call from my brother Collin, now a successful pro athlete on the AVP (Pro Beach Volleyball) Tour. Collin had an acquaintance managing an outfit in Gilroy called Buy Me RV. Drew and I drove down to meet this guy, Sandy Steinman, who knew Collin through mutual friends in the world of professional sports. The lot was stocked with hundreds of RVs parked in long rows, ranging from the smaller thirty-two footers to the stylish, thirty-eight foot luxury models one fantasized about in a wet motor home dream. These were the ones you passed on the freeway, the driver some fortyish IT champ with salt-and-pepper hair. As you whizzed by him in the fast lane, you thought to yourself: *I'm leaving you in the dust, you smug, rich bastard!*

Sandy, a handsome guy with wiry black hair, engaged us in the innocuous style of banter intended to soften the blow as you prepare to drop tens of thousands of dollars. He ran my credit report and then came back into the office wide-eyed, saying, "Hey, you pay your bills! I can get you approved." One of his sales cronies drove us around to look at some middle-of-the-road models. Nothing jumped out as a sure winner. We went back to Sandy's office, not certain what to do.

"Did you pick one?" he asked.

"Not exactly," I told him. He sat there for a minute, thinking. Then he bolted out of his chair, and Drew and I could almost see a light bulb materialize above his curly crown.

"I've got an idea," he said. "Go check something out. Then come back and tell me what you think."

His assistant drove us to the outskirts of the lot, beyond the small and midsize units. As we ventured into thirty-eight foot luxury territory, Drew and I shot each other a confused look. Where was this guy taking us? We couldn't come close to affording any of the vehicles out here in the stable of Class A, high-end motor homes.

"Take a look at this one," the guy told us. We stepped on board and found ourselves wandering through a comfortable, spacious motor home with plush interior and various amenities. We walked through the bedroom, bathroom, dining room, kitchen and lounge of this Monaco Dynasty home on wheels, leaving only one more question to ask: *Why are you showing us this?* The guy shuttled us back to Sandy's office. "What do you think?" Sandy asked.

"It's awesome," Drew said. "But that's not my point."

"What's your point, Drew?" Sandy asked.

"My point is this... We can't come close to affording it."

"What if I told you that you *could* afford it? That it belongs to someone who's not only a very good friend of mine, but an acquaintance of your brother?"

"Then I'd tell you to keep talking, Sandy," I said.

"The RV belongs to Jake Redwood, who used to play for the Los Angeles Lakers, among other NBA teams."

I knew of Jake Redwood, a near seven-footer who'd never made an impact in the NBA, but had lingered long enough to earn substantial cash. Redwood also dabbled in volleyball, which was how my brother knew him.

The next thing I knew, I was on the phone with Jake Redwood. He really wanted to sell that RV. After a brief, friendly conversation with

Jake, Sandy told us the Monaco Dynasty was ours if we wanted it. Drew and I were left in the office to ponder the possibilities. We told Sandy we'd sleep on it, and spent the drive back to San Jose pinching ourselves.

Could this really be happening? Were we on the verge of scoring a luxury motor home, a possession of value far beyond anything either one of us had ever owned in our entire lives? Were we finally catching a break, some fortuitous fluke to compensate for all the hardships?

The next day, we decided the Monaco Dynasty thirty-eight foot RV was the way to go. It was a once-in-a-lifetime opportunity. Plus, it was the only offer on the table. I arranged to secure about $9,000 for a down payment, and we showed up at the lot ready to do business. My mother Anne, concerned I might be making an irreversible mistake,[132] came down to the lot to meet Sandy and see what the deal was all about. After checking out the RV and talking to him, she had misgivings. She knew something wasn't right about the whole situation, and if I'd been smarter I would have listened.

In the end, however, Sandy convinced me that the wisest choice was to go with the luxury diesel motor home, rather than cut corners on a cheaper vehicle. The cost of this wisdom? $120,000.

I invited Woo and the Mayor to come down to assess the situation. We all sat in the lounge of the Dynasty, contemplating the decision. We all agreed that buying the Monaco was the best thing we could do.[133] We had a tour starting the next day, and there was no more time to jerk around. We needed a vehicle *now*. I might have thought we were making an informed decision, but in retrospect, we had no idea what we were getting ourselves into. None of us had the first clue about maintaining a complex, multi-system diesel RV.

We had not yet signed a binding contract with Jake Redwood or Buy Me RV, but I handed two checks to Sandy Steinman, one for $7000 and one for $2000. This was the down payment agreed on, and Sandy said we would handle the rest directly with Jake's lawyer, Dick Merck. The Dynasty was a 1996, but had only 30,000 miles on it. With its powerful Cummins diesel engine, the vehicle was going to give us several hundred thousand miles over the years. Despite this upside I must

---

[132] What's that expression… *Parents know best?*

[133] As I reflect back now, I realize that while I was sharing the decision with everyone, it was *my* ass that was on the line.

admit I felt an unmistakable wave of anxious doubt sweep over me, as Drew turned the ignition and drove us off the Buy Me RV lot.

We began the journey north on the 101 freeway to San Francisco, the destination of our kick-off gig for the next wave of touring. We'd been driving twenty or thirty minutes when trouble arose. Let me repeat that: *We'd been driving twenty or thirty minutes when trouble arose.* We're talking about $120,000 dollars here. We're talking about monthly payments for the next fifteen years. Off the lot for half an hour, and the Dynasty was broken down.

We made some calls and found friends to meet us off the 101, somewhere south of San Jose. They hurried us and our gear up to the Tongue and Groove nightclub. Had you told me this would be the norm, an average day in the world of Monaco Dynasty motor homes, as opposed to some freak occurrence, I would have left the lumbering hunk of fiberglass right there, cancelled my checks and rescinded the deal. Of course, I didn't know that. I was figuring everything out on the fly. I was wingin' it, man.

Sandy arranged to have the Dynasty towed to a mechanic and repaired, on his nickel. This instilled an early yet ultimately unfulfilled belief that relations between me, him and Jake Redwood were going to be positive.

We got through the show at the Tongue and Groove, and were scheduled to play Club Creation in Park City, Utah the following night. With the Dynasty breakdown, there was no chance we would get there in time. I knew the club owner personally, and thought he would understand the situation—but if there's one thing I've learned through my travels, and yes, here's another important one for you up-and-coming musicians: *Nobody understands nothin'.* You missed the show. Nobody cares why. You weren't there, period. *Hey, someone in my family was injured in a horrible car accident. I had to get to the hospital. You understand, right?*

NO. YOU MISSED THE SHOW. PERIOD. WHAT DOES YOUR EXCUSE HAVE TO DO WITH ME RUNNING MY CLUB?

Play music long enough, go through enough bands, survive enough tours, and you *will* become hardened. People in music like to pretend the scene is all about community. This was especially true in the JBS, which ostensibly echoes the peace and love sentiments of the sixties and seventies. The JBS is just like every other genre in music, however.

It is comprised of people and organizations looking out for their own self-interest, first and foremost.

I had hoped in the early, warm and fuzzy days that maybe one of the more established groups I'd interacted with would reach out to me at some point. I was waiting for someone to say, "Hey, man, you've been working hard, doing the same things we did when we started out. Why don't you open a couple shows for us, or at least connect with our management, so you can get some ideas how to refine your process?" Nothing like that ever happened. Don't hold your breath waiting for some kind of *deus ex machina* from fellow musicians.

I believe it's important to nurture creative people in this society. I aim to be supportive of anyone brave enough to be a full-time musician. A simple gesture of moral support or a little career guidance can be of great benefit to a young guy or girl seeking affirmation that their pursuit is worthwhile. Once you begin to make your mark, you're obligated to give back in some way—at least that's what I think.[134]

Of course, I can also understand why successful groups remain insular. When you have busted your ass for years, playing countless dumps and negotiating a continual obstacle course of ups and downs, your first inclination, once you find some success, is not to go out and save the world. The world didn't save *you*. You built your career the hard way, and you've earned the right to take a minute to smell the *ganja* cloud that permeates the green room.

As your band gets bigger, the job of managing everything gets more complex. There's more money changing hands, more people answering to more people, and the band becomes a business. For the musicians themselves, there are more decisions to be made than back when you were driving around in that first rental van. Managing your music, your career and your personal affairs becomes an all-consuming task. You don't have time to play Mother Theresa to some young band

---

[134] In Charles Barkley's book, *Who's Afraid of a Large Black Man?*, Morgan Freeman takes the contrary position: "Your obligation is to yourself. If you have talent for anything, your obligation is to that. Make that work the best you can, and I think everything else just falls in its own place. I don't know that you have to live your life outside the boundaries of your own needs." One wonders if there weren't people who extended themselves to Freeman when he needed a break, when he was struggling.

who thinks they're the next Moe. You're caught up in trying to build your own legacy, not figuring out how to lift up everyone else.

The further you get, the more you realize it's a unique process for every band. A group derives its identity from the collective personalities and talents of its individuals. From band to band, this chemistry is so dramatically different that it's impossible to compare one's process and evolution to that of another. An experienced group of musicians knows that a young, aspiring organization will have to figure things out for themselves. What works well for one group often doesn't work for another.

Another reason established musicians don't always lend a helping hand is fear of competition; they're afraid the younger band will steal their audience. It's a legitimate fear, because music fans are inherently restless. If they feel a group has lost its creative edge, they'll seek out something new that ignites a spark for them. There's only so much room at the top of the commercial heap—only so many fans in a given scene, and those fans have a finite amount of money to spend. If one band is blowing up all of sudden, starting to draw bigger crowds, another is falling by the wayside.

UCOLORTANAHO

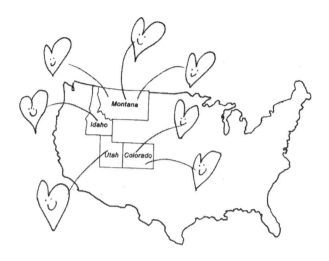

In the early GFC days, almost all the shows took place within the block of states that includes Utah, Idaho, Colorado and Montana. I started referring to it as *Ucolortanaho*. There are many beautiful sights to behold in this region, including spectacular mountains, lakes, valleys, and some of the nation's most unique terrain. Flathead Lake, for example, is part of a breathtaking area of Northern Montana not to be missed. I defy anyone to argue that Tahoe has anything on Flathead.

Colorado boasts a number of quaint ski towns, nestled within some of the most amazing mountains in the world. Personal favorites include Telluride, Crested Butte and Steamboat Springs. The gondola ride in Telluride lowers you into the town's tiny downtown from such a dramatic, vertical angle that you feel you're floating down from the heavens; it's a jaw-dropping experience.

Yellowstone Park, Glacier Park, Moab and Zion are also among the places you must see in this lifetime. Yellowstone sits above the world's largest caldera, or supervolcano, and is overdue for its once-every-600,000-year blow—an occurrence scientists agree might extinguish the human race.

The months of January and February are not the optimal time for musicians to enjoy the Ucolortanaho experience. The weather is harsh, leading to miserable road conditions and other logistical nightmares. Many of the mountain roads are not drivable at all, and therefore shut down for the winter season.

I was not equipped to deal with extended exposure to below-freezing temperatures and continual blizzards, having spent the majority of my life in the warm California sun. Neither were my Global Funk Council cohorts up to the challenge, as we grumbled through two months of icy misery. During the trip from San Francisco to Salt Lake City, the Dynasty's maiden voyage, I had my first glimpse of the myriad vehicular disasters to come. While trying to back up in a gas station near Truckee, California, Woo jackknifed the trailer into the rear of the vehicle, cracking the fiberglass and maiming the ladder beyond repair. When I took the wounded beast to a repair facility, the first question the mechanic asked was, "Why the hell were you driving that son'bitch with such a short hitch? You need a *much* longer trailer hitch than that!"

It would have been nice if old Sandy Steinman had tipped me off to that fact, back on the lot of Buy Me RV. I was learning quickly that the Dynasty came with not only bottomless stomach for diesel gas and propane, but a massive learning curve as well. I wasn't feeling up to the challenge.

We arrived in Salt Lake City without further complications and settled into the downtown Sheraton. (This particular hotel would provide comfort and refuge during frequent returns to the city in the coming years). T.J., a friend of Little Jesus, was part-owner of the Lazy Moon Saloon, and hooked up a discount rate every time we came to town to play his club.

The first night in SLC, I got a call from Dick Merck, Jake Redwood's lawyer. Merck was livid, and here's why: Sandy had just *given* me the RV in Gilroy, allowing me to drive off with no signed contract, hence no formal agreement with Redwood. "Those guys are my bros. It'll be fine." Those had been his words.[135] When Sandy tried to explain to Merck how he'd brokered a half-assed, under the table deal to some

---

[135] Months later, he would tell my brother Collin that it was "the worst deal I've ever done in my life."

414

scuffling musicians who needed a tour bus, the attorney had understandably blown a gasket.

This wasn't the main reason Merck was freaking out, however. The real reason he was fuming was that I had called him earlier that day and left a message saying: "I don't like the terms of the contract. The RV's breaking down already, and I don't feel good about the deal. I plan to return the vehicle to the lot in Gilroy." I realize now that I had the right idea. My instincts were solid. God how I wish I had trusted them. Had I stuck to my guns and returned the RV after that first tour, I would have come out of the whole mess okay.

Merck's return message was: "You think it means anything that you didn't sign a contract? That doesn't mean shit! You're *keeping* the RV."

There was one thing stopping me from dumping the Dynasty back in Gilroy and being done with it. That one thing, without which I might have spared myself a great deal of grief, was Woo's handiwork at the gas station in Truckee. It wasn't exactly his fault, but whoever's fault it was, it was a big mess. The damage was to the tune of at least a few thousand bucks, which I didn't have handy. Notice, as I'm recounting the GFC saga, how I *never have the dough?* Young artists, let this be a warning.

I came to the conclusion that the Monaco Dynasty—in actuality, more of a *Suck n' Blow Travesty*—and I were stuck with each other, for better or worse. Let me correct that: *for worse.* I knew I'd have to sign some kind of contract, but no way would I agree to a tacked-on $90,000 balloon payment at the end of the term. In terms of the negotiation, I still had an ace in the hole. Merck had cashed my $2000 down payment check, but I had stopped payment on the additional $7000 check. When he unsuccessfully tried to cash the second check, Merck called Todd Sherman and screamed that he was going to report the RV stolen.

After a couple more drafts of his shitty contract, I still didn't like Merck's terms, which included an interest rate of ten percent, and numerous clauses that clearly did not have my best interest in mind. Todd was tired of dealing with the whole situation, however, and it was his Monopoly money I was playing with. I very reluctantly agreed to sign my life away.

Once we'd jumped this hurdle, a new one appeared. Now Merck was barking, "Where's the insurance?!"

"I need to be able to register the vehicle first," I told him.

"Then register it!"

"I can't."

"Why?"

"Because you don't legally own it."

These guys had pulled a slick one on me. They were stuck with a long-term loan *of their own*, and in me they'd found a sucker to bail them out of their mess. They could charge me the amount of their monthly payment, then tack on interest and turn a profit.

I was getting pulled over by cops every few days, because the registration tags were expired. One time a Boulder, Colorado cop followed us around for two days, trying to force us out of town. "There's no camping here," he told us. We'd go park somewhere else to hide, only to hear his flashlight knocking on the Travesty's window once again. "I told you, you can't camp here." *We ain't campin', sir. We don't want no trouble.*

"Get moving. We don't want you here." In a re-imagining of *Shane*, he was Riker and I was Joe Starrett, but instead of quarreling over the rights of a courageous group of 19th Century Western settlers, the beef was over parking a giant RV along the congested streets of modern-day Boulder.

On top of all this I still had to pay the California sales tax and registration fees. Again, the particulars of this process had been curiously *overlooked* during negotiations on the Buy Me RV lot in Gilroy. The California DMV tacks on a hefty tax percentage; I believe the final price tag to register the Travesty, including both the tax and the year's fees, was around *thirteen thousand dollars*. This, of course, was on top of the nine grand down payment.

Todd somehow came up with the dough and cut me a check. When I handed over the payment to the ladies working the DMV counter in Stockton, California, their eyes lit up. *Oh my God, look at that check!!* I was thinking: *Don't be deceived, ladies. I'm just a broke guy driving around the country in a big-ass lemon motor home I just got coerced into buying.*

As 2002 arrived the country was still reeling from 9/11. The music industry was suffering, along with the symbiotically linked restaurant and club industry. I couldn't have picked a worse time to start a small business. The stock market was down, jobs were being lost, and people didn't have as much disposable income as usual. If you were the Rolling Stones this wasn't going to hurt you. If you were Dave Mathews you were going to pull through. If you were Global Funk Council your back was pushed yet a little further against the wall.

416

As a result of 9/11 there was a sense of anxiety surrounding the 2002 Winter Olympic Games in Salt Lake City. When GFC rolled into Utah for a string of shows to coincide with the Games, all kinds of crazy talk was circulating. People were murmuring about potential air attacks, suitcase nukes and other possibilities. Word on the street was that military snipers were hidden all over the city, watching your every move. It was hard not to believe the hype. After all, what better way for terrorists to follow up 9/11 than by decimating an American city playing host to the global community?

With the backing of the military, the F.B.I. and other federal agencies, Salt Lake City launched a security effort unprecedented in the history of the Olympics. Literally billions of dollars were spent in the process. The city had also undergone a massive, aesthetic facelift.

I managed to get swept up in the Olympic spirit. I watched from a rooftop as the torch was carried along Main Street in Park City. I sat in Salt Lake Stadium, freezing along with tens of thousands of other people while President Bush, Sting, Steven Spielberg, Michelle Kwan and R. Kelly[136] led an impressive cast in the opening ceremony extravaganza. This ceremony included an elaborate, ambitious presentation celebrating the heritage of Native Americans. Hundreds of tribal performers boogied around teepees and rode horses, while fashioning a colorful assortment of historically authentic getups. When this portion of the show concluded, a small army of chuck wagons rambled into the stadium. *Here come the pioneers!* The music morphed from Hiawatha to hillbilly, and the public address announcer might as well have declared: *Then, the white folks came along and plundered the land, obliterating Native American culture in one fell swoop!*

A few days later, Todd, a couple band members and I decided to experience the adrenaline-charged roller coaster ride that is *men's curling.* Curling consists of guys pushing stones along narrow strips of ice, screaming at other guys who are sweeping around the stones as they skid along. To my eye it's a blend of bowling, shuffleboard, and some of the various tasks normally associated with janitors. Curling is a huge deal in cold places like Canada and Northern Europe, but the magic doesn't quite translate for Southern dwellers like myself. Drew and I cracked up at the coach for one of the teams, who kept screaming

---

[136] Who would be indicted days later on child pornography and statutory rape charges.

at his players in some harsh foreign tongue and at the top of his lungs, as if the fate of the world would be determined by the outcome of this pivotal contest. The thing was, we'd tried to get tickets for hockey and other marquee sports, but those events had been sold out for months. I don't mean to slam curling. I'm sure you have to train your ass off for years to even be considered for an Olympic curling squad.

After our Olympic run, coined the Fresh Powder Funk Tour, we returned to California for a week's break. When we got home, Dan and Jenna decided they were leaving the project. In Sun Valley I'd asked Jenna to step off the road and concentrate on administrative tasks.

Jenna, however, had been adamant from the beginning that she wanted to stay on tour. I recognized her as a valuable asset—she'd worked in San Francisco as a promoter and publicist for various jam bands, and knew the scene inside out. Also, I didn't want to lose Dan, whose textural guitar work and great attitude were a pleasure. Despite Jenna being cool and also helping on numerous levels, it was also true that her relationship with Dan complicated the social dynamic of our mobile operation. When everyone was single, or had left their significant other back at home, it wasn't fair to have a near-married couple on board. There was also the basic matter of resources. Over time, even one person's expenses started to add up. On the road, everyone took up space, ate food, and needed money for various things. That was the reality.

Steve Adams, who I'd come to consider a friend, was also planning to leave the band, in large part due to a lack of chemistry with Drew. Steve and Dan had plans to resurrect their old band ALO.

Drew and I drove the RV down to San Diego to work on our first studio album. With Steve moving on, I made the decision to hire Jeffrey Whitaker, a bassist living in Boston. I'm going to refer to him as Wildman, because that's the nickname we called him by for most of the time he was in the band (I'll explain later). Drew had been given a nickname as well, after someone quipped in not-so-politically-correct fashion, "You kind of look like a black Colonel Sanders." We already had the Mayor, and now we had... *the Colonel.* Drew was a good sport and rolled with it for a while, but one day he calmly said to the whole band, "Guys, I'm not feeling 'the Colonel.' It makes me sound like a tool. Can you find something else to call me, please?" We gave it a rest, but it wasn't long before someone said, "Drew, with your dreadlocks, you sort of resemble an African-American Sideshow Bob."[137] Everyone laughed, including Drew, but no nickname resulted.

After fulfilling his obligations to Johnny A, a popular blues guitarist, Wildman flew out to meet us in San Diego. I was attracted to the fact that he was willing to walk away from a good-paying, secure sideman position to pursue his own creative ambitions. In other words, he was crazy enough, courageous enough, and perhaps stupid enough to be a part of Global Funk Council. We were sure to get along.

I expected Wildman to be a clean-cut, wire-thin guy with a backwards baseball cap. That's what I imagined based on his speaking voice. Instead I was greeted by a husky, long-haired dude with a scraggly beard. I had been expecting a youthful version of Andy Garcia, but the guy that showed up looked more like a young *Jerry* Garcia.

"Cool," I thought. "This guy's got the jam band look."

Vick Barerra, who was now the band's percussionist, was also present in the studio. If Wildman resembled the Grateful Dead's frontman, Vick's physical appearance and demeanor were reminiscent of a fictitious creature from *Star Wars: The Phantom Menace*. It had been suggested by someone, quite possibly me, that Vick was a human version of Watto, the unscrupulous slave trader and junkshop proprietor who is half parrot, half flying insect. As written by George Lucas, Watto is devoid of morals: *I sold your mother. I'm sorry. It was nothing personal. It was just beeeezness.* When you were doing a Watto impression, you not only mimicked the voice but also pretended you were frantically batting wings in the air, hovering in one spot like a helicopter. Vick was thick-skinned. He didn't seem to mind being compared to a Star Wars character.

In some ways the studio experience turned out to be a nightmare. I'd hoped to use pre-existing tracks from the incomplete, never-released Living Large sessions; I wanted to overdub new parts with my current band and turn it into a Global Funk Council album. Lincoln Norris, however, claimed he was the owner of the master tapes, citing the fact that he had written the checks for the studio time during which they were originally created. He had a point. The music wasn't his from a copyright perspective, but the songs had been recorded as Living Large material, with his financing. I admit, I wasn't thinking

---

[137] One of the more memorable *Simpson's* characters.

reasonably at that point: *Those are my songs. I can use the old Living Large tracks if I want, because they're my songs.* Steve Weatherbee, engineer and owner of Golden Track Studios as well as a personal friend, set me straight. He said that since Lincoln paid for the original performances, he was the proprietor of the original recording.

This meant that we had to start from scratch, beginning with the drums. Drew did a stellar job, nailing all his parts in less than two days. He was a real pro, one of the most exacting drummers I'd ever worked with. I re-recorded all my keyboard parts, and also brought in a horn section to play new ensemble parts I'd written. We added guitar, as well as multi-layered vocals on a few songs. I had the expertise to do this, I assured my benefactor Todd Sherman, but it was going to be time-consuming and somewhat expensive.

The band *had* to get a studio album out there. We couldn't keep promoting ourselves with a cheap, five-song demo. The bigger festivals weren't going to consider us unless we gave them a polished product.

Drew and I put our heads together to finish the album, saving as much time and money as we could without sacrificing quality. Dan Lebowitz and Dale Park contributed guitar tracks, Vick Barerra played percussion on some cuts, and Walt Williams sang on an intricate jam called *How Can I Be Down.* When all was done, it wasn't a watershed artistic statement, but the *Keep on Pushin'* sessions resulted in a nice collection of well-played and arranged tracks.

When it came to the live show, both Drew and Wildman were great players, so it seemed a foregone conclusion that they'd form an excellent rhythm section. Wildman had killer chops and could execute percolating, syncopated bass lines. Drew had stellar technique and time. Both were virtuosos, but when they played together, something was curiously missing. The groove lacked synergy. It lacked magic.

Drew and Vick, meanwhile, developed a bag of rhythmic phrases and tricks they would pull from arbitrarily, at times with little regard for what was going on with the rest of the band. They were tight within themselves, but their shared concept was failing to mesh with mine and Wildman's; the two of us were having long discussions about the stylistic direction of the music, and decided we wanted to head in a more adventurous, epic rock direction. This meant long, through-composed songs, more vocal material, and more jamming. It also meant no longer exploiting connections to funk bands we no longer wanted to emulate. Funk seemed like music you played in a bar, or maybe a small club, but not an amphitheater or arena. To play the big venues, the ones every aspiring band dreamed of, Wildman and I believed you needed epic, powerful music, and you needed vocal tunes as opposed to instrumentals. We also agreed, along with the Mayor, that we needed to put a stop to Drew's canned patter between songs. It was effective on some level, yes, but it made us seem like a bar band. Looking back now, I believe I was mistaken about Drew and his stage presentation. It was working, crowds dug his vibe, and the band would have been better served to just let him do his thing. *If it ain't broke...*

VOWS OF POVERTY,
ACTS OF BRAVERY

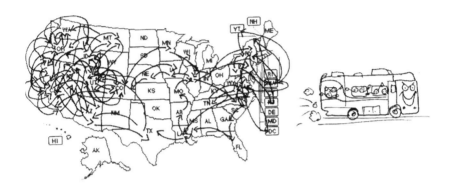

I spent the entire twelve months of 2002 on the road. Drew and I were determined to establish ourselves as a national group. We weren't going to be content to just loaf up and down the West Coast. Our goal was to have as big a following in New York as in San Francisco. We were getting decent bookings through our various associations with other proven acts, and also because despite being only six months old, we were a pretty good band. Once we played a new club, they usually liked us and wanted us back.

I had a core of committed people, but due to the grueling schedule I was attempting, musicians and crew members were dropping like flies: Nash, Gary, Dan, Jenna, Steve Adams. Despite this, Drew and I were going strong. We had fire and faith. Drew was a top-notch drummer, I was a versatile keyboard player, we both sang and wrote good music, and we shared a belief that we were among the best young musicians on the national circuit. To give you an idea of the amount of ground we covered in 2002, here is a list of the shows:

1/2	Breckenridge, CO	Sherpa & Yeti's
1/3	Denver, CO	Quixote's True Blue
1/5	Boulder, CO	Trilogy
1/6	(same)	
1/8	Park City, UT	Plan B

1/10   Park City, UT   Harry O's
1/12   Salt Lake City, UT   Lazy Moon Saloon
1/17   Park City, UT   Harry O's
1/21   Pocatello, ID   First National
1/22   Moscow, ID   John's Alley
1/23   Missoula, MT   The Blue Heron
1/24   Bozeman, MT   Zebra Cocktail Lounge
1/25   Whitefish, MT   Dire Wolf Bar
1/26   Missoula, MT   The Blue Heron
1/28   Portland, OR   Goodfoot Lounge
1/29   (same)
1/31   Tahoe City, CA   Sierra Vista
2/1   South Lake Tahoe, CA   Strange Brew
2/2   San Francisco, CA   Elbo Room
2/6   Park City, UT   Plan B
2/7   (same)
2/8   Salt Lake City, UT   Lazy Moon Saloon
2/9   (same)
2/10   (same)
2/11   Ogden, UT   Beatnick's
2/12   (same)
2/13   (same)
2/14   Breckenridge, CO   Sherpa & Yeti's
2/21   San Louis Obispo, CA   Mother's Tavern
2/27   San Diego, CA   Winston's
2/28   Santa Barbara, CA   Velvet Jones
3/1   Ben Lomond, CA   Henfling's Tavern
3/2   San Francisco, CA   Danzhaus
3/3   San Rafael, CA   Pete's 881 Club
3/4   Berkeley, CA   Shattuck Down Low
3/6   Las Vegas, NV   Legends Lounge
3/7   Flagstaff, AZ   Flagstaff Brewing Company
3/8   Las Vegas, NV   Legends Lounge
3/9   Tucson, AZ   Nimbus Brewery
3/12   Austin, TX   Empanada Parlour
3/15   Salt Lake City, UT   Lazy Moon Saloon
3/23   Breckenridge, CO   Sherpa & Yeti's
3/24   Denver, CO   Quixote's True Blue
3/26   Cedar Rapids, IA   Club Lab
3/27   Iowa City, IA   The Green Room

3/28   Madison, WI   King Club
3/29   Chicago, IL   Boulevard Café
4/1   (same)
4/2   (same)
4/3   Pittsburgh, PA   Pittsburgh Deli Company
4/4   Stanhope, NJ   The Stanhope House
4/7   Burlington, VT   Nectar's
4/8   Cambridge, MA   House of Blues
4/10   Bay Shore, NY   Da Funky Phish
4/12   New York, NY   Tobacco Road
4/13   Bay Shore, NY   Da Funky Phish
4/19   Blacksburg, VA   Baylee's
4/20   Asheville, NC   Asheville Music Zone
4/27   New Orleans, LA   Blue Nile
5/2   New Orleans, LA   Tipitna's French Quarter
5/3   Baton Rouge, LA   Chelsea's
5/4   Fayetteville, AR   Chester's Place
5/8   St. Louis, MO   Cicero's
5/9   Chicago, IL   Boulevard Café
5/10   (same)
5/11   Evanston, IL   Nevin's Live
5/12   Iowa City, IA   Gabe's
5/14   Omaha, NE   The Music Box
5/15   Denver, CO   Quixote's True Blue
5/16   (same)
5/17   Boulder, CO   Tulagi
5/18   Salt Lake City, UT   Lazy Moon Saloon
5/19   Missoula, MT   Caras Park
5/21   Seattle, WA   Tractor Tavern
5/22   Portland, OR   Mt. Tabor Theatre
5/23   Eugene, OR   Samurai Duck
5/24   San Francisco, CA   Boom Boom Room
5/28   San Diego, CA   Winston's
5/30   Henderson, NV   Whiskey Sky Bar
5/31   Flagstaff, AZ   The Alley
6/1   Tucson, AZ   Plush
6/3   Prescott, AZ   Lyzzard's Lounge
6/4   (same)
6/5   Phoenix, AZ   Rhythm Room
6/6   Prescott, AZ   Moctezuma's

6/7   Las Vegas, NV   Legends Lounge
6/8   Salt Lake City, UT   Lazy Moon Saloon
6/12   Portland, OR   Mt. Tabor Theatre
6/13   Richland, WA   Duke's Pourhouse
6/14   North Plains, OR   Horning's Hideout
6/15   Hood River, OR   Savino's
6/16   Mt. Shasta, CA   Mt. Shasta Community Building
6/19   Santa Barbara, CA   Soho Restaurant and Club
6/20   San Jose, CA   Plant Fifty-One
6/22   Berkeley, CA   Starry Plough
6/29   San Francisco, CA   Elbo Room

(Hang in there, you've made it halfway through the year)

7/2   Tahoe City, CA   Sierra Vista
7/3   Incline Village, NV   Jimmy Bongo's Velvet Lounge
7/4   South Lake Tahoe, CA   Strange Brew
7/5   Quincy, CA   High Sierra Music Festival
7/7   (same)
7/9   Chico, CA   LaSalle's
7/11   Stockton, CA   Alder Market
7/13   Squaw Valley, CA   Squaw Valley
7/17   Ketchum, ID   Ketchum City Park
7/18   Park City, UT   Harry O's
7/19   Steamboat Springs, CO   Levelz
7/20   Snowmass Village, CO   Janus Aspen Stage
7/22   Vail, CO   Half Moon Saloon
7/23   Colorado Springs, CO   Utopia Café
7/24   Denver, CO   Quixote's True Blue
7/25   Boulder, CO   Fox Theatre
7/26   Carbondale, CO   Carbondale Mountain Fair
7/27   Fort Collins, CO   Mishawaka Amphitheatre
7/28   Copper, CO   Copper Mountain Ski Resort
7/31   Minneapolis, MN   Cabooze
8/1   Chicago, IL   Boulevard Café
8/2   (same)
8/3   Mishawaka, IN   Mishawaka Brewing Company
8/7   Buffalo, NY   Nietzsche's
8/8   New York, NY   Lion's Den
8/11   Great Barrington, MA   Butternut Basin Ski Area

8/12   Winooski, VT   Higher Ground
8/15   State College, PA   The Brewery
8/16   Pittsburgh, PA   The Attic
8/17   Fort Wayne, IN   Sneaky Pete's
8/19   Chicago, IL   Boulevard Café
8/22   Asheville, NC   Stella Blue
8/23   Black Mountain, NC   The Town Pump
8/25   Richmond, VA   Cary Street Café
8/28   Great Barrington, MA   Club Helsinki
8/29   Allston, MA   Harper's Ferry
9/5   Burlington, VT   Club Metronome
9/6   Waitsfield, VT   Mad Mountain Tavern
9/7   Little Falls, NY   Beardsley Castle
9/8   Buffalo, NY   Broadway Joe's
9/10   Rochester, NY   Milestones
9/12   Indiana, PA   Brown Hotel
9/13   Pittsburgh, PA   The Attic
9/14   Williamsport, PA   Bullfrog Brewery
9/16   Charlottesville, VA   Orbit Billiards
9/17   Washington D.C.   Velvet Lounge
9/18   Richmond, VA   Cary Street Café
9/19   Bristol, TN   State Line Bar & Grill
9/20   Blacksburg, VA   Baylee's
9/21   Charlottesville, VA   Outback Lodge
9/24   Black Mountain, NC   The Town Pump
9/25   Raleigh, NC   Lincoln Theatre
9/26   Athens, GA   Georgia Theater
9/27   Lafayette, GA   Blue Ridge Harvest Festival
9/28   Jacksonville, FL   Jack Rabbits
10/01   Oxford, MS   The Two Stick
10/02   New Orleans, LA   Tipitina's Uptown
10/03   Baton Rouge, LA
10/04   Houston, TX   Fitzgerald's
10/5   Austin, TX   The Vibe
10/9   Tucson, AZ   Plush
10/10   Phoenix, AZ   The Rhythm Room
10/11   Flagstaff, AZ   The Alley
10/12   Fresno, CA   Club Fred
10/15   San Diego, CA   Winston's
10/16   Santa Barbara, CA   Soho Restaurant and Club

10/17	Santa Cruz, CA Moe's Alley
10/18	San Francisco, CA Boom Boom Room
10/19	(same)
10/20	Eugene, OR Joggers
10/21	(same)
10/25	Berkeley, CA Shattuck Down Low
10/26	Ashland, OR Siskiyou Brew Pub
10/28	Hood River, OR River City Saloon
10/29	(same)
10/30	Moscow, ID John's Alley
10/31	Missoula, MT Wilma Theater
11/1	Bozeman, MT Zebra Cocktail Lounge
11/2	Salt Lake City, UT The Zephyr
11/6	Colorado Springs, CO Utopia Café
11/7	Fort Collins, CO The Starlight
11/8	Vail, CO Half Moon Saloon
11/9	Boulder, CO The Fox Theatre
11/10	Denver, CO Quixote's True Blue
11/12	Nederland, CO I&I Café
11/13	Steamboat Springs, CO Wolf Den Tavern
11/14	Park City, UT Harry O's
11/15	Ketchum , ID Whiskey Jacque's
11/16	(same)
11/19	Chico, Ca LaSalle's
11/20	San Francisco, CA Great American Music Hall
11/22	Las Vegas, NV The Blue Note
11/27	Santa Barbara, CA Soho Restaurant and Club
11/29	Tahoe City, CA Sierra Vista
12/3	Eureka, CA Rumour's Lounge
12/4	Ashland, OR Siskiyou Brew Pub
12/5	Hood River, OR River City Saloon
12/6	Eugene, OR Downtown Lounge
12/7	Portland, OR Mt. Tabor Theatre
12/8	Seattle, WA The Rainbow
12/26	Tahoe City, CA Sierra Vista
12/27	Park City, UT Harry O's
12/28	Salt Lake City, UT Lazy Moon Saloon
12/30	Denver, CO Quixote's True Blue
12/31	(same)

There you have it, a whole year on the road. That's over two hundred performances. You probably have a few questions, such as...

What did you do between 4/20 and 4/27?

We camped out in the Wal-Mart parking lot in Asheville, North Carolina.

Is there really a place called Indiana, Pennsylvania?

Yes. Do not go there. Avoid any city named after a state in which it is not located. I'm not even going to get into what happened in Honolulu, New Mexico.[138]

Why are there so many places called the Velvet Lounge, and do they really have lots of velvet inside?

I don't know why so many places are called *velvet* this or that. In my experience, such establishments usually fail to deliver the plush interior you are imagining.

Did you really play a coffeehouse?

Yes, more than once. It's quite a morale builder.[139]

And a deli?

Guilty as charged. The deli, at least, had a stage, along with some damn good sandwiches.

What about the castle? What was that like?

It was a little bizarre. We actually played in a tent *next* to the castle. The one guy listening to our music that night handed me a card that read: gaypants@hotmail.com. He told me to *call him*. I passed the card around the band. To my knowledge, nobody called, but you never know... the road can get lonely.

Was Sneaky Pete really sneaky?

That guy stiffed us out of a thousand bucks, while lying to my booking agent. So yes, Sneaky Pete was a very sneaky bastard. Steer clear of Fort Wayne unless you're bringing Suge Knight along.

The band enjoyed successful runs through Colorado and Montana, two states known for being kind to jam bands. In Missoula, we were greeted like rock stars, packing the Blue Heron and *funking up* local college kids and hippies.

---

[138] Just kidding...

[139] Almost as much as when you're playing an epic composition called *Jazz Odyssey,* and you open for a puppet show.

During the soundcheck that evening, I told a couple guys to "please shut up," because they were making noise while we were trying to dial in our levels. Then, on the set break, one of them walked up to me and said, "Hey, man, you disrespected us by telling us to shut up earlier."

"Okay, I'm sorry about that. I was just trying to get things done. I didn't mean it to come out that way." He accepted my words and walked away. At the end of the night, as I was saying hello to people in the lobby, the same guy came back over.

"What's up?" I asked.

"My friend and I talked it over, and we still don't feel right about what you did."

"Oh yeah?" I answered.

"Yeah."

"Well, guess what? That's too fucking bad. I apologized already. Maybe your friend should apologize for disrupting our soundcheck. There's nothing more to talk about. You don't like it, don't come back next time we're in town."

How's that for customer relations?

In Whitefish we packed the house again, in spite of the harsh winter conditions. Our shows in Lake Tahoe and San Francisco were equally successful. Salt Lake City was perhaps our best market, a city where we had numerous friends and supporters. We made frequent visits to play both the Lazy Moon and Zephyr clubs.

Things were moving along, but the burden of holding it all together—the personnel changes, the attempt to keep everyone happy and to establish ourselves as a national act, the costs of the road—all this was too difficult to bear sober, and I began drinking too much. I found I could ease my daily stresses with booze and the company of the opposite sex, two vices which tended to accompany each other, and which were both readily available on the road.

The Travesty broke down constantly. Many of our gigs were poorly planned and promoted. I was going weeks without making much money. This was all exacerbated by an unstable musical roster. Todd was still committed to the project but was growing tired of bailing the band out of dire financial circumstances. I started floating the project with personal credit. It was that or watch everything fall apart, then return to life in San Diego—a scene I felt I had outgrown.

Woo stepped off the road and returned to his parents' ranch in Durham, a small town outside of Chico. He felt he could manage the band's affairs from home, and I agreed. All-star affiliations or not, we were a fledgling organization that lacked the draw to fill even medium-sized venues. Promoters offered only small guarantees, and we had to say yes. We didn't have the muscle of a major label behind us. We had to convince people to give us a chance. Sometimes we had to beg. In those early days Woo did an admirable job of holding things together. For years after I would sound like a broken record when I said, "There would be no Global Funk Council without Woo."

Woo's efforts were not enough to keep the band from suffering long, costly hiatuses in the middle of touring. We desperately needed a booking agent, and one materialized during a two-night run at Trilogy Wine Bar in Boulder. Rob Sarno's Mountain High booking agency had handled Living Large, and now was interested in working with GFC. The band had a great show at Trilogy, and we looked like we really had our act together. During the break, Little Jesus walked over and said, "Rob Sarno's blowing sunshine up my ass. He's gonna come over and blow some up yours too, T." Rob and I talked after the show, and agreed the timing was right to work together. I signed a booking agreement with Mountain High.

Even though some good things were happening, Drew was forever discontent with the band's progress. He would say, "We're doing okay, but everything could be so much better." Sure, things could have been better, but the complaining sounded like a broken record, and I was tired of hearing it. The truth was, Drew and I had both already paid a lot of dues as musicians. We weren't young kids taking a band out on the road for the first time, happy to lap up whatever scraps the scene threw our way. No, we were looking for an accelerated path to success. Neither of us was prepared to slug it out like teenagers in a garage band, even if that was *precisely what was required.*

Just because you might be older and more experienced doesn't mean you have value as a touring act. Music doesn't work like corporate politics. You don't automatically climb the ladder because you've managed to outlast the competition. There's no war of attrition in music. You might have been around for fifteen or twenty years, maybe even longer, but that doesn't mean you can pack a venue. Seniority doesn't entitle you to respect from the touring circuit. You have to create demand.

You can get up onstage and play a plastic kazoo for two hours, and if the club is packed and people like it, everyone will be happy. The owner, the manager, the servers and the bartenders will love every note you play on that kazoo, no matter how terrible it sounds. Every squawk will bring them pleasure. They'd rather hear you squawking on your kazoo in front of four hundred drunks (if they're drunk that means bar sales are kicking ass) than have the greatest virtuosos in the world playing to an empty room.

The problem with some musicians is that they feel clubs should willingly lose money on them, just because they've been around a long time. Because they've braved a tough life in show business and e*arned their wings.* If clubs subscribed to this philosophy, they'd be driven out of business faster than you can belt the first line of *Mustang Sally*.

Drew and I were blinded by ambition. We were dreaming in the clouds but camping at Wal-Mart. We thought things were just magically going to get better. If we kept rambling around the country, doing as many shows as possible with no concern for our sanity, good things would happen. You can work smart or you can work dumb, and when I look back on that first year of touring, I was working dumb. I figured you had to do this if you wanted to make it. You had to sleep in parking lots, play terrible venues, make shitty money, and sacrifice pretty much everything.

I did have a secondary agenda. I wanted to travel; to hang out in New England, New Orleans, Atlanta, Washington D.C., Philadelphia, Long Island, Montreal and Vancouver. I wanted to hit Yellowstone, Niagara Falls, Glacier, Yosemite, and the Gulf of Mexico. I was a natural seeker who had rarely ventured far from home, and it was time to get out there and experience the world. Global Funk Council was my vehicle.

Burp the Turtle

The Travesty, in all its (lack of) glory, was *also* my vehicle, in a more literal sense. One nice thing about having such a big motor home was that there was plenty of room for people's random stuff—the stuff they brought on tour, and the stuff they collectively accumulated as the band made its way around the country playing gigs.

Within reason it was okay for people to pick up random knick knacks, and sometimes one of these items would be "adopted" by the entire group. For example, at some point I brought on board a big, velvety stuffed animal, which happened to be a turtle. While initially intended to serve as a pillow, the turtle quickly was put to a different use...

I had at some point written a funk tune called *Burp the Turtle,* based on an inside band joke: a turtle is, in some circles, slang for *going number two.* Forgive the crude imagery, but there exists the saying, "got a turtle's head pokin'." One of us came up with the idea that if somebody passed a bit of gas, they were *burping the turtle.* Thus, when I came on board with a large, stuffed green turtle, the Mayor was quick to give the inanimate creature a name: "His name is Burp. Burp the Turtle." Everyone agreed, and the Travesty had itself a mascot.

Shortly thereafter, the Mayor, who did much of the driving in those days, came up with yet another fine idea. The turtle would be kept somewhere in the back of the motor home, in a spot accessible to everyone. Then, when one of the guys needed a bathroom break (for a project more involved than simply taking a leak), instead of announcing this fact to the entire crew, he would simply pick up the turtle and hurl it toward the front of the vehicle. The driver, seeing

Burp flying at his head through the rear view mirror, would know it was time to pull over. This proved a great way to eliminate unnecessary chatter in the vehicle, streamlining intra-band communication.

This Guy Must Sing His Ass Off

There were many good times on the road. It wasn't all lemons, even if the Travesty was proving to be a major one. We limped into Las Vegas, leaking oil all over the I-15, and pulled into Legends Lounge, a popular little dump along the jam band trail. It was here that a bleary-eyed, gambling addict degenerate told me, "You can really learn things watching Jerry Springer. With Springer you gotta read between the lines. Look beneath the surface."

Legends Lounge was located in the corner of a seedy strip-mall, miles off the actual Strip. Little Jesus had been off tour for a while, so when he showed up with a frizzy blonde from Utah, it was a surprise. Woo was back on the road, sporting a Hunter Thompson-style visor (what better place to do it than here?). Also in attendance were some characters from the Las Vegas Jam Band Society, a curious cadre of individuals who turned up periodically to get a dose of the funk. The crowd was rounded out by the usual farrago of hippies, hustlers and drifters. What really set that night off, however, was the presence of a luminous figure, the true master of this trashy domain. Ladies and gentlemen, *Elvis was in the building.*

I have reasonable expectations of anyone who endeavors to be an Elvis impersonator. If you have the hair, sing the right songs, and do at least a couple of the dance moves, you're cool with me. This particular character didn't look anything like the King. He was too short and too fat, for one thing. Also, he didn't have the hair right. *This guy must sing his ass off*, I thought. How else could he survive this cutthroat environment of omnipresent Elvis? I'll bet he croons the crap out of *Hound Dog.*

I invited this third-string Elvis up to do a couple songs, and also allowed Little Jesus to pound away on my Clavinet D-6 keyboard. He didn't know middle C from the Phish tattoo on his hairless chest, but in some run-down lounge out in the boondocks surrounding Las Vegas, it didn't really matter. You can't have Elvis start his set with a ballad, so we broke into *Heartbreak Hotel*. The problem was, none of us knew *Heartbreak Hotel*. I'd never played it in my life. We were up there feeding Elvis to the piranhas. To make matters worse, our fat, low rent Elvis couldn't carry a tune.

I expected him to redeem himself when we followed up the first song with *I Can't Help Falling in Love*. At least I *kind of* knew that one, and could guide him along. Wildman didn't have a clue, however, so it sounded like we were playing two different songs at the same time. Woo, meanwhile, continued his emulation of Gonzo, guffawing as he drunkenly stumbled around the dance floor, pointing in ridicule at our floundering frontman. After this collectively pathetic presentation, Elvis wandered off stage and I broke into *Sausage Party*, a little random ditty I'd written one night in Utah:

There's a feeling of excitement in the air
'Cause my homeys seem to think there will be ladies everywhere
So we're all dressed up in our Sunday best tonight
Got some jungle juice on and our gear's all looking tight
We pile into the car and we drive out to the spot

From the street, you can hear that they're bumping some loud hip-hop
So we get out of the car and we walk up to the door
And once we get inside, guess what's in store?

Oh no, not another sausage party!
Damn bro, I don't see a single hottie
All these dudes pushin' up now on me
Let's bounce to another spot now Lonnie
'Cause I don't think that I can stand another night of kilbasa
I just wanna take some honeys back to mi casa
But everywhere I look Jimmy Dean pork links surround me
So if you're swingin' sausage then you better not come around me
Or try to clown me

It goes without saying that *Sausage Party* does not represent the pinnacle of my achievement as a lyricist. (If it does, God help me). After I sang the chorus, I went into Frank Zappa mode, peripatetically canvassing the stage, microphone in hand, to allow each band member the chance to improvise his own verse. When it was Wildman's turn, he squawked like a chicken, no doubt prompting the manager of Legends Lounge to ask himself: *How much am I paying these assholes?*

The gig might have been a somewhat of a joke, but that didn't stop Drew and me from making the most of our couple days in Vegas. The next night we put on our suits,[140] hopped in a cab and hit the Strip for some fun and entertainment. In one casino I ran into an old friend, bassist Daryl Williams, who had lived in San Diego but was now living and playing out in Vegas. Years earlier Daryl and I had done a regular gig at the Loews Resort in Coronado, and he'd made enemies with a particular Coronado motorcycle cop. The cop would chase Daryl, in his red sports car, after he spotted the bassist speeding too fast down the road leading to the resort. Somehow Daryl had been able to *hide out* in the parking garage at Loews, evading the cop on more than one occasion. When I saw him at the gig, he'd have a smile on his face as he said, "I ditched that cop again." *High five, Daryl.*

Drew and I wound up at Rio, which had a rooftop club overlooking the whole strip. The view has been featured in many a movie. I balked

---

[140] Why were we traveling with dress suits, while playing in a funky jam band? I have no idea.

at the forty bucks cover charge for the two of us to get in there, causing Drew to huff, "What did you think it was going to cost? This is Vegas!" I reminded him that, although we had slapped on some jungle juice and were looking spiffy in our suits, we were living in an RV parked in a strip mall, in front of some crummy club in BFV (*bum fuck Vegas*).

The next day Drew and I decided to ride the elevator up to the top of the Stratosphere, Vegas's tallest tower. At the top of the Stratosphere, there's not only a restaurant and club, but also a rollercoaster and another thrill ride, which shoots you up an additional hundred feet in the air. We opted to give the latter ride a shot, and both nearly soiled our pants in fear as we were hurled high into the sky above Vegas. Before descending to street level, we decided to grab a cocktail in the restaurant, where we could enjoy the view.

As we were relaxing atop the Stratosphere, sipping a Captain and Coke (which was also Drew's beverage of choice), I got a call on my cell from Gary Klein, the bassist who'd fallen out of favor with GFC and had elected to sue me in small claims court. Gary spoke in a cordial tone, as if nothing negative had happened between us: "Hey Anthony, how's it going? I'm just calling to let you know that I won the court case, and you owe me nine hundred dollars." Since I had been traveling non-stop, I couldn't show up in court in San Diego to "defend" myself against Gary's claim. I had submitted a written defense, providing evidence of my "innocence," but was informed by someone knowledgeable in such matters that if you don't show up in person, a small claims judge will automatically rule in favor of the other party.[141]

---

[141] I decided not to pay Gary, because I felt the claim was chicken shit. But he got the money anyway—he was able to have some sheriff yank the funds out of my savings account.

Baby Blue Takes One for the Team

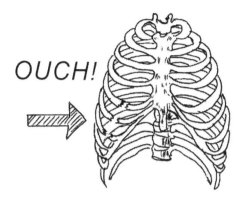

After Vegas, we continued east to Colorado for a short run. Dan was bailing from the project after the upcoming Chicago gig, so I put the word out that GFC was looking for a new guitarist. Two guys showed up to audition at Quixote's, a club in Denver. I wound up hiring one of them, Mark Reese, right on the spot.

Mark, a lanky, six-four white guy, asked "When do you guys need me?"

"We're leaving in the morning," I told him.

This is not uncommon in a touring band. People drop off along the way, and you pick up new ones as you go. It's not the most stable profession. Luckily, most musicians aren't tethered to anything that would prevent them from taking off on a moment's notice.

The tour moved east to Iowa. GFC was now in uncharted waters. We'd been on tour for several months, and as the Travesty rolled through the gloomy streets of Cedar Rapids, Iowa, I sensed my fellow band members were suffering acute cases of both philopatridomania and azygophrenia.[142]

---

[142]In other words, they were homesick, and they needed some action.

Club Lab was a shady looking joint, situated by itself along a remote strip of expressway. We waited in front of the building for signs of life... a promoter, a manager... anything. By the time it was dark there was still nobody around. I was getting nervous. What if this was a set-up? What if, like Santino in *The Godfather II*, we were about to get mowed down by a row of coldblooded gangsters, or in this case *gangstas*, who would riddle us with bullets and steal all our gear? I didn't like it.

Finally somebody showed up, but it wasn't the promoter. It was his girlfriend, who had no idea what was going on. Sensing a *shit sandwich*[143] in the making, I decided to pull the plug on the gig. We migrated to a nearby bar, drinking beer and watching Cedar Rapids' version of *local fight night.* This turned out to be a wonderful way to spend an evening. Local participants eagerly jumped into the ring to beat the living crap out of each other, while a crowd of rowdy louts, us included, egged them on.

A few of the guys appeared to have actual training, executing rudimentary mixed martial arts moves. The highlight of the evening occurred when a short, lightweight guy squared off against a beastly oaf, and the brawl played out like the Biblical tale it resembled; the short guy jumped on the behemoth's back, like a child getting a piggy back ride, and started pounding his massive, bald head. The place went wild. David slew Goliath, yet again.

I left the GFC crew and wandered to another bar on my own. This place was smaller, and empty but for a few weathered lushes scattered around the room. One was a long-haired Vietnam veteran, with breath smelling like a deceased, infinitesimal rodent had lodged in his gums. I was powered by a few Fat Tires by now, and got into a spirited, redneck conversation with the vet. I listened to his entire story and then bellowed, "You're a hero, man! I appreciate what you did!" He responded with a hearty pat on my back and the words, "You're a good old boy!"

This is a typical exchange in dive bars, between alcoholic war veterans and inebriated younger guys who haven't seen combat (and have no desire to see combat). It's a conversation between men of proven courage and untested poseurs. The hero is drunk enough to forego judgment of the wannabe, speaking to him as if he had been

---

[143] Thank you yet again, Christopher Guest and Rob Reiner.

there right beside him, dodging fire at Hamburger Hill, while the wannabe is drunk enough to have the nerve to talk to the war vet as if the two of them are *cut from the same cloth*... as if there is not a gaping chasm which separates the man who once laid his life on the line, and now lives with the psychological aftermath of combat, and the civilian who, despite being sheltered from danger his entire privileged life, thinks he knows something about war and valor.

The next day we continued on to Iowa City, to perform at a club called the Green Room. This would be a defining moment in my career as a touring artist, for it would be on this night that I would discover the extent to which I was willing to lay it all on the line to follow my musical dreams. Once I'd crossed the line laid out before me in Iowa City, there would be no turning back. The Elbo Room in San Francisco had been a major rite of passage, a stepping stone to artistic freedom and control of my destiny, but the Green Room would represent the next level of sacrifice, the point of complete submission to this ridiculous lifestyle.

The show went very well at the Green Room. The club was crowded and people reacted enthusiastically to our music. After the set, I was sitting at the merchandise table to relieve Woo, when the owner of the place, Neal, came over to compliment the band and buy a CD. I told him I appreciated his support, and we talked for a couple minutes. Woo returned from his break, and this is when things went awry.

"Well, should we settle out now, Neal?" Woo asked.

"Settle out? Whadda you mean?"

"You know, get paid." Neal's affability transformed into hostility. He stood tall, ast least six-six, arching his back like a grizzly bear preparing to attack. Make that a *hammered* grizzly bear.

"Bullshit!" Neal screamed, loud enough for everyone in the bar to hear. Woo timidly attempted to continue the dialogue.

"You said you'd give us the door,[144] when we talked on the phone."

"Are you doubting me? You're calling me a liar!" Neal screamed in Woo's face. Enter *me...*

"Were you planning on just not paying us *anything*? What kind of a deal is that?" I asked.

"I got you motel rooms at the Super 8! Fuuuuuuuuck!"

---

[144] Meaning, he'd pay us whatever money was collected at the door that evening.

This is where I lost my cool.

"Do you think I drove my ass all the way out here from California for a couple hotel rooms? Is that what you think?"

Neal opened up his mouth and puffed out his chest, like a grizzly that's consumed ten pints of Guinness, and let out a grotesque roar: "Aggghhhhhhhh!" This act was intended to scare me, but I squared up to him, at least a few inches shorter but not deterred, and called him out.

"You don't intimidate me. You think just because you're screaming in my face we're going to walk out of here without any money? We packed your club and you're giving us nothing?" The other GFC guys were over in the corner, nervously packing up their equipment. Nobody rallied. I was on my own. "How 'bout you just give us a couple hundred bucks, and we'll get out of here and forget about this," I reasonably offered.

"I'm not giving you a fucking dime."

I walked away from him to calm down, still level-headed enough to realize this was a brawl waiting to happen. The female bassist from the opening band was standing nearby; the opening act was a group of local kids who hadn't even known how to *hold* their instruments, much less play them. Usually with local opening acts there's some redeeming quality—a decent guitarist or singer, a catchy tune—*something*. It's rare to encounter an opening act that has absolutely nothing going for it, a group of amateurs that has no business performing in public. *This was that group.*

When I walked into the corner the bassist approached me, having overheard my exchange with Neal.

"Let's just all try to get along, okay? It was a fun night. We played good, you guys played good. We all made some money..." I shot her a malevolent glare.

"*What?* Did you say you *made some money?* You got *paid?*" She cowered, sensing my anger.

"Well, yeah, a little."

"How much did he pay you? Tell me!"

"Like a hundred and fifty bucks or something."

I stormed back over to Neal, sticking my finger in his burly chest.

"You paid those amateurs? You have a national touring band pack your club, and you choose to stiff them and pay some college hacks? You insult us like that?" Drew stepped in to diffuse the situation, steering the slurring club owner into a back room to discuss the matter. This left me standing there irate, while Woo sat crumpled in a chair.

"I didn't get a contract, T," Woo admitted. "Sorry." There was nothing to do now. Without a contract we had nothing. Several of the owner's friends were gathered over by the bar, and they began laying into me.

"Hey you, Baby Blue[145]... you fucked up! You shoulda got a contract. Now you got nothin'." Remarkably, I ignored this abuse for a few minutes. It was clear nobody else in the band wanted to fight. As the ridicule continued, I knew I would have to take a stand—a physical, possibly violent stand. Like Mookie at the end of *Do the Right Thing*, I simply couldn't allow this injustice to go unchallenged. You can view me as a principled warrior, a man unwilling to back down when he's been wronged... a sort of *Braveheart* of the Jam Band Scene, if you will... or you can look at me as a hot-head who doesn't know when to walk away from trouble. There's some truth in both assessments.

I'd had enough of the guy referring to me as *Baby Blue*. I walked over, stood inches from him and asked, "You think that's pretty funny, huh?" He was smirking, enjoying himself.

"Yeah, I really do."

With that, I cocked my arm and followed through with a hard, open-handed slap across the face. "How 'bout that... was that funny?" It should have been a punch, because if you're going to fight, you should throw the first punch, as Len had once taught me; but I wanted to shame this guy in front of his friends by, as such actions are referred to in street parlance, *slapping him like a bitch*. Stunned, he shook his head and stared at me in disbelief. He clearly wasn't going to retaliate, so I walked away and started packing up my gear.

The impact of what I'd done sank in for him after a few minutes, and he started cursing and challenging me. "I'll see you outside," he warned. He said that a few times before I finally took a cue from the Bob Weir playbook:

"Forget outside. I'm right here."

I continued packing my keyboards, and that's when the guy caught me off guard. I didn't think he had it in him, but he rushed me with all his force, throwing me off balance. I went reeling into a table. The next

---

[145] I was wearing a powder-blue, collared shirt with some kind of Japanese patterns.

thing I knew we were on the ground, writhing around in puddles of spilled beer, and I was stuck in some kind of wrestling hold—not a surprise since we were in the heart of Iowa—as the guy whacked at the top of my head. I was reaching up trying to grab him, but couldn't break free. He was stronger than he looked, and certainly ballsier than I had given him credit for being. I felt a mild twinge of panic, as I couldn't move. He wasn't hurting me, but I was stuck down there, immobilized. Before long we were separated by Neal and a couple other locals.

"Bet that hurt a little more than a slap, didn't it?" my opponent snickered as he rose to his feet. Not much. It probably hurt his hand more than it hurt the top of my head. What *did* hurt was the rib or two that I'd broken when I crashed into that table. That hurt a hell of a lot. I hadn't considered the fact that you can break something other than your nose when you get in a barroom brawl.

By the morning I was in serious pain, clutching at my right upper torso in agony. Good thing I only had another eight months of non-stop touring ahead! Playing keyboards with broken ribs is a bad idea. I don't recommend it. The next couple months would be pure hell.

Before the Green Room incident, I'd often wondered if I would ever find myself in such a situation. You always heard about these things happening. Some would say I acted like a jerk that night, but the Green Room became a personal badge of honor.[146] I took a stand against an unjust situation. I don't regret what I did, other than the fact that what I said about the opening band was too harsh. There are times when you have to rise up to defend something you believe in. If you

---

[146] I have come to believe that Iowa City is like a Bermuda Triangle of male violence. In 2006, I went back there with KD3 to do a show. Within seconds of pulling up to the entrance of the Sheraton Hotel, a belligerent, drunk, huge, corn-fed white guy tried to climb into our van, thinking it was a shuttle. Joe Cahill, the road manager, pushed him away from the vehicle. After this the guy started screaming horribly profane things, and punctuated his verbal attack by spitting in Joe's face. I stepped forward, and in an ironic role reversal, played peacemaker: "Come on, guys, violence isn't the answer here. Let's all be cool." The guy turned to me and said, "You're cool, man. I got no beef with you. It's this other cocksucker that I'm going to destroy!"

never do this, you're not the kind of person who's going to make a mark on the world.[147]

And on the Sixth Day, God Created Benadryl

In Chicago, I met a woman named Rochelle. She was a street-wise, big city type. I broke the ice at the Boulevard by asking Rochelle if she knew anything about the art museum downtown. I know what you're thinking: *Hahaha. The art museum! Nice work.* Actually, I had genuine interest in art museums while I was traveling. I admittedly didn't know much about fine art, but I enjoyed looking at paintings, and would visit museums in various cities, usually by myself.

Anyway, this ice breaker worked pretty well. I got some details about the museum, and Rochelle invited me over to her place after the gig. It may seem as if these road dalliances had no redeeming value and were mere hedonistic flings, but the truth is, they served a utilitarian purpose as well. Often, the band's accommodations were insufficient for five or six grown men. If we'd relied on them exclusively we would have been packed together like rodents, and would have driven each other to the brink of madness on a regular basis.

When you were in the middle of a grueling tour, and you met someone to spend time with away from the gang, your motivation was not only the desire to kick back with a girl and absorb some feminine energy, but also the need to get everyone out of your face for a minute; to get a respite from the guys you were driving around with every day, every week, every month. You were also doing *them* a service. Breaking from the pack was a healthy practice when you were attached to a group of male musicians who were, for all practical purposes, married without the fringe benefits.

When you think about it, being in a touring band is a subverted version of traditional marriage. In a normal marriage, you escape the monotony of spending every waking moment with your spouse by hanging out with your friends or buddies. On the road, you escape the doldrums of being constantly stuck with your buddies by hanging out with a girl.

---

[147] That's not to say there aren't other, more productive ways to make your mark on the world than getting in fistfights in shithole bars in Iowa City.

Brevan Maddox, a guitarist friend from Lawrence, Kansas, brought a small group to Chicago to open for GFC at the Boulevard. He had somehow coerced the former drummer of the Sun Ra Arkestra, a much older, veteran musician, to make the trek with him, for what must have been peanuts—if anything at all.

A six-foot-six stork with glasses, dreaded hair, hippie clothing and sandals, Brevan had done a short stint a few years earlier with Living Large. One night in Minneapolis, Brevan, by virtue of his fashion sensibilities, had put us all in danger. He was sporting a patched together, colorful skirt which draped down to the midpoint of his hairy calves. In the student center at UC Berkeley this would have been fine. At some biker bar in Minneapolis, with the city's angular, almost sinister-looking skyline looming in the distance, framed by ominous, dark cloud cover, it was not fine at all. In fact, it was a real problem. We paraded through the large, intimidating watering hole, which was packed with scraggly, bandana-wearing bad-asses, and I could clearly hear the words being muttered in our wake: "Hey Rocky, check out this faggot."

When Brevan went into the bathroom to heed nature's call, one of the biker bad-asses spotted the guitarist's checkered, patchwork dress crumpled on the floor underneath a stall. "What the hell, Jomo? There's some big chick with hairy legs droppin' anchor in here!"

Brevan had been the wrong fit for Living Large. His personality annoyed everyone in the group, specifically his inability to stop talking for more than five seconds at a time. I'd accepted an avuncular role in shepherding the kid along, however, so I had misgivings when an emergency meeting was called before the long drive from Salt Lake City to San Francisco, to determine how to shut Brevan up for the next ten hours.

"We've got to do something here," Woo noted. "We can't have this kid blabbering all the way back to California."

"We're gonna need drugs," someone suggested.

"I've got an idea," Woo said, grabbing Brevan's water bottle. He unscrewed the top and proceeded to drop a couple valiums into the water. There were snickers of delight. We began the drive, Brevan in the front seat. He began screaming the lyrics to *Respect* at the top of his lungs, prompting Woo, the driver, to shove a pillow in his face.

"Why'd you do that?" Brevan asked.

"You can't be butchering Aretha like that," Woo answered. An hour later, the valium still hadn't taken effect. Brevan stammered on about King Crimson bootlegs and other topics no one cared to discuss. When we pulled over for a pit-stop, Brevan hit the john.

"Give me that damn thing," Woo groused, grabbing the water bottle and unscrewing the lid. "The valium's not gettin' it done." He pulled a pair of Benadryl capsules from his backpack, cracked them open and emptied the contents into the bottle, which now looked like a freshly shaken snow globe. Like Rasputin, the fabled giant who failed to succumb to poisoning, here was this loquacious hippie giant, staving off the soporific effects of valium, droning on and on about obscure groups and albums.

"What's that floating around in my water?" Brevan asked as we got back on the road.

"It's Echinacea," Woo replied. "We all want you to get over that cough."

"Thanks, guys." Brevan pounded the comatose cocktail and, fifteen minutes later, finally passed out, avoiding the eventual strangulation that befell Rasputin. Once he was out cold, Brevan slouched in the front passenger seat, mouth agape and dead to the world, which is how he remained until the Golden Gate Bridge was visible through the van's windows. *And on the sixth day, God created Benadryl. And on the seventh day, Brevan slept... and that was good.*

I had a nice time with Rochelle in Chicago. We ate the best deep dish pizza I'd ever tasted, from a joint called Piquad's. We also went out for drinks with her hipster big-city friends. Late one night, she took me to a diner where there was seventies porn playing on a multiple TV sets. I ate a terrific meatloaf sandwich and watched some hairy, hung bastard service a tawdry chick with caked make-up and a curly perm. These are the random moments you remember from the road.

The Boulevard was a great little venue. The owner, John Glynn, was very supportive of musicians. He treated GFC like kings. The food was great, and we ate whatever we wanted for free. John could party with the best of them—a Chicagoan trait, for sure—and would keep the bar open for friends and musicians long past closing hours. Sometimes, he'd close up so we could head over to a downtown bar called Estelle's, which stayed open until four a.m. and was always packed. On more than one occasion I remember leaving the Boulevard, closing down Estelle's, and going *back* to the Boulevard to continue the party until the sun was up. When you played John's club, the party went on as long as you wanted it to.

We left Chicago, but not before John gave me the skinny on my friend Rochelle. He pulled me aside and said, "You know, man, Rochelle is a madam. She manages high-priced call girls. She's set up a couple of my friends." The next time I was at Rochelle's place, I delicately broached the subject: "So, Rochelle, do you run a brothel?"

"What?" she shot back.

"I just heard a couple things."

"What did you hear?"

"I heard you're somebody who can make... arrangements. If it's true, you know, I've got a couple friends that are really desperate —"

"I do not run a prostitution ring!"

"It's cool if you do. I mean, I don't really care, Rochelle."

"Who told you this?"

"I shouldn't say."

"Who told you?"

"John."

"That son of a bitch. My friends are *not* hookers... but I do have a couple I'd like you to meet."

"Really? Meet for coffee? Crumbcake? Some miniature golf?"

"I think you know what I mean," Rochelle whispered, reminiscent of Rebecca DeMornay's sultry character in *Risky Business*, another temptress from the greater Chicago area.

"Well, we'll see what shakes out next time I'm in town," I coolly responded. We're talking Steve McQueen cool.

Picture with Nectar

After a forgettable show in Pittsburgh, the band continued east for a show at the Stanhope House in New Jersey. We opened for the Bomb Squad, a funky ensemble featuring some members of another East Coast group called Deep Banana Blackout. The show went well, and the Bomb Squad guys complimented our music. We were getting tight, with Mark Reese finding his niche on guitar.

Our next stop was one of considerable JBS significance. Burlington, Vermont is to the jam band fan as Graceland is to the obese tourist from Oklahoma. This northeastern town, which borders Lake Champlain, is home to Phish, the king of post-Grateful Dead jam bands. The Mayor was excited about our journey to the vortex of jamming. Phish was the reason he was in the RV in the first place. Without Phish, I probably wouldn't have been in the RV either.[148]

Woo had concocted the idea of doing a show at Nectar's, the famous little restaurant where Phish got their start. Our gig would coincide with the airing of a new Simpson's episode featuring Phish. It was a great idea except for one fact: Everyone in Burlington stayed home to watch the Simpson's that night. Nectar's was near empty. After our *crickets*[149] set the Mayor and I chatted up Nectar, the owner, and subject of the album cover for *Picture of Nectar*, one of Phish's most famous albums. He joined us for a group photo, which we dubbed *Picture with Nectar*.

Burlington was beautiful. The weather was warming up, and the lake was resplendent with reflections of lush surroundings. It was a hip town, home to the University of Vermont and a thriving music scene. On a night off, I heard some number of excellent musicians playing in local bars.

The following night, we played the House of Blues in Cambridge, Massachusetts. This venue, next to the campus of Harvard, was the first installment of the House of Blues franchise. The gig was not successful. Besides being super loud, Mark had an off night, and the room, again, was practically empty.

Todd Sherman was on the East Coast for business, and came to see the show and hang out after. We scared up some late-night pizzas and took them back to the Travesty, along with a couple bottles of red wine. It was times like this that the Travesty was an asset on the road. It was spacious and comfortable, and could accommodate a dozen people for an impromptu party.

We stayed in Connecticut that night, holing up in a hotel adjacent to the campus of Yale. I spent the free afternoon walking around the campus, enjoying the dramatic, gothic architecture of the university's old buildings. I reflected back on my rejection by several Ivy League colleges when I was eighteen, and wondered how life would be now, had things turned out differently.

---

[148] Thus, I don't know whether I should be thankful to Phish or hate their guts.

[149] When a show is totally dead (nobody shows up), musicians like to say, "It was crickets, man."

After Connecticut, GFC ventured south to Long Island.[150] We were scheduled to play the Phunky Phish, which was owned by a crusty local, and was home of the most stunning *dready mama*[151] bartender of all time. Before the gig, I wandered into a neighboring cafe for a snack. On the east coast, little restaurants sell these meat pie pastries I've never seen anywhere else. I don't know what is used in the filling — looks like the stuff inside Chef Boyardee raviolis — but it sure tastes good. Once I was turned on to the East Coast meat pie, I devoured them with regularity.

I grabbed a couple meat pies from the Egyptian owner of the tiny eatery, and we engaged in a stimulating discussion about relations in the Middle East. He was assertive with his pro-Palestinian opinions, and unlike most of the drugstore pundits I encountered on the road, actually knew what he was talking about. The man had lived many years in Egypt before coming to the States and marrying a white woman, and it was an eye-opener to hear an informed perspective from his domestically unpopular viewpoint.

After the show that night, Todd and I picked up some brews and drove out to the beach with a couple girls we'd met at the club. It was too cold to hang out at the ocean, so we grabbed some breakfast back in Bay Shore, had a nice conversation, then dropped the girls off at their car. When we said our goodbyes, one of them said to me, "Thanks for being nice guys. It's refreshing."[152]

The prospect of maneuvering the Travesty into busy Manhattan on a weekend afternoon was something nobody looked forward to. Fortunately, the Mayor, who drove the beast with impressive agility, did a fine job of getting us over the George Washington Bridge and into the city. There was no place to park once we were in midtown, and I had to plead with law enforcement for permission to stop long enough to unload our equipment at a club called Tobacco Road.

---

[150] Typically pronounced *Long GUY'land*.

[151] A term coined by either Little Jesus or Mr. Peepers, in reference to young, attractive girls with long, crazy dreadlocks.

[152] This reminds me of my brother Collin's all-time classic pick-up line in a bar (before he met his wife): "You know, it's really refreshing to come to a place like this and meet a woman who's into sports."

As we unloaded, I noticed, out of the corner of my eye, a familiar figure hurrying up the street. It was Joe Locke, the vibraphone great I'd corresponded with via e-mail.

"Joe?" He stopped, but didn't recognize me (he'd never seen me before in person). I reminded him about our letters, and the Cult of Soul CD I'd sent him, and he perked up.

"Hey, Anthony! Of course I remember you. What's up, man?" I told him I was in town for a show, and introduced him to the guys in GFC. As we were talking, the guys in his band filed out of the adjacent rehearsal studios. Out walked Jeff "Tain" Watts, the great jazz drummer. Watts shook my hand and posed with me and Joe for a picture. This may not sound like a big deal, but these little moments reinforce an important sentiment for musicians: We're all part of the same fraternity. We might work in different genres, but we all deal with the same basic challenges of the artistic life.

The cops allowed us to park the Travesty in front of Tobacco Road that night, an act of great munificence, and we enjoyed a nice RV party before the show. This included the company of Mike Blanco, my bassist buddy from San Diego who was now a hard-working Manhattan transplant, drummer Mark Ferber, who I'd played with in Gilbert Castellanos's band in San Diego, and a handful of other friends.

On nights like this, the Travesty came through in spades. Not only was it comfortable for pre-set cocktails, but it gave the illusion that the band was far more successful than it really was. You could see in people's faces that they were thinking, *Wow, you guys are really making it.* In this sense, Global Funk Council was a fitting metaphor for life in America: *Everybody's living beyond their means.*

Wildman hit it off with the bartender at Tobacco Road that night, a pleasant-looking girl named Tia. The next day we returned to Long Island for a day off, and Wildman announced he would be making a solo trek back to Manhattan to hang out with Tia. This prompted Mark to quip, "Jeffrey, I can see you setting that up at four in the morning, when you're sauced after the show, but to actually follow through with it the next day? That's dedication."

After a second night at the Phunky Phish, the Travesty lumbered on to Blacksburg, Virginia for an evening at Baylee's, a club that catered to the Virginia Tech crowd. The show was great, a large group of kids turning out to check out the funk refugees of GFC. Drew was at his best, people responding positively to his stage presentation; and it must be said that his stock patter, which was bugging the shit out of me, Wildman and the Mayor, was actually helping the band get over.

Talking onstage was one thing that Drew could really do. He'd go off on tangents about drinking, faux racial banter... *I'd like to call attention to the fact that I'm the only black person in a hundred miles of this place...* or the Mayor's personal favorite: *Remember when you were at the eighth grade dance, and all the guys were on one side of the room and all the girls were on the other? That's what this crowd reminds me of.*

While this was a bit annoying, Drew counterbalanced his lounge shtick with some fine drumming and musical leadership onstage. I'll go so far as to say Drew carried the band some nights. We hadn't found a strong musical identity yet, and Drew compensated for it by laying down a serious groove at all times. If you make people get up and dance, you can offset many musical liabilities, and people will leave your show with a smile on their face. Drew could always get people dancing.

This in itself—making people dance and party—only took me so high. Wildman and I agreed there were loftier musical goals to set our sights on. This *party 'til you drop* vibe was not the ultimate musical statement the two of us wanted to make to the world. I was fascinated by the fact that while Drew possessed advanced skill as a musician, in his heart of hearts he was a barfly. He relished in raising his Captain and Coke high into the air between songs and bellowing into the microphone, in a raspy, deep tone that could never be mistaken for anyone else, *Cheers, y'all!*

The Birth of Wildman

Alas, we've come to the hiatus between April 20th, 2001, and April 27th, 2001. 4/20 is a notorious date in the JBS, due to its association with the marijuana subculture; it is also noteworthy in this particular tale, because it commenced a week of living in a Wal-Mart parking lot—something I'd never imagined was a possibility before I embarked on my JBS journey. Like the days spent toiling in a rock quarry in Chino Valley, this circumstance would prompt existential contemplation: *How did my decision to be a musician lead me to this moment, camping out for a week in the Wal-Mart parking lot in Asheville, North Carolina?*

The show at the Asheville Music Zone was not a good one. The night before, guitarist John Scofield had sold the place out. For our show, there was virtually nobody in the club. Maybe ten people. We were a last-minute replacement for some act that had cancelled, and nobody knew (or cared) about us being there.

The next night, Drew and I had a critical conversation back at the Wal-Mart, during which his future with GFC was determined. He wanted more free time to pursue his own project, and I told him we needed to keep hitting the road hard with GFC. We would need to work even harder next year than we did this year. I was adamant about this. Drew said he'd have to think about it, and then paced the parking lot while talking to his girlfriend back in California.

We'd spent a whole week parked in front of the Wal-Mart, and as lovely an experience as it had been, it was time for some new scenery. We still had a few days to kill before our shows at Jazzfest in New Orleans, so we found an RV park in Alabama, right on the Gulf Coast. We rented a space with electrical hook-ups, and camped out next to a number of similar motor homes, most owned by people twice our age.

The RV park proved a good time. One day, Woo asked me to cut his hair. I had no business cutting anybody's hair, and was forced to completely shave his head after I botched the job, leaving him looking like Private Pyle in *Full Metal Jacket*. One afternoon, we hit some basketball courts. Woo and I squared off against Wildman and Mark. Mark seemed like he'd be a good basketball player, if for no other reason than the fact that he was six-four and had long arms. Woo, under six feet and nearly as wide as he was tall, had played high school football, but didn't have much experience on the basketball court.

As the game began, Wildman demonstrated that he was a natural athlete, running around the court with the helter-skelter movements of a good soccer player, driving the ball to the basket and converting a few shots. Mark, with his awkward frame and slow feet, was inept, allowing Woo to establish physical and psychological dominance through a series of punishing screens. Like many ex-football players I've encountered while playing hoops, Woo was applying gridiron techniques to compensate for his dearth of roundball finesse. Since he was on my team, I encouraged him to continue to pummel the hell out of Mark, while I attempted to contain Wildman.

The game became heated, and Wildman, whose long, abundant hair was blowing wildly in the Gulf Shore breeze, grew more aggressive, butchering me with elbows and body checks every time I tried to take the rock to the hole. It was a good streetball tactic, because it was the only way he was going to keep me from driving in for a lay-up on every possession. I got very competitive, as I always do when the game is close, and became agitated by Wildman's rough play. We had agreed to play three games, and Woo and I had taken the first two. The third game was coming down to the wire, when Wildman launched a game-winning two-pointer from at least thirty feet out,[153] thoroughly pissing me off. I shouted at him as he marched off the court to have a post-victory cigarette, "You're a goddman wildman out there!" That's where the nickname came from. I'm not sure he ever liked it, but it's what I and everyone else called him for the next two years.

Our next stop was New Orleans, home of the popular Jazz and Heritage Festival. We weren't on the festival's official bill, but like dozens of jam bands from all over the country, had secured gigs at local venues to coincide with the fairground performances. For two weeks, New Orleans became a free-for-all gathering of music enthusiasts, international jazz fans, and JBS musicians and supporters. We had two shows scheduled, one at Tipitina's and another at the Blue Nile.

The night we got into town, I showed up at Tipitina's Uptown to hang out with my friends from Karl Denson's Tiny Universe. Dave Veith, Karl's keyboardist, was a friend from San Diego. Like me, he had studied with Rick Helzer at SDSU. Now, Dave was touring all over the world with Karl, playing festivals and nice venues. I was also friends with Brian Jordan, Karl's guitarist, who had been a San Diego musician before making a name for himself with KDTU.

I jammed with Karl and company that night at Tipitina's. Like The String Cheese Incident, KDTU was inspiring because they'd earned a loyal following across the country, without sacrificing the integrity of their music. After sitting in, I hung out at Tipitina's with John Staten, Ignacio Arango and Mike Travis, the String Cheese Incident's drummer. Sometimes you go for long stretches without seeing people in these circles, because everyone's constantly touring. The festivals give you a nice opportunity to catch up.

On April 27th, GFC played the infamous Blue Nile breakfast show, a gig that didn't start until 7am. You might be thinking, "Who would be up that early?" It wasn't a matter of who had woken up, but who had *never gone to bed.* At Jazzfest, people were wired for days on end, wandering the streets in a glazed stupor. If you were relatively sober, you might feel, while walking along Bourbon Street at six in the morning, as if you had dropped in on a scene from *Night of the Living Dead.*

---

[153] In streetball, a normal basket counts as one, not two points.

Mike Travis sat in during the Blue Nile show, which was raging. We got into some organic Latin jams, and pulled off a convincing version of our epic original piece, *New Century Suite*. This instrumental composition was about twenty minutes long and wove its way through numerous styles and grooves. It was the musical centerpiece of the band at that point.

Several of my friends from the scene were at the Blue Nile, including my old San Francicso pal, Debbie. She and her friend Miso were partying hard, sweaty and wide-eyed. After the show, Woo dragged a haggard, violently coughing Miso back to the hotel room of Big Noam, a friend of the band who was in town from New Jersey. Big Noam, uncannily, was the same exact physical dimensions as Woo, with a rivaling appetite for everything under the sun. We took to calling him *East Coast Woo*.

Noam had opened his hotel door to us throughout the festival, allowing the whole band to crash in his room and escape the heat; and now Woo traipsed in with this bedraggled bag of partied-out bones, hoping to get lucky. Noam was not amused. "What the fuck are you doing, Woo?" I was hoping for a showdown, a standoff right there in the Ramada: West Coast Woo vs. East Coast Woo… *Big Sweaty Brawl in the Bayou*. Instead, Noam stormed out, disgusted. I pulled Woo aside and said, "Dude, get Miso out of here. Noam's getting ready to kick us all to the curb." He complied.

Wildman wasn't around much during Jazzfest. He was in New Orleans, but spending most of his time with a woman from Washington D.C. She was a lawyer, had money to spend, and if you want to know what she looked like, Vick summed it up best: "She looks like you without the goatee, Wildman."

While in New Orleans, I connected with Eric Levy, the stellar keyboardist in Garaj Mahal. I invited Eric to sit in with GFC during our Tipitina's show on May 2nd, and he coaxed sounds out of my MS-2000 I didn't know were possible. Eric took a masterful synth solo that knocked out the Mayor and me alike. During that same gig, both Dave Veith and another solid keyboardist, Ethan White, took the stage to jam with me, creating a keyboard summit of sorts.

You'd think that after a long tour culminating in an eventful week in New Orleans, it would have been time for a break. Remember, however, this is Global Funk Council we're talking about—the band that never got off the road. We weren't even *close* to stopping. From New Orleans we hit Baton Rouge and Fayetteville, two shows that might as well not have happened. Then it was on to the band's debut in St. Louis. Spotting the famous arch along the Mississippi River, I crossed another item off *T's Must-See Tourist Curiosities.* Who knew I was about to encounter another American cultural treasure: the venerable Ron Jeremy.

Posing with the Hedgehog

Ron Jeremy remains the world's most recognizable male porn star. For guys of my generation, who were first exposed to porn in the eighties, Jeremy was a household name. A stumpy, hairy and unattractive guy, he provided hope to millions of young men in America: *If that dude can get some action, I can too.* As an actor, Jeremy possessed a subtle wit and charming propensity for self-deprecation, which, coupled with the fact that he was always in films with gorgeous young women doing things to him that most guys could only dream of, helped him become a pop culture icon. When I saw a marquee which read *Tonight… Ron Jeremy in Person,* as I walked the streets of St. Louis, I knew I had to be there. This was an opportunity I simply couldn't miss.

I had several hours to kill before seeing Ron, so I decided to head downtown to take a closer look at the Arch. Normally I would take a cab, but Wildman urged me to save a few bucks and hop on public transit. *Great idea,* I thought. I'll take the bus. Wildman was supposed to join me, but after waiting a few minutes, I got antsy and left without him.

I hopped on the bus, which wound its way into some pretty run-down neighborhoods; but I wasn't flustered. I'd once reared my Caucasian head in the heart of South Central without trouble, after all. As we trucked along, the bus filled up, and I was the only white person on board. Soon, the bus was at full capacity, crowded with African Americans of various ages... and me.

Visions of Reginald Denny danced in my head. Flashbacks to that unlucky sap getting dragged from his diesel rig, then having the crap kicked out of him on national TV. Various *payback for whitey* scenarios played on the silver screen of my insecurities, as I caught surly glares from fellow bus riders. If something ugly went down it would be deemed *my* fault; my fault for being white, and my fault for willfully entering hostile territory. Al Sharpton, speaking on CNN, would explain the actions of the vengeful mob: *These people were angry, and this man was in the wrong place at the wrong time. The people cannot be blamed, as they were driven to this act of outrage by over two hundred years of disenfranchisement.*

All this might sound irrational and paranoid, but I will tell you this: When I hopped off that bus in the heart of the 'hood, to look for a cab, I was stopped by two dudes who said, "What you doing in this neighborhood, bro? You better get the fuck out of here quick." This wasn't a threat but merely a *heads up*. I hunted down a cab, jumped in, wiped the sweat from my brow, and was greeted by another "What you doin' down here, bro? You're lucky I stopped," the cabbie continued. The Arch was cool, yes, but not cool enough to justify nearly becoming a sacrificial honkey lamb.

Back at the club a few hours later, I saw Wildman and said, "Thanks. I almost got crucified on that bus, but hey, I saved a few bucks in cab fare."

"You should have waited for me. I was going to come with you."

"Great, so it would have been my backwards-baseball-capped white ass, and your Jerry Garcia-looking hippie white ass together... we *definitely* would have got beaten down."

I set up my gear and we rehearsed Wildman's epic composition, *Out of the Darkness*. After that, I bowed out for a brief brush with greatness. It was time to meet Ron. The unlikely adult film icon, a human incarnation of Mario, the mustached midget that jumps barrels in *Donkey Kong*, was in town to promote his new documentary film, *Porn Star: The Legend of Ron Jeremy*. I watched the film, which was somewhat entertaining and humorous, then stuck around for a post-film Q&A session.

The questions asked by audience members were as entertaining as the film:

Ron, what was the key to your being discovered?

"My talent was that I could get an erection consistently. Now, guys just pop Viagra, so that's no big deal."

In the lobby, I took a picture with Ron, considerably shorter than me (but also considerably *longer*). I invited the Hedgehog, as he is known to some, over to Cicero's to check out my show, going so far as to invite him to jam with the band.[154]

"That's sweet. I'll try to make it." I wasn't sure how I felt about Ron Jeremy saying that my words were *sweet.* The Hedgehog didn't make an appearance, perhaps fatigued from his ambitious publicity campaign. I have a feeling our paths will cross again.

We returned to Chicago after St. Louis for a couple more shows at the Boulevard Café. Rochelle called while I was en route to the Windy City. She said, "Look, I've got a meeting in the afternoon tomorrow, so I need you to come over in the morning. It's an important meeting, and I'm going to need sex so I can go in there loose. Come over when you get to town." It wasn't an invitation—it was an order. I was still recovering from Jazzfest, and a bit put off by Rochelle's demanding tone.

"I'm not one of your employees, Rochelle."

"I'm not a madam, damn it!"

"And I'm not a gigolo. My job in life is not to make sure you're loose for meetings." The conversation ended abruptly, and I didn't see Rochelle until she showed up at the Boulevard, asking me to come over to her house. I said no. I had met another girl in Chicago at this point, Theresa. Rochelle was out, Theresa was in. I had a few nice times with Theresa, but was soon deflated back to the realization that every rose has its thorn. Thank you, Brett Michaels, for this pithy truth, which is right up there with *time marches on* and *love is blind.* As I was trying to figure out why Theresa had gotten weird on me all of a sudden, Woo informed me that the girl was taking a strong prescription medication called Calonopin. I don't know how he knew this, but my man Woo always had the pharmaceutical dirt on people. I've always been

---

[154] Jeremy supposedly plays some keyboard.

somewhat naïve about people on drugs. I just think they're acting bizarrely, until someone announces, "man, that guy's tweeking right now!" *Oh, really? I thought he was just in a peppy mood.*

Lipp Confronts the Homeless

After Chicago, we headed out for shows in Evanston, Iowa City, Omaha and Denver. At Quixote's in Denver, I got into a disagreement with the band when my intricate set list turned into a disaster onstage. The guys didn't like the segues and abrupt modulations I'd specified. Vick asked if he could write a set for the following night, which we were co-headlining with the Santa Cruz band Netwerk Electric. I told him to go ahead. Vick's set list, while lacking originality, worked much better than my intricate one. I've never quite been able to grasp the concept of *keep it simple, stupid.*

We continued our run with Netwerk Electric at Tulagi's, a club next door to the Fox Theater in Boulder. It was a packed show with about four hundred people, and our set went well. Kyle Hollingsworth was there to check us out, but disappeared before I could chat with him. I found Hollingsworth, in my several interactions with him, to be a rather introverted guy.

After a good show at our *home away from home,* the Lazy Moon in Salt Lake City, we hit Missoula, Montana for an outdoor park concert. Vick bowed out due to sudden illness, and we performed as a quartet. It went really well, prompting the obvious question: *Do we really need percussion?* Wildman, for one, was a strong proponent of the *no* camp. He disliked Vick personally, and felt Vick's playing was cluttered and obtrusive. He also thought Vick was more interested in showing off to women in the audience, so he might get an overnight invite after the gig, than making sound musical choices. There was no love between Wildman and Drew, either. Vick would aggravate this by rolling his eyes in collusion with Drew, when the rest of the band did something they did not like. Wildman loathed this dynamic, and as I became more aware of it, I began to share his feeling. These cliques within a band are always a harbinger of bad things to come.

We cut across Montana into Washington, for a show at Seattle's Tractor Tavern. It was a dud. That night we stayed with Mark's parents. His mother was a singer and pianist, and had a nice grand piano I took pleasure in playing for a couple hours, late that night, before raiding the refrigerator for leftover salmon. Ernie's father was quiet and polite; his parents seemed like a happy couple. I remember thinking, *I guess it really can work. Two people can stay together for many years and still like each other.* How disconcerting it would be, only a couple weeks later, when Mark announced to the band, "My parents are getting a divorce. My dad's moving to California to live with another woman. My mom isn't taking it well." You just never know what's going on with people.

We had a lousy show in Portland, Oregon at the Mt. Tabor Theatre. I never had a good show in that room, with either Living Large or Global Funk Council. I did, however, meet Terrell Brandon one night, the veteran NBA point guard. We wound up at a cocktail bar across the street (Terrell sipped a Coke while I had a real drink). He had come to the show to check out his cousin's band, our opener, who he was considering bankrolling. We talked a little basketball, but the hoops journeyman was in the twilight of his career, and was more interested in discussing investments and business enterprises he planned to pursue after his looming retirement.

In late May, we returned to San Francisco for a show at the Boom Boom Room, a popular club near the Fillmore. The Boom Boom Room had a consistent weekend crowd, which gave a band the illusion that they had packed the place. The place packs *itself.* The owner hired groups he personally liked, so you were playing as much for his benefit as the audience.

On one occasion, a friend named Lip got into a heated exchange in front of the Boom Boom Room. It started out with Lip exchanging antagonistic but harmless banter with a homeless woman. It became more abusive, and the woman slapped Lip in the face. After this happened once more, Lip, a husky, bald guy with a rough, unmistakable voice, said "If you touch me again, I'm going to knock you out." She slapped him yet again, and Lip had to be restrained from making good on his promise. In cities like San Francisco, there is a great economic gulf separating affluent professionals, who frequent the city's nightlife spots, and penniless vagrants who wander the same sidewalks, ask for money and sometimes just look to be disruptive.

GFC headed south for a show at Winston's in San Diego. San Diego was just another city now, another market to hit along the national JBS trail. We continued east to Las Vegas, a place that always got my creative juices flowing. It's just an interesting city. Movers and shakers love Vegas. Not just financial movers and shakers, but artists, writers, and creative people in general. I'm not a gambler, so I guess I'm drawn to Vegas's unique atmoshpere. There's something enticing about a place that's as alive at five in the morning as it is at five in the afternoon.

We played a spot called the Whiskey Sky Bar, in Henderson. Walt Williams, my vocalist friend from San Diego, joined us as a special guest. When he started to sing, I realized Walt's R&B style was a bit confusing for the JBS audience.

The band was the focus of everything in my life, but at this point in time I had an even more intense concern, a matter in which I'd made a huge emotional investment: the NBA Western Conference Finals between the Los Angeles Lakers and the Sacramento Kings. My hatred of the Lakers stemmed a fourth quarter comeback years earlier, when they had rallied to beat the Portland Trailblazers in game seven. I was guilty, along with many other adult males, of allowing a group of multi-millionaire athletes to wield great control over my state of happiness as a human being.

Fucking Derek Fisher

The Travesty lumbered into Tucson, for a show which coincided with the Lakers/Kings game seven. As this game would determine who advanced to the Finals, I was a mess. I'd been riding an emotional roller coaster the entire series, still furious after Kobe Bryant's flagrant foul nearly broke Mike Bibby's nose in game six (a referee had clearly watched the foul as it was committed, but chose not blow his whistle). This sham prompted Ralph Nader—yes, Ralph Nader—to call for an investigation of NBA officiating, to determine if the series was fixed.

The Mayor was a die-hard Laker fan, and I found myself truculently projecting my frustrations onto him as we traversed the country in the Travesty. We had a day off, so the guys settled into a bar in outer Tucson to watch the game. I'd sworn that after the injustices of the previous game, I would be boycotting the final contest. In late May, Tucson is about 120 degrees, so this decision meant I'd have to sit in the Travesty for three hours, while the guys watched the game in an air-conditioned sports bar.

I sat there in the parking lot, sweating, stewing, prepared to righteously sit out the entire game. After a while I couldn't help but think *what if the Kings pull it off? Is that something I want to miss?* I gave up my stand and reluctantly sauntered into the sports bar, promptly ordering a couple shots of Tequila. I was going to force myself to watch, but I wasn't going to do it sober. No, that would hurt too much. Watching Robert Horry drag what looked like a pair of prosthetic knees up and down the court at half-speed, lollygagging in the corner to wait for a late-fourth-quarter pass, so he could drive a knife into the Kings' hearts with another picture-perfect three, followed by his stupid little gallop/arm across the chest move, followed by commentators infuriatingly barking that *maybe this is destiny*... all this would be too excruciating to endure without the numbing effect of alcohol.[155]

Our show at Tucson's Plush was raging, but this did little to ameliorate my purple and gold-inflicted suffering. The Lakers had pulled it out in Sacramento, and I was really having a rough time with it. We were playing for a lively club of JBS enthusiasts, but all I could think was: *The fucking Lakers won again. There is no justice. Life has no*

---

[155]Some three hours later, the Lakers were victorious. At least in this game, the officiating was respectable and the better team won. This much I could not argue. The Mayor patted me on the back and said, "You were a good sport, T. Well, time to get my three-peat t-shirt." I was not a good sport. I was a terrible sport. I was merely holding my tongue, waiting for next season, when I would renew my contempt and root against the Lakers with every last bit of my very soul; and my patience would be rewarded that next season, for the Lakers would go down in just the way they'd scraped by this year—with a Robert Horry three-point attempt. Of all the maxims great literature has blessed us with over the centuries, is this not the greatest? *Live by the sword also die by the sword.* Beyond crumbling in glorious, ultra-satisfying fashion during the 2003 playoffs, the Lakers were also plagued by inner strife, as if to confirm my feeling all along that they were winning on borrowed time, didn't deserve their good fortune, and collectively possessed a smug sense of hubris which would, one day, be avenged in full.

meaning. Fucking Robert Horry and his prosthetic legs. Fucking Rick Fox and his curly hair, his appearances on Oz, his fashion ads in Vibe Magazine, and his marriage to Vanessa Williams. Fucking Phil Jackson and that pompous Zen grimace, and those pretentious books he wrote, and those mile-wide shoulders and big, up-turned butt. Fucking Mark Madsen and his fundamentally sound box-outs and crisp outlet passes. Fucking smirking Jack Nicholson and that guy in the shades that looks like Donald Sutherland. Fucking Kobe and his echoes of Jordan-like dominance. Fucking Shaq and his improved free throw shooting, and his free reign to barrel into the paint and dunk without drawing a charge. And most of all, that masterfully flopping, three-point dagnger delivering, incessantly hustling scrapper:

Fucking Derek Fisher[156]

The next stop was Prescott, Arizona. Len had been living there for a few years, and it was a little funny coming back after so much had happened in my life. The last time I was here, I'd shouted to the heavens asking, *God, why am I splitting flagstone in Chino Valley? What lesson am I to take from this?*

I never fell in love with Prescott. While living there I'd made cursory attempts to find new friends, but a pervading provincial aloofness discouraged any meaningful liaisons from materializing.

I got in a squabble with the Mayor while we were in Prescott. He booked a little gig on his own, and when I found out the details, I wasn't into it. He got mad at me, suggesting that I didn't appreciate his efforts. This lament was punctuated with his signature phrase, "I'm over it." I was over it, too. The road was wearing me down. Wildman didn't like Vick, Vick didn't help load the gear, Drew didn't like Wildman's playing, the Mayor didn't like my RV driving, I didn't like the Mayor's whining, nobody was digging Mark's guitar playing, and Woo was locking horns with Rob Sarno and Mountain High Booking. Things were starting to suck.

---

[156] Recently, I was playing a gig at a resort in Laguna Beach, and when I walked into the men's room on a break… there he was. My sworn enemy. The man who broke my heart. As he washed his hands, he made eye contact with me through the mirror. Here was my chance to come clean… to say the things I'd screamed at the television screen to the man's face. So what did I do? I grinned pleasantly and nodded. *What's up, Derek?* Pathetic.

Sea Biscuit

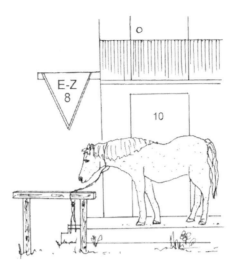

When we got to Phoenix for a show at the Rhythm Room, my conflict with the Mayor came to a head. While we loaded in, the manager greeted us with comforting news:

"Hey guys, just to give you a heads up… there have been a string of violent murders in clubs around here. Some guys in ski masks have been showing up at the end of the night, when the places are about to close, and shooting people and stealing all the money. Just want you to be aware of what's going on."

It's one thing to break a rib when some ex-wrestling, Iowan asshole throws you into a table, but another thing to get mowed down by an M-16 while you're trying to collect your two hundred bucks after the show. This wasn't the first time I'd heard about murders in the Phoenix area.

When I mentioned my concern to the guys in the band, the Mayor blurted out, "You're trippin', dude." That was the wrong combination of words. I called him outside.

"Don't tell me I'm tripping! People are getting murdered around here! You wanna be next? Excuse me for fearing for our lives, Tristan." The Mayor didn't take this too well, breaking down emotionally while repeating the refrain, "I'm over it!" I backed off, gave the guy a hug and told him to hang in there. I realized the road was kicking his ass hard, and he would need a break soon.

We returned to Prescott for another show. Late that night, in a moment of supreme selfishness, Mark monopolized one of the band's two motel rooms to service a groupie, while the girl's friend was passed out in the *other* band room, by herself, with the door locked. This left everyone other than Mark shacked up in the Travesty. If anyone was still of a mind to defend Mark's inconsistent guitar playing, these loyalties were extinguished as he mounted Sea Biscuit in that EZ-8 motel room.

We swung through Salt Lake City, Vegas and Portland before heading out to a festival in North Plains, Oregon, at a spot called Horning's Hideout. Here, we manipulated the Travesty through back woods and into an open, sloped grassy field. Talk about an adventure.

We were keeping good company that weekend, sharing the bill with Jerry Joseph and the Jackmormons and The Steve Kimock Band. Kimock was a household name in the JBS; A friend had explained to me that Kimock was considered part of the Jam Band Holy Trinity. This triumvirate consisted of Trey Anastasio (the dark prince of jamming), Jerry Garcia (the Great Almighty), and Garcia's successor, Kimock. Legend had it that Garcia once proclaimed Kimock his favorite guitarist, a gesture that galvanized the younger man's career.

Kimock's band featured the dynamic drummer Rodney Holmes, who played intricate, funky rhythms under Kimock's melodic guitar work. On bass was Alphonso Johnson, an alumnus of Weather Report. I liked the band's music.

We headed south for a show in Shasta City, a small town located at the bass of Mt. Shasta, near the border of Oregon and California. We were being hosted by a husband/wife promotion team, and the performance was at a local community center.

The show was a complete flop. For whatever reason, the good people of Shasta City didn't turn out for Global Funk Council. I had to go through the awkward but familiar post-gig routine with the promoter couple, shaking my head as I said "Wow, wonder what happened tonight? Must be something else going on in town." When the show tanks, verbal emollient is required to ease the sting the promoter feels while handing you a wad of cash you have not rightfully earned. I know how to play this game.

The couple put us up at their house, no doubt adding insult to injury—they'd lost money, and now had to deal with the six of us for another twelve hours. The wife was a salty character, entertaining the band with profane stories as we drank strong coffee the next morning. She humorously bickered about how Starbucks expects you to adhere to their contrived lingo: *grande, venti, frappucino.*

"You expect me to speak your fucking coffee language? Just give me my damn cup of Joe." You always meet colorful, outspoken people on the road.

It was always good to get back to California. Having grown up in the Bay Area, and rarely leaving the state throughout my teens and twenties, I'd fallen into the belief that California was nothing special. It was just like any other place out there. Wherever you went, the weather was temperate, the beach was near, and the geography was varied and beautiful. *The whole world is just like California.* After traipsing across the entire country for several years, I realized I had been wrong. The U.S., as a whole, is not like California. Few places rival California's weather and aesthetic beauty.

Living in California encourages a progressive world view. It's not a homogenous place, so you get used to mingling with numerous ethnicities—which I believe is a good thing. Also, there's a *wide open* feeling in certain regions of the state; there are still big, open spaces of undeveloped land, and you can drive for hours without encountering a heavily populated area.

No city better exemplifies the aesthetic beauty of California than Santa Barbara, the coastal town an hour north of Los Angeles, with its shimmering Pacific Ocean, dramatic mountains peppered with mansions and estates, and the never-ending parade of good-looking people making their way up and down State Street.

GFC first played Santa Barbara in June of 2002, at an upscale restaurant called Soho. The place catered to the affluent set without sacrificing a sense of youthful hipness, and the management was kind to musicians. When a club has exceptional food, dinner is comped, and a bar tab provided, it makes its way onto the Favorite Places to Play list. *What? You're going to be nice to us, give us a bar tab AND buy us dinner? We won't forget this!* Soho became a frequent stop for GFC. Our shows always went well there.

The next gig was in San Jose at Plant Fifty-One. It was a homecoming show for Drew. A bunch of his friends showed up to check us out, but the band didn't perform well. Afterwards, Drew's friends told him, "You don't look happy up there." Drew was becoming increasingly discontent with the band, because it wasn't progressing as quickly as he'd hoped it would. We were just running around the country, killing ourselves to do as many shows as Rob Sarno could book for us. At least we had the Elbo Room on Saturday night to look forward to...

This Is the New Groove

We had been partnering with a San Francisco promotion outfit called Sunset Productions. I knew the main guy at Sunset, John Miles, from the Living Large days. I'd stayed at John's house and we were casual friends. Another of the Sunset partners, Rob Kawal, was also a friend. He had been supportive when I broke away from Mario and Lincoln, encouraging me to pursue my own project.

Rob also was a DJ, and would always do an opening set for the shows Sunset promoted. The Mayor didn't feel Rob's turntable skills were up to snuff. Rob was a cool guy, but would get pissy right before his set began, shouting "We've got doors!" at musicians who were trying to finish soundchecking.

After his opening set, Rob continued dropping samples while we played. There were two snippets he repeatedly used: a trumpet sample that went *furn furn furn!,* and a deep voice that said *This is the new groove.* The rhythm was a little off when he mixed in the sounds, making it distracting to play along to, and prompting grimaces from the Mayor. The next day's ride to Lake Tahoe was riddled with humorous mimicry of *furn furn furn!* and *This is the new groove.* The Mayor and I ad-libbed a beat-box jam incorporating both tidbits, and also other inside jokes like *T's macking on my bitch,* a reference to Todd Sherman's mistaken notion that I was hitting on a female masseuse he'd hired in Boulder. The jam also incorporated *totally,* the calling card of Dan and Jenna, and a mainstay of the California slacker lexicon. The ditty went something like: *totally, totally, to-to-to-totally, furn furn furn, totally, totally, T's macking on my, this is the new groove, furn furn furn, this is the, furn furn, new, to-to-totally, T's macking on my, new groove, furn furn furn!*

The Mayor and I had many a great laugh along the roads of America, but the winds of change were blowing, and they were blowing him toward Boulder, where he now had a steady girlfriend. He was tired of truck stops, fast food, difficult personalities, power struggles, too many gigs and not enough success to show for it. His parents had remained supportive for a long time, but were starting to wonder what their son was getting out of driving around for months on end, engineering sound for a band that was struggling to break even.

I couldn't give them—or him—a convincing answer. It was a path you embraced for reasons hard to explain in practical terms. It wasn't that Tristan didn't believe. He just was burned out. He was beyond the point where a couple days off is going to recharge your battery. He needed a *new* battery.

Jazzfest had been a milestone for the band, but an even more critical rite of passage was around the corner: High Sierra Music Festival. This huge gathering of bands took place in Quincy, California between July 5th and 7th, and included Bruce Hornsby, Medeski, Martin & Wood, Karl Denson's Tiny Universe, Garaj Mahal, Michael Franti and Spearhead, the Yonder Mountain String Band, Sound Tribe Sector Nine, Umphrey's Magee, and literally hundreds of other groups. It was a who's who of the JBS, the most comprehensive festival of national JBS acts outside of Bonnaroo.

Through Jenna's connections, along with our name associations and positive buzz, we'd managed to secure not one but two choice slots at High Sierra. This was a major boon, and I was determined to make the most of it. We'd added a couple of Wildman's involved compositions to the repertoire, and could put together two sets of polished music. The band was sounding good.

Our first show was during the afternoon, and was jam-packed with people. The audience liked the music, and I was charged up by their energy. The following day was spent checking out music and entertaining friends in the Travesty. I listened to Medeski, Martin and Wood and some other big-name groups, mingled with friends and jammed with Dan Lebowitz's band, ALO, which he and Jenna had resurrected after their departure from Global Funk Council.

The next night, as we prepared to do our high-profile set on one of the big stages, I enlisted Eric Levy of Garaj Mahal to join us, along with KDTU guitarist Brian Jordan. We hit the High Sierra crowd with all our funky, up-tempo material, including *Keep on Pushin'* and *Too Much Funk*, and our guest musicians added excitement by playing great solos. My spoken-word verses during *Too Much Funk*, which I always wrote specifically for the occasion, were well received, and Drew delivered a good performance on drums, as usual. Wildman played well, psyched by the energy of the crowd, and Mark Reese and Vick came through with good performances also. It was a great show, prompting Michael Deeds, the entertainment editor of the Idaho Statesman to write "GFC funked me up more than Karl Denson." That was high praise.

Later, I sat in with Karl Denson's group during their relentless, four-hour late-night show in a big tent, and wound up staying onstage for about an hour. As the sun was rising, I walked back to the camp area with a friend and JBS die-hard, Heather Coleman. We sat in lawn chairs, watching the sunrise while drinking gin and juice. I basked in the triumph of GFC's two successful High Sierra performances. The band had come through when we really needed to, and word would spread in the scene that GFC was a band to be reckoned with.

Orange Jumpsuits and Huge Cellmates

Just a couple days after the glory of High Sierra, it was back to reality. Wildman and I found ourselves confined to the Travesty, which was parked beneath a freeway overpass in Stockton, California. A stray, vicious pit bull was circling the RV, waiting for one of us to exit the vehicle so it could attack. One day you're playing a prestigious music festival, the next day you're being hunted by wild dogs, while parked beneath a freeway structure somewhere in Central California.

We were in Stockton to play at a strange place called Alder Market. The show was a bust and the promoter, a young guy, lost some cash. I felt bad for him, but you never knew how well the show had been promoted, or how realistic it was for the promoter to book it in the first place. Promoting is tricky business, and it's easy to fall on your face.

We hurried out to Ketchum, Idaho for an outdoor show that was not exactly within our comfort zone—the crowd consisted of yuppie families that wanted to hear covers, not epic, twenty-minute jams. We continued to Park City to open for Bernie Worrell at Harry O's. Bernie was a living legend, an original member of Parliament Funkadelic, and an important contributor to Talking Heads. He was a talented keyboardist who'd made an impact on the music scene for four decades. By now, however, Bernie was nearly deaf, as he told me himself.

I realized this during his Woo Warriors soundcheck, which was so loud that had an F-16 taken off in the club as they were playing, nobody would have heard it. Our opening set went well, and Bernie and his band were complimentary. While certainly funky, the Woo Warriors were so loud that I couldn't endure more than a song or two. I took off to hang out with my Park City friend Chili Halprin, the Bagel King.

We continued on to Steamboat Springs, Colorado, for a show thrown in conjunction with a screening of the Widespread Panic documentary, *The Earth Will Swallow You*. After the film, we played on the same stage where Vince Neil, a couple months earlier, had berated an unsuspecting audience after only a couple songs, storming off without completing his set. The crowd had screamed for Motley Crüe songs, but Vince wanted to hit them with his *own* stuff. A sad story—not because Vince Neil was a glam metal dinosaur clinging desperately to his last vestiges of pop culture relevance, but sad because I was playing the same venues as Vince Neil.

As we left for Snowmass Village, the Mayor reminded me it was his twenty-fifth birthday. When we got to Snowmass, Wildman and I wandered off to some shops to pick out gifts for the Mayor, mostly of the gag variety. There was the Ken Movie Date doll, a hard hat that said Little Engineer, and some other worthless stuff we though would elicit laughs. I threw a little party for the Mayor at Pizza Hut, during which we presented him with the gifts and had some fun. Wildman acerbically noted: "Hey T, this is a fun time. You should have a party for yourself more often." I chuckled, realizing that perhaps I'd invested a bit too much ego in the Mayor's Pizza Hut celebration.

A couple days later, GFC played for the first time at the Half Moon Saloon in Vail. It was a slamming show, and the venue became one of our best spots in Colorado. The management treated us nicely, giving us open season on the bar and food menu. It's a good feeling when you establish a new relationship with a club that treats you well. You feel like you're making progress. Also, I met a kind, good-hearted girl named Jessenia at the Half Moon show. She and I would be good friends for the next few years, and she would host the entire band on multiple occasions.

We forged ahead to the Utopia Café, a hippie restaurant in Colorado Springs. There were a bunch of earthy, spirited kids at the show, including some attractive underage girls, who took an interest in Vick, Mark and me. Visions of orange jumpsuits and huge cellmates with morning wood skated across the icy tarn of my worst nightmares. Though flattered, I avoided the underage girls like the plague, and convinced my bandmates to do the same.

After the show, Drew, who'd consumed several strong Captain and Cokes, backed the Travesty *straight into a concrete pole.* A dreadlocked, Utopia Café employee had erroneously assured him that the coast was clear. This mishap nearly tore the entire back fiberglass panel from the body of the vehicle. I watched as it happened, and the image is still vivid in my mind today. All the little nappy-headed guy could muster was "Sorry, bro. Looked clear from where I was standing." Drew was upset with himself, and I was unable to mask my own utter disappointment. This was several thousands of dollars of damage we're talking about, and the Travesty would have to be repaired quickly to avoid *further* damage.

After all the breakdowns, mishaps, accidents, and the simple fact that I was a hundred dollars poorer every time we gassed up, I was having grave doubts about the Travesty's long-term value to the organization. It was sucking every last dime Todd and I could scrape together, which led me to consider alternatives...

THE VARIOUS SCENARIOS WHICH HAVE BEEN CONTEMPLATED, TO EFFECT THE DISAPPEARANCE AND CONSEQUENT EXTRICATION FROM THE FINANCIAL LIABILITIES OF A THIRTY-EIGHT-FOOT, 1996 MONACO DYNASTY MOTOR HOME

Faced with many more years of lofty payments for an RV which had already caused continual grief and near financial ruin, Woo and I began exploring creative solutions to our problem. The first and least messy would be to write a polite letter to our debtors—a seven-foot, ex-NBA big man and his ruthless lawyer—pleading for compassion, due to extenuating circumstances. Attached to this plea would be a detailed list of the myriad repairs, their costs, and a mention of the fact that all of it had occurred in less than a year's time. As much as I believe in mankind's basic capacity for kindness—yes, many people, in their heart of hearts, are good—Woo and I anticipated the following response, harkening back to that backyard code of business ethics outlined by Ray Liotta, via voice over, in *Goodfellas*: *Fuck you, pay me.*

As *option two*, we considered retaining legal counsel, then arguing the case that we'd been sold a $120,000 piece of garbage, a vehicle that looked impressive when you rolled up in front of a club, but had in fact undermined our business. Lawyers, however, cost a lot money, and if you get nothing else from this tale... if none of my anecdotes or hard-earned wisdom seeps into your cranium, please remember at least this one thing: *99.9% of musicians don't have money.*[157]

From here the options became, shall we say, less *legitimate*, as we entered an imagined realm of furtive machinations and scheming skullduggery. For example, consider this scenario: One harsh winter night after a show in Telluride, the RV driver loses control on a snow-covered, treacherous pass, sending the Travesty reeling over a ten-thousand-foot rocky cliff, exploding in a kick-ass fireball that would make Michael Bay green with envy. Can you say *full purchase price replacement coverage?*

What about the people in the RV at the time? *You can't send folks plummeting to their doom just to get out of a lousy contract, can you?* No, it would be preferable that the guys were evacuated *before* the Travesty did its dipsey-doodle over the ridges above Aspen. So, you would just let everyone out before you did it: *This is your Captain. Please step off the Travesty immediately, or face certain death.*

What about the driver? Would you recruit a suicide bomber from the hills of Afghanistan? Not necessary. Instead, you'd build a robot and program it to drive the Travesty. You'd control the robot with some kind of remote gizmo, follow in a trailing vehicle, then let out a menacing cackle when little R2D2 steered that propane-sucking pig to its glorious demise. You're not buying the robot part? Yeah, it's a stretch. Okay, then you could just hunker down and make like Dennis Weaver in *Duel*, steering the Travesty off the cliff yourself, diving out at the last possible second before it smashed through the guard rail and into the great wide open.

If you really wanted to go the *Duel* route, you could set the stage a couple hours earlier by pissing off a surly truck driver in an eighteen wheeler, then engaging him in a game of chicken. You'd flip him off, speed past him, allow him to catch up and pass you, flip him off again, and repeat this process several times. After a while, he'd decide you must die a gruesome death, and would devote the rest of his afternoon

---

[157] The people you read about in *Rolling Stone*... they make up the other .1%

to trying to run you off the road. You'd lull him into a false sense of security by allowing him to knock you halfway over the stretch of highly elevated road between Telluride and Durango (that incidentally has no guard rail), making a narrow recovery and barely avoiding disaster. This would only strengthen his resolve to finish the job.

Soon, you'd come upon that choice switchback you'd scouted out in advance. You'd let that diesel-drivin' mofo ram you, thinking he was just going to knock you over the edge and then go brag about it to his plebeian kith at the grease pit up the road. Oh yes, he was going to bump you right off there, but what he didn't know was that he was going down too! And as he went into freefall, in glorious Bruckheimerian conclusion, you'd stand on the edge watching, pumping your fist in the air like another distinguished Dennis: Dennis Eckersley, the retired Oakland A's relief pitcher, who would psychologically rub your nose in your own waste with exaggerated taunts and jeers, after he struck you out to secure the save.

Dennis is just a kick-ass name. Weaver... Eckersley... Farina... Franz... Johnson... Hopper... Miller... Leary... DeYoung... and let's not forget Rocky Dennis, and the triumph of the human spirit against great odds.

The final possible course of action discussed, and this was perhaps the most plausible and fail-safe, involved more of an abandonment than actual destruction of the Travesty. Let's say I was chilling in San Diego for a couple days. The Travesty was parked somewhere in the city, not too close to Len's pad in Rancho Bernardo. Let's imagine some very bad people decided to take the beast for a joyride down to Mexico. I didn't even realize it was gone for a few days. The Travesty wound up at a chop shop in Jalisco, picked clean like a coyote's carcass after the vultures have had their fill. It happens all the time. Can you say *full purchase price replacement coverage?*

The *pros* of this tack: I'd get a kickback from said bad people, once the Travesty safely made it across the border. It was, after all, a six-figure luxury item. Heap that on top of the fat check from the insurance company and I'd have myself a nice little nest egg. I could enlist a couple of the rough kids from the old group in Santa Monica. Hugo and DeRon would be about twenty-three by now—perfect age to pull off this kind of job. They owed me, after all. I gave them a farewell party they'd never forget.

The *cons:* The dealer claimed, at the time I bought the Travesty, which was still a Dynasty at that point, that he'd hidden a Lo-Jack somewhere under its belly. This meant it could be tracked wherever it went. Imagine Hugo and Deron in the Travesty, being chased down the I-15 by a flock of law enforcement helicopters, racing toward the border at high speeds, crashing into cars as they motored their ill-fated juggernaut towards Tijuana.

```
EXT. HIGHWAY - DAY

A large motor home races down the 5 Freeway,
wrecking everything in its path, as several police
helicopters speed along in tandem, like a flock of
determined birds.

                    POLICE BULLHORN
          Pull the Dynasty over!  This is the
          San Diego Police!

                    HUGO
          You'll have to kill me first, holmes!
          We goin' out like gangstas!
```

This moment brought to you by Lo-Jack, and the folks down at Buy Me RV in Gilroy, California.

We're not talking about pocketing a Whatchamacallit from the local 7-11. This was a serious crime; the kind where if you get nailed, you're going to that place mentioned in *Office Space*: the *Federal Pound-Me-In-The-Ass Prison*. Woo and I decided to hold tight for a while and see how things played out.

The band was gigging frequently in the Salt Lake City area—I was logging more time in Utah than at home in California. SLC was by no means a barren wasteland, but it was also no San Francisco or Seattle.[158] Besides getting hopped up on coffee and buying too many books at Borders, I was having a hard time finding things to do during my days off.

I decided to indulge a vice I'd been averting for obvious financial reasons: NBA basketball. It was ironic that the one NBA team I truly disliked, the one organization which consistently got on my nerves, was here in Salt Lake City, where I was suddenly spending weeks on

---

[158] I came to really like Salt Lake City over the years. It's got its own style.

end. The Utah Jazz was a hard group to dig; scheming provacateurs on the court, and the collective personality of a yellow squash off the court. The team's recent acquisitions of Scott Padgett, Andre Kirilenko and Matt Harpring—three more lanky automatons hand-picked to perpetuate owner Larry Miller's vanilla vision—did little to spice things up. Kirilenko looked like a cross between Dolph Lundgren and Gumby, Harpring was a *hatchet man*[159] that might have had success as an NFL linebacker, and Padgett, though a former college standout at Kentucky, looked like the poster boy for NBA affirmative action.

Even if I wasn't a Utah Jazz fan, I loved the NBA game, which is breathtaking to watch live. On TV you don't get the whole picture. You don't get the visceral thrill of watching the world's best athletes sprint up and down the floor, jump over each other for dunks and blocked shots, and make high-difficulty shots like they're nothing more than lay-ups.

I must have loved the game, because I opted on multiple occasions to drop a Benjamin or more, for the privilege of watching Dirk Nowitski lope up and down the court like a gazelle with a glandular disorder, or an aging Michael Jordan hobble around firing off-balance jumpshots, instead of stocking the RV with groceries and re-filling the propane tank.

During a couple games at the Delta Center in downtown Salt Lake City, I tested myself to see if I possessed the chutzpah to stand alone before twenty thousand adversaries and express myself verbally, and in the process I discovered a surprising thing: I was a natural-born heckler. I had a gift. I possessed the ability to get under the skin of both rival fans and players. I give you...

---

[159] A hatchet man is a guy who comes in off the bench for the express purpose of disrupting and annoying the other team, with fouls and overly aggressive play. In other words, the guy is such a roughneck, such a hack, that he might as well be wielding a hatchet out there on the court. Truthfully, Matt Harpring was better than that. He had legit skills. But he did look like a thug out there.

CONFESSIONS OF AN NBA ARENA HECKLER

The astute reader will recognize my blatant nod to Joe Queenan's *Confessions of a Cineplex Heckler*. Like Queenan, I elected to make somewhat of an ass of myself in the presence of a captive audience, specifically people who either paid a lot of money or were being paid a lot of money to be there, and thus could not simply get up and leave.

My aspersions were not cast within the dark recesses of America's cookie-cutter multiplex theater complexes, but rather in the well-lit, wide open forums of America's cookie-cutter, indoor professional sports arenas. There, I fired well-informed, close-range invective at many of the stars of the National Basketball Association, along with the loyal fans who love them, worship and fantasize about them, and pay their ridiculously inflated salaries.

My verbal barrages boasted an unassailable knowledge of the game I've loved my whole life; I was a good player at one time, a guy who could have made at least a minor impact at the Division I collegiate level, so when I opened my mouth at an NBA game, my barbs were infused with an understanding of the subtleties of basketball, as well as a trenchant wit that most specators—or players, for that matter—were unable to counter.

For example, one night I was screaming at Nene Hilario[160] of the Denver Nuggets, who had just missed another uncontested, five-foot turnaround: "This is the wrong scenario, Hilario! That's a shot you have to bury-o, Hilario! You're making your coach wary-o, so back to the bench you go, Hilario!" The towering specimen scowled at me, thinking, *You never played the game yourself, so shut up.* But Nene was wrong. I had not only played the game, but had shot the basketball better than Nene Hilario, who was being paid millions of dollars to miss five-foot turnarounds. In fact, I had shot the basketball better *in seventh grade* than Nene did right now.

Granted, I didn't have a clue what it was like to be out there on the court with adroit, muscular giants who were in your face every time you touched the ball, so my heckling combined an interesting blend of knowledge and experience, sarcasm, and the hallmark of all hecklers: no sense of what it's really like to be out there on the court under the competitive, physical conditions of an NBA basketball game.

In my mind, all this made me perhaps a little more risqué, if not nearly as literarily accomplished, as the author of *Balsamic Dreams*[161], because it took a lot more guts to traduce a guy like Karl Malone, who stood six-foot-nine and weighed two-fifty, than to insult the likes of Vincent Spano on the silver screen. Consider also that unlike Joe Queenan, who got paid a handsome stipend for his smack-talk, my courageous courtside billingsgate was entirely pro bono. I was doing it strictly for the love.

NBA heckling was a passion that offered many more interactive possibilities than cineplex heckling. You were close to the action (assuming you bought good tickets), hence the athletes, who unlike baseball and football players wear no protective headgear, could hear you loud and clear. This environment made possible a number of scenarios:

---

[160] He just goes by "Nene" now.

[161] Queenan's brutal take on baby boomers.

478

- Screaming something to upset a player.
- Screaming something to upset a coach.
- Screaming something to upset a player, who takes his frustration out on the coach.
- Screaming something to upset a coach, who takes his frustration out on a player, or if you're really lucky, the entire squad.
- Screaming something to upset a fellow fan, or group of fellow fans.
- Screaming something to encourage a fellow fan or group of fans to join you in heckling a player, coach, referee, or entire squad.
- Screaming something to entreat a fellow fan or group of fans to aggressively heckle the team you are rooting for—an effective way to level the playing field when your team is beating the crap out of the other team.
- Screaming something to turn a player against a fellow fan who is rooting for that player. This is a great way to break somebody's heart while destroying the rah-rah hometown momentum.
- Screaming something at a referee.
- Embarrassing a player to the point that he screams at a referee. When carefully executed, this tactic can have a wonderful domino effect: The player who screams at the referee receives a technical foul, provoking a heated reaction from his coach, who also receives a technical foul. The assistant coach attempts to calm down the head coach, who screams at him and tells him to back off, effectively undermining the delicate courtside pecking order of the coaching staff. The emotionally wounded assistant coach blames the player who got the original technical foul—shit floats downstream—yanks him from the game and relegates him to the end of the bench to think about what he's done—the professional sports equivalent of being made to sit in the corner with a textbook on your head by the fifth grade teacher, while your classmates hurl spitballs at your face—more publicly exposed and humiliating in this case, but derived from about the same level of psychological reasoning. Pull off this

impressive coup and you will have successfully compromised not only the player-coach relationship, the coach/referee relationship, the coach/coach relationship and the player/referee relationship, but also the flow of the entire contest.

- Screaming something so offensive at a player that he chases you into the stands.
- Screaming something so offensive at a player that he chases you into the stands, breaking the foot of an innocent bystander in the process. Rick Barry, Charles Barkley and at least a few others have brought this concept to fruition, looking like world-class assholes in the process.
- Screaming something so offensive at a player that he not only chases you into the stands, but catches you and then kicks your ass. Benefit to you? $$$
- Throwing something at a player on the court. A much dicier proposition. For one, your chances of a direct hit are close to nil. Those guys run fast out there. And if you do connect, arena security is going to swamp you quicker than you can say Thomas Hinckley. Unless you've snuck into the arena the previous night and scoped out some stealthy vantage point from which to launch your projectile, pass on this one.
- Throwing something at a fellow fan or group of fans. Now you're talking. This can be effected without security becoming involved, and at times can do much more to convey your sentiments, which might get drowned out in a noisy 20,000 seat arena. As they say, action speaks louder than words.
- Screaming something at a player while somehow managing to involve his friends or loved ones, who are conveniently within earshot.
- Engaging in lengthy stare-downs, either with fellow fans, players or coaches. This is a nice choice when your vocal chords are tuckered out from three-plus quarters of assiduous verbal abuse, and your arm is tired from chucking inanimate objects at fellow fans in adjacent rows and neighboring sections.

- Managing to be utterly intrusive and disruptive through appearance alone. You can accomplish this by painting your face and/or upper torso, shaving your head, waving insulting signs, or sporting the colorful regalia of the visiting team. You might get your two seconds in the sun on SportsCenter, also.

Combine a few of these tactics and you are assured to attract at least one physical confrontation by halftime. Now that I've given you a fairly thorough overview of the theoretical art of NBA heckling, let's take a look at some examples of these techniques in actual practice...

Fear and Loathing in the Delta Center

Accompanied by Little Jesus, my faithful companion... Goose to my Maverick, Hutch to my Starsky, Cash to my Tango, Vanilli to my Milli... I gingerly set foot in Salt Lake City's Delta Center, that nefarious den of Naismithian treachery and hardwood pettifoggery, eager to take my anti-Jazz stand. I got the impression that I, like Captain Kirk and the crew of the Enterprise, was *boldly going where no man had gone before*.

The Delta Center had maintained a hostile environment for opposing teams and their fans over the years, because nobody had ever possessed the temerity to go in there and challenge the pervasive brainwashing that had duped the people of Salt Lake City into believing their team represented a triumphant dynasty of some sort. The Utah Jazz, excluding the perennially inspiring play of all-time great John Stockton, were losers. They'd had their chances, time and again, and they'd squandered them away, time and again. Now, faced with the aging of its two best players, Stockton and the less likable Malone, the organization was in big trouble. For once, my timing couldn't have been more perfect.

Before Little Jesus and I could begin to prick holes in the inflated belief cultivated by the Jazz P.R. team, we would have to make it through the lobby and to our seats. My diminutive chum was suddenly ducking and dodging, asking me to *cover him.* It turned out he'd been arrested and detained in this same building a year earlier, when security suspected he was peddling dope during a Ben Harper concert. I suggested he was now being paranoid, but Little Jesus said, "No, T, I'm dead serious. They're gonna be looking for me."

"It was a whole year ago. You honestly think someone's going to remember you?"

"I'm telling you, T, these guys don't mess around. They probably still have my picture posted in their office." As I laughed off this notion, I noticed out of the corner of my eye a cavil of blue-jacketed security guards pointing and looking right at us.

"Come on man, we gotta move!" We ducked into a bathroom and hid in a couple stalls. The guards swarmed the area, reconnoitering the crapper like a multitude of Mr. Smiths on the trail of Neo. Somehow they overlooked us, and once they'd moved on we made our way to the lower loge, settling into seats that promised unimpeded heckling of Jazz coaches, players, and possibly even players' wives.

I warmed up with some basic, uninspired patter to get the juices flowing: "Hey Malone, let's see your ring." (Malone, of course, had no championship ring). This elicited a few groans and mini-scowls, but nothing more. Little Jesus decided to focus his energies on the relationship between head coach Jerry Sloan and rookie sensation DeShawn Stevenson. "Hey Jerry, why isn't DeShawn on the floor? Put… in… Deshawn! Did you hear me, Jerry? Put… in… Deshawn!"

The Jazz were facing the miserable Atlanta Hawks on this particular evening, and the fact that the Hawks were beating them handily gave me some nice angles. The Hawks did have one excellent player in Sharif Abdur Rahim, the smooth power forward with a deft shooting touch and good passing ability. Rahim was torching the Jazz, and every time he scored I would yell, "Sharif, Sharif, Sharif is on fire!" Or, if Rahim swatted some weak doo-doo from the clumsy hands of Greg Ostertag, the towering Jazz center, I would shout "Sharif don't like it… Rock the white boy, rock the white boy."[162]

I noticed I was starting to aggravate a middle-aged man sitting in the row in front of me, to the point that he appeared to be experiencing the early symptoms of a heart attack: sweating, red face, shortness of breath, etc.[163] There was only one thing to do now—*turn up the heat even more.* Causing a Jazz diehard to, well, actually *die,* was beyond one's wildest heckling dreams, but it looked like I had a shot of pulling

---

[162] Sung to the tune of *Rock the Casbah.*

[163] He wasn't really having a heart attack, of course.

it off. "Looks like it's gonna be a banner year, Jerry. You're getting spanked by the worst team in the league, and your best two players are fifty years old. Where do I buy my season tickets?"

This was more than the flush-faced homer could handle. He, after all, *did* have season tickets, which he'd been holding since the team arrived from New Orleans, many moons ago. He'd been forced by this franchise to come back every year with a renewed faith in guys like Greg Ostertag and Greg Foster— more than any team could reasonably ask of their faithful customers. The season ticket-holder remained quiet throughout the second quarter, either trying to think of some clever comeback, or maybe trying to catch his breath between aortic contractions. I countered his nonstop stink-eye by waving a giant, foamy Hawks finger in his ruddy face.

Much to his and everyone else's chagrin, there was nothing security could do to me or Little Jesus. We weren't cursing. We weren't threatening or assaulting anybody. We weren't vandalizing anything. Like Larry Flynt, we were simply executing our Fifth Amendment right to free speech and expression, in an environment where our words happened to be quite unpopular. Maybe Milos Foreman would make a movie about our exploits: *The People vs. Anth and Little Jesus.* The blurb on the poster would say: *Censorship always starts with the perverts... then it moves on to the sports hecklers.*

An NBA arena was one place where you could scream whatever you wanted, as loud and as long as you wanted, without breaking any laws or risking punishment. As long as you kept it clean, you were untouchable.

I decided to focus on Jerry Sloan's wardrobe for a while. "Hey Jerry, that jacket's too small! You can afford a nicer jacket than that. That jacket is much too small, Jerry! We need a little more Neiman Marcus and a little less Ross." Sloan was surely accustomed to a bit of heckling on the road, just not on his own turf here at the Delta Center. I really do believe I was the first person to ever sit behind the Jazz bench and lay into them. Sloan looked at me like I was nuts. *Do you know where you are?*

Midway into the third quarter, Little Jesus and I were really starting to make our presence felt. I say this because people were now throwing stuff at us. Guard Bryon Russell had been a major Jazz contributor a few years earlier, assigned the glamorous defensive task of guarding Michael Jordan in the NBA Finals; but now he was just riding the pine, picking at the raised bump on his shaved head.

"Bryon, stop picking at your head. Get out there and show us a bit of the old magic." Russell heard me and laughed it off, eventually shooting me that patented NBA smirk that says, "Haha, good one... so how much money do *you* make a year?"

By the fourth quarter, the Jazz had caught their second wind and were now beating up on the pitiful Hawks, who had nobody to help Sharif Abdur-Rahim. Every time Karl Malone drove to the basket he would kick his leg out, throw his arms into the air to draw the foul, and nearly castrate whoever was trying to guard him at the time. I'd always hated this little trick, which Malone had been exploiting throughout his NBA career. "Hey ref, if you're going to allow kicking, let's get Ken Shamrock and Royce Gracie out there. Some guys that know how to do it with style."

Malone, known as the Mailman, was getting to the line almost every time down the floor, and Little Jesus and I would count out loud while he prepared to shoot his free throws. You're only supposed to get ten seconds to release the ball once it's been handed to you by the ref, but this was another rule the power forward had been smugly disregarding throughout his years in the league. To make matters worse, Malone was hard to heckle. Being so disliked throughout America, by so many fans for so many seasons, he had developed a strong immunity to ridicule. You had to really come up with something special if you wanted to ruffle The Mailman's feathers.

Scottie Pippen understood this, and did it with great success. In Game One of the 1997 NBA Finals between the Chicago Bulls and the Jazz, Malone was preparing to shoot a free throw, which would have sealed a Jazz victory and given Utah a 1-0 lead in the series. Pippen, one of the NBA's all-time greats in his own right, walked up to Malone before he received the ball and whispered, "The Mailman doesn't deliver on Sundays." Rattled, Malone launched a terrible brick, the Bulls won, and the guy they used to say was the greatest power forward of all time cemented his reputation as a choker extraordinaire.

"You haven't said a word to John Stockton all night," Little Jesus noted.

"That's because John Stockton is a great player, a class act, and an example of how the game is supposed to be played, LJ. The man has my infinite respect, even in this hellhole." Any six-one white guy who'd been getting the best of fellow point guards who were exponentially quicker and more naturally gifted than himself, for almost two entire decades, was above reproach in my book. Stockton would have to do something really stupid or infuriating out there before I would even consider aiming an assault in his direction.

As Little Jesus and I left the arena after the game, he confessed that heckling the Jazz, his hometown team, had left him feeling conflicted. On the one hand, he wanted to have my back, as he always had, but on the other hand, to do so in this case meant railing against the ballclub his own parents had loved and supported for many years. I was forced to go *Dubya* on him: "You're either with me or against me, Little Jesus. The choice is yours." If he planned to sit with me at future games, he'd have to accept his role as my Jazz-loathing apostate. After some deliberation, he agreed—as long as I would allow him to retain his reverence for DeShawn Stevenson. I was cool with that. The six-five Stevenson had ridiculous hops, and had been cool enough to flash us the *universal hip-hop head nod of unspoken empathy* when becoming aware of Little Jesus's impassioned advocacy.

My next trip to the Delta Center saw the Jazz squaring off against the Denver Nuggets, the only other team in the league that could rival the Hawks' Herculean ineptitude. Since I was planning to raise the bar of ridicule, I decided I would need some extra muscle. We brought along Ryan Callisto, another Salt Lake native and buddy from the jam scene. GFC had sponged off Callisto's hospitality on numerous occasions, prompting him to suggest a new band name: *MWU (Mobile Welfare Unit)*.

Decked out with flashy clothes and scarves, and rocking a permed, receding hairline, Callisto seemed to be mimicking the fashion sensibilities of early seventies Elton John—cool at a hip nightclub, yes, but grounds for an ass-kicking at a professional sporting event. In addition to metrosexual swagger, he brought along props: scribbled signs he'd crafted for the occasion, such as one that read, in cheeky reference to the JBS druggie sub-culture: SMOKE THE NUGGETS!

Within the first few minutes of the game, Callisto managed to get into a hassle with a woman and her young son, apparently over a balloon. Callisto had borrowed the balloon, and began twisting it into random shapes, which the kid found amusing. After a while, the kid became concerned that Callisto was going to pop the balloon, and demanded it back. Callisto refused. He wasn't done with it yet. This led to a tug-of-war between a grown man and young boy, over a balloon, with the boy's mother scolding the grown man for stealing her son's toy. I pretended not to see any of this, and focused my heckling energies on the talented but cancerous lout that was Nick Van Exel.

Van Exel, like my old friend J.R. Rider,[164] was one of those guys who had fabulous physical gifts, but was considered a pariah by every team foolish enough to secure his services. After playing in a desirable market like Los Angeles, the six-three shooting guard had now been banished to the NBA's version of Siberia: the Denver Nuggets. Through impertinence and uncoachability, Van Exel had fallen out of favor with the game's behind-the-scenes puppetmasters, and this horrible sentence he was serving in Denver made him the Raskolnikov of professional roundball.

I wasn't going to lay into Van Exel too hard, though. He looked like the kind of guy who wouldn't chase you into the stands and administer a beat down—no, he'd *wait for you in the parking lot,* where it was very dark… *What was that you said about me during the game?*

We hit the concession stand for a snack. There, we ran into Bear, the Jazz mascot. Not Grizzly Bear, not Bobo the Bear… just Bear. I imagined the marketing meeting where they were first inventing the team's mascot:

How 'bout Jazzy the Bear?
No, that doesn't work.
Okay, how 'bout Rebound the Bear?
Sounds too close to Rerun… from What's Happening.
How 'bout Hungry Bear? Or Wounded Bear?
Maybe if we were in a giant wigwam instead of a sports arena. Too colorful, guys. We need something more bland.
How about… Bear?

---

[164] Isiah Rider, a.k.a. J.R. Rider, was a major talent when he came out of the Bay Area, went to UNLV, then swiftly jumped to the pro ranks. He also had the rep of being a jerk and borderline criminal, getting in trouble in Portland for cloning cell phones at one point early in his career. I met Rider at Crustacean, a restaurant in Beverly Hills, while the Blazers were facing the Lakers in the play-offs. Unlike his rep, Rider was totally nice. He talked to me like I was a member of his crew. I really liked the guy. The moral of the story is, don't judge a guy by what they say about him in the media. Short, intelligent white and Jewish male journalists with no athletic gifts are predisposed to dislike giant black guys that are naturally gifted and subsequently wealthy. Take my word for it… a lot of those cats are cool, one-on-one.

486

Bingo. That's what I'm talking about.

Bear came skipping over to play with some kids gathered nearby. I had a camera on me, and suggested a group photo: Bear, Callisto, and the youngsters. I lined up the shot, and just as I was taking the picture Callisto shouted, "Okay, everyone, let's all say *the Jazz suck,* on three!" Bear gave Callisto a hard shove, followed with a dousing of that stringy stuff that shoots from a can. Little Jesus took offense to being sprayed and charged the mascot, screaming, "I'm gonna kick your ass, man! You better start running!" This was problematic on multiple levels. First, it's just not cool to get into a heated altercation with a mascot. Second, I'm pretty sure Bear, underneath the costume, was a small woman. Third, one of the kids started to cry. I quickly wolfed the rest of my weener and guided the trio to greener pastures.

By the fourth quarter of this sloppy, forgettable contest—I'd participated in higher caliber playground games—Little Jesus, Callisto and I had burned so many bridges that we were now being forced to do a terrible thing: *Sit in the actual seats we had purchased.* These stinkers were all the way up at the Delta Center's highest section, next to the freebies for special needs kids and disgruntled war veterans. Not only could you not heckle from here... you could barely see the damn court.

Since these seats were unacceptable, we relocated yet again, back to the bottom of the upper deck. There, we waved Callisto's homemade posters and taunted the teeming mass of Jazz fans directly above us. My poster said JAZZ IS DEAD,[165] another clever word play from Callisto. It wasn't long before I felt a barrage of gummi sours raining down on my back. More pelts followed, consisting of Milk Duds, licorice bits and ice. We could no longer rely on the shelter of the affluent lower loge. No, we were deep in the slums now, and the rules were different up here. If you barked loud enough and long enough, someone was going to fire back.

The stakes were raised when I felt the breeze created by a quarter barely missing my head. I don't have to tell you, reader, that a quarter is not a gummi sour. A gummi sour is a fun, pliable little treat. A quarter is made out of metal. It can jack you up. I turned to the

---

[165] The name of an all-star Grateful Dead cover band, featuring former Dixie Dregs keyboardist T Lavitz, as well as bassist Alphonso Johnson.

faceless enemy and wagged my finger, Dikembe Mutombo style.[166] This was where it was good to have a guy like Little Jesus on your side. He was a master of schemes and ruses, he could pull off the short con or the long con, and he could read somebody like a children's book. If you needed help in a tough situation, Little Jesus was like the Wolf.[167] He had figured out exactly who was throwing coins at us.

"I'm watching them, T."

"Good," I said. "It's time to dance."

"Show them to me, Little Jesus," I said.

"Right there, T. Those two." I took a good look at the pair of them. Young college guys, maybe even high school seniors. They saw me looking in their direction and shrugged their shoulders in unison like a pair of smug, synchronized swimming fruits. Now I was irritated. Call me names, bounce gelatinous candy off my cranium as payback for me cheering against your team. Fine. I got no problem with that. *Throw quarters at my face and then proceed to tease me?* As my stepdad Terry would say, "Not cool, Jazz fans. Not cool."

Callisto returned from the snack bar, gripping a huge cup filled with soda and ice. I suddenly had a vision. "Hey guys, you about ready to split? This game's a joke. Let's get out of here."

"Yeah, let's do it," they agreed.

"Can I borrow that soda, Callisto?"

"Sure, man."

"I'll get you another one."

"Are you gonna drink the whole thing?"

"Not exactly."

With that, I marched up to the row where the culprits were sitting. Little Jesus and Callisto crept up the left and right aisles, a sort of poor-

---

[166] Mutombo, over seven feet tall and known as a defensive specialist, liked to mockingly wag his finger after blocking a guy's shot, as if to say, "Get that shit out of my village." After a while, the African center was widely criticized for poor sportsmanship, and got his comeuppance when Michael Jordan started a game by dunking right in Mutombo's face, followed by an exaggerated finger wave of his own. Jordan always got the last laugh… with *everybody*.

[167] In *Pulp Fiction*, the Wolf, played by Harvey Keitel, says to Vincent Vega (John Travolta), "If I am curt with you, it is because time is of the essence. Now, pretty please with sugar on top… go clean the fucking car."

man's secret service tandem keeping an eye out for danger. I kept going until I was literally a foot or two in front of the coin chuckers.

"Great game, huh?" They stared at me. *Does this guy really have the audacity to just walk up here and confront us, on our home turf?* Yeah, the guy really did... and it was about to get worse. I pulled the lid off the giant cup and held it high in the air for all to see—like a magician verifying the authenticity of his materials—and dumped the jumbo drink on both of their heads. All sixty-four syrupy ounces.

"Whadda you say, guys? Pepsi or Coke?" They sat there in disbelief, drenched in ice-cold soda. What followed was a barrage of every curse word under the sun, coming from Jazz fans in all directions. For a bunch of pious Mormons, the folks at the Delta Center could curse like the foulest-mouthed of sailors.

Before I could react, I was bum-rushed by that swarm of Mr. Smiths that Little Jesus and I had previously eluded. They handcuffed me right there, to the delight of the squabbling sea of Karl Malone lovers. The Pepsi taste test duo taunted me with "You're goin' to jail!" Callisto, standing nearby, bellowed, "You just got soda poured on your head!" I was led out to the walkway by the guards, who I realized had been watching my every move. I figured my actions might get me thrown out of the arena, but was pretty sure they weren't grounds for an arrest. Dousing someone in soda hardly like grounds for an aggravated assault charge.

Much to my chagrin, the security guards were even bigger idiots than the fans. They'd apparently been copping lingo from bad TV shows and movies because they said things like, "You're in a world of shit," and "You got a lot of explaining to do." Little Jesus jumped to my defense, trailing the guards as they led me to an unknown destination.

"Why didn't you stop those guys from throwing stuff at us?"

"I remember you. We busted you at the Ben Harper concert last year. You better watch your ass."

"As for you..." They turned their attention back to me. "You're lucky we're not throwing you in the hole."

"The Delta Center has a *hole?*"

"You wanna find out?"

"No, not really."

They escorted us to the exit, released me from the cuffs and said, "We don't want to see you in here again."

"I'm afraid I can't make that promise," I said, slipping into the Salt Lake City night. I would be back, and I would be back soon.

Ignoring the warnings of Mr. Smith and his Delta Center security clones, I returned to the arena a few days later to root for the Golden State Warriors, another lackluster organization that hadn't accomplished anything noteworthy in a long time. I did have a small affinity for the Warriors, at least, since I'd grown up in the Bay Area and attended some games. As a kid I watched Bill Walton (my boyhood idol), David Thompson, the flashy guard with an almost fifty-inch vertical leap, Pistol Pete Maravich, the greatest ball handler of all time,[168] and the New Orleans Jazz—that's right, the *New Orleans* Jazz, with Truck Robinson and Spencer Haywood. There's no damn jazz in Utah. The *Utah Jazz*... talk about an oxymoron.

The Warriors had gone out on a limb, using the third pick in the draft to take Mike Dunleavy Jr., the son of Mike Dunleavy, the NBA coach. Let me correct that: Mike Dunleavy Jr., the slow, white son of Mike Dunleavy, the NBA coach. If humanity is doomed to repeat the errors of history, then the Golden State Warriors were a wonderful metaphor for humanity. No other sports team had drafted so many dogs, complete wash-outs... *Washburn*-outs, if you will...[169] than the

---

[168] After Paul Reubens and George Michael.

[169] A 6'11" center, Chris Washburn was one of the top three high school recruits in the country in 1984. An incredibly gifted athlete, Washburn combined size with blazing speed for a big man; and soft hands. According to one of his former teammates, however, Washburn was a student in name only. He almost never attended classes, but coach Jim Valvano always managed to get him eligible to play. He was also caught stealing a stereo, which netted him forty-six hours in jail, a five-year suspended prison term and five years of probation. His work ethic was also called into question. Recruiting analyst Bob Gibbons claimed that Washburn was "never as good as his reputation," even as a high-school All-American. Washburn was selected by the Warriors with the 3rd pick of the 1986 NBA Draft. He looked like the next Karl Malone in physical appearance, but not in moral fiber or work ethic. On January 28, 1987, Washburn checked into a Van Nuys, CA drug rehabilitation clinic, admitting he had a cocaine problem. He is widely considered to be one of the biggest busts in NBA draft history. Sports Illustrated named him the second-biggest NBA draft bust. Washburn was banned from the NBA for life in 1989 after flunking three drug tests in three years. By the mid-1990s, Washburn was still trying to scrape together a basketball career in various minor professional leagues. He was last known to be in the mortgage business in Dallas.

perpetually unlucky Golden State Warriors. No other team had traded away as much great talent with nothing to show in return, either. Latrell Sprewell and Chris Webber were only recent examples.

Mike Dunleavy Jr. represented not only a continuation of a regrettable Warrior tradition, but his acquisition had the potential, according to an expert consensus of opinion, as well as my own gut, to take that tradition to staggering new heights. The Warriors had passed over several top prospects—explosive, athletic prospects—to give Dunleavy the privilege of lumbering around the league in a Golden State uniform. I was coming to the Delta Center that night to see if it was true. Was Dunleavy as vastly overrated as Charles Barkley said he was? Was he destined to be another Danny Manning, Joe Smith or Kwame Brown? My money was on *yes*.

Callisto was unavailable that night, so I showed up with Little Jesus and TJ, the part-owner of the Lazy Moon Saloon. Since TJ sounds very much like LJ, and TJ sported one of those neck-draping Saudi Arabian do-rags that makes one look a bit like a potential terrorist, we'll call him *Abdul...* in honor of Kareem and his sublime skyhook, also.

Abdul had the idea to get us all into the Delta Center for free. I liked this idea. I'd been shelling out upwards of a hundred bucks for me and my friends to line Karl Malone's ungrateful pockets, and it was starting to mess with my mind a little. Abdul said we could pretend we'd been smoking outside, than play stupid when the usher asked to see our ticket stubs. I had no faith in this ruse, but Little Jesus thought it had a chance. Sure enough, we waltzed right in with no problem. In fact, we waltzed *right down to courtside*, where we snagged a threesome of seats no more than a couple rows from the action. I decided to take it easy for a while, sip a Captain and Coke and scrutinize the game of Mike Dunleavy Jr., my potential new whipping boy. But Jerry Sloan did something I didn't see coming. He made a startling move that forced me to immediately shift gears. *He put Scott Padgett in the game.*

Padgett, a stand-out the previous year at Kentucky, was exactly what everybody feared would become of Dunleavy: a slow-footed, unexplosive swingman whose game didn't translate to the high-flying acrobatics of the NBA. Padgett was the kind of guy you expected to drift around the league for several years, picking splinters out of his pine-saddled posterior while cheering with feigned enthusiasm for his more capable teammates.[170] You'd see him at the end of a blow-out, running around out there giving a hundred-and-ten-percent, executing fundamentally sound box-outs and mad-dog, Mark Madsen-style D, even though the game was already long lost or long won... only he was in a different uniform than you remembered... *Hey, that's Scott Padgett... I thought he played for New Jersey.* One day, you'd no longer see Padgett at all, and if you did a little research would learn that he'd given up on the NBA and was now chalking up 7.5 ppg and 6.2 rebounds for Kinder Bologna.

The moment I saw the corn-fed, six-nine Padgett strip away his sweat pants and jog over to the scorer's table to report for duty, I jumped to my feet and shouted, "No, no, no, Jerry! Not now! Not Scott Padgett!" Padgett checked into the game, and managed in two minutes of play to support my thesis that guys like him just don't have a place in the NBA. The Utah Jazz always had players like this on the roster; Adam Keefe had been Padgett's predecessor, and had more or less stunk up the great indoors for several seasons before disappearing with no fanfare. I have to confess that I somewhat relished in watching Adam Keefe fail to meet expectations. The thing was, I had a bit of personal history with Adam Keefe...

When I was seventeen, I was selected by my high school coach to participate in an all-star showcase in Santa Barbara called Superstar Camp. A few of the guys at the camp would eventually play in the NBA, including Delano Demps, Rex Walters... and Adam Keefe. Six-nine, strong and competitive, Keefe was was being courted by many top college programs in the country. I was a few notches down the food chain, but determined to show the college scouts that I could hold my own. As far as I was concerned, the only thing Adam Keefe had on me was about six inches (of height).

---

[170] If you ride the timber in the NBA, you are expected to be a great "practice player": You push the marquee players to work hard in scrimmages, you suck up to them on the plane or in the hotel lobby (to the extent that when it comes time to renew your contract, Kobe Bryant says, "I like [insert name of timber-rider]. He's good for team chemistry"), and most important, you jump for joy like a high school cheerleader every time someone does something positive on the floor, to let everyone know that: *Gosh darn it, I may not get any P.T. (playing time), but I'm here for my teammates! We're in this together! When Coach needs me, he'll call on me. Until then, I'm gonna give my guys 24/7 support... from the bench. Right here next to the towel boy.*

During a game between my team and Keefe's, he received an outlet pass off a defensive rebound and charged down the court for a dunk. All the scouts were watching, and Keefe surely wanted to throw down a jam for the guys with clipboards. His only problem was the fact that I had sprinted back on defense, and was standing in the key waiting for him. Keefe assumed I would jump out of his way when he got to the hoop, but I wasn't going to budge. I saw that he was going to try and run me over, so I braced for a collision—I wasn't about to go out like Ray Fosse.[171] Keefe had a full head of steam and barreled into me with everything he had, sending us both crashing to the floor. The referee blew his whistle. "Charging!" The call went my way, and Keefe was livid, cursing me as we ran back down the court. "Jordan would have jumped *over* me. Guess you're not Jordan."

So I somewhat enjoyed watching Keefe struggle once he got to the NBA. His *lack-of-air apparent,* Scott Padgett, clearly couldn't guard whichever Warrior he'd been assigned to on this night at the Delta Center, and I was quick to offer suggestions: "You gotta move your legs on defense, Scott. Bend your knees and move your legs. What's Jerry teaching you guys?" When Padgett let the ball slip out of bounds on the next possession, I continued with, "Padgett, you're two turnovers from the CBA,[172] buddy. Two turnovers!"

At that moment, the woman sitting directly in front of me turned around. She looked at me with a wounded gaze.

"Hi," I said. "How's it going?"

"Can you please stop talking about Scott Padgett?" she asked.

"Why?"

"Because he's my husband."

I decided to re-direct: "Let's go, Scott! How about a rebound? Been a fan since the K.U. days. We're all in your corner up here, buddy."

A few minutes later, an attractive, impeccably dressed blonde walked over and said, "Look, guys, I know these aren't your seats. You can stay here, but you can't talk trash on the Jazz players. I'll have you removed." *Who did she think she was, anyway?* Little Jesus grabbed my arm.

"Don't say anything, T. Let it slide."

---

[171] The catcher Pete Rose famously mowed down at home plate, in the 1970 All-Star Game.

[172] The NBA minor leagues.

"Who is she to—"

"That's John Stockton's wife, man." There weren't too many people in the building who could shut me up, but John Stockton's wife was one of them. She had her three children with her, who were busy screwing around in the aisle. She would periodically scold them.

"Stop it. Come over here and watch your father play." *Yeah, kid, settle down and watch the great John Stockton in action. He'll be retiring soon.*

A couple Captain and Cokes closer to a legitimate buzz by the fourth quarter, I was disappointed in myself. I was just sitting there, watching the game. Mike Dunleavy Jr. was riding the pine, and when he did get in the game, he didn't do anything blatantly bad enough for me to lay into him. I didn't come to the Delta Center to be a polite spectator. I could have just sat in a bar and watched on TV. By appeasing Mrs. Stockton, I was not being true to my calling.

"I'm bored," Little Jesus griped, and then he got up and walked over to sit next to Mrs. Stockton.

"What's he doing?" Abdul wondered.

"No idea," I said. Bombay and Sapphire in hand, the diminutive, scruffy Christ clone had decided to strike up a chat with the spouse of Bob Cousy's modern successor. It went well—he managed to occupy the empty seat next to the woman for several minutes, before eventually re-joining his heckling homeys.

"What did you talk about?" Abdul asked.

"You know… this and that."

"No, we don't know. Whadda you mean, *this and that?* What the hell did you say to John Stockton's wife?"

"We just talked about basketball, the Jazz organization, Salt Lake City, the kids. What you might expect."

"How'd you end the conversation?" Abdul asked.

"I just said, 'It's great to talk to you, Mrs. Stockton, and hey… if things don't work out with John, give me a call.'"

As the Global Funk Council tour moved to Colorado for a string of shows, I set my sights on the Denver Nuggets and the Pepsi Center. The Pepsi Center was a wonderful, modern facility, outclassing the Delta Center in numerous ways. The Nuggets, however, were in last place. No team, to my knowledge, had ever sucked so badly in an arena so plush. This was speculation, of course. I'd never set foot in Philips Arena in Atlanta.

Even though they were a miserable ballclub, I didn't have negative feeings about the Denver Nuggets. I didn't feel anything for them whatsoever. They had some knuckleheads, yes, but nobody to rival Karl Malone. If I was going to heckle in Denver, I'd have to manufacture some antipathy—for antipathy is the clay from which the heckler molds his cantankerous verse. The building blocks upon which he constructs his biting, four-quarter diatribe.

I came up with a plan, but in order to explain it I must first take you back to Superstar Camp again, when I was a seventeen year-old buck with dreams of playing Division One college ball. One cool thing about the camp was the fact that the organizers brought in guys who were actual superstars. Well, maybe not superstars, but at least successful players in the NBA: Xavier McDaniel, Reggie Theus, and Kiki Vandeweghe, to name a few.

Xavier McDaniel, a power forward for the Seattle Supersonics, showed up decked out in sweet warm-up gear. He had a bad-ass attitude to augment his intimidating, bald head. There was no circumstance under which I would ever in my right mind pour a sixty-four ounce soda on Xavier McDaniel's shiny dome, then or now.

The coaches decided to have McDaniel square off for a little one-on-one with one of the campers. They chose a seven-foot white guy, a solid player who could really shoot. On the first play, McDaniel shoved the seven-footer out of his way like a rag doll, thundering a Daryl Dawkins-style jam that shook the whole basket.

Reggie Theus, like Bill Walton, had been something of an idol for me as a kid. Theus was a sharp dresser, and showed up in velvety warm-up duds. He was rocking a mean jerry curl, looking like Eric LaSalle in *Coming to America*. Deft ball handling was Theus's forte, and he started his clinic by demonstrating a dribbling technique using his individual fingers—kind of like playing *tabla,* the Indian drum. This was not an easy thing to do. (Try dribbling a basketball with each finger, like you're running up a scale on a piano, without losing control of the ball). Then, to further showcase his skills, Theus asked for the two quickest guys in the camp to come out and attempt to steal the ball from him. When the two quickest dudes obliged, Theus upped the ante by saying, "All right, now give me a second ball." *Was he serious?* One of these guys had picked my pocket at least three times in a game, and the other one was even quicker. They were going to make Reggie Theus look like a fool.

Jerry curl glistening, gold chains swinging, the NBA journeyman dazzled four hundred of us by dribbling two basketballs, while the pair of super-quick guards tried in vain to steal them away. The older man somehow kept the two younger players at bay, never allowing them to touch either of the balls. When Theus was done showing up the two campers, he smiled and said to the whole camp, "You all didn't realize I was doing that finger shit the whole time, did you?" *Ooooooooh. Ahhhhhhhh.*

Kiki Vandeweghe was known in the NBA as the consummate gunner. Every time down the court, it seemed, he was launching a jump shot. He was a great shooter, and could go for forty with no problem if he was hot. He walked out in front of the camp carrying a basketball, and began talking. "I remember when I was your age." Jump shot from the top of the key, *swish.*

"I wasn't very good." *Swish.* "In fact… *swish* … I was terrible. Then I started working on my game." Moves to the deep corner of the court… *Swish, swish.*

"I slowly began to improve." *Swish, swish, swish.* Vandeweghe demonstrated why he was able to rack up points in an NBA game.

Fast forward to the following school year, and I'm a senior at Mitty High School. I'm also the best player on the team, a minor college prospect, and currently dating Tracy Vandeweghe, Kiki's niece. One night, Tracy and her dad, Kiki's brother, bring me along to watch the Warriors play Kiki's team, the Portland Trailblazers. After the game, Tracy's dad takes me back to the Trailblazers' locker room. The guys are all showering, getting dressed. Tracy's dad starts introducing me to the players, saying I'm a promising high school player. I meet Maurice Lucas and Terry Porter. Porter asks me about my game, listens to my questions. He's got an indentation on his chest from what looks like either a bullet wound or a knife slash, but I resist the urge to ask which it is. Jerry Sichting walks over, and we rap for a few minutes. We discuss the fact that a heckler was yelling at him during the game, saying, "Hey Jerry, Ralph Sampson's looking for you!"[173] I

---

[173] The reason the heckler said this was because during Game 5 of the 1986 NBA Finals, Ralph Sampson, 15 inches taller than Jerry Sichting, had elbowed the much smaller Celtics guard, to which Sichting replied, "I'll get you for that." Sampson unleashed a couple right jabs at Sichting's head, and Dennis Johnson (R.I.P.) ran over to break it up. Sampson nailed D.J. with another

excuse myself to meet the superstar Clyde Drexler. Clyde is cool. I'm not looking for a date, but Clyde, in the buff, is a chiseled specimen.

Showered and dressed, Kiki joins Tracy, her dad and me on the ride over to the nearby Hoffbrau restaurant. This place is familiar to me — Len and I used to come here before or after Warriors and A's games. Kiki isn't too friendly, it turns out. I ask him a couple questions, but he's not in the mood for conversation. This season might be his swan song, so perhaps he's contemplating life after hoops. At the end of the meal, we drive back over to the arena to drop Kiki off. I decide to ask another question, and it is a fairly dumb one: "Kiki, when you were speaking at the Superstar Camp last summer, you said you were terrible when you were in high school. But you made it to the NBA, so it's hard to believe you were ever terrible. So why did you say that?" After an awkward pause, Kiki blurts in an irritated tone, "Because it was true! You think I was just making it up? I was a terrible player! I said that because it was true!" This is our last communication.

Ladies and Gentlemen, There is a Lost Child on the Court!

So now it was 2002, and I was a vagabond musician — not impoverished, but not living in a mansion in the hills either. Kiki Vandeweghe was the general manager of the Denver Nuggets. I was in the fourth row at the Pepsi Center, and Kiki Vandeweghe was perhaps twenty feet away, wearing an expensive suit while sitting on the end of the Nuggets bench. Next to him was the oft-disappointing, criminally overpaid Marcus Camby, whose only redeeming quality at that point in his stalled career was the bad-ass tattoo of some Chinese symbol on his arm. I wasn't a big tattoo fan, but Camby had a good one. Like Nick Van Exel, Camby was considered to be a head case, and had

---

right. Both benches emptied, and Johnson went toe-to-toe with Akeem Olajuwon. Bill Walton, who would be named the NBA Sixth Man of the Year at the end of that season (his last productive campaign in the NBA), and had sported a *Dance For Disarmament* t-shirt at practice the previous day, pulled the old *Iowa Dive Bar Special*, tackling Sampson to protect his Celtics teammates. Celtics radio announcer Johnny Most had this to say about Sampson's assault: "Ralph Sampson is a gutless big guy who picks on little people, and he showed me a gutless streak."

similarly been banished to this Siberian wasteland for gifted but troubled hoopsters.

The astute reader understands by now that at the core of my heckling... deep within the recesses of my former-jock psyche, was a desire to address and possibly vindicate my personal failure to make it to the NBA. I also was driven to settle the score with certain individuals who had crossed me at some earlier point in time. I'm talking about your Adam Keefes here. I had sour grapes, and there was no other way to vent them than by skewering those who had passed the test and joined this elite athletic circle.

Kiki Vandeweghe was on my list. I'd never forgotten his petulant retort in the parking lot of the Hoffbrau, back in 1988. It was still fresh in my mind, and now it was time to pay. "Hey Kiki, take a look at the man to your right. Marcus Camby. Do you see a bright future? Do you see someone who's going to turn the franchise around? No, you don't, Kiki. Whose brilliant idea was it to bring him to Denver, anyway? Wait... you're the general manager. That was your call. Nice one. How many times do you get to drop the ball, before they hand you a cardboard box and tell you to pack your stuff? The suit's nice, but your team is in last place. I remember the Hoffbrau, Kiki. I remember."

Vandeweghe pretended not to hear me, and truthfully, maybe he didn't. He certainly had bigger problems to worry about than a traveling musician/heckler that once dated his niece, and was now jawing at him from behind the Nuggets bench. Two of these problems were former Benetton Treviso standout Nikoloz Tskitishvili, acquired as the fifth overall pick in a moment of Golden State-like ineptitude, and awkward center Chris Anderson.[174] I was joined again by my trusty sidekick Little Jesus; the Bear to my B.J., Willis to my Arnold, Murdock to my Riggs. During warm-ups, the seven-foot Tskitishvili buried a bunch of threes in a row, and Little Jesus said, "That tall, skinny foreign guy can shoot."

"Yeah, in warm-ups he's incredible. Let's see what happens when the game starts. Twenty bucks says he can't buy a lay-up." I came up with a nickname for Tskitishvili: *Shish-kabob.* For Anderson, a six-

---

[174] Who knew that Anderson would evolve years later into some kind of cult hero, covering his body with crazy tattoos, spiking his hair up and earning the nickname Birdman.

eleven, white beanstalk with short, spiked hair reminiscent of Dolf Lundgren in *Rocky IV*, I came up with another flattering handle: *Frankenstein.* So we had Shish-kabob, Frankenstein, and a GM whose back was up against the wall after some poor decision-making, and was now receiving karmic comeuppance from yours truly. Not a bad start.

"Let's get Shish-kabob and Frankenstein out there at the same time! If we can't see a quality basketball game, at least give us some comic relief. And can we get Camby to at least take off his sweats, so I can see that tattoo? Kiki, you paid five hundred million over six years for a tattoo! If you got Damon Stoudamire, you could have a cool tattoo *and* someone who can hit a ten-foot jumpshot. Hey, here's an idea, Kiki… Why don't you just suit up yourself! You're already sitting at court level. All you need's a uniform. You shoot better than any of these guys. While you're at it, grab me a uniform too. I can shoot the rock better than these guys too! This is your chance to make amends for the Hoffbrau. You don't even have to give me a salary. I know you're broke after paying Marcus Camby. Just reimburse me for the scalped tickets and we'll call it even."

Little Jesus pointed out, shortly after the opening tip, that the Clippers point guard was like four feet tall. "He's shorter than me," LJ noted. Yes, Harold Boynkins was a little guy, especially by NBA standards. He was maybe five-foot-five. He wasn't a bad player, and certainly didn't embarrass himself, but I wasn't about to allow basketball's version of Mini-Me to run around on an NBA court for two hours, without capitalizing on the opportunity.

The obvious thing to do would have been to regale Boynkins with such uninspired fare as, "Hey Boynkins, how's the weather down there?" Or something like, "Hey Lollipop Guild, nice outlet pass!" But I managed to come up with something better. Much better…

"Ladies and gentlemen, can I have your attention please! There is a lost child on the court. Again, there is a small child running around on the court. Will the parents of Harold Boynkins please report courtside immediately. I repeat, will somebody please claim Harold Boynkins, before he shoots another brick. He is lost and needs his parents. Thank you for your cooperation."

Later in the spring, GFC made its way to New Orleans for Jazzfest. The first night we arrived, Wildman and I walked around downtown, and saw a sign on the door of a club which said: *Allen Iverson Party.*

He's in here right now! Iverson, the spectacularly talented shooting guard for the Philadelphia 76ers, was in town to play the New Orleans Hornets in the second round of the NBA Playoffs. We paid a cover and walked inside. There was Iverson, standing by the bar. He was taller than he looked on TV, with good-sized hands and feet. Wildman and I grabbed a Heineken—the same thing Iverson was drinking—and stood right next to him.

I feel I should take a moment to explain the significance of standing next to Allen Iverson. At that time, the guy was one of the highest profile athletes in the world. He was constantly in the news, for not just his exciting play on the court, but also his hip-hop attitude and defiance of NBA tradition. Iverson was one of the first big-name players to cover his body in tattoos, and embrace what some critics considered to be a *thug mentality*. Also, what Iverson could do with a basketball in his hands, at six-foot-one, defied not only logic but also the laws of physics. He was a creative, prolific scoring machine.

As the All-Star sipped his Heineken and watched ESPN SportsCenter on a TV directly above him, I contemplated extending my hand for a shake. I'd paid top coin to watch him play in person, and sung his praises to anyone who would listen. A handshake didn't seem unreasonable. Iverson's two bodyguards, whose necks and arms were thicker than my head, made it clear that if I invaded their boss's personal space, I might become the Rick Allen[175] of keyboard players. I decided against introducing myself.

Later that night—much, much later—I was walking past the same club, and saw a group of people hanging around on the street. There was Iverson at four in the morning, hours before an important playoff game, chillin' with his crew. As was noted in the Iverson biography, *Only the Strong Survive*, the 76ers organization had given up early on trying to curb their superstar's personal habits. He did what he wanted, and it was hard to argue with a guy that could drop thirty or forty without even thinking about it.

I went to the game the next day, and Iverson, not negatively affected by getting just a few hours of sleep, put on a clinic for the Hornets' hometown crowd. Heckling would have been impossible since it was the playoffs, and thus ear-splittingly loud inside the arena. Besides, I was too enthralled by Iverson's crazy shots to pay any attention to

---

[175] One-armed drummer for Def Leppard.

Todd McCullough, the injury-prone oaf keeping the Philadelphia bench warm.

It's 2012 now, and the latest news about Allen Iverson is that he's completely broke. This is supposedly due, in part, to the fact that for years he refused to travel with luggage. Instead, Iverson would buy a brand new wardrobe in whatever city he was in, leaving everything in his hotel room when the team moved on. Talented ballplayer in his day, but I guess nobody has all the gifts…

MULLETS, MISHAWAKA, MINNEAPOLIS
AND MIKAIL

After a long wait, Global Funk Council finally got an opportunity to play the Fox Theater in Boulder. Unfortunately, we had a bad night. The crowd was lukewarm, and our jamming lacked inspiration; and while I was comfortable belting out lead vocals in bars and smaller venues, sometimes in the bigger places I would become insecure and self-conscious. The truth is, I never had the right ego to be a lead singer. I was more comfortable hiding behind my keyboards, maybe singing a song here or there—but fronting a band for a whole show? Didn't really have it in me. I was too shy. I didn't have the natural pipes, either. I'd recorded my voice enough times to be aware of this fact. Try as I did in the studio to sound like Sting or George Michael, I just didn't have the tone. If you know you have a naturally warm singing tone, and that everything that comes out of your mouth is going to have that warmth, I would imagine there's a confidence that comes from that. The Mayor overheard someone in the audience at the Fox show say, "Oh man, this is a shell of a band." It hurt to have that snipe relayed to me, but it wasn't entirely false.

Next, we hit the Carbondale Mountain Fair, a gathering of local mountain folk in a town neighboring Aspen. When we arrived, a white woman in her fifties was squawking into a headset microphone, stiffly beating on a hand drum while leading an all-ages group in some kind of therapeutic drum circle. There was a nice backstage area with couches, a bar, and various snacks. An older guy with a flowing beard, sporting a white robe and sandals, was hanging around back there, and Vick and I decided he was a cross between Gandhi, Ron Jeremy and David Grisman. Later, Vick and I were reprimanded by a pair of prowling cougars in butt-hugging jeans, who took exception to us snapping their picture. We had been amassing a photo collection: Mullets of the Jam Band Scene, and couldn't resist. The next day in a local supermarket, we again snapped a photo of a woman, this one with a mullet that resmembled the glorious plumage of an exotic bird of paradise. She got wise to us and said, "You two are up to no good, are you?"

"Nope, we're not."

The next day at the Mishawaka Amphitheatre, located in the outskirts of Fort Collins, we opened for the Disco Biscuits, a popular East Coast band. On this night, we made the decision that Mark Reese wasn't going to work out as our permanent guitarist. Mark lived in Denver, and the time to make the move was now, before we headed east. We agreed to break the bad news to Mark after our opening set for The Radiators, at the Copper Mountain Ski Resort. Mark was shocked when Eric told him he was fired. He hadn't seen it coming. We gave Mark some money, helped him get his gear to his car, and made arrangements for him to clean his stuff out of the Travesty. That was that.

We set out east to tackle the last several months of the year, minus a guitar player. There were some enjoyable shows in that keyboard-dominated run, but our stop at the Cabooze in Minneapolis was not among them. While heading across South Dakota that afternoon, the Travesty broke down along a remote stretch of freeway. I was forced to call for a tow, and find us a ride to the nearest city. Chris Tanner, a lanky, six-foot-five friend from California, who'd I'd given the nickname Big Job, was now a member of our road crew. He, the Mayor, the band members and I all piled into the cab of a semi for the uncomfortable, thirty-mile ride to Sioux City. It wasn't like I was going to receive any good news once we got there, either.

At the Cummins repair facility in Sioux City, I was told the Travesty would have to stay overnight. I had to make a decision: *Do I cancel the show, or rent another vehicle and hurry to Minneapolis?* I hated canceling shows, and avoided doing it at all costs. Your reputation with clubs and promoters was everything.

GFC was not a household name, but among the venues where we worked we had good relationships. I bent over backwards to be professional and courteous. We would sometimes play for peanuts, and hold our tongues when things were not what they were supposed to be. I'd remain reasonable when there were discrepancies in contracts. I was sympathetic to the position of club owners, managers, and promoters, reminding myself constantly that a club could only stay in business if it generated profit. If my band wasn't bringing in money, we were of little use. The same was true with a promoter. If he didn't have something to show for his effort, after everyone else has gotten paid, there was no incentive for him to work with us again.

I decided to rent another vehicle and make it to the show in Minneapolis. But how were we going to get the Travesty to Chicago the following day, where we were scheduled for a two-night run at the Boulevard? How were we going to get the rental vehicle back to Sioux City? I came up with a plan: We would all drive to Minneapolis in a rented Chevy Tahoe, and play the show. Then, we would drive through the night to Chicago, getting there in the morning. The Mayor and Big Job would turn around and head back to Sioux City—a fifteen-hour drive. We would play the two-night run in Chicago while the two of them were returning the Tahoe, paying for and picking up the repaired Travesty, and driving back to Chicago. I know this much: it sucked to be them that weekend.[176]

It sucked to be me, too. By the time the Travesty was paid for, the Tahoe was paid for, and the gas for both was paid for, I had coughed up over a grand. This had been a one-time occurrence, either. Something like this was happening *every couple weeks*. I didn't know what to do. I was contractually stuck with the Travesty. Todd and I had dumped many thousands into it already, and I had no back-up vehicle. For a right-brain creative type, I've always had a logical side, an ability to analyze a situation –but this was an instance in life when I had a big problem, and no idea how to solve it.

---

[176] As if they didn't have it bad enough already, Wildman left his bass in the Tahoe, after the Mayor and Big Job were already several hours out of Chicago and on the way to Sioux City. They had to turn around and come back to drop off the bass, then start the drive all over again.

After Chicago, the repaired Travesty made it to Mishawaka, home of the Fighting Irish of Notre Dame. The show coincided with Big Job's twenty-fifth birthday, which provided a reason for everyone to get hammered. Had you been out on that leg of the tour, you would have gathered through such reasoning that almost every day was Big Job's birthday.

We played on an outdoor stage behind the Mishawaka Brewing Company, next to a miniature golf course. The owner of the Mishawaka, an older, friendly guy, was happy to have us there. He anticipated a big crowd. While we sound checked, somebody started screaming at us from the miniature golf course. We stopped playing, looked over and saw some old man standing there with his hands on his hips. "It's too goddamn loud! You're bothering my customers!" Our host jumped to our defense.

"Shut up, you old fart."

"Every time you do this, it's too loud!" the guy complained. It was obviously not the first squabble between the two seniors.

"They're not even that good!"

"Go back to your goddamn windmill. You know I have a permit."

"You're gonna drive me out of business," the miniature golf guy moaned.

"If I believed *that*, I'd have a concert every night," our guy quipped, sounding like Jack Lemon sniping at Walter Mathau in *Grumpy Old Men*.

Later, nobody turned out for our show. It was major crickets. The owner stood there shaking his head. "Whenever we have Umphree's Magee, the place is packed," he lamented. We managed to have a fun evening anyway, as several Mishawaka employees joined us in emptying the beer keg Milt placed at the side of the stage.

After the gig, Big Job, Vick, the Mayor and I joined some girls from the restaurant in hitting a nearby bar. After a few quick trips to the bar, Big Job was smashed. The rest of us weren't far behind him, either. Big Job whipped his shirt off, jumped up on a pool table, and started twirling the shirt in the air over his head, while spinning his hips and striking an effeminate pose. This was his patented move. He did it with a certain *je ne sais qua* that made you think he'd missed his calling as a Chippendale dancer. I led the bar in a drunken, out-of-tune version of Happy Birthday, as he worked the room with his spontaneous striptease. The dance, as entertaining as it was, did not help Big Job seal the deal with a waitress he'd taken a fancy to earlier.

She left without saying goodbye to anyone, leaving him puzzled. "Guess you got up in her grill too much," I speculated.

It was a long drive to Buffalo, New York, for a show at a place called Nietzsche's. I remember little about this joint, other than the fact that there was some graffiti in the urinal that read: *Mikail is a mean vodka drunk*. For reasons unexplained, I decided to turn this into a lyric:

Mikail is a mean vodka drunk
Mikail is a mean vodka drunk
He aims to fill your head with loads of existential junk
And he makes a nasty, mean, vodka drunk
Mikail is a mean vodka drunk
Mikail is a mean vodka drunk
He's wicked off the dribble but don't expect the man to dunk
And he makes a nasty, mean, vodka drunk
Mikail is a mean vodka drunk
Mikail is a mean vodka drunk
His mind a maze of theories you're not likely to debunk
And he makes a nasty, mean, vodka drunk
Mikail is a mean vodka drunk
Mikail is a mean vodka drunk
He ain't too big on country but he loves some Global Funk
And he makes a nasty, mean, vodka drunk

While in Buffalo, we rehearsed a new Wildman composition, *Sarah's Best*. This song was twenty minutes long, with seven or eight different sections— the most complex piece the band had thus far attempted. The rehearsal was terrible, the music a disjointed mess. I had learned, however, not to judge a piece until it had been fleshed out and tested in front of a live audience. As Gary Klein had taught me, if you dismiss someone's song prematurely, they might sue you in small claims court... and *win*. *Sarah's Best* evolved into an interesting pastiche, spurring GFC's ultimate transition from a funky bar band into an eclectic rock quartet.[177]

---

[177] I now believe this extreme musical shifting of gears, from palatable funk to quirky, eclectic rock was the beginning of the end for the band. It confused people.

We drove to New York City to play at The Lion's Den, a popular Manhattan rock club. As was the norm in both L.A. and New York, the club lumped us together with three other bands, creating a chaotic environment where everyone scrambles to get their gear off and onto the stage all night, overlapping into each other's scheduled time slots. I've always disliked this kind of herd-'em-in, herd-'em-out affair.

It turned out to be one of the best GFC shows ever. I was inspired by the presence of my friend Mike Blanco, a discerning listener I knew could not be bullshitted. I'd sat with Mike at big-name shows while he lambasted the presentation, saying it was *jive*.

The band still had no guitar player, so I was forced to cover all the rhythm parts with my left hand, while playing melodies with my right. I stretched out on long solos, guiding the band into unexpected, creative directions. I liked playing without a guitar, as it was less restricting; but I ultimately wanted the band to have a rock edge. I wanted a guitarist who would bring people to their knees with epic, wailing solos. I was about to find him.

We headed up to Great Barrington, Massachusetts for Birkfest, the East Coast equivalent of High Sierra. Birkfest rounded up the usual suspects: MMW, John Scofield, Soulive, Sound Tribe Sector Nine, Michael Franti and Spearhead, and Robert Randolph, along with less popular acts like The Motet, Jacob Fred Jazz Odyssey, and us.

I dug the MMW show immensely, while Soulive was less convincing; they were good musicians, but didn't have MMW's synergy. Soulive's presentation relied too much on gimmickry. Keyboardist Neal Evans, however, was talented and likeable. His left-hand bass lines were a true marvel of funkiness.

Evans endured a very embarrassing moment during the band's set at Birkfest. As he was finishing the last song by himself, the other band members already off the stage, a stagehand came over and *unplugged Evans' keyboard while he was playing,* leaving him standing there hammering the keys in awkward silence. Keep in mind that this was in front of thousands of people. The show had gone over the time limit, and the soundmen had become fearful of violating a local noise ordinance. Someone should have simply walked up to Evans and said "Hey man, you have to stop playing right now." That would have been better than just pulling the plug on the guy.

The GFC set went pretty well. We were joined by friends from the Motet and Tea Leaf Green, and also Casey Benjamin, the terrific saxophonist/keyboardist who'd blown me away a year earlier, with Project Logic in San Francisco.

The big festivals were good for getting the competitive juices flowing. You watched the bands on the main stage, and you secretly plotted how you were going to get there yourself. The whole point was to make it to the Big Stage. If you went around to the side stages and asked every band what their ultimate goal was, they would tell you they wanted to make it to the Big Stage.

The Big Stage was as much an idea as it was a tangible thing. It represented the upper echelon of success in the scene. If you were on the Big Stage, you were, in the eyes of organizers and promoters, a commodity. You had value, and you could milk that fact when you sold your band to future festivals. Promoters now realized they could enhance the attractiveness of their lineup by affiliating themselves with your name. Like most successful business transactions, it was a mutually exploitational relationship.

As an artist, being on the Big Stage meant there were people assigned to deal with travel logistics, media coordination, stage preparations, and general troubleshooting. Also, you could count on receiving a certain amount of respect—something that was more, shall we say, *sporadic* during earlier points in your career.

By the second day of Birkfest, there were horror reports circulating the lot (the area where people were camping out and raging, twenty-four-seven). Countless festival goers had passed out from ingesting too many drugs, and some were lying face down in the mud. This East Coast party crew was known for unmitigated debauchery; the kids had a *party 'til you puke* mentality, and for many, the drugs were more a motivating factor in coming to the festivals than the music.

Birkfest was also memorable for another reason: there were no bathing facilities available. Thus, the roughly five days I spent getting there, hanging out, and driving to the next destination represented the longest amount of time in my entire life that I'd ever gone without taking a shower. We really were the Global *Funk* Council during that stretch.

I KNOW I'M NOT ONE OF THE GREATS...
BUT I KNOW I'M TALENTED

Our next gig was in Winooski, Vermont at a club called Higher Ground. Winooski bordered Burlington, and the club was owned by Phish guitarist Trey Anastasio's brother-in-law. I know you'll find this hard to believe, but the Travesty broke down that day, just inside the Vermont border. We were opening for Ozomatli, a Grammy-winning Latin/rock group from Los Angeles, and we didn't want to miss the show. A good Samaritan spotted us and pulled over in his pick-up truck, offering Eric and me a ride to the nearest town. We accepted, and were able to rent a passenger van, which we drove back to the malfunctioning Travesty. We left Big Job there at the side of the road, to meet the tow truck driver and help haul the piece of shit to Albany, the location of the nearest repair facility. Now a couple hours behind schedule, I aggravated the situation by taking the wrong route—a smaller road that appeared quicker on a map, but actually turned out to be painfully slow. Note to touring bands: *Always* take the main interstate, not the winding road that looks like a shorter distance. That alternate route might look enticing on the map you picked up at the gas station, but believe me when I tell you you're going to get stuck behind Jethro and Beulah, doing twenty-five in their pick-up, battered Airstream hitched behind it, with no passing lane for eighty-six miles. Drive the extra twenty miles out of your way, hit the interstate, and haul ass. Guaranteed to be a less stressful and time-consuming experience.

We made it to the Higher Ground just in time to set up and do our opening show for Ozomatli. Vick knew a couple guys from the headliner, so they jumped up and played for a while. I played well, pulling off some cool synth solos with my MS-2000. After the set, we were packing up our gear in the alley behind the club, getting ready to head to a local motel, when Vick walked up and said, "I want to introduce you to somebody." I was tired and grumpy from the long, trying day, and didn't feel much like schmoozing. Vick said, "This guy really wants to me you. And you're gonna really want to meet him." I sighed and agreed.

I watched the guy descend the back stairwell and walk toward me. It was dark, but I got a sudden feeling he was someone I knew. As he got closer I realized I knew him, all right. I'd seen his picture hundreds of times, seen him in concert videos, seen him in magazines. He was Page McConnell, the Phish keyboardist. We shook hands and he complimented me on my playing. "I liked what you were doing. I noticed it right when I walked into the club." Those were nice words to hear. Page McConnell was an important part of arguably the most influential rock band of the nineties.

I thanked Page and told him I was a fan of his playing. The rest of the guys piled out of the van and joined the conversation. The Mayor, huge Phish fan that he was, stood there waxing blasé, not wanting to seem like he cared too much.

"Hey Page, Tristan's been to a few shows… one, two, couple hundred." Page chuckled and asked, "Where are you guys staying?" I told him we had rooms lined up, and that we were fatigued from the breakdown and all-day drive. We were heading to the motel. Page said he'd be around later, and that I should come find him if I made it back for Ozomatli's show.

After grabbing a shower at the motel, Eric and I returned to Higher Ground to watch Ozomatli. As the show ended, I spotted Page by the bar, and we continued our conversation from earlier. The club emptied, except for a handful of employees, Page, Eric and me. Eric had always been a vocal Phish detractor. He didn't like their singing, their groove... their whole vibe. He would always protest when the Mayor blasted Phish bootlegs, while we drove between gigs.

Page grabbed us a couple beers and we walked to the green room, where we continued talking. We discussed keyboard gear and other topics, and the older man surprised me by getting mildly defensive when I made a comment about all the great players out there that you never heard of, guys who wallowed in obscurity their whole lives. "I know I'm not one of the greats," he said, "but I also know I'm talented." I thought about it and realized it was a good, thoughtful statement. You have to genuinely believe in your ability, without being delusional about it. You have to acknowledge and respect all the talent in the world, without allowing the reality of a planet full of gifted people to overwhelm or discourage you from exploring and enjoying your own talent.

Phish hadn't yet returned from a two-year hiatus, and nobody knew if they were coming back at all. I knew many Phish diehards who were speculating on the matter. Page smiled and said, "I think we're coming back. I talked to Trey today for a long time. The four of us are getting together this weekend for a retreat, to plan it." Had I been a journalist, I would have had a prized exclusive story on my hands.

My hang with Page McConnell proved to be a pivotal moment in my JBS journey. I never crossed paths with him again, but the evening we spent talking was like an accelerated mentorship. His humility opened my eyes. If a guy who routinely plays multiple sold-out shows at Madison Square Garden is approachable and unassuming, there's no excuse for *anyone* to cop an attitude.

We had been hanging tough without guitar for over a month, when Vick procured a lead from Fareed Haque, the guitarist from Garaj Mahal. Fareed recommended his star student, Chase Holtzclaw, who he described as "my *Mini Me*."

Chase showed up at The Boulevard, our Chicago stomping ground, to sit in and check out the band. White, goateed, and no more than five-foot-six, he looked like Harry Potter—sleight of build and wearing glasses, and hard to imagine as a commanding musical presence. From the first solo he took, however, Chase blew us away. He was supremely confident, had a great time feel, and played with clarity and direction. We were sold. We invited Chase to join us on the road, and he accepted. He threw his amplifier in the trailer, and we made arrangements to fly him out to meet us on the East Coast the next week.

We returned to Asheville, North Carolina, after playing Chicago and a couple other Midwest dates... wonderful tour routing! Along the way, I bought several Phish records. I dug the studio albums, which were more satisfying than the live bootlegs I'd been hearing for the last couple years. I became well-acquainted with the Phish repertoire. In fact, I became a Phish fan, and their music began to influence my compositional ideas. The more I listened, the more I liked their ambitious blend of influences, their risk taking, and their sense of humor.

My newfound appreciation of Phish presented a serious problem for GFC, however, because Drew loathed them. He and I were the backbone of the organization, the creative nerve center of a group that, like many others out there, aspired to be, in terms of commercial success, the *next* Phish. Once I found Phish, there was no way Drew and I could get along creatively. He was anti-Phish, and I was suddenly Mr. Phish. It was only a matter of time before we would part company.

Sometimes the greatest show happens in the most unlikely of settings. When we pulled into Black Mountain, North Carolina, everyone had on their *this is going to blow* face. The Town Pump was a tiny hole in the wall, the town's population barely in triple digits. That night, however, the little place came alive and was packed from wall to wall. The band made more money than we'd managed in our last several shows combined.

Pumped by our showing at the Town Pump, Drew corralled us into hitting an after-show party at someone's house, out in the boonies. We piled into the Travesty and searched for the place, quickly getting lost. We wound up on a road with no outlet, no street signs, and no lights. There was no place to turn around, either. In the confusion, Drew pulled the Travesty down a random driveway, and we wound up not in front of somebody's house… but *stuck on somebody's front lawn*. Imagine coming out in your pajamas at three in the morning, in a rural area of North Carolina, to find a bunch of scraggly guys in a forty-foot diesel RV, camped on your grass.

The man was a patient sort, and helped us deal with the whole mess. We had to unpack the entire trailer, drop it off the hitch, turn the Travesty around, re-pack the trailer, hitch it, and finally drive out of there. This took an hour and a half. Then, adding insult to injury, as Eric was trying to make the turn, he drove onto a garden embankment, cracking the Travesty's fiberglass frame. To say I was pissed would be an understatement.

THREE CAPITOLS, FOUR DORKS, ONE DAY

After gigs in Richmond and Great Barrington, we returned to Burlington to play Club Metronome, which was next door to Nectar's. We had several days off before the show, so the Mayor, Drew and Wildman flew to their respective homes. That left me, Chase, Big Job and Vick to conquer New England on our own. Chase was still new, and his innocence brought a certain good fortune—for a while there, everything seemed to come up roses. When we pulled the Travesty into downtown Portland, Maine, there was a huge parking space waiting for us, as if God wanted us to hang in Portland for a while. We squatted there for a few days, remarkably never getting hassled by cops.

Portland was a great time. We hit local bars and mingled with young, salty girls and tattooed, thick-necked muscle heads. While observing the locals, I identified a new genus of mullet: *the Portland Lobster Tail*. I took a tour of the Portland Observatory, the last remaining maritime signal tower in the nation. The view from the top was breathtaking, offering a panoramic vantage point of the entire state, as well as the Atlantic Ocean.

We tooled along the coast of Maine, stopping to enjoy the crisp ocean air and mingle with fellow RV tourists. Unencumbered by the usual stresses and constraints that accompanied a relentless touring schedule, I relished taking it easy for a while. Vick and I got into a conversation with a couple in their fifties, fellow RV owners who were putting around the East Coast. "What's this?" Vick asked, pointing to a U.S. map painted on the back of their smaller vehicle. There were tiny RV's peppering certain states, along with little figures of animals.

"The little motor homes show you which states we've been to with this baby," the guy said.

"What about the little deer silhouettes?" I asked.

"Those are the places where I done some huntin'."

We stopped in Portsmouth to cruise around downtown. We walked past a blues bar, and Chase expressed an interest in hearing the band. I got an idea for a practical joke: We'd dress Chase up in a geeky college-boy outfit—pullover sweater, corduroy pants—give him a biology book, and sit him in the front row. After a couple tunes, he'd yell out: *Can you turn down? I'm trying to study.* Of course the band would angrily refuse, at which point Chase would yell out to the guitar player that he was lousy. The guy would almost certainly fire back, "Oh yeah? Then bring your little Harry Potter-lookin' ass up here and show us how it's done." Chase would put down the biology book, hit the stage, take the man's guitar… and proceed to play circles around him. *Don't let the look fool you.*

We decided to forgo the joke for safety reasons, and stopped for the night somewhere between Portland and Augusta. In the morning, we continued north. The capital monument in Augusta seemed like a ghost town. Perhaps the fact that it was a Sunday afternoon had something to do with it. As we walked around I got an idea: *let's try to see three capitals in one day.* Concord, New Hampshire was in striking distance, as was Montpelier, Vermont. I was taking countless pictures back in those days, going through portable cameras quicker than chilled cans of Red Bull. I had a pile of cameras waiting to be developed, hell-bent on documenting all my road experiences. I felt like Clark Griswald, refusing to return from a problem-riddled vacation without having something to show for it. *This tour may be a complete waste, we may end up broke, and the Travesty might break down another ten times before I get back to the West Coast, but damn it, I'm going to assemble one hell of a photo album and brag about all the places I've been. At least I'll have that going for me.*

We came back down through Maine and cut over to New Hampshire, where we continued our northbound journey; most of Maine was wilderness or tiny little towns along minor roads, so we had to backtrack a few hours. We arrived in Concord in the late afternoon, and the weather had deteriorated to a cold, foggy funk. The capital building was not as impressive as the one in Augusta, and the city itself did not seem upon first glance to possess a remarkable array of visual treasures.

Big Job had recently pioneered an activity that could be described as SSSD (Sexually Suggestive Statue Desecration). This entailed climbing and straddling statues of important historical figures, in the courtyards near state capitals and other sacred, revered monuments—followed by obscene gestures that either incorporated the statue or drew humorous contrast to the intention of the statue. The preponderance of such erections (no pun intended) to be found in historically rich New England allowed Big Job to further explore the homo-erotic themes he'd been pursuing as the band's merchandise salesman. Every night, I allotted a moment in the show for Big Job to take center stage, swing a GFC t-shirt over his head, and pivot his hips seductively to the techno rumblings of Drew, Wildman and me. This portion of the show was well received in hipper markets like San Francisco, but in Fort Wayne, Indiana, where puritanical notions still had the locals in a strong headlock, it was not nearly as effective.

After performing mock fellatio on a bronze likeness of some American Revolution-era political figure of great prominence, Big Job eluded the capital building security team, and we marched toward our third and final destination in central Vermont. I vividly recall the drive that evening, cruising in the well-behaved Travesty to the rustic, soothing sound of Phish's finest studio album, *Rift.* As I gazed out the Travesty's large side windows at the rolling blue and purple hills accenting a fine New England dusk, the melodic refrain of Trey Anastasio's *Fast Enough For You* mollified the cumulative angst of my oft-frustrating life on the road.

We coasted into Montpelier and pulled up in front of the city's regal capital building. Night had fallen, and the snow-white, domed structure was gloriously lit against a jet-black sky. There were two teenage girls throwing a frisbee on the lawn covering the sloped hill in front of the capital, and we introduced ourselves and joined them for a group photo. Three capitals, one day.

We capped our journey with a surprisingly good Chinese dinner, and then continued north, stopping when we reached Burlington. We parked on a street close to Nectar's, and slept without disturbance. Our brief New England expedition had been so free of hassle from the usual headaches associated with the Travesty, that I was starting to believe Chase had brought some good karma into the organization. He didn't have Harry Potter's lightning bolt on his forehead, but he did have some magic working for him. Everything was relaxed and easy. I started calling him Good Juju Chase.

I was sitting in the Travesty practicing keyboard licks on my MS-2000, when Big Job bolted in and said, "I just met Page (McConnell) and Mike (Gordon) from Phish!" They'd been eating dinner at Nectar's, and Big Job had run into them out front. He told Page we'd be playing at Club Metronome, and invited him to the show.

I'd never been to Canada, and decided to rent a car and drive to Montreal. The other three guys joined me, and we pulled into the thriving metropolis late in the afternoon. Montreal seemed like a combination of old European influences and modern architecture, and I was immediately intrigued by its multi-cultural, cosmopolitan feel. After we paid a visit to the awe-inspiring Notre-Dame Basilica,[178] I broke from the group to hit a couple museums. I didn't need to be around people all the time. In fact, I often preferred to be on my own, whether at home or in a new, strange city. I was always observing, taking things in. Trying to figure out what made a particular place tick. Watching people. Pondering life's big questions. Pondering the questions of my own life. I couldn't do this in a group of people. Even with good buddies, there was always the matter of being social. Being *cool*. I had, and still have, the temperament of a writer. A writer has to block out the world. Block out people, conversations. Noise.

After a few hours to myself, I checked the four of us into a hotel. Vick pulled his weight, combing the local youth hostel and finding a pair of foreign girls, Australian and Irish, that wanted to party with us.

---

[178] ...a neogothic church, built in 1829, which features a Casavant organ, as well as the le Gros Bourdon, the largest bell in North America.

We took them to a karaoke bar, offering up renditions of Prince and Michael Jackson songs. The festivities continued in a lounge uptown. There were no shenanigans that evening, but we picked up with the girls the following morning and commenced to cover the entire downtown area, on foot.

Later, Big Job went on a booze run, and we polished off his haul before hitting the town for another evening of barhopping. One club we hit resembled a European disco, with blasting techno music and a dance floor packed with a hodgepodge of ethnicities and funky hairstyles.

After a couple days, we piled into the rental car and drove back to Burlington. I made the grave error of telling officers at the U.S. border that we were traveling musicians--they proceeded to search the vehicle inside out. They also searched *us* thoroughly, barely stopping short of the feared *full cavity search*. We were all Americans with clean records, returning to our own country, but the officers were rude and surly. Let me rephrase that: they were total pricks. One of them said to me, "If any one of your friends has any shit on them, *you're* the one that's going down. Understand?" I hadn't even thought about it, and it was indeed possible that one of my cohorts might be toting a small quantity of some illegal substance in his luggage. Luckily nobody had anything on them, and after an hour of being searched and hassled, we were cleared to re-enter Vermont.

The rest of the band flew into Burlington, and we all convened at a Wal-Mart on the outskirts of town. With the return of Drew, Wildman and the Mayor, Good Juju Chase's harmonious vibes suddenly stopped flowing. The Travesty broke down right there at the Wal-Mart. We scrambled to figure out what was wrong, and the consensus was that one of the batteries was bad. In our confusion to determine the faulty battery's voltage, Vick became irritated. He pointed to the battery sitting in its tray and said, "Are you guys idiots? It's a twelve-bolt system. Count the bolts. One, two, three..." I've already confessed to not being mechanically inclined, but I did know the difference between volts and bolts. The Mayor laughed out loud at Vick's gaff, and Wildman and I concurred that while unintentionally funny, it was one of the most intellectually challenged things we'd ever heard come from the mouth of a fellow adult human being.

Vick had a reputation for such verbal blunders. On another occasion, he, Karl Denson and I were hanging out in a recording studio. Karl made a reference to someone being a "bean counter."

518

Confused, Vick asked, "Why would you call him that? Does he work in a jellybean factory?" Karl laughed, but then we both realized that the percussionist wasn't making a funny. *Guess he hadn't heard that expression before.*

Perhaps the best example of Vick's lack of familiarity with the subtleties of the English language was his becoming strained, one day, as he attempted to remember the word for a particular item: "What do you call that thing? You know, with the sand dropping down to the bottom. It's made of glass. Oh yeah... the time/sand jar." The Mayor had joked that this would make a great Rush song...
(sung in Geddy Lee's unmistakable cackle)

Time sand jar!
Slipping away, one grain at a time, through the
Time sand jar!

Our show at Club Metronome was lousy. One of Trey Anastasio's sidemen sat in on trombone, but nobody came out to see us, and the band didn't play well. I was disappointed, but it was just another night at the office. That's how you have to look at it. The soundman, at least, liked our music. He was a foreign, swarthy character who served as traveling soundman for Pork Tornado, the curious side project of Phish drummer Jon Fishman.

We traveled south to Waitsfield, a little town in lower Vermont. The girls from Montreal had surprised us by showing up in Burlington, and we let them tag along for a couple days. They sold more merchandise in two gigs than we had moved in the previous two months. Guys would approach them and, in an obvious attempt to appease (hit on) them, buy our shirts, CD's and stickers. Too bad we couldn't keep the girls around longer.

The following night at Beardsley Castle, Drew pulled me aside and told me he was he was going to bow out of the project. I sensed it was coming. I felt a mixture of trepidation and relief, if such a thing is possible. Drew was a good guy and a fine player, but we were going to lock horns if we stayed together. It was that simple. He knew it, I knew it.

Drew's departure was uneventful and, in a way, rather sad. I asked him to keep it on the down low, concerned that a formal announcement would undermine the momentum of the band. He graciously agreed, and finished out the next few weeks without any fanfare. I sensed that he was hurt that the band didn't make a gesture upon his leaving—a goodbye party, a final show celebration, or something like that—but he wasn't leaving under ideal circumstances. His relationship with Wildman was strained, and he was also having problems with the Mayor and me. Furthermore, he had co-signed with me on the RV contract. Legally speaking, we were still married.

We headed back west, stopping in Buffalo and Rochester for a pair of shows. Buffalo was forgettable, but Rochester was better. We played a jazz club not far from Eastman, one of the nation's best music schools, and we drew a decent crowd.

After a lame show in Indiana, Pennsylvania, one of the dreariest places I remember visiting on tour, we sunk even lower with a night at the Attic in Pittsburgh. I liked Pittsburgh—a pleasant, modern city-- but the Attic was a meatmarket billiards bar, with a blisteringly loud punk rock club directly above it. The vibe was crap, and it it was just a terrible place to make music. Wildman's dad came out to see us—I'd like to point out that for some reason, parents always come to the worst possible show. When you're rocking a nice theater in front of a thousand people, Mom and Dad are nowhere to be found. Play some empty pool hall with a punk club right above it, and there are your proud parents, sitting in the front row. Of course, coming to the worst show on the entire tour reinforces their unspoken disapproval of your questionable career choice.

A good show usually follows a string of crummy ones, but no… it still got worse! We did two nights in Williamsport, Pennsylvania at a restaurant called the Bullfrog Brewery. The place offered a fine menu and a courteous waiting staff, but in terms of its benefit to the project, the Bullfrog Brewery turned out to be a real *bullshit booking*. There was a pitiful sound system, no stage, and no crowd. Fortunately, things picked up a bit in Charlottesville the next night.

Dave Mathews Band hailed from Charlottesville, and the city prided itself on a thriving music scene. We played a room called Orbit Billiards which, despite the obvious concerns caused by the name, had nice ambience and a good clientele. Here, we premiered a new tune I'd just written called *Stupid Disease*. It had a *second line* New Orleans flavor, and represented my first effort to write in that style.

KEEP ON PUSHIN'

Anticipating Drew's departure, Wildman and I started looking for a new drummer. Woo and Todd were putting the word out back in California and had amassed a list of prospects. One of these was a kid from Toronto. We'll call him Augie. Augie sent us examples of his playing, but before we could even listen to his CD and respond, he took the initiative of booking a round trip flight to Washington D.C., hoping to audition by sitting in at our show. *You've got balls. I like balls.*[179] We encouraged him to make the trip. Then we heard his music. Oh, God. No, no, no. Wildman called him immediately.

"Augie, we listened to your stuff. Honestly man, we don't want you to spend seven or eight hundred dollars flying out here to audition. Save your money." But Augie's faith in self persisted.

---

[179] The blunt words of a Middle Eastern terrorist in *Team America: World Police*, which is not only on my top 10 all-time list of comedies, but is inarguably the funniest movie ever made with puppets.

"I was hung over when I recorded those tracks. I'm coming. I've gotten every gig I ever auditioned for. This one won't be any different."

"Okay, man. Can't argue with that kind of confidence. We'll see you in D.C."

We drove the Travesty into Washington and approached the Velvet Lounge, a beat up little dump that looked like it could hold maybe eighty people. A very short guy with a rather large head was standing in front, hands in pockets, looking around like he was lost. He had a *Time Bandits* vibe minus the pirate costume, and looked from a distance like he might be a dwarf. He was holding something in his hands.

"Is that kid holding a pair of drumsticks?"

"I think so."

"Awww, fuck."

"I don't care if he sounds like Tony Williams. We're not hiring a goddamn dwarf to play drums in the band." I hopped out of the RV and walked over to him.

"You Augie?"

"Yeah."

Wildman and I took him to a nearby bar for a beer. We talked music, and after an hour or so decided that we really liked the kid. He had a good attitude and liked all the right music. If he could play his ass off, we might look past the *Time Bandits* issue.

That night, the show was a bummer. The club treated us like chumps, the turnout was disappointing, and we got *paid* like chumps. During the second set we called Augie up for his big chance. During the count-off—the four beats before the band actually began playing—I knew Augie was in trouble. Moments later, so did the other twenty-five people in the joint. Watto, sitting to Augie's right, had to coach him along: "Don't rush it, man! Lay back!" Augie wasn't even in the ballpark. His groove was all over the place, and he compensated by filling the space with conviluted fills and inappropriate poly-rhythms. We all felt terrible. The guy had shelled out a grand to fly out and audition, after all. Augie slept in the Travesty with us that night, and flew back to Toronto the following afternoon. When he left, he knew his trip had been in vain.

A few days later I called Augie to offer him encouragement. I got his voice mail and decided to leave a message. Everyone in the band was in earshot. I delicately made some suggestions of things he might improve in his playing, also breaking the official news that we weren't going to offer him the job. Then, unsure how to sign off I said, "Keep your chin up, Augie, and hey... *Keep on pushin'!*" I meant it sincerely, but the second it came out of my mouth realized it sounded condescending. The guys started laughing. "I can't believe you told him to keep on pushin'!" the Mayor bellowed.

"Geez, kick the guy when he's down," someone else added.

On our way west we hit the Stateline Bar and Grill in Bristol, Tennessee. In these parts, NASCAR reigned supreme. The top drivers were treated like rock stars, and upcoming events were being advertised everywhere you looked. The show was good that evening; we got into some creative jams, breaking out of the rut we'd been in the previous week. It's easy to get stuck playing the same types of things every night when you're in a jam band. In order to find new stuff, someone has to throw a curveball—play something unexpected, maybe even *wrong*. Vibes master Bobby Hutcherson once told me, "A mistake is a beautiful thing." I knew it was some deep shit he was saying, but I didn't understand his words at seventeen. Years later I realized he meant that a mistake is a catalyst for change. It is spontaneous, forcing you to react differently, to go in an unexpected direction.

In the jam band world most groups improvise over one chord—a static vamp that never goes anywhere, harmonically speaking. This is because it requires extremely refined ears to be able to follow someone harmonically, if you have no idea what they're going to play in advance. Also, when you start using a lot of chords you run the risk of losing most audiences. Jalen Jones, my old Faze cohort, once told me, "Ant, people don't really like chords. They like bass and drums." I thought what he was saying was simplistic and dumb at the time, but it makes perfect sense to me now. He was right. That's what people like: repetitive bass lines and monotonous, loud drums. He's touring the world with the Black Eyed Peas. I'm playing B-52's covers at Viejas Casino in Alpine. Maybe I should have listened.

In order to break up the monotony of one-chord jams in GFC, I would often superimpose dense jazz chords over the top of the static bass line. This would create a sense of tension and excitement. Sometimes Wildman would deviate from the vamp and follow me harmonically. He had a good sense of when to stick with the original harmony, and when to drift into *outer space*. Chase and I developed a terrific guitar/keyboard rapport, intertwining single-note melodies between our respective instruments. Sometimes he would establish a riff and the rest of the band would react to it; other times it would be the drums and bass that laid down the foundation.

We were developing a reputation for innovative jamming. While there were times we fell into the trap of sounding like Phish, there were also times when we got into our *own stuff.* It was difficult not to sound like Phish—their influence was inescapable in our world. You heard their music everywhere, saw their posters, and hung out with kids who constantly brought them up in conversation, comparing everyone and everything to them. Many of the bands in the scene were struggling not to sound, act or otherwise emulate the legendary quartet from Vermont, for fear of being labeled Phish wannabes; but the truth was, we were all Phish wannabes. They were the kings of the scene. It was *their* scene. Most bands, GFC included, would have been thrilled to have a fraction of their success, and that's what we were all desperately clawing and competing for.

The band stayed at a large house owned by a middle-aged woman with a much younger boyfriend. I studied the family pictures in her foyer, from which I was able to construct a chronological outline of events: her husband had been a doctor, or something else that brought in a lot of bread. They had divorced, and she of course kept the house. They'd had children while married, then she got spaced out on prescription drugs, and her dependence had fueled the break-up as much as his indiscretions. Now, she had this beautiful house, the kids were grown, and she didn't have to do much of anything anymore. The doctor was remarried and living in a nice condo in another part of town. His new wife was twenty years younger, which pissed off the lady whose house we were crashing at, but not enough to keep her from continuing to cash those alimony checks, which he continued to kick down, even though the kids were out of the house. As Sir Charles would say, *I might be wrong… but I doubt it.*

A pair of girls, who'd first seen us play in Bristol, showed up in Blacksburg, Virginia to catch our show at Baylee's. One of them, Crystal, was a tall and attractive college student. *Crystal from Bristol.* We struck up a conversation after the show, and I found her bright and mature beyond her years. We wound up getting to know each other a bit, and I was happy when she told me she planned to come see the band again soon, at a festival we were scheduld to play in Atlanta.

We returned to Black Mountain, North Carolina. Remember how I said we were heading west? Cancel that. This was but one example of terrible tour routing. We were continually backtracking, going out of the way for shows that weren't worth the trouble. Of course, it's easy to see that now. At the time, I was just glad there was work, and I was willing to drive an extra eight hours with the hope that maybe we'd have a great show, and attract a new group of people to our music.

The Travesty broke down in front of the Town Pump, right after our stinker of a show there. We were supposed to open for Melvin Seals, at the Lincoln Theatre in Raleigh the following night, and I didn't want to miss it. I decided to have Vick hang in Black Mountain with Big Job, while the rest of us went ahead to Raleigh. Vick didn't like it—after all, he was a member of the actual band. I had learned in Missoula, however, that we could survive without percussion.

We might as well have cancelled Raleigh. Poor Melvin Seals, as established as he was, drew nobody. The theatre was empty the whole night. The onus wasn't on us to bring in a crowd, but it was still a pathetic scene. We played well, despite the empty room. The next morning we caught a ride to a rental place, to pick up a passenger van for the return trip to Black Mountain. There was some confusion at the office, and an officious employee tried to twist facts to make it seem like my fault the van wasn't ready. I remained patient, but after an hour or so, I finally spoke up: "*You* got your wires crossed, not us. Why do we have to suffer for your mistake? We made a reservation, and our livelihood depends on us getting that van. Right now." Once I took this tone, everything changed. A senior manager walked out from the back office and attempted to appease me.

"You're right, Mr. Smith. This isn't your fault. Can I buy you and your friends lunch?"

Thought you'd never ask.

One of the office workers brought us Chick Filet, which I instantly loved, and our van appeared within minutes. The manager told me to simply *say the word* if there was anything else the company could do to assist us with our needs. I learned something about customer service politics that afternoon: If you are weak, you will get pounced on. Even though you might be justified in being unhappy, you will be blamed for not reading the fine print. But if you are direct and demanding, taking on an air of entitlement nuanced with the potential threat of *formal complaint,* prepare for the red carpet. The royal treatment.

I was supposed to return the van in Asheville a couple days later, but called to ask if I might hold on to it an extra day. The manager from Raleigh said, "Sure! Keep it for a few more days. No extra charge!" I'm not kidding. It was hard to believe, but that's what he said—all because I had raised some hell in the office. I felt like Mr. White from Eddie Murphy's old *Saturday Night Live* routine.

We picked up the rest of the team in the rental van and drove down to Athens, Georgia for a much-anticipated show at the Georgia Theater. Athens was a famous music town—REM hailed from there—and was home to Georgia Tech University. The college area was complemented by nice restaurants, record stores, clubs and various shops. I found a music store with rare recordings by hundreds of great jazz and rock artists. I was in hog heaven there, and spent a couple hours scouring the selection before deciding on a handful of discs.

When we took the stage that evening, there weren't many people in the audience, but by the second or third song, another hundred and fifty heads had filed in. It was a solid turnout for our first time in town, and we played well. The night was a genuine morale builder, a bright spot on an East Coast tour otherwise riddled with disappointments.

We continued south to play Harvest Festival, a gathering just outside of Atlanta, organized by the High Sierra people. Like High Sierra, the event was staged on a large piece of remote, rural land. The area had just been pummeled by rainstorms, and when we arrived for our show, the whole lot was one massive mud pit. Vehicles were stuck everywhere, and we had to load our equipment through a brown/ orange, foot-deep quagmire to reach the our scheduld stage. I gave half a thought to canceling and hitting the road, but decided to tough it out. The performance was difficult, not just because of the weather and ground conditions, but also because we were deprived of a sound check. We couldn't hear each other, and had to perform on pure instinct.

Crystal from Bristol showed up with her friend Margie, who Vick volunteered to entertain. After the set, Vick and I threw our suitcases in the back of Crystal's car. We said goodbye to the rest of the guys, and they headed back to Asheville to await the Travesty's repair. Vick and I were planning to stay at the festival an extra day, then cruise around with the girls for a couple more days after that.

That night we enjoyed Steve Kimock's group, and also Soulive. I chatted with Neal Evans, Soulive's keyboardist, while Vick talked to Neal's brother Alan, who'd been the first drummer in Karl Denson's Tiny Universe. Neal and I discussed playing Hammond B-3.

"Yeah, organ is *aiiight*," he sighed, "but I'm more into producing hip-hop these days." This was interesting coming from a guy best known for his organ playing.

We left the festival and found hotel rooms somewhere in Atlanta. The next day, the girls began to act their age: giggling over inside jokes, talking about guys they liked, and playing stupid songs on the radio for hours on end. Vick and I were grown men, thirty-plus, and here we were hanging out with girls around twenty. Furthermore, we were at their mercy; riding in their car and adhering to their agenda.

There was nothing to do in Atlanta. We wasted a few hours in a mall, and then drove back to Athens with another full day to kill. Vick approached me and said, in his characteristically calm manner, "T, we've gotta get away from these chicks. They're getting on my nerves. Let's get back to the RV as soon as possible." I agreed. We convinced the girls to drive us back to Asheville to rendezvous with the rest of the band.

During the ride, I reprimand Crystal for her horrible driving. She had one hand draped over the bottom of the steering wheel, was blasting dance music and taking turns way too fast. I said, "Look, you need to pull it together and start driving better, or just let us out. This isn't how we wanna die."

"Okay, Grandpa," she said. Ah, the generation gap.

Back in Asheville, the band was camped out at the RV repair place, waiting for the Travesty. The shop was waiting on parts, so there was nothing to do but stand around in the parking lot and throw a Frisbee. I must say, my Frisbee chops really started coming together.

When the part finally arrived and the work was done, a gruff mechanic in his fifties walked over and asked, "All right, time to settle out. Which one of y'all is the big dick around here?" I stepped forward.

"It is I you refer to," I said, pleased to be the recipient of the title, even if it was figuratively intended. He handed me an invoice. *Big dick,* in RV repair parlance, meant *the guy who's paying me.* The big dick broke out his wallet full of high-interest credit cards and rolled the entrepreneurial dice, one more time.

We did a crappy show in Oxford, Mississippi, then headed back down to New Orleans to play Tipitina's Uptown. Tipitina's was a fixture of the national music scene, a hallowed institution that fostered great legends like Professor Longhair and Dr. John. But as luck would have it, we were returning to New Orleans during what was shaping up to be the worst hurricane to hit the Gulf Coast in a hundred years. Meteorologists speculated that if the hurricane arrived at the peak of its fury, the entire French Quarter—which sits well below sea level, would be completely wiped out. On the bright side, we would have a compelling excuse if the show bombed!

There were no hotel rooms in the deal that night, so we would be riding out whatever maelstrom Mother Nature might unleash on us from within the confines of the Travesty, which was hunkered down in a grocery store parking lot near the club. I had visions of our unreliable monstrosity converting into a submarine and floating down St. Charles Street, a combination of the amphibious contraption from *The Spy Who Loved Me* and the Partridge Family tour bus, as the deluged Quarter became a new version of the city of Venice.

Through great luck, the focal point of the storm missed New Orleans, and the city suffered only minimal damage. The gig was a joke, as people chose to stay barricaded indoors, rather than risk their lives to hear some funk/rock band from California. We made it out of the city and continued on to Baton Rouge, for a show at Chelsea's. Local businesses were boarded up, their windows covered with` crisscrossed masking tape. Most people had fled town, yet to return, making it a show that didn't need to happen. We played well despite the empty room. Touring musicians, keep this in mind: You don't just have to worry about your vehicle breaking down, other bands stealing your draw, or clubs double-booking and canceling you with short notice… no, you also have to worry about hurricanes.

While driving across Louisiana, we hit yet another automotive snag, and this time it wasn't the Travesty's fault. I was sleeping in the back bedroom when I heard a loud *thud* against the back of the vehicle. I walked to the front cabin and asked the driver, Big Job, if he sensed a problem. He said no, and the Mayor suggested we turn on the rear camera to make sure everything was okay. When Big Job did this we could see sparks shooting up from the trailer, leaving a wake of glowing embers as we motored down the freeway. The trailer was completely lopsided, scraping against the asphalt as we continued at full speed. I took a cue from the Neal Page playbook[180], laughing out loud at the absurdity of it all.

---

[180] One of the most classic scenes from *Planes, Trains and Automobiles* is when Steve Martin stands on the freeway, cackling with John Candy as his rental car becomes engulfed in flames.

Big Job pulled to the side of the road and we hopped out to survey the damage. One of the trailer's wheel wells had popped off while we were driving, and somehow had generated enough momentum to hurl *forward*, defying physics while slashing a chunk out of the Travesty's fiberglass frame. After this, the tire itself had popped off, leaving the exposed rotor to scrape directly against the road. The rotor was now worn to a nub, completely shot. We slept right there on the side of the freeway, and in the morning I called the nearest town, Crowley, in search of a repair facility willing to help us.

After a few hours a ruddy character with an infectious Cajun drawl showed up. He introduced himself as Mick Garvey as he hopped out of his ridiculous tow truck, which looked capable of hauling a small aircraft carrier. Crowley had been ravaged by the hurricane; laid to waste. Mick said there wouldn't be anyone working for the next couple days, so we were sort of screwed. He could tow us, but that was as much as he could do. I pleaded with the Crowley native to help us find the parts and get the repair done, so we could keep touring. He said he'd try, and he towed our trailer to his boss's yard.

Crowley was indeed a disaster area. Buildings were caved in, trees were blown over and scattered in the road like random toothpicks, and everywhere you looked there were smashed windows and overturned cars. I'd never seen anything like it in my life. Once we reached the yard, we parked the Travesty, and Mick directed us to an area in the back. A mean junkyard dog lapped green water from a corroded pond. I asked what the liquid was and Mick said, "It's a combination of coolant, old dirty water and some other poisonous shit."

"That can't be good for the dog, can it?"

"Ain't killed him yet. Just makes him more pissed off… which makes him a better guard dog."

Mick dropped our mutilated remains of a trailer down next to a couple other wrecks, one of which was a new Mustang. Mick saw Big Job and me eyeing the car, and offered some background on it:

"Guy that owned that one was a drug dealer. Hit a tree dead-on. Sonny Bono style. Was killed instantly." Big Job and I shot each other a scheming glance. *Drug dealer, huh?* Mick smiled, reading our minds.

"There ain't no money back there. I already looked. You think I'd be fuckin' around in this junkyard if that trunk had been full of cash? Me n' my wife would be sippin' cocktails on a beach in Mexico."

Mick managed to get our trailer all fixed up that night, God bless him, and we split for Austin. The show in Austin went well. My brother Collin and his fiancé Stacey were in town, so we partied after the gig, and I crashed in their hotel. The next stop was Tucson, at a spot called Plush. Pierce Piedmont, a drummer from L.A., came out to meet us and audition for the drum chair. Pierce looked like a *bobblehead* doll: narrow shoulders supporting a large, freely swiveling cranium.

It took all of five minutes to realize Pierce was not our man. Wildman was given the task of breaking the news: "Well, Pierce, thanks for making the drive. You've got a lot of determination, but it's not gonna work out. Sorry." We helped Pierce pack his drums, and he hit the I-10 back to Los Angeles. *You've got to keep on pushin' for what you want... You've got to keep on pushin' for what you need.* We still had no replacement for Drew. This was becoming drummer hell.

Some friends of the band threw a party in Fresno, and we played one of our best shows ever. The crowd was decked out in disco costumes, and the band laid down the funk with energy and soul. It was always great to play for people you knew. Even if it was only ten or fifteen friends, who had brought some of *their* friends along also, it changed the whole vibe. As a performer, you felt *loved...* and everybody needs love. We continued our California run with shows in San Diego, Santa Barbara and Santa Cruz.

It was impossible to have a serious relationship while living on the road, so I kept my options open—had some fun, while enjoying friendships mixed with a bit of romance. I've been asked, usually by men who are settled down (and whose wives are not in earshot), if life on the road as a touring musician is anything like the way it is depicted in film and pop folklore. The answer is yes, it is. Life on the road as a touring musician is exactly the way it is depicted in film and pop folklore. It's a tough grind for sure, but there are women, and then there are more women... if you're into that. At a holiday party one family member bluntly asked one time, "How's the (action) out there, man?" I explained that being a touring, single male musician is like being a traveling salesman. The goal is to establish *repeat customers in multiple markets.*

Once you've built a portfolio of accounts, you must tend to each of them from time to time—put in the occasional maintenance call, keep the lines of communication open. Otherwise, you roll into town unannounced, hoping to service an existing account, only to find that it has been closed without your knowledge. The customer has moved on, or in the musician's case, she's decided to take back Dylan, her ex-boyfriend, with his anger management issues, numerous piercings and tats, and part-time bouncing gig at a local dive bar. The musician plays his trump card: "I'm only here 'til tomorrow, then I'm off to Laramie, Wyoming." She counters: "I know, but Dylan's been really sweet to me lately." The musician, like the traveling salesman, realizes Dylan possesses scant capacity for genuine *sweetness*, but through proximity and accessibility wages an effective war of attrition that the musician, by virtue of his transient existence, is destined to lose. He also recognizes that the well has run dry, and thus re-focuses his energy on scouting new leads.

After winding through the mountains along Highway 17, we merged onto 280 towards San Francisco. The Travesty would not grace the great City by the Bay on this day, however. The monolithic splendor of the Transamerica Building would not be visible through her side windows, as we motored our way up the Peninsula. No, the Travesty sputtered to a stop on the freeway, close to San Jose City College.

I was not in the right frame of mind to deal with this latest contingency. I had an emotional meltdown, walking along the 280 as semi trucks roared past me with only inches to spare. I picked up a large piece of wood and started smashing it against the ground. I cursed the motor home gods with everything my lungs could muster. The guys in the band approached, sensing my anguish.

"Are you okay, T?"

I was not okay. I was livid. Why was this happening? What terrible things had I done in my life to deserve such a predicament? If God was watching over us all, cutting us a break every now and then, wasn't I about due? How much ill fortune would I have to endure, before finally spotting a flicker of light at the end of the JBS tunnel?

I now offer this timeline of events between 10/17/02 and 10/23/02:

10/18
1:15 pm: Leave Santa Cruz for San Francisco.
2 pm: Travesty breaks down on 17 freeway, near San Jose Airport.
2:15 pm: Park Travesty along residential street near San Jose City College.
3 pm: Tow truck arrives.
3:30 pm: Mayor and Big Job jump in a cab to get a rental U-Haul for our gear, so we won't miss the show in San Francisco that night.
4 pm: Tow truck leaves with the Travesty on its massive flatbed, heads for a repair shop in San Jose.

4:15 pm: The Mayor and Big Job return with U-Haul truck, we hitch the trailer to it, and they leave for San Francisco.

4:30 pm: Friends Vince and Gina LaForte show up on the scene, ready to drive me and Chase to San Francisco.

4:35 pm: Vince, noticing that the tow truck had uprooted a street sign that says "Permit Only Parking," snags the large piece of city-owned property and throws it in his trunk as a joke.

4:36 pm: Cop car follows us and pulls us over near Bascom Avenue.

4:37 pm: Officer asks Vince if he has the sign.

4:38 pm: Vince answers "yes," then retrieves it from his trunk. Officer decides not to arrest Vince.

4:40 pm: We drive past neighbors who ratted Vince out, and give a sarcastic wave to express our appreciation.

6:00 pm: Arrive at Boom Boom Room in San Francisco.

7:00 pm: After setting up gear, we can't decide what to do with the next five hours.

7:00-11:30 pm: Stand in front of Boom Boom Room and do nothing, other than wolfing down pad Thai from House of Noodles.

11:45 pm: Play first set as kids filter in from Sound Tribe Sector Nine show at the Fillmore.

1 am: I am approached by a tall, large-breasted brunette I have previously kept at bay during visits to town.

1-2 am: DJ and rapper do annoying set, thinning crowd considerably.

2:30 am: Second set goes better than the first. I'm enjoying playing the real B-3 organ.

4:30 am: Finish show.

5 am: Leave with Woo and Jersey Joe, hole up at Red Roof Inn by the airport.

10/19

12 pm: Wake up. Eat crappy meat raviolis at Leanne's diner.

1-8 pm: Do nothing. Stare at TV while Giants beat up Angels in Game One of World Series.

9:30 pm: Arrive at Boom Boom Room for second night of STS9 after shows. Stand on street, as usual.

9:45 pm: Watch friend Lipp get slapped in the face by a belligerent homeless woman. Listen to Lipp say "Bitch, you touch me again and I'll knock out your remaining tooth."

12 am: Play first set. It goes much better than previous night. Digging the B-3. People watching are so close they slobber on me.

2 am: DJ and rapper again thin out crowd with their jive-ass beats.

3 am: Second set. This is Drew's last hurrah, his final GFC performance. Vick pukes from food poisoning as we take the stage, and decides to duck out... with a chick. We never see him again that night.

3:30 am: Some yahoo wants to rap onstage. He starts rhyming into my ear while I'm taking an organ solo. It takes every peaceful bone in my body to resist the temptation to head butt him. I decide I'd rather have him get up and drop his *mad flava* on the crowd than continue to regale me with alcohol breath, so I bring him up. He follows his cliché-ridden rap by pulling out a harmonica, which is in a different key than the song we're playing. This doesn't deter him.

5 am: Take off back to hotel.

10/20

2 pm: Go back to Boom Boom Room to pack up our gear and load trailer, which is sitting on the street, chained to a lamppost.

3:30 pm: Having loaded thousands of dollars of gear—the prized tools of our trade—we drive off, leaving the trailer sitting there in plain view. The Travesty is undergoing surgery in San Jose, so we have no choice.

5-10 pm: Wander around the Haight, stumbling into a cramped pub to watch the Giants/Angels Game Two. While pouring a beer directly in front of me, the bartender gets in an altercation and is fired by his manager. In a burst of originality, the bartender screams "Fuck you... I quit!"

10 pm: Go to Todd's crib near the Presidio, nibble on burnt pizza crusts and drink red wine. Watch a bad movie starring James Gandolfini and Robert Redford. Carry out another installment of the *Todd Sherman Financial Bail-Out*.

11 pm: Drive back to Red Roof Inn and do absolutely nothing.

10/21

9 am: Wake, shower and drive to club to retrieve trailer, which, God willing, will still be there and intact.

10 am: Stop at bank, where I learn that Gary Klein has obtained a sheriff's writ and cleaned out my savings account, per a small claims lawsuit he has somehow managed to win against me, back in San Diego.

10:30 am: Speculate with Woo about possible legal, non-violent methods of exacting revenge against Gary. Come up with nothing promising.

11 am: Attempt, with no success, to remove a certain lock from the trailer—a lock the Mayor has dubbed the *iron cockblock*. This lock is designed to prevent criminals from stealing your stuff while it sits on a random street in San Francisco.

1 pm: Summoned from the sanctuary of the Red Roof Inn, the Mayor and Big Job arrive and proceed to remove the iron cockblock.

1:30 pm: Hitch trailer to Todd's friend's truck, and drive down to San Jose to drop trailer off at the RV repair shop. I follow in a rented Saturn.

3:30 pm: Leave trailer, head back to San Francisco.

5 pm: Eat burritos, stand in line at the post office in Burlingame.

6 pm: Take a nap at the Red Roof.

8-11 pm: Wander streets of San Francisco, eat a slice of mushroom pizza, scour the jazz room at Amoeba Records on Haight Street.

11:30 pm: Return to Red Roof.

10/22

Watch the World Series. Big Job's birthday surprise is a case of Sierra Nevada and a bottle of Jagermeister.

1 pm: Spend entire day trying to find a rental van, so we can get to Eugene for two heavily promoted SCI aftershows. Come up empty, have to cancel the shows. Resign myself to a couple more days at the Red Roof.

10/23

My thirty-third birthday.

6 pm: Sit in the room with the Mayor and Big Job. We get hammered in celebratory birthday fashion while watching *Austin Powers: Goldmember*. I laugh out loud during the rap video scene, when Mini Me sports a do-rag and drops a domino.

   As you can see, the events of these several days involve little that has to do with the performance of music. This is the real road experience. The hours you spend actually making music are but a small fraction of your time. Most of your days and nights are spent driving from one place to another, and hanging out in motels and hotels—unless you're crashing with some dude named Jimbo, his girlfriend Maya and their four dogs and three cats.

GROWN MEN ARGUING OVER VIDEO GAMES

The JBS was opening my ears to new musical idioms, including techno/electronica. I'd formed a friendship with Steve Molitz, keyboardist of the Los Angeles-based quartet Particle, who was incorporating techno concepts in the band's jam-rock approach. Steve appreciated my jazz background, and I appreciated his savvy with synthesizers. I wasn't much of a synth expert. I'd owned them for twenty years and had learned to get around on them somewhat, but I wasn't a natural. I was and still am more of a player than a gear wizard.

Particle, Sound Tribe Sector Nine and Project Logic were all bands incorporating electronica in their live shows. I jumped on the bandwagon, coaxing classic analog sounds from my Korg MS-2000, learning enough about programming to design my own textures. The jam band audience loved the mixture of funk and techno, a sound being used even by bluegrass groups like The String Cheese Incident.

Just as jazz had resonated with youthful hipsters back in the mid-Twentieth Century, the JBS served the same demographic of its era: young people with a sense of culture and artistic adventure, coming out to listen, dance and socialize.

Without any fanfare, Drew removed his personal items from the Travesty, said his goodbyes and was out of our lives. We had decided on a new drummer from Baltimore, Ben Carson, who'd received a glowing recommendation from some friends in a Colorado-based band. Todd Sherman flew Ben out to San Francisco, picked Ben up and brought him to the Travesty, which was repaired and road-ready. Ben was black, medium height and had dreadlocks. He was kind of a cross between Bob Marley and Adam Sandler. I think, looking back, that I was attracted and committed to the idea of having a funky African-American drummer in the band, as I was leery of traveling around with a crew full of only white dudes.

We were excited about Ben's arrival. The last month with Drew had been a drag; we knew he was leaving, he knew he was leaving, and everybody in the audience seemed to know. Still, I appreciated the fact that he gave notice and then stayed on long enough for me to find a replacement. He handled the matter professionally.

The first show with Ben was in Chico, an after-party for The String Cheese Incident. We rehearsed prior to the gig, and the first tune we worked on was *First Team All-Planet*, a simple funk jam with a few rhythmic punches. It wasn't a song anyone expected Ben to have problems learning, so I was taken aback when he butchered his way through the first couple passes. This guy was supposed to fill Drew Reed's shoes. He was supposed to ease stress, not compound it.

I stopped the band to go over the trouble spots a few times. Try after try, Ben couldn't get the hits right. Jeffrey and I shot each other a concerned glance. *Oh shit. What if this guy can't play?* Ben shrugged it off with a smile, assuring us it was "all good," but Woo and the Mayor, standing in the corner, telepathically sent me a message: *If he can't play this simple stuff, how's he going to deal with your complex, twenty-minute compositions?*

Ironically, Ben played his finest GFC show that same evening. Not knowing the songs, he just went for broke, jamming his way through the gig with all sense of form and structure thrown out the window. After the show, it seemed like there might be hope. Wildman said "Well, he's got good energy, and once he learns the music and executes consistently, he'll be fine." The key words there are *executes consistently.* Those two words would become my nightmare for the next entire year. I didn't know it then, but Ben would be the first of a string of failed drummers, a parade of flailing aspirants to the permanent GFC drum chair. This fruitless fiasco would not be held within the confines of a private rehearsal space, but would instead run its embarrassing course as an ongoing public spectacle, on the stages of some of America's finest small venues.

During the next couple months Ben continued to struggle with the music. To make things worse, he also failed to connect with the group on a social level. I got along well with him myself—he wasn't a musical heavyweight, but I found him to be a nice, easygoing guy. I enjoyed drinking beers and hanging out with Ben. He wasn't complex or moody, just the kind of normal guy you could shoot the breeze with and have a laugh or two.

Wildman didn't respect Ben musically, questioned his work ethic,[181] and didn't relate to him on any level. When the drummer started blowing important shows by playing poorly, things really got dark. We made such a pitiful showing at the Great American Music Hall in San Francisco that our longtime supporters, Sunset Promotions, put a moratorium on working with us—a moratorium that was never lifted.

We fumbled our way through another String Cheese after-party in Berkeley, where Kyle Hollingsworth happened to show up. I found myself apologizing to the SCI keyboardist after our set, but he said, "No, I dug it. You guys have a natural jamming rapport that I wish we had in our group." That surprised me, and I wasn't sure I completely believed it, but I accepted the compliment. Kyle was always supportive of my groups, and seemed to admire my playing.

We headed north to Ashland, Oregon, where the Travesty again proceeded to die. Todd had just shelled out five grand to a repair shop in San Jose, on top of the original down payment, the monthly payments, the exorbitant registration cost, and the thousands of dollars already lost in various repairs. Throw in the continual hundred dollars it cost to fill the gas tank, plus another forty or fifty for propane, and you're talking about one of the great vehicular money pits of all time.

After a two-night run in Hood River, our next scheduled stop was John's Alley in Moscow, Idaho; but this show would not happen. When we piled in to leave Hood River, the Travesty *would not start.*

---

[181] There could be no arguing this point. Wildman was right on the money.

This time she was going to have to be towed, and we would miss at least the Moscow date.

As we stood weathering the harsh cold of a Hood River street corner, figuring out our next move, I came up with a plan: Big Job would stay in Hood River to oversee the repair, while the Mayor, Ben, Chase, Wildman and I would throw our gear into a rental van and high-tail it to Missoula for our Halloween show. What about Vick, our percussionist? *Vick would have to return to San Diego until further notice.* I hated to do it. Didn't want to do it. I had no choice.

There wouldn't be room for five of us, soundman included, and all our gear in a passenger van. Vick became emotional as I broke the news. He felt betrayed, and I understood why. I felt really bad about the situation. I was the one who had brought him in. I knew his absence was going to create a musical void, also.[182]

Wildman had wanted Vick out of the band for some time, but I'd resisted the suggestion that we scale down to a four-piece. I felt Vick was making an important musical contribution, but Chase agreed with Wildman. Now, they would have their wish. I don't want to put it all on them, however. From a business standpoint, I thought it was a good idea to downsize.

Big Job stayed with the Travesty, Vick flew back to San Diego, and the rest of us continued our valiant pursuit of the dream. Once the beast was repaired, Big Job took a bus back to Santa Barbara. He also was now out of a gig. We'd lost our percussionist and our road crew, all because of that God-forsaken lemon. Despite all this I planned to persevere until GFC was a successful band and business. Nothing was going to stop me. It was about much more than the music or the scene. It was a personal mission to vindicate my past failures and validate my life in the arts, for once and for all.

After the Missoula gig, which we did luckily make, we continued to Bozeman, then Salt Lake City. It was hard to play with Ben. He only learned half the tunes, and you didn't know from one show to the next if he was going to deliver or flounder. We weren't an amateur band on their first tour. We'd logged many well-attended, sometimes critically

---

[182] Looking back, letting Steve go was one of the biggest mistakes I made in GFC—one decision I really regret. Sorry, Steve. Wish I could do that one over again.

praised performances, and there was a reputation to uphold. With every passing show, that reputation was eroding. Crumbling.

I hit my breaking point in Salt Lake City. I couldn't bear getting onstage in a nice venue like the Zephyr for a performance most likely going to be terrible. I'd been drinking a bit more than usual, retreating into the old handle of Captain for lack of a healthier form of therapy... but I *really* tied one on at the Zephyr that night. Armed with my drink of choice after sound check, I'd barricaded myself in the green room with a female friend from Ogden, and we proceeded to *fine-tune the set list*. I was three sheets to the wind when I hit the stage to begin the performance—perhaps the only time in my life when that's been the case.[183] The show licked elephant balls, as I suspected it would, and it would have tanked just as much had I been sober. That's how bad it was; it didn't matter if the band was loaded or not. We couldn't manage a decent night to save our lives. We were crusaders of crap, Ben our proud captain.

Word was getting out in the scene: Drew was no longer in the band, nor was Vick. The associations with KDTU and Greyboy All-Stars were gone. Our new drummer wasn't cutting it, and we were limping around with the same material we'd been milking for the last year. It was not a glorious moment in GFC history.

Morale was at an all-time low. I decided the Travesty was *through*. It had failed time and again, and only a fool would continue to throw money at that giant turd on wheels. After the tour I swung back through Hood River, paid for the repairs and picked up the vehicle, and drove it to Woo's ranch. There, I left it for dead, still littered with the personal items of a dozen band and crew members. Inside, it was a disaster zone. It smelled awful, too.

Chase, Wildman and I were getting on each other's nerves, bickering about the drum chair, whining specifically about Ben. We were already feeling the backlash of clubs and promoters that didn't want to work with us anymore. I heard through the grapevine that people were saying GFC was *Drew's project*—he'd been the reason for our early success. This steamed me.

The band's relationship with Rob Sarno was also souring. He wasn't getting us the choice bookings anymore, and claimed the clubs were low-balling because we'd had personnel changes. Also, Rob was

---

[183] I have definitely *ended* a few drunk, however!

deriding me for missing shows when the Travesty would break down. Rob went on to lament our lack of merchandise and production: "When I first started working with you guys, you had a crew, you had merchandise… you had your shit together. What happened?"

What could I say? Yes, people had left, people had been fired, vehicles had failed and been retired, shows had been missed, shows had been played poorly, and morale was bad. There was no money, no savings, nothing to fall back on. We were scraping by week to week. It was all true.

Rob stuck with the band through those grim times, and the band did somewhat salvage its reputation through sheer will and persistence. We stayed on the road the rest of the year, doing whatever we could to nurture relationships with club owners, promoters and fans, hoping things would somehow turn around. It took a lot of courage to hang in there, and the challenge brought the band's nucleus (Me, Wildman and Chase) closer together. We started to develop a collective musical personality—our *sound.* Circumstances had forced us to be empathetic with each other off the stage, and this started to benefit us *on* the stage.

There's no hiding your personal relationships with band mates once you take the stage. The audience quickly zeros in on the dynamic between members of a group. One reason people connect with certain bands is because those bands convey a spirit of camaraderie. They look like they enjoy playing music together. Listeners feed off this symbiosis, and they get excited when a group is really *talking* to each other through the language of music. As a player, it's not something you can fake. If you aren't getting along with the people in your band, you will communicate that to your audience; and they will not like it.

I knew Ben would not be making the return trip to the West Coast after his Christmas break in Baltimore, but what I didn't know was that Ben wouldn't just dissipate into the ether of GFC's past—no, he would go down in a blaze of disreputable glory, perpetrating a ruse that surprised even me.

In early December, we played a club in Fairfax, California called 19 Broadway. Kurt Kimmelman, a blonde, long-haired guy in his early thirties, promoted at 19 Broadway, and was an old buddy of Woo's from the JBS. He had an apartment above the club, where musicians and their friends could hang out, smoke pot, drink, eat and eventually sleep.

Through frequent visits to the club, Kurt and I had become friends. He was an acquaintance of Buckethead, the bizarre, towering guitarist who always wore a mask on his face and a KFC bucket on his head. I was intrigued by Buckethead, a jaw-dropping virtuoso who never revealed his identity to the public; I would ask Kurt various questions about him, usually over cocktails after the gig.

During this particular visit, Ben allowed Wildman and Chase to borrow his Sony Playstation. Somehow the pair managed to either break the Playstation, or, as they would insist, it simply stopped working. Whatever the case, Ben did not take the news well. He demanded that they buy him a brand new Playstation. Neither Wildman nor Chase was in a financial position to replace it, nor were they of the opinion that it was beyond repair.

I was not tickled that the other three grown men in my band were embroiled in a dispute over a video game machine, but nonetheless found myself in the middle of it. I was managing the band's money, and if a brand new Playstation was to be bought, it was coming out of the GFC survival fund.

After great deliberation, Ben agreed to let the other two pay for a repair rather than replacement. This went down as the tour was wrapping in Seattle. Chase cut a check to Ben for fifty dollars. When Chase got his bank statement, he saw that the check he'd written for fifty dollars had cleared for *one hundred and fifty*. The bank confirmed that somebody had written a "1" in front of the "50." I called Ben and mentioned that it's a crime to doctor a check. He insisted it was the work of some dishonest person in his father's law firm. I was insulted that he expected me to believe this. I still owed him a bit of money from the tour, but since I had to drop a big, unexpected chunk of cash to ship his drums back to the East Coast, I struck a deal with him: *I'm flying all your stuff home on my nickel, and I'll talk Chase out of pressing charges against you for doctoring his check. After that, we're even.* Ben agreed, and it was the last time we ever spoke. He was just one of numerous guys I'd gotten along well with on the road, but who didn't work out in the project.

Wildman and Chase flew home to spend Christmas with their families, and I began driving the rental van back to Hood River to meet Woo. It was a peaceful trip. I sorted through the chaos of the previous few months, and took in the sublime sights of the Northwestern landscape. I returned the van, grabbed a snack at Taco Time and picked up a coffee to go, hopped in Woo's car and we headed back to California.

Woo and I had a nice friendship throughout those Living Large and GFC years. His world view was more left-leaning and iconoclastic than my own, and we weren't exactly cut from the same cloth in terms of our appearance or background, but we had a bond; a musical and intellectual connection, and a shared sense of brotherly affection. You just know who your good friends are in life, and even though I rarely see or hear from the guy anymore, I'll always consider him one of mine.

I spent most of the break at Anne's house, resting, recuperating and writing. Writing was fulfilling me in ways music did not. With pen in hand, or fingers perched over keypad, I wasn't at the mercy of others. I didn't need anyone's help or approval. Managing and musically guiding Global Funk Council was a taxing job, requiring endless troubleshooting, analyzing, future planning and creative financing. Writing was an escape.

It also helped me make sense of the past. As I took inventory of the events of my life, from pleasant boyhood adventures to the struggles of early adulthood, I started to see patterns of behavior. Well-entrenched notions of who I was as a person were not always consistent with the decisions I had made over the years, or with the way I had generally lived my life. In other words, by writing about my life, I discovered, to some extent at least, who I really was, not who I *thought* I was.

Before I could begin another year of jam band madness, two obstacles laid in my path: I had no drummer and I had no vehicle. Without either one, the show could not go on. I talked to a young drummer from San Diego… we'll call him Rain Man… about joining the band. Rain Man was a protégé of my friend Tim McMahon. Tim assured me Rain Man was a very gifted individual. I met up with him to hear him play, and Tim was right, the kid had talent. After a chat with the new prospect, however, I became unconvinced Rain Man possessed the basic social skills needed to sit in a van with four other grown men, drive from state to state for months on end, and survive the general rigors of the touring life. The guy seemed to be barely functional in a social sense, and I wouldn't have the luxury of stopping so he could watch Judge Wopner re-runs every afternoon, nor the time to allow him to drive in herky-jerky circles in front of a Vegas casino. I needed Rhythm Man, not Rain Man.

ICHABOD

Rain Man's last-minute bailout from the running left me with all of four hours to secure a drummer for the upcoming tour, which included a lengthy run through Utah and Colorado. Nowhere else to turn, I fumbled through an old notebook and found a few drummers' phone numbers scribbled down. I began calling them randomly. The only guy who answered was a Los Angeles native we'll call Ichabod. The conversation went something like this:

"Hey, Ichabod, this is Anthony from Global Funk Council. I need a drummer for this tour. The pay is lousy. The band is really good, though. Think you'll have fun. Oh yeah—we leave immediately. I would need to pick you up in about four hours."

"Count me in. Let me give you directions."

Next thing I knew, I was pulling up in front of a storage building near an overpass for the 405 freeway, somewhere in the San FernandoValley. Ichabod invited me inside his storage unit/living space, and I stood there for ten minutes, watching him eat a bowl of grits with strawberry sauce. The guy was about six-seven, had short, wiry hair and thick, black-rimmed glasses. He looked like a throwback to 1942. We packed his drums and hit the road.

I had no idea what to make of Ichabod. We didn't know each other at all. I just started playing him our stuff, giving him the chance to learn at least a few songs before our first gig, which of course was the following day. Ichabod seemed confident he'd be able to handle any music we threw at him. I wasn't quite so sure, but I appreciated his pluck. After stopping in Fresno to grab a bite and catch up with my friend Gina LaForte, we continued driving to Santa Cruz, where we stopped for the night.

After only a few hours of sleep, we rose to face what was going to be an incredibly long, busy day. I had been approved for a loan to buy a new fifteen-seat passenger van, and the dealer was in Roseville, not far from Sacramento. Ichabod and I would pick up the new van, then he would follow me in my van to Durham, just outside of Chico. We would pick up Chase at Woo's parents' house and hustle to Lake Tahoe for a show that evening. Wildman was flying into Reno, and made arrangements to meet us at the venue, Sierra Vista.

This plan, as conviluted as it sounds, would have worked out fine had it not been for one thing: it was the day after Christmas, and traffic between Santa Cruz and Sacramento was worse than anything, including my two years in L.A., that I had ever experienced. It took eight hours to get to Roseville, which under normal circumstances would take three. The van transaction took another hour, and then we hauled up to Durham to get Chase and the equipment.

By the time we were on the road for Tahoe, we were way behind schedule, and I was worried we would miss the gig. It began snowing, and traffic was still pretty thick. I called the club several times to alert them to our situation. Of course, a huge crowd turned out at the club, and the manager began to panic when we still hadn't arrived by 10 pm. I was driving like a madman to make it, and we had just reached the Highway 89 turnoff, mere miles from the venue, when the call came: "They've cancelled the show."

Everybody was silently angry with me over the matter, as if it was my fault that the traffic was horrendous, or that it started to snow. I had found a drummer in L.A. with only a few hours to spare, left San Diego and picked him up, then driven straight to Northern California, slept for a few hours, hopped back in the car and sat in traffic for eight hours. Then I bought a thirty-five thousand dollar vehicle using my own credit, caravanned to Durham, removed the benches from the new van, loaded it up, and began driving to Tahoe, only to be the scapegoat when the plan—a questionable one to begin with—did not succeed.

We turned around and headed to Reno, where we picked up Wildman. The next show was in Park City, and it was not a throw-away. We were opening for Michael Franti at Harry O's. Ichabod was frantically trying to learn the songs, headphones glued to his wiry mop. We pulled into Park City with at least a little confidence that he'd get through the show. He had the work ethic, at least.

This hope was crushed the moment Ichabod sat behind his drums and started to play. At that moment, Wildman, Chase and I looked at each other and we knew: this was going to be a horrible night in our musical lives. The new drummer didn't have a clue what to do. Often, an opening set is of little consequence, the crowd slow to arrive for the headliner. As luck would have it on this night, the show was sold out, and Harry O's was already at full capacity when we took the stage. There were over a thousand people there.

In a musician's career, there are so many gigs where you play for nobody; nights when the band might be on fire, or you might personally be in the zone, but nobody gives a damn. Then, there is that rare occasion when the crowd is a massive, rabid throng of crazy fans, pressing up to the stage in anticipation of the show, but you realize you aren't prepared to satisfy their needs. You have been set up to fail, and it's too late to do anything about it.

The moment when I walked out on that stage, to play music with Ichabod in front of a thousand-plus Michael Franti fans, was surreal. He might as well have been playing another song and another tempo than the rest of us. There was no correlation between what we were doing and what he was doing. He was just cluelessly hammering away, trying to generate some energy. Chase and I took turns soloing over one-chord funk jams, hoping the audience wouldn't realize we were completely out of sorts, winging the whole performance. The agony ended quickly enough, but the damage was done. We'd made fools of ourselves, desecrating whatever was left of the good GFC name.

If all this wasn't bad enough, we were heading from there to Denver to play opposite Garaj Mahal, for a big New Year's Eve party. If there was any band in the JBS that was musically frightening, any band where each of the members was an accomplished virtuoso in his own right, it was Garaj Mahal. If you were doing a show with them, you wanted to be running on all cylinders. Forget cylinders—we were having problems with the starter. I was praying we could make it through the New Year's gig without completely humiliating ourselves.

Fortunately, we were friends with Garaj Mahal. Chase was Fareed Haque's former star student, and I was good friends with Eric Levy, the keyboard player. The night didn't go so bad. We set up on opposite stages and took turns doing sets. Chase and I hopped up with the Garaj guys and did some nice jamming. Eric Levy bowed out during the late set, having gotten sick all of a sudden, so I finished the show for him. In the end, the Garaj guys were supportive of our efforts, despite the lack of groove plaguing the band.

We continued with Ichabod for another month, including shows in new markets like Albuquerque; but he knew, as did we, that he wasn't going to cut the gig. He was a good guy—smart, down-to-earth, and easy to be around. Had he been more musically accomplished, everyone would have been happy to keep him. We dropped Ichabod in Berkeley at a friend's house, then made preparations to pick up our next drummer victim: Brad Wood, an old friend of Wildman's from Boston.

Brad had been in a popular East Coast jam band, which folded due to financial hardship. He was looking for a new project, so I flew him out to San Francisco, and met him for the first time at the Boom Boom Room, hours before our first show together. Wildman had high hopes for Brad, who'd been one of the bright young stars of the Berklee music program.

The show was terrific. Brad played great, Wildman connecting with him in a way he never had with the band's previous drummers. There was a look of joy on his face from the beginning of the show to the end, and I was having a blast too. For once, all my gear was working properly—I had the piano, the MS-2000 synth, the Rhodes, and the club's Hammond B-3. The house sound was excellent, also. These are the nights that make it worth it; the times when the sound is good, the music is good, the crowd is good, and if you walk across the street to the House of Noodles,[184] the food is good.

We headed east for a long run through Colorado, Utah and Wyoming. This included shows in Vail, Keystone, Steamboat Springs, Aspen, Salt Lake City, Ogden, Jackson Hole, Denver, Crested Butte, Dillon, Ft. Collins, Grand Junction, Durango and Winter Park. In the middle of March, Denver suffered one of its worst snowstorms of the previous hundred years. We had a few days off, and were staying in a budget hotel a few miles from downtown. The storm hit, and we got snowed in for three days. The hotel ran out of food, and all the nearby establishments were closed down. You couldn't drive anywhere because snow was blocking every road.

We found ourselves in an environment similar to a minimum security prison. Chase and I debated whether to share our last packet of Swiss Miss hot chocolate mix, or hawk it in the lobby to the highest bidder. We would have gotten a nice price for it. Since we couldn't go anywhere or do anything, the four of us immersed ourselves in the writing process, and it wound up being the most creatively productive three or four days in the band's short history. I wrote a handful of new songs and pieced together a huge composition called *Space*—a through-composed piece with a dozen different sections and themes—a funk/rock symphony. Wildman and Chase also worked hard on new music.

Once we finally got out of Denver, the tour took us through Kansas, Missouri, Illinois and Indiana. We did a two-night run in Chicago at The Boulevard, and then traveled south to Bloomington, Chase's hometown, for a show at joint called Uncle Fester's. After the gig, attended by Chase's family and old friends, we set up shop in his parents' garage loft, a small structure on a beautiful piece of property in rural Bloomington. We rehearsed for a few days, and I contributed more original songs to the GFC book, including *Rub* and *Spank*, a pair of funky instrumentals, and *Charlatan's Web*, an involved vocal composition with unmistakable echoes of Phish.

Chase's family (his mother, sister and stepfather) was delighted to have him home, and extended their hospitality to the rest of us. At night, we had dinner and all watched movies. I also met Chase's

---

[184] Now it's called the house of something else, but they still serve Asian cuisine.

biological father, who lived nearby on a golf course. He was an entertaining storyteller, and told me a good one about Bobby Knight, the legendary coach of Indiana's men's basketball team. Chase's dad had been at a breakfast for IU alumni, and saw Coach Knight sitting at a table with an assistant, eating. He walked over and said, "Coach, I don't mean to interrupt your breakfast..." Knight glared at him and said, "Then don't." Chase's dad hung in there, explaining that he represented a certain charity, and was wondering if Coach Knight could help. The tenor changed immediately. Suddenly Knight was interested and engaged.

"I'll be happy to help out, however I can." The story illustrated the well-known extremes of Knight's personality: he could be a gruff jerk, and he could also be a generous, great guy.

We made our way to the East Coast for a two-week run. I allowed Brad to drive one night, waking up early in the morning to find him taking hairpin turns at eighty-five miles an hour. Rather than scold him, I closed my eyes and pretended it wasn't happening. We made it to Boston alive, and managed to get through a forgettable show at Harper's Ferry. I hooked up with my old buddy John Staten, who had secured the drum chair in Karl Denson's band, and was also playing in Boston that night. John had left Living Large after a near-violent confrontation with Mario, and over dinner we recounted some good tales from our past experiences together. He told me one I must repeat here:

While playing with Living Large, John had been under the managerial guidance of a certain individual. The band did an opening set in Minneapolis for the legendary Wailers, Bob Marley's back-up band. Afterwards, John was approached by a few members of the Wailers. They told him they were preparing to do Lauryn Hill's next studio album, followed by a worldwide tour to support the album. They needed a drummer and they loved John's playing. Would he be interested? John said yes, of course, but they would need to talk to his management. He gave them the manager's card, reiterated that he was very interested, and asked them to call the manager. Not long after that, Lauryn Hill's representatives contacted John's "management" to inquire about his availability. Rather than close the deal for John, making the Wailer's gig a reality, John's manager said that John was under strict contract with him, and that the drummer was working exclusively with the manager's personal record label. Lauryn Hill's rep said "Oh, okay. Thanks, but no thanks. We'll look elsewhere." There went the opportunity of a lifetime, in one fell swoop.

THIS SESSION IS FOR PROFESSIONALS

After gigs in Boston, Northampton and Danbury, we headed to Manhattan for a show at Tobacco Road. Our previous performance there had been excellent, and I had high hopes for a repeat. It was a weird schedule that night: we were to play an early set, take a long break, come back and play until the wee hours. After the early set, Chase and I caught a cab to a club called Irving Plaza to check out Karl Denson's Tiny Universe. I was anxious to see John Staten play with Karl's band. I'd heard he was killing the gig.

John sounded great with Karl and company, his drumming style meshing well with Karl's soulful vibe. Karl invited up a young keyboardist with a growing reputation, Marco Benavento, and I was impressed with his chops. After a few tunes, Chase and I jumped on the subway to get back to Tobacco Road for our late show. We finished very late, maybe four in the morning. I decided to keep club hopping with a platonic local friend, Veronica, who wanted to keep the party going. We wound up at Small's, the legendary jazz club in Greenwich

Village. The name is not ironic. The place is tiny. The sun was coming up as we descended the steps into the dark cavern that had been home to countless jazz legends over the years. Veronica met some more friends inside, and we all sat to enjoy a jam session already in progress.

The group was playing a standard, some well-worn *real book* tune. The players were all competent. Not great, but decent. The pianist was a young Asian woman seemingly incapable of an original idea to save her life, but she had copped some old bebop clichés—what you would expect at six in the morning, on an off night at Small's. I was enjoying a drink, listening to the music when a strange thing happened. The trombonist, a young black guy with dreadlocks, stopped playing to say something to the sax player, a skinny white guy. The exchange was brief and seemingly cordial. Moments later, however, the trombonist lunged at the sax player and attempted to smash his head with a combination of punches. The saxophonist crumpled to the ground as the rest of the band stopped to intervene. The two brawlers were escorted out of the club, and the music stopped.

The stage was empty when a mildly attractive young woman walked up and said "Can anybody accompany me on a couple songs?" I was right there, and I could indeed accompany her, so I jumped onto the grand piano. Why not? The girl didn't have a bad voice, but knew nothing about stage etiquette. She didn't understand when to start singing and when to stop... two crucial tools for the aspiring vocalist. I laid down the chords to *Come Rain or Come Shine*, and we got through it without a major train wreck. A drummer jumped up to join us for a second song. He was mediocre, but I did my best to hold things together.

The host of the session, a very old black guy in a dated suit and bow tie, lurked near the stage. He fit an archetype I was a familiar with: the elder jazz statesman, elegant reminder of an era past. Noble ambassador of America's one true art form; never swayed by contemporary fads and trends, a staunch practitioner of the tradition. Purist. Preservationist. Experience had shown me that some of these guys were the real deal... and alas, some were full of shit.

When we finished the tune, this Keeper of the Guard walked to the microphone and cleared his throat. There was something on his mind. I'd done the best I could under the circumstances: *inexperienced singer, bad drummer.* The announcement began: "We apologize for the disturbance, and thank our guest musicians and singers for sharing their music with us. But let me point something out... This here is

New York City, the greatest jazz town in the world. And this here session... this session is for *professionals*." Yeah, I agreed, why let amateurs get up and perform in a venue with such a legacy? Let me sit in with some fellow pros. Then the old cat paused, turned in my direction and glared at *me*. I cracked a disbelieving smile. "Are you serious, man?"

"Like I said, this session is for *professionals*." I felt like Travis Bickle staring at himself in the mirror. *You talkin' to me?*

"Alright, man. Whatever." *You've got some Bud Powell wannabe Japanese chick up there the whole night, playing clichés as if they were fresh, inventive ideas... and you have the nerve to suggest that I can't play?* The whole scene was a little suspect; musicians stuck in a style of playing that had flourished sixty years earlier, thinking there was something noble about what they were doing. When I asked the pianist who her influences were, the only name she could come up with was Elmo Hope.[185] The house drummer, also a young Asian woman, gave me some sort of condescending, snooty jazz trip. *You better sound like Elvin Jones when you get up there, sister.* Of course, she didn't come close.

I wandered over to the bar, where the singer I'd accompanied proceeded to apologize for butchering the jazz standard repertoire. I said it wasn't a big deal; it didn't matter, so let's have a drink and forget about it. She asked what she'd specifically done that was wrong, so I told her: "Well, you didn't know when to come in, and then you didn't know when to stop. You cut me off right after I started taking my piano solo, and you unwittingly changed keys in the middle of a phrase. Then, you didn't know how to end the song, so we kind of train-wrecked. Other than that, you did great." *She began to cry.*

"Hey, it's cool. This is just a jam session. It doesn't mean anything."

"I just want to make it," she wept. What could I tell her? Music was a serious struggle for all but the very few and very lucky. She was in New York, where only the youngest and most gifted were going to be noticed. If you were a female singer trying to make it in jazz, you had to be good looking and under thirty, and you had to have undeniable talent.

I crashed at Veronica's apartment in the Village, while she went out to keep partying, wired on something that apparently made sleep

---

[185] Not to belittle the achievements of Elmo Hope... but if that's the most recent jazz piano player you admire, you're in trouble.

unnecessary. I woke up in the early afternoon, left a note to say thanks for the hospitality, and enjoyed a lovely solo drive out of Manhattan and up to Connecticut, where I met the rest of the guys to do a radio show called *Jam Nation*. We set up in the station's studio and played some songs, followed by an interview.

Brad had arranged the whole deal through the host, a friend of his who also wrote for Relix magazine, the premier jam band monthly. We spent the night at Brad's parents' home nearby. They seemed supportive of him being in the group, and I found out later they were pressuring him to quit the road life, get a normal job and settle down.

In the morning, we left to continue the tour. I was starting to have a hard time getting along with Wildman. We'd had a blow-up in Black Mountain, North Carolina, over something trivial, and now we continued butting heads over stupid little things. After a while the stupid little things started to mount, carry more weight, and become destructive. We'd become distant during a long stretch through Colorado, and neither of us wanted to confront our issues. Finally, we got it all out on the table, as a snow blizzard raged outside a venue in some mountain town I can't remember.

As I attempted to communicate and resolve our conflicts, I realized that it was a one-way street. I was trying to talk to Wildman openly, and he just kind of sat there and didn't respond much. It was like talking to a wall.

I came to the conclusion that Wildman and I were both complicated alpha male guys, strong-willed, highly analytical, and capable of ruthlessness. Unless we seriously worked on our communication, we would always lock horns.

Creative people tend to be intense and complicated, and when you throw a few together in a van for months at a time, there are going to be issues. Creative types aren't always the most communicative— they're accustomed to retreating into a private world, a place where they work everything out on their own. When creative people infringe on each other's personal space, problems arise.

After another night at Higher Ground in Vermont, opening for a popular reggae band, we drove back down to Trenton, New Jersey, where we had a show at an all-ages venue called Conduit. The club was nice, but the turn-out poor. I walked around the neighborhood, grabbed a couple meat pies and hustled back to the venue; the area was funky and felt unsafe.

From there, we hit Richmond, Raleigh, Asheville and Charlottesville. A few of the shows were String Cheese Incident after parties, and two of them went very well. Brad hadn't settled into a comfortable groove as the band's drummer, but he was connecting with Wildman's bass lines and playing with good energy.

Our return to the Georgia Theater in Athens was highly anticipated. It was 4/21, the pot smoker's holiday, and the promotional poster, plastered on storefronts throughout Athens, featured a photograph of Big Job taking a rip from a huge bong. As it turned out, the show was horribly attended. The door didn't even cover the production expenses, so we didn't make a dime. When I went up to the office to settle out and get paid, the manager didn't even look at me. He just grunted something about not covering expenses, and that was that. No *thanks for coming,* no *we'll do better next time.* Just *pack up and get out.*

We did a decent show in Black Mountain, during which Wildman and I avoided any repeat blow-outs, and then we drove to Boone for a gig at The Spot. The drive through North Carolina was beautiful, and Boone was an attractive, hip little town. The gig was another story. First, getting there was a drag. Chase had given me a bum steer on the directions, and didn't realize the mistake until we'd gone an hour-and-a-half *in the wrong direction.* I happened to be driving and—tired and worn down—lost it.

"You're kidding, right?"

"No. We should have gone the other way."

"How does that happen? You're looking at the map every half hour. Why did you tell me to go west if we're supposed to go east?" Chase resented my unsympathetic tone, and simply shrugged his shoulders. Chase never wanted to be held accountable for anything. He just wanted to wander through life, it seemed, riding from gig to gig and playing his guitar.

"Why can't you take responsibility for your actions? If you're going to fuck up, at least be a man and say 'I fucked up.' Otherwise, you can't be trusted to make decisions." We had been on the road for months now, and I was fatigued. I was snapping at people over inconsequential things like taking a wrong turn. I was losing my grip, being a jerk.

We continued to Decatur, a suburb of Atlanta, for a show at Jake's Toadhouse. *Can there ever be a good show at a place called Jake's Toadhouse? Is it even possible? Of all the places to play in Atlanta, why had God sent me to a toadhouse? If Jake's main mission in life was to harbor homeless toads, why did he also feel the need to present live music?* These are all valid questions.

The opening band was a quartet with guitar, bass, drums and vibes. I was intrigued to see someone playing a vibraphone, but as Wildman and I sat there watching these guys play, curiosity soon turned to boredom. Wildman concluded that the group was "terribly gay." The guitarist laid down heavy rock riffs while the vibes player noodled over the top—*Metallica meets Gary Burton*, if you will.

The next stop was New Orleans' Jazzfest. It would be our second consecutive appearance at the eclectic gathering. Like the previous year, we weren't scheduled to play the actual festival, but had arranged shows with promoters in local clubs. We were due for some good fortune. The touring had been difficult, and the four of us were in need of a morale builder.

Due to the poor economy, there were thousands less people in town than usual, and music promoters were in danger of taking big hits. One guy in particular had a nightmarish experience at Jazzfest, and his misfortune would trickle down to many artists, including us. His woes were so monumental that year that they became a cautionary JBS tale. I give you…

THE RISE AND FALL
OF KURT KIMMELMAN

During one of the band's several stops at 19 Broadway in Fairfax, Kurt Kimmelman shared with me his ambitious plans for the upcoming 2003 Jazzfest in New Orleans. Kurt planned to rent a club for the duration of the festivities, hiring numerous big-name acts, along with lesser known ones, and presenting a lineup of talent to rival all the top promoters at Jazzfest. This one, he said, was really going to put him on the map. He would finance the operation himself, using savings, credit cards, and the money he generated from the shows themselves. He might only break even the first year, but that was always the way it went with such enterprises. Eventually, if he kept it going and managed to become a Jazzfest fixture, the big bucks would roll in, and Kurt would realize his dream of being a big-time JBS mover and shaker. I've always admired people who dream big and ignore the naysayers; who have the courage to go after their ambitions, no matter how grandiose—so I was completely in Kurt's corner. I told him I thought it was a great idea. In turn, Kurt offered to include Global Funk in his plans. This would mean we'd get to share the bill with some heavy hitters, and I'd have an excuse to spend a whole week in New Orleans.

Kurt asked me my opinions about working with certain artists. I offered some ideas, and also suggested he secure Woo as his production manager for the full two weeks of Jazzfest. He liked the idea and hired Woo, who was delighted to learn he'd have a job during the festival, making money while rubbing elbows with some of his musical idols. This was good on more than one level; I had hustled a gig for my buddy, but also positioned him to help GFC once we got to New Orleans.

While driving to Louisiana for Jazzfest, the discussion in the van focused on a certain friend of ours (who shall remain nameless), whose appetite for partying knew no bounds. We knew this guy would be at Jazzfest, raging like there was no tomorrow, so we decided to create a pool. We each made a prediction about which drugs and what quantities our Belushi-esque buddy would consume, from Ecstasy to DMT (the stuff people lick off of frogs).[186] The conversation sounded something like this:

```
INT. VAN - DAY

The members of GFC banter with each other, while
driving down the freeway.

                    CHASE
          I say he's going to drop acid three
          times, do ecstasy twice, snort coke five
          times, and smoke pot at least three
          times a day.
```

---

[186] My understanding, or at least how it was explained to me, is that you have to scare the frog before you lick it. Actually, you have to scare the crap out of the frog enough so that it thinks it's going to die. When the frog enters this state of desperation, it secretes the stuff that gets you high. Then, you scrape the slime off its skin, dry it, smoke it, and off you go. I've never witnessed any of this, but you have to admit, the process sounds kind of fascinating.

```
                    ME
        You're overlooking a number of
        likelihoods, my friend. He's going to
        eat mushroom chocolates six times, smoke
        opium twice, drink half a bottle of
        Crown Royal a day, snort coke no less
        than four times, drop acid three times,
        do ecstasy twice, and use a THC
        vaporizer every chance he gets.  On the
        last night, he's going to do all the
        above, and also smoke some DMT.

                    BRAD
        I'll go with everything you said, but
        double.  And he's going to pay for
        female companionship, down at that
        Casino.

                    WILDMAN
        Come on, guys.  The dude's gonna do all
        of that stuff every day!  Plus, he's
        gonna take no less than five hundred
        bong rips during the week we're in town.
        And on the last night, he's gonna blow
        it out by doing a speedball, and he's
        gonna hook up with some girl who he gets
        completely blitzed on numerous
        substances, and she's not gonna wake up—

                    CHASE
        Whoa, you're getting a little dark, man.
        Let's leave it right there.
```

We pulled into New Orleans, anxious to find out who had correctly predicted the depths of our friend's narcotic gluttony, and also to play music, party a bit ourselves, and interact with many of the brightest stars of the JBS.

The first thing I did once we arrived was to catch up with Woo, who was already busy busting ass for Kurt Kimmelman. "I'm too busy down here to party. Kurt's got me running out to the airport three times a day. I just picked up Frank Gambale, T. Thanks for the tip. I spotted him right away." Uncertain what Gambale looked like, I'd told Woo to "look for the guy with the dead squirrel draped on his head."

Gambale was almost as famous for his hairpiece as he was for his monstrous guitar playing.

Kurt had set up shop at Mama's Blues, a club right in the Quarter. Like we'd discussed in Fairfax months earlier, he'd managed to book artists from all over the country, including well-known ones like ex-Journey drummer Steve Smith, keyboardist Bernie Worrell (Talking Heads), bassist Rob Wasserman, members of Moe, organist Ruben Patterson, guitarist Grant Green Jr., and a host of others. You had to hand it to him—he wasn't just talk. He'd actually made it happen.

In addition to two sets at Mama's Blues, I had a couple shows lined up at a different venue, so I was feeling pretty good about being at Jazzfest. For the first few days we stayed with a friend named Heather Coleman, an itinerant music lover who made her living selling arts and crafts at festivals around the country. Every year at Jazzfest, Heather rented a charming flat on Governor Nichols, and opened her door to friends and musicians. When we arrived, the members of Garaj Mahal were already squatting there.

I spent the first couple days enjoying music and relaxing with friends. Brad's girlfriend Tessa had come down from Boston to be with him, and we hit some local bars, Wildman hanging also. Brad and Tessa were a hard drinking, fun-loving couple; they threw back round after round until they could barely walk. I was drinking also, but mostly so I could keep my seat at the bar, in order to watch the Philadelphia 76ers square off against the New Orleans Hornets in the first round of the NBA Playoffs. Wildman slugged down a ridiculous number of Bloody Marys, one after another, all day long. He ate all the vegetables too.

When I checked in with Woo and the Mayor, I learned that things weren't going well at Mama's Blues. Kurt had scheduled several acts to play *every night*, and was now having great difficulty paying everyone. Numbers were down all around town—not nearly as many people had come to New Orleans for Jazzfest as in previous years. Kurt had both Woo and the Mayor on the payroll, and neither had seen a dime yet. After only a few days, I sensed disaster looming; if Kurt was unable to pay Bernie Worrell, Willie Waldman and the members of Moe, he was definitely not going to pay us.

Two of our four shows were with Kurt, and we needed the money to pay for the house we'd rented on the outskirts of the Quarter. When I approached Kurt at Mama's Blues to discuss the situation, I could see fear in his eyes. He was a man heading for a tragic fall… a man who was about to completely lose his ass. The guy had made a major mistake in his planning. He'd overextended himself by hiring far too many acts at far too high prices.

To make matters worse for GFC, the other promoter we were working with in town reneged on *his* deal, canceling our two shows at the last minute. It was a bad scene.

There was nothing I could do about Kurt Kimmelman. He was screwed at this point, and we weren't going to get paid. I wasn't the only artist who realized he would be leaving empty-handed. Bernie Worrell, legendary keyboardist, marched onto the stage at Mama's Blues, and interrupted a band in the middle of a song. He grabbed a mic and said, "Where is Kurt Kimmelman? He owes me money! I want my money now!" Kimmelman was nowhere to be found. Worrell was staying at the same hotel as the floundering promoter, so he decided to smoke him out. He set up camp outside Kurt's door, resolved to wait for him to come out of hiding. According to Woo, Worrell had stayed there for hours, getting liquored up as he watched and waited for Kurt's door to open. "I know the motherfucker's in there. He's got to come out some time."

There were at least a dozen other artists Kurt hadn't paid, and also his staff. Woo had not only worked day and night for Kurt, but had also rented a minivan using his parents' credit card, so he could drive the musicians wherever they needed to go.

One night, as Woo was standing in front of Mama's taking a break, a paintball whizzed past his head, missing by inches and splattering the club's wall. One of Kurt's unpaid, disgruntled artists had decided to exact revenge, Woo the apparent target.

We'd taken no other work for the two weeks of Jazzfest, and had shelled out a bunch of dough for the house rental, so when the second promoter cancelled on us, the situation became somewhat desparate. Out of desperation, Wildman and I repeatedly called the second promoter and demanded that he pay us.

This is where Wildman came through for the band—an instance when his verbal skills and slightly pushy phone demeanor really saved the band. He got on the horn with the promoter and insisted he meet us downtown to pay us for the cancelled shows, threatening to slander his reputation if he didn't comply.

Wildman and I went downtown to meet the guy and collect the cash. I was nervous. Despite our threats, we had no recourse if he decided to stiff us. When we got to the designated street corner, sure enough, the promoter came walking up the street. He apologized for the misunderstanding, said he hoped to keep the door open for the future, and handed me an envelope with a sizable quantity of cash. *Whew.*

Despite all the hassles I had a blast at Jazzfest. I saw lots of great music, including an intriguing solo performance by Buckethead, who combined macabre themes with Vaudeville to create a bizarre show incorporating numb chucks, break dancing and robotic pantomime.

Kurt Kimmelman's reputation was destroyed over the Mama's Blues fiasco. Some of the unpaid artists attempted to bring lawsuits against him, and he was now a JBS pariah. Nobody wanted to see his face at a show, a festival or anywhere else. I tried to contact him a few weeks after Jazzfest, not because I expected to collect any money but because I was concerned for the guy. I got his outgoing voicemail message, which said: *This is Kurt Kimmelman. I am no longer in the music business, and cannot be reached at this time.* I never saw Kurt again, or heard another word about him.

As we prepared to leave town, Mr. Peepers pleaded with me to give him a ride. When I probed his circumstances further I learned that beyond needing a lift out of New Orleans, he really had no place to go. His "friends" had abandoned him and he was broke. There was no room in the van, unfortunately. I realized Peepers was just a kid, wandering around, looking to belong to something. What was he doing out here by himself? He should have been home in Medford, Oregon, going to school, working, or planning for some kind of future.

There were thousands of Mr. Peepers, male and female, in the JBS. They traveled the country, attended hundreds of shows by their favorite bands and clung to a lifestyle free of commitments and responsibilities.

Another Day, Another Drummer

We returned west for a short run through Colorado and Wyoming. By the time we hit Vail it was clear Brad was going to quit the band. He had serious financial woes, and I was in no position to bail him out. Also, he almost apologetically told me, "You know, I'm going to marry Tessa one of these days." Brad was the fourth drummer in GFC, and his failure to fit the bill was especially disheartening for Wildman, who had hand-picked him. Before leaving Brad recommended a friend in Los Angeles, Manny Graham, and we decided to give the guy a shot.

I want to point out the logistics involved in replacing band members, particularly drummers. Every time you replace a drummer, it means you're flying somebody somewhere, shipping their equipment, and potentially flying in somebody else and also shipping their equipment. Flying in the new guy and shipping his gear is risky because you don't know for sure that he's going to work out. If you get him out on tour and he doesn't cut it, now you have to fly him home and ship his gear, and incur the same costs to repeat the process with the next candidate.

Manny was waiting when we pulled up to 14 Below in Santa Monica. He looked like Chase's twin brother: same height, same body type, glasses... the whole bit. It was uncanny. Manny scuffled through that first show, but he'd at least learned some of our songs. Like a guy who goes through a string of failed relationships, I was praying this next drummer would work out somehow.

After several shows in California, we headed out to Arizona for a run through Phoenix, Tucson and Flagstaff. There were a handful of fans that followed us around Arizona, and this was a nice morale builder. At the Flagstaff Brewery, Wildman hooked up with some girl who invited him back to her apartment. For reasons I can't remember now, the rest of us sat in the van in front of her place, listening to *The Best of Art Tatum*, waiting for Wildman to handle his business.

"How was it?" someone asked.

"Aggressive," he answered.

"Hmmm. Interesting. Hey, check out Art Tatum's version of *Yesterdays*."

We forged ahead to Rico, Colorado; a mountain town close to Telluride, and so small you could motor right through it and never realize you were there. The show was in the Rico Theatre, a good-sized venue with a reputable history. We decked out in wigs and funny clothes to celebrate Halloween, and the place got packed. Manny's family came out, including his father Jesse.

Jesse was a colorful character. A fellow keyboardist and singer, he'd made his living for years as a lounge act in posh Colorado resorts. His claim to fame was a squabble he'd had with Hunter S. Thompson, who lived near Aspen and frequented a club where Jesse performed. Jesse had recorded a song celebrating Thompson's infamous reputation, and Thompson, previously a friendly acquaintance, threatened to sue him for slander. On the wall of Jesse's den, he had a framed letter from Thompson—a hostile, handwritten note in which the famous beat journalist aired his grievances.

Jesse and I got along well. He understood the musician's life, and was supportive of his son joining the band and hitting the road. Jesse was generous, too. He bought me dinner, and housed the whole band when we passed through his little town of Rifle.

Manny had two sets of parents and a younger sister, and they all came to the Rico show. His whole family drank like fish, and I was right there with them, doing shots at the bar after the set was over. I made friends with Hanna, a pal of Manny's sister, and later booted a grouchy Wildman from one of the motel rooms, in order to procure a bit of privacy. This practice was sanctioned as per the *universal touring musician's code of conduct*, which states: If a bandmate has secured the affections of a member of the opposite sex, and is in need of the sleeping space you are occupying, you shall relinquish said sleeping space willfully, hereby doing unto others as you would wish them to do do unto you.

Chase was in another room making overtures toward Manny's sister, but Manny threw a nasty, sibling c-block, thwarting the eager guitarist's efforts.

The next morning, we headed out for Lubbock, Texas. It was a long drive, and when we arrived in Buddy Holly's hometown, it was blisteringly hot and humid. The gig was at Klusoz Coffee and Cigar Bar, a decent little club with a college clientele. We enjoyed a well-attended show, converting a number of kids to the GFC cause. Manny was doing okay on drums at this point, and the band was putting a good foot forward in its first tour through Texas.

With a day to kill, we decided to hang around Lubbock, and dropped in on a jazz jam session at the same venue. The promoter, pleased with the previous evening, got us a hotel, and after sitting in with the house band on some jazz tunes, I invited a new, blonde friend back to the room to kick back and relax. She was nice enough, but had some strange ideas about things. She went on a rant about not liking animals, because they required constant maintenance, and they smelled. I don't remember much else about the encounter, to be honest.

Meanwhile, Chase and Wildman were vying for the hand... well, maybe not the *hand*... of some young lady at a house party. Wildman was on the inside track, ready to close the deal. Chase swooped in and foiled the larger, bearded man's campaign with brooding, THC-induced grimaces. As the pair of them moped back to the van empty-handed, Wildman barked at Chase, "I'll never hang out with you again! You do this every time!"

The next show was supposed to be in San Angelo. It fell through, so we motored down to Galveston for a date at a joint called Yaga's. Like most islands, Galveston had a distinct personality. I corralled the guys into taking a tour of the Moody Mansion, a haunted, 28,000 square-foot structure bought by W.L. Moody Jr., after the great hurricane of 1900. Moody and his family built a formidable American empire based on cotton, banking, ranching, insurance and hotels.[187] It was Winchester Mystery House *Lite*. The tour was a snoozer, kind of like whale watching—but you can't just play gigs, sit on your ass in RV repair shops, sleep in Wal-Mart parking lots, drink and hang out with groupies all the time. You've got to attempt to *edify yourself* out there every once in a while.

I spent the rest of the day getting the van's alignment adjusted and some tires replaced. The show that night was not well-attended, but a handful of people really liked our music, and I sold some CDs. When you're roughing it out there in a jam band, making a few new fans and selling a handful of CDs might provide the morale boost necessary to make it from Galveston to Gary, Rochester to Rico.

While still in Galveston, I got in touch with Dick Merck. The Travesty had been collecting dust at Woo's ranch in Durham, California. Merck was responding to a letter I'd sent him during the previous week. He said, "Jake's not happy about the situation, but you make some valid points in your letter. Let's try to figure something out." I was finally communicating positively with these guys. I told Merck I couldn't keep the vehicle because of the incessant repair issues. He pressed me for the Travesty's whereabouts, so I divulged its location. I asked him for some time to clean the vehicle up and get a few repairs done, before he and Jake Redwood repossessed it, but Merck said his client wanted to take the Travesty back immediately. I informed Woo of the situation, and he arranged to rendezvous with Redwood at his family ranch in Durham.

We returned to Austin, where I met up with my old elementary school friend Chris Taylor, who now lived in Killeen with his wife and two kids. Chris stayed in Austin with me and the band, tagging along for the next couple gigs. Out of nowhere, Mr. Peepers, who I hadn't

---

[187] I Googled these extraneous details after the fact.

seen since Jazzfest, showed up and provided us with a crash pad after the Austin show.

I was excited to hit Houston, a place I'd always wanted to visit — but the city didn't live up to the image I'd created in my mind. The weather was bleak, the downtown area a bore. We co-billed with a local band in a hippie bar, and the show was a bust. GFC's stock had fallen with all the personnel changes, and my discontent over having to keep playing the same music must have been obvious to audiences. We were in a rut, and Rob Sarno wasn't getting us good gigs. Plus, with our relentless schedule, we had to play places where the JBS was not thriving. Places like Houston.

Midwest Misery

The next stop marked a turning point for the band. We finally did something we'd been threatening to do for a long time: *scratch the absolute bottom of the barrel*. Stillwater, Oklahoma sucked more than any other booking I could recall.

The only reason to be in Stillwater was to play for the college crowd, and school, as luck would have it, was not in session. The cleverly named College Bar didn't have so much as a meager P.A. system, and the staff *didn't even know we were coming*. It's one thing if a show doesn't get promoted properly. It's another if the club has never heard of you, and doesn't even have you on their calendar. I called Todd, urging him to bitch out Rob for setting us up to fail.

The next gig was in Lawrence, Kansas, and this time I had hope. I'd played fun shows in Lawrence with Living Large, and knew the JBS was strong there. Unfortunately, this night was, like its predecessors, a dud. No crowd, no cash. Things would surely pick up the following night in Columbia, Missouri, right? Wrong. We played a coffee shop doubling as a used CD store, and only a smattering of JBS diehards showed up. The highlight of the gig was finding a free place to stay.

By the time we got to St. Louis, everyone was feeling deflated. It had been a tough run. When we pulled up to a club called Off Broadway, situated next to a giant Budweiser factory in a grungy, industrial slum, we all laughed out loud. *Way, way off Broadway, man.*

Since we got to the club super-early, Wildman and I embarked on a mission to drink each cocktail on the specials list. We made it through the whole list, *twice*, before the opening band, whose goal seemed to be to fuse together smooth jazz and Vegas lounge R&B, had even finished sound checking. There were no more than six or seven people in the audience when we played, which was just as well, because we played like crap. When there's no one there to listen, why care how you sound? *If a band hits a riff together in a club, but there is no one in the club to actually hear it, did the band actually make any sound at all?*

Manny had a female friend in attendance, and to cap our triumphant showing near the Budweiser Factory, we all slept with her dog on the hardwood floor. The next morning, Wildman informed me that I had snored like a brontosaurus throughout the night. I blamed it on the dog.

We returned to a venue in Chicago where we were at least sure to receive good treatment: the Boulevard. There, we had good meals and a roof over our heads. Wildman and I took John Glynn, the owner, out for pizza the day after our show. We had a proposition for him: *How would you like to manage the band?* John was a JBS lover, a guy who helped certain acts he believed in. He had mentioned in the past that he'd be willing to do this for us; but things had changed. We were no longer viewed as a group to watch, a rising star of the national touring scene. Now, we were just another jam band with a passenger van, driving around the country hoping for lightning to strike. John politely said he was too busy to get involved.

We headed east again for a couple dates in Ohio. The first was in Columbus, a huge college town, at the Newport Music Hall. The place was massive and cavernous, and we played with two other bands, including Ray's Music Exchange, an interesting group in the Miles Davis fusion tradition. As luck would have it, Ben Harper and Jack Johnson were playing up the street the same night. Our show was dead as a doorknob. *Please, can somebody stop the bleeding?*

Cleveland was equally terrible. The venue was a dive—a long, narrow room that had been converted from a bowling alley—and the opening band, Kung Fusic,[188] was providing the sound system. I don't have to tell you that any group which calls itself Kung Fusic is to be viewed with a cautious eye. They weren't all that bad, really, but the sound was awful, and the only people clapping after our songs were Wildman's dad and stepmom. And they *had* to clap.

---

[188] Worst band name of all-time, I think.

We returned to Uncle Fester's in Bloomington, Indiana, for yet another mediocre show. It was a rough run, I tell you. Then, as if he instinctually wanted the tour's lowest moment to dovetail with his own drumming abyss, Manny played his worst show at the Ranch Bowl, a bowling alley in Omaha, Nebraska. Rob Sarno had plugged us into the Midwest coffee shop/bowling alley circuit, and I didn't like it one bit. It wasn't a sexy circuit.[189]

We made another run through Colorado — Fort Collins, Denver, Bond, Steamboat, Boulder, Telluride, Durango and Aspen. We stayed with Manny's mom and stepdad, who had a nice home near Aspen. Wildman and I watched with amusement, as Chase attempted to curry favor with Manny's sister by bouncing on a trampoline with her young son.

Manny's mom and her husband took us out to a nice dinner in nearby Glenwood Springs, and I found myself thinking, *what a nice couple… together for many years, and still in love.* Two weeks later, Manny told me his mom and stepdad were getting a divorce. The stepdad owned the house, and wanted Manny's mom to split, a move which would oust the daughter and her child as well.

---

[189] I believe Rob Sarno was trying to get one or more members of the band to commit suicide. He thought to himself, "Where can I send these guys that will make them want to slash their wrists or jump in front of a train? Aha, I've got it… a bowling alley in Omaha, Nebraska!"

The Shrine of the Dismissed Drummers

We completed another Ucolortanaho run then returned to California. Manny wasn't working out on drums, a fact that left Chase dejected. In early August we did a show at an L.A. club called Fais Do Do. This would be Manny's last GFC performance.

The show was advertised as a Galactic afterparty, with a local band opening. It so happened that my old pal from Faze, Nico Valencia, was in the opening band, which also featured the ex-drummer of a platinum-selling rock group called Cake. Nico and I got a chance to catch up, and much to my pleasant surprise, Jalen, on a break from the Black Eyed Peas, also showed up to say hello. I hadn't seen him for a few years, so we had a lot to talk about. He was still serving as musical director for the Peas, which had skyrocketed to become a globally popular hip-hop group.

Jalen was also writing songs with other big industry names. He'd always had an understated tone of voice, so when he drolly said, "Ant, I just wrote some songs over at Burt Bacharach's house," I cracked up. "You know that Justin Timberlake song that's all over the radio?" he continued.

"Yeah, I think so," I said.

"I co-wrote that one too."

I was glad Jalen was doing well for himself. He was a lot like me—never quite found a niche as a solo artist, but always had the fire, and was perpetually driven to *make it.*[190]

After the show, I was packing my gear with Big Job, who'd come down from Salinas to hang and help out. We were all sharing a house in Salinas now, a major improvement over relying on the Travesty exclusively for shelter. As we packed up my keyboards, the ex-drummer from Cake, a skinny white guy with glasses and wavy hair, was also packing up his drums. The stage was small, and everyone's equipment was intertwined in a mess of wires and speakers. As I went to lift my synthesizer, I accidentally bumped one of the drums. Bumped it *very lightly.*

"Those are really expensive drums. If you need me to move something, just ask," he scolded me.

"Okay. Sorry about that." I continued what I was doing.

"I mean, there's no reason to just start bumping into stuff. Just tell me, 'Hey, I need you to move your drums,' and I'll be happy to comply."

"Yeah, okay. I got it."

I kept my attention on the keyboards.

"Why would you just start knocking into my equipment without thinking about what you were doing? Like I said, these are expensive drums." The moment of *failed diplomacy* had arrived.

"Fuck off."

The guy stared at me.

"What?"

"You heard me."

"I'm a *touring musician.* Maybe if you did some touring you'd understand about respecting people's equipment!"

"If I was a touring musician, like you? A dude who used to be in some three-chord alternative rock band, and now is opening shows for *me?*"

Nico intervened to prevent things from getting any worse. Once we were done packing up, Wildman, Chase and I drove to Lipp's house in Ventura. During the brief ride, Wildman and Chase got in a bitter shouting match about Manny's drumming. I came to the conclusion

---

that Manny was going to have to go. His liabilities were causing fights among the rest of us.

We arranged to leave Manny's drums at Lipp's house, which was less than an hour from Manny's apartment in Venice Beach. Chase called Manny and told him the bad news. Manny was not the first drummer who, fired from GFC, would have to retrieve his gear from Lipp's house in Ventura. Lipp and I contemplated the construction of a memorial in the corner of his living room: *The Shrine of the Dismissed Drummers.*

We were starting to wonder if we'd ever find a drummer who played at the level of the rest of the group. We didn't have much to offer in terms of money or creature comforts—the most enticing thing about our group was the opportunity to be in a creative project, where nobody was telling you what or how to play. We were attracting players who were decent, but not stars, not guys who would make the group stand out.

We were all set to head home to Salinas, but Big Job asked us to stop in Santa Barbara so he could run an errand. We never made it to Salinas. While he was handling some business at a bar on State Street, the rest of us were treated to free micro-brews. Specialty beers typically contain a higher alcohol content than normal beer. If you don't factor that in, you can get happy in a hurry. I've never been a huge beer drinker, and I was sipping, so I was okay. Chase, on the other hand, weighed about one-fifty, and did have a passion for good beer. He was blitzed before he knew what hit him.

Chase and I wandered across the street to find another bar. As we walked, we started talking to two tall, attractive women, one blonde and one brunette. They invited us to hang out, and we followed them to an outdoor patio club. The brunette sat across from me, and as we talked, I started to get that feeling—the one you get every once in a while, as you take a closer look at someone you at first thought to be a complete stranger. I realized that I knew her. I couldn't figure out from where. She kept talking, and then, like a combat flashback, it swept across my mind in a montage of visceral images. Only this montage wasn't filled with cries of agony and dismembered limbs. I had spent a romantic evening with this girl after a jazz gig, years earlier in San Diego.

"Do you ever spend time in San Diego?" I asked her.

She had figured it out before I had, and was ready when I asked the question.

"Yeah… we know each other."

The four of us talked for a while and then I excused myself to use the restroom. I was gone for only a couple minutes, but when I returned Chase was sitting at the table all by himself, staring off into space.

"Where are the ladies?" I asked.

"They're gone."

"What happened?"

"A couple guys came over to talk to them… their friends."

"And?"

"I said, 'Who are these tools?'"

"How'd that go over?"

"Not too good, T. They all got up and left."

"Nice work," I said. I spotted the girls at the bar and walked over to them. The blonde saw me, wagged her finger and said, "You and your friend need to leave."

"Why?"

"He's belligerent. He called our friends *tools*."

"Are they?"

"Are they *what*?"

"Tools? In this place, I'd say the chances are pretty good."

It was time to pull up stakes and find a new watering hole. In the two minutes that passed while I was taking a leak, Chase had managed to turn an entire club against us. We rejoined Big Job and Wildman in front of the first bar, where Chase continued his verbal assault on the Santa Barbara locals.

"Look at these assholes!" he blurted as various people walked past us on the sidewalk. Finally Chase hit the wall. He realized he was drunk and out of sorts. "I'm sorry guys! I'm sorry! I lost control." We comforted him, as much as a group of weary, thirty-something jam band musicians can, and led him back to the van for a nap.

I corralled Wildman to go with me back to the patio bar. We had a cocktail (or two), then I got the brilliant idea to start *checking I.D.'s at the door*. There was no doorman, so why not? I was just joking around, standing at the entrance asking people for their driver's licenses. Suddenly some big bubba was in my face.

"Good night, sir!" He pointed at the sidewalk, my cue to get lost.

"Man, I was just kidding around. It's not a big deal."

"Good night, sir!"

Wildman grabbed me and we skulked back to the van, putting an end to a rather fruitless evening on State Street in Santa Barbara.

COUNCIL IS ADJOURNED

After a show at The Mangy Moose in Jackson Hole, we headed for Boise. In Boise I met with Michael Deeds, the editor of a Boise newspaper, who wanted to do a little story on the band. The conversation started awkwardly, with Deeds putting me to task about the band's name. This had become a sore subject for Wildman, Chase and me. We had evolved into an eclectic *jam project*, with forays into Latin, world grooves, free-form improvisation, and rock vocal material. Our music was more interesting now than when we started out, but it wasn't funk... and the band was still called Global Funk Council. We all agreed that if we could come up with something new that everyone liked, we would change the name. As we discovered, band names are tricky. We couldn't find anything that stuck, and I realized that unless someone had a stroke of genius, it wouldn't be worth it to start over with a name nobody had ever heard before.

We decided in the end to shorten the name simply to Global Funk. I even wrote a song called *Council is Adjourned*. Wildman thought the shorter name was cool, because it contained a second meaning: *we're all stuck in a global funk... how are we going to escape this predicament?* It was the kind of sentiment JBS fans could sink their teeth into.

When Deeds's article came out, Todd was a little bugged with me. I was quoted as saying we had milked early associations with other bands, in order to open doors for GFC. I also said that I was no longer interested in appeasing people who thought we were a funk act. When Deeds asked what happened to the band's "super-funk focus," I had answered: "That died." The music had evolved, I went on to say, and our audience would just have to evolve with us or move on.

I was happy with the article, because it was honest. I wasn't interested in being a dance/party band, playing simple funk grooves in order to keep people on the dance floor all night. If I was going to keep driving around the country, hanging by a financial thread, continually trying to instill enough faith in my fellow band mates to keep the project together long enough for us to turn a corner, I wanted to play creatively satisfying, challenging music. I wanted to feel like I was doing something to raise the musical bar, to elevate people's awareness of various styles. If you were just going to mimic the watered down dance bullshit on the radio, why bother to have a band, to fall on your sword for live music? For the arts?

If there was anyone I wanted to appease, it was the club owners and managers. I realize I slammed the whole notion of *the client* in an earlier passage of this book, but I understood that as a touring act, these people were our clients. I wanted them to have a good taste in their mouth when GFC rolled into town, and an even better one when GFC rolled out of town. This started with being punctual, friendly, and cooperative. You scored big points if you were courteous and generous with the staff of a given place. Then, if you managed to bring in some business—people who wouldn't have come to the show if you hadn't been playing—you really put a good foot forward. Most of the owners I talked to understood how difficult it was to do what we were doing, and they in turn appreciated it when you demonstrated your awareness that it was difficult for them as well. Touring is tough, but running a restaurant or a club is no walk in the park either.

It's important for bands to sympathize with the plight of the club owner. Many bands go out there viewing clubs as a stepping stone to bigger things. Once the stars align, the act will surely move on to theaters, then amphitheaters, and maybe one day even arenas. *Once we make it, we'll never set foot in those little clubs again.* Yeah, maybe. If you wind up being Coldplay. But what if you don't? You better hope you built some relationships at the club level.

Back in California, we stopped in Fresno to rehearse at the home of our friends, Kate and Rabbit. After working on music for several hours, we all migrated to a bar in a strip mall, where we drank and danced to a DJ friend of Kate's. Kate was attractive, with long, reddish purple dreadlocks, and an Irishman's alcohol tolerance. She had a tendency to get a little belligerent when she was liquored up, and enjoyed rough housing with the guys. On this night, I was the one she singled out. First, she threw my shoes over a fence. I responded by pouring booze on her shirt, and soon she was punching me (which kind of hurt), and then we wrestled on the pavement. The next morning, she had a big scrape on her face. I didn't remember how she got it, but figured it had something to do with me.

The next night we all went out to dinner at a Mexican restaurant. The food was tasty, and of course Todd, Kate and Rabbit ordered multiple pitchers of margaritas. For some reason I refrained, and in my sobriety noticed something: GFC and its network of friends could drink with the best of them. I guess I'd been trying to cut back at that point. I felt better when I didn't drink to excess, but it was hard to stop entirely. I enjoyed the buzz, as well as the escape from reality. I also found a bit of boozing to be therapeutic for my relationships with the guys. Wildman and I would have our most open, unencumbered conversations when we were throwing a few back. With men, the ego gets in the way of honest communication; but with some drinks in the bloodstream, the walls come right down.

Around this time we were in Vancouver, playing a show and hanging out for a couple days. I decided to buy some books at the Virgin megastore. Wildman was already sore that I had gotten myself a laptop using a new credit line, and the books compounded his distaste. I more or less understood where he was coming from. Nobody was getting a salary, so where did I get off buying shit, especially expensive items like a laptop? This was my rationale: I was the one whose family jewels were on the chopping block, should the band fall apart. The RV, the van, multiple credit cards… all of it was in my name. So where were my perks? If you pay the cost to be the boss, there should be some reward as well. I guess I figured my reward was the freedom to be able to buy something for myself here and there.

Maybe it was wrong, but nobody else was stepping up with lines of credit or big chunks of cash to keep the project afloat. As the old saying goes, *money talks and bullshit walks.*

When I faced a potential lawsuit from the owners of the RV, nobody was there to help. I got out of it myself by writing a series of letters and taking steps to extricate myself and consequently the whole project, from what could have been a complicated legal mess. If somebody got sued, it was going to be me. I had shouldered that burden. Todd never wanted his name on anything. Nobody else had the credit history to have their name on anything. If one or more of the guys decide for whatever reason that they want to leave the project, I would be stuck with a mountain of debt. I would be the one going down, nobody else.

FOURTEEN INCHES OF FAME

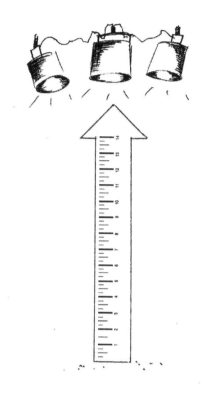

I picked up an issue of Rolling Stone one day, and found myself reading an article about a New York City native named Jonah Falcon. Jonah was about my age, seemingly intelligent, and shared my love of film. The article, of course, was not about how the guy was bright, loved New York, and had a passion for movies. No, the article was about the fact that Jonah Falcon had, by many people's accounts, the largest wiener on Planet Earth. The guy's equipment was supposedly so prodigious that he was known around the world for his rare physical endowment. People talked about him on websites, and European TV stations flew him across the pond to chat on their programs. Jonah claimed that porn producers had been approaching him since he was twelve, but he had always resisted their offers. God only knows why "porn producers" knew the anatomical particulars of a twelve year-old kid. Perhaps the adult film world works like professional sports scouting; future prospects are identified and courted early on.

Why had Jonah resisted the world of porn, when he surely could have been a star? Was it because of moral objections, perhaps? No, it seemed to be because the guy had aspirations as a bona fide thespian. He saw himself becoming a successful film actor. The article discussed Jonah's connections to Miramax, and how certain executives there felt he had potential to work as a serious actor. I read this, and something in me clicked. I had written a couple drafts of a screenplay about a white-collar sex addict living in San Francisco. I called it *Deviance,* and had gone so far as to pay for professional script analysis. It wasn't flawless, but it had a lot of potential. When I read the Rolling Stone article about this guy with a giant package, who was the same age as me, a film buff, and had Hollywood aspirations, it hit me: *I should get in touch with this guy and send him the script.*

This, it turned out, wasn't that hard to pull off. I found a valid email for Jonah via the Internet, sent him a letter introducing myself and telling him about my screenplay, and quickly received a favorable reply. He appreciated the note and said that he was indeed interested in checking out the script. He thought it sounded like something right up his alley, and he, in fact, had been working on a screenplay based on his life experiences. He again mentioned the Miramax connection, and said that if he liked the story, he would be happy to pitch it to the studio's executives.

It sounded good to me, but when I ran the whole thing by Len, he threw up a red flag.

"You don't know this guy, Anth. He might rip off your idea."

"That's paranoid, Pops."

"No, it's not. It happens all the time. You're not a proven writer. Somebody steals your concept, it will be very hard to prove it was your original idea. Imagine how heartbreaking that would be." Len had been a successful L.A. script writer back in the late fifties, writing episodes for such TV shows as *Lawman* and *The Blue Angels.* He gave up early on pursuing it as a career, but he knew more than a thing or two about the game.

I thought about it and Len was right. I would need to vet this freakishly hung character, before I was willing to send him the fruit of my creative labors. Just what did he intend to do with my material, and what was in it for him? During our next phone conversation, I came out and asked this very question.

"So what do you imagine your role being, should something happen with *Deviance?*"

"Oh… I thought that was pretty clear."

"Uh, not really. Enlighten me."

"I want to play the lead."

The lead character was Marty Price, a thirty-something graphic arts designer making a good salary in San Francisco, sharing custody of two small children with his estranged wife, and leading a double-life as a sex addict/porn junkie. It was a challenging role. The actor would have to negotiate a wide range of emotions, from joy to anger to utter despair, and also demonstrate sharp comedic timing. In my fantasy world, I imagined an A-lister tackling the part. A Cruise, Cage, or Damon.

Were Miramax to snatch up my script, attach a director and start casting it, I had no idea who would wind up playing Marty Price—but I was pretty sure it wasn't going to be Jonah Falcon, whose big screen credits amounted to a whopping goose egg. Yes, the Rolling Stone article said Jonah had appeared on some random television shows, and that he imagined his career one day amounting to more than that of a mere anatomical curiosity, but the fact of the matter was this: the guy had no substantial credits as an actor. He might get to play the proprieter of my fictitious adult bookstore, Sin Central… if he was lucky.

Of course, anything could happen, and many of the big names in Hollywood got their first break entirely by way of chance. One night while performing at Croce's with Hollis Gentry's jazz group, I got in a conversation with J.C. Quinn, the fine character actor known for his small but memorable role in *Vision Quest* (the famous Pélé speech). Quinn liked to talk about music, but also enjoyed chatting about acting and film. He told me that Tom Cruise's career had started in L.A. as a *mistake.* "It wasn't supposed to happen," he'd said. "It was total luck."

I didn't know if Jonah had any acting talent, but I knew he was starting from scratch. At least Ron Jeremy, long snickered at for his delusions of grandeur as a legitimate actor, had managed to appear in a smattering of cameos in mainstream Hollywood films; and this was on top of a multi-decade porn career, which, any moral qualms aside, must be viewed as one of the more prolific accomplishments in the history of American home video.

Jeremy, at times, was able to infuse his adult-oriented work with a sense of wry, self-effacing humor… sort of a *Groucho Marks with his pants around his ankles* quality. Sadly, this delightful nuance in Jeremy's bottomless (pun intended) oeuvre has not materialized in his PG-13 forays. In other words, his work in legitimate films more or less blows (pun intended).

In the Hedgehog's defense, he hasn't exactly been given the meatiest of roles to sink his serious-actor's teeth into—but perhaps this has been for the best. After all, one struggles to imagine the moustached XXX icon taking the stand while donning decorated U.S. general's garb, leaning forward and shouting at Tom Cruise, "You can't handle the truth!" Then again, maybe the hirsute lickmaster would have hit it out of the park. We'll never know.

I voiced my reservations about Jonah pitching himself as the lead in *Deviance,* but I also didn't want to deter him from opening doors for the script. The guy seemed to have ideas about location scouting—he dug my placement of the story in San Francisco—and I wondered if we might at least find someone to cobble together a meager budget for us, allow us to first perfect the screenplay, then co-direct a humble indie film in the City by the Bay. I know, it sounds far-fetched, but stranger things have happened. It was obvious from our phone conversations that Jonah knew a lot about film, and also "got" what I was trying to do with this particular story.

During one conversation, Jonah said, "Hey, I just sent you some pictures of me."

"What kind of pictures?"

"I guess you could call them head shots." Oh, okay, I thought, he wants me to have professional pictures of him, in case I'm pitching the project out here on the West Coast. I opened his email with the photos, but rather than focus on his face, they were shots *from the waist down.* I called him back.

"Dude, I think you might have gotten the wrong impression about my interest in working with you."

"What do you mean?"

"Well, how can I put this? You just sent me pictures of your dick."

"Oh, I just thought you'd find that interesting." One of the pictures featured Jonah—many years younger, I might add—holding his engorged equipment in his hand. Next to this was the inclusion of a photo-shopped ruler, demonstrating the length of his pride and joy.

"Well, it's impressive, man, but I want to make clear to you that I'm not cruising. I like women. I contacted you because of your interest in film, and thought you might find my script intriguing."

"I understand that. Can you send me pictures, so I can see who I'm talking to?"

"Yeah, but mine are going to be from the neck up, if that's cool. I mean, even if I was inclined to send photos like yours, which I'm not, they might pale somewhat in comparison." Jonah laughed, his voice a little smug with the assurance that very few men on the planet could compete with him in this regard.

"Yeah, I get it. That's fine."

I decided to send the guy the full script, in the end. I reasoned that it wasn't going to do anything for me sitting in a desk drawer. I had to get it out there, take that chance. Jonah read the script quickly and called me.

"The script needs work." *Of course. The script always needs work. Tell me something I don't already know.*

"Okay, what do you think needs fixing?"

"Some structural issues. And the mayor... that character doesn't work. And the deus ex machina at the end... that doesn't work either."

"I don't have a deus ex machina at the end."

"Well, whatever you did with the ending, it doesn't work."

"Okay, fair enough. Now tell me what you think *does* work." Jonah's tone changed a bit.

"Well, there are parts of it that are brilliant. Some great scenes, like the one where Marty's ex-wife Dana calls him and cuts him off from the kids, after she finds the kids playing with his box of sex toys... what was that little wind-up called?"

"Dino, the Walking Dick."

"Yeah, right, that's all brilliant. And the concept is great. But you're going to have to rewrite the script."

"If we're working on it together, then don't *we* have to rewrite the script?"

"I'm really busy. You're going to have to do it." *If you're so busy, why are we talking about it in the first place? And just exactly what are you busy doing? You don't work, you're not currently acting. You live at home. What's cluttering up your calendar, homey?* The conversation continued...

"I'm seeing the movie in black and white," Jonah said. "Kind of like the vibe in *Pi*, you know?"

I hated *Pi*, but I lied.

"Yeah, that could really work. Black and white."

"We can shoot this thing for cheap. The script doesn't have any expensive scenes built into it. And by the way, don't worry... that picture in *Rolling Stone* is nothing close to what I really look like. It pissed me off that they used that one."

"It was you, wasn't it?"

"Yeah, but I don't look like that," Jonah assured.

"But you did when they took that particular picture."

"The point is, I'm going to get in great shape for the role. My acting style and physical appearance has been compared to John Ritter."

We were getting ahead of ourselves, and truthfully, I found Jonah's phone demeanor a tad rude, a tad curt. He fancied himself an underground celebrity, and perhaps he was in New York, but as aspiring filmmakers we were on an equal level: the bottom! He had no justification for talking down to me. Especially when it was my material we were talking about.

During one chat, the conversation drifted to a discussion of his background and various exploits. I found myself asking gossipy questions like a teenage girl, because the guy seemed to have the dirt on lots of well-known people. When one very famous male actor's name came up, Jonah sighed and said, "He's such a size queen." I hadn't heard the term, and it took me a minute to figure out that it didn't refer to women's breasts. Jonah also mentioned his suspicion that his biological father, who hadn't been around while he was growing up, might be the one and only John Holmes. I pressed for details, but he didn't want to get into it on the phone.

"I'll tell you about that some time when we're hanging out in person."

Discussions with Jonah Falcon fizzled out. He had nothing tangible to bring to the table, and I didn't like the way he talked down to me like I was somehow inferior to him. I was traveling across America, playing my original music—a successful artist, at least on some basic level. I had a college degree and a long musical resumé. What had he done? He had a giant sausage and a Rolling Stone article. That, as near as I could tell, was about it.

Meanwhile, I had made a much more promising film industry contact: a Hollywood script analyst named Will Dreyfuss. Will, who I found through a screenwriting magazine, took great interest in

Deviance. He was intrigued by the lead character, and thought my first draft had many great moments. What I lacked, he told me, was an understanding of screenwriting format and structure. My script read more like a novel, he said; too much detail, too expository. The pages were too heavy, meaning there was too much ink filling them. An engaging screenplay, he told me, should be "light on the page." This means there should be plenty of white space. The majority of the script should be dialogue, and descriptions should be kept to the minimum space needed to convey only the necessary information.

With Will's help, I worked through a couple more drafts, attempting to make the improvements specified in his notes (also known as "coverage"). I refined my structure, adhering more successfully to the three-act format most successful films incorporate, but Will felt I now had a new, significant problem: Somehow my main character, whose balance of faults and virtues Will had felt was pitch perfect in the original draft, was reading as somewhat crass and less likable. This was the kiss of death. Unless the audience loves, or is at least totally intrigued by your main character, you have nothing. This paradigm might not apply to all independent and foreign films, but within the Hollywood system, you *must* create sympathetic characters that the audience will root for to succeed. If you don't, your script won't even get read, much less produced.

Will encouraged me to keep chipping away, to keep re-writing, because he felt I would eventually have a good enough property to get an agent and possibly a sale. But I didn't have it in me to keep trying at that point. I was discouraged. The rest of my life was already too hard: keeping the band on the road, juggling all the credit card balances, dealing with disgruntled musicians, searching for reasons to keep trying to make Global Funk successful. I was quickly figuring out that screenwriting was just as much of a rat race, a continual struggle with no guarantees of any success, and I just didn't have the energy and belief to plow forward. I sidelined the script, along with all my other ideas for stories, and focused my attention back on the band. I had great passion for writing, yes, and I would have loved to spend twelve hours a day or more working on it. Life had other ideas for me, however. It just wasn't in the cards. One day, when things were more settled, I would return to screenplays.

BEER AND LOATHING IN RENO

Once we returned to Salinas, the first order of business was to secure *yet another drummer* for the upcoming Northwestern tour. After some deliberation we settled on a guy name Micah, a friend of Chase who lived in Berkeley.

After a show in the Santa Cruz Mountains, we kicked off the tour with a late-night party in the wilderness near Yosemite, a rave-style gathering called *Rabbitfest*. Rabbit and his wife, Kate, were good friends of the GFC organization, and held this event every year at the same place, a large, flat rock formation in the middle of nowhere.

We caravanned to Rabbitfest in two vehicles; Todd, Woo and Chase in front, the van bringing up the rear. Todd drove like a lunatic along steep, narrow passes, as Wildman shadowed him in the E-350. I was nervous, peering out the passenger window at the sheer drop-offs we were hugging at every turn. Once we got close, we had to off-road over rocks and areas of thick brush. The sides of the van got scraped by twigs and branches.

Rabbitfest gave everyone the chance to blow off steam, which in jam band circles means drink, smoke, do drugs, and drink and smoke some more. In between our sets, I met a girl who was a friend of Kate and Rabbit, and spent most of the evening talking to her. Meanwhile, one close associate of the band was making up for his narcotic conservatism at Jazzfest. He arrived on the scene, pointed to his mouth and shouted, "DRUGS GO HERE!" (In the morning, I would find this friend passed out, face down, on a giant rock).

We had augmented the road crew to include Chip Cooley, a.k.a. Mr. Peepers, a ubiquitous presence in the national JBS touring scene. A young, long-haired Oregonian with a Taliban-like beard and front chompers that could puncture a thick piece of cowhide, Mr. Peepers was an alumnus of both the String Cheese and Karl Denson camp. He and I were friends from the Living Large days, and he was looking for a new cause. We needed a *roadie*—someone to help load the gear in and out of the clubs, and set it up on the stage. Mr. Peepers was strong as an ox, and also a terrific dancer—guaranteed to have a Pied Piper effect on a tentative crowd when he displayed his unabashed blend of spins, hoola-hoop gyrations and various Paleolithic gestures.

Around this time, I felt a strong desire to finish a draft of my memoir.[191] While off the road in Salinas, I bought a laptop and started writing around the clock. The Salinas house, rented in Big Job's name, served two purposes: first and most important, it was supposed to bring in much needed cash—Big Job had converted two of the bedrooms into a marijuana growing operation. Initially, the idea seemed dangerous to me, since the house was in a densely populated neighborhood, and police cars would frequently drive past. Also, there was an orange glow emanating from inside, due to the high-temperature light fixtures used to grow the plants. We had neighbors next to us on both sides and also behind us, and I was concerned somebody would figure out what was going on.

---

[191] In retrospect, I was nowhere close to being finished at that time.

Big Job, however, seemed confident in what he was doing. With Todd's help he acquired all the necessary equipment, and the plan was to harvest a new crop every few months, allowing Big Job to make a modest living and also support the Global Funk Council organization.

Things got off to a promising start. The operation seemed to be running smoothly, and the band and friends now had an off-the-road California sanctuary. I didn't fall in love with Salinas, a drab agricultural town without much going on. The house didn't have cable TV, so I had to watch NBA playoff games at the Round Table Pizza up the street. The place was overrun with Lakers fans, which was a real drag. I was the only white guy in there, and I was cheering for the San Antonio Spurs. I felt like I was in a foreign country—specifically, Mexico. I know it's not politically correct to say that, and I should learn Spanish and do my part to bridge the gap... Yes, I should, and yes, I will.[192]

The idea was to keep a low profile—we didn't want to draw attention to what Big Job was doing in the house. I was surprised when he and Woo, who moved in to work with him on both the growing operation and also the band's business, opened the door to a constant parade of friends and *business associates.* When we'd return from tours, the place had the feel of a frat house the morning after a big party. There was trash everywhere, dust and random junk littered around the joint. It reeked of marijuana and stale booze.

It was Big Job's ass that was going down if a bust happened. We all knew that, and this fact made him the king of the castle. It was his risk, so he was the boss. The only risk to me was if a raid happened, the contents of the house would be confiscated. That would include the majority of my possessions, stored in the garage.

My hope was that Woo and Big Job would harmoniously co-exist in the Salinas house, joining forces to elevate our business to the next level. They had a whole house to themselves, plenty of pot to smoke, and a lucrative crop approaching harvest time. Sadly, the two didn't click, and instead developed an antagonistic, distrustful relationship doomed to go nowhere in a hurry. Big Job accused Woo of hording product, breaking fictitious Miami kingpin Frank Lopez's rule of drug trafficking: *Don't get high on your own supply.* Woo accused Big Job of allowing his newfound position of power to go to his head.

---

[192] I bought the *Learn Spanish* CD's, now I need to start listening to them.

"You don't want me to smoke so much pot, but you buy your cigarettes and booze without thinking about it," Woo griped.

"Yeah? Well you just sit on your ass and take bong rips all day," Big Job countered. It was disappointing that the pair of them couldn't pull it together on behalf of the organization. Their grievances seemed trivial, and among band members there was a consensus that they were both to blame. I sat down with Todd and Big Job to discuss possible solutions, and Big Job offered only one: "Woo's gotta go." Todd agreed. I said, "No way, Woo's not leaving, and that's not negotiable." But it wasn't exactly my call. It wasn't my house, after all. My name wasn't on the lease. My ass wasn't on the line if the heat came down. I had to defer to the guys who had put this Salinas situation together in the first place, and they thought the best idea was for Woo to return to Chico.

Reluctantly, I called a meeting in the backyard and broke the news to the big fella. He was disappointed and angry. I didn't know if he would just walk away from everything, or accept the decision and continue working with the band from Chico. Somehow, I salvaged my personal relationship with Woo and he remained a part of the team, even after clearing out and heading back to his parents' ranch.

The Salinas house wasn't a comfortable place to be for more than a few days. Any time there was a knock at the door, you wondered if this was the *moment of reckoning*—if someone had tipped off the police, who were about to storm in with a search warrant. Also, things were going south with the growing operation. Mites had infested the plants, embedding themselves in the walls of the house. The place was getting trashed beyond belief. Numerous fixtures had been broken, and mold was growing in the nasty, dirty carpet. The place was in bad shape.

Todd, who had yet again coughed up his hard-earned savings to invest in this place, began to fear all would be lost. He no longer had faith in Big Job to salvage the situation, his own personal relationship with the Kingpin of Salinas well on its way down the toilet.

Wildman was no longer living in the band house. He had found himself a girlfriend, Ariel, who had completely swept him off his feet. Widman was growing darker and darker about the band's woes, and threw his passionate all into his relationship with Ariel, who seemed equally smitten. At one point, trying to acknowledge the fact that circumstances of his life had changed, and perhaps his priorities as well, I said, "I realize your relationship with your girlfriend fills an emotional void, man..."

Wildman shot back, an edge to his voice, "A huge emotional void... a HUGE void!"

This was the beginning of the end for Wildman, although he would continue on with the group for another year. I saw the writing on the wall, and there was nothing I could do about it. Truthfully, I was happy he found somebody. He'd been having a hard time with the organization's difficulties and failures, and rarely sought refuge, as I and others did, through short-term flings on the road. Excluding a few instances, he wasn't wired that way. How could I begrudge the man for finding someone to care for?

What I *did* begrudge was the extent to which Wildman transferred his passions and energies to his relationship with his girlfriend, leaving little for the creative progress of the band. He stopped writing music, and writing music was his greatest asset to the project. I felt he was giving up not only on our band, but on the scene in general. The guy got bitter. It was tough for all of us to watch other bands rise in popularity, make more money, and land the prestigious gigs like Jam Cruise, High Sierra and Bonnaroo. It hurt me, sure, but it hurt Wildman more. He was a competitive, intense guy, and it killed him that we were being passed by bands he felt were not as good.

The sad truth is that we had a chance to be something special. *We coulda been a contendah.* Between Wildman, Chase and myself, there was a lot of talent: playing talent, writing talent and producing talent. We had the potential, between the three of us, to make great albums. Hardships and life circumstances were getting in the way of the music by this point, unfortunately, and in the end, hardships and life circumstances would win. We didn't have a solid enough business infrastructure to showcase our collective abilities. We had no marketing plan, and no money to implement one.

We had been trying to play Vancouver for over a year, and finally got the chance when we were added to the Zoophorus festival, which also had Karl Denson's Tiny Universe, Garaj Mahal, and the popular eighties hip-hop group, De La Soul. After a strange show in Tacoma, Washington, we drove through the night to Whistler, the popular international ski resort community north of Vancouver. When we arrived we learned that Karl Denson's Tiny Universe was cancelling their appearance. Karl had been turned away from a flight in Colorado because he didn't have I.D.

We did a set on the festival stage the first day, then two more opening shows for Garaj Mahal at an adjacent indoor club. It went well—Micah was having problems with the music at times, but I liked his sense of interaction with the rest of us. There was an organic quality to his jamming. Also, he was intelligent and easygoing, qualities which made him pleasant to have on the road.

After a long dry spell with the opposite sex, Chase hooked up with Tabitha, a tall, sociable brunette he met at the Garaj Mahal shows in Whistler. After meeting, the pair had disappeared to enjoy a sensual romp of some sort, which had the effect of completely blowing Chase's mind. I was happy for Chase, and so was everyone else. He needed some female love in his life. Tabitha rode with us back to Vancouver, where we stayed for a day of rest and sight-seeing. I kept to myself mostly, pounding out prose at a downtown Starbucks. We dropped off Tabitha and picked up Fareed Haque, who I'd agreed to give a ride to the Seattle airport.

The drive with Fareed was full of levity. We joked about the music business, women and other subjects, and had an intelligent lunch discussion at a diner near the border. Somebody asked Fareed if he was familiar with mullets. He smiled and pulled from his wallet an old I.D., which showed him sporting a full-blown *ape drape*. I asked if the hairdo had a name. Fareed said no, so I thought for a moment, and then suggested one: *The Pakistani Possum*. Everyone laughed out loud, including Fareed. We stopped at a gas station before hitting the airport, and I sang the praises of Twix cookies to Fareed inside the convenience store.

"Everyone talks about the caramel and the chocolate, but you know, it's the cookie that really makes a Twix."

"Yeah... it's a damn good cookie."

Once we dropped off Fareed, we did a gig at the Ballard Firehouse in Seattle, followed by shows in Portland, Hood River, Moscow, and then a three-day stint in Big Fork, Montana. The presence of Mr. Peepers during the Northwest tour created an environment reminiscent of a junior high school camping trip. There was farting, crude lyrics sung over familiar songs, gay jokes, butt jokes, frequent, loud belly-laughter, rough-housing, and a general tone of adolescent mischief. Also, Peepers introduced a new form of drug abuse to my band members: *bubble hash knife hits*. Curious, I decided to watch a certain band member engage in this practice before the first show in Big Fork. He began by heating the end of a kitchen knife on the stove in the small, ratty apartment bequeathed to us for our stay on the banks of Flathead Lake. Once the knife was sufficiently toasty, the band member placed a small piece of hash on the end of the knife, and then pressed another heated utensil down against the substance. As smoke rose from the knife, he captured it in a sawed off water bottle, while pressing his lips against the rim of it, sucking up the fumes. He assured me that a couple of these hits would get you really messed up. I chose not to partake, but it was interesting to watch.

I felt like my keyboard playing jumped up a level around this time, for no reason in particular. I was suddenly playing more melodically than in the past, telling stories with my solos, avoiding clichés and familiar patterns.

A couple guys from a band called the Withdrawals sat in, adding interest to the second set. We funked out on *Underground* and embarked on long, Latin forays during *Groovebagg* and *Straight No Chaser.* A percussionist named Chongo stretched out on a couple long solos.

After the gig, a pair of drunks staggered out into the street and became violent. They were too wasted to cause any real damage to each other, and spent the next hour screaming, wrestling around on the ground, reconciling, and then trying to beat the crap out of one another again. Mr. Peepers, Micah and I watched from the apartment upstairs, laughing at the display of inebriated testosterone. This town needed more women.

Mr. Peepers was the quintessential alpha male. This was why a twenty-three year old kid was able to encourage men several years older to regress to such juvenile tendencies on the road. Back in the room, which was lined with bunk beds, Wildman, who was feeling no pain, chased Micah around, a hood pulled over his head to mimic the maniacal ghost girl from *The Ring.*

Micah giggled in short, giddy outbursts, and Chase was passed out on a couch. More than one guy was exhausted from the long gig and multiple bubble hash knife hits. I was on my bed, trying to concentrate on Joe Queenan and William Goldman books, despite the chaos caused by tripped out, grown men chasing each other around the room. I wasn't bugged—that was life on the road, and there were plenty of moments when I was the one running around acting the fool.

I felt like I was on a different wavelength at times. Not higher, just different. The band needed a cheerleader, a motivator, but I was introverted and self-contained. I wasn't interested in other people's issues and challenges. This doesn't work well in a band, particularly if you're supposed to be the leader. I didn't realize that my aloofness was hurting the group as much as it was. I began to feel separated from the rest of the tribe, ostracized in a way; but looking back, it was me who created the distance, not them.

The two-year anniversary of 9/11 occurred while we were in Montana. A woman on ESPN announced, "When we return, we'll take a look at how sports reacted to 9/11." That struck me as really stupid. Who cares *how sports reacted to 9/11?* 9/11 demonstrated how *unimportant* sports were in the big scheme of things. I'm a sports fan, but sports don't really mean squat. They're simply a diversion from the more quotidian aspects of life. I suppose some would say the same thing about music.[193]

We played in Missoula at a club called the Top Hat. The soundman was a character, introducing the band with a lengthy spiel about all the bands that were coming to the club after us, along with some canned patter that reminded me of the emcees in strip clubs. *Gentlemen, show some support for these lovely ladies… throw money.* The second set included some interesting jams, and happening versions of *Feel the Sun* and *Mr. Potatohead*, a clever Wildman composition.

Wildman had a unique songwriting style, taking great care with each composition as if it was a novel, an entire saga unto itself. He wouldn't write a new song unless he had a complete, fully realized concept. He was a huge fan of the *Lord of the Rings* books, a fantasy freak. His songs told stories of strange characters, both human and animal, that were the products of his imagination. While I believe his songwriting talents would have ultimately been recognized on a bigger level, Wildman suffered from the fact that his vocal delivery was excessively similar to that of Trey Anastasio. He had adopted certain inflections that characterized the singing style of Phish's frontman, and more than a few people took note of the fact. For example, Wildman had copped Anastasio's tendency to *drop off* at the end of phrases, from a singing tone into a spoken tone. Also, Wildman's lyric-writing approach… the incorporation of intellectual ideas and a certain, well, nerdy and quirky style of storytelling… was decidedly Phish-influenced. If he had continued writing, I believe he would have overcome this fact and developed his own identity. But he lost the fire. He lost his commitment and purpose, and thus only wound up contributing a handful of songs to the GFC repertoire when all was said and done.

---

[193] …although I feel music taps into something a bit deeper.

Mr. Peepers had taken a liking to the digital camera I picked up before the tour, and was now constantly taking pictures and shooting videos of everybody, attempting to catch guys in incriminating situations. After I spent one evening hanging out with a young woman of the plump variety, Peepers, who had gone to great lengths to snap shots of me socializing with the girl, who while overweight had a very pretty face, started referring to me as *Captain Ahab.* I, in turn, had begun teasing Mr. Peepers about his *cherkin.*

What's a cherkin, you ask? Let's start with Webster's definition of a peculiar item called a *merkin.* A merkin is a pubic hair wig for women. WTF?, you're wondering? Don't ask me. I don't make the rules. I don't work for Webster, and I have absolutely no idea what the practical applications of such an item could possibly be. Anyway, I took the word *merkin* and combined it with *chin* to come up with *cherkin*—a chin merkin, if you will, or long beard that looks like overgrown pubic hair hanging down from the face... precisely the style of nappy facial hair Mr. Peepers was sporting.

As was the case with mullets, I discovered there was a great variety of cherkins floating around in America. There was the cherk-a-farian, the Cherk Norris, and the Charles Cherkley, to name just a few. It was easier to capture images of cherkins in their natural habitat, because cherkin owners usually thought you were simply taking a picture of their face. With mullets, you often had to come up from behind to get the proper angle, a move which raised the subject's suspicion; typical mullet-sporters were well aware that their chosen hairstyle was prone to generate ridicule, and they were thus defensive and potentially hostile when they sensed that someone was attempting to document their plumage for inclusion on a website like mulletsgalore.com.

Somewhere between the middle of nowhere and Reno, I announced to the crew that I'd be hosting a scavenger hunt once we reached our destination. I'd made the decision to stop chronicling the band's ongoing saga—I was tired of keeping a mental inventory of everything interesting that happened from day to day—and the book would have to conclude with some colorful event; with a little *flair.*[194] I wanted to create a carnival atmosphere, with Mr. Peepers spearheading the festivities. Pumped up by this temporary promotion from roadie to

---

[194] Just like Jennifer Aniston in *Office Space.*

ringleader, the Bucktoothed Avenger[195] asked if he might procure some extracurricular recreation for himself, when we got to the California border.

"Sure... on your nickel," I replied.

Here's how I launched the scavenger hunt:

I will be your guide and your chauffeur. I will remain throughout the night at your disposal. Should you emerge victorious from your quest, you will be treated to a leisurely, all-you-can-eat breakfast at IHOP (crepes, bacon, orange juice, lousy service). If you lose, you will be treated to a five-minute pit-stop at 7-11 (frozen burritos, chocolate milk). Bring me:

- One pair of women's underpants.
- One cowboy hat (okay if stolen).
- A picture of Ted Kennedy, Toni Kukoc, and Tawny Kitaen.
- A short video featuring a midget or a dwarf.
- A photo of Mr. Peepers' face buried in cleavage of at least 40D caliber.
- A sample in a jar (use your imagination, extra points for creativity).
- A picture of somebody in the band's bare ass, with a casino security guard also in the frame.
- One birth control pill from a prostitute.
- One Del Taco employee mission statement.

As I was formulating all this in my mind, I was pulled over by a highway patrolman in Oregon. He had been perched on a bluff nearly a mile away, and nailed me with the long-distance radar gun. Our conversation went something like this:

Me: What's the word, my man?

Cop: License, registration, proof of insurance, please.

Me: Have you seen the movie *Supertroopers*? 'Cause you look like the one guy with the buzzcut.

Cop: You wanna play games? You want me to search your vehicle?

Me: Only if you plan on re-packing it when you're done, 'cause it's a real pain in the ass.

---

[195] As identified by Karl Denson.

Alright, I didn't really say this stuff, but this is the conversation I *wanted* to have. The cop gave me a ticket and we continued towards Reno. After shaking off the first ticket, I receive a *second* on the way into Winnemucca, a little gambling outpost a hundred miles out of Reno. Apparently the highway leading into Winnemucca had a 35 mph speed limit. Since I was going 67 mph, the officer informed me that he would be justified to write me up for reckless driving.

"I already got one ticket earlier today, Officer."

"I don't care." I resisted the urge to talk back, and my acquiescence was rewarded. The guy let me off on the reckless driving charge.

I was looking for some action in Reno. Something to rival the juicier moments of my story, and something that would provide a fitting "button" to my rambling, crazy tale. I came up a bit short. It seems you just can't manufacture these things. They have to happen organically. It wasn't a bad effort, however. These were the highlights: Mr. Peepers approaches female mullet at casino bar. Her male friend, a Vanilla Ice look-alike, steps in to defend her.

Mr. Peepers: I'm documenting mullets. I'm with a band, and we really like your girlfriend's hairdo.

Friend: Oh yeah? What's a mullet?

Mr. Peepers: Chop it on top, let if flow in the back.

Friend: (getting mildly angry) So whadda you call that mess *you* got goin'?

Mr. Peepers: My beard? It's called a cherkin. It's like a pubic hair wig for women, only it's real hair, and it's on my chin.

Fistfight narrowly averted.

In the elevator, Mr. Peepers realizes the scavenger list is nowhere near complete. He approaches a pair of female sexagenarians and asks, "Can you ladies lend me some underwear? Me and my friends are on a scavenger hunt."

We attempt to procure a copy of the Del Taco employee mission statement. Gwendoline, working the drive-through window as we pull up, hands us a piece of cardstock. It's not what we're looking for, but it's in the ballpark:

Hi! Would you like to try our new Tacoss Del Carbon today?

If you are on morning shift, use the Ultra Breakfast Sell: *Hi! Would you like to try our new hash-browns today?*

Micah yells out to me as he chases a pair of prostitutes up the street, "Hey T, are these ones big enough? You said 44 D's right?" We find a pair of open-minded, full-bodied ladies who allow Mr. Peepers to burrow in for the bosom shot. They keep their shirts on, unfortunately.

It's 3:15 am and we're at the Golden Phoenix Bar, where we meet some nice folks from Northern California. I wind up talking for a long time to a nice twenty-eight year-old named Rachel. I drink several beers in the process.

Micah has had enough, and announces he's grabbing a cab back to the Nugget.

The sun is up, Chase's head hurts from where he banged it in the elevator earlier, while asking a random prostitute for a birth control pill, and the three of us—Chase, Mr. Peepers and I—are very hungry.

Chase and I approach the front doors to McDonald's, but they are locked. Chase begins pounding frantically on the door, screaming "Open up now!" Inside, an employee holds up seven fingers. "It's always six! It's always six!" Chase protests.

We drive to Wal-Mart to steal some employee vests. I quickly grab a vest from an unattended back counter and return to the van.

I am now sporting a blue Wal-Mart uniform, and cannot resist pulling over on the freeway for a photo op. I jump out of the driver's seat and run back, against traffic, to an abandoned El Camino. I hop on the hood, strike a pose, and Mr. Peepers takes the picture. We head back downtown.

Chase has stolen a bag of mops from Wal-Mart, but we don't need any mops, so we discard them along the freeway.

It's snack time at McDonald's. As we case the wall near the registers, hoping to make off with an Employee of the Month plaque, we get made by the manager. We take off.

We return to the Wal-Mart for more vests. This time both Mr. Peepers and Chase are successful. Now we're all wearing Wal-Mart employee vests.

It's time to hit the strip clubs. The problem is, none of them are open at this hour, and I for one am completely exhausted.

There's still some unfinished business. We go back to McDonald's a third time. The sun is beating down, and the Jagermeister and Red Bull shots have worn off now. We're operating on pure adrenaline.

"We both know it is your destiny to go back into McDonald's and steal the *cool greens, warm chicken* sign," I tell Mr. Peepers.

"Face your calling, Oh Cherkin-Growing One."

"I know, T, I know."

I pull the van up next to the McDonald's, park illegally in a traffic lane, flip on my hazards and wait. I'm not there long before Mr. Peepers bolts from the fast food joint, jumps in with the sign and screams, "Go T, go!" In the background, we hear a whiny voice shouting "Come back! You can't keep that!" We screech out of there, and although I'm riding a sudden burst of energy once again, I'm also overwhelmed with a certain feeling of sadness. There are numerous items on the scavenger list which have not been gathered. Still, I'm proud of the guys. We've accomplished quite a bit here in Reno on a quiet Sunday night. We all need sleep desperately, and return to the Nugget to grab a couple hours before the Grim Housekeeping Reaper shows up to oust us from our dark, tenth floor lairs.

HOW MANY PEOPLE YOU GOT IN THAT VAN?

In September of 2003, Len broke the news that he was putting Bobby, our nineteen year-old cat, to sleep. Bobby had showed up on our doorstep one night in the mid-eighties, meowing for milk, and never left. His presence gave both Len and me something positive to cling to, something to focus on instead of our lingering sadness over the breakup of the nuclear family.

Bobby had been getting progressively sicker in 2003, and Len felt it was time to put him out of his misery. Many an evening had been spent in the family room, watching TV while Bobby rolled around on the carpet, rubbing his soft head against my leg. It was around this time the family also lost Aunt Erin to lung cancer. I regrettably missed the funeral, stuck down in New Orleans during Jazzfest.

GFC pulled into Monterey for the city's famous Jazz Festival. We got to the fairgrounds with a couple hours to kill, procured our credentials, and checked out the scene. I sensed the show was going to be a little rough with Gruden, our latest drummer,[196] who had flown out from his native New Jersey to replace Micah. Gruden was a handsome, stocky blonde guy with considerable musical talent. He played not only drums but also bass and guitar, and he had perfect pitch. It was unfortunate that his first show with the band was going to be such a high-profile appearance, a featured spot at one of the world's great music festivals. If he came out thrashing around like Ichabod at Harry O's, God help us.

Before our set we checked out a young, smoking all-star band from Berklee College. The college sent them around to various festivals to show the world what great musicians were being developed in their practice rooms. The group executed interesting polyrhythmic arrangements coupled with mature solos.

Earlier in the day Wildman, a bitter Berklee drop-out who felt the experience had been a major rip-off, walked up to the university's recruiting booth, where a representative was busy trying to convert a few young prospects. "Lies!" Wildman screamed. "It's all lies! Don't give them your money!" The guy was never afraid to rock the boat, to ruffle some feathers. He took pleasure in it.

We took the stage and proceeded to get through our hour-and-a-half set—not triumphantly but respectably. Our music was a bit rock-oriented for the jazz audience, but we managed to get over thanks to a cheering section of close friends and family members.

After the festival, we drove to Ojai to play a much humbler gathering, the Frequinox, held in Cuyama Valley. We were co-headlining with a Los Angeles band called Mama Sutra, and en route, stopped mistakenly at a compound called the Songdog Ranch. I'd never been to this part of California, somewhere between the 5 and 101 freeways. The ranch was on a remote lot of property with an old, decrepit windmill that moaned in the wind like a tortured animal. Dilapidated sheds and farming equipment peppered the grounds. I felt like I was in a Stephen King novel.

Looking for directions to the festival, I walked into the main entrance, where I was greeted by a bug-eyed lurch of an old man. The place, dark and musty, looked like it hadn't been cleaned in years, and I couldn't gather if it was functioning as some sort of fucked up bed

---

[196] I thought the guy looked a lot like John Gruden, the handsome NFL coach/TV analyst, so I started calling him Gruden.

and breakfast, a hostel for itinerant riff raff, or simply a private residence which had gone to hell. I thought of all the horror movies that started out this way... *Some unsuspecting guy walks into a remote, creepy place occupied by creepy people, ignoring the universally shared instinct to stay the hell away from abandoned properties in the middle of nowhere...* Fortunately the bug-eyed character had no designs on incorporating me in the evening's menu, and kindly pointed me in the direction of the Freaquinox.

The festival turned out to be appropriately named, as it took place during the summer equinox and was attended by a great number of *freaks.* Upon arrival we climbed up a winding dirt road, to a spectacular bluff overlooking the entire Cuyama Valley. There we were surrounded by men in dresses and other gender-bending costumes, sexy young female dancers, and a curious assortment of kooks, hippies and colorful partiers.

Mama Sutra was a friendly bunch, and liked GFC. They had recommended us for the Freaquinox.

As we were setting up to play, Mr. Peepers said something flippant that rubbed me the wrong way. I walked over and knocked a full beer out of his hand, then pushed him back a couple feet. He went over to my keyboards and snatched up his collection of magic crystals, which he always placed on my gear as little talismans of good vibes and funky jamming. Chase and Wildman marched over to tell me I "wasn't being cool," siding with Peepers in knee-jerk fashion. This just made me angrier and I stormed off. A tremendous orange sunset was taking form against the horizon. I found a quiet area and sat by myself, watching the sun fall as I cooled off. There were days when I loved and admired those guys in all their scruffy glory. Then there were other days when I couldn't stand being around the bastards, and I cursed myself for continuing so long and far down such an absurd life path. I'm sure they all felt the same way.

The show went well. Arlen, the long-haired, scraggly keyboardist for Mama Sutra, joined us for a few songs, lugging his B-3 organ onstage for the jam. He sounded great, coaxing interesting sounds from the drawbars. Gruden's energetic drumming propelled us into some sweet jams, including a spontaneous Afrobeat groove over a song called *Underground.* Wildman, Chase and I grinned at each other, heads bobbing with approval.

When another band took the side stage to play, Woo and I stood nearby chuckling to ourselves. The female singer looked like what would emerge from The Fly's mutation pod if you fused Teri Garr and Marilyn Manson, then handed the resulting creature a tambourine. The guitarist recited *new age* poetry over a generic tabla groove, the singer yodeling bizarre melodies in the background. These homegrown events were often rooted in the ripe-for-parody folk/psychedelic subculture, its practitioners expressing sentiments that might have packed more punch back in the days when LBJ was trying to salvage Vietnam.

I was fading, the six Red Bulls I'd chugged all but worn off. It was two in the morning and Mama Sutra hadn't even started their set. I stood by the side of the stage watching Arlen set up his extensive keyboard rig. I thought *I* had a lot of stuff. Arlen had at least seven keyboards, all old and beat up. The Millenium Falcon of keyboard rigs, I had little faith this hodgepodge of vintage wires and contraptions would produce any sound at all.

When Mama Sutra finally started, my skepticism was removed. Arlen's gallimaufry of gadgets and gizmos produced amazing textures. The B-3 sounded incredible, and his vintage instruments created growly rumbles at just the right moments. Arlen's playing itself was equally impressive, as he took some great organ solos. Gruden and I stood near the stage, digging it.

Someone introduced me to a woman named Vera, a Mama Sutra groupie from Marin County who had written a forty-five page poem inspired by Ginsburg's *Howl*. I glossed over the first couple pages and said, "Wow, that looks really cool," not having any idea what she was talking about, but appreciating the artistic spirit.

The night took a colorful turn when a cloaked guy with a lisp gathered everyone in a circle and launched into a spiel about the land, the elements, the gods, and most important, fire. He paraded around the circle repeating the words, "With salt and water, I bless this place." Actually it was more like, "With ssssalt and water, I blesssss thisss placcce." The guys and I shielded ourselves behind the van, cracking up. Everyone else was holding hands and waxing mystical.

"Let the gamesssss begin," the ringleader proclaimed. A woman in a white robe began mock-fighting a mostly naked dude, both wielding swords made of fire. This was presented as an authentic battle, but you just knew that in the end the chick was going to kick the guy's ass. Like an old WWF bout between Hulk Hogan and Andre the Giant, the result had been pre-determined.

There were several other robed individuals eating fire, snorting fire, dancing with fire, and doing everything else one can do with fire (without actually setting oneself *on* fire). Once the female ass-kicker polished off the inferior male combatant, a second male challenger appeared, this time wielding *two* swords made of... you guessed it, fire. This fight was longer and more intricately choreographed. Again it seemed the female fire warrior would emerge victorious, furthering the apparent feminist agenda of the behind-the-scenes firefight planners. There was an unexpected twist, however, and the two warriors killed each other simultaneously... a symbolic denunciation of all violence in the world. Our spell-casting emcee wasn't done: "To the lordsssss of the watchtowers of the wesssst, I ask you... blesssssss this place! To the lordsssss of the watchtowers of the north I ask you... blessssss this place!"

En route to Fresno the following day, I got a call from Chris Taylor, my friend in Texas. Chris had established an e-mail correspondence with Lincoln Marcinco, the author of the popular *Rogue Warrior* books. He'd pitched Marcinco the idea of adapting one of his stories into a screenplay, and Marcinco thought it could fly. He gave Chris his agent's contact information, and Chris called me to see if I wanted to collaborate with him. I agreed, but told Chris to check with the agent first, to make sure the rights weren't already controlled by someone else.

"Do you think we could get paid to write it?" Chris asked me.

"Not a chance in hell," I responded. I explained that we'd have to write the script on *spec.*

"What does that mean?" he asked.

"Don't spec to get paid." The rights to Marcinco's story were in fact owned by someone else, and that someone else was the Disney Corporation.

"The agent was kind of an asshole on the phone," Chris said.

"Of course he was. He gets paid big bucks to be an asshole." That was the end of that.

After Fresno, we returned to San Diego to play Winston's, one of my familiar haunts from the old days. At a late-night Chinese restaurant, Gruden unloaded on me for telling him what to do onstage. I explained that I eventually wanted him to set tempos and start the songs, but until he learned the music better I would have to do it myself.

As you no doubt realize, I have long found comic inspiration in the movie *Spinal Tap,* but the sad truth was that my real-life band, Global Funk, was mirroring many aspects of the film. The most obvious example of this was my inability to keep the same dude in the drum chair for any extended length of time. Gruden was the seventh drummer, and the band was less than three years old.

The other guys in the band jumped on the bandwagon, complaining that I became *dark* onstage when things weren't going well—I would visibly express displeasure, which they felt was a drag. Perhaps I was acting just a little like Buddy Rich, the late drummer/bandleader known for his abusive, profane tirades directed at the musicians in his band, but I couldn't accept being part of a mediocre product. I wanted the show to sound well-rehearsed, not like some haphazard crap thrown together in a garage. I would get angry when guys missed cues, forgot arrangements, sang out of tune, or lost their concentration in the middle of a jam. I wouldn't curse at anyone, but I would convey my frustration when people made stupid mistakes, or went on mental vacations in the middle of a performance.

In music, you get a lot of people who chose the path because it allowed them to avoid conforming or feeling controlled by anyone or anything, and this is particularly true of people on the road. I wanted to run a tighter ship, but I wasn't offering enough of an opportunity, in terms of salary, prestige or other incentives to expect the musicians in my band to hold themselves to an exacting standard of professionalism. I had mistakenly established GFC as a collective, rather than a benevolent dictatorship, which was Karl Denson's model. Karl had a way of getting what he needed out of his players, and was notorious for not suffering fools. If somebody was obstinate or otherwise incapable of doing what the music required, believe me, the benevolence ended quickly.

The next stop was in Los Angeles at the Knitting Factory, a great gig... *if you were playing the main stage.* We'd been demoted to one of the small side rooms. Arlen, my keyboardist friend from Mama Sutra, showed up with not one, but *two* B-3 organs, eager to jam. The two organs took up so much space that there was barely room for the rest of the instruments.

Before the show, we all grabbed dinner at a Mexican restaurant. A homeless guy approached as we ate, and Arlen, to everyone's surprise, stood up and barked "So, like, why you gotta be asking us for money, bro? Why don't you go get a job and take care of your own problems?"

The guy took exception to Arlen's mini-lecture and punched him, all 140 pounds of him, in the chest. Mr. Peepers rose to his feet, tensed his upper body and told the confrontational beggar to "Keep stepping, man." He listened.

One of Gruden's buddies, Rocky George, the original guitarist from Suicidal Tendencies, joined us onstage, along with not only Arlen, but also Stien, one of the rappers from my old hip-hop group Faze, who happened to be in the house. Surprise sit-ins were a pleasant way to break up the monotony of playing the same songs, show after show.

Wildman was livid about the booking. We had pilfered a perfectly good weekend night on a lame door deal, in one of the tiny side rooms at the Knitting Factory. He called Rob Sarno and let him have it. I wasn't so angry, and enjoyed the ragtag spectacle of an impromptu performance by Arlen, the hippie organ virtuoso, joined by Rocky George, aging punk rock guitar hero, and Stien, bespectacled hip-hop homey from the old San Diego days.

At the end of the night, Arlen explained to me his dream for the future of Mama Sutra: *to head out on a national tour with fifty buses filled with people.* I myself couldn't make it work with one bus, so I wasn't sure how Arlen planned to manage fifty of them. The Mama Sutra bus was a sight to behold—completely gutted, lined with all kinds of crazy stuff: musical gear, clothes, makeshift beds, band merchandise, leftover food, two B-3 organs. That's rock and roll.

The next leg of GFC tour took us to Zion, Utah. I'd wanted to go there for a few years, people having told me how geologically interesting it was. We played a restaurant called the Bit n' Spur, right in the heart of Zion National Park. We were treated to a great dinner, but due to lack of hotel room space I would wind up sleeping on the floor. I hated sleeping on the floor.

Little Jesus didn't make the trek from Salt Lake City, but had asked me to say hello to a pair of twin girls who waited tables at the Bit n' Spur. When I obliged him and said hello on his behalf, one of the girls began to cry... while taking our food order. I wondered what the scruffy little roadie could have done to upset her so much.

"He's a bad person!" she wailed. "Don't mention his name to me again." Little Jesus was my buddy, and there are two sides to every coin—so I didn't jump on her bandwagon.

"I'm sorry you're upset... and uh, I'll take the pork chops and a side of shrimp skewers."

The show that night was ear-splittingly loud, with Chase's guitar amp right by my head, but the music was enjoyable. Gruden's drum grooves packed the floor with attractive women, and the staff seemed to like the band.

The next morning, after getting booted from the El Rio Lodge, we followed Laney, an old friend of mine from Park City, out to a place called the Flyin' Zion Ranch. We had to scramble over at least a couple miles of unpaved road—always a treat—before arriving at the multi-acre spread, a variation on the middle-of-nowhere-hippie-compound theme with which I'd become quite comfortable through my travels.

A guy named Shave Deekley[197] showed us around. It was *Artist Week* out at the ranch, and people had come from near and far to set up shop and create woodwork, metalwork and jewelry. There was no actual house out there, only a scattered assortment of tents, hangars and work stations. There were tractors, dilapidated parts and random detritus, rusted barrels and fuel tanks, old beat up trucks with skulls fastened to their front grills, big stacks of chopped firewood, more skulls hanging from trees, a couple psychedelic school busses converted into living quarters, and a round clay structure I was told was an adobe sweathouse.

Laney interrupted the tour to ask if I'd like to take some organic peppers for our trek to Mystic Hot Springs later in the afternoon. I said yes. A friendly black dog approached, its tongue drooping out of his mouth, as a gentle zephyr blew through the leaves of cottonwood, ash and tamarisk trees surrounding the property. I typed on my laptop while sitting at a shaded, wooden picnic table. A man introduced himself as Gale; he was fortyish, sported a cowboy hat, had blonde curly hair and a tapered little half-goatee, and was shirtless. He informed me that the tamarisks were a nuisance out here and in similar desert locales. They swept across the land like a weed, wiping out cottonwoods and anything else in their path. They did provide shade however, which could be quite a commodity in this or any other desert.

I wandered around on my own a bit. I opened the door to the adobe sweathouse, and no less than half a dozen sizable lizards scurried in various directions. I took a look inside, giving half a thought to climbing in for a minute, but was overcome with sudden claustrophobic unease. Next to the sweathouse sat a tall, cylindrical

---

[197] That was his real name... I'm not making it up.

outhouse structure that looked like an old discarded nuclear warhead from the fifties. I could hear power saws in the distance. Somebody was hard at work over at the stone cutting table.

Laney cooked up a nice breakfast with eggs, salsa, cheese and tortillas. Her boyfriend Johnny was a tall white guy with long, dreaded hair stuffed under a white baseball hat, and big, round discs lodged in each earlobe. He looked like Kid Rock, post-conversion to an indigenous tribe in Zaire. Mr. Peepers returned from a short journey, dropping several pieces of alabaster next to my Toshiba.

My attention was directed to a spectacular view of the Kinesava Peak, a towering mass of red, jutting rock. I learned its name from Roger, a swarthy, fiftyish character with white, slicked back hair... the owner of this whole spread. Roger asked, not necessarily in the most cordial of tones, "Who are *you?*"

Zaire Johnny walked by with a plate of cookies and announced, "Here's our first bootie out of the solar cooker." I got a closer look at Johnny when he came over to tell me about the solar cookies. "They're loaded with THC," he warned me as I took note of the NBA-caliber tattoos he had on each sinewy bicep, along with a twisty, frizzy beard that seemed to shoot out in at least four directions. There was a black guy in overalls and nothing underneath sitting near me, soaking up the relaxed vibes.

Roger hopped into his truck to head back to his old trailer, telling the overall-wearing guy: "I'm gonna take a nap before I start getting grouchy. Then, I'm gonna get up and eat some beans." Life was simple on the Flyin' Zion Ranch.

Getting out of Zion proved a fiasco. Roger coerced Chase and me into helping him lift some heavy rocks. The day was getting long and we needed to leave for Mystic Springs, but Roger made us feel like were freeloading on his property, and should make some gesture to prove ourselves useful. It was a lot of guilt for a goddamn tortilla and some scrambled eggs, but that's the way it was. So, we piled into his old truck along with the black guy in suspenders, who never said a word, and drove back out that winding dirt road towards town. We crossed the main road and drove up onto a bluff, where there was a palette with long, angular pieces of limestone resting on it. Roger handed out gloves, and we lifted the heavy rocks onto his truck. I nearly smashed my fingers in the process, and everyone looked over in fear. "They're not broken," I assured. "But this *is* a fairly risky activity for someone in my line of work," I noted.

Once the limestone was secure in the truck, Chase and I realized there was no room for us to ride in back. We had no way to get back to Flyin' Zion. Roger said he'd alert the other guys in the band that we were waiting for them, and pass them my message to leave the ranch and pick us up, en route to our next engagement. We waited a couple hours, and I started to get concerned. Finally the van came rambling up the street as dusk approached. It was just Jeffrey. No Mr. Peepers.

"What happened?" I asked.

"We were waiting for you guys to get back."

"I told Roger to tell you to pick us up. Did he?"

"No."

"Where's Mr. Peepers?"

"He's still fucking around up there, looking for crystals."

"We gotta get outa' here. We have a show to play tonight." We booked it back to the ranch, and I hopped out to look for Mr. Peepers. There was Roger, lounging with a couple of his cronies.

"Hey man, why didn't you tell those guys to come get us?"

"Oh yeah… I said I'd do that, didn't I."

"Yeah, you did. I was sitting in an ice cream shop, waiting."

"I'm an old hippie. We space out sometimes." I tracked down Mr. Peepers, flying high after a successful hunt for crystals, and we hit the road.

We made it to Rustic Wells and played the show. There were more in attendance than usual, but this still only meant a handful. Rustic was so far off the beaten path that people had to be coming on purpose, and it they were driving from Salt Lake City, it was a three-hour journey. I made the effort to stop there a couple times a year because Tom, the owner, always treated us well. It wasn't a money or prestige gig, but more of a *family hang*.

After playing that night in the little performance room at Rustic, I stayed up until seven am. I was in a crazed creative mode, working to finish the outline to my rewrite for the screenplay *Deviance*. I had fifty-five notecards strewn all over the ping-pong table in Tom's lobby, and was studying them, shifting them around, adding things, consulting my notes, the laptop. Everyone was sleeping, so it was calm and quiet… a great time to write.

When I finished working at seven, I wasn't quite ready for bed. My mind was still going. I treated myself to a big bowl of Breyer's mint chip ice cream, and polished it off just before the sun came up. Once I lay down, I didn't fall right asleep. The creative wheels were still turning, and I stared at the ceiling for another hour.

On our way back to California, we stopped in Las Vegas to crash, at the Motel 6 on Tropicana Boulevard. The guys hit the Strip, but I stayed back. I was tired after my crazed writing session the previous night, and I'd done the Strip plenty of times. Unless you're going to throw money around and/or get hammered, there's not much to do on Las Vegas Boulevard except gawk at the lights, and saunter through ostentatious, labyrinthine casino structures like a tourist rube.

As I sat there in my Motel 6 cubicle—and when I say cubicle I mean it, because Motel 6 rooms are the size of a prison cell—I harbored some negative thoughts. I didn't like playing as loud as we did in Global Funk. My ears rang constantly. Furthermore, my keyboard gear was beat up after years of inevitable road abuse. We had to deal with a new soundman every night; sometimes the guy would be a downright dick, bitter about his job, bitter about having to pretend he cared about how we sounded... bitter that his career as a rock guitarist had crashed and burned years earlier. Sometimes the soundman was a cool guy, but the gear he was working with was dog shit. Bad speakers, not enough wattage, electrical problems that caused amps to buzz, inherently lousy acoustics, a club owner that didn't care enough to replace stuff when it was broken... I could go on.

If the soundman was a tool, you had to try and get what you needed from him without pissing him off, so that he wouldn't sabotage your show. I was never too great at dealing with recalcitrant soundmen diplomatically, and suspect I'm still not today. I just don't have patience for incompetence in the workplace, regardless of the milieu. *I'm sorry you don't like your job, man. I'm sorry you have to sit behind that little malfunctioning sound board in this crummy club in (insert city name), catering to low-rung touring musicians night after night. I'm sorry you're not chilling in an air-conditioned Prevost, doing front-of-house for Kings of Leon. But let's not forget, we are the architects of our own destiny.*

Further contributing to my woes was the fact that I'd gone through *six drummers in one year,* and had thus been forced to re-learn and perform the same repertoire over and over, month after month. This made me reconsider my original choice to become a full-time musician; I've never liked doing the same thing in the exact same way twice. I've always been most happy when creating something new. That's what I get off on: creating something out of nothing. Not many people can do this productively and consistently, but like my mom, I can do it all day.

So when I find myself in a situation where I can't be creative, for whatever reason, my soul suffers.

I had started GFC as a vehicle for creating new stuff, and in the beginning it was—but as I had come to understand the nature of leading a touring band, I realized that what I *really* signed up to do was develop and manage a small business. In a touring act, too much of one's time was spent caught up in the logistics of it all. The booking, promoting, planning, driving, fixing. Also, as a leader, the bulk of one's energies were directed toward managing other people. This is a valuable ability, as everyone knows, but I would argue that it isn't an artistically fulfilling one.[198]

After Vegas, we headed back to Southern California. What follows is the event that, looking back, I believe was the dagger in the heart of my complicated relationship with Wildman. Things would never be the same again, and the band, generally speaking, went downhill from there, never to bounce back. Here's what happened...

The band played a show in Santa Barbara, and then crashed at our friend Lipp's pad in Ventura. The following evening, I led a group up to the house of some new friends, not far from Lipp's. I'd met a couple nice girls at the Santa Barbara show, one in particular named Kristina, who wanted to hang out. She had invited us up to this house, so there we were. We stayed for a couple hours, listening to music, talking about the pop cultural relevance of *The Simpsons,* hitting the hot tub. I sat around watching everyone else smoke weed. It was a relaxing hang, and everyone was feeling good as we drove back toward Lipp's house.

When we pulled off the 101 to drive the final couple miles, we wound up at a red light next to a small, black car with four young guys inside. The one in the front passenger seat, a geeky kid who looked like a young Bill Gates, was trying to say something to me, so I rolled my window down. It turned out he wanted to *insult* us. He was drunk or high on something.

"Hey, how many people you got in that van? Is that a *special* van? Aren't you guys supposed to be wearing helmets?" I responded with a less-than-flattering comment of my own, and this initiated a war on

---

[198] I'm sure some self-help gurus out there would vehemently argue with me on that: *I beg to differ! Managing people is highly creative! Perhaps that's why your business failed!* Blah, blah, blah.

Victoria Boulevard between us — me, to be more specific — and a car full of aimless young fools. We pulled up next to them at the next few red lights, the verbal barrage continuing back and forth. I wasn't enjoying being cursed at by a twerp with glasses and a bowl cut, and without thinking I reached for a near-empty Starbucks cup. I hurled it at the kid, and its remaining contents splashed on his face. His friends laughed at him, and *my* friends laughed at him. I had raised the stakes, and the humiliated kid began throwing things back at our van. Plastic bottles, I'm guessing, which ricocheted off but didn't cause damage.

My guys were getting uncomfortable, yelling at me to get away from these idiots. The situation was getting out of control. I attempted to escape the late-night miscreants, but knew we were in trouble when Bill Gates Jr. popped up and out of the sun roof, cocked his arm back, and fired an unidentified projectile at our long back window, which then *shattered into a million pieces*. The little black car attempted to speed away at this point, but I followed them to get their license plate. Wildman called the police on his cell. As we tailed the culprits onto the 126 onramp, they did a sharp 180 degree turn, so they were now facing us, and sped back up the onramp *going the wrong way*. They could have killed themselves, and anyone else who might have been getting on the freeway.

Wildman scowled at me in disgust. This situation was more or less my fault, I agreed. I apologized once we made it back to Lipp's house, but it fell on deaf ears. Officer Gomez of the Ventura Police Department showed up to file a report, and I explained what had happened. He looked straight at me and asked, "Don't you think you acted foolishly out there?"

"Yeah," I said.

"It could have ended much worse," he continued. All the while, Wildman paced nearby, glowering in my direction. The cop dispatched another squad car to the Camarillo address matching the license plate of the black car — we'd scribbled down the plate during the chase. The officers at that scene knocked on the door, and a middle-age woman answered, the mother of one of the guys. She already knew what was going on, and the next day the kid who threw the rock through my window turned himself in at the Ventura police station.

I woke up at the crack of dawn to make arrangements to get the van's shattered side window replaced. I found a place to do the work, and drove the van over for the repair. Later that afternoon, once I'd returned to Lipp's house, Wildman marched in, announcing something along the lines of: "I have a right to surround myself with people who aren't going to endanger my life!" As he said this, he was carrying a new carton of cigarettes he'd just bought. I'd been inhaling his second-hand smoke for two years, so I said something like this: "Nice timing to accuse me of threatening your life... as you walk in carrying a fresh carton of cancer sticks." A snarky remark, yes—but with the exceptionally bright, quick-witted Wildman, you had to fight intellectual fire with fire, or be buried quickly. You had to be thinking a retort or two ahead, like in chess, or he would cut you off at the knees with one pithy, sarcastic quip to which you could mount no defense.

What I did that night was not cool. I knew it then, and I know it now. Let my behavior be an example of what *not* to do when you're on the road in a touring band. Even if someone looks like Bill Gates, they might still throw a rock through your window. I'd caused what should have been an easily forgotten exchange of words to escalate into a potentially dangerous situation. Put another way, I'd jeopardized the safety of my friends and colleagues by being a jack-ass. But the incident also led me to realize I was in a band with individuals who didn't have my back. A true friend stands by your side in the heat of battle, and only questions your motives once the storm is weathered, if at all.

When I sense that type of loyalty from a friend, I give it back in full. When I realize someone isn't capable of extending this virtue in my direction, and will instead look out for himself first and foremost, or even turn his back on me at a crucial moment, I can never look at him in quite the same way again. I don't think I'm alone in feeling this way. I would never reconcile the matter with Wildman. Just as he harbored his resentments, some of which were well-justified, I realized that he'd never genuinely supported my leadership role in the band, and that there had never been any real trust between us. And the real nail in the coffin: given what had now transpired, there would *never be* any real trust between us. I would have to chalk up my relationship with Wildman, in the end, as a profound failure—one for which both of us, I believe, were to blame.

We drove up to Meyers, a small town in the South Lake Tahoe area, to play a restaurant called Divided Sky. The owners were a young music-loving couple who made delicious, gourmet sandwiches. The place was too small to host the bigger fish of the JBS, but was perfect for a band at GFC's level. After the first set, Wildman almost got into a fistfight with some local guy, who'd unintentionally spit on him while they were talking. The men cursed each other, making a scene, and I found myself curiously thrust into the role of peacekeeper. Given the previous developments in Ventura, it goes without saying that I found this situation rather ironic. I separated them, walked Wildman outside to cool off, and found myself thinking: *Violence is not the answer. We must keep a calm head in these situations.* One day you're Ron Artest, beating people down in the front row at an NBA game, and the next day you're Meta World Peace, promoting global harmony and embarrassing yourself on *Dancing with the Stars*.

I went back inside to pacify the other guy, who was stewing near the bar. "I tried to apologize to your bass player," he said. "I didn't mean to spit on him. It just flew out of my mouth while I was talking. But when I said sorry, he wouldn't have it. He'd already made up his mind that I'm some kind of jerk. He seems a little unreasonable."

"I think I understand where you coming from," I answered. "Sorry for the misunderstanding, man. We're all about the love."

In the parking lot at the end of the night, we all stood around the van doing a re-cap of the evening's events—a typical ritual, which might include the puffing of a joint by various people. Wildman made a derogatory comment to Tabitha, who was riding along for that leg of the tour, about her alcohol breath; she didn't take it well. She called him an "asshole."

I myself have always had an inexplicable phobia about people's breath. My wife says I'm a *breath-a-phobe*. I sometimes keep my distance from people out of fear they will regale me with a foul odor, should I stand too close; or, I stay away out of the suspicion that my own breath might not be what the doctor ordered. This all most likely stems from something my sister Paula and I used to refer to in childhood years as *the Sniffs and Smees of Life*: a weird fascination with human smells, mainly those of the unpleasant variety.

THIS WASN'T IN THE BROCHURE

Once things fell apart in Salinas, I cleared out the garage and bedroom, dumped all my belongings in a storage unit, and holed up temporarily at Anne's home in Aptos. I knew I couldn't stay there long; I was thirty-four years old, after all. It was the holiday season, and Global Funk was taking a break from the road, so I had a little time to regroup and find a new place to live.

I researched some different areas to rent a house, realizing I'd probably wind up in another city like Salinas. The Bay Area was too expensive, and I had no intention at that time to return to Southern California. After perusing craigslist, it was clear that some of the cheapest rental opportunities were in a town called Merced. I'd heard of Merced but had never passed through. On a map of California, it appeared to be right in the middle of the state—south of Sacramento, north of Fresno, east of the Bay Area, and west of Yosemite—a great starting point for West Coast touring. I decided to take a drive out to Merced to check it out.

I've always enjoyed spending time on my own. I'm not a loner, and if I go more than a couple days without human contact, I miss it, but I do cherish the chance to do my own thing from time to time. Driving is a nice outlet for this, and on these occasions I often prefer silence. Driving alone is one of the few times in life when you can block out the incessant noise of the world around you, so why pollute this peaceful environment with more sonic clutter?

I took the 152 from Santa Cruz out toward the 5, a familiar route, with all the back-and-forth trips I'd made between Southern California and the Bay Area over the years. The difference this time was that instead of heading south once I hit the 5, I kept going straight through the town of Los Banos. Past Los Banos, a small farming city most famous, I believe, for its massive landfill, the 152 continued east toward the 99, a freeway that runs parallel to the 5, but goes directly through Fresno. I eventually hit the 58, a little known road that takes you north and, as I was about to discover, directly into Merced.

There was a "UC" campus under construction in the outskirts of the city, which meant that while the place might currently be rural and small-town oriented, it was going to enjoy major growth during the next several years. The presence of a thriving university changes many aspects of a town. The influx of millions of dollars, in the creation of new jobs and new businesses, can turn a podunk place into a modern, hip mecca.

I like small towns. While I'm attracted to the frenetic energy of bigger cities, it's the *idea* of such places that I'm mostly drawn to—the notion that lots of moving and shaking is going on in big cities, deals are being done, architects are planning new buildings, culture is being preserved and nurtured, writers are writing, artists are creating, and humanity, as it is prone, is aggressively progressing and evolving. It's a cool idea, after all.

The reality of *living* in a big city, well, that's another story. This entails constant frustration. Traffic, pollution, crime, rude people, waiting in lines, living in cramped spaces, scuffling to park your car... I could go on. My main gripe, and I realize this is a *western* thing, is the lack of personal space. In big cities, people are in your face all the time. There's no escape. Some seem to love this type of environment, but in anything more than small doses, I find it a bit uncomfortable.

During my visit to India, I realized that personal space is not a universally embraced concept. Though it is a large country, there is very little of this commodity in almost all of India. This is true even for the wealthy in Mumbai, who live not in mansions but bungalows and high-rise condominiums. There just isn't space in Mumbai for even the fabulously rich to seclude themselves from the rest of humanity. Nobody seems to mind in India. It's what they're used to. People identify as part of the whole, rather than as self-contained entities attempting to create isolation from other human beings. It is the West that has pioneered the whole idea that *the individual is king*.[199]

So I realize I'm somewhat full of crap in lamenting the human congestion inherent in big cities, but that doesn't change the fact that I love the open spaces of the country, the quiet pace of small towns, and the lack of the masses in places like Montana and South Dakota. Sometimes it's just nice to be able to think peacefully, breathe easy, and not be worried about someone riding your ass in the fast lane or cutting in front of you at the supermarket.

As I drove north on the 58 toward Merced, I passed through agricultural areas and wide open spaces, farming equipment accenting the landscape to both the west and the east. My blood pressure dropped back to normal. I rolled down the window, allowed the hot, manure-tinged Central California air to blow into my van, and broke into a welcomed sweat.

Once I reached Merced I drove into an actual town, with a movie theater, Starbucks, couple of restaurants and bars, and post office. The great thing was, there was only one of each! One movie theater, one Starbucks, and one post office.[200] The town felt old, vintage, anachronistic... and I *liked* that. I liked the fact that the buildings were weathered, that the whole downtown hadn't been razed to make way for slicker, more modern structures. I could relish the quaintness of the place, and I could also grab a Vanilla Bean Frappuccino.

The neighborhood streets in Merced were lined with big trees and old houses. The place had character. Plus, Merced was at that time the most depressed real estate market in California. You could rent or buy

---

[199] In the 2011 film *I Am,* successful Hollywood director Tom Shaydiac discusses the near-death experience which led him to realize that he had been living a lie, and that human beings were inherently much more connected than Western society had conditioned him to believe.

[200] I would learn in time that there was another movie theater, as well as one other Starbucks... but that still isn't bad!

612

a house there for dirt cheap. That would change when the university was completed, but for the time being it was a great opportunity.

I drove around Merced for the afternoon, checking out the whole town, and retired at the local Motel 6. The next morning I looked at a house inside a newer planned community. The place had cathedral ceilings, a nice backyard, and a big master bedroom, and since it was at the end of a cul-de-sac, there were neighbors on only two sides. Also, the monthly rental price was a reasonable $1100.

I needed a new pad, and the band needed a new home. Salinas had been a fiasco. Things had completely fallen apart, through a combination of incompetence, disorganization and social dysfunction. I had allowed someone else to control my destiny, and as often is the case when you do this, things don't work out well. When it comes to the big stuff—your relationships with family and friends, career moves, where you live, the long-term plans you make—you have to pull the trigger yourself. You can't allow other people to determine these things for you.

Tyson

I decided to get a roommate, in addition to the couple of band members that might live there. It so happened that my cousin, Tyson, was looking for a new living situation. Among my numerous cousins, Tyson was the one I was perhaps the closest to over the years. He was a couple years younger than me, but we'd always been kindred artistic spirits. Tyson was naturally talented, and had never caved into convention in his life, sometimes to the detriment of his financial well-being and general stability. Tyson's proud, lifelong denunciation of everything status quo, in terms of society's established values and expectations, made me, even with my checkered history of career-oriented mishaps, misadventures and otherwise questionable pursuits, look like a pillar of conformity and conservatism.

Tyson had gotten by in life on potential, and also good looks and charisma. He was six-foot-three, slender and undeniably handsome. In fact, Tyson had A-list movie star looks. Girls, for as long back as I could remember, had always loved the guy. He never even had to open his mouth. All he had to do was stand there and brood a little, maybe push his hair back with his hand, and before he knew it they were putty in his hands.

If he did open his mouth, it would usually help his cause further, because he could talk the talk of the maverick, the existentially complex artist, struggling to flourish in a dumbed-down society occupied mostly by small-minded simpletons. Tyson prided himself on an ability to think outside the box, to make his own rules, to scoff at suggestions that he was wasting his life pursuing meaningless passions.

I'd always liked Tyson, appreciated his artistic talent and deceptively sharp intellect (he could come across as dim-witted unless you pressed him to reveal his true colors), and believed he was misunderstood by most people. He was a diamond in the rough, and one day he'd surround himself with the right people, ones who would cultivate an environment in which his unique talents finally shined.

Tyson and I had funny memories together, too. There was the time our families vacationed in Lake Tahoe. I was about seventeen, Tyson fifteen, and my brother Collin twelve. The three of us spent the week chasing girls we'd spotted in the casinos and around the lake. I was the ringleader, of course, with Tyson and Collin just starting to learn the ropes. I hooked up with some troubled, older girl who was working at one of the casinos and living in a motel. The two younger dudes followed me around as I pursued this chain-smoking, hard boozing woman in her early twenties, who was much too world-weary for the likes of me. It wasn't entirely fruitless... we groveled around one night, while Tyson and Collin waited nearby for a full report... a scene reminiscent of a John Hughes movie.

Tyson's step-dad, my Uncle Rip, had noted as Tyson and Collin painstakingly coiffed their hair in the popular *feathered* style of the day: "If y'all don't have what it takes, I don't think that little bit of feathered shit is gonna make the difference."

Another day, the girl came marching up to our rental house, pounded on the door, and was met by Aunt Jean, Tyson's mother. After listening to a nonsensical tirade from the younger woman, who looked like she hadn't slept in a few days, Jean pulled me aside and said, "Anthony, I'm not questioning the girl's attractiveness... beauty is in the eye of the beholder... but what might we conclude about her mental faculties?"

Tyson had grown up in Orange County, me in the Bay Area, but those infrequent times when we got to hang out together had always been fun and memorable. Despite his spotty adult track record, I felt like sharing a house together now would be a nice experience. It was time to create some new memories.

Before anyone else in the band had seen the place, Tyson and I moved into the Merced house together. During the initial drive up the 58, he had a panic attack, fearful that I was taking him to some land of cow patties, farms and migrant workers. Merced did have that element, but it also had, as mentioned, the amenities normally associated with civilization. Once Tyson got a lay of the land, he was cool.

We pooled our money together to pay the deposit, pick up some furniture, and buy a lawnmower. Tyson didn't have a car, but I had two vans—the gray Econo-line E-350 I used for the band, and my own white Dodge Caravan, which Len had given me years earlier. I told Tyson he could use my white van for driving around town, until he could get his own car. Since Tyson had poor credit, I also agreed to hook him up with a cell phone, adding a second line to my long-existing Verizon account. Tyson assured me he would cover his part of the bill, and I had no reason, based on our personal history together, to think differently.

Initially, the only band member who moved into the house was Gruden. I took the spacious master bedroom, which included a walk-in closet, personal bathroom, and nice view of the surrounding area, Tyson took the second-biggest upstairs room, and Gruden claimed the downstairs bedroom next to the garage.

I made friends with a local club owner, Rudy, who owned and operated Rudy's, a jazz and blues club on Main Street. The club was right across the street from Starbucks and the movie theater. Rudy hired me to play solo piano for a couple private events at the club, and I was also able to hook him up with Tyson, who took a part-time job there as a bartender. Tyson worked alongside Earl, a big black guy who I gave some Global Funk CD's to check out. Earl loved my song *City to City*, and would sing it when I walked through the door.

The move to Merced created even more distance between Wildman and me. He remained in the band despite now living in Monterey with Ariel, who, to be fair, encouraged him to continue being a part of Global Funk, no matter what difficulties the band faced. Looking back, Ariel was an ally of the project, not an impediment, but I resented Wildman's withdrawal from the creative process; to some extent I took it out on his girlfriend by not being as friendly as I should have been.

At that time, I was bitter about women getting in the way of the band and the music. I viewed girlfriends and lovers as landmines — potential disasters I had to constantly step around in order to keep the project moving forward. They came to the shows, danced and sang the words to the songs, but they could turn on you in a heartbeat. If and when they got sick of the band and its requirements, you could be assured that the band member would soon be parroting the same grievances. Music is a powerful drug, but it's no match for sex. When a guy starts getting some regularly, everything else takes a back seat. I guess I expected everyone to remain single and poor until the band blew up and became superstars... very realistic, huh?

Your Greatest Asset Will Be Your Downfall

During a trip to Davis, California for a show near the U.C. campus, Chase, who was spending more and more time with Tabitha, dropped a bomb. He was going to leave Global Funk permanently. Gruden responded indifferently. He figured we'd just find another guitar player. Wildman reacted angrily. *How could that little shit do this to us?* And I, for reasons I still can't explain, became emotional. I cried, in fact. Literally broke down, while talking to Wildman about the future of the band.

The funny thing was, I wasn't that close to Chase anymore, nor very surprised by his announcement. And Wildman hadn't exactly been my shoulder to cry on... my bridge over troubled water... but there I was, literally crying on the guy's shoulder! Letting it all hang out on some random side street in Davis, California.

"Your friendship is important to me, despite the differences we've had," I remember telling him as I wiped away my tears. I'd fancied myself pretty tough by this point, after all that I'd been through in the past several years, but I'd come to my breaking point.

Todd, my close confidante for a long time, was now an absentee member of the organization, particularly since things had gone sour in Salinas. I hardly ever saw the guy anymore, and he'd ceased to be involved in the day-to-day decisions of the group. I was doing more and more of it myself, and now Chase, with whom I'd invested two years of time in establishing a musical rapport/creative partnership, was going to walk. I sensed the organization was going to suffer a major blow with Chase gone, and Global Funk was all I really had.

Wildman reacted to my emotional outpour with steely indifference. He was pissed off at Chase for his own reasons, resentful that the guitarist was quitting; Wildman, too, had invested a great deal of time and faith in the guy. As far as being sympathetic to my feelings, however, Wildman might as well have been a brick wall that day. He had nothing left for me, adding insult to my injury.

Had I been thinking more clearly, I might have expressed more frustration than sorrow toward Wildman, because more than anyone else, *he* was the one who had driven Chase away from Global Funk. He was the one who had chastised the guitarist for not being able to perform certain parts in the studio in Bloomington, Indiana. He was the one who psychologically tormented Chase's fragile ego, all the while encouraging the very indulgence that precipitated the guitarist's studio meltdown: excessive pot smoking. It was Wildman's own issues which had been a main cause of Chase's overall dissatisfaction.

Before the show in Davis, Gruden pulled me aside to give me some information. Chase had confided that he was mostly dissatisfied with Wildman—his bass playing, his attitude, his negative trip. Gruden agreed with Chase. Wildman was the band's musical weak link, he believed.

"I think the group would sound a lot better with a different bass player, man." Gruden suggested I talk to Chase about the future, keeping that in mind. I walked off with Chase to chat for a few minutes. Yes, he said, the root of the problem, for him, was Wildman.

"So if he wasn't around, you'd be inclined to stay in the band."

"Much more inclined, although I'd also want to revamp everything musically, and get a black singer to front the group."

I wasn't crazy about the singer idea, but Chase's words gave me pause. Maybe he and Gruden were right. Maybe it was time for Wildman to go. I reflected on this, but soon felt the tug of what I now realize, at least in a business sense, has been my Achilles Heel: *loyalty.* Karl Denson once said to me, "Your greatest asset will also be your downfall." I'm not sure where he heard this pithy truth, or if he came up with it himself, but it fit my life perfectly.

I realized that although we weren't a match made in heaven, personality wise, Wildman deserved my loyalty. He'd hung in there, through the same harsh shit that I had. He'd never given up on the band or the dream. It wasn't anyone's right to kick him out of Global Funk. It was his band. He'd earned the right to decide if and when he wanted to leave.

Furthermore, I was disappointed in Chase and Gruden for conspiring to break the band apart. *Get rid of him, or I'm leaving.* We were a band. Bands are supposed to stick together. We'd made a great record, and we'd been through a lot of crap together. Wildman had done many things, some questionable, but he'd never, ever said he wanted to quit. That meant something. It meant a lot, actually. Once you imply that you might quit, the dynamic is never quite the same. You've shown your hand. You've got one foot in and one foot out. You can never be completely trusted again. As much as we'd squabbled, and failed to become close personal friends, as much as we flat-out disliked each other at times, Wildman was still my musical soul brother.

I tracked Wildman down and told him the ugly truth: "Chase and Gruden want you out of the band. Chase is willing to stay if we fire you, and Gruden thinks your bass playing leaves something to be desired. I just thought you should know."

That ended up being a bad idea. It did nothing to repair any lingering ill will between Wildman and me, and my information only soured him further against me... I guess we always shoot the messenger. Furthermore, I completely betrayed the trust of Chase and Gruden by spilling the beans to Wildman, a mere hour after I'd heard it come out of their mouths. Now, everyone hated me.

When it was time to play, Wildman was a no-show. We had to start the gig without bass. After a while, Wildman sauntered to the stage, strapped on his bass, and left it hanging in front of him while he used both hands to flip off Chase and Gruden. Chase flashed a slight smile in return, smug in his psychological victory over the guy who had reduced him to a shell of himself in the studio months earlier. I sat in the corner, poking at my keyboards... the jerk who had managed to cry like a baby, while sucking up to the one guy who more or less disliked him, get steamrolled by the band's disgruntled guitarist and his list of non-negotiable demands, and then proceed to rat out the confidences of said guitarist and his co-conspirator... all in a day's work.

After the show, I apologized to Chase for betraying his confidence. It was I who had stirred up the shit storm, and I told him I would never do that again. He accepted. Wildman retreated further into his disillusioned shell, anxious for Chase to go away permanently.

The Mexican Yellow Pages

Back in Merced, Tyson began working a new sales gig. I walked in the house one day and he was sitting on the couch, head shaved, wearing one of my suits.

"You shaved your dome... and why are you all dressed up?" I asked.

"Got a new job, Anth."

"Doing what?"

"Selling ad space in the Mexican Yellow Pages."

"Huh... sounds different."

"I think I'm gonna make some serious cash doing this," Tyson said with confidence.

"I didn't know there *was* a Mexican Yellow Pages," I admitted. "I assume it's in Spanish..."

"Yeah, it's a new concept. I'll be going around to local businesses getting them to advertise."

"Cool," I said.

"Hope you don't mind I borrowed your suit."

"No problem." Tyson had been borrowing my car, my clothes, and just about everything else, but I didn't really mind. He was family. Before hooking up with me, he'd gone through an ugly divorce in L.A., kicked around between various dead-end jobs, and was—at least I thought—trying to figure things out and get a new focus in life. I had genuine love for him, and I wanted him to find his way. I hoped he'd discover a niche within the Global Funk organization; a band always needs fresh ideas, and in Tyson's case he had not only plenty of ideas, but artistic talent as well. He could serve as a creative consultant, poster artist, roadie and occasional booking agent. Unfortunately, there was little money to be made in the world of Global Funk, and at thirty-two years old, a man needs to make some money doing *something.*

Tyson met a young lady, Ivy, at one of the local bars. He began having her over to the house, and she fell hard for him quickly. Ivy was a hard-drinking, high-energy girl, and after a few weeks Tyson, as well as me and the rest of the people in the house, began to suspect she was a bit off her rocker.

Ivy had some sort of secret she was keeping from us. She'd left the country for a while and had a life-changing experience, but could not, for whatever reason, reveal any details.

"When the truth comes out, things are going to be different. People are going to recognize me." That was all Ivy would say, echoing Kevin Spacey's serial murderer in *Seven*, before Morgan Freeman has the misfortune of discovering Gwyneth Paltrow's severed head in a Fed Ex shipping box.

Tyson decided to cool things off with Ivy, who'd lived in Merced her whole life. It was such a small town that you saw people you knew everywhere. There was no hiding. We continued to bump into Ivy and her friends at Mahoney's, a downtown club that hosted karaoke once a week. Mahoney's attracted aggressive, belligerent dudes, who would resort to throwing pool balls at each other's heads. We began referring to the joint as *Mahomey's*.

Finally, Ivy's secret came to light—not through local gossip, but *on the cover of USA Today*. Ivy, it turned out, had been a contestant on a massively popular reality survival show, filmed on an exotic, uninhabited island. She had become a mini-celebrity overnight.

Non-disclosure clauses had prevented her from divulging information about the show, which was already wrapped when Tyson had begun dating Ivy; but now, every episode would be discussed in the national media. In one interview, midway through the television season, Ivy told the press, "I've been dating a guy in my hometown, and I'm crazy about him." I handed Tyson the article and joked, "You're famous, dude." Reminiscent of a certain TV commercial, in which a guy breaks up with his girlfriend, only to have her reveal that she's just won the lottery, Tyson learned that Ivy had finished second on the reality show competition, and had thus won several hundred thousand dollars. Too bad he'd already told her to take a hike.

It was decided that Chase was in fact leaving the band. "Even if everything magically came together in the next year, and we were playing arenas, I still wouldn't be happy," he confessed. He would finish out the last bit of touring, and then move to Canada to live with Tabitha. One morning, he and I stood in the kitchen of the Merced house, drinking coffee and arguing about politics. I'd just read Pat Buchanan's *Death of the West*, an excellent book about rising and declining birth rates, global population projections and political trends, and was sharing some of the author's insights. Buchanan noted, for example, that the U.S. birthrate was alarmingly low, compared with much of the world. In Europe, it was even worse. The implication was that Caucasian people weren't reproducing themselves, unlike other ethnic groups with burgeoning populations. Buchanan's argument was that Western culture—its philosophies, literature, and ideas—was going to die, if current trends continued.

"Well, maybe that's a good thing. Maybe it's time for white people to die out," Chase squawked.

"You're white yourself," I pointed out.

"I'm not proud of it," Chase answered.

"Why's that?"

"I would have been happier to have been born black," he continued. "So what if the West dies? Big deal!"

"Well, Chase, I think it *is* a big deal. Western culture embodies individualism, democracy, and many of the world's great ideas," I argued.

"I just don't give a shit," Chase huffed. At the end of the day, that was always his final argumentative stand; a conversation-killing, apathetic exclamation point. When he got tired of debating, he'd just say *he didn't give a shit.* I don't want to pick on the guy as I'm revisiting random conversations that took place in a kitchen in Central California years ago, but I do think it's fair to say that sometimes people with extreme political views are incapable of engaging in a discourse of ideas, and perceive any dissenting opinion as a threat to the dogma they've adopted as their religion. Chase, at least at that point in time, wasn't interested in expanding his ideological horizons. He believed what he believed, and that was the end of it. If you challenged his world view, he became pissed off and would shut down on you.

Wildman and Tyson discovered a new prospect for the guitar chair, a guy from L.A. named Orlando Stout. Orlando had phenomenal speed on the guitar, as evidenced by his audition disc. I was worried he might be someone who played too many notes—a common liability with rock guitar players—but we all agreed that Orlando possessed a quality essential for Chase's successor: the *wow factor*, the ability to make your jaw drop during one of his solos. I made arrangements for him to join us in Northern California, for an upcoming run of shows.

In the meantime, Chase still had another couple weeks he'd agreed to play with us. Tabitha was hanging with him, driving the two of them around in her old VW bus. Most nights, they camped out at beaches or rest stops.

Before his final few shows, Chase asked if he and Tabitha could hang out at the house in Merced. "Of course," I told him. "As long as you're playing in the band, it's your house too." They showed up the following day.

Merced was a conservative town in a conservative county; one of California's *red* regions. Tyson learned this the hard way while attempting to sell his Mexican Yellow Pages ad space to local business owners...

"Hi, I'm recruiting advertisers for an exciting new publication."

"What's that?"

"The Mexican Yellow Pages."

"We already got a Yellow Pages."

"Yeah, but this one's different."

"It's fulla Mexicans?"

"Not exactly. It's written in Spanish, and it caters to a Hispanic clientele."

"We don't believe in that around here."

"You don't believe in Hispanic people?"

"We don't think they oughta have their own Yellow Pages. Those people should speak English. Are you goin' down to Tijuana tryin' to sell the American Yellow Pages?"

"No. I'm not."

"This is California. Why do I have to learn Spanish just to make *them* happy? I was born here."

"In another twenty years, there will be as many people speaking Spanish as English here in California. You might want to prepare yourself."

"And you might wanna turn your ass around, take your Mexican Yellow Pages with you and get out of my store."

Tabitha Hates America

Merced did have a sizable Hispanic farmer/laborer community, but our cul-de-sac neighbors were all white and middle class, including various businessmen and a CHP motorcycle cop. As a hodgepodge of musical drifters from all over the country, we were fish out of water.

I was going out of my way to maintain an air of respectability, not only for myself but the whole household. I'd rented the place in my name, and was personally responsible for paying the bills and maintaining harmonious relations with the neighbors. I would garden both the front and backyard, mowing and pulling weeds in the sweltering sun. Two of the neighbors across the street possessed the most immaculately manicured, pristine front lawns I'd ever laid eyes on. These guys were lawn- maintenance virtuosos, nurturing and fine-tuning their masterworks on a daily basis. Oh, how I marveled at their rich, two-inch thick expanses of moist soil and velvety grass. At 1708 Poppy Hills Court, I'd been handed a horticultural shit sandwich—a patchy mess of weeds and dying, turd-brown plants—and I didn't possess the skill set to salvage the situation. I was out of my league.

One of the guys across the street snickered at me as I filled in dead earth with bark from Home Depot.
Pathetic, I could almost hear him say. The side of *his* house was garlanded with fancy rocks and perfectly tapered plants and trees. It wasn't just a home improvement solution—it was an artistic statement. Knowing we were musicians, he bellowed from his cookie-cutter

domicile one day, "So, you guys opening for Van Halen this weekend?"

No, but I am going to torch your house at some point.

Despite being domestically outclassed, I'd managed the respect of the neighbors by simply staying quiet. We didn't play our music too loud, didn't have obnoxious parties, and were on the road much of the time.

The day Chase and Tabitha arrived, all this changed. That night, the pair of them, along with Gruden, decided to have a crazy party. I don't know what they were partying *with,* but let's just say it wasn't cupcakes and fruit punch. They blasted loud music well into the night. I was dating a singer from San Diego, and she was visiting for the weekend. We hid out in my room, hoping the festive trio would settle down and eventually go to bed.

They didn't settle down, and instead got more rowdy as the night went on. When the sun came up, I was finally nodding off... but my friend was standing at my window, looking out into the cul-de-sac.

"You should see this, Anthony." I didn't want to get up. I was tired and pissed off that they'd kept us up all night.

"No, really. You gotta see what's going on out there." I stumbled over to the window to take a look. First, I saw one of our neighbors, dressed in a crisp suit and tie, walking to his car, his young son holding his hand, carrying a lunchbox. Then my eyes shifted up the street, where our CHP neighbor was straddling his bike and preparing to cruise off to work. Then my eyes returned to my own driveway, where they fixed on a most unsettling spectacle: Tabitha, running in the nude, laughing out loud. Chase and Gruden, not quite naked themselves, were tagging along also. The threesome frolicked across the front lawn as I stood there watching them from my upstairs window.

"Oh my god," my friend sighed. "How do you put up with this?" I marched downstairs and glared at them as they sat on the living room couch in a collective stupor. I didn't say a word, but Chase picked up my dark vibe and sneered, "Just go to bed! Go to bed!" As much as I wanted to tell him and his girlfriend to get there stuff and clear out, I held my tongue and walked back upstairs. They would be leaving soon enough, and there was no need for any more drama.

The next day, I calmly attempted to explain to Tabitha why I thought it was uncool for her to expose her unshaven private parts to our conservative yuppie neighbors. She responded by saying, "I feel sorry for you. I feel sorry that you have to live in this society with its stupid rules, in this stupid country. I feel sorry for you, Anthony. I can't wait to get back to Canada."

Despite the bad scene, Chase agreed to finish the agreed string of remaining shows. Orlando was learning our material down in Los Angeles, getting ready to jump on board. Wildman and I were counting the days until we could start fresh with some positive energy.

Perhaps in an effort to create forward momentum to counter the setback of losing Chase's guitar playing, I enlisted my good friend Lunabelle, from Missoula, Montana, to move to California and live with us in Merced. Lunabelle would take over the merchandise operation for Global Funk; it was risky, both for her and for us, as her presence meant another mouth to feed and another body taking up space in the van. Lunabelle was an energetic, fun person who loved music, however, and I knew her presence would be a positive. She had generously housed the band and countless other groups when they were passing through Missoula, and she was just the kind of cool chick you wanted to have around.

I met a woman named Teena Singh around this time. An old friend, Steve Minor, invited me to his wedding in the Bay Area. Steve and I were buddies as teenagers in Santa Clara in the eighties; we'd enjoyed some good adventures together, and also endured one particularly memorable ordeal…

In 1989, the San Francisco Giants squared off against the Oakland A's in a historic all-Bay Area World Series. I was able to score some tickets to Candlestick Park, through a relative, and elected to take Steve with me to watch the game. It was already exciting to be going to an actual World Series game, and then the seats ended up being right along the first base line. As I would later tell people, "I was so close that if (first baseman) Will Clark had picked his nose, I would have known it."

Steve and I settled in to watch the game, when we were suddenly overcome with a feeling of extreme disorientation. I literally sensed the tectonic plates of the Earth shifting underneath me, and the entire stadium began rocking back and forth. The press box began rattling like a box of Cracker Jacks, and the giant light towers rising above Candlestick Park began swaying, as if blown by a wind of untold strength. This continued for what seemed like a long time, but was most likely a matter of seconds. It was very surreal, to the point that I wasn't sure if it was really happening, or was instead some kind of strange dream. I sensed on instinctive level that we were in danger, and perhaps our lives were on the line, but I didn't panic. In fact, I felt no anxiety whatsoever. For reasons I can't explain, I was completely calm and accepting of the situation, whatever it was.

Of course, what was happening was a massive earthquake—the famous Loma Prieta quake, a 7.1 event that disrupted the World Series, and was viewed on television by millions all over the planet. The game was promptly cancelled, and thousands began wandering around both the field itself and the adjacent parking lot. Fans intermingled with ballplayers and commentators, everyone scrambling and trying to make sense of what had happened.

Steve and I realized we weren't going to get anywhere in my car for quite a while, so we walked toward the nearest area of the city, hoping to find a pay phone so we could check in with our families. Steve was a newlywed (first marriage), and was desperate to make sure his wife was okay. When we finally made it to an intersection with businesses, we found that local proprietors were guarding their establishments to prevent looting. Power was out throughout the Bay Area, and chaos was ensuing in the streets. The series, which Oakland swept in four games, was ultimately forgotten for the most part, but the quake is something that many still remember vividly. A high school friend, Erik Vaishville, had barely missed being on the Bay Bridge when it collapsed. To this day, surviving the World Series Earthquake of 1989 is one of my *claims to fame.*

Anyway, I was yet to meet Steve's bride, Caroline, who he'd hooked up with while working as a bouncer at a country bar in San Jose, the Saddle Rack. The wedding was on September 11, 2004—a curious choice for a matrimonial date. Steve, red-blooded patriot that he was, wanted to kill two birds with one stone, honoring America's undaunted courage while celebrating his union with Caroline. The speeches included a moment of silence for those lost on 9/11.

During the reception I met Teena, one of Caroline's co-workers at Oracle, the software giant based in Redwood City. We got along immediately, and after she had endured my pitiful attempt to learn a dance everyone else was doing, I realized there might be something special there.

The funny part of the story is the fact that Teena, as I later learned, had been dating a Bay Area fireman at the time. She'd contemplated bringing the guy, but when she asked Caroline if this was okay, Caroline had said in her thick British accent, "Only if he comes in uniform." The fireman declined, so Teena came to the wedding alone. The rest, as they say...

Teena was a music lover and took an interest in my career path, as well as the colorful cast of characters I'd assembled in Merced. She was supportive, but she wondered whether having Lunabelle relocate to Merced was the right move. I was already struggling to keep a roof over everyone's head, and this meant one more person to provide for. I was banking on my hope that Lunabelle, with her bubbly personality, crazy dreadlocks and hoarse, unmistakable voice, would give the Global Funk organization a much needed burst of energy. Also, having a girl sell the band's merch at shows might bring in some more revenue. Lunabelle moved in, taking the vacant bedroom next to mine.

We finished out the final gigs with Chase in Northern California. Gruden, so disgusted that we had again been passed over by the organizers of the High Sierra Music Festival, showed up for an outdoor tent show in Ukiah with his bass drum painted to read: *Low Sierra.* The guys in the band thought it was funny, but Todd wasn't laughing. He felt Gruden was undermining morale, and that he was talking shit behind Todd's back... which wasn't entirely untrue.

The Lightening-Fast Riffs of Orlando Stout

Once Chase played his final gig at the Ukiah Brewing Company the following night, we said some half-hearted goodbyes, and the remaining band made its way south to San Francisco, where we were picking up Orlando. After spending the night at a rest stop off the 280 freeway, right near the statue of Father Junipero Serra, we woke up early to go to SFO. After driving around the airport looking for Orlando, we realized we were at the wrong place—the new guitarist was flying into Oakland, not San Francisco. We hopped on the Bay Bridge, hustled over to Oakland Airport in rainy weather, and met our new guy.

We got back on the bridge, stopping in downtown San Francisco to grab coffee before heading back north to Caspar for a two-night run. Orlando, stocky, thirtyish, and in possession of a long ponytail and Eastern European visage, ordered a quad shot espresso, and gulped it while huffing a couple cigarettes in front of the coffee shop. The dude was wired.

Orlando's first show with the band was at the Caspar Inn, a charming spot in the tiny coastal town of Caspar, just north of Mendocino. The second floor of the club, purported to have been a whorehouse at one point, now served as a little inn, and each guy in the band had his own room. As I rested, I could hear Orlando practicing his guitar through the wall. He played a technique exercise that sounded like *Flight of the Bumblebee,* and he played it as fast as humanly possible.

That night, Orlando demonstrated that not only did he have the technical chops to hold down the guitar chair, but that he would also bring some infectious, positive energy to the situation. In between sets, there was a quirky, one-man show staged by an acoustic bass player, who told the story of a fictitious character named Folly Shenanigens. As he plucked the strings of his bass, he interjected little verbal updates:

"Folly Shenanigens was verrrrrrry happy..."

Orlando and I listened from the bar, impressed with the storyteller's playing and sense of imagination, while also chuckling at the childlike absurdity of it all.

The Caspar Inn was owned by a guy named Kirby, a fast-talking character with plenty of good tales to tell. After the show, we all sat at the bar drinking free cocktails, as Kirby gave us the history of the club, the building, and his life in the entertainment business. It's always fun to hang out with the owner of a club after business hours, get drunk and tell war stories—this is one instance in life where being a musician, a member of a band, is a position to be envied. Everyone else is getting kicked out as the bouncers scream, "Get the fuck out! *Unless you're in the band...*" Even if George Clooney is in the crowd, he too has to *get the fuck out*, but you... you're in the band, you're an insider, and so you get to stay as long as you want. In this instance, and only this instance, you're cooler than George Clooney.

In one entertaining installment, Kirby described an altercation he'd had with an unruly patron of his club:

"This guy didn't want to leave, and wouldn't listen to my bouncer. Big old son of a bitch. I get in his face... he's a foot taller and a hundred pounds heavier than me... and I tell him to beat it. He refuses, then he starts choking me. I break free somehow, and jump on his back."

"Then what happened?"

"I bit his face."

"You bit his face?"

"Well, to be more specific, I bit his nose off."

"You what?"

"I reached around, sunk my teeth into his nose, and bit the tip of it off."

"Holy shit, man."

"Yeah, dude tried to sue me, but he had instigated the fight, so I was cleared."

It's good to know that you can bite someone's nose off in self-defense...

After Caspar, we headed south to an obscure town called Rio Nido, right next to the Russian River. I can't remember the name of the club. The town had been a rest stop for such luminaries as the Grateful Dead, back in the day, and was still home to some die-hard, old school hippies. The show was forgettable, but afterwards, comedy ensued.

Wildman's lady took him back to her parents' house, which was nearby, and Gruden had a new girlfriend, who'd gotten a hotel room somewhere. That left Orlando and me to fend for ourselves... and there was little fending to be done in Rio Nido. It was a long drive back to civilization, and the club had no lodging for us.

"What are we gonna do?" Orlando wondered.

"Find yourself a comfortable spot on the dance floor, Sparky. I might have a couple blankets in the van." I'd affectionately referred to other people in the organization as Sparky, but with Orlando, the nickname really stuck—to the extent that he started calling me Sparky too.

"You mean we're gonna sleep *in here?*"

"Yeah, Sparky, that's what I'm thinking. I'm scoping out this little area behind the stage, myself."

Folly Shenanigens was verrrrry sad...

I was so accustomed to the hardships of the road that I wouldn't think twice, at that point, about sleeping on the beer-soaked, stinky floor of some backwater bluegrass bistro in Rio Nido, California.

"I think I'm gonna have one more cocktail," Orlando muttered, skulking back to the bar in disbelief. After packing up my keyboards, I walked over and saw that Orlando had made himself a friend, a middle-aged woman who'd lingered after the show. "I've got some good news," he said with a smile. "My new friend is gonna put us up in her hotel."

Folly Shenanigens was suddenly relieved...

The kind, local lady put us up for the night, and we both got a comfortable bed.

At the end of Orlando's first tour, he returned to Southern California to spend some time with his wife. To his credit, he wasn't disillusioned by the difficulties of touring in a struggling jam band. No, the guy was motivated by the original repertoire and musicianship of Global Funk. The band was a breath of fresh air, after all the horrible cover band gigs he'd done in L.A. So many fine players spent the prime of their careers playing in variety dance bands and corporate bands, and Orlando saw an opportunity to escape that fate. That's why he was out there.

Now that I had the house in Merced, I was able to compose music again. The living room served as a rehearsal studio, and I had all my keyboards set up so I could practice or write at any time. Orlando took the train from L.A. to Merced, and I picked him up at the tiny station on 24th Street. We spent several days working on new songs—just the two of us. Gruden joined us for the last couple sessions, adding drum grooves to the material Orlando and I had been fleshing out. We emerged from those intense writing sessions with ten or more new songs, including *Soul Searching, Zoyd, See, Look and Listen, Top Level Professional, Star Focker, One Damn Thing,* and *Dancing Around the Truth.* It was exhilarating to create a new body of material, after I'd been playing the same music for so long. The new repertoire, in fact, rejuvenated my interest in hitting the road and keeping the Global Funk dream alive. As long as there were new songs to play live, it would still be worth it to sit in the van for fifteen hours, listening to everyone's cell phone conversations while risking our lives on two-lane roads, with giant diesel rigs whizzing past us going eighty-five.

Cletus

Out of nowhere, Gruden announced that he'd have to leave the project for a while. He wasn't sure if his hiatus would be permanent or not. Orlando suggested a friend from Los Angeles, Rob Kawal. Rob drove up to Merced for rehearsals, and after a day or two Orlando pulled me aside.

"I'm concerned, T."

"Yeah?"

"I'm afraid this guy might be a tool."

"Well, Sparky, we're gonna find out real quick."

Rob did his best to learn the music, and he had a good attitude. Beyond that, I liked the guy. He was a genuine person—socially awkward, and not the greatest drummer in the world, but the type of guy who would help out with things off the bandstand. I wanted to start working with musicians who were easygoing and helpful, after sticking it out with talented but difficult people. I might have alluded to this before, but the words *talent* and *difficult* often accompany each other. I should know... I have a bit of talent, and I've been difficult to work with at times.

The following tour took us out to Colorado, a region that had been solid for the band from the beginning. It was a winter run, which meant we'd be dealing with harsh weather and unsafe road conditions. Logic would suggest that a band from California might bypass the mountain states during the dead of winter, but this is a time when a touring group can make good money. Colorado and Wyoming are huge ski destinations, and upscale ski resorts can afford to compensate you well for your services. Like in most businesses, you go where the work is.

It took Rob all of two days to completely annoy Wildman. Rob told long-winded stories about the years he lived in Kuwait, while his dad was working there, and also explained in great detail his plans to build some kind of high-tech ORV (off-roading vehicle). He had already completed the blueprint. Due to his monotone delivery, Rob had the ability to turn a story of already questionable entertainment value into the most boring monologue in the history of the spoken word.

"This guy's gotta get his road chops together, man," Wildman grumbled. When a guy isn't cutting it musically—and Rob just wasn't—any flaws in his personality become even more irritating. I'd seen this phenomenon occur with several ex-band members.

Somehow, we started calling Rob "Cletus." It seemed to fit. When he'd launch into his story about the beaches of Kuwait, you shrugged your shoulders and said, "That's just Cletus." At the Top Hat in Missoula, Cletus got into a discussion with an aggressive guy at the bar. The guy was drunk, bragging about his martial arts prowess.

"I've got some training myself," Cletus countered. They began demonstrating various moves on each other. Orlando and I chuckled, grabbed ourselves a cocktail and walked away. Moments later, Cletus hurried past us on his way to the bathroom, a large gash opened up on his forehead. The guy had smashed his head into a post. Accidentally, of course.

We moved on to Lander, Wyoming, for a two-night stand at the Lander Bar. The manager was a fast-talking, booze guzzling gal the Lord had blessed with, as they say in places like Lander, a *bodacious set of ta-ta's*. In order to get your free Lander Bar t-shirt, you had to drink a Jagermeister shot right off of these ta-ta's, not an unreasonable price to pay for free merchandise.

Rather than our usual Telluride booking at the Fly Me to the Moon Saloon, we had a show at the top of a ski mountain. A staff of guys met us at the bottom, loaded our instruments onto a flatbed snow vehicle, and transported us up the slope on small snowmobiles. It was quite an adventure.

We played to a decent-sized but lukewarm crowd, and by the time we finished, the sky was getting dark. A blizzard was materializing outside. For whatever reason, the vehicles that had gotten us up the mountain weren't available to get us back down, so one of the staff members came up with a solution: a giant snow plow/garbage truck, with a steel cage on top for waste, rambled over to pick us up. We loaded our equipment into the cage, and then piled inside. The guys looked at me like I was crazy to sign off on this. It was freezing, the blizzard was intensifying, and we were about to ride down a steep mountain in what looked like a cross between a snowplow and a Sherman tank.

Having no choice, we buttoned our jackets, pulled our wool caps down to cover our faces, and hunkered down. The ear-splitting motor drowned out all other sound, as snow pelted our cramped-together bodies. Orlando shot me a look of bewildered disbelief. I smiled and said, "This wasn't in the brochure, was it, Sparky."

"No, it really wasn't."

Sparky was so engaging onstage that sometimes the lines between performer and audience became blurred. This was the case one night at Whiskey Jacques in Ketchum, Idaho, a club that basically had no stage to begin with. The crowd was raging, and Orlando was taking an epic guitar solo. Several large guys were pressed up to the bandstand, pounding brews and doing the white man's jig. Inspired by the guitarist's animated gestures and fretboard pyrotechnics, one of the beer-swilling bubbas screamed at the top of his lungs, "Play that guitar, you Hobbit fag!"

We made our way back west, where we'd secured a New Year's run in the Sierra Mountains. There was a gig in Reno, at a funky but charming downtown dive bar. The city was hit by a huge blizzard that night, and in the morning I realized the van's snow chains were broken. Cletus and I drove around Reno for hours, unable to find the right chains in any store. Finally, we found a place that had the right model. When I went to pay, the guy shot me a very inflated price. Remember, the city was nearly shut down at this point—there was snow piled high in the streets, and the roads in and out of town were a mess.

"Are you kidding? The last time I bought these chains it was half that much."

"Maybe you should buy 'em from that place again," the salesman snickered. He had me by the short ones.

"I'll, uh, take them."

"That's what I thought."

Buying the chains was only half the battle. Then I had to drive back to Truckee, for a New Year's Eve show at the Bar of America. Under normal driving circumstances, this is maybe an hour drive. On this day, it would take seven-and-a-half hours.

The day's tribulations were not done. The new chains secure, Cletus and I pulled into a private driveway to turn around, only to become completely stuck in snow. Unable to break free, we started knocking on neighbors' doors, looking for a shovel. Once we found one, we took shifts, digging for what must have been an hour. It wasn't exactly sunny outside, either. Finally, we managed to create enough traction to get the van out. I was now officially in a shitty mood.

Once we made it to the Bar of America, I felt like I'd scaled Mt. Fuji.[201] Cletus and I had been through hell, and we needed some love. The manager of the bar barely acknowledged our arrival, unfortunately, relegating us to a back table to wait for the dinner crowd to subside. We had to beg a waitress to take our food order.

This manager and I had a personality conflict that had been established during a previous visit; I had smashed my head into a TV monitor that was mounted above the stage, not once but *twice*, leaving a big, painful egg on my forehead. The first time I'd sucked it up, but the second time I lost my temper. If there's one thing I hate in life, one thing that makes me see red in a heartbeat, it's hitting my head against a hard object. Some things are just downright infuriating: hitting one's head on low-placed, inanimate objects, getting a seatbelt ticket when

---

[201] In *Mr. S*, Frank Sinatra's valet claims that the Chairman, chilling in a hotel room in Japan, was alerted: "There's Mt. Fuji, Frank. Isn't it something?"

Sinatra's response:

"Who gives a shit?"

you're wearing your seatbelt,[202] the ubiquitous use of the word *veggies* as shorthand for vegetables, waiters and waitresses that come to your table and start their spiel with "Hey gang!", guys that quasi-masturbate in male sauna rooms at 24 Hour Fitness... I could go on.

The next day the weather persisted, and Cletus and I had to drive back to Merced on our own. I prayed to the heavens that the new chains would hold, and we'd have no further complications, but God apparently had bigger fish to fry. We'd been driving for about an hour when one of the chains snapped. The *brand new* chains I'd bought at exorbitant prices. They say God may not always solve your problems for you, but he will at least grant you the strength to deal with them. It was clear out there on the I-80 that God was not going to solve my problems, but he had at least blessed Cletus with the technical aptitude I gravely lacked.

We pulled off the freeway and found a gas station where I could buy new chains... *again*. This time, I had them installed by slicker-wearing guys with numbers plastered on their chests. These guys stood at the side of the road throughout a blizzard, charging hefty fees to fasten your snow chains so you could proceed along the highway. You could do it yourself, but you probably wouldn't do it half as well as a pro, and it wasn't the time to cheap out.

---

[202] This happened to me while touring with Trunk Fulla Funk. We were pulled over while I was napping in the passenger seat, with my seatbelt securely fastened. The cop walked up... I thought we made an illegal lane change or something. "Click it or ticket," he said.

"Yeah, click it," I responded, motioning to my fastened belt.

"You weren't wearing that when you passed me."

"Yes, I was. I always wear my belt."

"I'm not going to argue with you. Click it or ticket."

"Like I said, click it."

"I could impound your vehicle. You don't have proof of insurance. But I'm just going to cite you for the failure to wear your belt."

"But... I clicked it."

"Here's your ticket."

Now, that is some serious bullshit! They should change the slogan to *TICKET OR TICKET. DOESN'T MATTER IF YOU CLICK IT. WE NEED THE MONEY.*

Even with expert installation, I still had to pull over a couple times during the long journey home, to make adjustments. Cletus patiently fidgeted with the chains, even though his hands were frozen. By the time we got home, I realized that in Cletus I had found a real friend. I was happy to be working with him, even if he was more Del Griffith[203] than Dave Weckl. His character made up for any musical liabilities, in my mind.

Orlando and Wildman didn't share this belief. They wanted Cletus out, and they wanted him out quick.[204] Orlando had brought him to the grown-ups' table and fed him turkey dinner, but now wanted to banish him to the kiddie fold-out. There wasn't much I could do. Orlando had found a potential replacement, a buddy named Dom who, in a case of pure coincidence, hailed from Merced. Dom had been living in the Dominican Republic, but now was back in Central California looking for a new gig.

Dom sat in with us in San Francisco at the Connecticut Yankee, and he crushed it. I thought he played great. Wildman, however, thought his playing was stiff, and that he wasn't the right guy. Gruden, meanwhile, was insinuating that he might return from the East Coast to rejoin the band. I had the feeling Wildman would walk if I gave Dom the gig, and I still had a strong desire to keep Wildman in the mix. I gave the green light for Gruden to move in with us in Merced and take the gig back.

Upon his return, Gruden and I locked horns. He started criticizing my playing, and taking a generally dark tone about the project. We argued about the tempos of various songs. He wanted to play every song fast, and I wanted them slowed down to accommodate the lyrics I was trying to sing; some of my songs were lyric-heavy, with long verses and syncopated melodies. They were like raps, but with actual notes. If the tempo was too fast, you struggled to say all the words, and even if you did manage it, their meaning was lost on the audience.

I'd listen back to live recordings of some of our shows and it was a joke. We were rushing through the music, playing too fast and playing

---

[203] *See Planes, Trains and Automobiles...* the second funniest movie of all-time.

[204] Orlando called me a while back and informed me that Cletus had passed away. Orlando was uncertain of the cause. I was saddened by the news. Cletus was a great guy. RIP, my friend. I hope you're in a better place.

too many notes, and the singing sounded forced and rushed. I wasn't at all happy with how the band sounded.

Wildman had a new concern of his own. The new songs, he felt, were more pop/rock and not *jam-bandy* enough. The shorter forms of the new material were indeed less jam-band influenced and more pop/rock-oriented, but this was a calculated decision I'd made to write more accessible songs. I was tired of people saying our songs were too long, or weren't danceable enough, or that our jams sounded like Phish or the Grateful Dead. The jam band audience en masse had made it clear: they weren't waiting around to discover the next Phish or Grateful Dead. After three-plus years, Global Funk was still struggling to find a musical identity, and an audience who would embrace that identity.

Oh, Mickey, You're So Fine

Given my ongoing woes with the drum chair, and my affinity for *Spinal Tap*—two very connected things, if you have seen the movie—I guess it was only a matter of time before I would come into contact with someone from the World of Tap. The band made its usual pitstop in Missoula, Montana at the Top Hat. We always had a good show there, even if I hadn't exactly made a love connection with owner Steve Garr.

Garr was a short, gruff guy in his late fifties. He was a bass player himself, and supposedly of the belief that the only people who could really play music well were old, overweight black men. Thus, he quietly despised the "hippie jam bands" that packed his club and made him money. We were a nuisance he tolerated for business reasons. Things came to a head one night between me and Steve, who I nicknamed Mr. Sunshine, when I was settling business with him after the show. He said, "You might wanna tip the bartenders. I know guys like you never do that, but it would be a nice gesture." This was total bullshit. A slap in the face. I *always* tipped the bartenders. I held my tongue and went back to the stage to pack up my keyboards.

Garr came back over and made another flippant remark directed at me and the band, and that was where I lost it. I picked up one of my keyboard stands and flung it across the room. It was heavy, and landed with a loud thud, startling anyone left in the building. In Global Funk lore, this tale has been tweaked a bit, and is now told with me actually throwing the keyboard stand at Steve Garr's head. Let me clarify that this is not true. I hurled the stand in a direction where I knew it wouldn't hit anyone—and strangely, Garr didn't really react much to my act of aggression, as if he knew he was being a jerk. The man is no longer with us, and his club provided a venue for many an enjoyable evening, so let me say: Rest in peace, Mr. Sunshine.

One night at the Top Hat, I was hanging out at the bar with Matt Schumacher, a bassist friend who was a local. There were some other regulars sitting with us, and one of them struck me as very familiar. I just couldn't quite figure out where I'd seen him before. Matt introduced me to the guy.

"This is Ric Parnell. He's a really good drummer." I said hello, and noticed the guy, tall, pale and in his fifties, had a legit British accent. We talked for a few minutes, and then Matt whispered in my ear, "He's the original drummer from *Spinal Tap*. He was in the movie." I took another look at Ric, and sure enough, recognized him from my favorite comedy of all time. He had only one short, featured scene, in which he's taking a bath, wearing a hairnet, and talking about the rock and roll life. This was an older, much more weathered version, but it was him. I turned to Matt:

"He doesn't wanna talk about *Spinal Tap*, right? That's probably the last thing he wants to hear."

"No, he's cool. Buy him a drink or two, and he'll be reciting all the lines from the movie in no time." I began buying Ric drinks, and when I finally mentioned *Tap*, he said, "Yeah, that's my claim to fame... even after all these years. It's the only fucking thing I've got going for me. Cheers, mate." The rock and roll life had not been particularly kind to Ric Parnell. When I asked how the hell he wound up in Missoula, Montana, he chuckled and told me the story: He had come down from Canada with some random band, and when they hit Missoula, the whole situation fell apart. The others returned north, but Ric decided to stay. Missoula was now his home.

Ric told me that he'd originally been contacted by Christopher Guest, the comedic genius who not only plays Nigel Tufnel in the classic mockumentary, but also wrote the film, and would go on to write and direct several more hilarious offerings. Guest wanted a legitimate British rock drummer for Spinal Tap, because the band had to actually sound decent. Even though it was all a big joke, the music had to be believable. Ric was a top session drummer in London at the time, and admittedly had his ups and downs with drugs.

"I would send my girlfriend down to the street to blow the dealer for a couple crack rocks," he confessed. This was a hard comment to respond to.

"Wow, that's crazy man. So how do you like it here in Missoula?"

Ric had played on a lot of big pop songs in the eighties, many for which he was never credited. This, he explained, was because he always wanted cash up front, rather than points on the back end.

"You know that song, 'Mickey,' by Toni Basil?"

"Yeah, of course. *Oh, Mickey, you're so fine, you're so fine you blow my mind, hey Mickey... hey Mickey.*"

"That's the one. That's me playing. I could have had a piece of the publishing, but instead I got a hundred pounds up front. That's it. Every time I hear that stupid song, I think about a hundred fucking pounds versus hundreds of thousands of pounds."

Ric and I became friends. He respected that I was a good player and committed songwriter who had *sacked it up* and taken the show on the road, and I respected that he was an intelligent guy and talented player—even if his career wasn't currently setting the world on fire. One night Ric jumped up and played with the band. He was, as Matt had said, a very good drummer. Wildman and I thoroughly enjoyed jamming with him. Ric also hosted a radio show on one of Missoula's stations, and featured Global Funk one week. We showed up ready to talk, play some of our music and party. Ric looked at our bag full of beverages and said "Sorry, guys, we can't drink in here." *Yeah, right Ric. Come on, stop pulling our chain.*

"No, I'm serious. I'll get fired."

Matt and I contemplated putting together a side project with Ric, who was hungry to hit the road. "I've got the perfect name," I said.

"What's that?" Matt wondered.

"Shit Sandwich." This, of course, was in reference to one of the funniest one-liners from *Tap*. Shit Sandwich never got off the ground, and things took a downward slide for Ric. When I last heard about him, he was said to be living in a tiny trailer near the mall in Missoula, and someone thought they'd spotted him working as a greeter at Wal-Mart. I hope they were wrong.

The Award-Winning Lawn Mowing
of Anthony Smith

Back at home in Merced, Gruden asked me if his girlfriend, Sue, could move into the house. She would share his room, contribute to the rent, and otherwise do her part to keep the place in order. I couldn't see a problem with it, so I gave the okay. Sue packed her little car, left her parents' home in Laytonville (where Todd Sherman was now living with his girlfriend and her daughter), and joined the comedy of errors at 1708 Poppy Hills Court.

After a few weeks, Gruden and Sue started playing *house.* She took over the kitchen, cooking elaborate meals every day, flitting about like the domesticated housewife that she was not. She was nesting, and doing so in a band house full of musicians and neo-hippies. Sue was in Gruden's face twenty-four/seven, and began snooping and spying on him. For instance, she began checking the numbers on his cell phone, trying to determine who he was calling and receiving calls from. Gruden, exemplifying behavior I have described in previous chapters, had established *repeat clients in a variety of markets,* and was indeed making and receiving calls to some of these clients.

In an effort to appease his insecure girlfriend, Gruden decided to give Sue the opportunity to *re-imagine,* if you will, the entire backyard, as an elaborate vegetable and flower garden—sort of a horticultural performance art piece. The trouble was, the two of them launched into this project without giving me so much as a heads up, and I had signed a lease specifying that I do nothing to alter the interior or exterior of the property.

I came home one afternoon to find Gruden and Sue covered in dirt, manipulating a hoeing device rented from Home Depot. They were tearing up huge chunks of grass to make way for their new vision, whatever that might be. I have no doubt by now convinced the reader of my cool, calm level-headedness in dealing with adverse circumstances,[205] so you might find it hard to believe that my first reaction to this unauthorized demolition of the backyard of a house I was renting, and had been forbidden against altering in any way, was the inclination to pick up a small coffee table and throw it through the sliding glass doors leading to the backyard in question. I didn't do this, fortunately, and instead opted to call Anne for advice.

"Hi Mom. Guess what? Gruden's out back with his girlfriend, tearing up the backyard. There's clumps of grass everywhere. They're absolutely wrecking the place. What should I do?"

"What are they doing exactly?"

"Planting some kind of crazy garden."

"Did they ask you first?"

"No."

(Sigh) "Well, I'd let this one ride, Anth. It's just grass. You can always replant it before you move. Don't get too upset. Just let them have their garden."

"Okay," I agreed. "I'll take your advice." I let the garden fiasco roll off my back, and concentrated my energies on the *front* yard. Gruden and Sue had their little slice of paradise, but the area in front of the house was mine. I sneered at my sarcastic neighbor as I sprinkled fertilizer and seeds over barren patches of soil, pulled weeds, watered,

---

[205] Hehehe…

shifted around bark and swept away refuse. Gruden snuck out front with a camera, one blistering summer day, and snapped a photo of me lumbering across the lawn with the mower, sweat beads accentuating the bald spot to the left/front of my follicle-challenged cranium. He posted the photo on the *Internet*, titling it: *The Award Winning Lawn-Mowing of Anthony Smith.*

For entertainment, we would all pile into the E-350 and head down to Mahomey's for Wednesday night karaoke. As long as I had some Captain Morgan in the bloodstream, I was fearless. I made friends with a heavy-set black woman who was a good singer, and we did duets. We brought the house down with *Reunited,* by Peaches and Herb—I played the role of Herb. I even had the balls to tackle *Runnin' with the Devil.* I could nail the loungey David Lee Roth verses no problem, but the raspy, high-pitched wails at the end? Those were another story. Orlando, fresh from his ten-hour train ride from L.A., took the stage to join me for a rendition of the Stevie Wonder/Paul McCartney classic, *Ebony and Ivory.* Since we were both white, it seemed a slight change of lyric was in order; our version was called *Ivory and Ivory.* The first line went:
I am white, and you're not black
You're as pale as a ghost, and that's a fact

Tyson wasn't big on karaoke, and would hang at the bar and wait for girls to come up and talk to him. Lunabelle, gregarious hippie chick from Montana, was quite the commodity there in our little central Californian refuge, especially among horny Hispanic guys.

One night, after drunken duets and embarrassing solo performances, we took a group of partiers home to continue the festivities. Lunabelle invited back a young gentleman named Nestor, in town on business, who seemed like a nice enough chap. She was playing that game girls sometime play: they're flattered that a guy is interested, so they ignore the fact that he believes there's going to be a pot of gold at the end of the rainbow, a reward for all his hard work. Lunabelle had managed to keep Nestor at arm's length at the club, chatting innocently while pounding drinks and fiddling with her prodigious dreadlocks, but now we were all back at the pad, and Nestor was ready to collect on his investment of time and paid-for cocktails.

The Captain had worn off and I was retired for the evening, but Tyson was still hanging. Lunabelle pulled him aside and told him she needed help getting rid of this guy.

"Where is he?" Tyson asked.

"He's in my room... waiting." Nestor must have been disappointed when, instead of a cute hippie girl sashaying back into the bedroom, it was a six-foot-two dude with stubble. Tyson walked in, and in his words, "found this guy lying on the bed, wrapping his churro for action. I told him to stop. 'Not gonna happen, bro.'" Nestor covered up and got dressed.

"Guess she changed her mind, eh?" the foiled Don Juan said.

"Yeah," Tyson answered, "I guess she did."

THE LIZARD STAYS IN THE CAGE

I was the only one sober enough for the job, so I gave the guy a ride back to his motel.

"Seemed like I had that in my pocket," he lamented as we drove down Merced's main drag.

"I think George Michael said it best, my friend: *Sometimes you think you're gonna get it, but you don't, and that's just the way it goes.*"

Around this time, Gruden's father passed away. He was understandably devastated, but opted to continue playing in the group and living with us in Merced. In the weeks after the sad news, the drummer's temper became short, and he was having a difficult time holding everything together. One day, Gruden, Orlando and I were listening to some music, looking for new covers to learn. I'd taken a shine to a Widespread Panic song called *Little Lily*, which I thought would be a good follow-up to our other Panic cover, *Tall Boy*. I started to play the song on the stereo in the living room, and Gruden immediately shook his head and said, "You're not thinking of playing *that*, are you?"

"Well, actually I was," I answered.

"I'm not learning some candy-ass Widespread Panic song! Fuck that!" I was so insulted that I turned off the CD, grabbed my backpack and bailed from the house without saying a word. There was a Starbucks just a few blocks from the house, and I found myself escaping there with more and more frequency. Working with these people was really taking its toll. When I went home several hours later, Gruden had left me a note. Written in anger, it was the worst shit anyone has ever committed to paper on my behalf. Imagine the type of letters Bernie Madoff must have received, after his clients found out he had destroyed their fortunes. *It was that bad.* There were f-bombs, accusations, character assassinations… it was the harshest of the harsh.

Walking out on Gruden, after he mocked my suggestion of a new cover song, had opened up a vitriolic can of worms between us. At that moment, I was convinced he and I would soon be going our separate ways. He would move out and perhaps return to his home in New Jersey, and I would yet again, tragic-comically, start the search for a new drummer. I wrote a long, detailed response to Gruden's scathing diatribe, taking a more conciliatory tone. I slipped the note under his bedroom door.

Upset about Gruden's letter and the breakdown of relations, I split ten hours early for our show that night at Cooper's in Nevada City, driving alone in my own car. I called Teena to tell her what had happened, and that I had already left for the gig. She listened patiently and then said, "You might have left for the gig a little early."

That night at Cooper's, Gruden approached me before the show. He said he appreciated my letter, and that he wasn't going to quit. We talked things over, and it seemed like all would be cool. After the band finished playing, we sat around chatting about upcoming tours and future plans, also attempting to clear the air after the awkward vibe from earlier in the day. The perfect end to the conversation would have been someone asking, in understated Derek Smalls fashion: *Can I raise a practical question at this point? Are we gonna learn Little Lily?* (In thick British accent) NO, WE'RE NOT GONNA FUCKIN' LEARN LITTLE LILY!!!

We returned to the Caspar Inn, this time hoping to draw people by adding a novelty theme: *Global Funk Plays the Grateful Dead.* I'd conceived of this idea thinking it might stimulate Wildman's passion, at least temporarily. He was, after all, a Head. He'd been to shows, he'd lived the lifestyle. Wildman wasn't keen on the tribute idea, however. It was just too late in the game for him. Nothing was going to re-ignite his belief in the project and the scene.

I went ahead with the idea, learning some Dead lyrics so we could get through the show. I didn't learn them *well enough.* I stumbled through the evening, squinting to read small scribbles of lyrics on a barely lit stage. The handful of hippies in the meager audience weren't tickled. One white-haired cat, who probably knew the band personally, bickered to Kirby, the owner, loud enough to be heard from the stage:

"These guys don't know the lyrics, man! I came down to hear Dead songs, and they're butchering 'em!"

"Butchering" might have been an overstatement, but we weren't exactly doing the ghost of Jerry Garcia proud, either. Kirby managed to appease the grumpy Deadhead, resorting to less extreme measures than he had employed with a certain belligerent patron discussed earlier...

Deadhead: This is bullshit, man. These guys suck.

Kirby: I hear you man. I'm sorry they didn't learn the lyrics. Let me get you a free beer.

Deadhead: I drove all the way over here from Ukiah.

Kirby: Here's your beer, bro. Now, I need you to shut the hell up. Otherwise, bad things might happen.

Deadhead: Like what?

Kirby: Well, I might get mad and *bite your nose off.*

Phil Towle Saves the Day

The tour made its way up to the Northwest, a familiar route. While staying at a promoter's house in Seattle, the four of us sat and watched a documentary about the band Metallica, called *Some Kind of Monster*. The well-done film told the tale of the band's attempt to co-exist with each other in the studio, long enough to assemble a new album and get back out on the road. There was a great deal of dysfunction between the members, particularly Lars Ulrich and James Hetfield, who bickered constantly. One of them was always threatening to walk out.

I've never been a fan of Metallica. Not only does their music leave me cold, but let me remind you that they came off as pompous d-bags when I was working as an intern at A&M Records in the mid-nineties. My brief interaction with them had been at the height of their popularity, when they were no doubt believing their own hype.

Now, in 2005, Metallica were hard rock legends. By deciding to reunite, record and tour again, they had relaunched a giant machine of middlemen, promoters, producers and other peripheral players, all looking to secure their seat before the gravy train left the station.

One of these peripheral individuals was a high-profile psychologist named Phil Towle. Towle, who'd carved out a lucrative niche as a troubleshooter for professional sports teams, actors and musicians, was brought in by the band to mediate fights, help the aloof, moody Hetfield interact positively with everyone around him, and basically keep the whole situation from falling apart. Towle's group therapy sessions were videotaped, and served as a main focus of the film.

Towle came across as an opportunist, one of many looking to make a buck, or many bucks, off the comeback of a major rock band. Somehow on film, he looked and sounded like a bit of a weasel, at one point pleading with the band not to fire him. He didn't seem effective as a therapist, as the band was comprised of egomaniacs unable or unwilling to meet each other in the middle.

We watched the documentary in one sitting, concurring at the end that the whole thing hit a little too close to home. We too had dysfunction. We too had put up walls between each other, and were unwilling to work through our interpersonal conflicts. Wildman and I were most likely a lost cause. Gruden and I were heading that way also. Orlando and I were cool, but he hadn't been around long enough to be bitter. We came to a depressing realization: We were Metallica, minus the platinum albums, sold-out world tours and legendary status. We had all the bullshit, but none of the glory. All the same toils, none of the spoils.

Okay, you're probably wondering, why the hell am I spending so much time talking about a Metallica documentary? Don't worry, there is a reason...

Perhaps a month later, the band was back on the Ucolortanaho trail, having just played Jackson Hole. We cruised into Victor, Idaho for a two-night run at our familiar stomping ground, the Knotty Pine. Let me point out, if I didn't before, that this place is in the middle of nowhere. It's in a valley surrounded by the Grand Tetons and other mountains, in a tiny little town with nothing around it but beautiful, wide open space. Put another way, it's not a place where you expect to run into people you know, unless they're locals you met last time you passed through.

I parked the van in front of the Knotty Pine, just as I always did, and we started loading our equipment into the club. Orlando was the first to go inside, and when he came back out he walked over with a smile on his face.

"Hey, T, you're not gonna believe this. Guess who's in there?"

"Who?"

"The guy from the Metallica movie."

"One of the guys in the band?"

"No. The psychologist."

"No way, man. I'm sure it's someone who just looks like him."

"No, it's him. I'm positive."

I walked inside, and sure enough, there was Phil Towle, sitting at a table having lunch with his wife. I was friendly with the bartender, Adam, a nice guy in his late twenties, and walked over to chat with him.

"Hey, Adam, is that by chance Phil Towle sitting over there? The guy from the Metallica movie?"

"Yeah, that's him. He's my dad."

Phil, it turned out, came with his wife every summer to visit Adam. He was on vacation.

"Do you want to meet him?" Adam asked.

"Sure, that would be cool. We just watched the movie recently."

"Okay, I'll bring him over and introduce you guys."

A while later, the four of us were standing on the club's patio, chilling out before our sound check. The sound man at the Knotty Pine, incidentally, was a member of sound engineering most revered *royal family*. Jeff Lord-Alge was the brother of two of the most successful recording engineers in the history of popular music: Chris and Tom Lord-Alge. These guys had either engineered or mixed many of the biggest songs and albums of all time. Jeff had burned out on the L.A. scene early, and elected to continue his career in the more laid back environment of the Teton Valley.

As we stood there, Adam walked over to introduce us to his parents, who'd just finished eating.

"Hey guys, this is my dad, Phil." I shook his hand, and was immediately struck by how different his presence was in person. First off, the man was tall and solid. Also, he had an intensity about him, a sense of focus that was entirely lost in the movie's depiction.

For some reason, Wildman had no interest in talking to Phil Towle. After the greeting, he wandered off. I, Orlando and Gruden stayed.

"I hear you guys are very good," Phil said.

"Thanks," I responded. "We saw you in the Metallica film." Phil grimaced a little.

"You know, I don't feel the film did me much justice. The filmmakers had a certain viewpoint, but I don't think it accurately reflected who I am and what I do." We made some small talk for a couple minutes, and then Phil said, "So, how are you guys doing?"

"We're doing okay, having a decent tour." He looked directly into my eyes.

"But *how are you doing?*" The three of us looked at each other. We were doing shitty. We weren't getting along, and the band wasn't progressing in the scene.

"Not that good, man. Not that good." Gruden shook his head.

For the next forty-five minutes, Phil Towle proceeded to psycho-analyze our band. He asked us to each give our assessment of the situation, and offered thoughtful ideas about how we could improve our relationships, as well as our business. He was articulate and convincing. You could see why people paid him big bucks to help them with their problems. The guy was good—and he did this free of charge. I was friendly with his son, and he was relaxed and on vacation, so we'd caught him in the right frame of mind.

Now, here's the really funny part of the story. After watching the Metallica movie, I and the other guys in the band had more or less dismissed Towle's psycho-therapy sessions as jive—a bullshit, money-making racket. That's how the film depicted him, after all. But in person, Phil Towle was the real deal. What he said resonated with me. Laugh if you must, but standing on that patio of the Knotty Pine, in a middle-of-nowhere town somewhere in Idaho, Phil Towle made a *breakthrough.*

We thanked Phil and said our goodbyes. He admitted that he probably wouldn't be back to hear the band later that night. He would be taking it easy with his wife and their dog. After a frustrating first set, during which I felt Gruden was being an asshole on drums, something in me snapped. Phil had just told us that where people go wrong is in thinking it's better to bottle things up and avoid conflict... seemingly to keep the peace. When we do this, we're not keeping the peace at all. We're only allowing a manageable, reconcilable conflict to grow into a situation beyond repair.

I decided I was done walking on eggshells with Gruden. I was done pretending everything was okay when it wasn't. I walked over to where he was standing, by the club's little cluster of old-school video games like Galaga and Miss Pacman.

"Hey man, can we talk for a minute?"

"All right."

"So listen. I'm fucking fed up with you. I'm sick of your bullshit attitude. I took you back into this band, when my gut was saying not to. I know you've been through a lot of shit with your family, with your dad. I'm sorry, I really am. But I'm so sick of you being a prick, vibing me while we're playing like I'm wrong for wanting to make the music sound good. Fuck your attitude. If you don't want the music to sound good, and you don't want to work at this, then go home. Go back to fucking New Jersey. I don't need any more bullshit, man. I'm at the end of my rope. Just leave." After spewing all this, I felt an incredible sense of catharsis, like I'd just opened the floodgates of all my pent-up frustrations. I'd finally shot from the hip, without concern for the consequences, and it was liberating.[206] *Stay… leave… I don't care anymore. Here's the truth.*

I expected Gruden to turn and walk away. I was sure he would leave the project, and thought he might even split right then and there. But a strange thing happened. He paused, thought about what I'd said, and turned to look at me.

"You know what, man? That's the most honestly you've ever talked to me. I had no idea how pissed and frustrated you were. I'm sorry. I'll work on my attitude."

The band is a thing of the past in 2012, but Gruden and I are still good friends to this day. We keep in touch via phone, and occasionally get together to hang out. Every year on my birthday, he calls me (I share a birthdate with his older brother) and loudly bellows, "Happy birthday, asshole!" A big reason why we're still friends is Phil Towle. Without his advice in front of the Knotty Pine, I don't think we would have made it. Phil's therapy might not have gotten it done for Metallica, but it sure worked wonders for Global Funk.

Shortly after returning to Merced, Wildman called me from Monterey. "I can't keep doing this," he said. "I'm gonna have to move on." We had a frank chat about the band, the struggles, and our shared need to make money and deal with personal debts. I didn't exactly try to talk him out of his decision. After all, the two of us didn't get along

---

[206] My Uncle David recently wrote a self-help book called *Rude to Recovery*, in which he makes the same argument as Phil Towle: Just be honest. If your honesty is perceived as rude or upsetting, too bad for the other party. It's the healthier choice for *both of you*. We live in a society where people constantly lie to each other, and we collectively suffer for it.

much of the time, and I also believed the best thing for him would be to move on and figure out what he wanted to do with his life. We might not have been bosom buds, but I did care about the guy, and was saddened by the fact that Global Funk had led him to such dire straits. Wildman agreed to play for a short while longer, until I could find a replacement.

I already had one in mind. Matt Schumacher, a friend from Missoula, seemed like the right guy to take over the bass chair. I called him and explained the situation, and he agreed that he'd like to join Global Funk.

The next couple tours featured the lineup of Orlando, Gruden, Matt and me, and it was the most harmonious group of guys I'd ever taken on the road. We had a blast, and the music was sounding good, but the sad truth was that the damage was done; the organization was going nowhere, the business model had failed, and no matter how much fun we might be having on the road, the end was looming.

Yes, it was looming, but it hadn't quite arrived yet. We still had shows to play, we still had twelve-hour drives to make, and, as Orlando would say, we still had to do *terrible things to terrible people.* I never exactly understood what he meant by this, but it was a funny line, regardless.

Chariots of Fire **Meets** *Less Than Zero*

Before heading back out to Utah, we made a pitstop in Reno. I had an old friend, Leanne, who owned a music club downtown. Years earlier, Leanne had dated bassist Ken Dow, while Ken and I were playing together in Faze. Now she was in Reno, harboring musical vagrants who spanned every genre from foul mouthed, mysoginistic gangsta rap to veganed-out, vegetable oil-powered neo-hippie funk.

During our show at Leanne's club, Orlando hit it off with a pair of girls at the bar. Normally I wouldn't care, and would actually be relieved, because it meant I'd have one less person whose needs I would have to attend to after the music was done. When a guy came up and said, "Hey, T, I'm going home with (insert female name of your choice), see you in the morning," I'd say, "Great! Have a blast." *Handle your business well, Sparky, so the girl buys you breakfast before dropping you off in the morning.*

On this particular occasion, however, we had to drive all night to get to Zion National Park. We'd been hired to play a wedding reception in a hotel courtyard, and the fee for the gig was going to keep the van rocking for a couple more weeks. I didn't want to screw it up, in other words. I knew we'd have to split right after the show in Reno to make it out to Zion by the morning, with time to brush our teeth and hose ourselves off before we had to face the scrutiny of some uptight bride and her micro-managing minions.

When we finished playing at Leanne's place, Orlando walked over with a smile on his face.

"No, dude. Not tonight. Don't do this to me. We're on a tight schedule."

"T, I need half an hour. These girls live right up the street. Just give me half an hour." I sighed.

"Okay. We'll pack up the stuff and gas up... but don't fuck this up. Be ready to rock when I call you, and keep your cell phone on, all right?"

"Thanks. Deal." He disappeared with a pair of ladies who reminded me of the adage, embraced by a large number of men, which states that there are times in life when it's more practical to forget about perfect 10's, and instead settle for *two 2's and a six-pack.*

We packed the van, got gas, and I called Orlando's cell. No answer, straight to voice mail. I started blowing up his phone, but he wasn't answering. I had told him not to do this. He was partying, living the dream, and didn't want to be bothered until he was finished with his business. Normally, I couldn't care less what guys did in the wee hours of the night... *You say you hooked up with some members of a bestiality ring, and they're taking you back to their compound to huff super glue, then put a hurtin' on some farm animals? That's lovely... just make sure your ass is in the van before we split town. And be sure to shower.*

I waited and waited, but Orlando was *incommunicado.* Finally, I had to put my foot down. We simply had to start driving. I told the rest of the guys, "We gotta bail. He'll have to find a ride to Zion." I actually started to drive in the direction of the freeway. As I was getting ready to turn toward the onramp, Matt called out from the backseat, "Wait. I think I see him." I looked out the window and saw a lone figure, sprinting toward us from afar.

"It's him," Gruden said. Orlando's stocky silhouette was illuminated by streetlights as he strided through the fog, running as fast as he could to avoid being left behind. There was something both poetic and sad about the moment. It was kind of a cross between *Chariots of Fire* and *Less than Zero.* Orlando hopped in the van, offered up a muted apology, and we started driving.

Halfway to Zion, I remembered something. "Damn, we're supposed to play some INXS song for the first dance."

"Which one," Gruden asked.

"Never Tear Us Apart," I answered. Matt started laughing.

"That song kind of sucks, man. Who's gonna sing it?"

"Me, I guess." More laughs.

None of us knew the tune, so we stopped at a Wal-Mart in the middle of nowhere, and I picked up a copy of INXS's greatest hits album. I let Matt drive for a while, and I scribbled out the lyrics to the song. We would be faking our way through this one big-time.

We made it to Zion with barely enough time to clean up, change our clothes, set up our equipment and play. The father of the bride came over to talk to me, and seemed a little concerned by our appearance. The wedding party was wearing tuxedos, and the band looked like... well, the band looked like some scraggly dudes that just drove through the night from Reno.

The reception went fine, the crowd dancing to our funky grooves and enjoying themselves. Then, it was time for the first dance. I knew the INXS song from hearing it a million times on the radio, but singing it convincingly was another story. I could pull off certain tunes, but mimicking Michael Hutchence would be a real stretch.

We broke into the song, and I self-consciously mumbled my way through the lyrics:

I, I was standin'
You were there
Two worlds collided
And they could never tear us apart!

The bride and her father danced tentatively, shooting me concerned glances. The band hacked through the song unconvincingly, while I kept singing the same verse over and over again. Talk about a mockery! I felt a little bad taking the bride's father's money—but not bad enough not to take it. After the set Matt came over, deadpan, and said, "Hey, T, great job on that INXS song. You really killed it."

"Yeah... I downright murdered it."

While in Zion, I logged some hours at an internet café, doing research for a new screenplay I was excited about writing. After years of immersion in the jam band world, and much time spent in Sonoma, Mendocino and Humboldt Counties, I'd come up with a film premise I thought was truly inspired: the tale of a ruthless, Godfather-style mogul living a fabled, semi-reclusive existence in the hills of Mendocino, where he oversaw a huge marijuana growing operation. The character's name was Curtis Keats, and he was a West Coast, hippified version of Gordon Gecko; a personification of the dark side of the American Dream. I set out to write an epic tale, a commentary on numerous aspects of American culture, and a journey into the world of high-volume marijuana trafficking. I called it *The Sultan of Mendocino.* In retrospect, it was a great idea with some colorful characters and compelling scenes, but a structurally flawed effort.

My problem with screenwriting always tends to be in the area of structure. I'm passionate about creating a vibrant world, and I have a knack for writing strong dialogue, but I lack the stamina to rewrite over and over—precisely what you must do to beat any script into presentable shape. With screenwriting, there are carefully defined parameters you have to adhere to, at least if you hope to attract the film industry's interest. With a novel, or a free-wheeling, rambling memoir (haha), you can take many more liberties with the organization of your ideas. *The Sultan of Mendocino* remains one of several promising scripts I keep in a box in my garage, hoping I'll one day find the time and desire to rethink, rewrite, and present them to the world.

The Novacaine Should Kick In Any Second Bro

As if I didn't already have enough to deal with in Global Funk, I started having problems with one of my back molars. I found a dentist in Merced and went in to get it checked out. The guy was young for a dentist... younger than me, which seemed a little weird. He had good credentials and came recommended, so I went ahead. He took a look at the tooth and said, "You need a root canal." It would be a first for me. I figured it was inevitable; doesn't everyone need a root canal, sooner or later? I made an appointment to get the work done.

A couple weeks later I was sitting in the chair, and the dentist came in with his assistant, who was even younger than him. While they prepared the drills and utensils, they began chatting.

So, dude," the dentist began. Now, this is already problematic. Someone who is about to start boring holes in your mouth should not use the word dude under any circumstances. It got worse.

"So I'm at this bar last night, and I'm talking to this chick, right? She's vibing me like she's not down."

"Oh yeah, bro?"

Now, I'm getting nervous. These guys are talking like a couple high school knuckleheads, but they're also holding high-powered drills in their hands, getting ready to chisel away inside my mouth and gums. Not good. The dentist bent over to speak to me.

"You're going to feel some pressure now, okay? So anyway, it's not like she was super hot. She was maybe a seven. Feel anything?"

"Yeah, I feel it."

"The novacaine should kick in any second bro. So she's talking to me like she's Cristy Turlington, and dude, she's totally not." The drill hit my tooth. BUZZZZZZ. Shards of tooth started flying in various directions.

Excuse me, Doctor, do you think you can cut to the chase and tell your dumbshit assistant if you wound up getting laid or not, so you can get back to concentrating on my oral surgery? And I'd prefer that you don't call me bro.

Within a week of each other, Orlando and Matt both broke the news that they couldn't continue to be a part of Global Funk. Orlando wasn't making enough money to keep his home life in L.A. afloat, and Matt just didn't believe the band was a viable business. That left me and Gruden, along with Lunabelle, Tyson, Sue, and the house in Merced. Tyson announced plans to move to San Francisco. He hadn't been able to keep a job, and I had nothing concrete to offer him. Lunabelle also wanted out—she was going back to her old life in Missoula, which I thought was the right move.

I drove the streets of my little middle-of-nowhere city, pondering an uncertain future. I walked through the defunct Castle Air Force Base, now a museum, wondering how I would face the mounting debts Global Funk had dropped in my lap. The massive, gutted planes on display, including a rusted B-52, were a reminder that all things have a finite shelf life. Like those old war aircraft, my band, my business, my vision… was now but a shell.

I knew I could piece Global Funk back together, once again, if I so chose. I'd done it before, and I could do it again. I'd had people tell me, "*You're* Global Funk, man. As long as you're there, we'll come out to the show." As much as I appreciated such support from loyal friends and fans, however, I knew it was done. Global Funk was at the end of the line, and it was time to let go.

Woo, more than anyone else, was glum about my decision. He wanted me to keep the band going, replacing Orlando with a competent young guitarist from Chico. Gruden was willing to stay, and it wouldn't have been too difficult to find a new bass player. Woo had been there from the beginning, and I suppose he shared my sadness in watching the whole thing fall apart. Global Funk was his band, just as it was mine.

Todd was disappointed, but understood it was time to fold. Since the break-up dovetailed with the exodus from 1708 Poppy Hills, I opted to give up the house and move to the Bay Area. I joined Teena in her San Carlos apartment. Shortly thereafter, we took a fabulous trip to Thailand, Cambodia, Vietnam and India.

VULCAN, GOD OF GREAT SAX SOLOS
AND MUSCULAR BUTT CHEEKS

Upon my return from Southeast Asia, it was clear I needed a new path. Not an entirely different career, but a new direction, philosophy and plan. I decided to relocate, yet again, to San Diego. I would always consider the Bay Area home, but my entire network of music contacts was in Southern California. The idea of moving south was not what Teena had in mind. We were finally living in the same place, and I was about to complicate things again.

Time had healed old wounds, and I found myself back in contact with Lincoln Norris, the entrepreneur I'd worked with in Living Large. I know it seems unlikely that I would collaborate again with someone who had dumped me on a corner in San Francisco, but there had been much water under the bridge since 2001, and the Living Large blowout hadn't been entirely Lincoln's fault. He had continued to evolve as a businessman, and I felt comfortable giving him another shot.

Lincoln loved my photos from Delhi, India, which featured me sporting a turban and full beard. He was excited to create a new marketing campaign for me, incorporating the turban shots, as well as photos he snapped himself. Lincoln wanted to call my campaign *The Many Faces of Mr. Smith*. I thought it sounded cool, and was just happy somebody still wanted to invest energy in my musical career.

The anger I had felt toward Lincoln, after being released from Living Large, had been the driving force behind my leaving San Diego and establishing Global Funk Council on a national level. If he hadn't pushed me in that direction, I doubt I would have formed a group, bought an RV, and experienced many of the highs, lows, and colorful circumstances detailed in these pages.

Toward the end of the Living Large days, I had been hard-headed. I wanted to be the boss, and I wanted to call the shots. *I got what I wanted…* and as you have learned, I paid serious dues for that privilege. I made major mistakes. My lack of business experience and effective leadership, as well as my self-centeredness at times, led to the inability of the band to turn a corner. Yes, the ultimate failure of GFC was partially due to my personal shortcomings. There are other people and factors I could blame, also, but I'd rather just take responsibility for my part and resist pointing fingers elsewhere.

Wisdom in the entertainment business is hard-earned. There's no substitute for the gritty experience you accumulate in the trenches. The reason Lincoln Norris and I could now have a harmonious partnership was that we had both evolved. We were better at our respective jobs, and able to communicate more effectively than in the past. One consolation of aging is that you don't do as many dumb things as you used to. That's as good a definition of maturity as any: the learned ability to avoid doing dumb things.

The first project I tackled with Lincoln was a reunion with Mario Walker. Mario was teaming up with Roscoe Church, a well-established drummer from New Orleans, to present a show called Re-New Orleans… a post-Katrina tribute to the city, I guess. The trouble was that Mario didn't have a band. That's where I came in. I knew the end was near for Global Funk, and the bookings I was getting from Ain't Too Proud to Beg were a joke. Mario's Colorado tour seemed like a way everyone could walk away from Global Funk with a good taste in their mouths. The tour was sure to be well-attended, and included a stop at the spacious Boulder Theater.

After all that had happened in the past, working with Mario again was a decision that flew in the face of common sense. I knew, for one reason or another, it was going to wind up being a fiasco. It was always a fiasco, no matter how well organized or structured the tour might have been. At some point, the guy was going to lose his mind and do some questionable, strange shit. Like I've said, I loved his trumpet playing, and I even had love for him as a person, but I'd seen the same scenario unfold too many times.

Nonetheless, sticking with the pathetic winter tour Ain't Too Proud's Jarvis Fogarty had cobbled together would have been the greater of two evils. It would be better to watch Mario lose his mind in front of a packed house at the Boulder Theater, than to play for the crickets in some tiny dump in a remote mountain town. After four arduous years on the road with Global Funk, I wanted to go out with an obnoxious bang, not a whimper. Working with Mario was going to be a roller coaster ride, and the odds of Mario managing a harmonious working relationship with Roscoe, also a notorious wild card, were basically zero.

I'd gone through seven or eight drummers, a few guitarists, and now three bass players. It wasn't that JBS fans didn't like Global Funk[207]... after all the personnel changes, they just didn't know what Global Funk *was* anymore. How many times could I keep reassembling the lineup, reworking the same repertoire for new musicians? If it was essentially *me*, with whomever else was still standing, or whoever I'd grabbed for a particular tour, why was I calling it Global Funk? Maybe it was time to put my own name on it. People in the scene would come up and say, "Man, you've really hung in there. I've seen you with so many different players. The one thing I know, when Global Funk comes to town, is that you'll be sitting behind those keyboards."

I also realize our business model was inherently flawed. Todd Sherman, Woo and I had been starry-eyed dreamers. Short of a minor miracle, there was no way Global Funk was going to be profitable. Given the amount of money it costs to tour and to make basic provisions for people's living needs, contrasted with the often meager

---

[207] Although there are always those out there who think you suck, no matter who you are.

wages a touring band earns, unless it breaks through to a higher level of popularity, taking a group on the road is going to be a money-losing proposition. That's the plain truth.

Of Rats and Yes Men, Starring Jarvis and Amir

Things had been getting ugly with Ain't Too Proud to Beg Booking. Global Funk was going nowhere and I knew it. I bailed out of a succession of lame Ain't Too Proud engagements so that we could do the gigs with Roscoe and Mario, aware that the relationship with Ain't Too Proud would likely be severed as a result. Since Global Funk was locked into a pair of lucrative New Years shows in Jackson Hole, and the Re-New Orleans tour was committed to a New Years gig in Bozeman, we agreed we'd use two vehicles: my van, and Lincoln Norris's RV.

The first show of the Re-New Orleans tour was at the Mangy Moose in Jackson Hole. We did a few Global Funk shows on the way out to Wyoming, as I was trying to appease Jarvis after canceling several Ain't Too Proud bookings. Upon arrival at Teton Village, we checked into our band condos—the usual drill—and relaxed for a while. This group of guys had no problems getting along. Matt and I clicked much better than Wildman and I ever could. Gruden and I had resolved our differences (thanks to Phil Towle!) and were better friends now than ever before. Orlando, while high-strung and somewhat crazy at times, was an easy guy to be around.

One of the greatest laughs I've ever had in my entire life occurred while we were driving between gigs, somewhere in Northern California. Gruden and I launched into spirited impersonations of Jarvis and Amir, our nincompoop booking agents at Ain't Too Proud to Beg. I'd just recounted my latest phone conversation with Jarvis, who spoke with a thick Southern drawl, when the floodgates of humor opened wide. Gruden grabbed the ball and started doing Jarvis, with a Southern drawl that was downright Foxworthian. I began doing Amir, copping a stereotypical Jewish agent's delivery. We played out a mock conversation between Jarvis and Amir, reminiscent of Lenny and George in Steinbeck's classic.

Jarvis: Aynthonay, you boyz urr really on the right track out thar. Let me get off the horn so I can check in with Amir. I'll call yew back layter.
Jarvis walks over to Amir's office and enters.
Jarvis: Hey, Amir. Just talked to them boyz from Global Funk. Got 'em booked for a saayfood festival out in Monterey.
Amir: A what?
Jarvis: A saayfood festival.
Amir: A *seafood festival?*
Jarvis: Yep.
Amir: What the hell are you doing, Jarvis? I entrust you with handling one of our most important acts, and you book them at Cannery Row?
Jarvis: It's a really good gig, boss.
Amir: How can that be a really good gig, Jarvis? Are they playing for the fish, over at the aquarium? Are they going to serenade the monkey-faced eels?
Jarvis: Why ya always getting' on my case, Amir? Ahhm tryin' ta do what you asked me to, that's all.
Amir: What you're doing is ruining my business, you damn redneck! I gave you a specific strategy to follow, and I must tell you, I am not pleased!
Jarvis: Ah, come on, Amir. I been there with you from the beginning.

Amir: Yes, and you're keeping me down! I've carried you on my back, friend!

Jarvis: Whatchoo talkin' about, Amir? Golly, I'm the one doin' all the dirty work!

Amir: That's because you're a retard! I'm the brains behind this operation!

Jarvis: Hell, all you do is sit around n' cook them books. Any Jewish fella can do that.

Amir: Don't you get racial with me, you cornfed hick!

This continued pretty much the entire distance from Northern California to Wyoming. Laughter is therapy.

When Mario knocked on the condo door in Teton Village and entered the room, it took me all of five minutes... wait, make that one minute... to realize he was just as *out there* as ever. He started trying to teach us a bunch of songs, haphazardly jumping from one to the next before we had a chance to even comprehend what he was talking about. Matt shot me a rolled-eye expression that said: *This is going to be a long tour.*

As showtime approached, the Mangy Moose got packed with hundreds of people. Word came down that Roscoe wasn't even in Wyoming yet. Due to severe winter weather, his plane had been delayed out of New Orleans. By 10 p.m., it was time to take the stage one way or the other. Gruden was not with us—he'd flown back to the East Coast temporarily—so we had no drummer without Roscoe.

"I've got an idea," Orlando said. He'd just bought a new Mac computer, and had programmed some drum loops. We did our first set using the loops, Mario fronting the band with his characteristic offbeat charisma. The audience responded well, and we made it through an entire set in this fashion.

Shortly before the beginning of the second set, when it looked like we were going to have to do the whole night without a drummer, Roscoe waltzed in, took the stage, removed his jacket and sat down behind the drum kit. He nodded at me at and the other musicians, cracked the snare drum with one of his sticks, and we proceeded to spend the rest of the night laying down some very funky grooves. The crowd loved it. I was impressed with Roscoe's drumming immediately.

The following day, we convened at a diner in Jackson before heading on to Colorado. Perhaps as an outgrowth of his military experience,

Lincoln liked to conduct briefings and debriefings at different points in a given tour. The guys in Global Funk were adamant about riding in our own van, as opposed to jumping in the RV with Mario, Roscoe and Lincoln. I would not be so lucky—Lincoln asked me to ride with him, so we could talk business. I agreed, and the caravan hit the road.

About five minutes into the journey, Roscoe made his presence felt.

"Yo, Lincoln…" We all turned to listen.

"We gotta talk about this money, man. Mario told me one thing, and now I'm gettin' the impression it's somethin' else. What up? What are you paying me for this tour?"

"A thousand dollars."

Roscoe's eyes lit up, the glare of a man who's just been thoroughly disrespected.

"Oh, hellllllllll nooooo! A thousand fucking dollars for twelve gigs? Are you out of your fucking mind? Hellllllll nooooo! Put me on a plane! Take me to the airport! I'm goin' home. You out your mind! Thousand dollars? Hellllllll naaaaaahhhhhhhh!!!" Lincoln, as was his m.o., attempted to respond with phlegmatic nonchalance.

"It seems we have a misunderstanding, Roscoe. But I'm sure it can be resolved."

"The misunderstanding is that Mario told me he was givin' me twenty-five hundred dollars."

"Well, that's between you and Mario, I guess."

"Pull this motherfucker over! Now! Let me get out on the side of the road! I'm callin' my lady in Boulder! I'm getting' picked up at the next gas station! Fuck this!"

Mario was quietly listening, while also attempting to light a joint as he drove the RV. The RV was careening across lanes of icy slickness as Roscoe continued his tirade.

"Roscoe," Lincoln softly intoned, "Relax. I'm sure we can work something out. There's no need to raise your voice."

Roscoe began digging into the bag of pot sitting on the island between the two front seats, and started to roll himself an impressive fatty. Lincoln's facial muscles suddenly twitched into a feral, murderous glare. The look was a combination of puzzled irritation, contempt, and craziness. I'd seen it before; I'd been its recipient on a couple occasions.

Lincoln paced toward the front of the RV, Mario still struggling to both light his joint and avoid driving the RV off the road.

"I know you're not smokin' my weed. I know that's not my fucking bag of weed," Lincoln barked. It was Roscoe's turn to be diplomatic.

"It *is* your bag of weed, Lincoln, and I am in fact smoking it. Please make note of the quantity which I have consumed, and make the appropriate reductions in my salary accordingly." Lincoln eyeballed Roscoe and replied, "Oh, you can be sure I'll be making the motherfucking appropriate reductions, dawg. That you can count on."

"Which leads us back to original issue of compensation, and what that number is in fact going to be, brah. I didn't get off my couch in N'Orleans to fly out here and risk my ass in this snow and shit for a thousand dollars."

This banter continued for a couple hours without resolution. Perhaps Lincoln's weed had impeded Mario's navigational judgment, because the trumpeter meandered off the freeway and into the parking lot of an abandoned warehouse complex. He needed to pee, and when he realized there was no public restroom anywhere, Mario tried to back the RV up and go back the way we came. With a trailer, this can be tricky. Lincoln fixed his trademark puzzled/irritated scowl on Mario, and I sat on the couch, quietly shaking my head. There I was again, on the road with Mario Walker and friends... a circus on wheels... or, as Matt Schumacher aptly coined it, the *Mobile Clown Service*.

When we finally made it to a gas station, I was at wit's end. I had to get out of that RV. I bee lined it for the comforts of my own van. There were footsteps behind me. I turned around and saw Roscoe, cigarette drooping from his mouth, sauntering behind me toward the Global Funkmobile. He'd had enough, too. I made the rare exception of allowing someone to smoke cigarettes in the van. Roscoe was something of a star, so he got star treatment. We motored on toward Whiskey Jacques in Ketchum, Idaho, Roscoe two-fisting it with a joint in one hand and cigarette in the other. We listened to music, teaching the colorful drummer a few of our songs, and had some good laughs.

I recognized the tour as an opportunity to develop a rapport with a player who had scaled the heights of the JBS, seemingly without ever giving it much thought. Roscoe had recorded and toured with Page McConnell... Page McConnell was one fourth of Phish... and Phish was the biggest jam band that ever was, excluding the Grateful Dead. By gleaning what I could from Roscoe, I might tap into the magic: that intangible ingredient that catapults some to the pinnacle, while everyone else languishes below.

At one point, Roscoe pulled out his cell phone and dialed a number. I heard a nasal male voice on the other end. I knew that voice. I'd heard it on records many times.

"Page, it's Roscoe. What's up, man?"

"Hey, Roscoe. How are you doing?" Roscoe skipped the small talk and got right to the point.

"Hey man, you gotta book some gigs, man. I gotta make some fuckin' money. I gotta get paid. Book some gigs, Page!"

Page didn't seem receptive to Roscoe's suggestion. He muttered something about having to get back to looking after his daughter, and he was gone. I figured that relations might have soured between the two men during the Vida Blue days. It was clear, after only a few gigs, that Roscoe, talented and charismatic as he was, was also a handful.

My speculation about Vida Blue's interpersonal dynamics was confirmed later, when Roscoe launched into a monologue about what he had demanded from Page's management, before Vida Blue first hit the road.

"I told him, 'I gotta have a nice hotel, unlimited room service, and I just wanna be left the fuck alone when we're not sound checking or playing the show. I know y'all can afford to pay me what I need, and I ain't playin' games. Don't be messin' with me.'" According to Roscoe, Page had listened to his demands and responded by saying, "I think we can work together, Roscoe." The Vida Blue record was released by Epic Records, the same label which had put out all of Phish's studio albums over the years, so it was probably true that McConnell had had a decent budget to work with. I liked the Vida Blue record, a techno-oriented concept album which was a major stylistic departure from Phish. I particularly liked the track, *Most Events Are Not Planned.*

After successful shows in Boulder and Denver, Roscoe decided it was time to go home. He'd had enough of the Re-New Orleans experience. He and Mario hadn't made a love connection, but Roscoe had managed to bond with me and the Global Funk gang. He liked our material and enjoyed hanging with us. The door was open for future projects.

We weren't quite done with the tour, even though Roscoe was bailing. Gruden flew back out west and met up with us in Grand Falls, Idaho. We also temporarily hired a mandolin player from Pocatello,

Idaho named Leland Hackworth. Leland and I were old friends from high school band camp in Yolo, California.[208]

In Vail, we played our usual spot, the Sandbar: a glorified sports bar with good food. The night went well, and as it was winding down, I found myself at the bar sitting next to a drunk woman in her late twenties. I talked to her for a while, and then made my way back to the stage to pack my gear. Later, she walked over with Mario in tow, stating that she was leaving. Mario had a smile on his face.

Leland, meanwhile, had put in some serious legwork with a blonde skier at the bar. The guy was good. He would get right up in a girl's face, propping his chin against his hand and staring intensely into her eyes as if she was blowing his mind with dazzling intellectual flurries and rare gems of inspired storytelling. He had stamina, too. He'd sit there for a solid hour or more if necessary, never wavering. When it was time, four whiskey and Cokes later, to close the deal, he seized the moment like a single-minded predator.

The ski bunny had led Leland to believe she would be spending the night with him after the show. As he gloated in this seeming victory, a tall meathead, rocking the obligatory backwards, fitted ball cap, walked over with his arms folded. "You ready, Sara?"

"I'm talking to this guy right now."

"It's time to go."

The meathead backed off, and Leland turned to the girl.

"Who's that dude?"

"That's my ex. He just looks out for me, makes sure I don't get into any trouble."

"Well, I'm not going to cause you any trouble. He doesn't have anything to worry about."

"I know, it's just that James is really protective of me." Leland was getting flustered.

"If it's over between you and him, what business is it of his—" James the Meathead reappeared, grabbing Sara the Ski Bunny by the arm.

"Sorry," she murmured, shrugging her shoulders as if the decision was out of her hands. James led her away.

"Did you see that? What a son of a bitch! I had that locked up. I *had* it!"

---

[208] :-p

"The locals always have the upper hand," I tried to explain. "She's cried on that guy's shoulder. He's paid her rent, maybe even her delinquent parking tickets. Sorry, man. You win a few, lose a few." I put my arm around Leland's shoulder and we all left the club, proceeding toward the van. It was bitter cold, and the ground was icy and dangerous. As we got to the van we saw the couple walking to a nearby SUV.

"Just keep walking, Leland. Don't say anything." Suddenly, Sara the Ski Bunny stopped, turned and faced us.

"Hey Leland!" she called out. His eyes lit up. Maybe she'd changed her mind. Maybe Eric the Meathead was the one who would be leaving empty-handed, after all!

"Yeah?" Leland responded, cracking a smile.

"See this?" In one quick maneuver, she unzipped her pants, pulled them down to her knees, and flashed her naked rear end for Leland and the rest of us to behold. A couple of us gave approving whistles.

"Yeah, I definitely see it," Leland answered.

"Well," she continued, "This is what you *won't* be getting tonight." Leland's face turned red, as the rest of us tried not to laugh. There would be no love for the mandolin player on this night. Mighty Leland had struck out.

The next morning, I called to check up on Mario. He invited the whole band to join him at an upscale Italian restaurant before we left for Aspen.

"I don't think we can afford it," I said.

"The whole meal's gonna be comped. I'm friends with the owner. I play there sometimes."

"Say no more, Mario. We're there." We met up at the spot, had a delicious lunch, and were still at the table when our server brought over a bill.

"This meal is comped," I noted, grimacing at the numbers on the paper.

"Not to my knowledge."

"Mario said the owner would kick us down a free lunch."

"Mario doesn't work here, and I've heard nothing about it." The other guys in the band quietly slid out as I spoke to the girl, who was clearly irritated. I rose, wiped my chin with my napkin and said, "You'll have to work it out with Mario. He said he had it covered." Mario, of course, was nowhere to be found. I waltzed out, leaving only a tip.

I heard comp, not cap…

As we were hanging up there in the Rocky Mountains, it somehow came up in conversation that Mario was contemplating a side career in porn. He was not the first of my musical colleagues to consider such a foray (as you'll recall). Mario had brought along some pictures he'd shot with a tall, attractive blonde in San Francisco, and he decided to show them to us one afternoon. The pictures started out fairly tame, and got more and more provocative. I seem to remember one of Mario scaling some kind of rock formation, while naked and in a state of semi-arousal… but perhaps that's my memory playing tricks on me, and that was just a bad dream I had at some point.

By the time we made it to Aspen, Mario was tired; tired of the tour, tired of Lincoln, and tired of just being out there. He was probably tired of me, too. He didn't seem interested in "renewing" New Orleans anymore—it had never been clear just what the tour had to do with New Orleans or Hurricane Katrina anyway.

We got to the Belly-Up, a club modeled after the Belly-Up in Solana Beach, California, and loaded in for soundcheck. Ralph, the sound engineer, had worked for years at the original club in Southern California, and now was living in Aspen. Ralph remembered me from San Diego, and was happy to see Mario, who arrived with his new girlfriend and her heavy-set, British female sidekick.

When I first walked in, I'd spotted a familiar figure near the bar, watching football on a big screen TV. I thought: *I know that face. But what happened to the bushy, porno moustache? Why, it's John Oates from Hall n' Oates!* I knew it really was Oates, because I remembered the Hall n' Oates *Behind the Music* episode, in which Oates discussed the old glory days… the fame, the women, the money. At the end, Oates had said he now lived in Aspen, Colorado. I caught his eye at the bar, and he gave a friendly nod.

I mentioned to Mario that John Oates was in the house, pointing to where he was sitting. His face lit up, and… I'm not making this up… he reached into his jacket and pulled out a *Hall n' Oates' Greatest Hits* CD.

"We were just listening to this in the car! I'm gonna go say what's up!" Before I could advise him against bugging the guy, Mario pounced. He was at Oates' table, thrusting the CD at the eighties pop icon, who was hanging out with his young son. From what I could tell, the Top 40 craftsman was polite, receiving the trumpet player's giddy enthusiasm with a diplomatic bent he had no doubt refined during his hirsute heyday. The show was good that night, a reminder that if Mario, Lincoln and I had somehow been able to create a stable environment in which to work together, there was much we could have accomplished.

The phone rings…

Me: Hello?
Jarvis: It's Jarvis, Anthonaaay. Y'all still on the road?
Me: No, we just got back to California.
Jarvis: Yeah, well, listen, me n' Amir's real mad y'all cancelled them shows.
Me: Those shows were lame, Jarvis. I could have booked those myself.
Jarvis: Well, you boyz been makin' some bad decisions. Me n' Amir are gonna let you fellers go.
Me: Fair enough. I trust Amir will do the final numbers and remit any remaining balance, considering you guys took half our New Year's Eve money, and deposits on other shows also.
Jarvis: Amir's real tight with them numbers. I'm sure you'll be hearin' from 'em rayl soon, Anthonaaay.

A month later, the phone rings…

Amir: Hello?
Me: Hi, Amir. It's Anthony from Global Funk. I still haven't received those final numbers from you, much less a check to settle our business from the last tour.
Amir: I must tell you, our lawyers have informed me that you breached our contract with you. You cancelled several shows without our consent.
Me: You took a massive deposit on the Mangy Moose gigs, which *our manager* booked, while the shows *you* booked were all losers.
Amir: The fact is, we are not indebted to you at this juncture.
Me: Not by my calculations.
Amir: I think this conversation is over, my friend.

In early 2006, I moved back to San Diego. Lincoln agreed to pay me a monthly stipend to serve as musical director for various projects under his Next Groove umbrella, including my own, and to play keys for a Memphis-based singer named Greg Higgins. I listened to Greg's album, which, while slickly produced, struck me as a pedestrian R&B effort. His voice was technically sound but also rather generic.

I wasn't jazzed about backing Greg Higgins on a long tour, but Lincoln felt it would be a good springboard for my solo project. At the first meeting all the musicians showed up to discuss a rehearsal schedule. Greg, just off the plane from Memphis, immediately struck everyone as arrogant. Lincoln was billing the band as the Greg Higgins Experience, so the guy must have been thinking he was the focus of everything. In actuality, Lincoln wanted him to simply be the frontman, while showcasing all the other talent in the group as well.

There was quite a bit of talent: John Staten, on extended hiatus from Karl Denson's Tiny Universe, held down the drum chair. Jesse Molloy, a Living Large alumnus and accomplished soloist, was on saxophone. LaTanya Lockett joined the group on vocals. The McKinney Brothers, two of San Diego's finest gospel musicians/R&B producers, played guitar and bass. There was also a back-up vocalist named Diane. I don't remember her singing, but I remember John Staten having a crush on her.

It wasn't a jam band, but it was a powerful sounding group. The rehearsals were held at the Community Actor's Theater, the place where it had all started with Living Large years earlier. It felt strange being there again, after so much had happened in my musical journey. It also felt strange being in San Diego again after leaving and returning so many times.

I got a feeling of déjà vu when Lincoln asked me to be the musical director for the tour, only to arrive at rehearsals and watch Greg Higgins start marshaling us around like he was Prince or Lenny Kravitz. He was saying things like, "I need you to give me more," or "Y'all need to get this tighter." Nobody wanted him in charge, but the tour had his name on it.

Nobody was enamored of his Greg's music, either. The tour was organized with a typical jam band routing, heading out through Arizona and Colorado; but the show we were assembling, with Greg's guidance, was the kind of thing you'd hear in a lounge in Vegas: rigid arrangements, played exactly the same every time, with corny segues and a generally dated approach.

Greg did have talent, to be fair. He played nice keyboards and sang well. What he *didn't* have was frontman charisma: the kind of personality that would endear him to a new crowd and win over fans. LaTanya, on the other hand, had this in abundance. Greg's portion of the show was tight and strained, an outgrowth of the unease with which the rest of the band related to both him and his material, while LaTanya's couple songs were funky and well-received.

After lukewarm shows in Tempe, Flagstaff, Tucson, Boulder and Durango, Lincoln concluded that he'd made a mistake bringing Greg out west to front the band. It would have been one thing if the singer's music simply wasn't going over, but Greg compounded the problem by being aloof, even churlish at times.

In Vail, while hanging out in the plush, cozy lounge of the Holiday Inn after a show at the Sandbar, Lincoln apologized to me, John and Jesse. "I'm sorry about this, guys. When we get home I want to make the three of you my top priority."

Back in San Diego, Lincoln held his usual wrap-up meeting at his office in South Park. We all sat around his long, varnished wood table, reviewing the tour and settling unfinished business. Once the meeting concluded Greg approached everyone individually, asking, "Will you go out with me again?" After ignoring most of us for the entire tour, he wanted to know where he stood. Everyone, myself included, told him, "Yeah, sure, Greg. We'll play together again." He was heading home anyway, so why say something negative?

A couple days later I learned that Lincoln and Greg had parted on bad terms. Greg believed his travel expenses were being absorbed by Next Groove Records, but Lincoln informed him this wasn't the case. The conversation turned to future touring prospects, with Lincoln saying, "You didn't make a love connection with the guys."

"But they all said they would go out with me again," Greg countered.

"Well, Greg, how can I put this... they lied to you."

Shortly after my return to San Diego I received an unexpected phone call, like the one I'd gotten from Mario Walker in 1999—the one that launched my life as a road dog. This call was more auspicious, however. It was from Karl Denson himself.

Over the years, Karl and I had become acquaintances. Guys in GFC had come from KDTU, and guys who wound up in KDTU came from Living Large. Our paths crossed often out in the scene, and GFC even opened shows for the Tiny Universe every now and then. When both bands were at a festival, I would jump onstage and join keyboardist David Veith to do some impromptu jamming.

In addition to getting to play with KDTU here and there, I was able to chat with Karl from time to time about the realities of the business:

the challenges of leadership, grass roots marketing, and other subjects of concern. I considered him a mentor. He was ten years older and his career was further along.

Back in 2004 I'd filled in at a KDTU wedding reception performance in Boulder, Colorado. It was only the second gig David had ever missed in the history of the band. I'd been on the road when I got the call, and made arrangements to get recordings sent out to me, so I'd put a good foot forward on the gig. Once I received Karl's music I charted out all the songs, and listened to the music incessantly as GFC drove around the Northwest. Because of my respect for Karl and his organization, I wanted to nail the job.

I flew out to Boulder to meet up with the band, the day before the wedding. At the airport in Denver, a limousine was waiting to take me, John Staten, bassist Ron Johnson and Karl to a hotel in Boulder.

"Wow," I said. "This is how you guys roll?"

"No," Karl chuckled. "This is just a fluke with the limo." During the ride, the jokes started flowing as we drank Sprite from champagne glasses. There was a lot of history between John, Karl and myself, and we delighted in recounting humorous past episodes.

The road manager, a middle-aged Southerner who would go on to annoy everyone with ceaseless movie references[209], handed me per diem and an itinerary, then directed me to my room. The whole thing was so *organized*. This was in sharp contrast to the way things typically ran in the GFC camp.

When we rolled into the wedding reception, a complete keyboard rig awaited me: Hammond B-3, Fender Rhodes, Clavinet, Triton synth. It was all set up and ready to play. I didn't have to do anything but sit down and start jamming. I realized how badly I'd been roughing it during the last three-plus years in my own band. The client, a friend of Karl's from the scene, provided us with generous hospitality.

My preparation paid off. I nailed the job, surprising my friends in the band by knowing transitions and specific keyboard parts. Karl thanked me for putting in the time, and John and I hit Denny's for a late-night feast.

---

[209] Including an extended revisiting of the *Sexual Chocolate* scene from *Coming to America*, which, unbeknownst to the guy, actually featured Karl Denson himself!

I didn't realize that by doing a good job for Karl on the gig, I'd opened the door for a future collaboration with the sax master. It was now 2006 and here I was in San Diego again, just back from an unremarkable tour with Tim Terry, getting another call from Karl. This time, it wasn't for a one-off gig. It was to put together a new band:

"Hey, Anthony, I've got this idea. What do you think about doing an organ trio with me?" Without thinking I replied, "I think that sounds great, Karl." I was immediately receptive to any musical configuration Karl might have in mind. Plus, this one sounded like a true musical challenge—something I hadn't had in a long time.

Karl had also been feeling uninspired by his musical surroundings. He too was looking for something to push him to evolve artistically. Tiny Universe had become stagnant. Like GFC, only on a more accomplished level, the group was headed in the wrong direction. The guys in the band were getting jaded, ticket sales dwindling.

Karl asked me to focus on playing Hammond B-3 organ in the new group, something I'd never done on a consistent basis. I knew how to fake my way around a B-3, just from playing it occasionally at festivals and on recording sessions. I didn't have a command of the instrument, however.

I'd played left-hand keyboard bass on a bunch of low-profile gigs over the years, but it wasn't something I'd ever really concentrated on. This wasn't going to be some jive hotel lobby job. This was going to be big clubs with good sound systems and well-lit stages. Marquees with our names on them. Headline festival appearances. I was going to have to really *bring it* to pull this one off.

Like acoustic piano, Hammond B-3 has a rich legacy. Jimmy Smith, Lonnie Smith, Jack McDuff, Jimmy McGriff and the younger Larry Goldings and Joey DeFrancesco are but a few of the artists who have defined the jazz/funk organ tradition. Organ is its own animal, with both technical and idiomatic particulars. In other words, there is a *right* way to play the B-3 and a *wrong* way. The wrong way is to approach the instrument like an acoustic piano. Organ players hate hearing a piano player fake his way through a gig on B-3. You can't play B-3 if you're strictly a piano player. You have to become an *organ player*. It's like learning an entirely new instrument.

I was a little scared at first. *What if I can't cut it? What if I'm not good enough, and Karl gives me the heave-ho?* I decided it was a chance I'd have to take. It was too good an opportunity. We began rehearsals at Karl's house in San Diego.

I didn't have my own pad yet, and was crashing at Len and stepmom Ann's house in Rancho Bernardo, a suburb north of San Diego. I would drive over to Karl's place and work on all the new music he'd assembled for the new group, which he'd decided to call KD3. On drums, Karl chose Brett Sanders, a creative jazz player I'd known for many years in San Diego. Brett could swing hard, and his solos were inventive. Brett was also notorious for losing people onstage; he had such a free, unique sense of time that some musicians struggled to keep the form straight, particularly during fast swing tunes.

This made my task even more challenging; not only would I have to get my left-hand act together in a hurry—I would also have to hold it all together against the tricky drumming style of Brett Sanders.

When I look back on my life, it's been during the times when I was afraid to fail that I made the most progress. There's no better incentive than the fear of being terrible. When you're a single guy trying to meet women, you constantly struggle with the fear of rejection. When you're trying to get credit or a bank loan, you struggle with the fear of being denied because your finances are weak. When you're a musician who plays in bands, you live in fear of being fired and replaced.

With Karl Denson or any act on his level, there wasn't going to be much tolerance for mediocrity. As I said earlier there's not much affirmative action in the arts. Either you cut the gig or you don't; and if you don't, a good bandleader, which means a musician who is also a good businessman, isn't going to keep you around very long. There's minimal job security when you're a sideman in a band. You might merely turn in one lousy show and be told to take a hike. Buddy Rich, perhaps the most infamous tyrant to ever lead a band in the history of show business, was known to fire guys for missing *a few notes*, first berating them on the bus in front of the entire band, then kicking them off the bus when they got to the next town.[210]

Lack of job security is a good reason to keep your chops up, bring enthusiasm to every performance, and most important, try not to ever miss a gig. When you miss a gig, even just one, you open the door for someone else to come in, play better than you and take your spot. One

---

[210] There is a famous bootleg tape, recorded on the bus without Rich's knowledge or consent, during which he irrationally (and profanely) attacks the entire band, accusing them of being amateurs and threatening to fire them all.

time I couldn't make a job in Orange County, and I got a pianist friend named Shep Meyers to cover it. When I called the agent to check on more upcoming work she told me, "Sorry, they really liked Shep. He plays lots of the old standards people want to hear."

When you're a sideman, the best assurance against being replaced is constantly being available—saying yes to every gig and every tour you are offered. The minute you start becoming unavailable is the minute the bandleader starts contemplating a change. I know this because I've worn both hats. I've been canned, and I've done the canning.

KD3 began its performance life with a string of shows at Winston's, the beloved watering hole in Ocean Beach that had been a San Diego institution for years. Right off the bat the place was jammed with people eager to hear Karl's new project. Brett and I, if we hadn't realized it before, saw firsthand how loyal Karl's audience was. We would joke, in fact, that Karl could get up on stage and start beating on pots and pans and people would eat it up. He was one of those entertainers people just loved to watch.

With KD3, Karl wanted to return to his jazz roots. The band's repertoire included several straight-ahead swing songs, such as Thelonious Monk's *Off Minor* and Cannonball Adderly's up-tempo version of *Fiddler on the Roof*. It was a risky move for Karl because his core audience expected him to play funk and dance music, like he did in both KDTU and The Greyboy Allstars.

After the first batch of Winston's appearances we did a show at Boulder Station in Las Vegas. Brett and I drove out there with Aaron Bleiweiss, a guitarist friend of mine first introduced to me by Lincoln. While not on or even near the Strip, Boulder Station was a sprawling casino and hotel complex, with a mid-sized showroom for national acts.

We played one set, for middle-aged couples sitting and sipping cocktails. Karl left after the show, leaving me the luxury high-roller suite given him by the promoter. Before retiring to this penthouse overlooking the entire valley I joined Aaron and some locals in checking out a cover band called Yellow Brick Road. I wasn't too excited to sit and listen to a cover band with such a cheesy name, but one of the locals said "No, man, these guys are really great. It's not what you expect." After listening to an entire set of classic rock ranging from Zeppelin to Boston, I was blown away. The group sounded awesome—the best cover band I ever heard. If you're in Vegas looking to hear the cover band of all cover bands...

In the late summer of 2006 I started hitting the road hard with Karl. We did runs along the East Coast, across the South, and around Colorado. It was a four-man operation, consisting of the three band members and road manager Joe Cahill, or, as I began calling him, *Crazy Joe*. Crazy Joe and I hit it off quick, falling into an *intelligent white clown in his thirties* shtick inspired by Vince Vaughn and Owen Wilson, à la *Wedding Crashers*. When we launched into this mode at afterparties we either had the room in stitches, or completely cleared it.

I played mostly organ on Karl's gigs, holding down the bass lines with my left hand. Given Brett's free drumming approach, it was a challenge to make the bass groove, nail unison melody lines with Karl, and hold down song forms without spacing out. I developed a newfound respect for bass players, realizing the bass player can make or break a band as much as a drummer can. If the bass player doesn't keep the form together, the whole band sounds discombobulated. My challenge was to keep the bass rock solid while coming up with interesting things with my right hand.

Brett's drumming wasn't the only thing about him that was quirky. We came to view him as a food squirrel: someone who eats very small portions and always has a few half-eaten meals in his backpack, ready for the next nibble. Sometimes Brett and I roomed together, and after a gig, even late at night, he would venture out into whatever town we were in to "find something to eat." He'd come back an hour later carrying a takeout bag. He'd sit down, open up the package, take a few small bites and go to bed. I would think to myself, *that's a lot of work for a couple bites! Wouldn't it be easier to just grab a bag of chips from the hotel vending machine?* But that was how Bretty Brett rolled.

Brett also had the habit of pulling the hood of his sweatshirt down tight around his head, covering any exposed skin on his face. We could never be sure if he was cold, afraid of germs, or maybe a bit of both.

A frugal guy who seemed to live a relatively Spartan existence outside of his enthusiasm for high-performance cars, Brett surprised me one day by asking if I would help him pick out some new clothes. I thought he was maybe going to get a shirt or two, but a couple hours later I had helped the dude choose and then purchase an entire new wardrobe. He had to buy an extra suitcase just to get everything home.

When it came to women, Brett was very shy. He liked them, for sure, but he simply didn't have a predatory bone in his body. One night we were driving somewhere on the East Coast, and made a quick pit stop to grab Italian takeout from some joint in a strip mall. We didn't have much time; we were just getting our food and hopping back in the van. Brett managed to start chatting with a girl working at the place, and before we left he pulled me aside and asked, "What should I do, Anth?"

"I don't understand what you mean," I answered.

"I'm not sure how I should proceed." I realized Brett was interested in the girl... *despite the fact that we were in some random strip mall in New Jersey, and would never return there for the rest of our lives...*

"Well, Brett, whatever you're going to do, you better do it quick. Our food just came up."

Despite these idiosyncracies Brett was, at least for me, a real pleasure to tour and make music with. He was a sweet, thoughtful guy, a man of devout Christian faith, and a monster drummer in many ways.

When Karl informed us we'd be playing a night at the Blue Note in New York City, I was excited. Many fine musicians live in New York for years and never get the chance to play the Blue Note, one of the world's most famous jazz clubs. Moreover, not every kid who takes piano lessons winds up headlining the Blue Note in later life. I'd survived the initial challenge of cutting it in KD3, and would now have a performance opportunity that would, at least in part, validate the many years of hard work and sacrifice I'd devoted to a career in music.

I was a bit nervous about this high-profile gig, but also realized that nervousness wouldn't hamper me the way it had when I was younger. As a college student I would get downright scared to perform at recitals. It was such a pressure-filled situation. Now, in my thirties, I might get a little nervous in the days leading up to an important performance, but once it was time to hop up on that stage and handle my business, I just played and forgot about nerves. When you've done something a few thousand times, you find some inner peace.

One of the keys to overcoming nerves is to realize you're never as good or as bad as you think you are while you're playing. When you listen back to a recording of yourself, sometimes the music sounds better than you thought it was at the time; and sometimes, you thought you were *killing it*, but it turns out what you played wasn't that special. The lesson is this: the range of quality in your performances is probably not as great as you think it is. You play the way you play, or you sing the way you sing. *It is what it is.* Put another way, when someone listens to you while you're on you're *A game,* it's more or less the same listening experience as when you're having an off night. I know this sounds ridiculous, but I do believe it to be true.

Another thing to consider is that the experience of playing music is very different than the experience of *listening* to that same music. When you play, you're thinking about a lot of different things. You're trying to execute, and to feed off of and react to what the other musicians are doing. When you're just sitting and listening, you hear what's really happening... not what you *thought* was happening while you were playing. If you are excited during your performance, this might result in nervous sounding music. If you are relaxed, to the point of even being bored, the music might actually sound great... because you're not pressing the issue. Things never sound good when you press or force. Maybe that's a good credo for life in general.

You're going to play the way you play, regardless of your mindset, so it's better not to invest too much ego in the process. Ego interrupts the flow of inspiration—the connection between the abstract realm of ideas, the brain and the fingers.

Experienced musicians know that one performs in the same manner one practices. If your practicing is patient and controlled, your performance will reflect this. If your practice is frantic or schizophrenic, that's what will come across when you play in front of people.

Abandoning Global Funk and joining KD3 entailed a return to sideman status. I wasn't responsible for anything other than playing the shows and contributing a creative idea here and there. All the logistics were handled by Karl's management, Q Prime, and booking was done by the William Morris Agency. It was nice to not worry about all that—to just get paid for doing my job. Being the leader brings a variety of stresses. If the tour loses money, and there are plenty of reasons why it might, *you're* the one losing money. The sidemen, the road manager and the booking agent get paid either way.

I was learning a great deal from Karl, not only in terms of his bandleading approach, but also his understanding of the business of touring. Karl didn't confuse camaraderie with the financial bottom line. If a band wanted to open for KD3 or do a co-bill—even a well-known band—Karl would ask, "Why should we play with them? Are they going to bring enough people to justify the expense?" Unless a band had proven draw, Karl wasn't interested in sharing the pot. As Todd Sherman would say, *this isn't a charity.*

He was a shrewd businessman, but at forty-nine, Karl had also managed to remain passionate about music. He brought his i-pod on the road, and would plug it into the van stereo and share albums, ranging from punk rock to hip-hop to jazz. We'd discuss the intangible ingredients that make a song, an album or a band great. Karl would dissect the integrity of a groove in order to clarify what made it special. If someone played a record that didn't move him, Karl would grimace and say, "That shit's not funky."

Brett Sanders wasn't available for one East Coast tour, so Karl hired a well-traveled New Yorker named Bruce Cox. Bruce bore uncanny resemblance to the pop singer Seal, and was soft-spoken and chill. We got along well from the beginning. We had a great show at the Blue Note, Bruce and I connecting on cool rhythmic patterns and recurring motifs. Afterward, we drove up to rural Vermont to stay in someone's empty house. Bruce played bootleg copies of current theatrical releases, created by someone sneaking a video camera into the theater and keeping it fixed on the screen for the entire film. You'd see silhouettes of people getting up to grab popcorn or hit the restroom. The sound was so terrible that you couldn't follow the plot. I asked Bruce why he collected these crappy bootleg DVD's, and he said, "The price is right, man."

After shows in Vermont, Maine and New Hampshire, we were driving down some freeway, heading to another gig. We'd been passing around a bag of cookies. Bruce was asleep in the back seat, when Karl and I realized we were approaching a major accident ahead. When we got to the scene, there was an eighteen-wheeler overturned, completely ablaze. It was quite a spectacle, smoke billowing high into the air. As we gasped at what we saw, Bruce, groggy from his nap, sat upright and took a look.

"Can you believe that, Bruce?" I asked.

"Yeah, that's somethin'. Yo, where 'dem cookies?"

On another run, we made our way across the South, starting with the Carolinas and working our way to Birmingham, Alabama. The show in Birmingham was at a place called Vulcan Park, home of the world's largest cast iron statue, which happens to be a likeness of… you guessed it, Vulcan, the Roman god of fire and forge.[211] The park sat on

---

[211] In case you're wondering, as I was, a forge is a shop with a furnace where metal is heated and hammered out into useful items.

top of a hill overlooking greater Birmingham, which contrary to my preconceived notions, appeared to be a lovely city.

The Vulcan Park website explained:

> Birmingham is unique because of the availability of the raw materials necessary for making iron: coal, iron ore and limestone. By 1900, Birmingham was called the "Magic City" because of its rapid population growth due to the larger number of workers needed to produce iron. City leaders wanted to advertise Birmingham and Alabama at the St. Louis World's Fair and decided a statue of Vulcan would best highlight the area's growing industrial abilities.

That's all fine and dandy, but not what made the massive cast iron construction interesting to *me*. As we drove our rented passenger van onto the ten-acre park property, I looked up at Vulcan, right arm extended, holding a hammer in his hand, and saw not the Roman god of fire and forge, but the jam band god of great sax solos and muscular butt cheeks. That wasn't a hammer… it was a *flute*. That statue was Karl Denson himself!

I pointed this out: "Hey Karl, Vulcan looks just like you, or… you look just like Vulcan." Everyone chuckled and Karl had to admit, "Yeah, he's got the same butt and calf muscles."

"From the back, his hair's the same, too," Crazy Joe noted.

From that point on, Karl's KD3 nickname was Vulcan; or, if you want to be thorough, *Vulcan, God of Great Sax Solos and Muscular Butt Cheeks.* When Brett[212] and I were waiting in some hotel lobby the morning after a show, hurting for coffee and food, Crazy Joe would saunter downstairs, black bags under his eyes, and mutter, "Vulcan's still in the shower."

I found it interesting that the crowds for KD3 were consistently enthusiastic in 2006, despite Karl's emphasis on extended, free-form jazz forays. He expected his audience to embrace this esoteric musical direction, and for the most part they did. Perhaps he was such an interesting character to watch, or his audience was so irrepressibly loyal, that it didn't matter what type of music Karl chose to play. Or

---

[212] Due to his previous stint as a competitive boxer, Brett earned the nickname Southpaw Sanders.

maybe I underestimated the concert-attending public's insatiable appetite for complex, cutting-edge improvisational music?[213]

All I know is, I had tried mightily hard with GFC to appease the audience. I slaved over writing a different set list every night, and went to great lengths to make the shows danceable and well-paced. I wrote lyrics and hooks I believed were catchy and accessible, and constantly came up with new ideas to keep the performances fresh. Despite all this, the band never broke through to the next level.

Karl, on the other hand, quickly assembled a trio—an instrumental organ trio, nonetheless—patched together a repertoire of simple originals, his and mine, along with a handful of obscure jazz standards, booked a tour, and immediately had the attention of the national jam band community. This underscores a basic truth of the music business: When it comes to a performing act, and how that act is perceived by an audience, *it either works or it doesn't. People either dig your stuff or they don't.* Taking it one step further, *people either dig YOU or they don't.* I wasted a lot of time pursuing projects doomed to fail from the beginning. I didn't realize that the basic brilliance, the mysterious spark or whatever that intangible thing is that makes lots of people like you, just wasn't there. So my advice is this: Watch your audience carefully. Watch how they respond. When it's clicking, when it's working, there's a tangible sense of it. You can feel the energy. When you don't feel the love, don't allow yourself to come up with justifications or excuses. Just accept the truth: *This shit isn't working.* You'll save yourself a lot of struggle.

Also consider that there are thousands of bands out there; a whole army of driven people who believe as much in their creative ideas as you do, and who are equally or more committed to making their mark. Therefore, you better have something interesting to offer. You better have some novel element working for you. If you're just a carbon copy of other established acts, you're doomed to get lost in the shuffle.[214]

After a year Karl decided to make a change in the drum chair. Bret, for all his creativity and improvisational brilliance, just wasn't laying down the funk to KD's liking. If you asked Karl who his favorite drummer on the planet was, he wouldn't bat an eye before answering,

---

[213] Hahaha.

[214] Of course, being entirely derivative might work to your benefit if you're shooting for a career in mainstream pop or rock.

"Zak Najor, hands down." Zak was an original member of Greyboy All-Stars and had played with Karl all over the world. A tall, fair-skinned guy of Middle Eastern descent, Zak was a jokester, a fun character who never took himself too seriously. He took his music very seriously, however, which was one of the reasons Karl loved him. To Zak, the groove was sacred. He didn't even like to take solos. He preferred to find the perfect groove for a song, and then lay it down with as much conviction and consistency as possible.

Zak had had his ups and downs with Karl. At some point his Christian faith had led him to feel that the road was not a savory environment, and not where he belonged. It was hard to fault him for this—the road, after all, was a wild place where anything could happen. There were temptations galore, and if you weren't grounded you could get into trouble out there.

In addition to this spiritual disconnect with the scene, Zak had a reputation for backing out on gigs at the last minute. He'd only done it a few times, but it was the kind of sin that was not easily forgiven; the kind of sin that stuck to your name like a virus for a long, long time. I'd learned this lesson the hard way myself. The thing is, you can do everything right ninety-nine times, but that hundredth time, when you drop the ball… that's what people remember. It's shitty, but that's how things work, and that's how people think; at least in the business I know, which happens to be the music business.

Zak had fallen out with Karl over such a situation, and was no longer the drummer for Greyboy All-Stars. He immersed himself in his faith, migrating from San Diego to Portland, Oregon, then to L.A., and ultimately back to San Diego, each time to pursue involvement in a particular church. Zak and I were friends going back to the Fried Bananas days, when he had auditioned for the drum chair, only to announce at the end of the audition that he liked us individually but thought the band was kind of, well, *stupid*. His candor was part of his personality, and it had never really bothered me about him. In fact, one of the things I liked about Zak was the fact that he never put on airs or pretended to be someone he wasn't. I wish I could say that about more people in the entertainment business.

Karl and Zak had parted company, but Zak's younger brother, Jake, was also a very solid, funky drummer, and available to hit the road. Like his older sibling, Jake was a treat to play with. He was a huge guy, and supported my theory that big guys get a richer, deeper sound out of the drums. Jake, in fact, was big enough to be an NFL offensive lineman—that's the type of natural frame he had. His playing had a big, round pocket, so while he might not have been as rhythmically sophisticated as some players, or as laden with "drummer tricks," he delivered what really mattered: good time, a good sound, and a groove that was always fun to play over. If I'd had him at the beginning of Global Funk Council, I might have saved myself years of grief.

Unlike Zak, who was like a big teddy bear, Jake had more of an edge. He could be witty and fun, but he could also be pessimistic at times. He was intelligent and perceptive, but his observations sometimes led him to cynical or nihilistic conclusions.

Jake was living with his folks, didn't have a family to feed, and was making good dough on tour with Karl. Crazy Joe, a short, fiery Irishman, was a guy who had *man problems*. He was divorced, had a daughter, and was trying to make a living and provide. He had a hard time with Jake's attitude at times, and consequently didn't relate to him. Jake, on the other hand, didn't understand why he should have to appease or take orders from Joe, who was more or less a glorified roadie. Jake's attitude was, "You don't dig me? Fine, now go do your job and set up my shit, Crazy Joe."

I began locking horns here and there with Jake also, and this wasn't good, because we had to get up on stage and make music together every day. It wasn't a musical thing; I loved Jake's playing, and considered him one of the best groove-oriented drummers I'd ever worked with. Karl pinpointed the problem one day: "Jake, you have a strong, aggressive personality, and Anthony, you have a strong, aggressive personality. That's what's going on here." Karl wasn't exactly Mr. Rogers-in-a-wimpy-sweater himself, but he was the boss. His job was to steer the ship, and our job was to get along with each other.

One night in Orlando, after Jake and I had bickered in the van during the drive, he took it out on me on stage, playing super loud and obnoxiously, so that I had a hard time hearing my bass lines, Karl's sax, or anything other than his cymbals and snare drum. After the show Karl asked us what had happened. Jake admitted he was pissed off at me, and was venting during the performance. Without so much as raising his voice or even saying anything particularly negative, Karl made himself crystal clear: *Don't ever do that shit on my gig again.*

Karl was a good leader and a level-headed guy, but didn't shy from conflict. He wasn't afraid to speak the truth, even to a cop who had pulled us over at three in the morning for no apparent reason. Karl was behind the wheel, and after handing over his license and insurance asked, "Why are you sweating me, man? We're just doing our work, minding our own business." This seemed to give the officer pause, and within a minute or two we were back on the road. It dawned on me on more than one occasion that Karl would have made a great military general. He had a commanding presence, and a way of making you want to give him what he was looking for. You didn't want to fall short of his expectations, and it wasn't just because he was writing your checks.

Another time we were pulling into Bloomington, Indiana for a show at the Bluebird. I was behind the wheel this time. A car raced in front of me at an intersection, and as it did the driver and passengers all flipped me off and cursed horribly at us. They apparently thought I was going to cut into their lane—I wasn't.

As luck would have it, we pulled up beside them at the next light. The passenger window came down and the woman riding shotgun went nuts. #&$%#$, you $@$#*ing $#$%*&er!!! I don't remember exactly how I responded, but let's just say my words wouldn't have made Desmond Tutu or Mother Theresa particularly proud. When the light turned green the car sped ahead, cut in front of us, and stopped. Right there in traffic. It was like a dare or something: *What are you gonna do?* I looked back at Karl. He was completely unbothered. Not mad, not nervous. Just chillin'.

"What should I do, Karl?" I asked.

"Go around those stupid idiots. We gotta get to soundcheck." It was good advice.

Later that night, in between songs at our packed show, Karl took the mic and said, "Bloomington, you got some crazy fools in this city. There's some serious road rage going on. I thought we were gonna have to throw down earlier today, when we were driving into town." The crowd reacted with awkward laughter.

On the break, I was heading to the green room when I was stopped by a couple. They asked if they could get me a drink. I said yeah, sure, not thinking twice about it. I ordered the usual, and the guy left and returned a minute later with my Captain and Diet. Then the woman said, "Look, we're really sorry about earlier today." It clicked… they were the ones!

"That was you?"

"Yeah, unfortunately."

"Oh well. Thanks for the drink."

One night in Chicago, we played a fun show for an enthusiastic crowd, at an interesting spot called the Abbey, or something like that. Jake pounded two whole Rockstars before we hit the stage, and I asked him, "Why did you do that?" He answered in his typically droll voice, "I gotta drive the train, bro. I kinda gotta bring the energy, you know?" Later that night we were all hungry, so we made our way across downtown to a late-night hot dog joint. I didn't know at the time that the place was famous for its profane, insult-slinging servers, but I was about to find out.

As we approached the window to order, the guy in front of me said, "Go get me two hot dogs, bitch." I was taken aback. Did he really just say that? The large, African-American woman behind the counter glared at him and said, "Shut up, punk ass. I'll get your fucking food when I feel like it." All of us looked at each other and started cracking up. This was going to be fun.

When it was my turn to order, one of the women grimaced at me and said, "What the hell do *you* want?" I was a little shy and said, "Gimme one of those goddamn footlong dogs."

"Shit, is that the best you can do?" She brought me the dog, and it was Jake's turn. "What you want, Big Dawg? Twenty hot dogs and ten orders of fries?" Jake, not in the mood for late-night verbal abuse, quietly answered the large-busted, belligerent server, "It's kind of not cool."

"What?"

"It's not really appropriate."

"You know where you are, bitch?"

"Why don't you just shut up and get my food," Jake said. She wasn't done, though.

"Hey, y'all, check it out. This dude's titties even bigger than mine!" Gales of laughter at the late night hot dog stand.[215]

KD3 was a challenging, rewarding band, providing me the chance to play nice venues all over the country, but it wasn't panning out business-wise for Karl. He wasn't clearing enough dough after paying everyone else and covering road expenses, and a large percentage of his core audience missed the larger, more dance-orienced Tiny

---

[215] Jake and countless other recipients of this woman's legendary mouth would have their revenge, when she was paid a visit by Triumph the Insult Dog, who proceeded to rip the razor-tongued server a new one.

Universe configuration. The band would continue on for a while, but I sensed change coming.

Meanwhile I decided to take another stab at being a bandleader. KD3 gave me a solid platform from which to launch a new project, and Lincoln Norris was backing my pursuit of a solo career, or at least a band of which I was the leader and main songwriter. Lincoln had even tried to sign on as Karl's manager, assuring the veteran saxman that if given the chance, he'd "hit it out of the park." We were driving somewhere in the South, doing a KD3 run, when Karl gave Lincoln his answer via cell phone. Karl had been listening patiently while Lincoln went off on numerous tangents, explaining his vision for the future of Karl's career. I'd had these types of conversations with Lincoln myself, and knew he had a tendency to get sidetracked, or to try and cover too many ideas at one time. I could see Karl's patience thinning. Finally, Karl had heard enough. "Lincoln, I'm gonna stop you there. Listen, man, I'm out here trying to run a business. I've got a family to provide for, and I don't have time for a bunch of jibbety jabber. Just because you say you're going to 'knock it out of the park' doesn't mean you have the ability to manage me or make me more money. Those are just words." Karl ended the conversation, and with it, any hopes Lincoln might have had to manage him.

After that, Lincoln became frustrated with my participation in KD3. I was spending a lot of time on the road with the band, and Lincoln had no piece of the action. He told me, "You're just riding Karl Denson's coattails, man." But I wasn't. I was gaining invaluable performance experience, building my national reputation, and writing and arranging lots of new music for my next project. Also, I was getting paid well for my time.

One thing Lincoln was right about, however: it was time to get back out there with my own thing. I'd known Chicago-based guitar virtuoso Fareed Haque for a number of years, and had always hoped to do a project with him. The opportunity finally arose, when I conceived of the idea for Anthony Smith's Trunk Fulla Funk. Both Fareed and Roscoe Church agreed to be a part of the band.

SO YOU WANNA BE A BANDLEADER...

In the winter of 2006, I got the Trunk Fulla Funk trio up and running. I wasn't sure if Fareed and Roscoe would get along, but Fareed was *gung ho* about playing with him. Lincoln and his booking associate, Harley Kirk, put together a small run along the California coast: San Diego, Santa Cruz, and two nights in San Francisco. Lincoln encouraged me to be the bandleader — to put my name in front of the band name, and feature my own picture in publicity materials.

"You gotta get your name out there, man. Build yor own marquee," he maintained. I wanted that to happen, but felt pangs of anxiety about being a leader again. The leader has to answer to everyone, the leader does twice as much work, and the leader gets paid last, if at all. I knew this, but I also knew it was a special opportunity I had here — a chance to play with two great musicians, in a situation where I would be running the show. I knew I might not make money on the tour, but it would still be worth it to get the word out in the scene that I was playing with Fareed and Roscoe.

The day before the first show, I called Roscoe to make sure he was prepared for the tour. The following is a loose but essentially accurate transcript of what he said when he answered the phone:

Hello? Hold on… Who the fuck is this? Who? Oh, hey, it's you… Listen, brah… there's somethin' you need to know. If we do this again, and I'm anticipating that we will, 'cause it's probably gonna be the shit… don't ever, ever, ever, ever, ever, EVER book me on motherfuckin' Southwest again! I can't fly no fuckin' Southwest! I'd rather stay home and lie in bed, with one hand on my dick and the other on the remote control. If you don't get to the airport three hours early to change your seating assignment, you get stuck in the middle between two fat fuckin' assholes. I just can't have that happen… I'm a nervous person. I'm fidgety. I get real nervous, real stressed. I gotta be movin' around a lot. Can't be all confined and shit. I hate to fly, dude. I'm just a nervous person. That's just the way I am. Couple fat-asses all up on my armrests and shit… no can do. Gimme the goddamn window. I have missed flights over this very shit. Missed flights! And another thing: I do NOT want to go directly to the club when I get off the motherfuckin' plane! Do NOT do that to me! After I've been stuck between two fat fucks for four hours, I ain't goin' to no goddamn club to soundcheck! I need to rest. I need to recover. If I'm gonna be sittin' between two fat-asses all morning, after I had to get to the airport at five fucking o'clock a.m., do you think I wanna go deal with some load in, soundcheck shit? I need to go somewhere I can chill, brah… after surviving that ordeal… that CRISIS. That's if the plane even makes it to San Diego, after my fucking layover in Phoenix. If you already made some arrangements, and you're gonna force me to go down to the club right when we leave the airport, there better be a good fucking bag of weed waiting for me when I get through baggage claim. I am totally serious. Have that shit ready and waiting, brah. Light it up and stick that shit in my mouth before anyone says a word. Once I get some smoke in my lungs I'll be able to calm down. I'll smoke that shit and then I'll be straight. That's my routine. That's how I roll. That's WHAT I DO. And don't forget, man… it's my birthday. There better be a big fucking cake with icing waiting for me in your van, with a fat splif stickin' out of it, lit up like a candle. And don't be throwin' any crazy musical shit at me. Keep it simple. I don't wanna be getting' all tired out. You feelin' me, brah?

I decided to make my main mission insuring Fareed's comfort, and let Lincoln and company worry about Roscoe. I picked Fareed up at the San Diego Airport and we rolled over to Winson's to set up our gear. Once we got to Ocean Beach, we grabbed a bite at a Mexican restaurant and discussed the musical direction for the tour. He talked about the ups and downs of Garaj Mahal, his acclaimed funk/fusion group. The group had four strong personalities, and they'd all struggled to get along at times. In fact, there'd been a meltdown during a show, when a couple of the guys had a full-blown altercation on stage. The incident necessitated a formal Internet apology from the band.

When professional musicians sit down to break bread, the main topic of discussion tends to be the difficulties of sustaining a career playing music. Even for the very talented, like Fareed Haque, there's rarely a time when you can simply coast along. You're always hustling for new opportunities; better gigs, better publicity and management, a bigger fan base, more critical acclaim, more visibility, and of course, a higher income. It never ends.

I took Fareed back to my place near San Diego State. I was renting a charming little house less than a mile from the university. It was tiny, but quiet and affordable. Most important, it was a house—I wasn't sharing common walls. I could practice piano, play CD's, and enjoy the seclusion not afforded an apartment dweller.

Fareed and I ran over some material. I sensed he was used to moving fast, and didn't have patience for people struggling to learn music. He expected you to run through something once or twice and have it down. Some musicians would be threatened by such pressure, but I welcomed it. I like to have people pushing me, testing my skill level. If things are completely comfortable, you're not learning anything. The kiss of death in the arts is complacency. You can't allow yourself to get to a point where you say, *Okay, I'm good enough now. I can relax.* You can never relax. You have to keep pushing yourself, with every new project you take on. That's *my* philosophy, at least.

Roscoe encountered difficulties trying to get out of New Orleans. We'd purchased his tickets using the wrong name, it seemed. His real name was Darren, not Roscoe. You would think that a musician who traveled as much as he did would know to alert anyone buying plane tickets for him that his real name was something different than what everyone called him. And you would think that such a musician would know better than to wait until the morning of the flight to check his itinerary. But you would be wrong. Musicians are last-minute, fly-by-the-seat-of-their-pants type people.

The latest news I had was that Roscoe had missed the scheduled flight, but had managed to get on one to Houston, and then was going to attempt to get on another to San Diego. Concerned that we wouldn't have a drummer for the show, I called Brett Sanders and put him on stand-by.

Roscoe managed to make it to San Diego in time to do the gig. He was picked up by Harley, who gifted him with the bag of weed he had so vehemently demanded. My original plan had been for everyone to get to San Diego the day before, so we could learn some material and put on a tight show. This, of course, was thwarted when Roscoe missed his flight out of New Orleans, so now we were going to be jumping up there and winging it. Faking it, which is exactly what I had *not* wanted to happen. I figured that just getting both Fareed and Roscoe to San Diego at the same time to play a show was an accomplishment unto itself. If the music actually gelled, that would be icing on the cake.

When I saw Roscoe at Winston's, he was moody and quiet. There was no time to talk about music, so I said hello and left him alone. He'd just hop up there and do his thing, and people would like it because he was Roscoe Church, New Orleans' funkiest drummer.

We got a good turnout that night. For a Wednesday, Winston's was crowded. People liked the music, which, while loose, was organic and funky. My suspicion was confirmed: if you get great players on a stage together, and let them do what they do, an audience will respond positively. Even people with an untrained musical ear can recognize advanced musical talent. If someone can play an instrument exceptionally well, it's obvious.

After the show, we had to pack up quick and hit the road for Santa Cruz. We drove through the night, me doing the majority of the driving. Fareed, suspicious of Lincoln's navigational abilities, snapped at one point, saying, "Why don't you just let Anthony drive? He knows where he's going." Fareed was the kind of guy who, while nice to everyone, didn't have even a little bit of tolerance for bullshit. If something was going a way he didn't like, he was going to let you know about it; and you were going to listen, because you respected him and wanted him to be happy.

I realized Fareed and Roscoe would be tired and possibly irritated when we got to Santa Cruz, having slept in the van all night, so I tried to get them to sanctuary as quickly as possible. Lincoln's wife Diana, who handled administrative tasks for tours, had booked a hotel room for Roscoe all the way down at the beach, near the Boardwalk. By the time we got down there, Fareed's patience was waning.

Lincoln gave me a wrong direction, and we got lost. Fareed snapped, "You should have Mapquested it, man! What the fuck are we doing?" I could see Lincoln's face twisting into the *Norris scowl of intimidating animosity*... but he caught himself, relaxed, and let the moment pass. I was relieved, because the last thing I needed was a heated altercation between Lincoln Norris and Fareed Haque on the seedy sidestreets of Santa Cruz.

We found Roscoe's shitty motel, only to learn that the joint didn't have a smoking room available. We had to hunt down another motel, where Roscoe could chain smoke to his heart's content. We dropped him off and headed back to Anne's house in Aptos.

The Aptos house had always been a point of pride for the family. It was like a little white castle, perched at the top of a hill. From its windows, all of lovely, wooded Aptos was visible, along with the Pacific Ocean. I'd always relished the opportunity to bring friends and musical associates there, not only because the house and surrounding property were impressive, but also because Anne and Terry were, without fail, incredibly warm and inviting, no matter who I was bringing into their home. They always got a kick out of the colorful individuals I'd worked with over the years.

Often, I'd come out of the downstairs bedroom in the morning to discover one of my bandmates or friends engaged in animated conversation with Anne, who loved to discourse with fellow artists about business, the creative process, or the challenge of reconciling the two.

After everyone slept for a few hours, Fareed and I sat at Anne's out-of-tune upright piano to go over a few arrangements. Lincoln, always energized by observing musicians in the midst of the creative process, sat nearby, absorbing my interaction with Fareed.

I was impressed with Fareed's ability to learn music so quickly. He not only had great technique, but an amazing ear as well, which meant that once he'd played through something one time, he owned it. I was throwing some challenging harmonic progressions at him, and he played inventive solos over them immediately. For him, it was second nature.

Just as we were wrapping up the spontaneous rehearsal, I decided to show Fareed one more sketch, an arrangement I'd started writing for the Police song, *King of Pain*. I played a little bit of it and Fareed perked up.

"I love that. That's amazing! We gotta do that!" We fleshed out the arrangement, which was a reharmonized take on my favorite Sting song (and one of my favorite songs of all-time), and there was a vibe of excitement in the air. We were collaborating, and it felt good. Lincoln was psyched by what was happening, and exclaimed in characteristic fashion, "That arrangement is a muuuutherfucker!"

The Santa Cruz show was at Moe's Alley, a club specializing in blues acts. I'd played there numerous times with Global Funk, and had rarely drawn a crowd. The owner, a guy named Bill, liked Global Funk, but had become frustrated with our inability to draw people. He'd called Todd Sherman and said, "You must not be doing your job, because the band sounds good. They have good material and they're good players... so where's the following? Where's the crowd? What are you doing as their manager?"

I figured it would be easier to draw people with names like Fareed and Roscoe, and I was right. Trunk Fulla Funk did well for its first time at Moe's, and Bill was pleased. We had some rough musical moments due to the lack of rehearsal, but again the vibe was funky, and the audience seemed to dig it. Or so I thought...

After the show, Roscoe split with a woman he had met at the show. We'll call her Gracie. Gracie said she'd get Roscoe to San Francisco herself the next day.

"That makes me nervous," Fareed said.

"It makes me nervous too," I replied. Nonetheless, Roscoe was a grown man, and he was going to do what he was going to do. I don't have to speculate for you what his reaction would have been, had I said, "Hey Roscoe, Fareed and I would prefer you hang with us, rather than someone you just met an hour ago."

As we drove up the 17 freeway en route to San Francisco the next day, Fareed got a call from Alex, the owner of the Boom Boom Room. Someone who had been at our Santa Cruz show had tipped Alex off that we weren't musically tight. Alex was calling to say we better get our shit together somehow—he was paying us a good guarantee for a two-night run, and he expected it to be slamming.

Hearing this pissed me off. Getting Roscoe to the venue was enough of a challenge, but an actual rehearsal? That would take a miracle.

Plus, I'd never really gotten a warm feeling from Alex. I'd played the Boom Boom Room many times, with Global Funk and also a group called the San Andreas Experiment. He paid well, but always seemed to have some axe to grind, a reason to be dissatisfied with your performance. So hearing he was again disgruntled with one of my projects, because some random guy at a show had emailed to say this new group wasn't tight, was just some extra bullshit I didn't feel like dealing with.

We arrived at the Boom Boom Room, set up our equipment, and waited for Roscoe, who'd been apprised of the necessity of a last-minute rehearsal. Roscoe kept us waiting, so Fareed and I worked on material without him. Most people, when they arrive late after leaving people hanging, are apologetic. The first words out of Roscoe's mouth, once he'd sulked onstage to join us, were, "Okay, now that I'm here, what the hell is it y'all are so desperate for me to learn?"

We went through a couple tunes, and then I started to play the new arrangement of *King of Pain.* Roscoe lit up. "I love that song!" he said, and started playing a groove underneath the bass ostinato I was laying down. Fareed joined in, and the trio sounded great. There were certain things Roscoe would do, certain signature riffs and patterns, that you just didn't hear other drummers doing. He had his own style. Nobody could deny him that.

After two nights at the Boom Boom Room—two musically strong, well-attended nights—Alex was singing a different tune. He invited me to join him at a table with Fareed and some attractive girls, the first time he'd ever extended himself to me socially. We smoked weird cigarettes, drank some obscure liquor and chatted about the music scene. He was finally welcoming me into his circle.

Later, Alex pulled me aside and we had a lengthy conversation about the business of promoting music. He gave some strategic suggestions for how to tour intelligently in the jam band scene. I appreciated his thoughts, and realized he didn't have the low opinion of me I had previously suspected. He was just the kind of guy who remained inaccessible to you until you demonstrated to him that you were worthy of his energy.

The next morning, Lincoln, Fareed and I headed for Scotts Valley, where we were scheduled to spend a day in the studio recording. Anne and Terry had put hardwood floors in their house, and the guy who did the installation job was named Hal Diaz. He'd mentioned that he owned a recording studio, and when I heard about it, I contacted him.

When you're a musician, people often tell you that they or someone they know has a recording studio, and you should check it out. Studios, of course, range from elaborate complexes with multiple rooms and millions of dollars worth of equipment, to someone's nasty studio apartment with a cheap-ass multi-track recorder, a ghetto drum machine and some crusty pasta sauce stains on the carpet. I happened to follow through on the lead with Hal, and we began working on projects together.

A lumberyard manager and contrator by day, Hal was also a hard-partying rock and roller who had decided, at forty, to fulfill the lifelong dream of building and running a studio. Like me, he was a big horror buff; he owned the complete set of action figures from *House of a Thousand Corpses*, along with a large, rather scary Captain Spaulding doll.

Hal was green as an engineer, so the first few sessions we did together had been frustrating. He hadn't mastered his equipment yet, but was trying hard, and giving me a *really, really ridiculously reasonable rate*[216]. I brought in John Staten and Garaj Mahal bassist Kai Eckhart, who lived in the Bay Area, to lay down some of my compositions. John drove all the way up from San Diego. Eckhart didn't come cheap, so I wanted to maximize my time with him. I got three or four solid tracks with Kai and John, but when I came back the next day to do some mixing, Hal had a frown on his face. "Sorry, brother. "

"What's up?"

"I was learnin' how to use this hard drive, and I accidentally erased some of your music." I was bummed, but I couldn't really get mad at Hal. He was a nice guy, he was working with me for next to nothing, and it had been an innocent mistake. When Matt caught wind of the incident, he turned it into a running joke: *I'll make you a deal, brother. For every piece of new gear you buy for the studio, that's one of your tracks I won't erase.*

Hal had dealt with substance issues in the past, and was now on the wagon. He'd replaced alcohol with energy drinks, and his new beverage-of-choice was 24-ounce cans of Rockstar. I'd get a call from Hal saying, "Stop at the market and pick me up some Rockstars,

---

[216] As Derek Zoolander would say…

brother!" He guzzled the stuff like it was bottled water. His ticker must have been palpitating like Mahmoud Ahmedinejad's at a Holocaust sensitivity retreat, but I guess it was better than further pickling his liver by swilling Jack Daniels.

One of my projects at Crazy Licks Studios involved the Global Funk guys, who I gathered for one last recording date. I was living with Teena in Redwood City, and no longer able to harbor musical refugees the way I had in Merced. Matt, as a result, had to crash at Hal's pad. Hal's pad, of course, was not a pad at all, but a storage unit resourcefully converted into a studio/meager living space. Hal didn't have the room (or the desire) to have Matt, as cool a guy as he was, hanging with him in his "living area," so Matt slept on a couch in the studio itself. I called him to see how it was going.

"I woke up in the middle of the night, and that fucking Captain Spaulding doll was staring at me, man. It freaked me out."

"Sorry, Matt. Let's remember, it's just a movie." Hal seemed to be okay with Matt being there. He walked into the studio in the morning and said, "It's a good thing I like you, Matt. Otherwise, this arrangement just wouldn't be workin' out."

Now, many months later, Hal had refined his engineering chops, and had also lifted his moratorium on booze. He was partying again, but no longer accidentally erasing entire tracks. Hal, as I liked to joke, was a dead ringer for Vince Neal, minus the good fortune of joining Motley Crue and becoming a millionaire. Hal, in fact, had bumped into the *real* Vince Neal at a lakeside resort in Northern California.

Neal was there to make some kind of "celebrity appearance," and was sitting by the pool with a couple women (read: bleached bimbos). Hal worked up the nerve to walk over and say hello.

"I don't want to bother you, Vince, but I'm a big fan."

"Jesus! Can't you see I'm in the middle of a conversation?" Neal blurted, not in the mood to be bothered as he discussed Arab/Israeli relations with a pair of bikini-clad hotties from Sacramento. In one fell swoop, a loyal fan became a sworn enemy.

"Fuck that guy," Hal would say if you mentioned Vince Neal. "He's a major asshole." Without having met Neal myself, I can't say for sure, but based on Hal's experience, and information I gleaned from Neal's own book, *The Dirt*, it seems the dude indeed has the capacity for some pure, unadulterated douchiness.

Fareed, Lincoln and I pulled into Hal's studio, located on the ground floor of an industrial warehouse behind a carwash. Once again, we sat around waiting for Roscoe, who was being chauferred by Gracie, his new Bay Area squeeze. After an hour or so, Gracie's little car pulled up by the big garbage dumpster next to the studio. Roscoe was reclined in the passenger seat, sporting his characteristic backwards baseball cap and hooded sweatshirt, a cigarette dangling from his mouth.

"Yo, Anthony! Come here!" I walked over, afraid of the conversation that was about to take place.

"Hey, Roscoe. Nice show last night. What's up?"

"How am I getting paid for this session? I don't just play on people's records for free."

"We talked about this, remember? Before the tour? I asked if you'd mind staying an extra day to record, so that I could make an album to promote the group. You said okay."

"Well, whose band is this? If I'm just playing on your shit, then how is that my band? If you want me to play on *your* record, pay me."

"It's your record, too, if you want it to be. Do you have a song you wanna record? 'Cause that's fine."

"I tried to teach you my song, and you never fuckin' played it!"

"Dude, you came an hour and a half late to the rehearsal. There wasn't any time."

"So how are you gonna pay me?"

"Look, man, I just want you to do this. We're here, the studio's ready, the time is booked. You tell me. You wanna sign a release relinquishing your rights to the music, and let me make some payments to you, or do you wanna profit share and have more of a stake in what we're doing?"

"I don't know nothin' about relinquishin' and all that bullshit. Look, brah, just get me a bag of good weed and I'll be straight."

"Seriously?"

"Yeah."

"Consider it done." I called up an old friend who shall remain nameless. He now lived in the Santa Cruz Mountains, and if anyone could deliver me some good weed in a hurry, he was the guy. I reached him, and he agreed to come down immediately.

"You going skiing?" he asked.

"No, just gardening." I informed Roscoe that his payment was en route, and we proceeded with the session.

We recorded several songs in a matter of a few hours. Roscoe, for all his bickering and dissatisfaction, delivered the goods within one or two takes. Fareed was further impressing me with his guitar mastery, assembling an entire album's worth of beautiful rhythm and lead tracks in a one-day session. Hal had begun the morning with a potent, blended eggnog and Vodka concoction, and now was putting a hurtin' on a twelver of some microbrew his new gal pal[217] had fetched from the local liquor outpost.

Fareed and I were drinking with him, and also taking a couple puffs off the old *peace pipe*. I wasn't much of a smoker, but here I was in the studio with Fareed Haque and Roscoe Church. *Shit, I might as well let go and enjoy myself.* Roscoe smoked one thing or another constantly, all day and every day, so it was impossible to know if he was sober, completely stoned, or somewhere in between.

It looked like we were on our way to finishing a very productive day at Crazy Licks Studios. We'd laid down several songs, and still had a few hours to get the remaining material recorded. That was when Roscoe started to crack. He was angry that we weren't recording his little song—not a song, really, but a four-chord progression with an R&B groove—and threatened to walk in the middle of the session. He also got on my nerves by snapping at me and Fareed, as we were practicing before laying down a particular song.

"I didn't come in here to hear you fucking noodling on your instruments, running weird scales and shit. Let's play some music." Fareed and I looked at each other in disbelief, having a hard time fathoming that this guy would have the nerve to address his colleagues in such a manner, but we kept quiet. My friend had arrived earlier with the weed, which he'd generously kicked down for free. I still had it in my pocket, the plan being to give it to Roscoe at the day's end.

Fed up, I said, "I'm just going to give him the weed, Fareed. Just to make him happy so he stops complaining and stays for the rest of the session." Fareed walked over to me, got right in my face and looked through me with piercing, intense eyes.

"Anthony, do not give him that bag of weed now. Do not do that."

"Why?" I asked.

---

[217] This gal pal, it turned out, had just gotten sprung from county lock-up, and wasn't, in fact, *new*. When asked about the nature of the relationship, Rick had offered, "We get together every now and then and do our thing for a couple days... when she's not in jail, that is."

"Because the minute you give him the weed is the minute he walks out of here. You want him to stay and finish the session? Keep the weed in your pocket." I smiled.

"Fareed, that's some sage wisdom. I appreciate your guidance."

Roscoe lasted for a couple more songs, then Gracie whisked him out to her car and they disappeared. I gave him the bag, which he snatched out of my hands and shoved in his pocket. *No thank you, no nothin'.* I gave Roscoe a half-hearted pat on the shoulder and said, "Take care, man." *No response, no nothin'.* I walked back into the studio, and that was that.

Fareed and I decided to keep working for a few more hours. We recorded a ballad I'd written, kind of a lullabye, as a duo. We also cleaned up some of our guitar and keyboard tracks. By this point, the beer was gone, the whiskey bottle was empty, and Hal was breaking into the Crazy Licks Studios Private Reserve: two bottles of cheap-ass red wine. As Fareed overdubbed a killer solo, Hal let out a loud "Woooohoooo!" and threw his head back and guzzled the vino straight down his ever-thirsty gullet. One hand was on the mixing console, the other wrapped around the bottle. One false move and Hal's expensive gear would have been doused in bargain bin Cabernet, but hey, it was his studio and his stuff. As the Vince Neal hater had once announced, much to the delight of saxophonist Jesse Molloy and yours truly, "My studio, my rules, brother."

Later that night, Lincoln and I dropped Fareed at a hotel near the San Jose Airport, and began the long drive back to San Diego. When all was said and done, I lost a good chunk of change on the whole Trunk Fulla Funk affair. I didn't make any salary, and also didn't get reimbursed for flights, hotels or vehicle maintenance. All the money went to Roscoe and Fareed. What I *did* get was a full-length studio album with Fareed Haque and Roscoe Church, and a solidified relationship with Fareed, a world class guitarist I'd long wanted to work with. I felt like Roscoe had pretty much acted like a jerk during our brief California tour and recording session, but I respected his drumming, and still appreciated the good times we'd had playing and hanging out in the past.

EPILOGUE

It took a number of years to complete this book—a long haul, when I reflect back on the numerous stops and starts—periods when I either lacked the resolve to continue writing, or simply didn't have the time or energy. Of course, my hurdles were nothing compared to those of Gregory David Roberts, author of the epic novel *Shantaram*. The first two versions of Roberts' manuscript were destroyed by German prison guards... and that was after he'd survived lengthy stints in Australian and Indian prisons, during which he was routinely tortured and forced to participate in brutal knife fights. Writing is already difficult enough without such added challenges.

I wondered how I might tie everything together, making sense of my two-plus decades in the creative rat race. Would this sprawling patchwork of insider tales, cultural observations and random tangents hold up as a cohesive statement, and more importantly, amount to a worthwhile investment of the reader's time? I'd like to think so, but you can decide for yourself and shoot me an email.

As I read through the manuscript one last time before calling it a "wrap," I marveled at some of the inexplicable things I'd done over the years; and now that I'm removed from the road environment and settled into a more grounded existence, I see not only where I went wrong, and where I chose courses of action doomed to fail, but also how committed I remained in such a difficult career path for so long. I might have made some missteps, but I also demonstrated perseverance and courage. Also, though I never made a big commercial breakthrough, I think I accomplished quite a bit creatively speaking. I took some shots, I rolled the dice. I definitely didn't play it safe.

Now that I've gone to great lengths to share my journey via the written word, I view my life and career in distinct phases or chapters. There was the SDSU chapter, the Young Man with a Gig chapter, the Lizard chapter, the L.A. chapter, the jam band gypsy chapter, and so on. I suppose each was a rite of passage, presenting a unique test that, once passed, led to a few new nuggets of wisdom.

There are a handful of things I regret, yes—I don't feel great, to cite one example, about my decision to allow the teenagers in a state-subsidized group home to drink, smoke marijuana and watch adult videos. I also wish I hadn't poured a not-quite-empty Starbucks mocha on some kid's head, while sitting at a red light in Ventura, California. I wish I had been ready to defend myself, when that mouthy local tackled me at the Green Room in Iowa City, so that I might have spared myself the agony of touring with broken ribs. I wish I hadn't set my apartment in Santa Monica on fire, igniting a pile of used acne pads belonging to my roommate (who would later go on to make a memorable cameo on *Curb Your Enthusiasm*). I wish, I wish, I wish.

It took me a long time, in both life and the arts, to become a realist. In youth, I excelled at school and sports, and this led to the belief that it would always be that way for me. I would skate through life because I was good at things; I got good grades, I was athletic, and I was imaginative. I had no idea, like most young people, just how competitive and cutthroat it would be out there in the real world. It wasn't until my mid-twenties that I realized I'd chosen a very difficult field, in which only the very few were lucky enough to enjoy financial comfort. Society *needed* plumbers, accountants, teachers, construction workers, doctors, and lawyers... not musicians. I'd rolled the dice by going into music, and now the dice had landed. The rewards, at least for the vast majority, were not commensurate with the struggle. I decided to accept this disheartening fact and keep trudging forward.

My story, ultimately, has been about one thing: living an interesting life. By interesting I mean taking chances, traveling, continuing to learn and evolve, developing new abilities, and assembling a rich collection of experiences and memories. The arts aren't the only arena in which this is possible; many walks of life generate extraordinary experiences. In fact, most people's lives are orbited by fascinating characters and circumstances. One might not, however, have the motivation or desire to observe and comment on the curiosities of his own environment. To be a self-chronicler, you have to recognize novelty in the seemingly mundane, complexity in the commonplace.

I ignored my grandfather's advice to choose a career more stable than music, even though his opinion was based on seventy years as a professional keyboardist. Having now logged twenty-five years of my own, I have to admit that he might have had the right idea. There have been a number of times when I wished I had another way to make money, so I could pick and choose the artistic projects I wanted to focus on, instead of having to say yes to just about everything that landed on my plate. Based on my life in the arts, I cannot in good conscience encourage a young person to pursue this field as his or her sole livelihood. I'm not saying you shouldn't develop you artistic talent—I hope you do—but betting the bank on it is a risky proposition, unless you are someone who has negligible interest in the material world. (If that's the case, you probably don't want to live in Southern California).

My travels as a musician taught me that I like the road life. I like the freedom of it. I never minded the long drives, or packing and unpacking in a different motel every day. I always met interesting people on the road, and had memorable times not only playing music but also just experiencing the world. There is something about the road that speaks to the heart of a true musician; a feeling when you're out there that it's where you belong. Perhaps this is because to be truly appreciated for doing something original in music, you have to take your show on the road. Every city has at least a small community that values originality, and will come to a venue to hear you make your personal statement. There is also a sense of respect you feel from people when you're a *touring artist*, because you believe in yourself enough to take your talents out to the world.

Since 2008, when I stepped off the road and re-established myself in Southern California, I've become a jack of many musical trades. I play jazz piano and vibraphone, solo piano, pop/rock keyboards, I produce demos for songwriters, and I work in musical theater; I've played keyboards and musically directed shows at the La Jolla Playhouse, The Old Globe, and the San Diego Rep, working with seasoned conductors, directors and actors. I've even written for the stage, with the hopes of one day getting my original material produced. I also went back to school at San Diego State University and got a Masters degree in music performance, and teach part-time at my alma mater.

I'm now married and have two young kids, and must say it didn't take long to realize that raising my sons will be the most important thing I ever do, overshadowing anything I've attempted in music and the arts. Free time becomes a precious commodity when you have small children, and I have to pick my creative spots more judiciously these days. If I'm going to write a new screenplay, it better be a damn good idea I'm working with… something that, if well-executed, *just might fly.*

My interest in songwriting, particularly pop songwriting, has waned in recent years. If I have a specific project or artist to write for, cool, but writing songs on spec, just for the pure joy of the process? Been there, done that. Never made me money, and never opened any major doors. I'm not bitter about it. That's just the truth. I'm not crazy about most of what's played on mainstream radio these days, and feel like I've kind of heard it all before. Excluding the occasional tune that catches my ear, it sounds like the same old recycled stuff. I'm not sure if this is the result of getting older and having a jaded ear, or if there's just a lot of crap on the radio. My suspicion is that it's a bit of both.

As my wife perceptively noted one day, pop music plays a major role in your life when you're young. You feel certain songs very deeply, as if they were written just for you. You don't just follow certain bands and artists… you worship them obsessively. But as you get older, you've got more important stuff to worry about. The sentiments expressed in the typical pop ditty don't have much resonance when you're forty years old, with a full-time job, marriage, kids, aging parents and a mortgage. That's not to say you can't still have fun listening to pop music, but you're probably not losing sleep waiting for the release of the latest Bruno Mars single.

I still like playing jazz, but admittedly have a hard time imagining who's going to *listen* to jazz in the future. I suppose I must accept that it will always be an acquired taste for a small, sophisticated audience. The irony is that there are tons of great young improvisers out there, playing better and better at earlier ages. These young lions have absorbed the entire Twentieth Century jazz language, and are pushing the music forward, developing fresh ideas in the new millennium. I admire artists who've stuck to their guns and pursued jazz exclusively, although I often wonder how they survive. If all I played was jazz, I would have no doubt starved to death at some point in my twenties.

If you have a burning desire to be a musician, actor, writer or some other pursuit conventional society deems a pipe dream, you owe it to yourself to take your best shot, keeping in mind that some people do in fact make it happen. It *is* possible. Once you've decided you're *all in*, the real question becomes: How long can you hang in there? Do you have a contingency plan, or are you laying it all on the line without a safety net?

We all read magazine articles about famous artistic people who say, "I was either going to make it doing this or wind up working in a drugstore." I remember the successful film director Tim Burton once quipping, "If my film career hadn't panned out, I would have wound up living in a trailer somewhere." This underscores the cold reality of the arts: It's a total crapshoot. There's no surefire way to make it, whatever "making it" means. If you have talent and you're smart about how to leverage it, you can surely find some success on a local level, at least. If it's fame and fortune you seek—and I would advise you to do some soul searching, if this is the case—you'll have to pray the stars align, because this is a phenomenon that requires a great deal of luck, regardless of your gifts. You might get your fifteen minutes in the sun by doing something outlandish, like sticking your child in a hot air balloon and calling up CNN, but let's not confuse fame with shame.

If you're going to make a go of a creative life, be smart about it. Don't just jump into the fray with no plan and no direction, hoping it will all work out. Have specific goals, be realistic about your strengths, and work hard to improve your weaknesses. Narrow your focus and find a *niche within a niche,* one that puts your best foot forward and gives you the best chance to succeed.

I knew early that my gift was composition. I could write music in a variety of different styles, and I could do it prolifically. I never found the right vehicle to allow this ability to truly shine, unfortunately. I made demos, put together bands, and crisscrossed the country for years, but what I lacked, looking back, was business and marketing chops. Any time you assemble a team of people and try to manage them, regardless of the product, you are a business person. You need a certain skill set which has little to do with artistry, and in fact is the antithesis of the mysterious, right-brain nature of the creative process.

Throughout my twenties and thirties I had creative energy to burn, but wasn't a savvy businessman. Sometimes I wasn't a good leader, either. People who know me, and understand how hard I worked at various projects over the years, might say I'm being too hard on myself. After all, I did manage to create several bands and make them viable in both local and national marketplaces, inspiring talented musicians to accompany me on my journey. I've got numerous recordings and other tangible products to show for my efforts.

Creative content, whether we're talking about music, books, films or whatever, is continually produced in great abundance, by both amateurs and professionals alike. Thus, an individual artistic entity (song, book, script, painting) tends to have little value, or put another way, provides little if any leverage for its creator, ninety-nine times out of a hundred. Creative people, unless they rise to the top and start wearing other hats, are low on the totem pole. An actor, once she makes it onto the A list, starts a production company, so she can develop a higher volume of projects and generate income from a variety of sources. A popular novelist creates a series, and then employs a team of ghost writers to turn his outlines into finished products.

I suppose my point is this: if it's money you're after, don't hang your hat on the arts. It's a rough go, my friend. For every person you read about in Rolling Stone, there are thousands who will struggle their entire lives to be recognized and rewarded. Many of them have more talent than the person typically on the cover of Rolling Stone, and that's just the way the world works. You've heard it said before, but I'll reiterate the notion that the only good reason to be a full-time artist is because you have no choice; you'd be miserable doing anything else. It's your calling. It's simply what you must do with your life. If that's the case, nobody's going to talk you out of it, and they shouldn't. The world, after all, will always need music, books, movies, and the many other artistic mediums that make life more palatable, meaningful, and enjoyable for us human beings. If someone's going to make it, it might as well be you.

It's popular these days to drop the word maverick in conversation. A maverick is a cool person who doesn't care what people think, who chooses his own destiny and sets the trends others follow. Artists and mavericks are closely related. Perhaps they're one and the same. But it's only hip to be a maverick if your uncompromising stance has paid off. The maverick ideal is glamorized by the media and entertainment industry, but true individualists are not typically rewarded by the society in which we dwell. The stability of our society, and maybe any society, relies more on conformity than individualism. We're rewarded for buying into the existing program, not creating our own program (excluding Steve Jobs and a small group of transcendent individuals). The powers that be want you to think you're a unique individual, marching to the beat of your own drum. Look at your life and ask yourself, is it really the case? Are you running your own show, or is someone else running it for you?

Most of us are not compelled to brave the risks associated with being a maverick or, for our purposes here, uncompromising artist. When it comes down to it, we're driven by a desire for security and creature comforts, an impetus which dictates that we get what we can for ourselves, while we have the chance. We might love to cheer the *lone rebel fighting the big machine,* that irresistible theme that turns up over and over again in Hollywood movies, but we're rooting more for an abstract idea than for something that actually exists. It took me twenty-five years to fully grasp this.

I'm not the world's greatest maverick, but I have lived for the things I care about, for better and worse. Eventually, you have to accept your circumstances. They're not the result of what you did yesterday, or last week. They're the cumulative result of the complex person you are, the many decisions you've made throughout your life, and the manner in which the world has reacted to all this.

A great life is not a safe life. *Crime and Punishment's* Raskolnikov, one of the most fascinating characters in all of literature, was hell-bent on distinguishing himself at any cost. In *Zorba the Greek,* Kazantzakis said that "to be alive is to undo your belt and look for trouble." I say, keep your belt buckled... people these days might get the wrong idea... and look for trouble.

I'd like to thank the many talented and fascinating people I've had the opportunity to work with over the years, and also the wonderful friends and family that have constantly supported me, and who made it possible for me to be an artist and musician in the first place. It's been quite a ride so far. I don't imagine the next twenty years being quite as quirky or colorful, because one, I'm not going to sit in a van or RV with a bunch of dudes and drive aimlessly around the country for months at a time, and two, I'm becoming less of a risk-taker in my middle age. Like any committed family guy, I want to create a nice life for my wife and kids.

I've had the chance to follow my heart, to pursue any and every whim. I'm grateful for that, because a lot of people throw in the free-spirited towel way too early in life, jumping on the stability treadmill before they've had the chance to figure themselves out. I didn't switch gears until recently, and when I finally did, it was a welcome transition. I'd taken my shots, I'd done it "my way," and I was ready to move on to a new existence. I'm still a freelancer, so I'm not exactly mired in conventional malaise, but I'm also no longer eating burritos from gas stations in Montana at three in the morning—do you realize just one of those puppies has a week's worth of your suggested sodium intake?[218]

One of my best friends has a theory that a man has a better chance of sustaining a happy, monogamous relationship in middle age if he's spent his earlier years dating as prolifically as possible. I'll take the Fifth on whether or not I agree with him—I've already incriminated

---

[218] An exaggeration, but not by much.

myself enough in this book—but I think his idea applies perfectly to the evolution of an artistic life. If you don't give it everything you have when you're young, full of energy, and unencumbered by the need to sustain a certain standard of living (and possibly provide for others), you'll never know, when you're older, and less inclined to jump without a net, how much you might have accomplished.

ABOUT THE AUTHOR

Anthony Smith has been a professional musician since his late teens, performing on piano, organ, keyboards, and vibraphone with literally hundreds of bands and artists in a wide variety of genres. He holds a Bachelor of Arts degree from San Diego State University, and also a Master of Music degree from the same institution. He has recorded several of his own albums, and appeared on dozens of additional recordings as a sideman. Anthony has played extensively throughout the U.S., and also in Asia, Latin and South America. In addition to his reputation as a world-class jazz performer, he is also in demand as an arranger, producer, and musical director. Though he has been writing album reviews, essays, short stories and screenplays for years, *The Lizard Stays in the Cage* is his first published book. Anthony lives in the San Diego area with his wife, Teena, and their two sons.

For additional information about Anthony and his various projects, visit:

Website: anthonysmithcreations.com

ABOUT THE ARTIST

Anne Ormsby is a California artist and designer whose paintings have sold to private and corporate collectors both nationally and internationally. She works in a variety of media from pen and ink to watercolor, pastel and acrylics. Her style is most associated with a bright, colorful palette and a sense of humor. Anne has licensed her designs to gift manufactures for over a decade. Her art has been applied to over sixty gift products ranging from stationary and beach bags to tableware collections, in a variety of colorful patterns. Additionally, she has contributed art to book publishers.

For more of her artwork and design go to

Website: ormsbyeditions.com

Made in the USA
Charleston, SC
02 November 2012